LOOKING AT LAW THROUGH CHILDREN'S EYES

School of Human Rights Research Series, Volume 93.
The titles published in this series are listed at the end of this volume

LOOKING AT LAW THROUGH CHILDREN'S EYES

Marieke J. Hopman

INTERSENTIA
Cambridge – Antwerp – Chicago

Intersentia Ltd
8 Wellington Mews | Wellington Street
Cambridge | CB1 1HW | United Kingdom
Tel.: +44 1223 736 170
Email: mail@intersentia.co.uk
www.intersentia.com | www.intersentia.co.uk

Distribution for the UK and the rest of the world (incl. Eastern Europe):
NBN International
1 Deltic Avenue, Rooksley
Milton Keynes MK13 8LD
United Kingdom
Tel.: +44 1752 202 301 | Fax: +44 1752 202 331
Email: orders@nbninternational.com

Distribution for Europe:
Lefebvre Sarrut Belgium NV
Hoogstraat 139/6
1000 Brussels
Belgium
Tel.: +32 3 680 15 50 | Fax: +32 3 658 71 21
Email: mail@intersentia.be

Distribution for the USA and Canada:
Independent Publishers Group
Order Department
814 North Franklin Street
Chicago, IL60610
USA
Tel.: +1 800 888 4741 (toll free) | Fax: +1312 337 5985
Email: orders@ipgbook.com

Looking at Law through Children's Eyes
Marieke J. Hopman

ISBN 978-1-83970-101-6 (paperback)
ISBN 978-1-83970-102-3 (PDF)
D/2021/7849/6
NUR 828

British Library Cataloguing in Publication Data. A catalogue record for this book is available from the British Library.

To my parents

CONTENTS

LIST OF ABBREVIATIONS

APE	(CAR) Association des Parents d'Elèves
CEA	(Dutch) Compulsory Education Act (*Leerplichtwet*)
CEDAW	Convention on the Elimination of All Forms of Discrimination against Women
CRC	Convention on the Rights of the Child
CSOs	Civil Society Organizations
CRPD	Convention on the Rights of Persons with Disabilities (CRPD)
ECHR	European Convention on Human Rights
GCs	Greek Cypriots
HAVO	(Dutch) Higher general secondary education (*Hoger Algemeen Voortgezet Onderwijs*)
ICCPR	International Covenant on Civil and Political Rights
ICERD	International Convention on the Elimination of All Forms of Racial Discrimination
ICESCR	International Covenant on Economic, Social and Cultural Rights
ICJ	International Court of Justice
ICLF	International Community of Legal Floors (a fictional community, see §1.4.3)
LEC	(Dutch) Law on the Expertise Centers (*Wet op de expertise centra*)
NGOs	Non-Governmental Organizations
NSA	National Security Agency (USA)
NVvTO	Dutch organization for homeschooling (*Nederlandse Vereniging voor ThuisOnderwijs*)
OECEANP	Order on Exemption CEA Nomadic Population
ONPPEA	(Dutch) Order on nomadic population under PEA (*Besluit trekkende bevolking WPO)*
OOSEA	Order on the organization of the SEA (*Inrichtingsbesluit W.V.O*)
PEA	(Dutch) Primary Education Act (*Wet op het primair onderwijs)*
RCCL	Republic of Cyprus Citizenship Law
RCCRL	Republic of Cyprus Civil Registry Law
RoC	Republic of Cyprus
SAO	the municipal "school attendance officer" (*leerplichtambtenaar*) who, according to Dutch law, is charged with enforcing the CEA on the municipal level

SEA	(Dutch) Secondary Education Act (*Wet op het Voortgezet Onderwijs*)
TCs	Turkish Cypriots
TR	Turkish Republic (Turkey)
TRNC	Turkish Republic of Northern Cyprus
UDHR	Universal Declaration of Human Rights
UN	United Nations
UNCAC	United Nations Convention against Corruption
VMBO –T	(Dutch) Lower Vocational Education – theoretical track (*Voorbereidend Middelbaar Beroepsonderwijs – Theoretische leerweg)*
VWO	(Dutch) pre-university education (*Voorbereidend Wetenschappelijk Onderwijs*)

INTRODUCTION

On 20 November 1989, the UN General Assembly adopted and opened for signature, ratification and accession the Convention on the Rights of the Child (hereafter: CRC). Since that day, all 197 UN member states have signed the convention, of which 196 have ratified/acceded to the convention, the only exception being the United States of America.[1] This means that children's rights are universal – at least in theory. The idea behind the Convention, as stated in its preamble, is that, since "childhood is entitled to special care and assistance", the child "for the full and harmonious development of his or her personality" should "grow up in a family environment, in an atmosphere of happiness, love and understanding", should be "fully prepared to live an individual life in society", and should to this purpose be "brought up in the spirit of peace, dignity, tolerance, freedom, equality and solidarity".

Concretely, the Convention therefore states that a child is "every human being below the age of eighteen years" (art. 1)[2] and grants children, among others, the right to non-discrimination (art. 2), the right to life and healthcare (art. 6, 24), the right to a name, a nationality and preservation of her/his identity (art. 7, 8), the right to protection against: sexual abuse and violence (art. 19), economic exploitation and child trafficking (art. 32, 34), abduction (art. 35) and torture (art. 37), the right to participation and freedom of expression (art. 12, 13), and the right to education (art. 28, 29).

Meanwhile, although positive trends have been reported, children's rights are still grossly violated on a daily basis and on a global scale. According to UNICEF data, worldwide at least 1 in 3 children is not growing well due to malnutrition[3], 3.9% of children die under the age of 5[4], 9% of children do not learn how to read and write[5], and 30% of children do not have access to safely managed drinking water service.[6]

Children's rights researchers work to understand why these rights violations happen and what can be done to improve the protection of

---

1 United Nations Human Rights Office of the High Commissioner (n.d.) "Status of Ratification: Interactive Dashboard". Available at: http://indicators.ohchr.org/.

2 "unless under the law applicable to the child, majority is attained earlier" (CRC (art. 1)).

3 UNICEF (2019a: 8).

4 UNICEF (2019b).

5 UNICEF (2019c).

6 UNICEF (2019d).

children's rights worldwide.[7] However, their research does not always lead to an in-depth understanding of the causes of children's rights violations, nor to an understanding that would be useful for intervention by practitioners, on behalf of children. At least two factors may contribute to this situation. First, when trying to understand why children's rights are being violated, children's rights researchers usually (if not always) depart from an adult's perspective. Not only does legal power in society lie with adults, for it is adults who constitute the sovereign, who vote, who are judges and teachers and parents, but also it is mainly adults who are legal researchers.[8] The adult perspective on situations in which children's rights are violated may leave out important information on the how and why of children's rights violations, which may only be understood when looking at the situation from a child's perspective. Second, studies that are currently trying to understand children's rights violations from a legal perspective usually do not go beyond formal written law. Legal researchers often engage in analyzing international conventions and analyzing national law, court proceedings and de facto reality in terms of compliance with international legal provisions. This type of analysis is also the usual approach of the UN Children's Rights Committee in their review of state practices as regards children's rights. However, an understanding of law that is limited to formal written (black-letter) law that addresses children and the people around them seems to be too limited a perspective if we want to have an in-depth understanding of why children's rights violations occur.

Therefore, the working hypothesis of this research is that, to acquire a better, more comprehensive understanding of children's rights violations, one has to look at law through children's eyes. For children, law is not necessarily limited to what is stated in state legal codes, of which they are generally unaware, rather it is what their parents or their teachers tell them. When looking at law through children's eyes, the rules of the household, the classroom, and other legal orders which they are members of, can in many instances be classified as law. This law, that we find when looking at law through children's eyes, has to be recognized as part of a complete picture of law influencing the protection and/or violation of children's rights.

Take for example a situation of domestic sexual abuse of children. This practice clearly goes against both national and international law. So why do

---

7 When trying to understand why children's rights are being violated, of course it is equally relevant to focus on its antonym – when children's rights are being protected. Therefore, while in this thesis I will mostly – but not exclusively – focus on "children's rights violations", this can also be read as "when children's rights are not protected", and the question when and under what circumstances, children's rights are protected (not violated) is equally relevant to the question when and under what circumstances they are violated.

8 Cf Darbyshire et al.: "Children also have no political 'clout'. They most certainly 'consume' but do not vote, lobby, organize or campaign and thus possess what Mayall (2002: 154) has called 'non-citizen status'. The 'exclusion of the voices of children from the political culture of the public sphere' is therefore commonplace." (2005: 419).

children sometimes "agree" to have sex with their caretaker, especially when they detest this practice? Why do they not just go to the police or generally ask for help?[9] I suggest that, when we look at law from the child's perspective, we can understand some of these instances as the child in fact *complying with the law*. The child complies with the law of the abusive parent, who rules over the child: "you are not allowed to talk about our little game to anyone". If children's rights are analyzed in this way, if we truly listen to children, we might be able to understand much better what rights and laws are for children and, consequently, why their formal rights are being violated (and perhaps use this knowledge for social change). To this end, a far-reaching legal pluralist theoretical framework is necessary, which includes not only international and national law but also legal orders closer to the child that are usually left out of legal pluralist studies, such as the household and/or the classroom.[10]

The main question for this research is therefore:

> How can violations of children's rights, in different cultural, social and political contexts, be better understood, if analyzed within a legal pluralist framework, taking into account the child's perspective and the relations of power inequality corresponding to the different legal orders surrounding children? And, consequently, how can this understanding be used to improve the concrete situation of children?

Sub-questions include:

1. What is law; what is a legal order?
2. What different legal orders apply to children?
3. How can we understand children's rights with regard to local, national and global legal orders?
4. What/who are the different legal actors in relation to children's rights and how do they relate to each other?
5. What is the role of power inequality within the legal order as related to children's rights?
6. How can children's rights researchers understand children's rights violations in different cultural, social and political contexts?
7. How can children's rights researchers capture the child's perspective on their rights, and how can this contribute to understanding the violations of children's rights?
8. How can a possibly better understanding of children's rights violations, informed by the child's perspective, be used to improve the day-to-day situation of children?

---

9 Kitzinger (1997: 168, 175).

10 "Legal pluralism" will be understood throughout this thesis to refer "a situation in which two or more legal systems coexist in the same social field" (Merry (1988)).

These questions will be answered in three parts. The first part of the thesis is the theoretical part, which consists of four chapters. In this first part, a definition of law is developed which can be used for the legal pluralist study of children's rights (chapter 1). It continues with an analysis of the relations between children and the law from both an adult and a child perspective (chapters 2 and 3) and a methodology for finding law for children (chapter 4).

The second part presents three case studies, in which the theory of the first part is put to the test:

- The child's right to education in the Netherlands (chapter 5)
- The child's right to education in the Central African Republic (CAR) (chapter 6)
- The child's right to nationality in the Turkish Republic of Northern Cyprus (TRNC) (chapter 7)

Each of these case studies includes empirical data from field research as well as data from literature research.[11]

Finally, the third part of the thesis is the conclusion, which includes an answer to the main research question, divided over two chapters: first, a reflection on whether the theoretical framework and methodology as developed in this thesis do indeed lead to a better understanding of children's rights violations in different cultural, social and political contexts and, if so, in what way (chapter 8). Second, whether this understanding can indeed be used to improve the concrete situation of children (chapter 9).

A more detailed and elaborate description of the different parts and their different chapters can be found in the introductions to each part of the thesis. It may also be useful to indicate that some parts of the thesis have already been published. Both the part of the theoretical framework that proposes an alternative definition of statutory law (§1.4) a shortened version of the legal pluralist theory (based on §3.2 and §3.4) and the methodology (mostly §4.3) illustrated by the findings in the CAR case study (chapter 6), have been published in peer-reviewed journals.[12] A selection of relevant results of all three case studies has been published in three popular scientific reports (one per case study).[13] A selection of relevant research findings of the last case study in Cyprus has been published in a UPR report submitted to the UN Human Rights

11 A general discussion of the methodology can be found in chapter 4. The specific methodology, including the number of participants, their ages, sex, background etc., will be described in the methodology sections of the respective chapters.

12 See Hopman (2017a; 2019).

13 See Hopman (2016b); Hopman et al. (2017b; 2018a).

Committee.[14] Lastly, much of the research process has been published on the research website[15] and on social media.[16]

Ultimately, the aim of the research is to create a new understanding of children's rights violations which opens up (possibilities for) social transformation. The hypothesis here is that a better understanding of different legal orders relating to children and children's rights will provide information that is useful for policy. As in the situation of domestic sexual abuse of children described above, to improve the situation of children, politicians might decide to amend national or international law. However, if we find through legal pluralist research that the family legal order here operates relatively independently from the national legal order, we might conclude that such a policy change has a limited effect. In exchange, one could construct a policy that targets the family legal order and its inherent unequal power relations more directly.

---

14 Hopman et al. (2018b).

15 Www.childrensrightsresearch.com.

16 Facebook: www.facebook.com/researchonchildrensrights; Twitter: www.twitter.com/marieke_hopman.

PART I

FINDING LAW FOR CHILDREN

To ask "what is law?" leads us to an old, never-ending philosophical discussion to which there seems to be no definitive answer. However, since this research is attempting to understand children's rights violations in different cultural, social and political contexts, we do have to start at this point. Children's legal rights are necessarily understood in the context of a legal order and form a part of the laws of the legal order. If there is anything we can say about children's rights violations, we have to start by understanding what laws apply to children, who makes these laws, in what position children stand in relation to these laws, what legal order children are part of – if any, and how we can empirically study these laws.

These are therefore the central questions in the first part of this thesis. It is only after we have answered these fundamental questions that we start with empirical research on children's rights. We can then examine empirically, for example, what laws exist for children, how we can study these laws in relation to children and what happens when children's rights are violated (or how they are protected).

The first chapter of part 1 focuses on defining law. This chapter contains a reflection on what makes a law a law and how a law is different from a social norm. Although the chapter does not attempt to solve the unsolvable philosophical question regarding the essence of law, it does attempt to give a comprehensive definition of law and legal orders that can be used for the purpose of the study of children's rights. Zooming in on statutory law, I will construct a new conceptual framework for understanding statutory law that outlines a broader understanding and application of statutory law.

Chapters 2 and 3 contain a hypothesis on the relationship between children and the law. In the second chapter, the unequal power relations between the child and the adult is analyzed from an adult perspective, including the role of law as instrumental to the civic education of children. The chapter will contain a critique of the underlying idea of normalization of children through laws. In the third chapter the perspective is turned around, analyzing the unequal power relations between the child and the adult and its corresponding laws from a child's perspective. I will examine what legal order a child is a part of (either as subject and/or legislator), entering the discussion on legal pluralism.

Lastly, in chapter 4, I will examine how we can find law for children. Based on the first three chapters, I will design a methodology which can be used to empirically study law in relation to children. The entire theoretical and methodological framework will be put to the test by conducting the three case studies in part II of the research.

CHAPTER 1
FINDING LAW

As indicated in the introduction to part one of the thesis, this first chapter focuses on defining law. In this chapter, I will reflect on what makes a law a law and how a law is different from a social norm. This definition will be the first building block of the theoretical framework at the core of this thesis. It is important to keep in mind that the chapter does not attempt to solve the philosophical question regarding the essence of law, nor does it attempt to enter the debates in legal philosophy about the exact, correct interpretation of the works of the different legal philosophers discussed. Instead, the chapter and its discussion of the question "what is law?" has to be read as instrumental to the overall purpose of the thesis, which is to find a new way to better understand children's rights violations. With this purpose in mind, the chapter aims to give a comprehensive definition of law and legal orders that can be used for the purpose of the study of children's rights. Lastly, it has to be remarked that the chapter may seem somewhat to focus on the state legal order to find definitions of law and the legal order. This impression is given mostly because most legal philosophers discussed focus on the state legal order in their discussions of law. However, throughout the chapter, a legal pluralist approach has been kept in mind so that the elements of law and the legal order presented in this chapter are considered to apply to state and non-state legal orders equally (see also §1.4 and chapter 3).

1.1. LAW AS A SOCIAL FACT

The question "what is law?" is a conceptual question that needs to be answered in order to create a strong foundation for any legal research.[17] The question does not refer to a reality "out there"; it does not relate to facts that exist in an

[17] Allott (1977: 2) starts his legal analysis in the following way: "We must begin with some definitions. Like all definitions, these are unsatisfactory, but they are not so much prescriptive, still less analytical, as programmatic or explanatory. In other words, they explain how the terms defined will be used by the author. When one remembers the mass of juristic writing on the nature and definition of law, there is attraction in this limited objective". To this argument I would add that the definitions given by authors, including hopefully this one, may be useful and applicable in a similar instrumental manner to other studies as well.

objective reality regardless of human conventions (so-called brute facts). We do not ask "what is law?" as we ask "is there a tree outside?", or "why do things fall down and not up?" The answer to the question 'what is law?" is necessarily dependent on an understanding of social convention, because laws are social facts.[18] They are created by men; they do not exist objectively and externally to human understanding, as do trees and stones and stars.[19] Laws exist only where there is a relationship between people, a specific sort of relationship that takes on a certain character, so that we define it as legal. It is therefore that, to understand law, we have to understand it as a social fact.

A law cannot be understood without its context, both the context of social reality and of a network of laws. A man alone who does not live in society has no law.[20] If law is a human creation, we need a norm posing the conditions for its creation and a law that has been created.[21] We only notice that there is a law, because someone (an individual or a group of people) has created a rule that we (the legal community) perceive as law, only because we understand this individual or group that created the rule to be authorized to create laws.[22] The law posing the conditions for the creation of law is what Kelsen calls the "basic norm" and what Hart calls a "rule of recognition".[23] As Lindahl formulates this point, following Kelsen: "[...] to view [an act] as a legal act implies that the act is authorized by a higher-level norm".[24] The being authorized by the legislator or the (attribution of) empowerment of the legislator leads back to a basic norm: the norm that presupposes that one ought to behave such as has been commanded by the legislator; or that the legislator is a legitimate legislator; or that indeed this

---

18 For a philosophical analysis of the distinction between brute facts and social facts, see Searle (1995, 2011).

19 In Turley's article on Critical Legal Studies, Unger is quoted to argue that "[o]ne of the great accomplishments of modern social theory, be it Marxist or liberal, is the recognition that society is a creation of the human imagination and not 'the expression of an underlying natural order'." (1986: 611, referring to Unger (1987)). In general, the view that law is a matter of social facts is attributed to legal positivism (see for example Raz (1979/2009), Twining (2009)).

20 See also Lindahl, who holds a view of law as a species of joint action, defining a legal order as "a form of joint action in which authorities mediate and uphold who ought to do what, where, and when with a view to realizing the normative point of acting together." (2013: 5, 8).

21 For this point, see Raz's discussion of Kelsen's first axiom: "[...] two laws, one of which directly or indirectly authorizes the creation of the other, necessarily belong to the same legal system" (1979/2009: 123).

22 For a discussion on the meaning of authorization in relation to law and creation of law or why and how a people subject themselves to a legislator, see §1.3.

23 Kelsen (1945/2007: 115-18), Hart (1961/2012: 100). In other places in his work Hart refers to these rules as "accepted fundamental rules" (62) or as "secondary rules" (81). There is a discussion in legal philosophy about whether this norm is a preconception or a social convention (Marmor (2006: 347)). However, I do not think this discussion is relevant for the current inquiry, and thus I will not address it here.

24 Lindahl (2013: 147).

individual or group has been authorized to create laws.[25] Therefore, no law can stand alone.[26] Laws are recognized as laws by the relevant legal community.

We can thus only answer the question 'what is law?' in relation to society and in relation to a network of laws. The legal community, the law(s) and the sovereign together form a legal order.

A law would then be defined, following Kelsen, as a valid legal norm, which is valid within a legal order, by virtue of the fact that it has been created according to a basic norm.[27]

1.2. HOW IS A LEGAL NORM DIFFERENT FROM A SOCIAL NORM?

A norm is a prescriptive statement, a rule that describes how one should act, how one ought to behave, etc. Or, adjusting Kelsen's definition a little, we could define a norm as a rule by which a certain behaviour is commanded, permitted or authorized.[28] When defining a law as a valid legal norm, the question then arises how we can distinguish a legal norm from a social norm.

25 See: Lindahl (2013: 146-55), Kelsen (1934/2002: 8-9, 1945/2007: 115-17).

26 When arguing that no law can stand alone, I want to keep in mind that Lindahl argues that here we find "a paradox at the heart of the law: ultimately, the legality of legal acts cannot be established from within the legal order itself [...] an act can only initiate a legal order if it is retroactively interpreted as an authorized or empowered act". He therefore argues that who institutes a legal collective must claim to act as an authorized representative, and this "would-be empowerment [...] only comes about if individuals retroactively identify themselves as the members of a collective by exercising the powers granted to them by that inaugural act". He refers to this as the non-legal emergence of the distinction between legality and illegality (2013: 146-55). Since Lindahl refers to the basic norm as a-legal, it is quite likely that he would argue that the basic norm is not a law, or that it only becomes a law when the members of the legal community retroactively identify it as such. The latter does however conform with my other statement, that law can only be understood in the context of social reality – a law has to be recognized as such by the legal community before it even is a law. Kelsen does recognize the basic norm as a law, when he states that "it is a most significant peculiarity of law that it regulates its own creation and application". (1934/2002: 71). See also Raz (1979/2009: 123-24).

27 Kelsen (1934/2002: 31).

28 Kelsen defines a norm as "the meaning of an act by which a certain behavior is commanded, permitted or authorized" (1934/2002: 5). However, I think the concept of a rule is clearer, because the act already implies the legislator or at least fixed decision, while norms can also change gradually in a process of changing tradition. See for example Glenn (2010), who relates this idea of emerging normative rules in tradition to legal orders. Kelsen mentions this point too when speaking about custom, which he describes as: "a tendency within the men to behave as the members of the group habitually do. [...] when these acts have existed for some time, the idea arises in the individual member that he ought to behave in the manner in which the other members customarily behave, and at the same time the will arises that the other members ought to behave in that same way" (1934/2002: 9).

1.2.1. THE NORM AS A RULE

Starting with the concept of a rule. Imagine you are playing chess. You know that your horse is supposed to move in direction A and your tower is supposed to move in direction B. There are rules that determine the possible movements of the pieces, as there are rules that determine the possible interactions between the pieces, etc. Then, suppose you are playing with your friend and you decide that, instead of moving your horse according to the rules, you start with moving your horse from b1 to b5 (see image 1 and 2).

Figure 1.

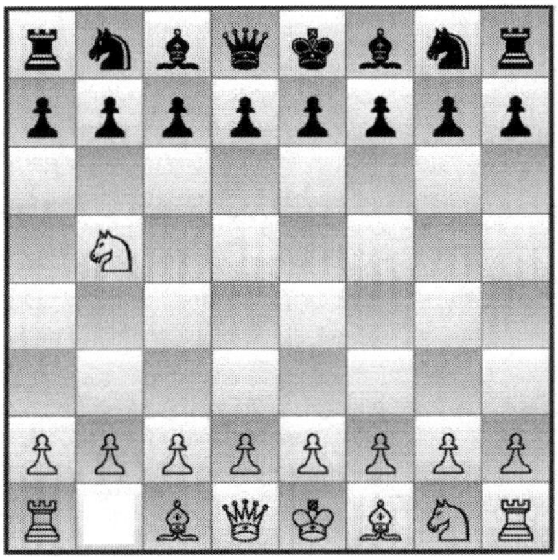

Figure 2.

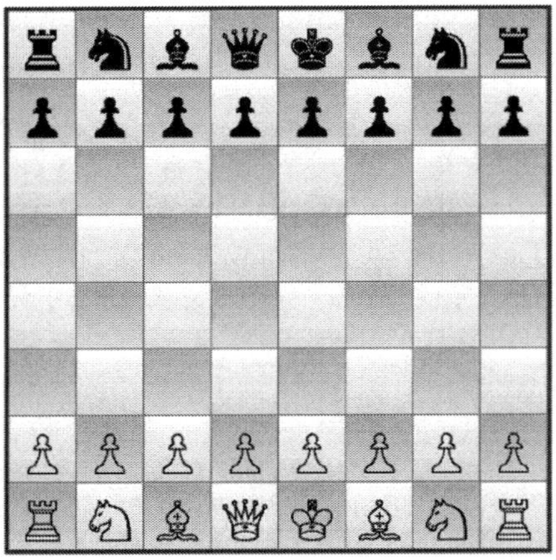

By doing this, you are (literally) not playing by the rules. Specifically, you are not abiding the ought-rule or norm, "when playing chess, you ought to move your horse in direction A". By doing this, you are effectively ending the game of chess. Either your friend continues playing and you invent new rules, so that you can still play a game (but not chess), or you stop playing.

The rules of the chess game, even if they do form a network of related rules which relates to a certain community (people who play chess), do not form a legal order and are thus not legal rules. There are two main differences between a non-legal social norm and a legal norm. One difference is that, in a legal situation, you cannot end the situation (or the game) by acting against the rules. The second is that, when considering a legal norm, the consequences of acting against the norm are imposed by an authoritative power. I will elaborate on both of these differences below.

1.2.2. IN A LEGAL SITUATION, YOU CANNOT END THE GAME

Both the law and the consequence related to acting against the law are inherent to the legal order. In some instances, it is possible to leave a legal order. For example, you can leave a state legal order by giving up your nationality after which you become stateless. In this way, at least from your perspective, you end the game of your previous state legal order. However, first, this is not always possible, especially not for children and, second, most state laws apply to anyone within the state territory regardless of their nationality and, third, you can certainly not do so after you have acted against a legal norm within this legal order and you have not yet suffered the consequences of this action as prescribed by the legal order.

Anyone who commits an illegal act is subject to the legal consequences within that legal order. In a social situation, if you act against a non-legal social norm, you can walk away and thereby end the social situation.[29] Of course, it may not be easy in a psychological sense to walk away when acting against a social norm, but it is physically possible. On the other hand, if you commit an illegal act within the legal order, you will generally be required by the executive powers of this legal order to suffer the consequences of violating a law, even if you declare that you want to leave the legal order. Compliance to the law will be ultimately enforced in a physical sense through use of physical force. Even if you physically manage to leave the legal order (if this is possible, since a legal order is a social and not a physical given[30], this will be forcefully prevented by the executive), you will always continue to be under the threat of a coercive act against you by the executive power of your semi-former legal order. The force of this threat and the level of prosecution differs depending on, among other things, the gravity of your illegal act, as perceived from the internal perspective of the legal order, and on the strength of the legal power of the executive, including available resources. However, theoretically you will always be perceived as being subject to a coercive act against you for having committed an illegal act. You will certainly not be allowed by this legal order to leave the legal order, to end your membership of this legal order before your debt is paid (if this would be allowed at all), while in non-legal social situations such as friendship or a game it would be possible to

29 In legal theory it is often debated whether we do not also suffer consequences of acting against social, non-legal norms, for example when your friend becomes angry at with you for not playing chess according to the rules. On this point, Kelsen writes that the moral order is usually considered as an order in which the principle of retribution is not applied and that it is therefore distinguished from a legal order. "However approval and disapproval of fellow members of the community are often sensed as reward and punishment" (1934/2002: 27, 28).

30 If you manage to leave the territory of a state, for example, this does not directly mean that you manage to leave the legal order.

leave.[31] Of course, as a legal consequence of your illegal act, you can be expelled from the legal order. This is a legal consequence you can suffer, which is imposed by the legal order and is independent of your individual wish.[32]

I can think of only two ways to leave the legal order after you have acted against a legal norm. One is to commit suicide and the other is to start a revolution and thereby overthrow the old legal order. Both these acts are usually illegal from the internal perspective of the legal order. Therefore, the only two ways to leave a legal order in this situation seems to be to end the existence of either yourself or the legal order, neither of which perhaps even constitutes "leaving". However, the important point here is that, generally, leaving a legal order by choice is often impossible (especially for children, as we will see later), in particular when you have acted against the order's legal norms.

Surely some examples come to mind of non-state normative orders that adhere to the above given description of the impossibility of leaving the legal order, such as in the situation of honour killings. If someone who has acted against the family's normative rules tries to escape to avoid an honour killing, this person will be forever under the threat of a coercive act against him or her by the executive power of her/his semi-former (family) order.[33] I would argue that the family in this sense can be understood to be a legal order. This is a perspective that I will elaborate upon more in chapter 3 on children and legal pluralism.

1.2.3. THE POWER INEQUALITY BETWEEN SOVEREIGN AND SUBJECT

As was argued in §1.1, one of the reasons we consider a rule a law is because it has been created by an individual or group that the relevant community understands to be authorized to create laws.

In the chess example and the above paragraph, it was shown that not abiding by non-legal social norms has different consequences than not abiding by a legal norm. This is because the consequences of not abiding by legal norms are based on power inequality.[34] In the chess example, you and your friend, as players of the chess game, are on equal footing. No one is imposing the rules on the other and no one is inflicting consequences on the other. It may very well

31 An exception here is when you made (part of) your social situation into a legal relationship, such as in the situation of a legal marriage.

32 Sometimes, of course, one might suspect that the legal consequence (A) of illegal act (B) will be expulsion. Therefore, anyone wanting to leave the legal order might commit an illegal act (B) with the aim of activating legal consequences (A). However, the judicial decision on the legal consequence is always uncertain and depends on the will of the sovereign and not on the will of the individual, which are in an unequal power relationship to one and another.

33 See, for example, Dorjee et al. (2013).

34 See also §1.3 on law and power.

be that next time your friend will not want to play with you, but this is a social consequence (and a logical one, since you make it impossible to play chess). It is a social consequence, because it is dependent upon personal, subjective relations between equal subjects. There is no power inequality in the example. Legal norms are therefore different from non-legal social norms in that if you choose to ignore legal norms, you are to suffer legal consequences imposed on you by an authoritative power.

1.3. LAW AND POWER

The power inequality that we find when analyzing the relations between the sovereign and the subject of the law seems to be another defining aspect of law, since it is one of the ways in which we can draw a line between non-legal and legal norms. Therefore, I suggest we take a better look at the relations between (social) power and the law.

As we found in §1.1, law is a social fact. It is considered law because it has been created by an individual or group that the relevant community understands to be authorized to create laws. Therefore, a certain inequality has been created between the sovereign and its subjects.

1.3.1. AUTHORITY AND THE POWER OF THE SOVEREIGN

If we say that the relevant community understands an individual or group (in short, a sovereign) to be authorized to create laws, what does it mean "to be authorized"? In *Leviathan* (1654/1996), Hobbes explains the etymology of the word "authority", and the action of authorization, in the following way:

> A PERSON is he whose words or actions are considered, either as his own, or as representing the words or actions of another man, or of any other thing to whom they are attributed, whether truly or by fiction. When they are considered as his own, then is he called a natural person: and when they are considered as representing the words and actions of another, then is he a feigned or artificial person [...] Of persons artificial, some have their words and actions owned by those whom they represent. And then the person is the actor, and he that owneth his words and actions is the author, in which case the actor acteth by authority. [...][35]

Hobbes is saying that having authority means that an actor (fictional person) bears the actions of the author (natural person). Authority means the right to represent a natural person and an authorized act means that the natural

35 Hobbes (1654/1996: 157).

person has "licensed" an actor to represent her/him. Concretely, for Hobbes this means that the relevant community, as a group of people that consists of natural persons such as you and I, creates an artificial person, the sovereign (Leviathan). The sovereign is artificial. It is not a real, natural person. It is like an actor.

Just to make the point clear, even if the analogy does not work completely, consider that Shakespeare's Romeo is an artificial person and Shakespeare, as a natural person, is the author of all that Romeo says and does. In this relationship, Romeo is authorized by Shakespeare to declare his love to Juliet. Shakespeare is the author of Romeo's actions and words and, in this capacity, he is completely responsible for all of Romeo's utterances and actions. The difference here is that Romeo's actions and words are directly prescribed by Shakespeare, whereas the sovereign, as an artificial person, does (at least in part) act independently of the author. In the relationship between the subject towards the sovereign, the author (subject) is nevertheless still responsible for the actions and words of the sovereign according to Hobbes, because a subject enters into a covenant with an authority to which he transfers his right to self-govern.[36] For Hobbes, this relationship originates from a state of nature, because, in a state of nature, you are never completely safe, since every man has a right to everything, which also includes taking your possessions, killing you, etc. People institute a sovereign because, in a state of nature, "every man has a right to every thing; even to one another's body. And therefore, as long as this naturall Right of every man to every thing endureth, there can be no security to any man".[37] Since man's passions incline men to peace, out of fear of death[38], and in a state of nature, which is a state without law[39], there is a war of all against all and men live in continual fear[40], they covenant amongst themselves to submit to a sovereign. In other words: by covenant they create an artificial person, a Leviathan, and they appoint one man to bear the responsibility for their person of whose actions they are the author.[41]

I want to raise the question of the legitimacy of the sovereign, for which Hobbes needs the idea of the insecurity in the state of nature, between brackets for the moment. What is important for now is the idea of authorization. Without the sovereign, men have no law.[42] By the act of authorization, they erect a "common power". They

36 Hobbes (1651/1996: 120).

37 Ibid: 91.

38 Ibid: 90.

39 Ibid: 90.

40 Ibid: 88-90.

41 Ibid: 120.

42 Except for natural law, which in Hobbes is a concept different from the notion of "law" that we maintain here. In fact, Hobbes seems to agree when he writes: "Where there is no common Power, there is no Law: where no Law, no Injustice" (1651/1996: 90).

> [...]conferre all their power and strength upon [the sovereign][43], [...] that may reduce all their Wills, by plurality of voices, unto one Will [...] This is more than Consent, or Concord; it is a real Unitie of them all, in one and the same Person, made by Covenant of every man with every man, in such manner, as if every man should say to every man: I Authorise and give up my Right of Governing my selfe to [the sovereign] [...] This is the generation of that great LEVIATHAN [...] And in him consisteth the Essence of the Commonwealth; which, (to define it,) is One Person, of whose Acts a great Multitude, [...] have made themselves every one the Author, [...] And he that carryeth this person is called Soveraigne, and said to have Soveraigne Power; and every one besides, his Subject.[44]

The people then subject themselves and they give up their right to govern themselves. By doing this, they confer *power* upon the sovereign; this is to say that the power of the sovereign over its subjects derives from the authorization of the sovereign by the subjects. Do not forget that this sovereign is an *artificial person* and not a *natural person*. This means that, even in a pure democracy, the people all together (although in practice this always excludes certain groups of people such as, notably, children) can constitute the sovereign. When, in a Rousseauian fashion, they gather together to discuss matters of law and politics, and establish a new law in this meeting, this law is the will of the sovereign to which all subjects (natural persons) of the relevant community must submit their individual will.[45]

1.3.2. RECOGNITION OF THE BASIC NORM

In the terminology of Searle, the power of the sovereign is derived from the fact that the status function of the sovereign is accepted by the relevant community, whereby "acceptance" does not mean "approval". According to Searle, acceptance in this context means anything from enthusiastically embracing to begrudgingly endorsing. To avoid confusion, I will use the term "recognition".[46]

---

43 Hobbes speaks here of "one man, or an assembly of men", thereby indicating that a sovereign as an artificial person can consist of one person or several people, even of all in a democracy (ibid: 120).

44 Ibid: 120-21.

45 For Rousseau (1762/1977: 184), every person of the people is an indivisible part of the body of the sovereign. The people as individuals are called "citoyens" as participants in the authority of the sovereign, and "subjects" insofar as they are subjected to its laws (for Hobbes, citoyens are those who together form the artificial person of the sovereign, whereas subjects are natural persons)).

46 Searle (1995: 39-41, 69; 2011: 8). Searle argues that this also includes the situation in which someone finds himself helpless and unable to do anything about the situation in which s/he finds himself. Recognizing thus does not mean approval. Hate, apathy and despair are consistent with the recognition of what one hates, is apathetic about or despairs of changing (2011: 8).

In Searle's terminology, for the continuation of the existence of a social fact, the individuals involved and a sufficient number of members of the relevant community have to keep recognizing these social facts. If they are to function, it is essential for there to be a continuing recognition of the status (in this case, of the sovereign as sovereign and of the law as law). In the event of the refusal of a social fact (and therefore its status function) it ceases to exist.[47] That is to say that the sovereign exists and has its power only because it is recognized as such by the relevant community[48] or because it is authorized to be the sovereign and to rule over the relevant community by this community. Alternatively, in Kelsian terms, the authorization of the legislator or the (attribution of) empowerment to the legislator leads back to recognition by the relevant community of the basic norm.

This same notion of recognition of the basic norm is connected to the generation of power, which is made most clear by Barnes' notion of the "ring of reference".[49] This concept refers to a relevant community that attributes meaning to a certain object, event or person. It is the ring of reference that creates legal power. Haugaard illustrates this with the following example:

> what distinguishes the actual Napoleon from the "napoleons" who are found in psychiatric institutions is not internal to them but the fact the former (unlike the latter) had a substantial ring of reference which validates his power.[50]

Although there are probably more differences between the actual Napoleon and "napoleons" in psychiatric institutions, the example clearly shows is that (legal) power is not self-referring. In other words, believing you are the sovereign does not make you sovereign. The sovereign is made by the recognition of this status function, the authorization, by the relevant legal community or, as Haugaard explains this point, "[...] power is not a zero-sum phenomenon which exists 'out there' in the world as a pre-given entity. Rather, power is created by social order".[51]

Maybe the point becomes clearer if we imagine the inverse happening. When in history class I learned about the Second World War, I often thought about the following. In 1940 the German forces invaded the Netherlands. After five days of fighting, the Dutch forces surrendered and the Netherlands was occupied by Germany, including having control over the Dutch legal administration.[52] Imagine that the Dutch people, collectively, would not have recognized the

---

47 Searle (1995: 117).

48 See also Weber: "it should be kept in mind that the basis of every authority, and correspondingly of every kind of willingness to obey, is a *belief*, a belief by virtue of which persons exercising authority are lent prestige" (1922/1978: 263).

49 Barnes (1988).

50 Haugaard (2008: 122).

51 Ibid: 119.

52 Warmbrunn (1968: chapter 2).

authority of the German occupier. Imagine that they would have collectively treated the German legal administration (legislative, judiciary and executive) as if they were "napoleons" in psychiatric institutions. Imagine that the Dutch people would have understood all the German Decrees as a madman's fantasy (surely the "napoleons" spend some of their time writing decrees in their institutions). This would leave the German government completely powerless in the Netherlands. Surely compliance with proposed norms could still be enforced using (physical) violence by the German executive forces, but this would then, at least in the eyes of the Dutch people, be no more than a criminal forcing an individual to comply with his command at gunpoint.[53]

1.4. STATUTORY LAW[54]

Since it was argued that law derives from the sovereign, an artificial body who is recognized by the relevant community as having legal power and therefore being able to create law, we refer here to statutory law.

In this section, I will start with questioning whether law needs a sovereign. If this can be answered positively, I will continue to construct a new conceptual framework for understanding statutory law that outlines a broader understanding and application of the concept than is common in modern legal theory.

1.4.1. DOES LAW NEED A SOVEREIGN?

In this chapter, the sovereign has been understood as the artificial person (consisting of one or more natural people) who has legislative power due to the acceptance by the relevant community of the basic norm regulating its legal power. Which persons exactly constitute the sovereign is a very complicated question to which the answer is different for every legal order.

Still the question is left open whether a legal order in general needs a sovereign or whether laws can exist without a sovereign. Obviously, the answer to this question depends on the (often implicit) definition one has of a sovereign. Rodolfo Sacco argues that the "lawgiver" is a recent innovation, in the actual meaning of a central authority entrusted with overall legislative powers:

---

53 In fact, this is what happened more and more towards the end of the war. While in the first years following the occupation, German power was relatively recognized, "[...] from 1943 on many German regulations increasingly remained empty paper gestures frustrated directly or indirectly by the Resistance, patriotic officials, and the population at large" (Ibid: 28).

54 A large part of the argument as presented in this section has been published, in a slightly different version and form, in the Journal of Legal Pluralism. See: Hopman (2017).

> It is a premise of modern legal theory that there is such an authority empowered to create whichever legislation it deems appropriate [...] This has not always been the case. The function of creating law was left, in time too recent to be ignored, to God [...] In other legal traditions, the rules of social interaction were thought to mirror a cosmic order [...] More often law preceded any individual design (mores mark the origins of Roman Law and customs those of the Common Law). Human power intervenes to regulate and improve the rules [...] or to reduce all existing laws to a unitary body of written law [...] This power of marginal intervention should not be confused with the power of destroying an existing body of law and replacing it with new one. [...] The idea of an overall legislative power is asserted only after the French Revolution [...] Before the end of the 18th century, law lived without a lawgiver.[55]

Whether he is right that law existed without a lawgiver, really depends on the definition one adheres to of a sovereign. Sacco identifies the sovereign power with the state.[56] Under that definition, many of these sources of law would not be sovereigns. However, we have identified the sovereign as an artificial person, who has legislative power due to the recognition of the basic norm regulating its legal power by the legal community.[57] Under that definition, God and his representatives on Earth can also be a sovereign, as well as the wise members of the community who explain which laws are to be obeyed to correctly mirror the cosmic order. In addition, Sacco argues that, in the past, law preceded any individual design. In reply, I would argue that for a social non-legal norm to turn into a legal norm, it needs an authority, a sovereign who decides what is law and what is not a law (even if the rule itself is not explicitly designed by the sovereign, as in the chthonic tradition described by Glenn (see below)). I agree with Sacco that rarely, if ever, law emerges out of nothing. A sovereign never starts from zero, but instead it works with existing social norms. For the legislator, there is no reason to intervene in existing social practices when there is no discrepancy between the norm and the de facto social situation. Only when there is a discrepancy, the legislator (sometimes) moves from apathy into action.[58] Moreover, often a sovereign emerges from the relevant community and this person or group of people therefore, as a natural person, has already internalized great parts of normative tradition (including the legal tradition) of the relevant community. If not, the sovereign at least has to take in account the existing social normative practices.

55 Sacco (1995: 455-56).

56 "The sovereign power – which, where it is found, is stable and operates through specialized and technically competent agencies – is the State. The State has not always existed. It was created when the sovereign power started to be exercised over society in a coherent way" (Ibid: 467).

57 See §1.1 and §1.3.

58 I explained this point more elaborately in my MA thesis, see Hopman (2014a: 62-65).

Glenn seems to argue that the earliest Chthonic legal traditions[59] lacked a sovereign, when he argues that "[a] chthonic legal tradition simply emerged, as experience grew and orality and memory did their work".[60] However, he also points out how in a wide world of chthonic peoples:

> the most common feature appears to be a council of elders, individual people who, by their assimilation of tradition over a longer period of time, often speak with greater authority [...] Councils of elders may be supplemented, or even replaced, by chiefs, but rule by chiefs is also necessarily a consultative form of rule.[61]

While arguably the form of sovereignty here differs greatly from the sovereign in a modern state legal order, I would argue that the council of elders and/or the chief would in these instances constitute the sovereign, possibly together with their ancestors. Even if the elders/chiefs only have a consultative form of rule, meaning that they answer the questions of the people with regard to the law without assuming they created the law (because the law was created in the past, by their ancestors, and they are simply asked to *remember* the law), they are the direct legal authority of the relevant community. The position can be compared to that of a priest who represents God on earth and who translates the will of God into earthly laws.[62] Since society is always changing, the representative of a legislator who is not physically present has legal power (in a way, he or she is *authorized* to represent God, which confers legal powers upon the representative). This is expressed for example by means of selection (rule A is a law, rule B is a tradition but not a law), its adaption of the traditional rules to more modern times, etc.

I want to argue that every legal order has a sovereign. This sovereign may differ greatly in form and substance. However, without a sovereign there is no difference between social non-legal norms or legal norms. Without a sovereign, in my opinion, there is no law.[63]

---

59 According to Glenn, Chtonic people were people who lived ecological lives, who live in or in close harmony with the earth (2010: 63).

60 Glenn (2010: 63).

61 Ibid: 66-67.

62 Sacco also identifies non-human authorities or sources of law, such as a deity or pharaohs (who often perceived themselves, and/or were perceived, as Gods) (1995: 455). I would argue that these constitute the sovereign, with the annotation that obviously they do not function alone; deities will need a human representative on earth, which can be magicians, priests, etc.

63 I understand that by this statement I argue indirectly against a lot of literature on customary law. However, it seems to me that for customary law to be labeled as "law" by the relevant community to which the law applies, they need an authority who is authorized to determine which possible rules are considered law and which are not. I have explained this point more at length under §1.7.

1.4.2. BEYOND THE DE JURE / DE FACTO DISTINCTION

To understand the socio-legal position of the child in the international legal community, understanding law as (any kind of) formal written law that addresses citizens seems to be too limited a perspective.

To give an illustration, consider the following situation: a child has a formal right to education but is deprived of education by a government whose unwritten rule is, for example, that Muslim children are not allowed to enter schools. When reflecting on what this tells us about the legal order, one is inclined to conclude that there is a large discrepancy between the formal law and the reality on the ground. At least, this is the common view of legal scholars who often distinguish between de jure and de facto reality.[64] However, this de jure/de facto distinction seems dissatisfying for explaining the socio-legal situation that we are trying to understand in the example. In fact, I feel that applying the de jure/de facto distinction to the legal situation of the Muslim child actually obscures the *legal* understanding of the situation. In particular, the distinction leaves out common instances in which there is a difference between the formal, written law and (rule-based) policy actively pursued by the sovereign, both when this is and is not publicly known. Since the sovereign has legal power conferred upon it by its ring of reference, due to the recognition of the relevant community of the basic norm installing the sovereign, the rule of the sovereign that Muslim children are not allowed to enter schools has legal significance and legal consequences.

In many countries, formal laws related to children are in perfect harmony with the 1989 Convention on the Rights of the Child (CRC) and other international treaties and yet discrepancies between formal law and government policy are common. The government (in some cases) actively pursues a different policy than is written down in formal law, and this is well-known publicly, including the consequences of transgressing this unwritten law (as is the case with the example of the Muslim child).

I therefore propose a new conceptual framework for the understanding and study of statutory law. I argue that statutory law within a legal order can take on three different forms: 1) formal written law, 2) law for the community and 3) non-public law.

---

64 See, for example, the 2012 report by Haveman "The Hiil Rule of Law Quick Scan Rwanda", in which the current de jure legal situation of Rwanda is described and compared to the current de facto situation (using data from several reports by NGOs, government, research institutions). These two taken together result in "positive trends" and "main challenges" in relation to the rule of law in Rwanda. In the context of international law and statelessness, Laura van Waas has criticized the de jure/de facto distinction (2008: 20-27).

1.4.3. THE LEGAL ORDER OF THE SIXTH FLOOR

Consider the following scenario. I am sitting here at my desk, on the sixth floor of the building of the law faculty. For some time now, I have enjoyed the privilege of being the sovereign of this floor. All other colleagues on the sixth floor are my subjects (they recognize my position as a sovereign). You, as one of my subjects, come into my office. I immediately notice that you are wearing bright red lipstick. As you are well aware, because I have recently told all subjects, the only colour lipstick allowed on this floor is blue. I created this law a few months ago and, in fact, two people have already been fined and have paid these fines for wearing non-blue lipstick. Just as I am about to tell you to change your lips to blue and go to see law enforcement to pay your fine (third office on the left), Harry enters. Harry is from the seventh floor. He works for the International Community of Legal Floors (hereafter: ICLF), of which we are members, having signed the charter. Article 3c of the ICLF charter states that "anyone is free to use make-up in any way they please". Harry looks at me and says "I just came in to see how you are doing on freedom of lipstick colours these days. Do you have that report for me?" I point at the wall where "The Laws of the Sixth Floor", our constitution, is on public display. Two months ago, I took down this document to score out the old article 6 and write it anew. I had been hoping that Harry would pop in ever since. "Article 6, Harry", I say with a slight sneer. Harry lifts up his glasses, turns to the wall and reads our constitution. Article 6 states: "Any person is free to wear any make-up they like". Harry looks at me, nods happily, and walks away. Meanwhile I am thinking that I have to visit the ICLF soon to see about some donations, since we are doing so well concerning human rights. Then I realize that you are still in my room wearing red lipstick and I call law enforcement to come to pick you up.

Next, Sally enters. Sally is one of my closest advisors. She is wearing green lipstick. Being a state advisor, Sally falls under the protection of a secret legal act that I have written down on a document known to few, which I keep in my bureau drawer. On this document, it is stated that certain highly valued government officials are officially exempted from the blue-lipstick law.

After this exposé, what would you say is the law? Harry clearly thought the law of the sixth floor could be known completely by studying the formal written law. Would you agree if you nevertheless had to pay a fine in the law enforcement office? If you are courageous enough, or foolish enough, to go upstairs to ICLF to complain, they would probably argue that there is a de jure right to wear any colour of lipstick on the sixth floor, although the de facto situation is different (and unfortunately there is not much they can do for you). You on the other hand might argue that "The Laws of the Sixth Floor" is just a document, a meaningless piece of paper and that, in fact, the law states that you can only wear blue lipstick.

I would agree with you (although not publicly, for obvious reasons). In fact, I want to argue that, within any legal order, there are three distinguished forms of statutory law, with statutory law understood in a broad sense as law created by the legislature. These three forms of law will be called "formal written law", "law for the community" and "non-public law".

1.4.4. DEFINING THE THREE FORMS OF STATUTORY LAW

I will distinguish statutory law according to the three forms it can take on. In our legal order, of which I am the legislator, there are three different forms of law. One is the formal written law, the constitution, which is the law that is recorded on the document on my wall. Secondly, there is the law for the community which I have declared to all my subjects, namely, that the only colour of lipstick allowed on the sixth floor is blue. Thirdly, there is the non-public law that one can find on the secret document that I keep in my bureau drawer, which states that government officials are exempted from the lipstick law. All three are statutory law, which is law created by the legislator, because they are created by the sovereign (legislator) who is legitimized, through recognition of the basic norm stipulating this legislative power, by the relevant community to create laws.

For any legal order, statutory law can thus be analyzed in relation to these three forms. Taken together, they constitute the statutory law of the legal order. The three forms and their respective categories can be schematized as follows:

	Formal written law (A)	law for the community (B)	hidden law (C)
Written	+	B1	C1
Unwritten	–	B2	C2
Public	+	+	–

In general, the first form of law, the formal written law (A) is found in official legal codes. It can be defined as rules found in official, formal legal texts, that are created by the legislature and open and available to the public. This form of law is necessarily written and necessarily public.

The second form of law, the law for the community (B), refers to what the subjects of a legal order believe the law actually is and what the law tells them, under the condition that this belief is the result of a relevant legislative act. It can be defined as rules created by the legislator, known by the subjects of the legal order. There are two kinds of law for the community: written and unwritten laws (B1 and B2). In case the formal written law and the law for the community overlap, the formal written law is the written law for the community (B1). To say that they overlap amounts to saying that the relevant community knows the formal, written law. In practice, the only situation in which (A) and (B1) completely overlap is in a situation of direct democracy or when a legislature is equal to its subjects. In any other legal order, legal codes are usually full of laws that the community is unaware of and therefore it is not law to them in this sense.[65] The conceptual distinction between formal written law (A) and written law for the community (B1) can be a useful epistemological distinction to research these instances.

The unwritten law for the community (B2) is more complicated. This can occur in two situations: either in a situation of a legal order that has no formal written law (B2i) or in a situation when a unwritten law for the community contradicts the formal written law (B2ii). When a legal order does not have formal written law (situation B2i), laws can be merely unwritten and in some sense non-formal. In this case, there is no A law. In order to study such a legal order, one has to engage in qualitative research with both the legislator and the subjects of the relevant order.[66] This kind of legal order will not likely be found among current state legal orders. It can be the situation in a more primitive legal order or a non-state legal order in a situation of legal pluralism or in a state of nature.[67] For example, when one views domestic law as law and the family as a legal order, this order usually consists of informal and unwritten law.[68]

The second situation in which unwritten law for the community occurs, namely when a unwritten law for the community contradicts formal written law (situation B2ii), comes to the fore when the subjects of a legal order have knowledge of a law, issued by the legislator, that contradicts the formal written law. In this case one finds that there are unwritten rules created by the legislature, which the people of the relevant community recognize (which means that they have a relation of recognition to the law, meaning: they abide, relate to, believe to be, live up to, break, etc. the law). It is not about the choice of the individual who breaks or abides the law, it is about what law is recognized by the subjects of a legal order, based on a justified belief in the legality of this rule.[69] So when a group of psychiatric patients belief the government is ordering all citizens to kill birds, yet no such law has been created, this is not an unwritten law for the community. My law that forbids the wearing of non-blue lipstick for all subjects

65 See for example van Gestel (2008) who describes the utopic idea that the relevant community of a state legal order knows its laws completely. According to van Gestel, there is a distance between law in the legal codes and law in practice (3). Ehrlich in this context argues that "[a] juristic science which conceives of law as a rule of conduct could not consistently have laid down a principle that men are bound by the law even though they do not know it; for one cannot act according to a rule that one does not know" (1936/1975: 12).

66 See also chapters 3 and 4.

67 Hobbes, for example, defines the family in a state of nature as a "little Monarchy", wherein the dominion that parents have over their children is analogous to the dominion of the sovereigns over their subjects (1651/1996: 142).

68 See e.g. de Sousa Santos (2002: 385-388) and further chapters of this thesis.

69 Where "justified belief", following Kelsen relates to the fact that the law is created by the legislator, receiving its validity from the constitution (basic norm).

of the sixth floor, is an unwritten law for the community that contradicts formal written law.

A real-life example in modern society of an unwritten law for the community that contradicts formal written law (B2ii) would be the Dutch soft drug law. According to Dutch formal written law, the "Opium Law" (A), it is forbidden to sell (among other things) hash, weed and magic mushrooms, which are categorized as "soft drugs".[70] This same law designates which executive powers are responsible for the enforcement of this law[71] and how enforcement should happen.[72] Punishment for anyone selling drugs can be either a prison sentence of two to five months or a fine.[73] However, as most Dutch citizens (and non-Dutch, for that matter) know, "coffeeshops" selling all kinds of hash, weed and magic mushrooms, are thriving in the Netherlands. This is not due to the inefficaciousness of the legislator; it is the unwritten law of the Dutch legislator that allows for the selling of soft drugs by coffeeshops under certain conditions. This policy is called "gedoogbeleid" ("tolerance policy") (B). Information about this tolerance policy can be found in several places, such as in academic writing[74] and on the government website[75], although it directly contradicts the formal written law.[76]

70 Dutch Opium Law (*Opiumwet*) (art. 2(b), 3(b)(1)).

71 Ibid: art. 8(j), 8(k).

72 Ibid: art. 9.

73 Ibid: art. 11.1-11.3.

74 See for example Buruma (2007). Buruma distinguishes "legal tolerance" and "cultural tolerance". Tolerance as a legal concept, according to Buruma, "[o]rdinarily [..] means that administrative or punitive reactions are postponed if the perpetrator agrees to act according to precise instructions. In certain fields – for instance, environmental law – there exists something called a 'tolerace order' (gedoogbeschikking), which means that the local or provincial authorities promise to not punish for a certain period under certain conditions. Such an order is legally binding on the relationship between local authorities and citizens. However, it is not the same as a permit (and if the Public Prosecutor finds out, he is free to prosecute)" (85-86). According to the author, this system is clever from a pragmatic and especially from a rule-of-law perspective, because of the public character of tolerance compared to secret tolerance in other legal orders (87). Legal pubic tolerance, then, in general is a category of law for the community, whereas legal secret tolerance would be a category of non-public law. Bruinsma (2003: 60) explains the Dutch practice of "*gedogen*" by saying that they apply to crimes without victims. In these cases, "the law in the books symbolically keeps up moral condemnation, while the law in action formulates a policy of non-enforcement".

75 See: Rijksoverheid (n.d.) *Gedoogbeleid softdrugs en coffeeshops.*

76 The example of Dutch *gedoogbeleid* illustrates that unwritten law does not necessarily have to be orally communicated law (such as a direct verbal command by the legislator). Instead, there can be (informal) documents describing the law, without actually stating the unwritten law or recognizing the law as law. An example of this is the information on *gedoogbeleid* provided on the website of the Dutch government. It describes the workings of an unwritten law, to which it implicitly refers. For example, its first line states that "Soft drugs are less harmful for public health than hard drugs. Coffeeshops are allowed to sell cannabis under strict conditions", thereby referring to an unwritten law which states that coffeeshops are allowed to sell cannabis. The document further lists these conditions. The same kind of documents explaining the workings of formal written laws can be found on the government website – usually these documents are used to turn complicated formal written law into law for the community.

The third form of law, the hidden law (C), constitutes the level of hidden power and corruption. It can be defined as non-public rules created by the legislature, known only to a specific group of people. There are two kinds of this form of statutory law; written and unwritten non-public laws (C1 and C2). The written lipstick law that I created for government officials, that I keep in my bureau drawer and that Sally knows about, is an example of a C1 category non-public law. To give an example in real-life modern society, I would like to refer to the USA/National Security Agency (hereafter: NSA) practice of domestic surveillance before this was revealed to the public by E. Snowden. In this case, the formal written law (A) stated that the collections of communications without a warrant are allowed when at least one end of the communication is a non-US person.[77] However, for the NSA, a "top-secret document" was created, under legal authority enabling the agency to warrant read emails and tapping phone calls between US citizens (C1).[78]

A possible example of an unwritten non-public law (C2) might be the rule-based permission for certain high party officials to take public money and use it for their personal gain, which is said to happen and/or have happened in Uganda. A recent report by Human Rights Watch and the Yale Law School argues that corruption in Uganda, benefitting the high-positioned government officials is indeed allowed by the legislator. They imply the existence of an underlying unwritten non-public rule when they argue that "[y]ears of evidence indicate that Uganda's current political system is built on patronage and that ultimately high-level corruption is rewarded rather than punished".[79] In fact, the report is a good example of how the ever-implicit de jure/de facto distinction obscures the actual legal situation of finances and corruption, in this case in Uganda. All the report can state is that there is a law (A) and what the law states does not de facto happen. For example, according to the report,

> Existing Ugandan laws require 'leaders' to disclose financial assets. This is an enormously important obligation that, if implemented, would greatly enhance the transparency of public officials' finances and likely deter public graft. The public also has a right to information (deemed in the public interest) under the constitution and the Access to Information Act. Despite the numerous laws, however, Uganda's regulatory framework to combat corruption fails to apply the requirement of asset declarations to presidential appointees and other high level officials, the tribunal to challenge the content of declarations has never been established, and there is no system for the public to access information regarding financial assets of officials.[80]

---

77 Fisa Amendments Act of 2008.

78 Ball & Ackerman (2013) "NSA Loophole Allows Warrantless Search for US Citizens' Emails and Phone Calls", The Guardian (2015) "The NSA Files", Waterman (2013) "Documents on Secret Court Rulings for NSA Operations to be Released".

79 Human Rights Watch (2013: 2).

80 Ibid: 27.

This kind of analysis implies that the law is "correct" and that it is only a matter of enforcing the law by, for example, setting up a proper system for the public to access this information. However, the problem is not necessarily a question of lacking resources or lack of practical solutions, but rather the cause of corruption here lies with Ugandan unwritten non-public law, created by the legislator for an elite group. This law, judging from the analysis in the report, would, in written form, be something like "the president and other high-level officials are exempted from law (A) that requires existing Ugandan leaders to disclose financial assets". The corrupt government high-level officials do not just take money on their private initiative; they abide by unwritten, non-public rules. In general, corruption usually falls under this category of unwritten, non-public (C2) laws.[81] Obviously, C laws, and in particular C2 laws, are extremely difficult to research.

1.4.5. WRITTEN AND UNWRITTEN LAW

On the Sixth Floor, I am the legislator and the laws that I establish are valid because I am authorized to be the legislator (by the constitution or basic norm). If you question the validity of the lipstick law, asking "why am I not allowed to wear red lipstick?", the answer will be "because you have to obey the rules of the sovereign" or "because you have to obey the law". Note that this answer does not answer the ethical objection that you might have to the lipstick law and maybe even to my position as sovereign.[82] The legitimacy or validity of my authorization lies in the constitution of the Sixth Floor that is recognized by the relevant community. This recognition renders my laws on the whole efficacious.[83]

However, you might argue that the lipstick law is not a law, because I did not write it down in a law book. Many western-centred legal researchers and legal practitioners insist on the formal written law as a condition for understanding it as "law". Kelsen for example, expressly states that "the law as the product of the legislative procedure, a statue in the formal sense of the term, is a document

81 For a discussion on corruption in relation to the legal order, see: Nuijten & Anders (2007). The editors argue that "[...] most important, we take distance from the commonly held view that corruption is simply the law's negation, a vice afflicting the body politic. Instead, we argue that corruption and the law are not opposites but constitutive of one another. Thus, we propose an approach that transcends binary oppositions and explores the hidden continuities between corruption and its antonyms law and virtue" (2). See also, among others, Schneider & Schneider (2005) on Italian governments "looking the other way" in relation to criminal activities of the Maffia; Shore (2005) on nepotism and corruption within the European Commission; Lazar (2005) on corruption on local and state level in Bolivia.

82 See §1.3.3 – 1.3.5.

83 The recognition of the basic norm, and the resulting efficaciousness of my legal order, can be deduced from the fact that there is an operative law enforcement and the fact that several people have already paid a fine for wearing the wrong color lipstick.

containing words, sentences [...]"[84], challenging the possibility of both law for the community that is not in conformity with the formal written law (since this needs to be unwritten law or, at least, not written in formal legal codes) and for unwritten non-public law.

Kelsen is in this respect exemplary for modern legal scholars. Although being written and formal is mostly not explicitly mentioned as a requirement of statutory law, it is often implied.[85] This is especially apparent in legal research methodology, which generally focusses on the study of legal codes, or on the effect of formal written law on the subjects addressed.[86] The underlying and, in my opinion, false assumption of modern legal scholars is that, for law to be law, for a statute to be legal, a law created by the legislature needs to be a written document filed in legal codes.

Since the issue at stake here is at least partly an issue of semantics related to the concept of "statutory law", I will address its etymology. Beatrix Weber researched evidence of language contact in the parliament rolls of medieval England, comparing occurrence of Latin, French and English nouns. In French and Latin, the most frequent co-occurent noun was *estatut* or *statutum* respectively. In English, on the other hand, the most frequent complement by far was the word *act*.[87] According to Bennion, the English word statute was first used in a political / legal context by Matthew Paris in 1246 to describe a meeting of the first English parliament, when prelates gathered to

> [...] discuss the state of the realm. When this body's decrees became formal they were called Statutes, from the late Latin *statutum* a decree, decision or law. In this way we got the earliest statutes, from which we get the current term *statute law*. Shortly afterwards it became the custom to call a piece of such legislation by the name *Act* of Parliament from the medieval Latin *actus*.[88]

---

84 Kelsen (1945/2007: 123).

85 Boaventura de Sousa Santos writes about the meaning that Western culture attributes to writing as a ceremony and to the written product as expression of commitment. "It appears," he concludes, "that the writing and the written are a rhetorical topos in our socio-legal culture". This may explain the inclination of legal scholars to identify law with written formal (state) law. See de Sousa Santos (2002: 107-08). Allott in this context mentions "[...] the 'black-letter' lawyers who see law as norms and rules in books [...]" (1977: 3).

86 Of course, there are many exceptions to this general practice in law schools. However, often when legal researchers do look further than formal written law to understand the law, they often pass by "statutory law" to look for "common law" or other forms of non-statutory law. For an overview of the history of legal research methods, see for example: Nolasco et al. (2010); Siems & Sithigh (2012).

87 Weber (2011).

88 Bennion (2001: 29). According to Bennion, "statute law" has a double meaning; "One meaning is law in statutory form, that is the body of enacted law sometimes referred to (inaccurately) as the statute book. I shall refer to statute law in this sense as 'legislation'. The other meaning

Originally, the word *statute* refers to the decision of the sovereign and not to written legal documents. In much of the not western-centered legal theory oral legal culture is widely recognized and unwritten legal norms are often considered law.[89] In addition to unwritten customary law, which is not under discussion here, statutory law (understood as law expressing the will of the legislator) can also be unwritten.

1.4.6. THE THREE FORMS OF STATUTORY LAW, LEGAL PLURALISM AND SOCIOLOGY OF LAW

Lastly, I will address how the definition of the three forms of statutory law relate to debates on legal pluralism and sociology of law.

Since legal pluralism is generally defined as "a situation in which two or more legal systems coexist in the same social field"[90], and debates on legal pluralism usually amount to a discussion of the status of different legal orders within a single social field – a notion that at the very least requires different legislators, or sources of law – it does not pose a challenge to the current theory. In fact, if one adheres to the idea of legal pluralism, the currently proposed epistemology of law can in fact be a useful epistemology for researching these different forms. The distinction between the theory of the three forms of statutory law and the theory of legal pluralism is based on the fact that the legal order discussed is one legal order by virtue of having one sovereign. This is the defining feature that takes the current theory away from Pospisil's notion of legal levels[91], which addresses subgroups within a particular society. Pospisil argues that:

> [a]ny human society [...] does not possess a single consistent legal system, but as many such systems as there are functioning subgroups. Conversely, every functioning subgroup of a society regulates the relations of its members by its own legal system, which is of necessity different, at least in some respects, from those of other subgroups.

Provided one agrees with Pospisil, for each of these subgroups, the legal order can be analysed according to the three forms of statutory law. In fact, the conceptual framework at hand can be used to support what Oomen calls "the central mission of legal pluralism"; "[o]n the one hand, it is about setting out [...] that there are many different orders and systems that essentially perform the same function as law, and should thus also be studied and even recognized as

is the area of knowledge and skill concerned with the nature, functioning and interpretation of legislation" (Ibid: 7).

89 See for example Allott (1984: 59, 66); Sacco (1995: 460); Leman (2011: 28-29); Bishop (2008: 3).

90 Merry (1988).

91 See: Pospisil (1967).

such. In addition [...] to point out the limits of state law, and how law in action very rarely corresponds to law in the books".[92]

The current theory is likewise distinct from a theory of sociology of law. It is in fact a theory of normative jurisprudence and not of sociological jurisprudence or sociology of law. It is not concerned with observing actual human behaviour, discussing for example in what way the law influences what individual human beings actually do or how they perceive themselves; rather, it aims at "a structural analysis of law as a system of valid norms".[93] It does in part discuss attitudes towards law if we study the law for the community, but it does not question whether or not these attitudes influence human behaviour. The object of the study of statutory law is norms issued by law-creating authorities and not patterns of actual behaviour.[94]

Ehrlich and Isaacs argue that "the whole law is incapable of being included in legal provisions". They hereby refer to "social laws" that regulate social order in the absence of legal provisions.[95] Clearly, according to the proposed current theory, there is no law that is not a legal provision. The current conceptual framework denies the possibility of "social laws". There are indeed social norms and these are specifically non-legal, insofar as they are not statutory law as has been defined in this section.[96]

Pospisil in some way recognizes this when he argues in reply to Ehrlich, that Ehrlich's "living law" failed when he inquired into the nature of the inner ordering of society's subgroups, that "he failed to uncover within the associations formal or informal leaders who actually influenced and moulded what he called 'living law'".[97] Clearly, to understand a legal order, we need to understand its statutory law.

1.4.7. A NOTE ON CUSTOMARY LAW

For the purposes of the current research, I will focus on statutory law and leave customary law out of the analysis. At first it might seem that, by leaving out customary law, I will give an incomplete account of the law, because customary law seems to be an exception to the idea that laws are legal rules that derive from the legislator, since for customary law the source of law is social custom. However, I think that the following conceptualization of statutory law raises

92 Oomen (2015: 105-06).
93 Kelsen (1945/2007: 162-63).
94 Ibid: 163.
95 Ehrlich & Isaacs (1922).
96 See §1.4.7.
97 Pospisil (1967: 7).

great doubts over the role and existence of customary law. What has been defined as "customary law" would be understood, within the current conceptual framework, either as non-state statutory law or as non-legal social norms.

The laws of local tribes in several African countries, for example, were often labelled "customary law" by the colonizer. These laws were created by a legislature (for example a group of elders in the village) and shared orally, or by means of performances, with the relevant community[98], while these laws were "being lumped together under the single title of 'native customary law' by the colonial rulers.[99] Under the current framework, these laws are (non-state) unwritten statutory law for the community (B2) (see more below).

In international law, according to Shaw, "the existence of customary rules can be deduced from the practice and behaviour of states".[100] According to the framework presented in this chapter, this would be classified as either law for the community (if the legal community is aware of the unwritten rule-based practice of the state) or as hidden law (if by "the state" is meant a certain part of the state apparatus such as a specific part of government, and its rules are not made public). Alternatively, the latter could refer to illegal behaviour, depending on what is meant by "the state" (for example if the national police acts against the laws of the governments on its own initiative). Shaw writes that "the essence of custom according to article 38 [(1) of the statute of the International Court of Justice] is that it should constitute 'evidence of a general practice accepted of law'" (58). In explaining this "acceptance", he refers to "the psychological factor, the belief by a state that behaved in a certain way that it was under a legal obligation to act that way" (59), in other words, the principle of *opinio juris* (59). Leaving aside the difficulty of attributing such subjective attitudes, such as a belief about an abstract entity as "the state", this again does not solve the difficulty of distinguishing between a social and a legal norm. The state, according to this definition, has to believe that it was under a *legal* obligation to act in a certain way. Therefore, how does "the state" distinguish between a legal and a social obligation? I have elaborated on the criteria for distinguishing a social norm from a legal norm under §1.2. According to the current legal framework, therefore, a law is a statutory law or there is no law but only a social norm. A last option is that "the state", or anyone, may hold a false belief about the legality of a certain norm or rule. That does not make a certain rule a legal rule, as legality cannot be based purely on subjective belief.

However, if social orders do exist that possess all the characteristics of the legal order except the sovereign, whereby the relevant community considers this order a legal order with laws – as I heard may be the case in some Kenyan villages – this might be an exception to this general statement and, in that case, perhaps in the future this theoretical framework might have to be expanded.

98 Allott (1977: 26).
99 Allott (1984: 57). See also Ehrlich (1936/1975: 15).
100 Shaw (1997: 57).

CHAPTER 2
LAW FOR CHILDREN, AN ADULT PERSPECTIVE

When discussing laws concerning children, we usually (if not always) depart from an adult's perspective. This is not very surprising, since academic researchers are usually (if not always) adults. It is not very recent either; even Plato wrote about the child as a becoming-adult, who needs to be educated, because its soul is still incomplete (lacking the element of reason).[101] Laws in this sense are supposed to be instrumental to both the child in the process of becoming an adult and to society for its protection against the irrational acts of children. To understand laws that potentially violate a child's right, the chapter will start by studying the relationship between children and the law from the adult's perspective. In the next chapter, the perspective will be changed around, whereby the relationship between children and the law will be examined from a child's perspective.

This chapter will start with a general reflection on the distinction between the adult and the child (§2.1) and it will continue with a comparison of the child and the madman in relation to society (§2.2). It will end with a discussion of what this means for the relationship between law and children, and specifically for children's rights.

2.1. THE CHILD/ADULT DISTINCTION

In children's rights research, as well as in society in general, a categorical distinction is made between the child and the adult.[102] We (both adults and children) understand the child as necessarily distinct from the adult. Whether this is a universal fact has been debated in academic literature; both the historical[103]

101 Plato (381 B.C./2012: Books V, IX, XIII).

102 Skolnick argues that in part this "gap" between childhood and adulthood might be enlarged by Rousseau. She writes: "There is [..] another side to the Rousseauian celebration of childhood. Rousseau's assertions of the natural childishness of the child emphasized the distance between children and adults [...]" (1975: 46).

103 Notoriously, by Ariès who defines the idea of childhood as "an awareness of the particular nature of childhood, that particular nature which distinguishes the child from the adult, even the young adult" (128). According to Ariès, this awareness was lacking in medieval society,

and the cross-cultural[104] existence of the child have been discussed at length. As this is not the place to enter into this discussion, I want to simply point out that, across all times and places, it is impossible not to notice the difference between a new born baby and a full-grown man. As argued by Rutter and Rutter: "no amount of training will cause, say, a four-month-old to walk or talk, or a six-year-old to learn differential calculus".[105] Anthropologists Levine & New conclude that: "every human society studied recognizes a distinction between children and adults and the age-linked emergence of children's abilities to learn, work and participate in community activities as they grow and develop".[106]

We perceive a great distance between the child and adult. To overcome this distance is the task of the child. The goal of childhood is to transcend its temporary condition; it is socialization, normalization and the becoming of an adult.[107] This position is not just the adult perspective; it is the child's perspective too, expressed by children accusing each other of "childish behaviour", by children studying at school because "I want to find a job later", etc. Adults may sometimes express the wish for children to "enjoy childhood while they still can" and to play and have no worries. However, at the same time, (almost?) no parent would agree with their child not going to school but instead to focus completely on play and fun, out of concern for the child-as-future-adult.

2.2. CHILDHOOD, MADNESS AND SOCIALIZATION

When wondering about the relationship between children, the law and society, and how children as newcomers to society can nevertheless be considered obliged to respect laws that they did not make nor consent to[108], I think that a comparison between childhood and madness as perceived categories of "otherness" in society may offer a partial explanation.[109] I do not want to argue that in some sense children are mad. What struck me when studying Foucault's

"that is why, as soon as the child could live without constant solicitude of his mother, his nanny or his cradle-rocker, he belonged to adult society. (…) The infant who was too fragile as yet to take part in the life of adults simply 'did not count'(…)" (1962: 128). In another passage he claims that there is "no doubt the discovery of childhood began in the thirteenth century" (47). For a reply to Ariès' arguments, see Archard (1993).

104 E.g. Mead (1928); James & Prout (1997/2005).

105 Rutter & Rutter (1993: 195).

106 Levine & New (2008: 3).

107 Cf. Anderson & Claassen (2012: 510):"'surely a regime of childhood should enable a process of maturation".

108 Although here "law" still seems to refer to state law, it can refer to any kind of law in society, including law in the household.

109 Cf. Smith (2011: 35): "Discourses of childhood can be deployed in ways which simultaneously obscure and reinforce unequal relations of power such as those based on class, race or gender. We know from Foucault (1977) that discourses are 'normalizing' in that they operate to differentiate between the 'normal' and the 'abnormal'".

work on madness and civilization were the similarities between society's reaction to the mad and society's reaction to the child.[110] Both categories of otherness have been argued to be purely socially attributed status-functions to people[111], although it seems that biological/physical functions play a role too (and thus that both categories are status functions assigned to people not *just* based on sociological assumptions but also based on brute facts).[112]

To begin our exploration of the similarities between childhood and madness, I want to start with presenting two case studies. Case study 1 originates from Foucault's work, drawing on a situation described by psychiatrist Diemerbroek, while case study 2 originates from my personal experience.

Case study 1: Demon

A man ...his mind was attached to a fixed idea, and this idea was for him the occasion of a constantly renewed sadness. He accused himself of having killed his son, and in the excess of his remorse, declared that God, for his punishment, had assigned a demon to tempt him, like the demon which had tempted the Lord. This demon he saw, spoke to, heard, and answered. He did not understand why those around him refused to acknowledge such a presence. Such then is madness: this remorse, this belief, this hallucination, these speeches; in short, this complex of convictions and images which constitutes a delirium. Now Diemerbroek tries to find out what are the "causes" of this madness, how it can have originated. And this is what he learns: this man had taken his son bathing and the boy had drowned. Hence the father considered himself responsible for his son's death [...] judging himself guilty, the man decides that homicide is execrable in the sight of God on High [...] he tells himself "that a horrible demon is assigned to him." [...] he imposes in his brain a certain image of this demon; this image is presented to his soul by the action of the brain and of the spirits with such insistence that he believes he continually sees the demon itself.[113]

---

110 It is important to note that Foucault's work is, for a big part, based on a historical analysis of the relationship between madness and (non-mad) society. Therefore, the several elements of madness as perceived by society, indicated by Foucault, relate to different periods in history. To me it is not completely clear from Foucault's work which of these elements remain in the current relationship between madness and society and which belong to the past. Thus, in the following discussion, I have chosen to highlight several elements of madness, as indicated by Foucault, that I feel are recognizable for a large group of people in their perception of, and relation to, madness. In addition, the following elements of (society's perception of) madness are highlighted because they bear a resemblance to (society's perception of) childhood.

111 Jenks (1996: 7), Brocklehurst (2009: 265).

112 On childhood: Fortin (2009: 83). See also Rodham 1973, as quoted by Skolnick (1975: 41): "Obviously this dependency [of children on adults] can be explained to a significant degree by the physical, intellectual and psychological incapacities of (some) children which render them weaker than (some) older persons. But the phenomenon must also be seen as part of the organization and ideology of the political system itself". "Brute facts" are facts that exist in an objective reality regardless of human conventions (see §1.1).

113 Foucault (1961/2001: 90-91).

Case study 2: Fetje
I used to know a four-year old child who was afraid of a shadow on the wall. Around bedtime, she would begin to stall; she did not want to go to bed because she was afraid of this shadow that she called "Fetje". Her parents could not see this figure, but they did believe that the child saw it. They noticed a connection between days with more stress and the occurrence of the evil shadow and explained this as a child's way of dealing with emotions, fear, anger and perhaps a feeling of lacking control. In addition, the parents were sometimes annoyed by the "presence" of this figure, since it made the going-to-bed ritual complicated. The mother gave the following description: "I did not see Fetje, but I could tell that for my child it was real, my daughter was really scared […] Fetje could be pretty coercive, for my child and for me, because he kept asking for attention. Sometimes my daughter after going to bed kept calling for us to come and see her. Sometimes I wasn't sure whether he was really there, or whether it was just a call for attention". When asked whether she ever thought her daughter displayed signs of madness, she answered, almost insulted: "NO. I think that every child has a similar phase. Children see ghosts, monsters, they have no grip on the world. Maybe they don't have words". The father agreed, arguing that "all children have fears. About what happens to them when they close their eyes, if they're still there, whether others are still there. An explanation or interpretation obviously uses words that a child does not yet possess". The parents ultimately found the following "solution": "We acknowledged the existence of Fetje. We started sending Fetje away by telling him to go away. We taught our daughter to do the same. Then one day, he was gone".

In both situations the description from the internal perspective would be similar. For the man who sees the demon and the child who sees Fetje, this figure is real and threatening. It is as Foucault describes:

> […] only the mind can turn what is given in the image into abusive truth, in other words, into error, or acknowledged error, that is, into truth […] Madness is thus beyond imagination, and yet it is profoundly rooted in it; for it consists merely in allowing the image a spontaneous value, total and absolute truth. The act of the reasonable man who, rightly or wrongly, judges an image to be true or false, is beyond this image, transcends and measures it by what it is not itself; the act of the madman never oversteps the image presented, but surrenders to its immediacy […].[114]

According to Foucault, it is the mind that turns a fantastic image into an erroneous truth. We can all think about ghosts and then we take a reflective position in relation to this image. We think, "is it real or not?" According to Foucault, the madman lacks this moment of reflection. He "never oversteps the image presented, but surrenders to its immediacy", thereby staying inside the imagination as if it is the real world.

Another observation by Foucault on the erroneous worldview of the madman corresponds to both accounts of erroneous beliefs, the demon and

114 Ibid: 88-89.

Fetje, namely that "[t]he reasonings of the madman are in themselves neither absurd or illogical".[115] In itself, the reasoning of the man ("I have killed my son – this cannot be forgiven by God – God was tempted by a demon – so I am being followed by a demon who wants to tempt me") is not illogical, and neither is the reasoning of the child ("there is an evil shadow on the wall in my bedroom – it is better not to go to bed").

Both descriptions from the external viewpoint of both situations show several similarities. Notice how both the parents in the second story, and the psychiatrist in the first, take a rational and distanced position in relation to the "erroneous belief". They acknowledge the feelings of the person who is unreasonable; for the man, the "idea was for him the occasion of a constantly renewed sadness", the child was "really scared". Both resort to rationally explaining the causes of these erroneous beliefs; the man "imposes in his brain a certain image of this demon" because "he considers himself responsible for his son's death". For the girl, Fetje is "a child's way of dealing with emotions, fear, anger and perhaps a feeling of lacking control", possibly caused by the child's lack of control and lack of language.

The difference between the two cases is that, from the external perspective, the madman is qualified as "mad" and as radically "other". The child, on the contrary, is perceived from the external perspective as in "a phase" that is typical for children. Therefore, even though the child has an erroneous belief that is in some sense similar to the erroneous belief of the mad, the child is perceived as normal *within its childhood*, which is understood as a temporary situation. An adult seeing a "Fetje" would be considered mad, whereas for the child it is externally perceived as something normal and something that belongs to (the category of) childhood.

What does this "strangeness" of childhood and madness consist of as a social phenomenon and what are the consequences of these social distinctions?

2.2.1. UNREASONABLE, IMMORAL AND UNSOCIABLE

Foucault starts his research on madness and civilization with a similar question; he argues that

> [w]hat is constitutive is the action that divides madness [...] the caesura that establishes the distance between reason and non-reason; reason's subjugation of non-reason, wrestling from it it's truth as madness, crime, or disease, derives explicitly from this point [...] we shall have to speak of this act of scission, of his distance set, of this void instituted between reason and what is not reason [...].[116]

115 Ibid: 89.
116 Ibid: xii.

According to Foucault, man understands himself as a "man of reason"[117] and, understanding the mad as the radical other, places him in the world of unreason.[118] Even if, as a human being, the madman was "originally endowed with reason"[119], it seems that the madman has lost (or never realized) his capacity for rational reflection sometime during his life. However, unreason is "only one of madness's modes of appearance".[120]

Similarly, the child is, by definition, excluded from the adult world of the reasonable man, because one of the defining differences between childhood and adulthood is the lack of reason or rational capacity. Plato, for example, refers to the child as unintelligent[121], as "before the age of understanding"[122], having no understanding[123], not possessing rationality[124], etc. In general, this distinction between adult and child based on rationality is common in classical philosophy.[125] Moreover, the idea of the child as irrational is not just a philosophical notion, but it is an idea that lies at the basis of most research on childhood (the disciplines of pedagogy and developmental psychology, for example, often focus on mapping the cognitive development of children, starting with Piaget, Kohlberg, etc.), which is widely shared in everyday common sense. The question that was posed by Piaget: "How does the child think? [...] What are the characteristics of his judgement and his reasoning?"[126] clearly expresses this implicit assumption that the child's thinking and reasoning are radically different from adult's reasoning. Unreason is *normal* when observed in the child, such as in the child that sees Fetje. Obviously, Piaget's work is somewhat outdated, and his answers to questions on childhood may be contested, but his questions remain.

The unreason of childhood and madness seems to be connected to immorality. We can find the origin of this line of thinking again in Plato, who connects knowledge and morality in a stronger way than we usually do these days. For Plato, the highest form of knowledge is knowledge of the Good.[127] This connection between knowledge and morality can still be found when analyzing

117 Ibid: 235.
118 Ibid: 62.
119 Ibid: 234.
120 Ibid: 78.
121 Plato (385-370 B.C./1961c: 181d).
122 Plato (385-370 B.C./1961b: Book II 653a).
123 Plato (385-370 B.C./1961a: 197b).
124 Plato (381 B.C./2012: 138).
125 Rousseau (1762/1979: 107) for example argues that childhood is "childhood is reason's sleep", or Hobbes (1651/1996: 36) who argues that "Children[..] are not endue with Reason at all, till they have attained the use of Speech: but all are called Reasonable Creatures, for the possibility apparent of having the use of Reason in time to come", or (Aristotle (350 B.C. / 1932: book VII part I) writes that a man is not happy who "[...] is as feeble and false in mind as a child or a madman".
126 Piaget (1926/1959: vii).
127 Plato (381 B.C./2012: 232).

the morality recognized in childhood and madness, in the idea that, to be morally good, one has to know the difference between right and wrong.

The idea of innocence resonates in both conceptions of madness and childhood. The mad and the child have no knowledge of the distinction between good and evil. They are often marked as "innocent"[128], a view that is reflected in the diminished responsibility for both the mad and the child in relation to the legal system.[129] They have no shame[130]; the child and the mad do not mind walking around naked in public. The lack of shame and fascination for its otherness sometimes results in the displaying of the child/mad by "rational man". Foucault describes how, for example, the mad were displayed to the public in the English hospital of Bethlehem, where on Sundays one could go and see lunatics for a penny. In this practice, madness becomes "pure spectacle".[131] A similar practice occurs in the social context around children, at birthdays, family gatherings, etc. Who has not had the experience of visiting a family with young children, where the child is summoned to do something it considers "normal" (from the internal perspective) for the public of spectators, who laugh at the strangeness of this action (judged from the external perspective)?[132] For example, we put on music to show the visitor how the child dances funnily, as was done for the visitors of the Bicêtre, where "[c]ertain attendants were well known for their ability to make the mad perform dances and acrobatics [...]".[133]

There is a second way in which the child and the madman are perceived as "immoral", namely in the sense that their actions are void of morality. Violent action, for example, is "normal" for the child and the mad. This is not to say that violence is allowed to both these groups; it is perceived as normal within the otherness of the child/mad, but at the same time it needs to be corrected. Therefore, "madwomen seized with fits of violence are chained like dogs at their cell doors'[134] and children who hit other children are corrected. In fact, the immorality of certain behaviour may classify someone as mad; paedophiles, psychopaths and criminals, in general, are usually understood as

---

128 Foucault (1961/2001: 19); Smith (2011: 27); Skolnick (1975: 44).

129 Cf. Allen (2009: 276): "Arguments for increasing the age of criminal responsibility fall into two broad categories. The first relates to autonomy and capacity. Children are not able to evaluate their actions morally, anticipate the consequences of their actions or control their behavior in the same way as adults [...] Indeed the criminal justice system itself recognizes that parents should be responsible for crimes committed by their children.'

130 Foucault (1961/2001: 198).

131 Ibid: 64-65.

132 The digital age provides many more opportunities to share, display and enjoy the strangeness of childhood. Several websites are dedicated to this purpose, displaying children who "lick grocery carts", "wiping boogers on the shower wall", "refusing to flush the toilet", etc. See: Rockwell (2014) 'He Did What? 17 Hilarious Strange Kid Habits'; No author (2015) 'Akward and Strange Things Kids Say and Do'; No author (2015b) 'I Used to Believe...the childhood beliefs site'; etc.

133 Foucault (1961/2001: 64).

134 Ibid: 68.

"mad" (assuming the illegality of the behaviour is sufficiently *strange*), in fact because s/he has not internalized morality in accordance with social norms. Both the madman and the child are in this sense unsociable.[135] Often they do not master language, or not in a way that is understandable by adults. They do not participate fully in society; they do not work and do usually not possess financial means, they pay no taxes, and they do not vote.[136] They cannot or do not comply with social norms; they do not naturally refrain from screaming in airplanes, they do not refrain from touching themselves and/or others intimately in public, they are often not toilet-trained, etc. As Foucault writes, referring to the mad: "[...] they distinguished themselves by their inability to work and to follow the rhythms of collective life".[137] The view of the child as unsocial is most clearly expressed by Rousseau in his Émile: "the child is a natural being, born in the unnatural condition of civil society. There is no escaping this condition of society, because men left the state of nature, and has thereby forced others to do the same."[138] In this sense, the child is an unsocial being who has to be socialized.

In law too the child and the mad are categorized as "abnormal", as "other", and therefore existing in some way outside of civil society.[139] This is expressed in a general lack of legal responsibility (because *they don't know any better*) and it is the basis for denying children and madmen their freedom (see below).

2.2.2. (IM)POSSIBILITY OF FREEDOM

From the perspective of rational man, due to its irrationality, immorality and unsociability, both the child and the madman have to be restricted in their freedom. If set loose, they would form a danger to society and themselves, and therefore they need to be restrained, which is argued to be in their best interest.

The basis of the argument for restricting the freedom of the child/madman usually follows the following pattern:

1. Personal freedom (1) consists of the ability to rationally control inclinations, emotions, etc., or to reason (correctly) and act morally (correctly);
2. Political freedom (2) consists of autonomy;
3. Political freedom, or autonomy, can only be granted if the individual is free in the sense of (1);

135 Obviously, the child in the process of growing up, and the madman in the process of being cured, become more and more sociable.
136 Foucault (1961/2001: 59).
137 Ibid: 54.
138 Rousseau (1762/1979: 193).
139 Hobbes (1651/1996: 208) for example writes that "only Children, and Madmen are excused from offences against the Law Naturall".

4. The child/mad (animal, savage) are not free in sense (1), they do not possess personal freedom, and therefore they cannot be granted freedom in sense (2) (political freedom).

In philosophy, this argument can be found, among others, in the writings of Kant[140], Rousseau[141] and Hegel.[142] In developmental research, this pattern of development is widely recognized (from "primitive, direct, impulsive, and noncognitive" to "more controlled, thoughtful, and logical").[143] In the children's rights discourse, both in research and legal practice, this line of reasoning is often echoed. To give a few examples; Anderson & Claassen argue that "there is a need for tutelage for the child [...] they need a safety net – and here we find the justification of parental authority and responsibility"[144], and Fortin argues that "[...] many theorists see little need to rule out paternalistic interventions to restrict the actions of adults or children; indeed, they consider them justified by reference to the rights of those constrained. On this basis, it is right to restrain or require activity simply because this will better promote that which the individual is interested in".[145]

Children and madmen lack personal freedom (1) as they are unreasonable, immoral and unsocial. The consequent impossibility of political freedom (2) due to lacking personal freedom (1) of the child/mad is the legitimation for externally restricting the freedom of the child/mad, by rational man. Therefore, the child/mad suffer from the constant restriction of their physical freedom; the mad are confined in hospitals; they are "kept on a leash, chained to walls and to beds"[146], "the doors to their rooms are closed, the windows barred so they can enjoy daylight but will not escape".[147] Children are subject to similar forms of confinement, although maybe less rigorously, since they possess less physical strength and are easier to control. Children's movement is restricted by adding barriers that they are physically unable to cross, such as the barred windows and closed doors for the mad. For children, there are closed doors too, in addition to

---

140 Kant, 'The Metaphysics of Morals', Kant (1797/1996: 6, 213-216, 230, 237, 280, 282, 399-400, 405, 408; 4771781/1996: 5-27, 29-30, 48, 78; 1795/1996: 120 footnote).

141 Rousseau (1762/1979: 85, 128-130, 137, 178, 190, 193, 205, 235, 247). Rousseau would perhaps not agree with statement 3. His account of the situation of the child in society is more descriptive, and he seems to regret the situation that the child find himself in; the child is pure of itself, but s/he is obliged to adapt to the social and legal rules of society. However, Rousseau recognizes the necessity of this situation when he admits to the impossibility of a return to a state of nature (1754/2002: 144-45).

142 Hegel (1820/1991: 35-36, 45).

143 Skolnick (1975: 68), referring to survey by Baldwin (1967) who compared the major theories of child development (Freud, Piaget and Werner) and found that, despite their differences, there was in this sense a consensus among the theories.

144 Andersson & Claassen (2012: 511).

145 Fortin (2009: 22).

146 Foucault (1961/2002: 67).

147 Ibid: 70.

other objects used as obstacles to free movement. In the baby crib we see a copy of the model of barred windows (figure 3).[148] Physically, children are kept on a leash, swaddled, strapped in car seats, etc.

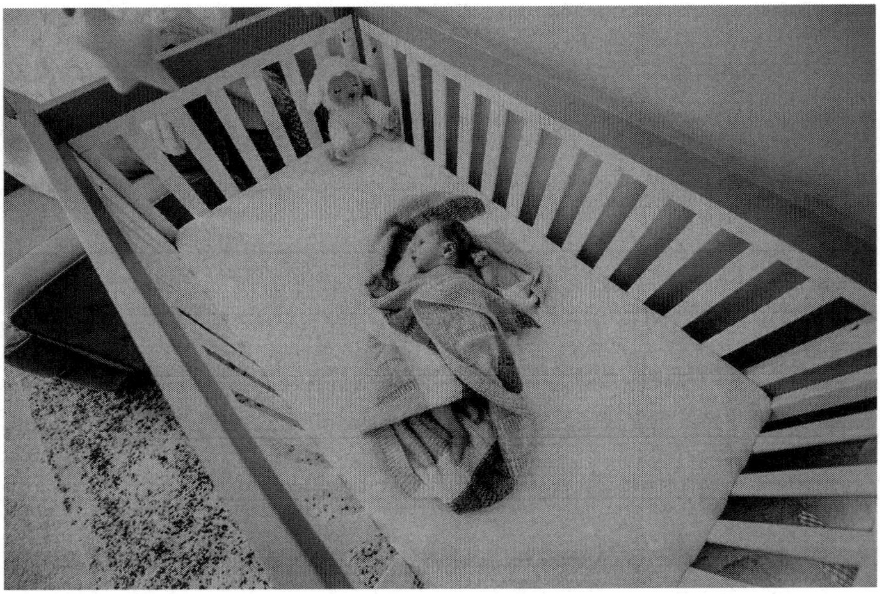

As has been said, for the child/mad, these measures of confinement are taken in their (externally determined) best interests. These interests are often not the child's/mad's interests *right now*[149], but an interest reasoned in reference to their future, socialized (cured) state.[150] This applies to all stages of childhood, not just early childhood. For example, when discussing childhood autonomy versus parental authority in relation to decision making, Fortin asks: "[b]ut what if adolescents foreclose on their future opportunities by reaching decisions which

148 Source: https://images.pexels.com/photos/971435/pexels-photo-971435.jpeg?auto=compress&cs=tinysrgb&dpr=2&h=650&w=940.

149 In this context, an interesting example is the following situation described by Foucault. He describes the situation often occurring in the asylum of Pinel, where "insane persons carried away by a sort of turbulent and reasoned humor" were corrected by a shower, for him to return to manual labor (Foucault (1961/2001: 253). The madman who is laughing and enjoying himself has to be corrected to get back to work, to literally work on his liberation (see Hegel below), based on the idea that this work will cure him, because "[d]isobedience by religious fanaticism, resistance to work, and theft, [were] the three great transgressions against bourgeois society, the three major offences against its essential values [...]" (Ibid: 255).

150 Cf Mayall (2001: 244) "In the first place, childhood is a political issue. Theories about what children need, about how they develop and what input from adults is therefore appropriate, are indeed theories or stories (rather than facts) and practices that derive exclusively from adult perspectives".

adults consider unwise of even dangerous? [...] many theorists are reluctant to allow them the freedom to make life-threatening mistakes".[151]

The requirements for the child's/mad's happiness are determined externally and in this way they are unfree. As Kant writes:

> As for the *freedom* [of every member of a state] as a human being I express its principle [...] in the following formula: No one can coerce me to be happy in his way [...] instead, each may seek its happiness in the way that seems good to him, provided he does not infringe upon that freedom of others to strive for a like end [...] A government established on the principle of benevolence toward the people like that of a *father* toward his children – that is, a *paternalistic government* [...] in which subjects, like minor children who cannot distinguish between what is truly useful or harmful to them, are constrained to behave only passively, so as to wait only upon the judgment of the head of state as to how they *should be* happy and, as for his willing their happiness, only upon his kindness – is the greatest *despotism* thinkable (a constitution that abrogates all the freedom of the subjects, who in that case have no rights at all.) [author's italics].[152]

Foucault calls madness "an absolute freedom" by which rational man feels threatened[153], because madness is the denial of everything the rational man stands for; the restriction of his emotions, desires and passions to be judged rational and normal in the eyes of his fellow man (which he then calls "personal freedom (1)"). The madman does not care about social conventions; madness is a "blind surrender to [..] desires".[154] In children we can observe the same kind of absolute freedom. To give an example: the other day I was at a village celebration in Portugal. It was around ten o' clock in the evening and everyone was waiting at the side of the large basketball court for the local band to begin its show. While the band members were preparing their set and everyone was drinking and talking, there was some music playing on the speakers. One girl of about six years old entered the basketball court and started dancing exuberantly. She seemed mostly to enjoy throwing her long hair around and turning around in circles with her arms wide. My friend sighed and said, nodding at the girl: "that is a great age, when you have no shame, when you can do just exactly what you want, what you feel like. That is absolute freedom".[155]

---

151 Fortin (2009: 27).

152 Kant (1792/1996: 290-91).

153 Foucault (1961/2001: 79).

154 Ibid: 80.

155 Here we see again the difference between social norms or rules and legal norms or rules. For the adult who does not feel free to go to dance on the basketball court if s/he wishes to do so, this freedom is not limited by fixed rules and related (legal) consequences. It is rather a consequence of internalized shame. The possible consequences of the hypothetical action are uncertain. They might be internal (shame) and/or external (gossip, as the anonymous action of the masses).

According to Foucault, we view the mad as unfree because we have "now got in the habit of perceiving in madness a fall into a determinism where all forms of liberty are gradually suppressed"; madness is nothing more than actions determined by nature, and in this sense the mad is like the animal, having no freedom in relation to its inclinations.

2.3.3. CORRECTION AND SOCIALIZATION

As the child/mad is unreasonable, immoral and unsociable, from the perspective of rational man/adult, they have to be socialized. To this end, the child/mad has to be limited in their political freedom and they are subject to physical restraint, because otherwise they would pose a danger to themselves and society. Obviously, the strongest physical restrictions are considered legitimate only for the least socialized; the extremely mad or the very young child. Confinement gradually disappears as the child/mad shows "improvement" (increased socialization), insofar as the mad becomes less mad, the child becomes less childish, insofar as they move towards being rational men. The "treatment" of children in this sense is usually very successful. An example is given by Skolnick. When discussing weaning and toilet training, she argues that this is an area where no room is allowed for innovation on the part of the child. "All children are eventually weaned and toilet-trained – in these struggles the culture always wins, and the child always conforms".[156] However this is not necessarily true. Some children are never toilet-trained and they risk moving from "child" to "mad", without ever becoming socialized. In general, if the child does not go through this process in the order and pace that is expected of it by his surrounding society, he can move straight from "child" to "mad" and never become "rational man".

Jenks observes this in childhood research: "being a child, having been a child, having children and having continuously to relate to children are all experiences which contrive to render the category as 'normal' and readily transform our attribution of it to the realm of the 'natural' [...]".[157] However, he observes that this is a false kind of normal or natural, as childhood is always researched in relation to adulthood and always with a project of socialization in mind. Therefore, childhood is perceived as normal/natural only in itself and, in fact, as abnormal in relation to the adult/society. He continues:

> All contemporary approaches to the study of childhood are clearly committed to the view that childhood is not a natural phenomenon and cannot properly be understood as such. [...] the widespread tendency to routinize and 'naturalize' childhood, both

156 Skolnick (1975: 51).

157 Jenks (1996: 6).

> in common sense and in theory, serves to conceal its analytic importance behind a cloak of the mundane; its significance and 'strangeness' as a social phenomenon is obscured.[158]

In general, childhood/madness is not a permanent state; rational man wants the mad/child to become rational man too. This is what Jenks calls "a universal cultural desire to both achieve an account for the integration of that difference [of childhood] into a more broadly conceived sense of order and generality that comprises adult society".[159] Here the process of correction and socialization and of education and discipline starts. This process is (externally) perceived as necessary because, as Rousseau observes, the child cannot stay pure and natural. "In the present state of things a man abandoned to himself in the midst of other men from birth would be the most disfigured of all".[160] "[The child] is not a savage to be relegated to the desert. He is a savage made to inhabit cities. He has to know how to find his necessities in them, to take advantage of their inhabitants, and to live, if not like them, at least with them".[161] The mad/child has to be educated to arrive at "more sensible and true ideas".[162] To this purpose of socialization, the child/mad have to become rational, moral and social.

For the child, this process takes place mostly in the family and in school (but also in the village, tribe, religious community, sports club, music association, peer group, etc). Rationalization works by replacing "false beliefs" with "true knowledge". Moral education works in the same way, in the sense that children are taught "correct morals" and forced to act accordingly.[163] Socialization works, in addition to internalizing rationality and morality, by applying these to daily behaviour in relation to others. An important aspect of child socialization lies in physical training; the child is taught how to move correctly (to walk, to move in general, its specification depending on which tasks the child is expected to perform in the future)[164], which will enable the future adult to perform in this way in employment.

Why do the child/mad have to become socialized? I think this has to do with the externally determined best interests and the external determination of happiness, as Kant says: coercion, based on an external judgment of how

---

158 Ibid: 7-8.

159 Ibid: 3.

160 Rousseau (1762/1979: 37).

161 Ibid: 205.

162 Foucault (1961/2001: 247).

163 The content of "correct reasoning", "true knowledge" and "correct morals" may change over time and among cultures, however all cultures seem to have some body of truisms in relation to these concepts that are taught to the unsocialized.

164 Erikson, for example, describes how Dakota boys in early childhood learn how to throw pieces of rope around objects (as a lasso around a bull) (1950/1987: 143).

someone should be happy.[165] The idea here is maybe that personal freedom (1) renders a person happy as does belonging to the social order.[166]

This is surely what Hegel has in mind, when he writes that:

> [w]hen reflection applies itself to the drives [...] and [to] a sum total of satisfaction – i.e. [to] *happiness* – it confers *formal universality* upon this material and purifies it, in this external manner, of its crudity and barbarity. This cultivation of the universality of thought is the absolute value of *education* [author's italics].[167]
> *Education*, in its absolute determination, is therefore *liberation* and *work* towards a higher liberation; it is the absolute transition to the infinitely subjective substantiality of ethical life, which is no longer immediate and natural, but spiritual and at the same time raised to the shape of universality. Within the subject, this liberation is the *hard work* of opposing mere subjectivity of conduct [...] it is through this work of education that the subjective will attains *objectivity* even within itself [...] By educated people, we may understand in the first place those who do everything as others do it [...] Thus, education irons out particularity [...] [author's italics].[168]

Or, in other words, education is socialization (ethical life) in the sense that the individual subject learns to align its actions with the actions of others, in this sense not to act on pure inclinations (following the drives directly) but opposing these subjective inclinations for the higher goal of "universality", which is doing as others do. This leads to liberation and happiness. In other words, education teaches you not to do as you wish in a selfish, immediate way ("I want to dance now") but to align your actions with others.[169] This then is the idea of socialization, maturation and liberation.[170] According to Hegel, it is not only the adult who wants this liberation for the child, it is the child itself who wants it: "[t]he need for an upbringing is present in children, as their own feeling of dissatisfaction within themselves at the way they are – as the drive to belong to the adult world whose superiority they sense, or

165 Kant (1792/1996: 290-91).

166 Cf Mayall (2001: 248): "[..] adults justify their control over children through a naturalisation of the condition of childhood: it is for the good of children that their school-days are as they are; if children do well at school, the argument goes, jobs, security and happiness lie ahead".

167 Hegel (1820/1991: 52).

168 Ibid: 225-26.

169 Cf. Dewey (1938/1997: 17): "the history of educational theory is marked by opposition between the idea that education is development from within and that it is formation from without; that it is based upon natural endowments and that education is a process of overcoming natural inclination and substituting in its place habits acquired under external pressure". Dewey in 1932 refers to "new education" which is criticizing "traditional education" by saying that traditional education "imposes adult standards, subject-matter, and methods upon those who are only growing slowly toward maturity" (ibid: 18-19). However, he also notes later that "there is no intellectual growth without some reconstruction, som eremaking, of impulses and desires in the form of which they first show themselves" (ibid: 64).

170 For a discussion on this idea of liberation through becoming an ethical actor and controlling inclinations, in relation to childhood, see Shapiro (1999).

as the desire to grow up".[171] For Jenks, this socialization is the assumption of the desirable adult world[172], and for Foucault, it is a pursuance of the myth of social happiness.[173]

A similar idea can be found in Haugaard. Children have to learn "true knowledge", because in this way children can enter the social ring of reference.[174] They start sharing an interpretative horizon with other members of society, which gives them "power to"[175]:

> A shared interpretative horizon gives actors a capacity for action, which they use to realize autonomy. [...] While the dominated may, at times, perceive the reproduction of the social order as reprehensible, acceptance of the existing social order does usually empower the dominated [...].[176]
> Meaning is not created singly. Part of the process of socialization is learning how to dovetail your individual acts of structuration with those of society as a whole [...] socialization entails the internalization of constraint [...] State education is the mass socialization of social subjects – a Panoptical project on a mass scale.[177]

If the child/mad would not be socialized, society runs the risk of returning to savagery, as Foucault writes: "[M]adness threatens modern man only with that return to the bleak world of beasts and things, to their fettered freedom".[178] Jenks argues that socialization theories:

> [...] [begin] from a specific and given model of the dominant social and cultural formation (which enshrines the theorist's purpose) and relentlessly strive to subvert and restructure the child's potentially dangerous and disruptive difference into a form that equates with the unexplicated grounds of the initial theorizing.[179]

---

171 Hegel (1820/1991: 212).

172 Jenks (1996: 9).

173 Foucault (1961/2001) writes that "For the Catholic Church, as in the Protestant countries, confinement represents, in the form of an authoritarian model, the myth of social happiness [...]" (59). In addition, in chapter 7 he explains how in the 18th century, people started fearing the mad, a fear that was based on a "moral myth" (192); the idea that madness as monstrous, evil, rotten and morally corrupted (193). Social reaction to this was both repugnance and pity (193). In the 18th century, happiness is "part of the order of nature and reason", from which madness is a deviation (202). Based on his work, it seems that this myth of social happiness is not only strived after by Catholics or Protestants but by society in general.

174 Haugaard (2010: 58).

175 Ibid: 58.

176 Ibid: 60, adding "except possibly in extreme cases, including slavery".

177 Ibid: 63, 65.

178 Foucault (1961/2001: 78).

179 Jenks (1996: 13).

2.3. CHILDHOOD AND CHILDREN'S RIGHTS

This binary distinction between adulthood and childhood is the basis for all law for children. Children do not "just" possess human rights, they have special children's rights. This is not to say that children are not human, but that human rights are in fact for a great part adult's rights that are not applicable to children.[180] What rights children have is decided by adults. Notoriously, no children were involved in the drawing up of the 1989 Convention on the Rights of the Child[181], and what is "in the best interest of the child" is decided by adults.[182] Generally, children have no legal power *because they are children.* They have no state legal power; they are not allowed to vote; they are not part of any sovereign; they are not judges; they are not policemen.[183] It is important to understand this child/adult distinction, because policies and decisions concerning children (by adults) ultimately derive from conceptions of childhood that are often unstated and implicit.[184] Even the desire to grant children rights and to make sure that these rights, as codified in the UNCRC, are not violated, may be an idea of development motivated by "a specific and given model of the dominant social and cultural formation"[185] which suits the adult researcher's purpose.

Interestingly, the adult's perspective is taken up as universal in research on childhood and children's rights.[186] An important example here is the 1980 Melton study.[187] In this study, Melton set out to measure empirically "children's concepts of their rights". To this end, 90 students from first, third, fifth, and seventh grade participated in semi-structured interviews. The research started from the hypothesis that "children's concepts of their rights can be expected to

180 Such as the right to freedom of movement (*The Universal Declaration of Human Rights (hereafter: UDHR)* (1948) art. 13.1), the right to marry and found a family (ibid: art.16), the right to take part in the government (ibid: art. 21), the right to work (ibid: art. 23).

181 Sandberg (2014: 2).

182 Mayall (2001: 243).

183 There are some exceptions to this, such as the situation where a child is the legal heir to the throne. In this context, Hobbes writes that "it is an inconvenience in Monarchie, that the Soveraigntie may descend upon an Infant, or one that cannot discerne between Good and Evill: and consisteth in this, that the use of his Power, must be in the hand of another Man, or of some Assembly of men, which are to governe by his right, and in his name; as Curators, and Protectors of his Person, and Authority" (1651/1996: chapter XIX).

184 Skolnick (1975: 38). She writes: "[…] the distinguishing feature of all of childhood is incompetence. The legal system not only reflects and codifies this conception of childhood, but shapes the social reality in which children – and adults – live their daily lives".

185 After Jenks, see §2.3.3.

186 Of course, there are some exeptions, however, this seems to be the general tendency, as explained below. Cf Mayall (2001: 143): "It is hard to peer beyond the tangle of adults who pronounce on children's 'needs' […], and to look clearly at children themselves. It is still more difficult to listen to children seriously. And it is yet more difficult to include children into society rather than excluding them".

187 Melton (1980: 186).

develop along a progression of three levels of reasoning".[188] These three levels are based on a theory of legal development by Tapp and Levine[189] and are formulated as follows:

> Level 1: "children believe that whatever one possesses or can do is by right bestowed by authority. Whether or not one has the right to do something is dependent on whether the action would result in punishment. [...] children have rights only if adults allow them".[190]
> Level 2: "rights are based on elementary fairness".
> Level 3: "rights are conceptualized on a higher plane of ethics and 'natural law'". "Within this framework, then, one may adhere to a system of rights not recognized in law or by social convention. Justifications for rights are based on abstract universal principles".[191]

The relationship between these levels is such that a level 3 concept of rights is conceived as the "higher level", which is hypothesized to occur more in responses of children in higher school grades and from children in higher social classes.[192] These hypotheses were both confirmed by the research.[193] In addition, the children were asked an open question, namely: "What is a right?" Answers to this question were reported in the following way:

> When asked "What is a right?", the average child had *some understanding of the concept* by the third grade (see Table 5). The modal first grader, however, was unable to give *a correct definition* or example. High-SES [Socioeconomic Status] fifth graders had somewhat lower scores on the definition than did High-SES third graders [my italics, MH].[194]

Table 1. Mean Scores on Definition of "a Right"[a]

	Grade			
	1	3	5	7
High-SES	0.2	1.1	0.7	1.4
Low-SES$_1$	0.3	0.9	1.0	1.3
Low-SES$_2$	–	–	–	0.9

Note. Possible range: O·2
[a]n = 10/cell.

188 Ibid: 186.
189 Tapp & Levine (1971).
190 Melton summarized the three levels in a subsequent article. All descriptions of the levels are taken from this article (1982: 535-36).
191 Last quote from Melton (1980: 187).
192 Ibid: 187.
193 Ibid: 187.
194 Ibid: 188.

Clearly, the child's answer to the question "what is a right?" is categorized according to an adult conceptions of rights, arguing that there is such a thing as a "correct" response to this question or a "more mature view about rights"[195], against which children's ideas are measured. It is interesting that Melton finds beyond questioning that there is a correct answer to the question "what is a right?", a question that legal theorist and philosophers have been debating for ages. Note that, according to Melton's model, the current research displays a level 1 "immature" concept of children's rights[196], as would definitions of rights of Kelsen[197], Bentham[198], or in general anyone who does not have a natural law concept of rights.

It is really a shame that the research overlooks the value of the actual responses from the children. The actual responses are reported a little in Melton's 1982 article on the same study. He writes that "many children, especially those in the younger age groups, cited a right to recreation (e.g., to watch television, go outside, etc.).[...] Similarly, the authoritarian school climate in one of the lower-class schools was reflected in the responses of two youngsters who mentioned that they had the right to go to the bathroom at school".[199] This is classified as level 1 understanding of rights, or: incorrect. When looking at law through children's eyes, anticipating what will follow in chapter 3, this seems to me like a *correct* (again, if there is such a thing) answer to the question "what is a right?" If we really want to understand children's conceptions of their rights, this is what we should be interested in.[200]

The Melton study is not exceptional in its approach to children's rights. Firstly, the model used in this particular study has been dubbed the "Children's Rights Inventory" (CRI) and the study has been repeated in many different countries,

---

195 Ibid: 189.

196 See chapter 1.

197 Kelsen (1934/2002; 1945/2007).

198 Bentham (1782/1970).

199 Melton (1982: 536).

200 Interestingly, the Melton study is perceived as doing exactly that. For example, Walker et. al. (1999: 59) write: "What do children themselves think about their rights? Melton (1980) was the first to ask children directly about their perceptions". In Melton's defense, it might be the case that his intention was only to know "when children can meaningfully participate in a legal defense of their own interests" (1980:186), the idea of uncovering children's conceptions of rights might be simply ill-formulated. It can be very interesting and useful to know to what extent children of certain ages and socio-economic backgrounds are capable of defending their rights in a court of law, for example. However, even when taking up this interpretation, I cannot help but wonder why then the "highest level" of understanding of rights is a level where "rights are conceptualized on a higher plane of ethics and natural law", where "one may adhere to a system of rights not recognized in law or by social convention" (1982: 535-36 and 1980: 187). What use is a conception of rights that is not recognized by law or by social convention, when participating in a legal defense of one's own interest?

such as Canada[201], Norway[202], the United States[203], Israel[204], and Estonia.[205] Its conclusions are echoed by many other research articles[206], arguing for example that "research suggests that children [...] are less likely to understand how they can exercise their rights"[207], "a conventional grasp of the nature of legal rights typically has developed by mid-adolescence"[208], "research suggests that by mid-adolescence teenagers have the cognitive capacity to make informed consent decisions"[209], "studies have highlighted that children from disadvantaged populations are likely to believe that they do not have meaningful choices"[210], "[m]ost of Melton's 14-year-olds [..] were able to provide a conventional definition of a right as an entitlement guaranteed by social agreement"[211], etc. Secondly, the general tendency to approach children's rights from an adult's perspective is widespread in children's rights research. It is already present in the research design, which departs from state or international law concerning children. Theoretical discussions on children's rights do not involve children and, when children are interviewed, their answers are "explained" by adult researchers. Rarely are children asked *why* they hold a certain view.[212]

2.4. THE ADULT PERSPECTIVE AND CHILDREN'S RIGHTS RESEARCH

Finally, I want to argue that the adult perspective in children's rights research is a form of ethnocentrism that is not sufficiently recognized as such.[213] I think that this form of ethnocentrism keeps us away from really understanding the socio-legal position of the child. Take, for example, the situation of domestic

---

201 Helwig (1997: 484).

202 Melton & Limber (1992).

203 Cherney & Perry (1996).

204 Khoury-Kassabri & Ben-Arieh (2008). These authors, however, decided not to use the scaling system of the three levels.

205 Limber et al. (1999).

206 According to google scholar, the 1980 article has been cited 172 times.

207 Redding (1993: 726).

208 Scott & Grisso (1997: 169).

209 Fisher (2010: 306).

210 Fundudis (2003: 20).

211 Grisso (1997: 10).

212 For more on research with children and research on children's rights, see chapter 4.

213 There seems to be a similar problem in developmental research and here the problem seems to be more recognized. Skolnick for example notes that "[o]ne surprising limitation is that most developmental research has little to say about children and their daily lives" (1975: 52). This is not surprising, as the role of developmental research in informing children's rights research and policy is important and authoritative (in the sense that it is perceived as possessing a high truth/knowledge-level). Mayall even argues that developmental psychology is "the discipline which has achieved dominance, as providing authoritative and factual knowledge for [child] professionals about children [...]" (2001: 244).

sexual abuse. This practice clearly goes against both state and international law. So why do children sometimes "agree" to have sex with their caretaker, especially when they detest this practice?[214] Why do they not just go to the police, or generally ask for help? I suggest that we can understand this situation as a legal situation, when looking through children's eyes. Possibly the (existence of) state and international laws are unknown to the child or, if the child is aware, the rule of the caretaker ("you are not allowed to talk about our little game to anyone") is perceived as a *law* that is not to be violated. Generally, I suggest that we can better understand the socio-legal position of the child when looking at law through children's eyes. The current research is not a study of the child's behaviour; I simply suggest that we can understand certain behaviour because it is influenced by and determined by law.

214 Kitzinger (1997: 168, 175).

CHAPTER 3
LAW FOR CHILDREN, A CHILD'S PERSPECTIVE

After having defined law (chapter 1) and having analyzed the relationship between children and the law from an adult's perspective (chapter 2), the current chapter will combine both insights to understand what law is for children and, consequently, how we can understand children's rights.

Since law is a social construct[215], its meaning can only be determined in relation to subjectivity. In the first chapter I answered the question "what is law?" by designing what Weber would call an "ideal type", a theoretically conceived meaning and the construction of a purely rational, ideal concept.[216] This leads, as Ehrlich would say, to a concept arrived at "by abstraction and deduction", which creates "a bloodless shape that loses contact with reality".[217] Now, the intention of the current chapter is to get back to reality, to design a framework of what law actually *is* to children. Designing a framework of what law is for children will be done by combining the ideal-type definition of law with the daily socio-legal realities of children. This means that we will investigate the legal orders surrounding children, its corresponding sovereigns and its legal rules, insofar as they apply to children. To do this, we have to look through the eyes of children.

The tentative analysis presented in this chapter is still grounded in rational reflection combined with literature study. A more grounded check with empirical social reality will take place when studying the case studies on children's rights by means of qualitative field research, as can be found in chapters 5–7.

3.1. DEFINING THE LEGAL ORDER

To find which legal orders apply to children, we have to start by defining the legal order. In chapter 1, a number of characteristics were distinguished which a social

---

215 See chapter 1.

216 Weber (1922/1978: 6). Weber, as a sociologist, speaks specifically about the type as a tool for sociological research; sociologist can use "the construction of a purely rational course of action" as "a type (ideal type)" (6). For more on Weber in relation to the current research, see chapter 4.

217 Ehrlich (1936/1975: 9-10).

order has to possess for it to be a *legal* order. If for any social order we find that these are met, we can speak of a legal order. To begin with, below, there is a short overview of these characteristics of a legal order mentioned earlier (as discussed in chapter 1):

A legal order consists of a legal community, a network of laws and a sovereign.

- The legal community is the person or group of people to whom the laws of the legal order apply, who ought to obey and who recognizes the basic norm authorizing the sovereign to create laws.
  - The basic norm is the rule or law posing the conditions for the creation of law within a legal order.
- A law is a valid legal norm, which is valid within a legal order, by virtue of the fact that it has been created by the sovereign.
  - A norm is a prescriptive statement, a rule by which a certain behaviour is commanded, permitted or authorized.
- A sovereign is an artificial person, consisting of one or more natural people, who has legislative power due to recognition of the basic norm regulating its legal power, by the legal community. A sovereign has authority.
  - Having authority means that a fictional person bears the actions of the author (natural person).
    - A fictional, or artificial person is a person whose actions or words are considered as representing the words and actions of another.
    - A natural person is a person whose actions or words are considered as her/his own.
  - Authority is the right to represent a natural person.
  - Authorization is the conferring of legal power upon the sovereign.

There is an unequal power relation between the sovereign and the subject.

- The sovereign has legal power over the subject.
  - Legal power is the power conferred upon the sovereign by the legal community, through recognition of the basic norm. It is the power to create laws and to enforce compliance with laws through coercive acts.
    - A coercive act is an act that ought to be executed even against the will of the individual and, if s/he resists, by physical force.
  - Legitimate legal power is power resulting from the recognition of the basic norm by the community.
- Anyone who commits an illegal act is liable for legal consequences posed within the same legal order.
  - An illegal act is an act that goes against a law of the legal order.

- Legal consequences are the debt(s) a member of the legal community has to pay for committing an illegal act. Legal consequences are imposed upon a member of the legal order by an authoritative power (sovereign).
- Legal consequences are imposed in the sense that the person is liable to be subject to a coercive act against the person, ordered by the sovereign.
- One cannot end the legal situation by committing an illegal act.

The laws of the legal order are statutory laws.

- Statutory law are laws created by a sovereign. Statutory law can be analyzed according to three different levels: formal written law, law for the community and hidden law.
  - Formal written law are rules found in official, formal legal texts, created by the legislature and open and available to the public.
    - Written laws are rules found in official, formal legal texts, created by the legislature.
  - Law for the community are rules created by the legislator, known by the subjects of the legal order. There are written and unwritten laws for the community.
    - Written laws for the community are written laws, created by the legislator, that are known by the subjects of the legal order. An example is when the subjects know the formal written law.
    - Unwritten laws for the community are unwritten laws, created by the legislator, that are known by the subjects of the legal order. They can occur in a situation of a legal order who has no formal written law (example: primitive legal culture), or in a situation when an unwritten law for the community contradicts the formal written law (example: Dutch soft drug law).
  - Hidden laws are non-public rules created by the legislature, known only to a specific group of people. There are written and unwritten hidden laws.
    - Written hidden laws are written laws, created by the legislator, that are known only to a specific group of people. Example: USA/NSA top-secret legal document warranting domestic surveillance.
    - Unwritten hidden laws are unwritten laws, created by the legislator, that are known only to a specific group of people. Example: corruption.

3.2. ELEMENTS OF THE CHILD'S LEGAL ORDER

In the above overview, several elements of the legal order are distinguished that must have empirical reality for there to be an actual legal order. These elements are: a) the legal community, b) the sovereign, c) laws and the basic norm as objects of subjective belief, d) the possibility of a coercive act through legal power, e) statutory law (valid legal norms created by the sovereign). Clearly, these elements have to be seen in connection to each other and can only be separated artificially. In practice, they are interdependent; for example, the possibility of a coercive act by the sovereign (d) is in great part dependent on the subjective belief of the legal community in the basic norm of the legal order (a+c). Keeping this in mind, I want to look at how we can find these elements of the legal order in relation to children.[218]

a) *The legal community*

The legal community has been defined as "the person or group of people to whom the laws of the legal order apply, who ought to obey, who recognize the basic norm authorizing the sovereign to create laws". To empirically identify this community, we will have to take up the perspective of the child in relation to law.

The first and most obvious member of the legal community of children is the child itself. Whoever the child believes is authorized to make law over her/him, to tell her/him what to do, is thereby designated as sovereign. This relationship can constitute a legal relation, on the condition that the sovereign takes up the legal power and creates law over the child. For example, a child who recognizes the state law which prohibits the child from using drugs as a law, belongs to the legal community of the state legal order.

Second, the legal community of children's legal orders has to be extended to include the people that decide for the child in legal situations. In other words, what people in an unequal power relation to children recognize as law for the child includes what law is for the child, as it directly influences (decisions about) the child's life. A parent who recognizes state law prohibiting the child from using drugs and who identifies her/himself and the child as members of the state legal order, for example, thereby indirectly includes the child in the legal community of the state legal order.[219]

From the child's perspective, the second situation does not necessarily include the state as a legal order. Imagine the child who asks her/his father why s/he is not allowed to use drugs. The father might reply "because I say so", implying his legal power over the child and his position as legislator. The father might alternatively reply "because it is against the (state) law", implying the child's membership of the state legal order.[220]

---

218 The following is written from the child's perspective, yet it also applies to adults in relation to the legal orders surrounding them.

219 This can be seen for example in the case study on the child's right to nationality in the TRNC. The child's nationality is a state legal concept whereby parents understand their children as addressed by, and members of, the state, whereas (young) children often are not aware of this at all. See chapter 7.

220 Note that the same argument can apply to the adult citizen, for example in its relationship to the state sovereign, in relation to international law.

b) *The sovereign*

The sovereign has been defined as "an artificial person, consisting of one or more natural people, who has legislative power due to recognition of the basic norm regulating its legal power, by the legal community".

From the perspective of the child's legal community, the sovereign is any artificial person who they recognize as having legal power over the child. It is the artificial person who legitimately creates law over the child. However, from the child's perspective, the existence of any sovereign depends solely on her/his individual recognition of a sovereign as an authority legitimized to create law over her/him. If, for example, the child does not recognize the state government as sovereign, the state government is effectively not a sovereign over the child (except in the indirect manner, through, for example, the parents), and the enforcement of its rules by means of coercive action will, from the child's perspective, be considered mere violence, undistinguishable from the criminal forcing the individual to comply with his command at gunpoint.[221]

c) *Laws and the basic norm as objects of subjective belief*

As has been argued above, the existence of a legal order for the child depends on its recognition of the basic norm and subsequent laws.

Firstly, the child has to believe in the sovereign as sovereign.[222] This means that s/he has to recognize the legal power or authority of a sovereign. This constitutes recognition of a basic norm. For example, the child who argues with a stepmother who tries to set a household rule that "you cannot tell me what to do, because you are not my real mother!"[223] recognizes the legal power of the "real mother" and denies the sovereignty of the stepmother.

The same is true for the law as the object of subjective belief. Even if the child recognizes the "real mother" as sovereign, s/he still has to believe that rule X has been created by the sovereign. Therefore, when a sibling argues "mother says that from now on you have to be home every evening at 6 p.m.", the child might not believe that this is an actual law as s/he doubts the origins of the norm. Note that this is different from believing that a certain law is unjust. If the child does acknowledge that the mother has created the law that s/he has to be home every evening at 6 p.m., and if s/he believes that the mother is authorized to create such law, s/he might think that the law is unjust and therefore not decide to abide it. In this case, the rule is still a law. As Searle writes: recognition (of a social fact, such

---

221 See §1.3.2 and §1.3.3.

222 Obviously, this is the case for each potential member of a potential legal order – yet since in this part the aim is to look at law through children's eyes, to find legal orders looking from the child's perspective, I only refer to the child here. For a discussion on whether state law still applies to children even if they do not believe in it / know about it, see §3.4.3.

223 I thank my friend Kila v.d. Starre for coming up with the example.

as a law) does not mean approval. Hate, apathy and despair are consistent with the recognition of what one hates, is apathetic about or despairs of changing.[224]

d) The possibility of a coercive act by the sovereign

Being a member of a legal order means that you are liable to be subject to a coercive act against you if you commit an illegal act. A sovereign must have the possibility to enforce legal consequences against its members, even if this goes against the will of the individual and even if this is done by physical force.

This means that, if there is a greater power than a person that the child recognizes as an authority, which completely takes away the possibility for a coercive act by this person, there is no legal order. Although this is a theoretical option, in practice, this will probably not be found as the recognition of the basic norm by an individual confers legal power upon the sovereign and therefore the possibility of being subjected to a coercive act by the sovereign. For example, if a state government takes the child away from her/his parents and puts the child in foster care, this would seriously diminish the possibility for a coercive act by the parent against the child, even though the child recognizes the parent as a sovereign. Yet, it would not completely rule out the parent's legal power over the child, which would still be present in the mind of the child as a threat and could potentially be realized, unless the parent has died.

e) Statutory law (valid legal norms created by the sovereign)

A condition for the existence of a legal order is that the sovereign creates valid legal norms, or, in short, law. As I have argued before, the law does not have to be necessarily written and not necessarily public. It can even be inferred from policy, as long as it is rule based.

From the child's perspective, the belief in the authority of a sovereign is therefore not enough to identify a legal order. The person believed to be authorized to create law has to effectively create these valid norms. A norm has been defined as "a prescriptive statement, a rule by which a certain behaviour is commanded, permitted, or authorized". For a statement to qualify as a rule, or norm, it has to command, permit or authorize behaviour, and it cannot be arbitrary, because then it is not a rule but a mere opinion.

For example, if a father says to his daughter "you shouldn't be wearing that skirt", this is not a legal norm but a statement of opinion, even if in general the daughter considers the father a sovereign. This is because rather than to command, permit or authorize the wearing of the skirt, the statement actually recognizes the autonomy of the daughter to choose whether or not to wear the skirt. The father says that in his opinion, the daughter should not be wearing the

[224] Searle (2011: 8). See also §1.3.2.

shirt, but grudgingly accept that apparently she has chosen to wear it. A different situation would be if the father says "you are not allowed to wear that skirt".

3.3. PLURALISM OF CHILDREN'S LEGAL ORDERS

When trying to identify legal orders for children, we have to wonder whether children are only members of one legal order (if at all), or whether there are multiple legal orders for children. This relates to the central discussion around legal pluralism on whether it is possible to say that multiple legal orders coexist in the same social field.[225] As the conventional concept of "law" usually refers to "state law", the first position taken up by legal pluralists is to argue that the state is not the only legal order and that there are other laws except state law. If we find that two or more legal orders coexist over the same social field, we can conclude that there is a situation of legal pluralism.[226]

In the following paragraph, I will analyze the central arguments to legal pluralism as they relate to the empirical legal reality of children. After discussing the question whether for children there is only the state legal order, I will zoom in on three ideas for the understanding of law and the legal order, by three great thinkers: the idea of the legal order based on living law by Eugen Ehrlich, the idea of the legal order understood as a semi-autonomous social field by Sally Falke Moore and the analysis of the legal order according to legal systems and legal levels by Leopold Pospisil.[227]

3.3.1. THERE IS (NOT) ONLY THE STATE LEGAL ORDER

Conventional understanding of law is that law is written, formal state law.[228] In the first chapter I argued for a broader understanding of statutory law, to include written and unwritten, public and non-public laws.[229] This argument still leaves open the possibility for the limitation of the legal order, which issues statutory law to state legal orders. Therefore, according to this view, the question "what is law for children?" can be answered by looking at which state laws relate to

---

225 Merry (1988).

226 See definition of legal pluralism, §1.4.6.

227 These three authors have been selected because they are generally understood to be the most important, basic authors of legal pluralism. In addition, I find it important to discuss them, because they each posit positive theories of legal pluralism, rather than (solely) critique of other people's work. They were also selected by Griffiths (1986) in his famous article "What is legal pluralism?" Ehrlich will be discussed at length, because he has written most about what legal orders are from a theoretical perspective. Moore's theory is presented in a journal article, while Pospisil's work contains for a large part the presentation of empirical data.

228 See §1.4.5.

229 See §1.4.

children. However, many researchers have argued for an understanding of law that recognizes laws other than those rules issued by the state.[230] Some even argue that the tendency to identify law with state law adheres to "the ideology of state centralism"[231], and call for an "uncoupling of law from the state".[232]

Based on the definition of law and the legal order as set out in this chapter, it follows that any social order of people which includes a sovereign, a legal community and a network of laws constitutes a legal order.

Several authors identify different legal orders apart from the state legal order. De Sousa Santos, for example, distinguishes six main legal orders which, according to him, are anchored in, constituted by, and constitutive of the six structural clusters of social relations in capitalist society. These are:

1. The household place, which has as its legal form "domestic law". Domestic law tends to be informal, unwritten and embedded in family relations.
2. The workplace, which has as its legal form "production law".
3. The marketplace, which has as its legal form "exchange law".
4. The community-place, which has as its legal form "community law". Community law seems to relate to something as the law of a local legal order that is bigger than a family but smaller than a state legal order; examples mentioned are the marginalized community of Pasargada, gangs or mafia groups or ancestral laws of indigenous peoples.
5. The citizenplace, which has as its legal form "territorial or state law". Territorial or state law refers to the modern idea of state law.
6. The worldplace, which has as its legal form "systemic law", which is "the sum total of rules and normative standards that organize the core/periphery hierarchy and the relations among the nation-states in the interstate system".[233]

Although I believe that de Sousa Santos' clusters are still not sufficiently clear to be used in empirical legal research on children's rights, because it is unclear what kind of empirical elements one should exactly find to find any of these forms of law, and his definition of law focuses on dispute settlement which is not always relevant for understanding children's rights violations[234], I do believe that, when

---

230 Among others: Oomen (2002: 25); Davies (2010: 805-06); Favali & Pateman (2003: 1-2); de Sousa Santos (2002); International Council on Human Rights Policy (2009: V); Weber (1922/1978: 316).

231 Griffiths (1986: 3).

232 De Sousa Santos (2002: 68, 85).

233 Ibid: 391-393.

234 Ibid: 86. In his 2002 work, de Sousa Santos did not apply the theory to empirical research. In later work he did engage in the empirical study of legal pluralities, for example. in Mozambique. The focus here, however, is on disputes that are brought to court, whether these are state courts or traditional courts. The household place, workplace, marketplace etc. are not included (de Sousa Santos (2006)).

looking at law through children's eyes, we will find a pluralism of legal orders, similar to the list created by de Sousa Santos. To see how other legal pluralist scholars have developed these theories, below I will discuss some of the most important works on legal pluralism and, under §3.4, use the theoretical idea of legal pluralism to identify possible legal orders for children.

3.3.2. EHRLICH'S LIVING LAW

Eugen Ehrlich is often celebrated by legal scholars for having reconnected the notion of law to social reality, in a time when lawyers and jurists were almost exclusively occupied with the black-letter state law.[235] Mostly, legal scholars are intrigued by his notion of "living law", even though there is no consensus on the exact meaning of the concept.[236] However, Ehrlich has also been heavily criticized for confusing facts and norms (most notably by Kelsen).[237]

In general, I feel the appreciation of Ehrlich's work, by myself personally and legal scholars in general, is best stated by Roger Cotterrell's comment on Ehrlich's main work, the *Fundamental Principles of the Sociology of Law*: "[t]he book has many faults: it is poorly structured, gets mired in diversions and distractions, and is repetitive, ambiguous and sometimes seemingly self-contradictory, but it is a virtuoso performance nonetheless".[238]

The virtuoso of Ehrlich's works, insofar as it is relevant to the current research, consists of: 1) his alternative conceptualization of law and the legal order; 2) his insistence on a scientific methodology needed for the understanding of law in a broader sense than solely black-letter state law.

Ehrlich's conceptualization of the legal order

Eugen Ehrlich was a jurist and an academic teacher in law. What he saw around him in the law schools of the early 20th century, of his students and colleagues, was that their education and research were only aimed at what he thought was only a part of the legal field: they studied "practical juristic science", which "had been designed for the use of the judge [since the 16th century] [...] It was to teach the judge how to apply the general propositions to the specific cases".[239] Consequently, according to Ehrlich, the modern jurist did not have a conception of law, because

---

235 See, among others: Hertogh (2009); von Benda-Beckmann & von Benda-Beckmann (2009); Pospisil (1967: 5-7); Griffiths (1986: 23); Nelken (1984).

236 Most notably set forward in Tamanaha (2011).

237 For an overview of the discussion, see van Klink (2009).

238 Cotterrell (2009: 78).

239 Ehrlich (1936/1975: 9-10).

> the jurist does not mean by law that which lives and is operative in human society as law, but, apart from a few branches of public law, exclusively that which is of importance as law in the judicial administration of justice.[240]

Jurists, according to Ehrlich, studied only state law, caused by the monopoly of creation of law which the state had acquired since the 16th century.[241] Although they recognized the existence of customary law, which had come to mean the same thing as non-state law, they saw it as an "inferior kind of law", whose validity was "conditioned upon authorization [...] by the [state] legislator".[242]

In response, Ehrlich devoted his work to sketching a theoretical map of the total legal field, which he grounded in sociology. This was a framework that he thought could serve as a map for researching the legal field in its totality. His life's hope was that this framework would be used to empirically investigate the legal field, specifically that, in addition to the practical juristic science, states would fund institutes that would research the "living law", the law which lives and is operative in human society as law.[243]

Ehrlich has never made a clear scheme or overview of his theoretical framework of the legal field and different elements of this framework have to be searched for throughout his work, which often presents the reader with inconsistencies. However, based on several of his writings, I think his intended overview of the legal field looks like this:

240 Ibid: 9-10.

241 Ibid: 13.

242 Ibid: 15.

243 Ehrlich (1920/1986: 239-40).

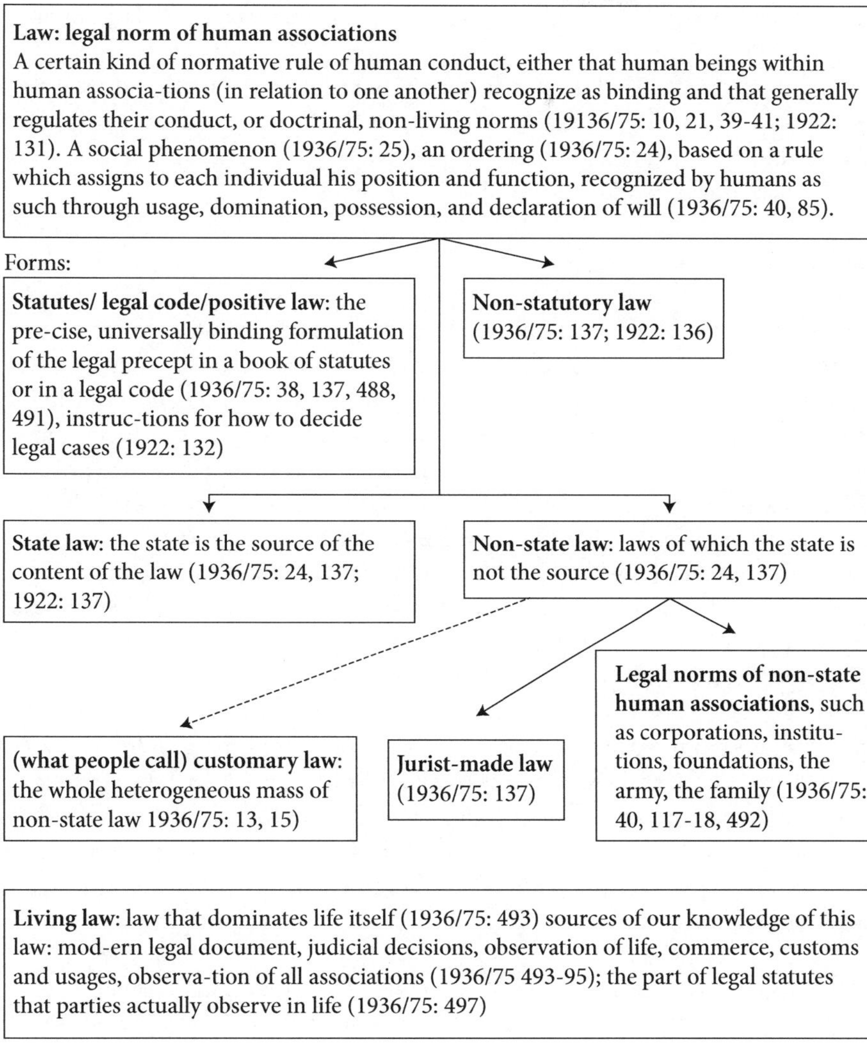

For Ehrlich, since law is a social phenomenon, every kind of legal science is a social science[244], and all laws are rules of conduct within the social order or association.[245] Basically, human beings live together in social groups or associations. In most cases, they regulate their conduct within the group according to certain rules of conduct that they recognize as binding.[246] Of these rules of conduct, there are legal rules of conduct and non-legal rules of conduct, of which the latter are non-normative rules of conduct (language,

244 1936/75: 25.
245 Ibid: 21-42.
246 Ibid: 39.

rules of hygiene) and non-legal normative rules of conduct (ethical custom, tact, etiquette).[247]

Legal norms appear in different forms, namely as statutes or non-statutes. What exactly counts as a "statute" is a little unclear – it seems that the concepts statute, legal provision, legal code and positive law all refer to the same form of law (written down in official legal code).[248]

Living law

To describe legal rules that affect life, as opposed to "dead-letter state law" (legal statutes that are not actually observed or applied in society), Ehrlich used the term "living law". Despite wide enthusiasm for Ehrlich's concept of living law, the concept has led to much confusion as it, too, lacks a clear definition or description. In secondary literature, many definitions of living law are given; it is "the law made and maintained by people themselves"[249], "the law that lives in citizen's experience, which may not even be law at all from a lawyer's perspective, but merely non-legal social norms"[250], "the inner ordering of the associations"[251], "the law which dominates life even though it has not been posited in legal propositions"[252], etc. I will try to shed some light on the understanding, and consequent value, of the concept of living law.

Firstly, living law is mostly, if not always, posited in secondary literature as opposite to legal provisions. A rule is either a legal provision or a living law.[253] I think this is a fundamental confusion that Ehrlich caused when he wrote that, as Griffiths quoted, living law is "the law which dominates life even though it has not been posited in legal propositions". However, this quote is taken out of context. In the passage where Ehrlich makes this statement, he is discussing the law of the family. He writes:

> I doubt whether there is a country in Europe in which the relation between husband and wife, parents and children, between the family and the outside world, as it actually takes form in life, corresponds to the norms of the positive law; or in which the members of the family, [...] would as much as think of attempting to enforce the rights against one another that the letter of the [state] law grants to them.[254] It is evident therefore that in this case, too, the [state] law is far from

247 Ibid: 39, 61.

248 On the other hand, Ehrlich does distinguish "legal propositions" from "legal documents" (Ibid: 498), which begs the question of what exactly a legal proposition or a legal document is.

249 Van Klink (2009: 128).

250 Cotterrell (2009: 77).

251 Pospisil (1967: 6).

252 Griffiths (1986: 26).

253 See for example Nelken (1984: 161); Urinboyev & Svensson (2013: 376); Tamanaha (2011: 298). The latter indicates this flaw in discussions on Ehrlich's living law.

254 Erhlich writes "the law" here; I added "state" to avoid confusion.

> giving a picture of that which actually takes place in life. [...] This then is the *living law* in contradistinction to that which is being enforced in the courts and other tribunals. The living law is the law which dominates life itself even though it has not been posited in legal propositions. The source of our knowledge of this law is, first, the modern legal document; secondly, direct observation of life, of commerce, of customs and usages, and of all associations, not only of those that the [state] law has recognized but also of those that it has overlooked and passed by, indeed even of those that it has disapproved. In our day, doubtless, the most important source of knowledge of the living law is the modern legal document.[255]

Even though the quote, when taken out of context, seems to imply that living law stands in opposition to legal provisions, I think we should read it as "living law is the law which dominates life itself even [in a case when] it has not been posited in legal provisions [such as in the case of some laws of the family]". Proof for this interpretation is mostly the fact that Ehrlich insists on the source of our knowledge of living law being primarily the modern legal document – which to my mind cannot be other than the legal provision. Living law is thus a legal rule of conduct, regardless of the source of this rule (state, family, ...) that actually, concretely, affects life.

This interpretation of "living law" seems to be confirmed in other texts by Ehrlich. For example, in his essay *Gesetz und Lebendes Recht*, he defines living law as "the rules, that people themselves while living together consider as binding on them".[256] Obviously people can experience all kinds of rules as binding upon them, including state law insofar as they are members of the state as a social association. A law is defined as "the inner order of human associations"[257], but not all law is necessarily living law. A state, for example, may hold a legal provision in its law books that is no longer followed by society; it then becomes a "dead letter".[258] Even though Ehrlich highlights a difference between the living law and the law in legal codes, he admits that "often enough norms from the living law permeate state law and sometimes the [state law][259] withdraws in face of the living law".[260] In this sense, the notion of living law seems to come close

255 Ehrlich (1936/ 1975: 491-93).

256 Ehrlich (1920/1986: 233). I could access these texts as combined in the 1986 collection of Ehrlich's texts, only in German. As I am not a German scholar, I include the German wording: "Die Regeln, die die Menschen selbst in ihrem Zusammenleben als für sich verbindlich beobachten, sind das lebende Recht [...]" (Ibid: 233).

257 Ibid: 181 "In seiner ältesten und ursprünglichen Form ist das Recht die innere Ordnung der menslichen Verbände"; Ehrlich (1936/1975: 24, 85).

258 Ehrlich & Isaacs (1922: 142).

259 Ehrlich uses the term "legislation" here, which I think is confusing.

260 Ehrlich (1920/1986: 233): "Da jedoch Gerichte und and andere Behörden doch shclieβlich nur verhältnismäβig selten angerufen werden, so dringen die Normen des lebenden Rechts of genug selbst gegen das Gesetz durch [...] Oft ist es aber die Gesetzgebung selbst, die sich vor dem lebenden Recht zurückzieht [...]".

to what I defined as "law for the community"[261]; sometimes state law and lived experience of law by the relevant community can overlap, as in a situation when the relevant community knows the state law.[262] Although Ehrlich seems to add as a criterion that people actually live by this law[263], his criterion that living law is the law that "parties actually observe in life"[264] can be taken to mean any form of observation, even knowing the law is A and acting in illegal way B.

However, it must be noted that, due to Ehrlich's inconsistency, elsewhere he does argue that the living law stands in contradiction to statutory law[265], so perhaps the above interpretation that I give of Ehrlich's living law should be read as a statement on what I think Ehrlich should have written, had he been consistent in his treatment of law, especially in the context of his general discussion of law (see also below).[266]

Law as the inner ordering of associations

For Ehrlich, laws are always and necessarily connected to the social order or association.[267] These human associations "include at least in part the clan, the family and the household. On top of these bigger, combined associations are built, who in part cross each other, in part include each other: the tribe, the people, the community, the state, the church [...]".[268] A law is then a rule of the association that a member of, or members of, the association consider as binding on them.

A legal order originates in man's need for protection and its inequality in strength. According to Ehrlich, weak people, such as women, children, a poor man, the vanquished, etc. are "unable to bear arms" and unable to "form an association capable of self-defense".[269] Therefore they place themselves under the protection of another, they subject themselves to a master and, from then on, an attack on them will be an attack on their master.[270] This relation of

---

261 §1.4.4.

262 Which can be compared to situation B1 under §1.4.4.

263 Ehrlich (1920/1986: 233).

264 Ehrlich (1936/1975: 497).

265 Ehrlich (1920/1986: 233): "Dieses lebende Recht, das so zum gesetzlichen in einen Gegensatz tritt, ist jedoch weder das interessanteste noch das wichtigste".

266 For more interesting suggestions on what Ehrlich should have said, see Van Klink (2009).

267 Ehrlich (1936/1975): 21, 39, 42.

268 Ehrlich (1920/1986: 181) "Unter den Verbänden, auf denen so die Gesellschaften beruhen, müssen vor allem die urwüchsigen hervorgehoben werden, die infolge des Waltens natürlicher gesellschaftlicher Kräfte überall wenigstens teilweise vorkommen: Die Sippe, die Familie und die Hausgemeinschaft. Erst auf diesen bauen sich die gröβeren, zusammengesetzten Verbände auf, die sich teils kreuzen, teils umfassen: Der Stamm, das Volk, die Gemeinde, der Staat, die Kirche [...] In seiner ältesten und ursprünglichen Form ist das Recht die innere Ordnung der menslichen Verbände".

269 Ehrlich (1936/1975: 89-90).

270 Ibid: 89-90.

subjection and domination is however not a relation of possession; it is "a legally regulated relation between the person who has the power and the person who is subjected to the latter".[271] Because domination cannot generally be permanently maintained as possession, as this would require constant surveillance, domination presupposes "a certain state of mind, a certain placing and fitting oneself into the relation of domination and subjection".[272]

This is the basis of the associations or order that human society creates self-actively. Ultimately, historically, smaller associations (such as the family) are combined into larger associations (such as the state).[273] These smaller associations are generally still left in their original form.[274] Some of the inner rules of ordering within associations are laws[275] and some associations are not regulated by legal norms at all.[276] Among legal associations, Ehrlich lists corporations, foundations, the state, the army, the various classes, the family, the household, and the clan.[277] An example of a law within the family is the law of marriage, which even if it is not regulated by state law, inertly orders the family legal order.[278]

Law within the association is a means to generate power over people; "power over men can be maintained and exercised permanently only by uniting them in associations and prescribing rules of conduct for them within the association, i.e. by organizing them".[279] Rules are made by the dominant person or group of people of the association and obeyed by those subjected, although they always contain elements of mutual interest.[280]

A scientific method for researching the whole legal field

To find and understand law, as scientists, legislators and legal practitioners, we have to be interested in the whole legal field and not solely in state legal provisions. According to Ehrlich, the jurist has "to look not only at the law, but at the whole of legal life, whether it accords with the law, whether it runs contrary to the law or whether it fills the gaps of the law".[281] This means that we have to look at both the state legal provisions as well as the inner legal ordering of the

271 Ibid: 90.
272 Ibid: 92.
273 Ibid: 27-28, 64, 118; Ehrlich (1920/1986: 181-82).
274 Ehrlich (1936/1975: 64, 118, 492).
275 Ibid: 39.
276 Ibid: 40.
277 Ibid: 40 64, 492; Ehrlich (1920/1986: 181-83).
278 Ibid: 229, 232: "Zweifellos entsteht ein groβer Teil des Rechts unmittelbar in der Gesellschaft: das ist die innere Ordnung der gesellschaftlichen Verhältnisse, der Ehe, der Familie […]".
279 Ehrlich (1936/1975: 61).
280 Ibid: 61.
281 Ehrlich (1920/1986: 232). "Der Jurist wird also nicht bloβ das Gesetz, sondern das gesamte Rechtsleben ins Auge fassen, ob es mit dem Gesetze im Einklange steht, ihm zuwiderläuft oder die Lücken des Gesetzes ausfüllt"(1986: 234). "[…] es wäre ein groβer Irrtum, wenn

smaller associations. For example, if we want to know family law, in addition to legal provisions, we have to study "which laws man and woman, elderly and offspring appeal to in relation to each other". To this end, we have to take into account

1. The immense amount of family law that has not been summarized in legal provisions yet;
2. whether the provisions of statutory family law have penetrated family life at all, or whether they enjoy validity only in the relatively rare cases where a judge decides over family disputes.[282]

In this way, legislators can legislate more effectively, because they will be better aware of the consequences of rules they install[283], scientific research on law will become much more relevant[284] and jurists can use real life in the courtroom.[285]

How can we find law? It is clear that we can find state law in legal propositions, judicial decisions and writings of jurists. But, how do we find laws of the social order that are not legal provisions, the living law and the legal provisions that are not state law? Here Ehrlich's refusal to define criteria that distinguish other social norms from legal norms is a death warrant to the development of an empirical scientific methodology for finding law. He gives a few hints on how it should be done; for the jurist, for example, the most important faculties are his eyes and ears.[286] The standard against which legal propositions and the legal document must be tested is actual life.[287] But what should the jurist see and what should s/he hear? The inner ordering of the association is empirically perceptible, because the people who are members of these orders direct their acts according to the norms of the association.[288] But then, they also direct their acts

---

man annehmen wollte, daβ Ehe und Familie in Deutschland wirklich so aussehen, wie sie im bürgerlichen Gesetzbuch normiert werden".

282 Ibid: 234. "Für das Familienrecht wird er nicht beim Gesetz stehen bleiben, sondern beobachten müssen, welche Rechte Mann und Frau, Eltern und Nachkommen einander gegenüber ansprechen und welche Rechte sie eindander freiwillig gewähren. Daraus wird er entnehmen 1. die ungeheure Menge des Familienrechts, das überhaupt noch nicht in Gesetzen zusammengefaβt ist; 2. Ob die Bestimmungen des gesetzlichen Familienrechts überhaupt in das Familienleben gedrungen sind oder nur in den verhältnismäβig seltenen Fällen zur Geltung gelangen, wo ein Richter über Familienstreitigkeiten entscheidet".

283 Ibid: 238-39.

284 Ehrlich (1936/1975: 493); Ehrlich (1920/1986: 237).

285 Ehrlich (1920/1986: 237).

286 Ibid: 238. "[...] das wichtigste für den Juristen sind Augen um zu sehen und Ohren um zu hören".

287 Ehrlich (1936/1975: 498).

288 Ehrlich (1920/1986: 242). "Die gesellschaftliche Ordnung beruth auf den grundliegenden gesellschaftlichen Einrichtungen: Ehe, Familie [...] Eine gesellschaftliche Einrichtung [...] ist [...] sinnlich wahrnehmbar dadurch, dass die Personen, die in diesen gesellschaftlichen Verhältnissen stehen, sich in ihrem Handeln nach bestimmten Normen richten."

towards ethical norms that are not legal norms[289], so how can we tell whether what we are observing is compliance to a non-legal or a legal norm?

The only way out of this dead end in Ehrlich's theory seems to be his insistence on the individual responsibility and inventiveness of the scientific researcher. He argues that:

> production of a work of science requires the same qualifications as production of a work of art; both require a certain receptivity of mind, imagination, and power to give shape to one's material. For this reason every independent investigator must create his own method, just as every creative artist must create his own technique. He who employs another's method, just like the person who employs another's technique, may possibly be a great disciple, but never more than a disciple [...] For the mind which thinks and works independently will be ever seeking new methods and new techniques which correspond to his individuality.[290]

Elsewhere he argues that: "The first and foremost function of all research is to find a method adapted to its subject matter. The life of many a great scholar has been spent in the endeavour to find a method. Once the method was found, the work could be carried on by inferior minds".[291] If he adheres to this conviction, then designing a method for other scientists would be more or less hypocrite, because researchers should do this themselves. But obviously this is a very shaky and meagre out. Ehrlich even argues that "ultimately, even the analysis of the spectrum is nothing more than a method"[292], and therefore if the researcher has to find her/his own method, why does Ehrlich supply us with such a rich analysis of the spectrum? The remark is interesting, however, because it does highlight that which is the key problem for the lack of methodology in Ehrlich's work; as soon as we define the distinction between legal and non-legal social norms, for the purpose of methodology, we thereby define the spectrum under research. In defining law, we risk leaving out the lived experience of people. Perhaps it is the privilege for the people themselves to say what is law (to them)?[293] In the end, all that Ehrlich tells us is that "there is no other means but this, to open one's eyes, to inform oneself by observing life attentively, to ask people, and note down their replies".[294]

---

289 Ehrlich (1936/1975: 22).

290 Ibid: 472.

291 Ibid: 9.

292 Ibid: 9.

293 This is also implied by Ehrlich's criterion for law as "opinio necessitatis"; people know a certain rule as a norm because in them it triggers a specific feeling of revolt (see Hertogh (2009: 3-4); Nelken (1984)). However, this criterion has been heavily critized to a point where it is hardly taken seriously (see Hertogh (2009: 6-9); Nelken (1984: 163)).

294 Ehrlich (1936/1975: 498). Allegedly, Ehrlich gave a very succesfull lecture about how to research law empirically during a seminar called *Seminar für lebendes Recht* (Ehrlich (1920/1986: 238). Unfortunately, the text of this seminar is nowhere to be found. According to Ziegert, at the seminar Ehrlich "taught his law student show to collect empirical data on

3.3.3. MOORE'S SEMI-AUTONOMOUS SOCIAL FIELDS

Ehrlich's notion of law as the inner ordering of associations may find a more concrete and clear expression in Moore's notion of the semi-autonomous social field – a notion that she describes in an article from 1973, in an attempt to reunite "law and the context in which it operates"[295] and to establish a concept as "a way of defining a research problem".[296]

Coming from anthropology, Moore proposes an approach:

> that the small field observable to an anthropologist be chosen and studied in terms of its semi-autonomy – the fact that it can generate rules and customs and symbols internally, but that it is also vulnerable to rules and decisions and other forces emanating from the larger world by which it is surrounded.[297]

The semi-autonomous social field, as defined by Moore, has three distinct features: 1) it has rule-making capacities; 2) it has the means to induce or coerce compliance; 3) it is "set in a larger social matrix which can, and does, affect and invade it".[298] Semi-autonomous fields "have" a legal order.[299]

Moore continues in her article to take the notion as a framework for analyzing the garment industry in New York and the Chagga tribe of Mount Kilimanjaro. In relation to the garment industry in New York, Moore describes the different relations that the different actors in the industry have to each other and what parts they play, including and exposing a system of corruption where the union business agent does not enforce the union contract (regulating wages and hours) to the letter, in exchange for gifts from the contractor such as whiskey and dresses.[300]

However, Moore does not identify the unwritten rules governing these and other transactions within the "system of exchange" of this semi-autonomous social field as law. She argues that they are not based on legally enforceable obligations, for which there is no need "where there are such strong extra-legal sanctions available".[301] Her analysis of the New York garment industry implies equality – in terms of relations – between different parties, such as when she argues that "the inducements and coercions involved in this system of

---

the social practices and usages of the 'tribes' populating Bukovina" (Ziekert (2009: 232)). However, it would seem that this is then about the "social practices" of the tribe and not about their law.

295 Moore (1973: 719).

296 Ibid: 742.

297 Ibid: 720.

298 Ibid: 720.

299 Ibid: 721. One wonders why Moore chose the term "have" and not "are".

300 Ibid: 724-726.

301 Ibid: 726.

relationships are founded on wanting to stay in the game".[302] I would therefore argue that this particular order she is describing is in fact a social order governed by social norms and not by legal norms – an observation that she seems to adhere to, because even though in her general definition a semi-autonomous field has a legal order[303], she identifies the rules of the field as extra-legal.[304] Moreover, when she writes that "law is obviously a part of this picture", she is referring to state law.[305]

When Moore discusses the Chagga Tribe, a similar picture emerges in the sense that she points at the several rules that are, in this case, situated in unequal hierarchical structures as "non-legal arrangements such as the allocations of land by fathers and uncles to sons and nephews" which contradict the "legal rules". Legal rules are not defined, but seem to refer to state legal rules, for example when she argues that "relationships long established in persisting semi-autonomous social fields are difficult to do away with instantly by legislative measures", illustrated by an attempt of the Tanzanian government to abolish chiefship in 1963.[306]

It seems that Moore does not understand the state itself to be a semi-autonomous social field[307], because she continually contradicts the semi-autonomous social field to the state and its inner regulations to state law.[308] In fact, therefore, even if very often referred to in discussions on legal pluralism as an example of legal pluralist theory[309], I would argue that Moore's theory of the

302 Ibid: 727.

303 Ibid: 721.

304 Ibid: 727.

305 Ibid: 728-29.

306 Ibid: 739.

307 Although some scholars argue otherwise, see for example Griffiths (2003: 24): "under normal conditions, the state – one of the most prominent and for many purposes the most inclusive of the [semi-autonomous social fields (SASF)] in a modern society – substantially constrains the regulatory autonomy of other SASFs. The autonomy of the state is of course also limited by other SASFs, as the reader of political news in the daily newspaper will be aware", although in an accompanying footnote he nuances slightly by arguing that "strictly speaking, the concept 'state' does not refer to one but to a whole complex of SASFs: legislative, administrative and judicial institutions".

308 Moore (1973: 721, 723).

309 See for example Woodman (1989: 1): "Social groups have their own rules for the ordering of members' relations, generated within the group or adopted from external sources. The non-state groups found throughout Africa, such as the "tribe" and the adherents of a religion, order the activities of members by such rules for most of the more important aspects of their lives. These groups are, in Moore's much-used and helpful phrase, "semi-autonomous social fields." Their rules may be appropriately termed "law": there is no empirical distinction between them and state laws other than the practice of certain institutions of the state to differentiate between them". See also Griffiths (1986: 29-37), who argues that 'Moore defines a 'semi-autonomous social field' as an identifiable social group which engages in reglementary activities. This also provides her with a criterion of the 'legal' (which as we have seen is missing from Ehrlich's account): all reglementation by a 'semi-autonomous social field' is, for purposes of a theory of legal pluralism, 'law' (36). '.

semi-autonomous social field is in fact not a theory of legal pluralism, but rather a theory on how state law interacts with social norms of certain social fields. Her concept of the semi-autonomous field may however be adapted to adhere to a more legal pluralist framework, if it is stated to include (and if so, in what case) legal norms.[310]

3.3.4. POSPISIL'S LEGAL SYSTEMS

Leopold Pospisil's interpretation of legal pluralism seems to be most useful to and coherent with the legal theory posited so far in this thesis, in addition to being most useful for understanding law for children. Pospisil distinguishes four criteria for law:

1) law is manifested in a decision made by a political authority
2) it contains a definition of the relation between the two parties to the dispute (*obligatio*)
3) it has a regularity of application (intention of universal application)
4) it is provided with a sanction[311]

In his research on disputes among the Kapauku Papuans, Nunamiut Eskimo and Tirolean peasants, he found that:

> the decisions of the leaders of the various subgroups bore all the necessary criteria of law (in the same way that modern state law does): the decisions were made by leaders who were regarded as jural authorities by their followers [...] these decisions were meant to be applied to all "identical" (similar) cases decided in the future [...] they were provided with physical or psychological sanctions [...] and they settled disputes between parties represented by living people.[312]

He therefore claims categorically that "every functioning subgroup of a society has its own legal system which is necessarily different in some respects from those of the other subgroups".[313] An individual is simultaneously a member of several subgroups, such as the household, the lineage, etc., and consequently the same individual may be subject to different and sometimes contradictory laws of different legal systems.[314] Within a legal system, one can find different

310 For a discussion, see Tamanaha (2008: 392-95).
311 Pospisil (1974: 8).
312 Pospisil (1967: 9).
313 Posipisil (1967: 9; 1974: 107). I personally disagree, because there are certainly also functioning subgroups of society that function based on shared social norms and not necessarily on enforceable legal norms. However, of course this depends on how one defines a "functioning subgroup of society"; Pospisil did not provide a definition.
314 Pospisil (1967: 9). The term "legal system" is used interchangeably with "legal level".

legal levels and different conflicts are adjudicated on different legal levels. For example, for the Kapauku, breaches of etiquette are punishable only on the family level, whereas war crimes will be adjudicated at the level of the entire confederacy.[315] Legal sanctions are different for each legal level too: slapping as a punishment for delicts is confined to the family and household levels, whereas confiscation of all property as a punishment belongs to more inclusive groups than the household.[316]

Pospisil sees the same kind of legal systems operating in Western society. In the USA, for example, "there exists, besides the federal or national legal system that is applied to the whole society (nation), the legal systems of its component states".[317] But he goes even further and controversially argues that "even a small grouping such as the American family has a legal system administered by the husband, or wife, or both, as the case may be. Even there, in individual cases, the decisions and rules enforced by the family authorities may be contrary to the law of the state and might be deemed illegal".[318] Other examples of legal subsystems are the criminal gangs, the province, the village, the clan, and guilds.[319]

The terms "legal system" and "legal level" seem to be used interchangeably by Pospisil in some instances. I think we have to understand the legal system as the legal order of a specific subgroup, a body of law that exercises social control over its members.[320] In another formulation: "the totality of the principles incorporated in the legal decisions of an authority of a society's subgroup" (because for Pospisil the authoritative ruler is one of the essential elements of law).[321] Legal levels refer to a hierarchy between these different legal systems, based on inclusivity.[322]

Griffiths criticizes Pospisil by saying that:

> [Pospisil's] "legal levels" within which the self-regulating subgroups of a society are arranged are conceived of as an orderly – one is tempted to say, an idealized – structure of the whole society, and the subgroups are conceived of as more or less inclusive building blocks within that structure.[323]

I disagree with this analysis. Pospisil gives examples of situations where different legal systems coexist on equal footing (such as the two legal systems among the Nunamiut Eskimo).[324] He does speak of a hierarchy, but this only relates to the

---

315 Ibid: 13.
316 Ibid: 13.
317 Ibid: 13.
318 Pospisil (1967:13-15; 1974: 112).
319 Pospisil (1967: 13).
320 Ibid: 24.
321 Ibid: 9.
322 Ibid: 9.
323 Griffiths (1986: 17).
324 Pospisil (1967: 5).

legal system's level of inclusiveness and not to a hierarchy in legal power. Even though a state legal system can be more inclusive (including more different legal systems) than the family legal system, for example, and is therefore higher up in the hierarchy, this does not mean that the state legal system has more legal power over the individual. This is precisely because, as Pospisil argues, the center of power is not necessarily located at the most inclusive level.[325] Where the center of legal power lies, with what legal system, depends on the perspective one takes. For example, for a member of a gang in the USA:

> the law of the criminal gang is usually provided with sanctions much harsher and infinitely more effective and immediate in application than sanctions of the official law of the country; therefore members of such organizations conform primarily with the legal system of their illicit organization. Thus, as far as the gangsters are concerned, the legal center of power is located in the gang rather than on the level of society as a whole.[326]

Whether something is legal or illegal also depends on the perspective one takes, from which legal system. "In individual cases, the decisions and rules enforced by the family authorities [Husband, or wife, or both], may be contrary to the law of the state and might be deemed illegal [from a state law perspective]".[327] The center of power is not fixed; it may shift its position over time.[328]

3.4. CHILDREN'S LEGAL ORDERS

Based on the above considerations and, in particular, the definition we have of the law and the legal order (§3.1), it seems increasingly clear that, when looking from the child's perspective, there are several legal orders of which the state legal order is not necessarily of primary importance.

Three legal pluralists that have been mentioned here (Ehrlich, Pospisil and de Sousa Santos) each recognize different legal orders of different social subgroups or associations. They recognize that legal orders can be of different degrees of inclusiveness – meaning that, for each legal order, the size of the legal community is different. Some legal orders can be small and local, such as the household or the family. It seems to me that smaller and more local orders will be most immediate and important to children; children may not know about state law (yet) but they sure know about the rules of the household at a young age. This is where I expect to find what Pospisil calls "the center of legal power".

325 Pospisil (1967: 17; 1974: 115).
326 Pospisil (1967: 17).
327 Ibid: 14.
328 Ibid: 18.

Recognizing that children all over the world live in very different circumstances where they encounter different legal orders, I want to sketch three legal orders that are ideal type legal orders that I expect apply often and generally to children. These are: the household, the school and the state. Other possible legal orders for children include, for example, the orphanage, the workplace, the gang, and the peer group.

3.4.1. THE HOUSEHOLD LEGAL ORDER

Tamanaha in his 1993 famous and quite genius critique of legal pluralism, wrote that:

> many legal pluralists have degrees in law and hold positions in law faculties. Law is what they know and are experts in; talking about law is their living. They are refugees from the study of doctrinal state law who tend to see law even when they look away [...] After all, it would only occur to persons trained in the law to conceive that the normative relations within the family constitute a 'legal' order.[329]

On this point, I have to disagree. In fact, it is philosophers who, long before the "existence" of legal pluralism as an academic approach, argued that the family or household community[330] comprises a legal order. For example, Aristotle wrote around 350 B.C. that, although the state differs in kind from other communities, "every family is ruled by the eldest, and [...] each one gives law to his children and to his wives".[331] According to Aristotle, within the household management[332], we find three relations: of master and slave, husband and wife, father and children.[333] The father rules over the child "exercising a kind of royal power"; because the child's soul is immature, the father is the natural superior to his subjects, alike the king.[334] In contract theory, we also find the idea of the household as a political and legal order. For Hobbes, for example, the father acquires sovereign power over his children "when a man maketh his

---

329 Tamanaha (1993: 205).

330 In the following, I will take the household community as point of focus, as "the family" is a much wider and harder to define concept. With "household" I refer to all the members of the legal community of the household, which will usually, but not necessarily, be connected to one house. In principle, it is about the rules that the head of the household installs for each person that lives in the house (although they might still apply to, for example, children who have moved out of the house – although then we might call it the family legal order rather than the household legal order).

331 Aristotle (350 B.C./1932: Part II Book I).

332 In Greek: *"oikonomia"* is used, which means "the management of the household", and with is the etymological origin of our word "economy". See Rousseau (1755/1994: 3).

333 Aristotle (350 B.C./1932: Part III).

334 Ibid: Book I part XIII.

children, to submit themselves, and their children to his government".[335] This results in a relationship between sovereign and subjects equal to the situation in a commonwealth by institution.[336] Rousseau speaks of "domestic government", which is the government of the father over the family[337], and argues that the family is the most ancient society, the first model of political society, where the father is leading and the children are obeying.[338]

When looking from the child's perspective, the child within the household encounters household rules that are imposed on her/him, usually by the caretaker. As long as the child accepts the authority of the caretaker in the legal sense, s/he imposes legal power upon the caretaker by recognizing the caretaker's being authorized to create laws and enforce compliance (at least in certain areas of household life). Then the household forms a legal order for the child. This recognition can be observed empirically for example in a child who argues that a step-parent "cannot tell me what to do because s/he is not my real parent" (implying sovereignty for the biological parent), in children who tell their caretaker that "you cannot tell me what to do – I am not a child anymore" (implying sovereignty of the caretaker over the child up until a certain age), in a child who argues that "I cannot talk to strangers because mom says it's not allowed", etc.

There is a difference between legal norms and social norms within the family[339], a difference that is perhaps not always immediately clear in words but rather becomes clear when we research the meaning the subject attaches to these words and sentences. Imagine for example a 17-year old boy who is going out on a Saturday night, whose mother has told him to be home at 1 A.M. The boy may feel that, in fact, the mother does not control him anymore (at least in this respect) and therefore there is no law for him that "his mother tells him what time to be home" (for example). However, he might still choose to be home at this time because it pleases his mother and he does not want to hurt her. If the boy feels that he is obliged to be home at 1 A.M., because his mother says so and if he feels he has to obey his mother because she is his mother, then this is a legal situation rather than only a social situation. But if he feels he wants to be home at the time his mother told him, because he does not want to hurt her feelings, this amounts to a social rather than legal relationship.

We can also imagine households where the caretakers do not control the children; they might form a democratic unity where decisions are taken through discussion and a voting procedure, for example.

Empirical research in childhood development has a large body of research on household laws. They are mostly discussed under "parental authority",

335 Hobbes (1651/1996: 121, 41).

336 Ibid: 138.

337 Rousseau, *Discourse on Political Economy and The Social Contract* 3.

338 Ibid: 77.

339 For the difference between social norms and legal norms in general, see §1.2.

"household rules", "control theory", etc.[340] To my knowledge, these researches have never been connected to a notion of legal pluralism or to children's rights research in general. However, the research fields are closely related, as we can see for example in Tisak's article on "children's conceptions of parental authority", who found it:

> possible to assess how subjects think about the jurisdiction of parental authority in making rules that inhibit or restrain child behaviors (e.g., a rule prohibiting hitting) and then, once the rule exists, how subjects evaluate children's obligations to obey the command.[341]

In his article, based on interviews with 120 children of ages 8–12 years old, we see that it differs per subject area whether children feel that their parents are legitimized to make rules. For example, 98% of respondents "thought that it was all right for parents to make a rule prohibiting an act when it pertained to stealing", and only 10% "stated that it was all right for parents to regulate friendships". When asked whether one has an obligation to follow the rules once they are formalized, 100% felt they had "an obligation to adhere to the rules pertaining to stealing" and 35% felt that they had to obey a parental rule that stated that they could not interact with one of their friends.[342]

The household as a legal order clearly has a great influence on the socio-legal reality of most children and should therefore be researched whenever we want to understand children's rights violations. As Ehrlich says, if we want to improve the situation of the child, knowing the living law for the child is "infinitely more important and interesting" than the dead letter (state) law.[343]

3.4.2. THE SCHOOL

Another possible legal order, as seen from the child's perspective, is the school. Clearly not all children go to school, as not all children live in a household community. However, many do and, for them, the school and the classroom are perceived as legal orders.

In his analysis of the history of the institutions of discipline and punishment, which includes the school, Foucault shows how, at least in the West, schools in particular have evolved as institutions where children (bodies and souls) are subjected to power through which they are disciplined.[344] He describes how

---

340 See, for example: Smetana (1988; 1995); Mayes et al. (2006); Smetana & Asquith (1994); Wright & Cullen (2001); Tisak (1986).

341 Tisak (1986: 166).

342 Ibid: 170.

343 See §3.3.2.

344 Foucault (1975/1995: 29, 30, 138).

gradually "but especially after 1762"[345], the educational space emerges which functions "like a learning machine, but also as a machine for supervising, hierarchizing, rewarding".[346] This happens through the organization of the space by assigning individual places, through organization of subjects and questions treated according to an order of increasing difficulty, through classification of knowledge (e.g. "tables"), through organization of time by using timetables, through the classification of behaviour by assigning to the pupil good and bad marks, etc.[347] The ultimate control being the dressage of the bodies through discipline: to install in children's bodies such obedience that whenever they perceive a "signal" that attracts "at once the attention of all the pupils to the teacher" and makes them

> attentive to what he wishes to impart them [...] Whenever a good pupil hears the noise of the signal, he will imagine that he is hearing the voice of the teacher or rather the voice of God himself calling him by his name.[348]

Foucault further describes the different techniques the school and the teacher use to discipline students, such as punishment and reward.[349] In the end, through education, enforcement of laws is no longer necessary, because students will have internalized the norm that was taught in school and they will self-discipline.[350]

Empirical research on school as a legal order is mostly found in educational research, which researches "classroom rules", "teacher authority" and "school rules". Classroom organization can take different forms, from authoritarian to democratic, but for all forms of organization these rules can be understood as laws according to the current definition (§3.1).[351]

3.4.3. THE STATE

When looking for a child's perspective on state law, for example, when wondering what relation children have to state law – are they even aware? – there is an overload of literature of adults discussing state law over children, but hardly anything about what children themselves have to say about state law.[352] In the

345 Ibid: 146.
346 Ibid: 146-47, 65.
347 Ibid: 147-51, 80.
348 Ibid: 166.
349 Ibid: 2. 'the means of correct training'.
350 Ibid: 184, 201-3, 16, 20-21.
351 See for example Johnston & Lubomudrov (1987); Thornberg (2008; 2009); Boostrom (1991); Davies (1984); VanderStaay et al. (2009); Mokhele (2006).
352 To illustrate: when searching google scholar on "state law child perspective", you find, in order of appearance: 1. ***Guidelines for child custody evaluations in divorce proceedings*** (American Psychological Association (1995)), 2. ***The child and the state in India: Child labor***

following paragraph, I will present the academic discussion on whether children are citizens in relation to the child perspective, followed by empirical research available on the child's perspective on state law.

Children as citizens

The question about the relation of children to state law is mostly addressed in terms of the popular academic question whether children are citizens. In ancient philosophy, the answer to this question was clear: children, like slaves, servants and women are not citizens. They might become citizens one day.[353] Citizens are male adult people who can participate in politics, who engage in deciding state law over all members of the state legal order, including non-citizens who are nevertheless subjected to the relevant state (or *polis*) legal order. In ancient times, thus, one could be a member of the legal order, without being a citizen; one could be subjected to state laws without having any legal or political power.

This distinction reappears in social contract theory. For Hobbes, for example, the father is the sovereign of the family and, when the father is the member of the commonwealth, children automatically become subjected to obligations from both the family and the state.[354] For Rousseau, children are not yet citizens; this they will become citizens "when they are men", and for children to become citizens, "it is necessary to educate them when they are children".[355] Rousseau takes this a step further than Hobbes. For Rousseau, until the age of 16, the child is not able to understand the [state] law. Consequently, the child is not subjected to duty.[356] Hobbes also recognizes that if someone lacks the means necessary to know the law (such as the ability to speak), they are excused from having to obey[357], but he does emphasize obedience of the child to its parents and indirectly to the state sovereign.[358]

and education policy in comparative perspective (a comparative study on goverment action by Weiner, (1991)), 3. ***Hatching the Egg: A Child-Centered Perspective on Parent's Rights*** (Wooudhouse (1992)), 4. ***From property to person status: Historical perspective on children's rights*** (Hart (1991)), 5. ***A policy perspective on child labour in India with pervasive gender and urban bias in school education*** (Chaudri (1997)). None of these discuss the child's perspective or relation to state law. A search for "law child perspective" amounts to similar results.

353 Aristotle (350 B.C./1932: Book III Part V; Book VIII Part I): "children are not citizens equally with grown-up men, who are citizens absolutely, but children, not being grown up, are only citizens on a certain assumption". Therefore, they have to be educated, to "be moulded to suit the form of government under which [the child] lives".

354 Hobbes (1651/1996: 62-63, 98-99). However, Hobbes gets into trouble here because, for him, the relationship between the sovereign and its subject can only be a relationship of subjection and obligation if based on a voluntary contract – and the question how children would be able to contract with parents and subject themselves is left open.

355 Rousseau (1762/1979: 165, 79).

356 Rousseau (1762/1797: 210, 312).

357 Hobbes (1651/1996: 208).

358 Ibid: 140.

Both these notions still apply to modern society. Whether anyone is a citizen of a legal order depends on two conditions: 1) whether they form part of its legal community (they recognize that the laws of the legal order apply to them) and 2) whether they have some form of legal power – of which the minimum threshold seems to be that they are allowed to vote (in a situation of a state legal order). Citizens, following the old Greek view, are people who are members of the legal community and who are part of the sovereign. Non-citizens of the state legal order are all others who are members of the legal community but do not have legal power (for example stateless people, asylum seekers in relation to the host country's legal order, people under dictatorial regimes, children).

In children's rights research, these two categories (citizenship and membership of a legal community) seem to overlap, leading to confusion. Ruth Lister argues, based on her 2003 empirical study with children in the UK, that "the most common model to which [young people][359] subscribed was that of citizenship as a 'universal status', enjoyed by virtue of membership of the community or nation".[360] When citizenship and membership of a legal community are used interchangeably, a plea for children's citizenship amounts to all kinds of wild statements. For example, in Lister's article she calls for children's citizenship, because children are able to "treat others with respect", which, according to Lister, is "seen by the general public as a key responsibility of citizenship". She continues to compare a child's quest for citizenship with the feminist movement.[361] Clearly, here we are confusing the discussion when we forget the distinction between citizenship and membership of a legal community.[362] The feminists in the 20th century were fighting for citizenship: a say in matters of legislation, some legal power. Children generally are not fighting for this at all.[363]

Manfred Liebel does a similar thing when he argues that "those who take children's rights seriously are bound to imagine citizenship also of children and to take action for it".[364] Clearly, children can enjoy all sorts of legal rights as members of the legal community, without necessarily possessing citizenship – with the exception of a right to legal or political power (they do not have the right to vote, to found a political party, to run for president, etc). Liebel presents

---

359 Based on interviews with 110 "young people" aged 16-23 (Lister et al. (2003: 236)).

360 Lister (2008: 10-11).

361 Ibid: 13-18.

362 For an interesting discussion of the meaning of "citizenship" and in particular its empirical understanding, see: ibid.

363 According to Lister et al. (2003: 251), children mostly view citizenship as a non-active role "rooted in membership of the community or nation", and good citizenship is identified with civic duties and communitarian membership. In my discussions on the subject with several groups of adolescent philosophy students, when I was a philosophy teacher in a Dutch high school, most children indicated that they did not want the right to vote. They argued that they enjoyed being children, not having to carry adult political responsibility.

364 Liebel (2008: 34).

a picture of children as disempowered victims of the adult political system, arguing that it is a "fact that children and young people have a profound feeling of impotence and exclusion" (without reference to empirical study), feelings that are connected to adult refusal of their political rights.[365] This argument could make sense if we are talking about older children – for example, adolescent street children who want to engage in the political discussion on legislation for children living on the streets.[366] However it does not make sense if we are talking about children in general, because what four year old would ever want political influence on the level of the state legal order?[367]

The 1998 UK Crick Report on *Education for Citizenship and Teaching of Democracy in Schools*, as discussed by Andrew Lockyer, does seem to draw this distinction between citizenship and membership of the legal order. Interestingly, they recommend practicing political engagement (active citizenship) in school, which they see as "the place to engage with politics both in the classroom and in the school community as a whole [...] to prepare all for civic and political participation"[368], implying that children are not yet citizens of the state legal order, but can be citizens of the school legal order.

Children and the state law

There is very little empirical research on children's relationship to state law, from a child's perspective. Do children even know about state law and the state in general and, if so, from what age? Do they view themselves as subjects of state law? Do they know the content of state laws? Are state laws for the community (chapter 1) laws for adults, or for children too?

Some empirical material is available on children's experiences of court proceedings, thereby testing their knowledge of the legal court system and subsequent legal terms.[369] This is done for example through a Children's Court Questionnaire that tests children's legal knowledge by asking questions such as "what does a child's attorney do?", to which the answer is rated according to "correctness", with the correct answer here being "He tells the judge what you

365 Ibid: 37-38.

366 See for example van Daalen & Mabillard (2018).

367 Liebel advocates for children's "citizenship from below", "expressed by children themselves setting goals they want to reach and choosing the way they want to act" (2008: 42). For this to happen on the level of the state legal order, at least a minimum of understanding of the state legal order is required. No one who does not have a minimal knowledge about the workings, reach, system, etc. of the state legal order can "set goals [for participation in legislation of the state legal order] they want to reach".

368 Lockyer et al. (2008: 24).

369 See for example Block et al. (2010: 660-61), who give an overview of empirical research on children's knowledge of court proceedings. Children's knowledge of court proceedings has been studied mostly with respect to criminal court (e.g.: Saywitz et al. (1990); Warren-Leubecker et al. (1989); Quas et al (2009a; 2009b)).

feel and what you think should be happening and helps the judge decide".[370] Tests of children's knowledge of courtroom legal language often prove that they do not know many of the concepts used in court.[371] Whether children are able to use this linguistic knowledge, when present, in a legally relevant manner (in court proceedings) is less researched.[372]

The only empirical research on children's understanding of state law that I could find was a 1969 article titled "Growth of the Idea of Law in Adolescence".[373] The researchers held qualitative interviews with 120 adolescents from fifth to twelfth grade (ages from 10–18 years old).[374] They show that young adolescents cannot think abstractly about concepts such as government and laws. Moreover, young adolescents have a very limited understanding of law as concrete, individually restrictive ("law is there to keep people from doing things they're not supposed to do like killing people" (13-year old)).[375] According to the authors:

> before the age of 15 (or thereabouts) the adolescent, lacking a differentiated view of the social order, cannot grasp the needs, present and future, of the total community; when the child thinks of law, he refers to it only to individual conduct, and, more specifically, to the constraint of anti-social conduct. Once a sense of the community has been established, it penetrates all phases of political and social thought.[376]

In addition, young adolescents did not understand the fact that laws can be changed. Around age 15 they come to understand the concept of amendment.[377] For younger adolescents:

> it was as though law emerged from the empyrean; once it has arrived, man's sole duty is to obey it. If he does not, the authorities are right to coerce him, using whatever means ingenuity will allow. Younger adolescents rarely imagined [...] that a law is absurd, mistaken or unfair.[378]

The only tacit explanation the authors suggest for the shift in understanding of law during adolescence, is that:

---

370 Block et al. (2010: 69-70).

371 See Saywitz et al. (1990).

372 See Peterson-Badali et al. (1997).

373 Adelson et al. (1969).

374 Most disturbingly, the authors added race as a selection criterion: "To reduce incomparability of age samples due to differential dropout rates, the authors decided beforehand not to include Negroes" (ibid: 328).

375 Ibid: 328.

376 Ibid: 329.

377 Ibid: 329.

378 Ibid: 332.

> the young adolescent is locked, matter of factly, into benignly authoritarian relationships to his milieu, both at home and at school [...] with the [older] adolescent's sharp surge toward autonomy, there is a gradual yielding of this way of looking at the politics of household and schoolroom, and ultimately of politics at large.[379]

James, in a similar manner, argues that "although children *are* seen as members of [...] societies [...] their membership is skewed. As a consequence of adults' particular ideas about what children can and cannot do, young people take little active part in shaping the societies to which they belong".[380]

It might therefore be a two-way situation. Because children do not understand the abstract concept of the state, of state law, of society at large, they are not allowed to participate in its creation and its amendment – they are not (yet) citizens. They are however members of the legal community of the state legal order, and state laws apply to them increasingly as they come of age.

3.5. CHILDREN'S LEGAL ORDERS (CONCLUSION)

Under the current theoretical framework, there are three main elements to a legal order: 1) a legal order consists of a legal community, a network of laws and a sovereign; 2) there is an unequal power relation between the sovereign and the subject; 3) the laws of the legal order are statutory laws.

When we look at law from a child's perspective, it seems that different social orders to which children belong can contain these elements and are therefore potential legal orders – most notably the household, school and state legal order. Taking a child's perspective on law therefore automatically leads to a legal pluralist perspective. In fact, state law in most cases seems to be far from children's daily lives and most children might not even be aware of such abstract concepts such as "the state". This means that, if we want to understand children's rights from a bottom-up perspective, we will have to engage in field research and identify the different legal orders to which children are subjected, which possibly influence the respect or violation of children's rights.

Other authors have developed theories for a broader understanding of law, which goes beyond a state-centric perspective. Of these authors, Ehrlich, Moore and Pospisil have been discussed at length in this chapter. Each of these have provided useful theoretical input, yet none of them have really developed a methodology for finding law of these legal orders. Therefore, while they provided useful theoretical concepts that can assist in data analysis, such as "living law" and the idea of the "center of legal power", the question how to find law for children still remains. This question will be the subject of the next chapter.

---

379 Ibid: 329.

380 James (2011: 170), referring to Lister (2007).

CHAPTER 4

FINDING LAW FOR CHILDREN: METHODOLOGY

After having created a theoretical framework for finding law for children, including a definition of law (chapter 1), an adult view of law for children (chapter 2) and a theory of children's legal plural orders (chapter 3), the current chapter will focus on how to empirically find law for children.

The chapter will start with a general methodology for understanding social action – of which legal action is defined as a subcategory – following Max Weber (§4.1). In §4.2, I will give an overview of how the child's perspective has been incorporated into academic research so far. After discussing developments and methodologies for listening to children / child participation in academic research, a methodology will be designed for looking at law through children's eyes. This section will argue that we have to engage children directly in the research and engage in research together *with* participants as equals. To realize this, I will use the educational methods of inquiry learning (§4.3.1) and philosophy for children (§4.3.2). Under §4.4, I will work out in detail a step-to-step guide to finding law for children.

4.1. FINDING LAW: MAX WEBER'S METHODOLOGY FOR UNDERSTANDING SOCIAL ACTION

Since in chapter 1 we concluded that law is a social fact, and that a law is a valid legal norm created by the sovereign, who is sovereign because of the recognition of the legal community of the basic norm[381], what is law ultimately depends on the community. If not, rules are like the rules created by a man in a psychiatric institution who thinks he is Napoleon; they are not recognized as legal by the relevant community and therefore they are not laws.[382] In this sense, we can understand Ehrlich who says that, to find law, there is no other way but to observe and ask people.[383]

381 Chapter 1, §3.1.

382 See §1.3.2.

383 See §3.3.2.

How then should we do this? A possible answer to the question of methodology might be found in the writings of Max Weber. Weber tells us that the human individual engages in social action; this is the action of an individual to which s/he attaches subjective meaning and, in this subjective meaning, s/he takes into account the behaviour of others, by which the action is oriented in its course.[384] Social action, according to Weber, "may be guided by the belief in the existence of a legitimate order". When a plurality of actors do so in relation to each other, they engage in a "social relationship"[385], which is called "an order" if this behaviour is "oriented towards determinable 'maxims'" (i.e. rules or norms).[386] An order is:

> "valid" if the orientation towards these maxims occurs [...] because it is in some appreciable way regarded by the actor as in some way obligatory or exemplary for him [...] even in the case of evasion or disobedience, the probability of their being recognized as valid norms may have an effect on action [...] a thief orients his action to the validity of the criminal law in that he acts surreptitiously.[387]

Basically, what Weber is saying is the following (see scheme below – although obviously "legal action" is not necessarily in the middle point of human behaviour):

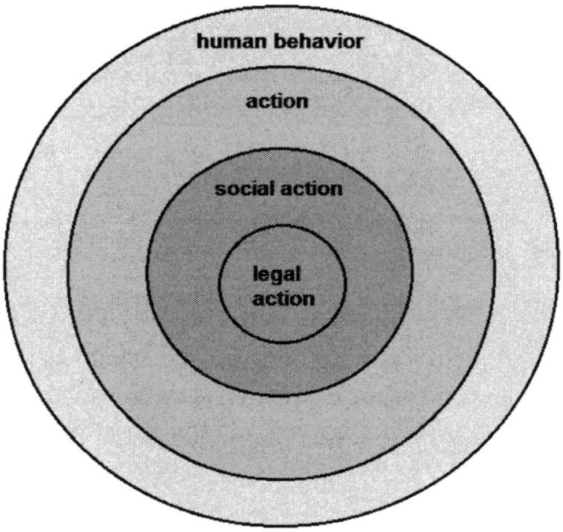

Of all the ways in which people move, there is certain behaviour to which a person attaches subjective meaning. For example, when I unconsciously move a pen over a piece of paper, while thinking of something else, I am behaving but I do not attach meaning to this behaviour, so I am not acting. However, when

384 Weber (1922/1978: 4).
385 Ibid: 26.
386 Ibid: 31.
387 Ibid: 31-32.

I take a pen to write down some of my thoughts on paper, this behaviour has meaning for me. Only the latter behaviour is what Weber labels "action". Of all human action, some is "social action". This is when I take the subjective meaning of another into account in my action, for example when I take up my pen and write a funny note for my colleague. Then, some of a human being's social action is guided by the valid norms of an order. "Valid norms" may refer to legal and non-legal social norms. Weber does not define this further. When we zoom in on legal social norms, we might find our action to be guided by the same legal norms, such as the laws of the Dutch government. Therefore, when I am in the Netherlands and I pick up my pen and stick it in my colleague's eyeball, I might lie and say that it was an accident, as I know we are both assigning subjective meaning to my action and we are both subject to the rules of the same order. We feel obliged by, or subjected to, the legal norm set by the Dutch government that we are not to do harm to another. Weber did not name this type of action; I will label it "legal action".[388]

Instead of sketching and explaining the rest of Weber's theoretical framework for economy and law in society, which I do not think is necessarily useful for the current research[389], I want to focus on the methodology that Weber designs for research in the social sciences. His approach basically consists of three steps: 1. Creating a theoretical framework, where relevant concepts are defined in the form of "ideal types"; 2. Relating the ideal-type constructs to individual subjective reality; 3. Drawing conclusions, using and judging the concepts from (1) in relation to qualitative data from (2).[390]

4.1.1. SOCIAL SCIENCES: ITS SUBJECT AND PRESUPPOSITIONS

In his essay, "the methodology of the social sciences", which Weber originally wrote to introduce the direction he and his fellow editors were planning to take for their scientific journal *Archiv für Sozialwissenschaften und Sozialpolitik*, Weber spells out most clearly his ideas on a methodology for the social sciences.[391]

For Weber, the social scientist (a term he uses interchangeably with "cultural scientist") looks at social reality and realizes that it presents to us an infinite multiplicity of constantly emerging and disappearing events.[392] Because we

---

388 Ibid: 4, 23, 26, 31-32.

389 In part, because I agree with Trubek, who writes that "despite his predilection for careful definitions, I do not believe Weber had one, clear-cut notion of 'law.' While he specifically defines law at several points, the discussion at other places in his work overflows the neat boundaries he himself sets up" (1972: 725).

390 Analysis mostly based on Weber (1904/1949). See specifically p. 75-76 for these three steps.

391 Weber (1904/1949).

392 Ibid: 72.

want to understand this social reality, and because we are limited by the finite capacities of our human mind, we can only make a portion of this reality the object of our investigation and so we have to make a selection.[393]

Social scientists, first, choose to direct their attention towards those phenomena of reality that are social or cultural (which is the same thing). They depart from their transcendental presupposition, namely that human beings are "*cultural beings*, endowed with the capacity and the will to take a deliberate attitude towards the world and to lend it *significance*".[394] A following presupposition, which is implicit in Weber's writing, is that the ideas that these cultural beings have about the reality in which they find themselves cause, at least regularly, their empirical behaviour.[395] Only when they do so are they acting rather than just behaving. In more philosophical terms, Weber's social science presupposes a principle of free will; there is a causal connection between the idea "I want to be nice to my sister" and the concrete action, for example, "*therefore* I make her a cup of tea". In Weber's terms: human beings can *act* and, what is more, they can *act socially*.

It is exactly this part of reality, the "small portion of existing concrete reality [that] is coloured by our value-conditioned interest" that is significant to human beings in general and to the social scientist in particular as the object of his studies.[396] To be more precise, it is these ideas guiding social action that social scientists want to understand, because they want to understand "the relationships and the cultural significance of individual events [...] and [...] the causes for their being historically *so* and not *otherwise* [author's italics]".[397] For example, in relation to my first case study (chapter 5), we ask: why do children go to school? By what value-idea is this action guided? In what sense, if any, is this a legal action (an action which is guided by the orientation towards the binding maxims of a valid (legal) order)?

4.1.2. WEBER'S THEORETICAL FRAMEWORK: IDEAL TYPES

To scientifically understand social reality, according to Weber, we need to construct a theoretical framework and, in particular, ideal types.

Again, we find ourselves confronted with an infinite multiplicity of constantly emerging and disappearing events. Moreover, these events that

---

393 Ibid: 72.

394 Ibid: 81.

395 Ibid: 95, "an ideal type [...] which can be abstracted from certain characteristic social phenomena of an epoch, might [...] have also been present in the minds of the persons living in that epoch as an ideal to be striven for"; "[...] those 'ideas' which govern the behaviour of the population of a certain epoch [...]" (ibid: 96).

396 Ibid: 76.

397 Ibid: 72.

social scientists want to understand are caused by ideas, and the ideas which govern behaviour empirically exist "in the minds of an indefinite and constantly changing mass of individuals and [assume] in their minds the most multifarious nuances of form and content, clarity and meaning […]".[398] We therefore need concepts, generalizations based on individual ideas, and mental constructs that are:

> formed by the one-sided *accentuation* of one or more points of view and by the synthesis of a great many diffuse, discrete, more or less present and occasionally absent *concrete individual* phenomena which are arranged according to those one-sidedly emphasized viewpoints into a unified *analytical* construct […].[399]

These concepts are what Weber calls "ideal types". An ideal type is "a purely ideal limiting concept with which the real situation or action is compared and surveyed for the explication of certain of its significant components".[400] The ideal type is "a mental construct for the scrutiny and systematic characterization of individual concrete patterns".[401] As an example, Weber discusses the ideal type "state":

> the problem of the logical structure of the *concept of the state* […] when we inquire as to what corresponds to the idea of the "state" in empirical reality, we find an infinity of diffuse and discrete human actions, both active and passive, factually and legally regulated relationships […] all bound together by an idea, namely, the belief in the actual or normative validity of rules and of the authority-relationships of some human beings towards others […] the scientific conception of the state […] is naturally always a synthesis which we construct for certain heuristic purposes. But on the other hand, it is also abstracted from the unclear synthesis which are found in the minds of human beings.[402]

To understand human social action, we have to construct theoretical ideal types and use them as guidance to construct hypotheses.[403] We cannot understand social reality otherwise;

> [t]he *significance* of a configuration of cultural phenomena […] cannot [..] be derived and rendered intelligible by a system of analytical laws […] since the significance of

398 Ibid: 96.

399 Ibid: 90.

400 Ibid: 93.

401 Ibid: 100.

402 Ibid: 99.

403 Ibid: 90. In Weber's biography, Gert and Wrightdefine Weber's ideal type as "the construction of certain elements of reality into a logically precise conception" (1946: 59). According to them, "Weber did not mean to introduce a new conceptual tool. He merely intended to bring to full awareness what social scientists and historians had been doing when they used words like 'the economic man', 'feudalism', etc". (ibid: 59).

> cultural events presupposes a *value-orientation* towards these events. [...] Empirical reality becomes "culture" to us because and insofar as we relate it to value ideas.[404]

This framework including its ideal types are construed by the social scientist and are therefore dependent on the quality of her/his estimations, to the extent to which the social scientist "can perform this imputation in a reasonably certain manner with his imagination sharpened by personal experience and trained in analytic methods"[405] and construct hypothetical causal relationships between concepts "which our imagination accepts as plausibly motivated and hence as 'objectively possible' and which appear as *adequate* from the nomological standpoint"[406] (i.e. according to rules of reasoning). This ability "varies with the individual case".[407] However, we cannot judge the quality of the framework and its ideal types *a priori*; they are the means towards an end, which is an understanding of a particular portion of social reality. We use these means as tools with which we approach empirical social reality.[408]

4.1.3. RELATING THE IDEAL TYPES TO INDIVIDUAL SUBJECTIVE REALITY

It is with this framework that we approach social reality. Here, in social reality, the scientist finds the "concrete, individually-structured configuration of our cultural life"[409], which are "psychological and intellectual phenomena".[410] S/he collects these "various very disparate *individual* types of cultural elements"[411] through qualitative research[412] and brings order into this "chaos of 'existential judgments' about countless individual events"[413] by relating it to the framework of cultural values "with which we approach reality".[414] We can use the constructed ideal type as "a heuristic device for the comparison of the ideal type and the facts".[415]

For example, the first chapter distinguished three forms of statutory law: formal written law (A), law for the community (B) and hidden law (C). These are all three ideal types that I constructed based on my personal experience

404 Weber (1904/1949: 76, 92).
405 Ibid: 80.
406 Ibid: 92.
407 Ibid: 80.
408 Ibid: 80, 92.
409 Ibid: 74. In Weber's biography Gert and Mills formulate this as follows: "the ultimate unit of analysis for [Weber] is the understandable motivations of the single individual[...]his point of departure and the ultimate unit of his analysis is the individual person" (1946: 55).
410 Weber (1904/1949: 74).
411 Ibid: 89.
412 Ibid: 74.
413 Ibid: 78.
414 Ibid: 78.
415 Ibid: 102.

(mostly after my field research experience in Rwanda and the Netherlands), on my analytical training (mostly consisting of studying the writings of several legal theorists) and I hope to have presented it in a manner that seems plausible to the rules of reason; i.e. in a coherent, logically consistent manner. This will be the viewpoint from which I will approach the part of social reality that I selected for my study, in this case two different international children's rights articles in three particular socio-cultural contexts. In this regard, I will look for people's "purposes"; their "conception[s] of an *effect* which becomes a *cause* of an action [author's italics]".[416]

There are two kinds of understanding, according to Weber: one is the "direct observational understanding of the subjective meaning of a given act as such, including verbal utterances", such as when the researcher asks a participant about her/his motivations.[417] The second is explanatory understanding; "we understand in terms of *motive* the meaning an actor attaches to the proposition twice two equals four, when he states it or writes it down, in that we understand what makes him do this at precisely this moment in these circumstances"[418], such as when the researcher infers from the remark of the participant (i.e. "I have to do this because my father says so") that there is a certain pattern and/or relation (i.e. "the father generally makes law over the child"). According to Weber, "it is the task of the sociologist to be aware of this motivational situation and to describe and analyze it, even though it has not actually been concretely part of the conscious intention of the actor [...]".[419] I would add that, to come closer to a true understanding of social reality, we should try to check these inferences we make with the research participant.

There is an ongoing mutual interaction between the framework and qualitative data obtained in social reality. The framework gives direction to the questions we ask, the respondents we choose and the things that we do not see. Neither is however static or rigid; both the framework and the qualitative data are subject to a certain amount of alteration by the researcher. On the one hand, when the researcher finds qualitative data that is significant for her/his research project but that does not fit well into the designed framework, s/he might use it to inform and alter the framework. On the other hand, "those elements in each individual event which are left unaccounted for by the selection of their elements subsumable under the "law" [will be] considered as scientifically unintegrated residues [...] alternatively they will be viewed as "accidental" [...]".[420]

Clearly, the researcher, as a human subject with value ideas, plays a great, subjective role in the quest for knowledge of social reality. This is necessarily so

416 Ibid: 83.

417 Weber defines a motive as "a complex of subjective meaning which seems to the actor himself or to the observer an adequate ground for the conduct in question" (1922/1978: 11).

418 Ibid: 8.

419 Ibid: 9-10.

420 Weber (1904/1949: 73).

and could not be otherwise. As Weber explains, "there is no absolutely 'objective' scientific analysis of [...] social phenomena", because "the cognitive goal of all research in the social science" is "to transcend the purely *formal* treatment of the legal or conventional norms regulating social life [author's italics]".[421] It is precisely *because* the researcher is a social actor, that s/he can empathically understand the ideas that motivate people's actions. And it is "reality under the guidance of values" that we are interested in here.[422]

4.1.4 DRAWING CONCLUSIONS

Even though a social scientist uses her/his personal subjectivity as a social actor to empathically understand the social action of others, this does not mean that s/he is writing a personal, individual subjective evaluation of a situation in social reality. The social scientist does not state ideals, which is the task of social policy, rather s/he analyzes facts.[423] It is never the task of empirical science "to provide binding norms and ideals from which directives for immediate practical activity can be derived".[424] On the other hand, "value-judgments do not have to be withdrawn from scientific discussions".[425] It is simply so that, when the researcher expresses value judgments and ideals which motivate him as a researcher, that s/he keeps "the readers and [her/himself] sharply aware of this [...] if this obligation is rigorously heeded, the practical evaluative attitude can be not only harmless to scientific interests but even directly useful, and indeed mandatory".[426]

The third and final step of the research of social science is to draw conclusions, based on the framework and its included ideal types as constructed under step 1, combined with the results from our observation of social reality, in particular the individual subjective value-laden ideas that motivate social action, as found under step 2. This conclusion can take different forms:

1. Technical criticism, of which there are two kinds:
   a. We can criticize the setting of the end itself as practically meaningful or as meaningless with reference to existing conditions – for example, when the government sets as its end (the idea guiding its social actions) that it wants all children of state P to have breakfast every morning, but there are no financial means available with any state party (including

421 Ibid: 72.
422 Ibid: 77.
423 Ibid: 60.
424 Ibid: 52.
425 Ibid: 52.
426 Ibid: 59.

the families) to realize this end. In this case, we can show that the end becomes meaningless with reference to existing conditions.[427]

b. We can determine the consequences which the application of the means to be used will produce – for example, the government of state P intends to introduce law Q, which states that all parents must provide their children with breakfast every morning and the social scientists engages in qualitative research to find what consequences this law would have and provide the acting person (government official) with the ability to weigh and compare the undesirable against the desirable consequences of his action.[428]

2. "We can also offer the person, who makes a choice, insight into the significance of the desired object. We can teach her/him to think in terms of the context and the meaning of the ends s/he desires [...] through making explicit and developing in a logically consistent manner the 'ideas' which actually do or which can underlie the concrete end".[429] This is what happens when we engage in a philosophical investigation of ideas; we look for ideas and ask whether they are logically consistent, among themselves and in relation to the end posited. For example, if I encounter a teacher who says it is most important for students to feel safe in the classroom, this is the end s/he poses her/himself. I can then ask: "why do you follow this end?" S/he might argue that s/he wants the students to speak freely, so they can develop an independent skill of critical thinking instead of following mass opinion out of fear for repercussions. In this case, following a logical deduction, the researcher could point out that, apparently the *real* end is for the students to develop to develop an independent skill of critical thinking and the safety in the classroom is only the *means*, a condition.
3. The scientists, after having understood and empathically analyzed the desired ends and ideals that underlie value judgments, can also judge them critically. "This criticism can [...] have only a dialectical character, i.e. [...] a formal logical judgment [...] a testing of [...] internal consistency". This critique can elevate the ultimate standards of value, which the person does not make explicit to her/himself, to the level of explicitness. This is "the utmost that the scientific treatment of value-judgments can do without entering into the realm of speculation".[430]

From this, it "does not follow that research in the cultural sciences can only have results which are 'subjective' in the sense that they are *valid* for one person and not for others. Only the degree to which they interest different persons varies

427 Ibid: 52-53.
428 Ibid: 53.
429 Ibid: 53.
430 Ibid: 54.

[author's italics]".[431] Any conclusion drawn by combining the framework with qualitative data must be understandable, logically coherent and seem at least plausible to all. Weber explains this as follows:

> [A] [German] systematically correct scientific proof in the social sciences [...] must be acknowledged as correct even by a Chinese – or [...] must constantly *strive* to attain this goal, which perhaps may not be completely attainable due to faulty data. Furthermore, the successful *logical* analysis of the content of an ideal and its ultimate axioms and the discovery of the consequences which arise purely from pursuing it, [...] must also be valid for the Chinese [author's italics].[432]

Of course, research in the social sciences presents culturally situated, historically particular conclusions and its conclusions will therefore most likely not be eternally true, because life, people and history change in "the eternally inexhaustible flow of life".[433] As Weber said in his lecture "On science as a vocation": "In science, each of us knows that what he has accomplished will be antiquated in ten, twenty, fifty years [...] Every scientific 'fulfilment' raises new 'questions'; it asks to be 'surpassed' and outdated. Whoever wishes to serve science has to resign himself to this fact".[434]

4.2. FINDING LAW FOR CHILDREN

Although the Weberian social science methodology of understanding the respondent's motivations for social action has been used widely, research on children and on children's rights in particular has, until recently, not seen the necessity for engaging children themselves in research.[435]

In general, children are often not heard by adults. It is inherent to the culturally determined vision of children, the idea of the child as irrational, immoral and unsocial, which determines that children's voices are not to be taken seriously.[436] This point is well illustrated by the following episode from Jodi Picoult's novel "Leaving time". The story is about a 13-year old girl, Jenna, who is trying to find her mother who went missing ten years previously. In the following scene, Jenna is with a (hungover) detective who formerly used to be on the case. They discuss why she did not go to talk to the police about her mother before this day.

---

431 Ibid: 84.
432 Ibid: 58.
433 Ibid: 84.
434 Weber (1919/1946: 134).
435 According to Powell et al. (2020), although since about 10 years there is "growing consensus around the value of engaging children in social research", in practice researchers report difficulties in recruiting and involving children in research. See also §4.2.1.
436 See chapter 2.

> A waitress walks by, and I signal to her, trying to get her attention, since Virgil needs coffee if he's going to be of any use to me. She doesn't see me at all.
>
> "That's what it's like to be a kid," I say. "No one takes you seriously. People look right through you. Even if I'd been able to figure out where to go when I was eight or ten... even if I'd managed to get myself to the police station...even if you hadn't left your job and the sergeant at the front desk told you a kid wanted to get you to reopen a closed case...what would you have done? Would you have let me stand in front of your desk talking while you smiled and nodded and didn't pay attention? Or told your cop buddies about the girl who showed up and wanted to play detective?" [...] "It's like that old saying," I tell him. "If no one hears you, are you even talking?"'[437]

I would argue that children's ideas are generally not to be disregarded and especially not in research.[438] If we want to know about children's lives, about their ideas, beliefs, experiences, about law for children and children's rights, we (adults) have to truly listen to them. The underlying idea is that "children are reliable informants of their own experience".[439] However, the above story carries a warning with it as well, for truly listening to children is not as easy as just sitting down, letting children talk and engaging in conversation. Even if we are totally committed to the idea that we have to take children's voices seriously, in general and in research in particular, we may accidentally engage in adult ethnocentric bias.

An example can be found in the work of Mullender et al., in their book titled "Children's Perspectives on Domestic Violence".[440] The authors of this book are totally committed to the idea of listening to children.[441] In addition to talking to children as respondents, they decided to engage children in the design of the research by engaging them in the pilot phase, asking for their feedback on questions. Some of these children were reported to feel that "their statements would not count because they were 'just something that children think'", and therefore these children "had to be reassured that this was very far from the case".[442] The research consisted of two phases; during the first phase, 1,395 children aged 8–16 years old completed a questionnaire about "what they knew and thought about domestic violence". In the second phase, 54 children who

---

437 Picoult (2014: 123-24).

438 A similar case can be made for the mad, the savage, the woman, and any other minority group that finds itself silenced by people in power. See for example "Filosofie van de waanzin" ("*philosopy of madness*"), a book by philosopher Wouter Kusters, who "suffered" two psychoses and wrote a book in which he defends taking the (voice of the) "patient" seriously. He describes several conversations with doctors similar to the dialogue Jenna has with the detective, in which he, because of being a psychotic, is not listened to at all (Kusters (2014)).

439 Danby & Farrell (2005: 49). See also Scoot (2008: 88); Hendrick (2008: 57); Christensen & James (2008: 6); Alderson (2001: 9).

440 Mullender et al. (2002).

441 Ibid: 2-13. The point is repeated continuously throughout the work.

442 Ibid: 22.

were known to have lived with violence against their mothers were interviewed individually and in groups.[443] The authors write:

> [w]e endeavored to work with children at all stages of research design. Our questionnaires were developed in conjunction with groups of children, who also helped to draw out the themes for the in-depth interviews. Thus we were open to children's own agendas and understandings.[444]

Their book meticulously describes this process, including difficulties encountered and it is therefore a very worthwhile study of how to engage children in research. However, in some instances, I feel that the researchers still, unconsciously, incorporated an adult bias. For example, when they describe how in the questionnaire they explore "individual and psychological explanations of the use of violence", which they explored through the statement "men who hit women are 'crazy'/mentally ill". According to the researchers:

> a clear majority of both sexes agreed with this although at age 11 to 14 more girls agreed than boys (almost three-quarters as against between a half and two-thirds). Perhaps boys are less ready to condemn men with these labels whereas, for us as the question-setters, there was an implication of offering men an excuse for their violence if it were to be explained in these terms. These findings echo a study undertaken for the Zero Tolerance Trust (Burton et al., 1998) that also asked young people aged over 14 a similar question, using the term 'sick' rather than '"crazy"/mentally ill'. Nearly two-thirds of that sample agreed with the statement, a figure remarkably close to that in the present study. This widespread perception amongst young people that men's use of violence against their female partners is linked to some form of mental disorder is not supported by the literature on male perpetrators […].[445]

An alternative explanation of these results, which seems more likely to me, is that the terms "sick" and "crazy/mentally ill" do not exactly refer to "mental disorder", a medical psychiatric condition, for children. These terms are used much more broadly by children in their everyday language. Think of a child who talks about how he was skating and he fell over. His peers could reply by saying "that is sick, dude!" / "that's totally insane", etc. It may also refer to a normative statement, for example when a teenager complains that his parents do not allow him to drink at all, a friend may say "man, your parents are crazy!". In neither of these example do children mean to say that anyone has a mental disorder. In general, concepts such as crazy, mental, sick, insane, etc. can mean a lot of things to young people, ranging from positive (cool) to negative (horrifying).[446] So we

443 Ibid: 25.
444 Ibid: 35.
445 Ibid: 72.
446 See also: Urban Dictionary (n.d.) "Crazy", available at: https://www.urbandictionary.com/define.php?term=Crazy.

cannot conclude that if most children agree with the statement "men who hit women are 'crazy'/mentally ill", they think that "men's use of violence against their female partners is linked to some form of mental disorder".

Another example from the same study is when children were asked about what they understood by violence:

> Children were provided with a list of possible actions and asked to say whether they thought these did or did not constitute violence [...] We also asked children to say if they thought the same acts constituted violence if the perpetrator was male and the victim female and if the sex of the actors was reversed. Primary school girls were slightly more likely to define various acts (such as pulling hair) as violence when committed by men towards women than by women towards men, but such distinctions were not evident in the responses of other children. Clearly, children and young people's own view is that violence is equally wrong, whoever commits it.[447]

However, the children did not say that they thought violence was *wrong*, they simply argued that the same act constitutes violence whether performed by a man or woman. There were no questions in the study related to the normative evaluation of violence. Therefore, as we can see from these few examples, there is warning here: listening to children might not be easy at all.[448]

4.2.1. A CHILD'S PERSPECTIVE IN (LEGAL) RESEARCH

What law is for children has so far mostly, if not always, been determined by adults. It is not only adults who constitute the sovereign, who vote, who are judges and teachers and parents, but legal researchers are also adults.[449] Therefore, the question "what is law for children?" has been decided by adults too, mostly by adult researchers answering questions about legal concepts such as laws and rights, analyzing state and international statutory law and connecting this to an idea of childhood as found in philosophy or developmental psychology or another academic discipline that provides a picture of childhood.

I have not been able to find one study that questions the notion of a law together with children (either as respondents or as child-researchers), neither

447 Mullender et al. (2002: 47).

448 Cf. Alderson on "interpreting evidence and responding to children's views": "Once children have expressed views, there can be further challenges in deciding how to interpret and respond to them [...] Research material which seems to support an obvious conclusion may have another explanation" (Alderson (2008: 152)).

449 Cf. Darbyshire and others: "Children also have no political 'clout'. They most certainly 'consume' but do not vote, lobby, organize or campaign and thus what Mayall (2002: 154) calls 'non-citizen status'. The 'exclusion of the voices of children from the political culture of the public sphere' is therefore commonplace" (Darbyshire et al. (2005: 419)).

in general nor on law on a specific legal issue (for example, education).[450] Why would this be? I suspect that, since the traditional idea of "law" is a concept that is viewed as being so thoroughly opposed to the irrational, immoral and unsocial subject that cannot (yet) be granted autonomy, that children cannot be invited to reflect upon law. Law stands in opposition of the unsocial subject, it rules over the irrational and the immoral in order to correct them.[451] Law rules over the child.

Involving children in research – something to which children have a legal right, according to the UNCRC art. 12[452] – has until recently not happened in academic research in general, although this is now changing. In the past, children have been excluded from the research process, both as researchers and as respondents.[453] According to Christensen and James, "traditionally, childhood and children's lives have been explored solely through the views and understandings of their adult caretakers who claim to speak for children. This rendered the child as object and excluded her/him from the research process".[454]

They and other authors argue that, in recent times[455], there has been a "paradigm shift", through which nowadays children are much more recognized as social actors.[456] This emerging point of view, which seems to submerge in history[457], (childhood) sociology[458], development psychology[459], and educational studies[460], raises new methodological and ethical issues.[461] Several authors argue that, if we want to know about children, about their lives, their development, their legal situation, we have to involve them in research.[462] As

450 The Oxford Handbook of Empirical Legal Research, for example, makes no reference to empirical research with children, and issues concerning children (child abuse, child protection, child care, etc.) are discussed only in terms of adult perceptions and adult analysis (Cane & Kritzer (2010)).

451 However, obeying the law requires awareness of law, which requires a certain form of socialization (learning the rules). But, of course, from an external perspective, a subject can still be subjected to laws of which this person is not aware.

452 CRC (art. 12.1): "States Parties shall assure to the child who is capable of forming his or her own views the right to express those views freely in all matters affecting the child, the views of the child being given due weight in accordance with the age and maturity of the child".

453 Powell & Smith (2009: 125).

454 Christensen & James (2008: 2). See also Alderson (2008: 155), Morrow (2005: 151).

455 According to O'Kane, "[s]ince the late 1980s there has been an increasing interest in listening to children's experiences and viewpoints, as separate to, and different from adults. Changes reflect an acknowledgment of children's rights to participate as promulgated by the United Nations Convention on the Rights of the Child" (O'Kane (2008: 125)).

456 Christensen & James (2008: 5); Mullender et al. (2002: 3); Alderson (2001: 1-2).

457 Hendrick (2008).

458 Among others: Sommer et al. (2010: 25-68).

459 Among others: Ibid: 25-68; Woodhead & Faulkner (2008).

460 Tangen (2008).

461 Christensen& James (2008: 1). See also Scott (2008: 89); Tangen (2008: 159).

462 In addition to all 19 authors of the chapters of book on Research with Children (Christensen & James (2008)), see also Mayall (2001:248); Woodhouse (1994: 323): "By paying attention to

Scott argues: "the best people to provide information on the child's perspective, actions and attitudes are children themselves"[463], a point that seems so self-evident, yet has not sufficiently been appreciated by most researchers until recent times. In general-purpose surveys, children have often been excluded as respondents, with survey researchers preferring "to ask adult respondents such as parents or teachers to report on children's lives, rather than to ask children themselves".[464] In psychology, according to Woodhead and Faulkner, "[w]hile research transcripts are often rich in [material on children's experiences, beliefs and concerns], they are generally analysed and interpreted in terms of more abstract questions which, as a rule, reflect the beliefs and priorities of researchers, rather than children".[465] Research methods are designed and carried out by adult researchers and research data is interpreted in relation to adult discourses about children's development. "In short, power relationships in the research process are traditionally weighted towards the researcher as the expert on children, and on how to study children, on what to study about children and about how to interpret what children say and do".[466] In traditional science, children have obtained an objectified status, because they are identified as experimental "subjects".[467]

Even in more recent studies on childhood and/or children's rights, children are still often left out as participants. Even when researchers are committed to the idea that children should be involved in the study, they still encounter methodological and practical difficulties, and may therefore in the end decide to do their study without involving children.[468]

---

children's lives and to what they say and do, as opposed to merely listening to what others say *about* children, perhaps we can begin to reduce the dissonance between dependence and autonomy and connection and individualism. By incorporating children's perspectives and stories in our deliberations, we can move children's rights towards a discourse that nether assumes a premature autonomy nor denies children the respect necessary for their growth toward autonomy".

463 Scott, 'Children as Respondents: the Challenge for Quantitative Methods' 88, see also Hendrick, 'The Child as a Social Actor in Historical Sources: Problems of Identification and Interpretation' 57 and Christensen and James, 'Introduction: Researching Children and Childhood Cultures of Communication' 6.

464 Scott (2008: 87). Scott even writes about "[t]he quarantine of childhood is represented in the exclusion of children from statistics and other social accounts", reffering to Qvortrup 1990, "and there exists very little material that directly addresses the experience of childhood, at the societal level" (ibid: 87). See also Darbyshire et al. (2005: 419): "The predominant approach to researching children's experiences is grounded in 'research on' rather than 'research with'or 'research for' children, ignoring the views of children as active agents and 'key informants' in matters pertaining to their health and wellbeing".

465 Woodhead & Faulkner (2008: 13).

466 Ibid: 13.

467 Powell & Smith (2009: 124).

468 Powell et al. (2020); Carter & Coyne (2018); Coyne & Carter (2018);

4.2.2. METHODOLOGIES FOR CHILD PARTICIPATION IN RESEARCH

Since this paradigm shift, how have children been included in academic research? Generally, the idea is to engage in "research *with*, rather than, *on* children, in our desire to position children as social actors who are subjects, rather than objects of inquiry".[469] When looking at the research process, research can usually be divided into several stages, all of which can involve certain levels of child participation.[470] These stages include:

1. Creating/designing/preparing the research
2. Conducting the research: collecting data through interviews, activities, etc.
3. Analyzing collected data
4. Reporting research / presenting outcome

Children who participate in these stages, other than as respondents, participate as "child researchers".

Children as researchers

Within the model of the child-researcher, child participation is often restricted to one of these phases of research – mostly the second phase. In the designing phase of the research, children sometimes participate by commenting on an existing research design (usually by participating in a pilot) or working on a research design together with professional researchers. However, in general "research questions and research agendas are still largely the province of adults, [therefore] children's narratives tend to be edited, re-formulated or truncated to fit our agendas".[471]

Child participation in the second, data collecting phase of the research is a little more common. There are several examples of children conducting data-collection, mostly by interviewing children, peers and family.[472] This however does not occur very often and it is not without issues; Simon Warren for example, found that after he had invited children "to take on the role of researcher, to design research tools, collect and analyse data", that "there was no consistency

469 Christensen & James (2008: 1).

470 Cf. Thomas & O'Kane (1998: 342).

471 Roberts (2008: 264).

472 To give an example of research on children by children: Warrington (2006) trained six young Gypsies and Travellers, aged 11-15 years, to interview their peers and families. Warrington felt that, given more time, the young people could have been more fully involved, although they actively disseminated their findings and presented them at the House of Lords (hereby also engaging in the "reporting research/presenting outcome" phase of the research) (As described by Alderson (2008: 280)).

in the recording of the data", and therefore it seemed impossible to read the response sheets "in any meaningful fashion".[473]

The third phase of research, of analyzing data, is not often done by children either. Mostly it is adults who interpret the responses of children, who find patterns and draw conclusions. Thomas and O'Kane tried to engage children in this phase. They write:

> there were several ways in which we tried to create opportunities for children to participate in the interpretation and analysis of research data. First, by selecting research instruments that enabled children to choose subjects for discussion and decide what they wanted to say about them, and by giving them a choice over which instruments were used [...]

Then, during a second interview:

> we gave them a chance to review and refine what they were telling us. Third, by using group processes we created space where children could collectively reinterpret the research questions and do further work on the material brought from the individual interviews [...].[474]

However, I would argue that "enabling children to choose subjects for discussion" and "giving them a choice over which instruments are used" does not happen on the level of interpretation of research data, but rather in the first or second phase of research. The group discussion does create some opportunity for children to engage in drawing conclusions together, thereby analyzing in a way their own data.

The presentation of research by children is (also) particularly hard to realize and perhaps not even wanted, as child language for example would rapidly disqualify any research report from being "academic". However, children can and do sometimes play a role in valorization, such as working with NGOs to advocate for change, based on a research report.[475]

Lastly, sometimes there are child-researchers who are involved in all phases of the research.

Children as respondents

By far, the largest occurrence of child participation in research is when children are engaged as respondents. There are many different ways in which children

473 Warren (2009: 127-28).

474 Thomas & O'Kane (1998: 346).

475 For example: Natascha Klocker (2006) trained three former child domestic workers aged 14-18 in Tanzania in research skills. "Working with legal experts, the research team is liaising with the Municipal Council to introduce a new bye-law, besides helping to set up an NGO 'Listen to the Child' to promote child workers' rights, and a weekly radio programme, which will employ young researchers" (as discussed by Alderson (2008: 280)).

are and can be engaged as respondents. This is usually labelled "participatory" only when the child-respondent is actively engaged in the research, rather than passively as a research subject (for example by filling in a survey).

Participation is often guaranteed through research activities, such as making time lines, drawings, games, group discussions, mapping, "photo-voice" (giving children a camera and asking them to take pictures of certain situations in their lives), diary method, role play, etc.[476] Thomas and O'Kane argue that the use of these participatory techniques in their research with children:

> greatly assisted in breaking down imbalances of power, not only by giving children greater control over the agenda and more time and space to talk about the issues that concern them, but also by creating an atmosphere in which there were no right or wrong answers and even some opportunities for children to interpret and explain their own data. In addition the meetings were more fun![477]

Davies engaged in conversations with primary school students, by just being present in the classroom and giving children "the freedom to come to talk to me whenever they wished".[478] Her experience also emphasizes the difficulties an adult researcher might encounter when including children as participative respondents, especially in the phase of analyzing data:

> The task I set myself in interviewing, and then in analyzing the interviews, was to learn to see as the children saw and thus to discover the relevancies of their world, the sense-making that they engaged in in their daily lives in the classroom and in the playground. I found this an enormous task since what I was discovering was a culture of childhood. I discovered this through the eyes of children who could translate their understandings so that they became available to my understanding. They were able to be both informers and translators [...].[479]

Lastly, research of Piaget also falls into this category, since during interviews with children he encouraged them talking freely, "thus allowing their thinking to unfold and reveal itself to an attentive researcher [...]".[480]

4.2.3. PARTICIPATION?

The above, and in general the literature on child participation, suggests a normative stance: the more children participate in research, the better the

476 Thomas & O'Kane (1998: 343); Darbyshire et al. (2005: 419-23); Scott (2008: 94-95); Mayall (2001: 110-11); O'Kane (2008: 129); Woodhead & Faulkner (2008: 32-33).
477 Thomas & O'Kane (1998: 344).
478 Davies (1984: 279).
479 Ibid: 279.
480 As discussed by Woodhead & Faulkner (2008).

research (in terms of representing children's views, lives, experiences, as well as in terms of fairness). Several authors mention in this context "the right to be researched".[481] To realize this right for children, either as respondents or researchers, a conceptual tool that is often used is the "participation ladder" as developed by Hart in 1992.[482] The ladder distinguishes several levels of participation, ranging from manipulation (1) and decoration (2, such as "children singing at adult conferences") to child-initiated and directed (7) and child-initiated, shared decisions with adults (8). There is some discussion on the highest levels; some argue that independent, child-initiated and directed projects (including research) have a higher level of participation than when children cooperate with adults.[483]

Hart himself discussed the participation ladder again in 2008. In this paper, he argued that his initial paper was written in a time where there was:

> little written of a conceptual nature on the theme of children's participation in [..] programmes, projects, or organisations. The book was simply meant to stimulate a dialogue on a theme that needed to be addressed critically. But many people have chosen to use the ladder as a comprehensive tool for measuring their work with children rather than as a jumping-off point for their own reflections.[484]

Hart points out that "a child may not want at all times to be the one who initiates a project.". However, he argues that "they ought to know that they have the option, and to feel that they have the confidence and competence to do so on occasion".[485] He further emphasizes that he never wanted to "argue naïvely that we should think of children as repressed individuals who [need] to be liberated through a series of steps whereby all adult engagement [has been] removed".[486] Instead, "what is now needed are programmes of collaboration between academics and those who work directly with children as well as with children and youth themselves".[487]

Based on these considerations, I would argue that, to enable genuine child participation in academic research, it is not necessary to eliminate the adult researcher. According to Pretty et al. "participation does not simply imply the mechanical application of a 'technique' or method, but is instead part of a process of dialogue, action, analysis and change".[488] This is how I propose to understand meaningful participation of children in the current research, as realized in such a process, which is shared between adult and child or, in general, between the

481 Beazley et al. (2009).
482 Hart (1992).
483 Ibid.
484 Hart (2008: 19).
485 Ibid: 24.
486 Ibid: 24.
487 Ibid: 29.
488 Pretty et al. 1995 54, as quoted by O'Kane (2008: 129).

researcher and respondent. This means that the child is actively listened to and allowed to be actively involved in the different stages of the research – allowed, but not obliged.[489]

4.2.4. ETHICS

As has been mentioned before, the active participation of children in research poses new ethical challenges.[490] A view on children as active participants[491] means, for example, that adult researchers cannot "use" them as passive objects of study. Rather, children themselves have to consent to participate in research and have to be informed about issues of confidentiality and possible risks and benefits.[492]

Generally, when discussing the ethical aspects of research with children (participants), three key ethical principles can be taken into consideration[493]:

1. Respect for persons: treating participants respectfully, taking them and their views seriously, respecting their privacy and confidentiality
2. Beneficence: balancing of harms and benefits for both participants and society as a whole, taking care of welfare of participants
3. Justice: making sure that inclusion and exclusion of participants is fair and fairness in (access to) benefits of the research

Consent

One of the difficult questions when deliberating on research ethics in research with children is the question of consent. Sometimes researchers feel that, when they are dealing with children, they do not need to ask for anyone's consent[494], and often consent is acquired only from an adult caretaker or legal guardian.[495]

---

489 The willingness of the child to participate in research will also help the quality of the research. As Scott (2008: 97) argues: "Asking questions that are meaningful to the child's own experience is not, however, sufficient to guarantee that children will give meaningful answers. A second factor that is fundamental to improving data quality concerns the child's willingness and ability to answer the questions and articulate his or her subjective experience".

490 See §4.2.1; Water (2018).

491 I will use the term "participants" in the broad sense, including both the child as respondent and the child as researcher.

492 Cf. Farrel (2008: 5): "Our understandings of research with children and, indeed, of ethics in research with children, are embedded within our understandings of children and childhood".

493 Farrell (2008: 4); Allen (2008: 19); Australian Government et al. (2007/2018: (section 1).

494 Alderson (2008:28): "watching or questioning children without asking their or their parents' permission first, is still widely accepted".

495 Cf. O'Kane (1998: 340): "the first principle of consent which we adopted was that inclusion in the sample would depend on active agreement on the part of the caretaker"; Danby & Farrell (2005: 53); Water (2018: 51-52).

I would argue that consent to participate in research can only come from the person who is asked to participate in the research. Moreover, simple consent is not enough; for consent to be meaningful, it has to be so-called "informed consent". This means there has to be a positive answer to the question "[i] s the research explained clearly enough so that anyone asked to take part can make an informed decision about whether they want to consent or refuse?"[496] Obviously there might sometimes be difficulties realizing the possibility of informed consent; this seems most difficult to achieve when doing research with babies or other groups of respondents who do not master language. I would argue that, for that purpose in general, we have to make sure that at least this group does not experience any harm during the research and perhaps then consent can be inferred during the research process whenever respondents seem content to participate (and the opposite, meaning that consent can be inferred to be withdrawn as the respondent clearly shows signs of discontent during the research, related to the research).[497]

Generally, the researcher has to make sure that the participant is well-informed before consenting to participating in the research, by informing the participant by means of appropriate language and leaving room for questions.

Is consent from the child-participant sufficient or do we need to obtain consent from legal guardians too? Many researchers opt for the latter, both because of existing legal constructions[498] and because adults often function as "gatekeepers": they decide, allow or restrict, access to children.[499] O'Kane, who chose to take as a principle of consent "that inclusion in the sample would depend on active agreement on the part of the caretaker", argues that "because of existing relationships of power and responsibility we had to accept that some children would be prevented from taking part because of adult concern [...]".[500] However, if we argue that children have to be respected as active participants and not as passive objects of study, we cannot rely on adult consent. The assumption of the researcher that an adult decides about the child's participation reinforces the idea that children cannot make their own choices. As is stated in the UNCRC art. 12, we have to "assure to the child who is capable of forming his or her own views the right to express those views freely in all matters affecting the child". As the question of participation in research is clearly an issue affecting the child, and not (directly) the caretaker, the child's view on this has to be taken seriously, taking into account the earlier mentioned principles of informed consent.[501]

496 Alderson (2008: 31).

497 See David et al. (2005: 129) for an example of a boy understood by the adult researcher as withdrawing his consent, through his silence and body language.

498 See for example Danby & Farrell (2008: 52).

499 Water (2018: 46-52).

500 O'Kane (1998: 340).

501 In fact, children have reportedly reacted very positively to being asked to consent to participating in research. See Danby & Farrell (2008).

If child participation in research is dependent on adult consent, adults can misuse this power. An abusive parent might, for example, not allow her/his child to participate in a research on child abuse.[502] Lastly, research has found that children are capable of acting as gatekeepers of their own accounts, "able to withhold or share their experiences, [..] able to clarify aspects of the study, and ultimately [to decide] whether or not they chose to participate".[503]

Concluding, although it will sometimes be inevitable to ask for an adult's consent for children to participate in research, primary consideration and weight has to be given to the child's consent.[504]

Confidentiality

Another related issue is the issue of confidentiality. Confidentiality has to do with trust and respecting confidentiality includes making sure that the respondent is, and feels, safe.

Partly this issue is related to the issue of consent; it involves the idea that consent is not a once-and-for-all decision, but instead respondents are allowed to withdraw consent at any point in the research, including after the data collection.[505] Consent does not necessarily concern the whole research or the whole set of data; respondents might simply refuse to answer a certain question or to investigate further into a certain subject. As Alderson writes: "children need to know that they can refuse to reply, and that they need not give a reason".[506]

Security is also created by taking the ideas of respondents, and children in particular (as this seems to be "harder"), seriously. Lipman formulates the confidentiality in relation to philosophical discussion with children, which I think we can directly apply to research with children in general: "students engaged in philosophical discussion should feel free to advocate any

502 Cf. Graham et al. (2015: 65-67).

503 Ibid: 61; MacNaughton & Smith (2005: 119-20).

504 This point of view seems to be in line with the UK government's policy on protecting the confidentiality of the health and social care services. In their Code of Pratice on Protecting the Confidentiality of Service User Information, they state that "Children have the same rights to privacy as all other persons and there is the same duty of confidentiality to them as there is to adults" (art. 5.1) and that only "where a child is not competent to consent, the consent of a parent or person with parental responsibility should be sought" (art. 5.3) (Department of Health, Social Services and Public Safety (2012)).

505 MacNaughton & Smith (2005: 119); O'Kane (1998: 340). However, this possible withdrawal of consent is limited to the moment the research report is finished, as it cannot be the case that respondents withdraw consent simply because they are not happy with the research results. Therefore, the researcher does have to set a certain clear ultimatum or deadline for respondents to react to the report of the individual research conversation. Also, it does not mean that caretakers can withdraw consent on behalf of their child because they worry that their child said things that they do not agree wit, or they do not want to come out (both situations presented itself during the field research on the right to education in the Netherlands).

506 Alderson (2008: 27).

value position they choose, without the teacher having to agree or disagree with each and every point".[507] To allow for respondents to speak freely, a "mutual relationship of trust and empathy"[508] should be established between researcher and participant as much as possible.[509] This will help in creating "an environment which fosters question-asking and question-answering", which is greatly dependent on mutual confidence.[510] Therefore, the researcher has to be open to input from participants in the research and not let fear of questions asked by the participant, or fear of what the participant might do which might invalidate the research data, impose limits on the (level of) participation.

Elements that can be helpful in creating and respecting confidentiality in research are:

a. openness and honesty of the researcher[511], especially by expressing personal insecurities and doubt[512] and avoiding manipulation[513]
b. taking time, especially in the beginning of the research conversation or whenever appropriate, to discuss topics of interest unrelated to the research, such as hobbies or pets[514]
c. preserving of anonymity of the respondent
d. choosing a safe environment[515]

Confidentiality is yet another area where respect for the privacy of the respondent seems to weigh less heavily when regarding children than when regarding adults, influenced by the fact that confidentiality of the respondent sometimes conflicts with the child's perceived need for protection. Thomas & O'Kane describe the discussion they had in their research team on this issue;

---

507 Lipman et al. (1977: 62).

508 Ibid: 65.

509 Watts et al. (1997: 1028).

510 Ibid: 1028.

511 However, as Campbell and Wasco remark in relation to feminist research methodology, this "openness" should not be taken too far, as "the focus of the interview (and the research more generally) must remain on the participants' lives" (2000: 786).

512 Especially in "not knowing", see §4.2.2.

513 Here the warning issued by Kvale might be useful; "Creating trust through a personal relationship [sometimes] serves as a means to efficiently obtain a disclosure of the interview subjects' world. The interviewer may, with a charming, gentle, and client-centered manner, create a close personal encounter where the subjects unveil their private worlds. A quasi-therapeutic interviewer role [...] can, as expressed by therapist Jette Fog (2004), serve as a "Trojan horse" to get behind defense walls of the interview subjects, laying their private lives open and disclosing information to a stranger, which they may later regret. Close emotional relationships between interviewer and interviewee can open for more dangerous manipulation than the rather distanced relationships of an experimenter and experimental subjects (Kvale (2006: 482-83)).

514 Alderson (2008: 144).

515 Cf. Tonkin et al. (2005: 130).

> In relation to confidentiality and to protection from abuse [...] is the important question of "what do we do if a child discloses that she or he is being abused?" The dilemma can be acute, especially with younger children, and we thought long and hard before arriving at our approach to the question. Again this was based on allowing children the autonomy to decide what they wanted to say and who they wanted to say it to. It was important for us to be able to give children an assurance that we would not repeat what they told us to other people, and for children to know that they could trust us.[516]

However, they felt the weight of their responsibility, as adults, towards children:

> If the information indicated that the child was being harmed, it would be our responsibility to support the child in telling someone who was in a position to do something about it; but this would have to be done with the child's consent. We could envisage circumstances in which the information was so alarming that we would have to insist that someone else be told notwithstanding our commitment to confidentiality [...].[517]

I disagree that there can be information shared by a respondent that is judged so alarming that the confidentiality agreement can be breached, because this makes confidentiality finally dependent on the personal judgment of the adult researcher. The promise of confidentiality as given to the child respondent turns into a lie, therefore being manipulative, in violation of principles a) and c) of confidentiality as described above, as well as the key ethical principle of respect for persons.[518] An adult researcher who hears about an alarming situation that the child finds itself in can openly share her/his ideas on the subject and especially possible solutions (b), one of which can be the sharing of the information by the adult researcher with a professional aid worker. However, for any step to be taken, the child's consent has to be obtained.

Child-adult inequality, researcher-respondent inequality, and research ethics

When engaging in research with active (participating) or passive (observed) respondents, as researchers we should be alert for engaging, consciously or

516 Thomas & OKane (1998: 339-340).

517 Ibid: 340.

518 In addition, the consequence of "conditional consent" may be that certain information which could be useful to the research is not shared by the respondent, as experienced by Roberts: "It was agreed that near the beginning of the interview, the researcher would say something like: 'Sometimes a person might talk about a situation where they have been harmed by someone. If this happens, I may need to talk to someone else, especially if it is something awful which is still happening to you, or if the person who harmed you may still be harming someone else [...]' ...The response of one young man to this was, 'Well, that's one part of my life I'm not going to talk to you about then, isn't it? I'm not having you deciding who to go and talk to about me'" (2008: 272-73).

unconsciously, in interaction based on an unequal power relation.[519] Part of this awareness is addressed by ethical principles such as have been discussed above. However, these ethical considerations often only stipulate threshold conditions and thereby do not address the underlying power relations. Not every morally charged research decision can be taken beforehand, especially in relation to unequal power relations, as it relates to personal conduct and presence.[520]

Therefore, even if we cannot anticipate all occurrences of ethical issues, especially in relation to the unequal power relation between researcher and participants as subjects, it is important to at least be aware of this issue.[521]

This unequal power relation between researcher and respondent can influence all stages of the research, ranging from the researcher who decides in what way a certain topic will be discussed in the preparing phase of the research, to respondents who try to give the "right" answers, to researchers who impose their analysis, their meaning, on the utterances of respondents and decide how to report their outcomes (which Kvale refers to as "the interviewer's monopoly of interpretation").[522] This is of particular concern when considering doing research with children. Both the participant and the researcher, when engaging in research together, are usually culturally primed by the idea of power inequality between academic researcher and participant[523] and, when considering adult-child research, the child-adult unequal power relation is another extra factor of culturally primed inequality.[524] As O'Kane argues: "Working within a historical and cultural context in which children's voices have been marginalized, researchers face great challenges in finding ways to break down the power imbalance between adults and children, and in creating

---

519 Cf. Campbell and Wasco: "Traditionally, a hierarchy has existed between the researcher and the researched: the researcher is the 'all-knowing' expert, the participant is not; the researcher has access to all information about the study, its designs, and questions, the participant does not [...]. This hierarchy does very little to facilitate trust, and in fact, seriously undermines the building of an open relationship" (2008: 785-86).

520 See also: Hewitt (2007: 1151).

521 For a discussion on power inequality between the researcher and respondent related to adult-adult research projects, see, among others: Baxter & Eyles (1997); Hewitt (2007); McDowell (1994: 656-66); on feminist social science: Campbell & Wasco (2000); Richards & Emslie (2000); Thapar-Björkert & Henry (2004); Kvale (2006). Interestingly, in these articles, children and adults are often taken together under the heading of "respondent", with "age" identified as one of the factors influencing the power relations between the researcher and respondent. From the perspective of children's rights research, Thomas and O'Kane argue that ethical issues related to research with children are not very different from those encountered when doing research with adults. According to them, "there are important ways in which such issues present themselves more sharply when the subjects are children [...] Above all [this] is due to different power relationships [...] Part of the task is to redress the power imbalance between child participant and adult researcher, in order to enable children to participate on their own terms" (Thomas & O'Kane (1998: 337)).

522 Kvale (2006: 485).

523 Karnieli-Miller et al (2009: 280-81); Richards & Emslie (2000: 72-74).

524 See chapter 2.

space which enables children to speak up and be heard. Questions concerning adult-child relationships must be carefully considered".[525]

Even if we cannot completely avoid having a power imbalance influence the research process and outcome, how can we at least minimize it? In addition to the research methodology that I design under §4.1 – §4.2, into which my answer to this question has been incorporated, for anyone wishing to minimize the power inequality during qualitative research, literature offers some general advice:

- Do not let others, adult or child (especially parents or teachers) be present during research interviews, as (power) relations between different people might influence responses; the more people that are present, the more possibility there is for answers to become politically laden[526];
- Reflect on the way in which the researcher relates to the research subject in terms of power relations and make conscious decisions on how to share this reflection[527];
- Beware not to strengthen the unequal power relation between researcher and participant for example by "talking down". As Alderson writes, in relation to research with children: "[o]ne major obstacle in conducting research with children concerns infantilizing them, perceiving and treating them as immature and, in so doing, producing evidence to reinforce notions of their incompetence. This can include 'talking down' to children, using over-simple words and concepts [...]".[528]
- Do not assume that the researcher has more knowledge on a certain subject. As the subject is the respondent, no one has more knowledge about her/his experiences, values, ideas, etc. than the participant her/himself. Respect participants and their views.[529]

---

525 O'Kane (2000: 126).

526 In relation to child-parent, see for example Meloni et al. (2015), although Meloni et al. argue that, in their experience, precisely the hesitation and fracture in the daughter respondent's language in response to being with her mother, in relation to certain questions, "urge us to acknowledge youth's lives as embedded within the family dynamics they are entangled with" (118); in relation to child-peers, see for example Scott (2008: 92).

527 Cf. David et al. (2005: 127): "As researchers, we must consider how our own experiences in childhood and our practices in adulthood of engaging with young children (as researchers, parents, [..] teachers [...]) contribute to our views about the 'needs', desires, abilities, skills and experiences of young children"; O'Kane (2008: 126). Mayall addressed the issue as follows in her research with children: she tried "to work with generational issues, rather than to assume adult superiority or to downplay these issues. I am asking children, directly, to help me, an adult, to understand childhood. I want to investigate directly with children the knowledge they have of their social position, the status of being a child, and child-adult relations [...] I present myself as a person who, since she is adult, does not have this knowledge" (Mayall (2008: 110-11).

528 Alderson (2000: 140).

529 Cf. Scott (2008: 96); Lipman et al. (1977: 62-66).

- Consider allowing different modes of expression, such as talking, drawing, writing, etc.[530]
- In general, consulting literature on philosophy with children can be most helpful, as in this educational practice power equality between adult and child is tantamount.[531]
- Lastly, some very practical points of advice by Alderson:
  - Sit at about the same eye level
  - Adapt the volume, tone and pace of talking to suit the other person
  - Use a simple or more complex vocabulary as appropriate
  - Word and rephrase questions clearly
  - Wait attentively for answers
  - Respect what is said and try to pick up and continue themes the person introduces
  - If they do not reply precisely to your question, do not say so, but listen to their reply and then rephrase your question
  - Respond to funny or serious moods
  - Tolerate silences and pauses
  - Try not to interrupt or dismiss what is said, be interested, and thank the other person[532]

Effects of the research: Benefits?

According to the ethical principle of beneficence (see above), in engaging in research with participants, an ethical consideration includes the balancing of harms and benefits for both participants and society as a whole and taking care of the welfare of participants.

The good news here is that children who are actively involved in the research, as active participants, have reported positive experiences.[533] In addition, authors argue that involving participants as co-researchers empowers them, as it acknowledges their agency.[534] Therefore, it seems that, during the research, the well-being of participants can be guaranteed relatively easily, precisely because of their active, participative role, including the conditions for informed consent.

However, the goal of the research is not just to gather data that will then remain in the researcher's private possession. Obviously, the goal is to share data and findings, in different forms, such as books, articles, reports, lectures, lobbying activities, etc. In this respect, there are several ethical risks involved.

530 Cf. Scott (2008: 91): "For children under 11, visual stimuli can be especially useful in the questioning process, because pictures make the issue far more concrete than verbal representation alone".

531 Cf. Vansielegem & Kennedy (2011: 175).

532 Alderson (2008:13-14).

533 Powell & Smith (2009: 131); Thomas & O'Kane (1998: 344); Harvey (2018: 61).

534 Beazley et al. (2009: 369); Powell & Smith (2009: 129-30).

Most importantly, these are 1) when participants share sensitive information, they might suffer consequences from people in (legal) power; 2) participants might have high expectations about the impact or effect of the research. These might turn out to be unrealistic. As Alderson writes: "Much research remains unpublished, which lets down the children and adults who contributed data, the research team, the funders, and everyone who might benefit from the findings".[535]

The first problem can be solved most simply by taking care to keep participants anonymous. This does not only concern excluding use of names but also to beware of other ways in which combined information might lead to identification (for example, place of birth, current place of residence in combination with political position). It also considers storage of data, in secured places, both on- and offline.

As regards the second issue, one has to take care to temper participant expectations. In general, if research will lead to any practical consequences, these will most likely not benefit the participants directly. If participants wish so, it is recommended to inform them of the actions taken based on the research and possible practical consequences.[536] This can be done for example by keeping a (possibly restricted) weblog, ideally in child-friendly language.

4.3. A METHOD FOR RESEARCH ON LAW WITH CHILDREN: MICRO-RESEARCH

To find law for children, I propose a combination of participant involvement in the first three phases of the research simultaneously, by treating each "interview" as a micro-research. This means that the (academic) researcher takes a moment with the (participant) researcher to jointly engage in a research activity.

The research conversation begins with a certain theme and perhaps the legal issue that the academic-researcher wants to know more about. The academic-researcher starts the micro-research session by naming the theme of the research and perhaps the legal issue, thereafter the academic and participant researchers engage together in a research of the theme/issue. They pose questions, search for answers, test hypotheses, share ideas, reflect on the research process, and formulate (tentative) conclusions. In this way I believe we can best capture the participant's view on a certain legal issue.

I take the technique used to perform this joint micro-research from education studies: the Socratic method as a method of giving space to the participant's view, a method for engaging in meaningful research dialogue (truth finding), and the method of inquiry-based science instruction to provide a framework for how to engage in a micro-research activity (that is not necessarily philosophical).

---

535 Alderson (2008: 157).

536 Cf. Australian Government, National Health and Medical Research Council & Australia Research Council (2007/2018: 12).

I hope to argue convincingly that this empirical legal methodology adequately solves the issues of both capturing the participant's perspective, and the ethical issues involved as posed under §4.2. The hypothesis here is that both educational techniques combined solve the above-mentioned issues in quite a natural fashion.

4.3.1. INQUIRY-BASED SCIENCE INSTRUCTION

In education, we find the idea of the child researcher[537] as a didactic practice; children are encouraged to engage in scientific inquiry, because in this way they will both construct factual knowledge and develop skills such as problem-solving, cooperative skills, critical thinking, etc.[538] This didactic practice is usually referred to as "inquiry learning" or "inquiry-based science instruction"[539]

Alderson's thesis that "research is part of everyday life in the projects every school child does"[540] is the central idea of inquiry-based science instruction. The instruction in inquiry science makes use of "the investigation cycle"; a cycle that teacher and student move through together (see figure 2).[541]

Figure 3.

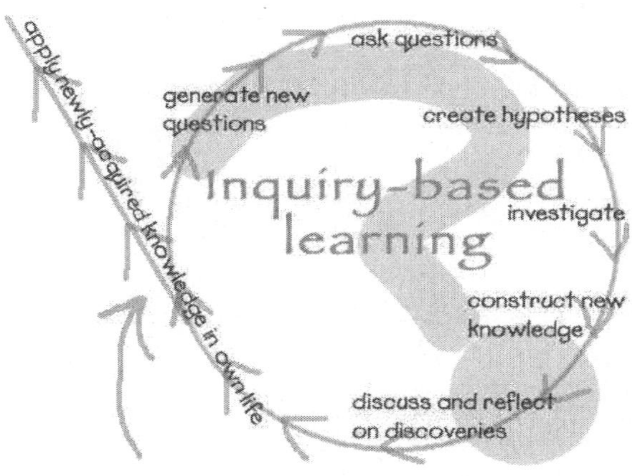

[537] The literature on inquiry-based science instruction considers the didactics only in relation to children. I would argue that the didactics are not specifically suited only for children, and I personally use them in teaching adults as well as children. However, to reflect the literature truthfully and, as I focus on law for children, I will use the notion of the "child researcher" here, knowing that generally the same applies to adult human beings.

[538] See Minner et al. (2010); Clark & Linder (2006); Cremin et al. (2015); National Research Council (1996).

[539] Cf. Minner et al. (2010: 474): in the US alone millions of dollars have been invested by several organizations into developing inquiry-based science instruction in primary education; similar investments have been made in Australia, England and on the international level. However, the didactics also occur in education in non-western societies, see for example Clark & Linder (2006).

[540] Aldesron (2001: 3).

[541] Ibid: 479. See also Bryan & Keys (2001: 632).

Questions are central to inquiry-based learning. Asking questions is not only done in the first two phases, but it forms an integral part of the whole research process.[542] According to Woodward,

> by posing questions, pupils are shaping and exposing their thoughts and hence opportunities will be provided for teachers to have some insight into children's thinking and conceptual understanding. Questions asked by children can lead teachers towards making appropriate assessments of children's understanding or, alternatively, their misconceptions.[543]

When we read "(academic) researcher" instead of "teacher", the method might very well lead to insight into children's (participant's) thinking and conceptual understanding and, consequently, into children's understanding of and thinking about law.

What kind of questions are used? If the researcher determines the questions beforehand, they will be imposed, and the participants will not be able to freely engage in research. In fact, the role of posing questions is an important one in the process of doing research. However, participants (students) need to be enticed to reflection. Watts et al. argue that "many questions are probably more in the way of open 'thought experiments' [...] These are the 'What would happen if...?', 'Why is it that...?', 'If this, then why not...?' kind".[544] The technique of engaging in research with children through asking questions has been developed more in the theory of philosophy with children (see below).

4.3.2. SOCRATIC DIALOGUE

Philosophy with children[545] is a subject in which a technique of engaging in research dialogue with children, as equals, has been fruitfully developed. The different programs for philosophy with children all offer different versions of the "Socratic method", a dialectical method for engaging in dialogue, which has as it goal to research certain convictions, opinions, ideas, etc.[546] In philosophy for children, the different variations of the dialogue follow a more or less fixed pattern[547]:

---

542 Cf. National Research Council (1996: 33): "In the science classroom envisioned by the *Standards*, effective teachers continually create opportunities that challenge students and promote inquiry by asking questions".

543 Watts (1997: 1027).

544 Watts et al. (1997: 1027).

545 Also often referred to as "philosophy for children".

546 See for example Lipman et al. (1977), Dewey (1938/1997); Lipman (2003); Matthews (1995).

547 Derived from the works of Lipman et al. (1977), Dewey (1938/1997); Lipman (2003); Matthews (1995). There are similarities with the investigation circle used in inquiry-based learning.

1. A theme or research subject and a specific question are found through discussing possible options and deciding on the theme and (research) question together.
2. Participants engage in a common research of the chosen question, that is conducted by means of a Socratic dialogue; meaning, rather than each participant giving his or her subjective opinion and having a discussion, participants engage in cooperative research, trying by means of questioning, dialogue, discussion, to find an answer to the (research) question. The principle of dialectic reasoning plays a key role.
3. The participants formulate a tentative or hypothetical answer to the (research) question. It is tentative, because all answers in philosophy are tentative and open to further research.[548]

The equality between the (academic) researcher and participant is in some sense essential to philosophy; as the philosopher, and Socrates in particular, departs from a perspective of not-knowing and therefore s/he does not know more than the participant.[549] Engaging in Socratic dialogue means not knowing the "right" answer or, even, doubting the existence of such a thing as a right answer.[550] However, it is of course true that an adult is in a sense "more developed" than a child, which plays a role when engaging in research together. As Lipman says: "Small children can *reason* [...] but they're painfully short on *information* and experience".[551] Nevertheless, this inequality of information and experience does not influence the power relations during the research process. It is essential to philosophy with children that the adult and the child are "equal companions in thought".[552] Children and their views have to be respected.[553] As Lipman argues, and I think this can very well serve as a guiding motto for anyone engaging in research with children (or, in general, engaging in research with anyone):

> If you think you already know all the answers, if you think you have a direct line to the truth, then it will be rather hard for you to respect children's opinions (or adult opinions for that matter) should they differ from your own. However, if you realize that you are still searching for more comprehensive answers in all of the educational disciplines as well as in your own personal life, and further, if you realize that

[548] Cf. Vansieleghem & Kennedy (2011: 174).

[549] Cf. Kvale (2006: 483084) who argues that research interviews are often misleadingly referred to as dialogues, whereas often an interview is "a one-way dialogue, an instrumental and indirect conversation, where the interviewer upholds a monopoly of interpretation". Kvale suggest as an alternative the Platonic dialogue (which is another term for the Socratic dialogue), "a conversation where two persons understand each other, where it is not the will of the individual persons that matters but a law of the subject matter", involving "an approximate egalitarian power distribution" (ibid: 483-84).

[550] Areeda (1996: 911-12).

[551] Lipman et al. (1977: 16).

[552] Vansieleghem & Kennedy (2011: 175).

[553] Matthews (1982/1995: 32); Lipman et al. (1977: 62-65).

> knowledge itself is endlessly being created by human beings to explain the world they live in, then you will be more apt to listen to all people, including children, for ideas that might lead to more comprehensive and meaningful explanations than you now possess.[554]

To arrive at these meaningful explanations, the teacher has to get children to think for themselves, for which the method is "dialogue coupled with reflection".[555] Lipman distinguishes three conditions for teaching philosophical thinking[556]:

1. Commitment to philosophical inquiry: the teaching of philosophy consists of recognizing and following very closely what children are thinking, helping them to verbalize and objectify these thoughts and then aiding the development of the tools they need to reflect upon these thoughts.
2. Avoidance of indoctrination: teachers insist that participants in philosophical discussions try to be coherent, consistent and comprehensive in their thinking.[557] Students engaged in philosophical discussion should feel free to advocate any value position they choose, without the teacher having to agree or disagree.
3. Respect for children's ideas and opinions.

The process of inquiry, the combination of dialogue coupled with reflection, in my view is a useful technique to use in engaging in research with respondents. It is not "a theoretical activity separated from the world, but rather [..] a potential that has to (and can) be developed in order to get a grip on one's interactions with one's environment, and to influence change".[558]

The academic researcher posits itself as Socrates; it is her/him who,

> through questioning, can introduce alternative views with the aim of always enlarging the [respondent's] horizons, never letting complacency or self-righteousness take precedence. In this sense, the [researcher] is a gadfly, encouraging the [participants] to take the initiative, building on what they manage to formulate, helping them question underlying assumptions of what they arrive at, and suggesting ways of arriving at more comprehensive answers.[559]

This is therefore the interview technique that I propose for the current methodology. The most interesting thing about the technique is that it goes

554 Lipman et al. (1977: 65).
555 Ibid: 60.
556 Ibid: 62-65.
557 As Scott argues, on research with children: "it seems good practice to include internal consistency checks, where possible, when interviewing children" (Scott (2008: 98)).
558 Vansieleghem & Kennedy (2011: 175).
559 Lipman et al. (1977: 60).

beyond mere question-and-answer format, exploring deeper the convictions, ideas, experiences etc. of the respondent. As Areeda argues, it is a method, a specific form of engaging in a dialogue, which has as it goal to "force [the participants] to think or to use the knowledge [the participants have] to get beyond it". In this sense, it goes further than mere opinion survey.[560] It might just turn out that, in this way, we come to embrace completely new perspectives.[561]

4.4. DESIGN OF THE MICRO-RESEARCH OF LAW

To find out about law for children, within the current framework of law (chapters 1 and 3), we do not start completely blank – which is in fact impossible, as has been demonstrated by philosophers of science.[562] We start with a framework which provides an answer to the question "what is law?", that defines law as a social fact, and we look for law in social relations and personal belief. As there are probably many laws governing a person's life, too many for one research project, the researcher has to be more specific. S/he can choose a specific legal subject, perhaps taking a specific state law as inspiration or a legal or moral subject, etc. and the researcher has to pick a specific context (cultural, territorial, etc).[563]

---

560 Areeda (1996: 912).

561 As has been practiced and explained by Smith (2013): after two children age 4 had consented to her watching them play, she analyzed the play situation. She then shared her analysis of the situation with the two children. As this was the first time when she asked them *why* they were in fact engaging in certain behavior (a question that could easily start a philosophical investigation), here she engages the children in the analysis phase of the research. She feels that this is the only way in which children really get a voice, as opposed to adult analysis of children's words (104-8). She even found that her own adult analysis, although beforehand she had been "quite confident that [she] was adept at using multiple theories to unpack recorded observations of children's play behaviors, and that this provided a complete understanding of what was happening" (107-8), after asking the why-question she is forced to admit that she had "failed to recognize that children are also political and strategic" (108) the important point here being that she could not have understood the situation if she had not discussed its meaning with the children involved. I would argue that this is equally true for research with adults as with children; we do not just ask them questions as in a questionnaire, if we truly want to understand a legal situation. We have to ask them why, too.

562 Karl Popper famously started his class on philosophy of science by telling his students "[t] ake a pencil and paper; carefully observe, and write down what you have observed!", to show how research without a theory is absurd and impossible. He writes: "Observation is always selective. It needs a chosen object, a definite task, an interest, a point of view, a problem. And its description presupposes a descriptive language, with property words; it presupposes similarity and classification, which in their turn presuppose interests, points of view, and problems" (Popper (1962: V).

563 For the selection of case studies for this thesis, including criteria, see introduction part II.

4.4.1. PREPARING THE MICRO-RESEARCH

When preparing the micro-research, it might be useful for the researcher to sketch a tentative, expected legal field as related to the particular legal issue. One can sketch expected legal orders involved (see chapter 3) and expected relevant types of law (see §1.4). If the legal situation is expected to involve formal written law, this can be studied separately from the field research (possibly as a preparation).

To identify possible legal orders, the leading question is: "Who are the potential legislators over the relevant community and the legal issue under research?" There can be one or multiple legislators involved (if you find none, it means the issue at stake is in fact not a legal issue). If it is uncertain beforehand whether something would count as a proper legal order in relation to the legal issue (for example the family), it is better to include it and the field research will reveal in a later stage whether it is in fact a legal order.

For each legal order, the researcher can try to identify the potentially relevant kinds of law; which forms apply? This starts by defining who is (are) the legislator(s). For level A law (formal written law), one has to search whether there are formal written documents that state the laws of the legal order. To find level B law (law for the community), one has to find the relevant legal community; these will be the addressees of the law and the sovereign. To find level C law (hidden law), the researcher must try to define potentially excluded or included communities, or communities otherwise potentially addressed by special non-public laws. This might be done by studying statistics (for example, does any group stand out in the number of convictions?), NGO research documents (for example, does Human Rights Watch identify special groups being targeted or prosecuted?) or other research documents (for example research on corruption).

4.4.2. INVESTIGATION WITH CHILDREN (FIELD RESEARCH)

After preparation, the researcher can engage in field research, especially to find levels B and C law. To avoid bias (adult ethnocentric bias or other bias derived from power inequality between the researcher and the participant), I have proposed to put the respondent in the position of a co-researcher, making the researcher and the respondent "equal partners in thought", as is central to both the didactics of inquiry-based science instruction and philosophy with children.

Concretely, I propose to do so by engaging in a shared micro-research. This means that researcher and participant (co-researcher)[564] move through the investigation cycle together (as explained under §4.3.1), whereby the researcher

[564] For convenience, I will keep referring to "participant" in the rest of the paragraph.

takes up the position of Socrates (as explained under §4.3.2). The researcher starts by telling the participant the legal subject under discussion, explaining the methodology and the fact that the researcher and participant are engaging in research together. As with inquiry-based science instruction, it is important here to stress the responsibility of the participant, including establishing a relation of mutual trust and openness.[565]

Example: investigating the child's right to education in the Netherlands

For example, I want to know about law for children on education in the Netherlands. I will then tell the participant that we will engage in research together on this subject. In the first, exploring phase, we discuss the subject, including questions such as "what is education?", "do you get education?", "what do you learn?", etc., ending with the question "what is the meaning of the child's right to education?"[566] From the answer to this question follows the hypothesis. For example, a respondent says: "I have to go to school". We then both engage in an investigation of this particular hypothesis. I will ask questions such as "why do you have to go to school?", "who says you have to go to school?", "what happens when you don't go to school?", etc. Here I will keep in mind the definition the framework gives of law (see §3.1), because I do not just want to find the opinion of the child on education, but rather what laws the respondent knows and/or experiences in relation to education.

For every aspect of education as identified during the explorative phase, I might have to move through the investigative cycle to find related laws and legal orders (for example think of a child who identifies both school and music classes as education). To end the investigation, I engage with the respondent in drawing a conclusion; we look back at the initial question and we formulate a tentative conclusion, which can include multiple aspects.

Note that this kind of research can be performed in this fashion with both subjects of law and with legislators, in which case the questions will be slightly different (see §4.4.4).

4.4.3. ANALYSIS OF DATA

In some sense, the analysis of data is done together with the participant, during the interview and especially when drawing conclusions. However, the researcher who oversees the whole research project and engages in several micro-researches has to compare these data.

565 See also §4.2.4 on ethics.

566 Although some small talk is nice and sometimes necessary, including exploring the subject, not too much time should be spent on this phase, as it is already clear what the main question for the conversation will be. For more on this, see the reflection on the methodology in chapter 8.

Following Weber, the researcher takes the theoretical framework and includes ideal types and tests these in relation to research data. In particular, we can look for regularities in the participant's responses and compare these to the hypothesis, the predicted regularities in ideas (as reasons for action), the following concrete social actions and its consequences. We might also want to adapt our theoretical framework as a result of empirical findings.[567]

According to the given framework of law, data can be analyzed. We can define the different forms of law found, where we can find the written, formal law by researching law books applicable to the relevant legal society.[568] Then we can distinguish different laws affecting the subject of laws on the same legal issue, by defining different legislators, the corresponding different legal orders and its laws.[569] Combined, we arrive at a "map" of law applying to a certain group of legal subjects on a certain legal issue.

4.4.4. PARTICIPANTS

So far, the text has mostly been about research with children. But if you go back and read the complete methodology, you can read "adult" or the more general "participant" in every place where it now says "child". In general, both subjects of the relevant legal community and legislators of all legal orders (as identified under §4.4.1) have to be involved in the research.

Although researchers argue that anyone can participate and that "listening is not limited to the spoken (or written) word"[570], participation in the current research will be limited to respondents that master language – at least those who are able to speak and understand verbal communication.

Example: Participants for the study of children's right to education in the Netherlands

The respondents will include: children who are residents of the Netherlands, caretakers of children living in the Netherlands, teachers who teach in the Netherlands, members of school boards in the Netherlands, politicians who are involved in making municipal and state law about children's education, politicians who are involved in making regional and international law over children's education, potentially excluded children (such as children that are home-schooled), adults involved as possible sovereigns with potentially excluded children (such as home-schooling parents).

---

567 See §4.1.

568 §1.4.

569 §4.4.1.

570 Tangen (2008: 159).

4.2.5. THE MICRO-RESEARCH STEP-BY-STEP

To summarize, if a researcher would like to find law for children according to the methodology of the micro-research as developed in this chapter, s/he would have to go through the following steps:

1. Define the legal case you want to study and corresponding context (e.g. the right to education for children in Central African Republic)
2. Identify potentially relevant legal orders
3. For each legal order, identify the potentially relevant types of law
4. Research literature to find mainly A law, but possibly indications for B and C laws
5. Identify participants for field research
6. Decide on ethical issues
7. Engage in micro-research
8. Report

Note that all the steps need a certain level of plasticity. While doing field research one might find that the legal case you want to study is not well defined after all, that there is a relevant legal order that you did not define in advance, or that there is a C law that you did not anticipate. Therefore, the initial answers to these questions and the initial methodological plan has to be open to adjustment through the process. For validity purposes, it is important to take notes of these adjustments and account for them later in the process.

PART II

LAW FOR CHILDREN IN PRACTICE: THREE CASE STUDIES

As indicated in the introduction to part I, while part I presented the theoretical framework and methodology for finding law for children, the second part of this thesis will present three case studies wherein the theory and methodology of the first part will be applied to actual cases, to try to understand the different laws, in different legal orders, involved in the protection/violation of a certain child's right in a specific socio-legal context. The three case studies in this part of the thesis are:

- The child's right to education in the Netherlands (chapter 5)
- The child's right to education in the Central African Republic (CAR) (chapter 6)
- The child's right to nationality in the Turkish Republic of Northern Cyprus (TRNC) (chapter 7)

Each chapter includes an overview of the situation of that particular child's right in that particular socio-legal context, followed by an analysis of the different legal orders and laws found during the case study. Before presenting the first case, I will elaborate on the selection of these cases.

THE ORIGINAL PLAN

According to the original research proposal[571], the idea was to apply the theory to six different case studies, studying different children's rights articles (derived

571 Hopman (2014b).

from the UNCRC) in different social and political contexts, to test the hypothesis that, in order to understand violations of children's rights more, one has to look at law through children's eyes. This understanding of the laws and legal orders surrounding children was hypothesized to create a new understanding of children's rights violations, which could open up (possibilities for) social transformation. To this end, then, the theoretical framework and methodology proposed had to be tested in relation to different children's rights violations, in different cultural, social, and political contexts.

The case studies selected were:

1. The child's right to education (art. 28, 29 CRC) in the Central African Republic and the Netherlands
2. The best interests of the child (art. 3 CRC) in the Turkish Republic of Northern Cyprus (TRNC) and the Netherlands.
3. The right to be protected against sexual exploitation (art. 34, 35 CRC) in the United States, in Massachusetts and in the Netherlands.

These cases were selected to create qualitative context dependent knowledge and test the theory and methodology developed in part 1 of the research. In addition, these particular case studies were selected based on:

1) Their potential to provide new information about children's rights violations
2) The cultural, social and political diversity of different locations
3) The non-Dutch situations for their lack of presence in research and media and for existing ties the researcher had developed with organizations in these countries
4) The Dutch cases because of practical reasons (as the researcher lives in the Netherlands) and because of strong connections of the researcher to Dutch children's rights organizations.
5) Dutch and non-Dutch cases for the possibility of comparison[572]

CHANGE OF PLANS

The original idea was to conduct approximately 25 interviews per case study during 6 weeks of field research per case, amounting to a total of 150 interviews.[573] However, as the theoretical and methodological framework developed further, it became clear that, to understand a case truly, 25 interviews and 6 weeks in the field was not nearly enough. According to the way in which

572 For a more elaborate justification see Hopman (2014b).

573 See the original budget plan (Hopman 2014c), available at: http://kinderrechtenonderzoek.nl/wp-content/uploads/2014/09/Budget-PHD-Hopman.docx.

the methodology was developed, it was necessary to identify different legal orders, and the researcher had to engage in interviewing a sufficient number of people in all of these different (possible) legal orders. As there were several (possible) legal orders involved, the total number of interviewees became much higher than the projected 25.

For example, for the first case study, on the child's right to education in the Netherlands, participants included: children, parents (caretakers), teachers, education inspectors, scientists/specialists, and local and national politicians. Because of the focus of the case study, participants had to include (families with) children in and out of school, (families with) children with and without home-schooling and Roma families. For this case study I identified 6 different legal orders and I carried out 51 interviews, supplemented by several participatory observations.[574] For the CAR case study on the other hand, for which much less information/research was available beforehand, I decided I needed (much) more data. During three months of field research, I engaged in 87 formal interviews with children, caretakers, teachers/school directors, APE, NGO/UN employees, religious leaders, and local and national politicians, in addition to 50 informal, documented discussions, 20 observations and a questionnaire via text message which was answered by 2,984 young people.[575] Lastly, for the TRNC case study, for which also little to no information/research was available beforehand, we[576] conducted 87 formal interviews, 79 recorded informal interviews, and several observations.[577]

It was only during the first case study that it became clear that it would not be possible to research six different cases within the time limit of the PhD research, unless I would choose to seriously compromise the quality of understanding of the different cases in exchange for quantitative results in terms of the number of cases. Therefore, although the total amount of research conversations (222 formal interviews and 129 informal, recorded discussions) greatly outnumbers the original projected 150 research interviews, the number of case studies taken up in the study has been limited to three case studies.

As a consequence, the three case studies that were selected cover three socio-political contexts that are extremely different, as intended. However, they only cover two different children's rights articles. The child's right to education is discussed twice, and one case concerns the child's right to nationality. With hindsight, for the sake of testing the theoretical framework of the current research, it might have been better to pick three different CRC articles. This change would, at the time, have meant changing the CAR case study by either focusing on a different CRC article or even choosing a different socio-legal

574 See §5.1.2.

575 See §6.1.2.

576 A team of five bachelor students was involved in the execution of the field research of this case study.

577 See §7.1.4.

context altogether. However, I decided not to do this because: 1) it was clear that CAR was greatly neglected in research and media and, at the time, it was made clear to me how much my research on the topic would be appreciated, and 2) there were different indications (such as the UN Human Development Index) that education in particular was a pressing issue in the country, with its poor quality hypothesized as hindering the peaceful development of the country as a whole.[578]

These choices amounted to the fact that, in the end, only very tentative conclusions can be drawn on the applicability of the proposed theoretical/methodological framework to different children's rights cases in different socio-political contexts. Within the limited time and research available for the PhD research, taking into account all factors and interests involved (not in the least the possibility for the research to make an actual change to the lives of children – see chapter 9), I am convinced that I made the right choice concerning the case studies discussed in this thesis. In my view, the current thesis is only the beginning of a larger research project on children's rights. Hopefully, there will be an opportunity to continue this research by testing, adjusting and refining the theoretical/methodological framework more as it will be possible to study more and different CRC articles in many different socio-political contexts.[579]

One last, practical note: while you are reading the different chapters on the different case studies, you may notice that only in the CAR case study (chapter 6) information is referenced by specific reference to individual interviews. The choice to include these very specific references, which is generally uncommon in presenting field research data, was because the data for this case study relies heavily on the field research data, more so than in the two other cases in this thesis. There is virtually no academic research on (the child's right to) education in the CAR, and the subject itself depends greatly on the daily experience of the people involved. This is in contrast to the formal written law, which plays a greater role in relation to the right to nationality and the fact that there is much more relevant research and legal documentation available in relation to the other two case studies.

---

578 Another pressing factor in the CAR seemed to be the right to health. However, there seemed to be a little more (Anglophone) research at that topic at the time. EG: when you search google scholar for "health Central African Republic" there are several studies on different health issues in the CAR context, such as fever, AIDS, rotavirus, respiratory infections, etc (see: Google search (2017a)). However, if you search for "education Central African Republic", the first page of results gives you articles about wildlife in CAR, AIDS, politics, Ebola, etc. and none on education (see: Google search (2017b)).

579 In fact, Prof. Fons Coomans and myself received an NWO/WOTRO SDG grant to do a four year study on the development rights of children living in unreconigzed states, a study that in part builds on the theory and methodology as developd in this study. The new project is called "Invisible Children" and runs from April 2019 to October 2023.

CHAPTER 5

THE CHILD'S RIGHT TO EDUCATION IN THE NETHERLANDS

With a focus on children out of school, home-schooling and Roma children

DEFINITIONS

In this chapter, the following terminology will be used:
"CEA" refers to the Dutch Compulsory Education Act ("*leerplichtwet*")
"CSOs" refers to Civil Society Organizations
"NGOs" refers to Non-Governmental Organizations

"SAO" refers to the municipal "school attendance officer" (*leerplichtambtenaar*) who is charged with enforcing the CEA on the municipal level

"children out of school" will mean children who are missing school education for more than four weeks in one school year

"the Netherlands" refers to the Netherlands in Europe. The Caribbean part of the Kingdom of the Netherlands is excluded from this research.

"public schools" (*openbare scholen*) are schools which are founded by the Dutch state, while "independent schools" (*bijzondere scholen*) are schools that are founded by any non-state party (religious group, group of parents, etc.). Both types of schools are financed by the Dutch state.

"home-schooling" refers to education which has the family home as its main location, where, except for family members, no other children are following this education. This includes both when parents are teachers, as well as when children learn independently or with online teachers, private teachers, etc.

5.1. INTRODUCTION

The first case study of this thesis concerns the child's right to education in the Netherlands (CRC art. 28 and 29). Although the Netherlands is among the richest countries in the world, with a GDP of $ 52.799 per capita[580] and a stable political climate (there has been no armed conflict since the end of the Second World War in 1945), according to media, 10,000–15,000 children are out of school annually and potentially not enjoying any education.[581] In this case study, I chose to focus on this group of children who live in the Netherlands and who are not in school, because these children's right to education seemed to be at risk of being violated. When I made this choice in 2014, children out of school were a prominent subject of political debate as well as media coverage. Specifically, of all children out of school, I chose to focus on three groups which I learned might be particularly at risk, namely: 1) children out of school ("*thuiszitters*", literally: "those who sit at home"), 2) home-schooled children and 3) Roma children.

The chapter is built up as follows. The first section is an introductory section, which will present first a short overview of the history of education and education law in the Netherlands, in order to sketch the relevant context (§5.1.1), followed by a specification of the methodology specific for this case study (§5.1.2).

580 The Organisation for Economic Co-operation and Development (2017) "Netherlands". Available at: https://data.oecd.org/netherlands.htm.

581 Kuiper & Bouma (2015), Trouw (2016), Keultjes (2016). Please note that, since a large part of the research for this case study, including the field research, took place during 2014-2015, I use the facts and figures relating to those years. For a discussion on how the case developed, see an update at the end of this chapter.

Section two will present general findings on the child's right to education in the Netherlands. It will start with a discussion of who "children out of school" are in the Netherlands and will present the conceptual framework of the discussion as seen through the eyes of children, based on the findings of this research (§5.2.1). This will be followed by the same conceptual framework as seen through the eyes of adults (§5.2.2). The third subsection will present a literature review of the large body of research on the child's right to education in the Netherlands, specifically as concerns the three focus groups of the case study. This will be followed by a review of recent reporting to the UN human rights bodies, as concerns the subject of this case study (§5.2.4). The fifth subsection will give an overview of the general findings from the field research for this case study and, lastly, I will share a short reflection on the meaning of law in the Netherlands (§5.2.6).

The third section will present an analysis of the different legal orders and its laws as regards the child's right to education in the Netherlands. This will include the international legal order (§5.3.1), the regional (European) legal order (§5.3.2), the Roma legal order (§5.3.3), the state legal order (§5.3.4), the municipality legal order (§5.3.5), the school legal order (§5.3.6), the household legal order (§5.3.7), and the autonomous child (§5.3.8).

Lastly, the chapter will end with an update on the situation regarding the right to education in the Netherlands since the data collection for this case study (2015–2020) (§5.4).

5.1.1. THE CHILD'S RIGHT TO EDUCATION IN THE NETHERLANDS: A BRIEF HISTORY

Historically, education, and in particular state legislation on education, has been an important topic of political debate in the Netherlands. Even before the birth of the nation state in 1815, since the 17th century, different regions obliged parents to pay education fees whether they sent their children to school or not, while in other regions financial aid was reduced for poorer families if they did not send their children to school.[582] Home-schooling was common for richer families.[583] In the early 1800s, the first national education laws were introduced, which stated that public elementary school should be accessible to everyone and also that school education and religion should be separated.[584] The latter would be the subject of the political "school struggle" (*schoolstrijd*), which lasted for over 100 years, during which religious groups (Protestants, Catholics and Jews) fought for the right to school children according to their religion and have this

582 Storimans (2006: 9); Boekholt & de Booy (1987: 24).

583 Van Bijsterveld (2013: 18); Boekholt & de Booy (1987: 94).

584 Schools, however, were "general-Christian" (Boekholt & de Booy (1987: 98-101)).

paid for by the state, while other leading figures opted to separate church and education in the spirit of enlightenment.[585] In the 1848 constitution, "freedom of education" ("*vrijheid van onderwijs*") was introduced, which meant that, in addition to public schools, everyone, including religious organizations, was allowed to start a school, called "*bijzondere school*" ("*independent school*") and provide education.[586] Both public and independent schools were subject to government control, but it was not until 1920 that public and independent schools started receiving equal government funding.[587]

In 1900, the Compulsory Education Act (hereafter: CEA) (*leerplichtwet,* literally: law on the duty to study) was introduced in national legislation for the first time – famously accepted by 50 votes in favour and 49 against, after an opponent had fallen off his horse and could not come to vote. At the time, this law entailed a duty to send children to school, imposed upon parents, meant to combat child labour.[588] The law made it mandatory for parents to send children aged 7–13 to school.[589] Enforcement was put in the hands of the municipalities. In case parents did not comply, they would have to appear before a judge.[590]

Baron Schimmelpennick en zijn biek	*Baron Schimmelpennick and his steed*
Deden beide aan politiek:	*Were politicians both indeed:*
De baron zie: 'Tegen, zonder manco.'	*The baron would vote: 'no'*
De schimmel zei: 'Wij stemmen blanco'	*While the horse said: 'we won't go'*
Zo werd Borgesius' Leerplichtwet	*So Borgesius' compulsory education*
Door paarde-politiek gered.[591]	*Was saved by a horse-politician.*

More and more schools were set up by religious groups, until around 70% of schools were "independent schools". This development was part of the "pillarization" (*verzuiling*) in Dutch culture, during which, up until the 1970s, every religious subgroup had its own schools, its own radio and tv stations, sports clubs, etc.[592] Starting in the 1960s, this religious segregation became less prominent, however the independent schools continued to exist. In addition to religious schools, most of which started to provide increasingly secular education, over the last 50 years, the right to start independent schools with government funding has been used to start all kinds of schools with less conventional didactical systems, such as Montessori, Jenaplan, Democratic,

585 Ministerie van Onderwijs, Cultuur en Wetenschap (no date); Boekholt & de Booy (1987); van Bijsterveld (2013); United Nations (1996: para. 28).
586 Boekholt & de Booy (1987: 144-45); Ministerie van Onderwijs, Cultuur en Wetenschap (no date); van Bijsterveld (2013).
587 Boekholt & de Booy (1987: 150, 221-22); United Nations (1996: para. 28).
588 Storimans (2006: 11-12); Boekholt & de Booy (1987: 154-155).
589 Boekholt & de Booy (1987: 155).
590 Ibid: 171.
591 Translation by Bavo Hopman.
592 Boekholt & de Booy (1987: 234-36).

Dalton, Steiner schools, etc.[593] More recently, an increase in migrants from Islamic countries has led to the establishment of several independent schools by Islamic groups.[594]

In 1969 the second *leerplichtwet (*CEA) came into effect. This law provided for a municipal "school attendance officer" (hereafter: SAO) (*leerplichtambtenaar*) who was tasked with enforcing the CEA and the period for compulsory education was extended to 9 years in school or until the age of 16.[595] The obligation was still aimed at the parents. Justifications allowing for an exemption from this obligation were if the child would not be able to be accepted in a school on physical or psychological grounds (art. 5a), if the parents objected to the "orientation" (*richting*) of the schools in their direct environment (art. 5b) or if the child received education in a school in another country (art. 5c). Home-schooling was taken out of the law and thereby rendered illegal, although in the explanatory memorandum to the law it was indicated that the practice "hardly exists anymore"[596], while the law did include the option for the minister to, on the ground of special circumstances, exempt parents from the obligation to send their children to school if it could be demonstrated that the child enjoyed sufficient education in another way.[597]

In 1994 the CEA was amended to add an obligation for children aged 12 and older to attend school[598], whereby the responsibility for the child's school attendance became shared between parents and children.

In 1999, researcher Veneman first "discovered" *thuiszitters* in the context of children who would go to special needs education establishments yet were placed on a waiting list and therefore had to wait at home instead of going to school.[599] This discovery was taken quite seriously by national politicians and the national education inspectorate. Based on several commissioned studies on the subject[600], in 2014 this led to the law on "Appropriate education" (*passend onderwijs*), which aims at the following:

- for all children to get an appropriate, or fitting, place in school education
- for every child to attend a regular school if possible

593 Ibid: 252-54. From a legal perspective, a school can be founded on religious and/or philosophical grounds – a requirement which the government is planning to change. See: Rijksoverheid (n.d.(d)) "Oprichten nieuwe school" ("*Founding a new school*"). Available at: https://www.rijksoverheid.nl/onderwerpen/vrijheid-van-onderwijs/oprichten-nieuwe-school.

594 For a discussion see Sunier (2004).

595 Compulsory Education Act (CEA) (*Leerplichtwet)* 1968(a) (art. 2(3)).

596 In the explanatory memorandum, it is argued that, since homeschooling "hardly exists anymore", it was not necessary to replace "duty to learn" (*leerplicht*) by "duty to go to school" (*schoolplicht*), because both expressions were now – in contrast to 1900 – basically identical (Tweede Kamer (1967: 13)).

597 Tweede Kamer (1967).

598 Eerste Kamer (1993-1994: art. 2); CEA (art. 2(3)).

599 Van Batenburg (2006: 5).

600 See §5.2.3.

- for children to attend special education if intensive support is necessary
- for schools to have the possibility to receive tailored support
- for the possibilities and educational needs of the child to be in first place, rather than the disability
- for children not to be at home for longer periods anymore[601]

With this law, schools are now responsible for finding appropriate education for children (they have a "duty to care" (*zorgplicht*)).[602] However, researchers point out that changing the reality for children out of school is still a "work in progress"[603], and media coverage is also critical.[604]

Another group of children that are often out of school in the Netherlands are Roma children. The Roma people are a people who live(d) nomadic lives and are said to have their own internal social (and perhaps legal) order. They travel, or used to travel, throughout Europe. Historically, because of their nomadic lifestyle, they did not participate in the forming of nation-states and therefore, even though they lived in European states, they were excluded from national communities.[605] In addition to social exclusion and attempts to destroy the culture through settlement programs and prohibitions on the use of the Romani language, during the Second World War the Nazi regime committed mass killings of Roma.[606] To date, many Roma have an illegal status and/or are stateless.[607]

In the Netherlands, it is not clear which people are understood as "Roma" (potentially because the nomadic background of Roma is a challenge to academic/popular indicators of cultural identity).[608] Some make a distinction between gypsies who have been living in the Netherlands for centuries (*Sinti*) and those originating in Eastern Europe who were given permission to legally reside in the Netherlands in 1977 and some who arrived later, for example from Yugoslavia (*Roma*)[609], yet others identify *Sinti* as a subgroup of Roma.[610] This research focuses on (children of) people who self-identify as Roma and/or those who are identified by research participants as Roma.[611]

---

601 Rijksoverheid (n.d. (b)).

602 Ibid.

603 Ministry of Education, Culture and Science (2015b: 2) "Kamerbrief met reactie op onderzoeken passend onderwijs" (*letter to the second chamber with reaction to researches appropriate education").*

604 See for example Kuiper (2016); Rutten (2016); ANP (2015); NOS (2015).

605 Bogdal (2014); Sollie et al. (2013: 23-25).

606 Bogdal (2014: 18-20); Sollie et al. (2013: 24-25).

607 Sollie et al. (2013: 25); Parra (2011); Warnke (1999).

608 Bhopal & Myers (2008: 5-6); Wijkhuijs & Sollie (2014: 74).

609 Van der Ree et al. (2001: 4); Sollie et al. (2013: 25); Timmermans (2016: 3).

610 Sollie et al. (2013: 36-37).

611 In line with Bhopal & Myers (2008: 8).

As regards education, historically, Roma children in the Netherlands did not attend school. In the 1960s, special Roma schools were set up in caravan camps where Roma resided yet, since the late 1970s, the policy focus changed to include Roma children in regular education.[612] However, school attendance has been limited. Roma children are often sent to special needs education, are absent from school or are not enrolled in any school.[613] SAOs have often "looked the other way" in these situations.[614]

5.1.2. METHODOLOGY

The main question for this case study was: "what is the meaning of the child's right to education in the Netherlands?" In line with the described methodology in chapter 4, in preparation for the field research, the following possible legal orders related to the case study were identified:

Legal order	Legislator (sovereign)	Relevant legal community
International legal order	United Nations	All residents of the Netherlands (including non-Dutch nationality), the Dutch state and its local offices and administrations
Regional legal order	a) European Union b) Council of Europe	All residents of the Netherlands (including non-Dutch nationality), the Dutch state and its local offices and administrations
Roma legal order	Rom Baro	All Roma
State legal order	Government of the Netherlands	All residents of the Netherlands (including non-Dutch nationality), local offices and administrations of the Dutch state
Municipality legal order	Local government	All residents of the relevant municipality
School legal order	Principal / board	Teachers, students of the school (and indirectly their caretakers)
Classroom	Teacher	Students of the classroom
Household	Caretaker (Father, mother, …)	Children of the family
Autonomous child[615]	Child	Child

612 Van der Ree et al (2001: 5); Rodrigues & Matelski (2004: 45).

613 Van der Ree et al (2001: 6-7); Sollie et al. (2013: 26-27).

614 Rodigrues & Matelski (2004: 44); see also research findigs §5.2.5.

615 This level was actually added after doing field research in the CAR. I realized that this level may also apply to the Netherlands. I went back to the data and decided to add the level at least

Based on this initial scheme, over the period of a year (2015–2016) I engaged in 51 qualitative interviews with the following respondents:

Role[616] / experience	Regular education	Special education	*Thuiszitters*	Home-schooling	No education	Roma	Physical disability	Psychological disability[617]	Total (roles)
Child (0–25)[618]	21	7	7	12	8	5	2	10	**24**
Parent / caretaker	18	9	13	12	13	4	4	13	**18**
Teacher[619]	6	3	3	4	4	–	3	3	**6**
Municipality employee[620]	5	4	3	3	5	3	3	4	**5**
Politician (national)	2	2	2	2	2	–	2	2	**2**
Education inspector	1	1	1	1	1	–	1	1	**1**
Education expert[621]	2	2	2	2	1	–	1	1	**2**
Scientist specialized in education	2	2	2	2	1	–	1	1	**2**
Total (experience area)	**57**	**30**	**33**	**38**	**35**	**12**	**17**	**35**	

Of the 51 participants, the youngest was 4 and the oldest 62 years old. 45% was male. 55% was female. Sampling of these participants happened in different ways: some were approached through snowballing sampling, some were approached via social media (mostly home schoolers and *thuiszitters*). Some people got in touch because they had heard about the research, for example

to add the discussion on in what sense the child is autonomous in relation to education in the Netherlands.

616 Some participants had several roles, for example when the politician was also the parent of a child. When this occurred, this was counted double only in cases where both roles were relevant in the research conversation. For example, in a conversation with a participant who works at the municipal level with Roma, it transpired that the participant was also the parent of a child who is out of school, and therefore both situations were discussed at length.

617 "Disability" is understood here as different from the norm, according to participants themselves. This includes gifted children, those with learning difficulties and low IQs, because in relation to education these characteristics are often experienced as disabling. It is a psychological factor that makes you as a child different from the rest of the group. Dyslexia is not included, because the participants who were dyslexic (or their parents) did not experience this as a disability in relation to education (perhaps because in the Netherlands the assistance in this respect in education is quite well developed).

618 I chose to include participants up until the age of 25, and to include them under "child", so that the experiences of young adults could be taken into consideration, when they looked back on their recent education experiences such as homeschooling, being out of school, etc.

619 This includes everyone with a teacher diploma and/or who was teaching in a school, including remedial teachers. Homeschooling parents without a teacher diploma were not included.

620 This includes: SAOs, education policy makers, employee of Roma programs, and youth care employees.

621 This includes: education consultants, education lawyers.

through the research website[622] and they wanted to share their story. Lastly, several institutions, such as municipalities, children's rights organizations and schools, helped to find participants.

In general, all children were allowed to participate, although I did aim to find a balance between children in regular education and those out of school, of the specific interest groups (*thuiszitters*, home-schooled children, Roma), and between participants in different parts of the country. Adults were allowed to participate if they had an active role in the lives of their children.[623] Parents who wanted to participate, but who would not allow their child to participate (if s/he wanted to), or whose child could not participate, were excluded from the research. Because of Dutch legislation and strong social norms, unfortunately I could not include any children whose parents did not give permission for the child to participate. In general, the priority in the decision on whether or not to allow someone to participate was the aim of the case study to present a child's perspective on the subject matter.

Interviews usually took around 45 minutes, although some were a bit longer or shorter. All conversations were recorded (unless the participant explicitly asked for it not to be recorded) and transcribed in the form of a conversation-report. After each interview, if the participant wished so, a report of the conversation was sent to the participant together with a form, on which they could write remarks and/or extra information.

In addition to formal interviews, I collected data from the following sources:

- Literature study: a general review of academic literature and more popular-scientific research (for example research reports published by NGOs) on education in the Netherlands and in particular on the subject of children out of school, home-schooling, Roma and *thuiszitters*.
- Legal doctrinal study of: relevant formal, written laws of different legal orders (see §5.3), relevant, recent evaluative cycles of UN human rights bodies, relevant court cases on the regional and state level, cases before the national complaints committee education, and lastly relevant policy documents.
- Participatory observation of:
  - "home-schooling café", organized by the Dutch organization for home-schooling (NVvTO)
  - Debate about the child's right to education and home-schooling with a group of 4 children's rights specialists
  - For a year I actively followed social media about home-schooling and *thuiszitters*, including Facebook groups for parents of children out of

622 Www.childrensrightsresearch.com.

623 Meaning that parents who did not live with their children, for example, or who were not allowed to see their children, etc. were excluded.

school and/or parents who wanted to, or were already, home schooling their children

- Study day organized by the Ministry of Justice together with the Ministry of Social affairs, titled "Work in Progress: Program Approach Exploitation Roma Children"[624]
- A visit of the SAO together with a Roma mother and her son, who had been summoned to appear at the municipality office because her son was not enrolled in any school.

– Observation of a meeting of the Committee Education, Culture and Science (Second Chamber, national level politics) on "appropriate education", March 16, 2016.

5.2. THE CHILD'S RIGHT TO EDUCATION IN THE NETHERLANDS: GENERAL FINDINGS

Before getting into the analysis of the legal orders involved in the child's right to education in the Netherlands, I will first present a general overview of the findings on the child's right to education in the Netherlands, specifically as concerns children out of school, home-schooling and Roma children.

In the Netherlands, a highly bureaucratic, organized state, much of public opinion, media and research is guided by concepts, statistics, numbers, and figures. The child's perspective is (almost) completely left out in determining these measurements and concepts. During the case study, I quickly found that the child's reality does not match the known concepts and statistics. Therefore, when looking at law through children's eyes, and in particular the right to education, much confusion arises when comparing the field research data to available sources. In terms of categorization, it is therefore difficult to align this study, in some sense, with the available data, law and research.[625]

In the hope to remedy this difficulty and to be able to discuss existing research and law as well as the lived reality of children, I will start by presenting the conceptual framework of the discussion as seen through the eyes of children (§5.2.1), followed by the conceptual framework as seen through the eyes of adults (§5.2.2). These sections will be followed by a review of existing literature on the right to education in the Netherlands, specifically as concerns home-schooling, out of school children and Roma children (§5.2.3), and a review of recent reporting to the UN human rights bodies, as concerns the subject of this case study (§5.2.4). To end, I will present the (other) findings of the field research (§5.2.5) and, lastly, I will share a short reflection on the meaning of law in the Netherlands (§5.2.6).

---

624 "Werk in Uitvoering: Programma Aanpak Uitbuiting Roma Kinderen", 18 February 2016.

625 See also: Sleeboom et al. (2009: 5) and van Batenburg et al. (2006: 5-8).

5.2.1. THE CHILD'S RIGHT TO EDUCATION IN THE NETHERLANDS THROUGH CHILDREN'S EYES

In general, most children in the Netherlands go to school.[626] However, there is also a group of children who are not in school. For the purpose of this research, "children out of school" will refer to children who are missing school education for more than four weeks in one school year.

From the child's perspective, we can distinguish children who are going to school and those who are not. Among children who are not going to school, we can further distinguish between children who receive education at home and those who do not.

Therefore, the basic division from the child's perspective is:

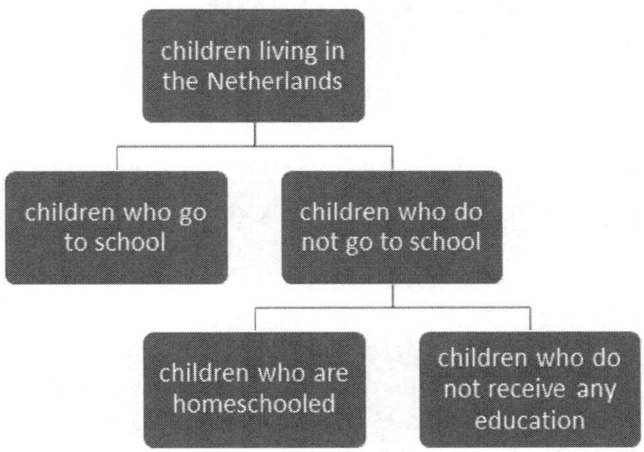

If we differentiate further, among children who go to school, we can differentiate between children who go to regular schools and children who go to "special schools" (schools for children with special needs). Of children who are home-schooled, we can differentiate between when this is the deliberate choice of the parents who prefer home to school education or when this is a consequence of being out of school. Of the children who do not receive any education, we can differentiate between when this is the choice of the parents, of the school, or of the child. Lastly, there is one in-between form, when children get both home-schooling and school education. Of course, children who do not receive any education may move into the category of children who are home-schooled

626 In 2015, 99% of 14-year olds attended fulltime education, and 98% of 16-year olds (Ministry of Education (n.d.) *Onderwijs in cijfers: Ontwikkeling van aantal deelnemers* ("*Education in numbers: development of the number of participants*"). See also United Nations (1996: art. 350-355) *Core document forming part of the reports of States Parties: Netherlands (European part of the Kingdom)*. According to my calculations (see §5.2.2), it seems that > 2% of children who fall under the CEA are potentially not receiving education (50,000 out of 2,372,256 children who fall under the CEA (Ministry of Education, Culture and Science (2016)).

because they are out of school. In this situation the diagram can be extended as follows:

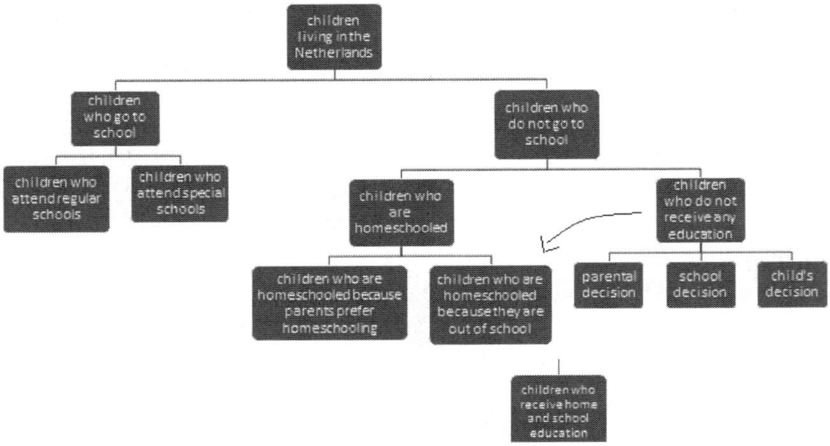

Based on the research for this case study, in particular the interviews, the following can be said about the different categories[627]:

1. Home-schooling: parental decision

An unknown number of parents in the Netherlands decide to home-school their children. They do so for two main reasons: either they have decided that they can offer better education at home than the child would be able to receive at school (group 1a) or they feel forced to do so by circumstances (group 1b). Group 1a can be further subdivided between parents who feel it is better to home-school their children because they want them to be taught according to their specific religious and/or philosophical principles (1ai) or parents who prefer home-schooling for non-religious/philosophical reasons (1aii). Group 1b includes parents who are travelling abroad for work or fun (group 1bi), parents of children who cannot attend school due to sickness (physical and/or mental, including children with disabilities) (group 1bii), parents of children who are not allowed to attend school, by school, for different reasons (for example because they seriously misbehaved and thereby put other children in danger) (group 1biii), and lastly parents of children who themselves prefer home-schooling to school education, such as in the case of Laura Dekker who wanted to sail the world[628] (group 1biv).

---

627 Please note that this is probably not an exhaustive list, yet only a reflection of the cases that I encountered (directly, or indirectly through interviews with school attendance officers and employees of the education inspectorate).

628 See, for example, Anderson & Claassen (2012).

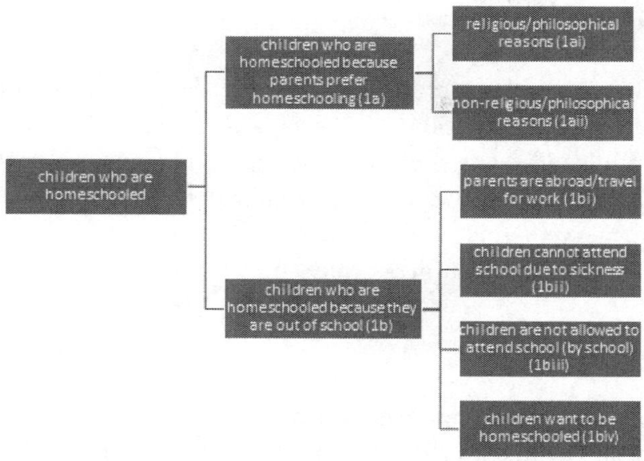

2. *No education: parental decision*

An unknown number of parents in the Netherlands decide to stop their children from attending school education – or never enroll them in the first place – yet they do not provide alternative education.[629] This group, too, can be subdivided between parents who deliberately choose to take their children out of school, for example because they feel that girls over age 12 should not receive school education (group 2a) and parents who feel forced by circumstances to take their children out of school (group 2b). These circumstances include when the child is unhappy at school for example because of bullying (group 2bi), because the child is sick, physically and/or mentally and parents feel that a focus on healthcare is prioritized above, and excludes, education (group 2bii), or because they are concerned about possible legal and/or financial consequences of sending the child to school, for example because they are illegal migrants (group 2biii).

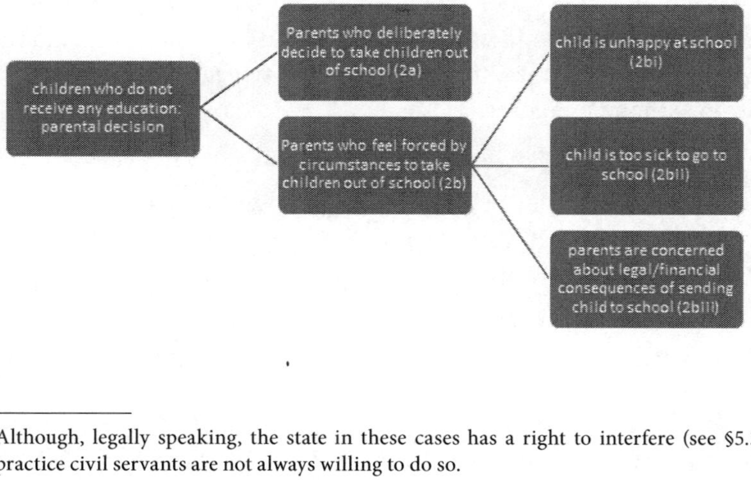

629 Although, legally speaking, the state in these cases has a right to interfere (see §5.3.4), in practice civil servants are not always willing to do so.

3. No education: school decision

Sometimes school authorities may decide to send children home without providing alternative education, for example because they feel they cannot educate the child adequately, because of the child's mental and/or physical disabilities. Since 2014, schools are legally obliged to accept these children and provide them with alternative education[630], however in practice this does not always happen, or at least not successfully.[631]

4. No education: child's decision

Sometimes children decide not to go to school, for different reasons, for example because they do not like it or because they do not feel safe. There seem to two be main groups; either older children who decide to skip school without their parents knowing about it ("truants") or younger children who want to stay home. For the latter, it seems that it is usually the parent taking the final decision for the child to not go to school.

5. Combined education: home- and school education

Sometimes when a child is not able to go to school, different authorities (teachers, school management, parents, municipality, inspectorate) work together to make sure that the child's right to education is still respected. In some of these cases, a combination of school- and home education may be put in place. For example, when, due to sickness, children have to spend a lot of time in the hospital, they may still be able to follow education in their regular classroom through a livestream and classmates visit the hospital and share homework.

Of course, these are all "ideal types", whereas in practice children do not fit neatly into one of the categories – rather many seem to move in and out of different categories. In general, children who do not go to school seem to fall into a "grey area" of the highly regulated education (school) situation in the Netherlands and often the different authorities struggle with the question of what to do with these children.

5.2.2. THE CHILD'S RIGHT TO EDUCATION IN THE NETHERLANDS THROUGH ADULT EYES

Dutch adults seem to take the Dutch formal written law as the point of departure for discussion. According to the Dutch Compulsory Education Act (CEA),

630 Primary Education Act (*Wet op het primair onderwijs)* 1981.

631 See Kuiper (2016), Rutten (2016), ANP (2015), NOS (2015), Ministry of Education (2015b: 2).

parents have the obligation to send their children aged 5–18 to school[632] and children aged 12 and older have the obligation to attend school. Both parents and children from age 12 and above can be punished through legal proceedings if they do not fulfil this obligation (parents usually receive a fine of around € 250, while children are sentenced to do community service).[633]

There are quite a few exceptions to this rule. A child does not have to attend school if:

1. A child is not considered fit to be accepted into school, proven by a declaration of a doctor, pedagogue or psychologist[634]
2. Parents object to school education in the surroundings of their home, based on their religious/philosophical beliefs[635]
3. There are special circumstances, and it can be shown that the child enjoys sufficient education in another way[636]
4. A child is expelled, or the school is closed[637]
5. A child cannot visit the school due to sickness[638]
6. A child is not able to visit the school due to obligations following from religious or philosophical beliefs[639]
7. Parents have a specific type of profession and therefore get permission to take the children on holiday outside of the school holidays[640]
8. The child is not able to visit the school because of other severe circumstances[641]

Reasons 1 to 3 result in parents obtaining an official exemption from the obligation to send their children to school, issued by the municipal school attendance officer (SAO), which is valid for one school year.[642] Reasons 4–8 are usually arranged between parents and the school (director), whereby the latter decides whether there is a good reason for the child to miss out on school.[643] In all these cases, children are exempted from the obligation to go to school and

---

632 All children aged 5-16 have to go to school, children aged 16-18 have to go to school as long as they do not have a "starting qualification"; a diploma that could get them started on the job market, by which any diploma starting at level VMBO-T (VMBO 4) is meant.

633 1969 CEA (art. 2.3, 26.2). For an overview of court cases, see Hopman, M. (2016a) "Rechtszaken en overige uitspraken over recht op onderwijs in Nederland" (*"Court cases and other judgments about the right to education in the Netherlands")*. The fact that these cases usually take a long time and have a very limited effect, shows that this is a very ineffective means of enforcement.

634 1969 CEA (art. 5a, 7).

635 1969 CEA (art. 5b, 8).

636 1969 CEA (art. 15).

637 1969 CEA (art. 11 a-c).

638 1969 CEA (art. 11d. 12).

639 1969 CEA (art. 11e, 13).

640 1969 CEA (art. 11f, 13a).

641 1969 CEA (art. 11g).

642 For reason 3, there is no known practice in terms of for how long the exemption is granted.

643 In addition to the above-mentioned articles, see also Rijksoverheid (n.d. (a)).

parents are exempted from the obligation to send their children to school. In Dutch state law, there is no legal provision that says that the child has a right to education and so children who do not go to school under these legal exceptions do not have such a right to education under Dutch law.[644]

Children who are out of school are in the Dutch discourse usually referred to as "*thuiszitters*" (literally: "those who sit at home"). The Ministry of Education, in its definition of "*thuiszitters*" excludes all children who are absent from school due to "permitted absenteeism" ("*geoorloofd verzuim*", meaning: absent based on reasons 1–8 mentioned above).[645] To the Ministry, "*thuiszitters*" means children who are absent for more than four weeks in one school year, without permission to be absent. They make a further subdivision between "long relative [unpermitted] absenteeism" (children who are enrolled in school) and "absolute [unpermitted] absenteeism" (children not enrolled in any school).[646]

Due to this policy approach, unfortunately it is impossible to count the number of children out of school, because the cases where school absenteeism is permitted by the school (reasons 4–8 above) are not registered on a central level.[647] In these cases, the school does not have to report the *thuiszitters* to the municipality and, therefore, for example when parents register their children as being sick for longer periods, these children are relatively off the radar. The situation would only be considered further if 1) the child's teacher would have the idea that perhaps there is no legitimate reason for the absenteeism, 2) the parents cannot submit a declaration by a doctor or psychiatrist, 3) the school reports the case to the school attendance officer (SAO), and the SAO investigates the case, or if 4) there are different regulations on the municipal level between the SAO and schools.[648]

Based on the limited available statistics on sick children in the Netherlands, we can estimate that this amounts to (very) roughly 36,500 children who miss school more than four weeks in a school year due to "permitted absenteeism".[649]

---

644 Zoontjens (2003) indicates that, because the Dutch state legal system is a system of legal monism, the international right to education is a part of Dutch law since the Netherlands signed several human rights agreements stating this right, including the ECHR. However, he also indicates that "the attention for this right in Dutch legal circles is limited" (3) and that many provisions of international law cannot be envoked by individuals in Dutch courts, accrding to a ruling of the Surpreme Court (9-11). For a discussion of the legal obligation potentially resulting from international law, see §5.3.

645 In addition, another form of "permitted absenteeism" is when the child receives education at a school abroad, provided the child visits this school regularly (1969 CEA (art. 5c, 9).

646 Ministry of Education, Culture and Science (2015a, 2016).

647 See also Verhoef et al. (2011: 15).

648 Vanneste & Lanser (2010).

649 Based on numbers of 2008, where the National Bureau of Statistics reported that in the period of 2001-2007 of children between aged 4-11, 0.1% suffered from cancer, 0.8 suffered from a congenital heart condition, 0.2% suffered from spasticity, 10% suffered from asthma, chronic bronchitis, emphysema or another respirational condition, 1.8% suffered from serious or chronic bowel conditions which lasted longer than 3 months (Centraal Bureau voor de Statistiek (CBS) (2008: 37)). Taking into account that there were 2,400,000 children in this age group in 2005 (the only available number) (Centraal Bureau voor de Statistiek (CBS) (2015)), we can make a

Based on the figures of the Dutch education inspectorate, we know that during the school year 2014–2015, 9,972 children were absent for more than 4 weeks per year without permission from school. The number of children whose parents were exempted from the obligation to send their children to school by the SAO, based on reasons 1, 2 and 3, figures are also available. We can therefore give a rough estimation of the total number children out of school over school year 2014–2015:

Long relative [unpermitted] absenteeism (absent from school > 4 weeks)	4,016
Absolute [unpermitted] absenteeism (not enrolled in any school)	5,956
Total considered "thuiszitters" by Dutch Ministry of Education	**9,972**
Exempted from compulsory education under CEA 5(a): unfit to enroll in school education on psychological or physical grounds	5,077
Exempted from compulsory education under CEA 5(b): parents have objection to school education in the surroundings, based on their religious/philosophical beliefs	619
Total known number of children out of school	**15,668**
Estimated number of children missing >4 weeks school due to physical illness, under "permitted absenteeism"	28,500[650]

very rough estimate to say that about 4% of these children (taking 15% with lung conditions (compared to numbers by Spee-van der Wekke et al. (1998: 359), who found that 12% of school children aged 4-15 had respiratory problems, more frequent in younger children, and of those 28% reported school absence more than one week due to illness)) will have missed >4 weeks school due to sickness, amounting to 0.04 x 2,400,000 = 96,000 between 2001-2007. Since this is over 7 years, per year this would amount to around 14,000 children of ages 4-11. Since this excludes children of ages 12-18, we should probably double the number, amounting to 28,000 children who have these specific sicknesses and therefore have to miss out on school for >4 weeks. This still excludes: a) children with other kinds of physical illnesses. The amount is very difficult to estimate and probably low because these children are not researched, but say these account for 500 more children, b) children who are out of school because of psychological reasons, which may cause parents to keep their children at home, and who may either visit a psychologist/ psychiatrist or not. In 2009, 267,700 children aged 0-17 were treated by a state mental healthcare institution (Verbeek et al. (2012: 48)). It is unclear how many of these children missed longer periods of school. If we say, similar to physical conditions, that 4% of these children missed >4 weeks of school, this would amount to around 10,000 children; c) the number of children who are reported sick to the school management for longer periods, yet they are not officially reported sick outside of school and/or receiving medical treatment - for example because parents report children who do not want to go to school as being sick or for children that they do not want to send to school. This number would probably not be too high, but I did encounter these cases in field research, which leads to an estimate of about 2,000 children per year in this situation.

Another research concludes that at least 14% of children in the Netherlands have a chronic disease (Mokkink et al. (2006: 41)), which would amount to a much higher figure – however, this would also include the children whose parents were exempted from the CEA under art. 5(a).

650 In 2017, a report was published that shared numbers of children in hospitals (aged 4-18) in 2015. Although this report is not used in this case study because the research for this case study took place in 2015-2016, the numbers in the 2017 report indicate that this estimation is probably too low. See Walraven et. al. (2017: 16), who found that, in 2015, of children aged 4-18: 46,556 were in the hospital 1-5 days, 6,783 children were in the hospital 6-28 days, and 819 were in the hospital 29 or more days. 2,395 children received education in the hospital (ibid: 28). Respondents in this research also indicate that some schools are not aware of their (legal) responsibility towards the education of (their) students who are ill, and these children

Estimated number of children missing >4 weeks school due to psychological illness, under "permitted absenteeism"	10,000
Estimated number of children missing >4 weeks school due to parents who register the child as being sick and keep them at home for different reasons	2,000
Total Estimated number of children missing > 4 weeks school due to "permitted absenteeism"	**40,500**
SUBTOTAL: children out of school 2014–2015	**56,168**

We can therefore very carefully conclude that the number of children out of school is around 56,168 per year. For all these children, their right to education does not seem to be a primary consideration under Dutch law. They are excluded from the education system and there is no control over their education. It is unclear whether they receive any education or not and, if they do, what the quality of this education is.

There is no research available on this whole group of children that are out of school in the Netherlands. Researchers tend to focus on specific subgroups, such as disabled children, children whose parents are exempted from compulsory education under the 5b rule, *thuiszitters* (according to the Government definition, or those who fall into the category of "unpermitted absenteeism")[651], etc.

It was only during the research for this study that I started realizing that this group of "children out of school" (*thuiszitters*) was in fact much bigger than expected. This insight was caused by children themselves, from whose perspective it does not matter at all how they are labelled in law and statistics. the children all have the same experience: they are at home and not in school, contrary to most children in the Netherlands. Most of the time, they are lonely; they feel bored and excluded. Some of these children are educated at home by their parent, a private teacher or via online education material, while some do not receive any education. This is the distinction that really matters, both according to children themselves as well as according to the normative legal perspective of the international child's right to education.[652]

5.2.3. LITERATURE REVIEW: THE CHILD'S RIGHT TO EDUCATION IN THE NETHERLANDS

In general[653], a lot of research is done in the Netherlands in relation to education. Areas that this research focuses on are, for example, the quality of education,

are less visible due to their "permitted absenteeism" (ibid: 25). They indicate children with long term illnesses as a "forgotten group" (ibid: 40).

651 Ministry of Education, Culture and Science (2015a).

652 For the international legal perspective, see §5.3.1.

653 For this general overview, I searched google scholar for publications under "education Netherlands", "children out of school Netherlands", "right to education Netherlands",

studied through factors such as innovation in education[654], teacher/school leader knowledge and education[655], and academic prestige of children and factors which may predict this[656], such as ethnic and gender factors.[657] In some studies, the outcome of education in children is measured for example through the analysis of test results.[658] Another area for education research seems to be the political organization of education in the Netherlands, in terms of finances, law and policy.[659]

As regards school attendance, there is quite some research discussing the integration of children with special needs in regular education[660], some research on school dropouts[661], and some studies on child well-being in schools, especially as regards bullying (although authors often seem not to couple this with school attendance as such).[662]

A last general point to notice when considering research on education in the Netherlands is that there seems to be many more quantitative studies with results based on questionnaires and statistical analysis, while qualitative studies are rare.[663]

Children out of school

Most of the research on children out of school in the Netherlands seems to be government-financed and focusses on what the Ministry of Education defines as *thuiszitters*, namely those who are out of school more than four weeks per

---

"*onderwijs*", "*onderwijs Nederland*" and "*recht op onderwijs Nederland*". I also looked through a database for academic books, and I searched the publications of the Kohnstamm Institute by hand (who do much research on education in the Netherlands) and the National Education Inspectorate.

654 E.g. Admiraal et. al. (2007).

655 E.g. Rohaan et al. (2010); Heyma et al. (2017); Schenke et al. (2018).

656 E.g. de Graaf et al. (2000).

657 Leeman & Volman (2001: 369) summarize this research as follows: "Dutch research on ethnic differences in education has concentrated on identifying factors that explain the generally poorer achievements of pupils from ethnic minority groups at school in comparison with those of pupils from the ethnic majority. Quantitative research has sought generally applicable conclusions on pupil and school characteristics in relation to academic success in the basic skills. By far the most attention has been paid to social-economic characteristics of pupils as an explanation for poor performance at school."

658 E.g. Inspectie van het onderwijs (2010); Torbeyns et. al. (2002).

659 E.g. Hartog & Oosterbeek (1988); Biesta (2012); Schuman (2007).

660 E.g. Koster et. al. (2010); van der Veen et al. (2010).

661 E.g. Traag & Van der Velden (2011); Kalmijn & Kraaykamp (2003).

662 E.g. Fekkes et. al. (2006).

663 When searching google scholar for academic publications on education in the Netherlands, I did not find one qualitative study. An exception to this rule are the studies performed by the National Education Inspectorate. See also Leeman & Volman who characterize existing research as having the structure "pupil characteristics x educational characteristics = educational outcomes" (370). I think this is true for all research on children out of school in the Netherlands and perhaps even in general for research on education in the Netherlands.

schoolyear without permission by the SAO or school director. As shown under §5.2.2, this includes only an estimated 18% of all children who are out of school more than four weeks per schoolyear. I will discuss a few exemplary studies.

One of the earlier studies on *thuiszitters* was the 2006 report by van Batenburg et al., who indicate different types of children out of school due to different reasons, yet they continue to focus solely on the unpermitted absentees. At the time, the registration systems of different municipalities were still quite diverse so that the problem could not be analyzed as precisely as in later research.

In 2010, Ingrado, the Dutch national organization of school attendance officers, did one of the first national studies on *thuiszitters*, financed by the Ministry of Education.[664] They studied the files of 110 *thuiszitters* in 24 municipalities.[665] Based on this study, they concluded that there were in total around 2,500 *thuiszitters* in the Netherlands, that the situations were very diverse and each case usually displayed a combination of multiple problems (such as psychological problems, behavioural problems, and/or problems in the household).[666]

In 2011, a research team of the National Ombudsman looked into the issue and wrote a report based on complaints that the office received over the years.[667] Their research therefore is a study mostly of the group "children who are out of school because of a decision by the school" (see first scheme under §5.2.1), since it is the parents who call the Ombudsman to complain that their child is not receiving any education. They conclude that, in many of these cases, a child displays signs of behavioural and/or psychological problems. Different actors within the school usually go to great lengths to try to find a solution for the child. However, if this fails, the child stays at home while an official "indication" (by a doctor) is obtained, which is necessary for extra financial support. Regular schools then often refer the child to special education, to which the parents do not always agree. At the end of the day, although many professionals are involved during many phases of this procedure, no one seems to take the final responsibility to find a solution for the child.[668] These situations often include conflict between professionals and parents, whereby professionals argue that parents do not have a realistic image of their child and unrealistic expectations of schools, while parents argue that they know what is best for their child.[669] Lastly, the researchers notice that, in these situations, the adults involved tend to forget about the child.[670] They recommend to put the municipal SAO as the "spider in the middle of the web" and to put the interest of the child first.[671]

---

664 Van Eekelen (2010).
665 Ibid: 7.
666 Ibid: 8.
667 Verhoef et al. (2011: 33).
668 Ibid: 15-18.
669 Ibid: 18.
670 Ibid: 23.
671 Ibid: 28.

In 2013, the children's ombudsman did a study also based on the complaints they received in their office. In their research, they take *thuiszitters* to mean "the child who is out of school due to her/his specific educational needs, while s/he would like to receive education" (thereby excluding children who do not want to go receive education).[672] In the study, they spoke to many children and clearly represented their voices throughout the report. However, rather than a more academic research, the report is focused on giving political recommendations, of which the most important are to change the mindset of school boards and teachers from compulsory education to a right to learn, to appoint a "learning right director" (*leerrechtregisseur)*, much like the "spider" mentioned above[673], and to make legislation more flexible to allow for combinations of options such as part-time home-schooling and part-time school education.[674]

Another exception to the limited interpretation of "children out of school" (*thuiszitters*) is the national mental health organization GGZ whose local office "Rivierduinen" (they are the main mental health care provider for the North and Middle of the province Zuid-Holland) did a study among their (almost 3,000) clients between ages 5–19, because they signalled that many of these children were not receiving any education.[675] This research took the child's perspective and therefore studied *thuiszitters*, irrespective of whether the children were out of school with or without official permission. Among their clients, they found that being out of school was the result of a process that started with some hours of absence and ended with not attending school anymore at all. The reasons for the absence included personal issues, bad experiences with other students, the wrong choice of school, and practical issues (for example not being able to combine therapy with school).[676] 23% of their clients, 690 children, were out of school, at least 45% of them without legal permission (and 33% unknown). Almost all children did not have any contact with a SAO.[677] In terms of daily activities, most children (42%) indicated that they "do nothing", followed by gaming/online surfing (31%).[678] 12% received home-schooling.[679] Support from school, such as efforts to still involve the child in school and/or to provide education, were very limited.[680]

One last subgroup considered under the heading of children out of school, is (research on) children with mental and/or physical disabilities. Research

672 Stam & van der Laan (2013: 31).

673 Ibid: 37.

674 Ibid: 8-10.

675 Sleeboom et al. (2009).

676 Ibid: 20. However reasons of "parental decision" or "school decision" were not part of the questionnaire (ibid: 40).

677 Ibid: 36-37.

678 Ibid: 42.

679 Ibid: 42. If this is indicative of the percentage of children out of school that receive homeschooling, this would mean that 12% of all children out of school, or 6,740 children, receive homeschooling in the Netherlands.

680 Ibid: 46.

in this field is related to the policy of "Education for All" on the international level, the policy of "appropriate education" (*passend onderwijs)* on the national level, and the question if children with disabilities have the right to be included in regular education rather than special needs education. Again, although "education for all" implies for all children, this discourse and research themes are specifically focused on a subgroup of children out of school, namely children with disabilities (although in international research "inclusive education" seems to be increasingly approached in a broader sense, defined for example as 'that schooling is organized in such a way that all pupils can, as far as possible, be educated together, even though they are different', referring to the 'education of *all* children, not just those with disabilities').[681]

Research in this area shows that, under international law, inclusion in regular education indeed seems to be a right enshrined in several conventions as well as jurisprudence.[682] In 1994 during the world conference on *special needs education: access and equality*, the Netherlands signed the "Salamanca Statement and Framework for Action on Special Needs Education" (Salamanca Statement), whereby states recognize "the necessity and urgency of providing education for children, youth and adults with special educational needs within the regular education system" (art. 1). The right to inclusive education has to be balanced against the best interest of the child (CRC art. 3), whereby a recurring question is whether including the disabled child in regular education is in the best interest of that child.[683]

Research in the Netherlands shows that, while parents are generally positive towards the idea of including disabled children in regular education[684], teachers in regular education are reluctant to include children with disabilities. The latter feel that they lack the necessary skills and knowledge to do so.[685] This is relevant in relation to children out of school, because one of the reasons why children are out of school is when there is a difference in opinion between parents and the school about what type of education would be the best for the child, as a result of which children end up at home (see §5.2.5).

In sum, while there is disagreement among researchers on whom to include in the category of "children out of school" (*thuiszitters*), outcomes are not very

681 Leeman & Volman (2001: 368); Thomas (2013: 473).

682 See: Waddington & Toepke (2015); Schoonheim & Nieuwboer (2015).

683 In this context, Ruijs et al. (2010) found that in the Netherlands among primary school students, having or not having children with special needs in their classroom did not have an effect on the academic prestige of students without special needs. Koster et al. (2010) also found that young students with special needs in Dutch primary schools have a satisfactory degree of social participation, although they do have a significantly lower number of friends, and fewer interactions with classmates. Opertti et al. point out that "Most often, the [Education for All] agenda focuses on the expansion of access to primary education, rather than guaranteeing equitable and quality processes and learning outcomes" (2009: 206).

684 De Boer et al. (2010b).

685 Pijl (2010); de Boer et al. (2010a).

different. While quantitative data is more diverse because it is more dependent upon categorization, on the more qualitative side, researchers agree that children are generally out of school due to (a combination of) several issues (physical disability, behavioural problems, family circumstances, etc). They also agree that there is currently no working solution for these children since actors with authority (SAO, state, parents) cannot agree on what is best for the child, and no one has the final say. In these processes, the child is marginalized and excluded.

Home-schooling

As shown under §5.2.1, home-schooling in the Netherlands happens either because parents prefer home-schooling to school education or because children are out of school and this is an option for them to still receive education (see scheme §5.2.1). Available research only discusses home-schooling insofar as this is a choice of the parents (1a) and, even more specifically, empirical research is limited to the group of parents who received an exemption from the obligation to send their children to school based on CEA art. 5(b) (officially based on parents' religious/philosophical beliefs).

The only study on what empirically happens in these families, are two studies that have been performed in relation to the "5b group", referring to the group of parents who have obtained a legal exemption from the obligation to send their children to school, due to their religious/philosophical objections to publics schools in their neighbourhood (in accordance with CEA 5(b)). The two studies were commissioned by the Dutch Ministry of Education, with the assignment to study how home-schooling is organized in the Netherlands, as regards:

1) the quality of education
2) in what sense there are children exempted from the duty to learn who do not receive any education
3) whether the parents would be willing to submit their home-schooling to quality control[686]
4) what education or professional trajectory young people follow after home-schooling[687]

The researchers answered these questions through (voluntary) phone interviews with parents who have obtained this 5b legal exemption. Based on these interviews, they show that all parents to whom they spoke (36% of all 5b parents) provide some form of education for their children. Most parents (80%) would not

686 As cited in Blok & Karsten (2008: 2).
687 As cited in Blok et al. (2010: 1).

mind some kind of quality supervision in the form of advice, yet 100% objected to an inspectorate that could impose sanctions.[688]

Another finding was that home-schooling parents, compared to parents of children attending regular school, have a significantly higher level of education – similar to findings among US home schoolers.[689] As concerns social development, all parents, with one exception, were positive about the social development of their children, saying that the children meet many people of all ages, for example in church and during sports and other classes (music lessons etc).[690] They do indicate, however, that they are concerned about prejudices they encounter from other people (the neighbourhood, family, government institutions), due to which they feel somewhat isolated or threatened.[691]

Regarding the trajectory after home-schooling, only 9 respondents provided information and, in most of these cases, children went to regular schools either because the child her/himself wanted to mostly to be in contact with peers (5 cases) or because the parents felt the child should have more contact with peers (3 cases).[692] However, since a significant number of parents did not participate in the study (65% of the target group)[693], and since participation was on a voluntary basis, it is not possible to answer the question whether the children whose parents have this legal exemption do indeed receive any education at all.

From a legal perspective, the most voluminous study on home-schooling in the Netherlands is the doctoral study of Sperling on the legal aspects of home-schooling in the Netherlands. Although, on the one hand, Sperling shows how on the European level (both ECtHR and European Commission of Human Rights), the ECtHR ruled that the child's right to education trumps the parents' right to respect for their religious and philosophical convictions[694], she argues that the Dutch ban on home-schooling is a violation of art. 23 of the Dutch constitution, which states that "all persons shall be free to provide education" (art. 23(2)). According to Sperling, the intention behind the article was, historically, to realize the right of parents to choose the form of education that fit their wishes for the upbringing for their children, provided the quality of this education is checked by the state, and so home-schooling should be legal.[695] Since home-schooling is not legal in the Netherlands, Sperling writes that:

---

688 Blok & Karsten (2008: III-V).

689 Ibid: 7, 25. It has to be noted that, also in international research, there is a severe lack of studies on homeschooling which involves children themselves. As Clery writes: "It is clear there is a lack of studies which have as a major focus examined the interpretation and understanding children have of their home learning experience". In her research, she speaks to only two homeschooled children (1998: 3).

690 Blok & Karsten (2008: 48, 50).

691 Ibid: 63.

692 Blok et al. (2010: 14).

693 Ibid: 29-31.

694 Sperling (2010: 142-51).

695 Ibid: 283-86.

> Since the abolition of home education as a legally recognized form of education did not end the demand for home education, parents who wanted to home educate their children had to find another legal basis. The only other basis available is a provision in the compulsory education law exempting parents from the obligation to enrol and send their children to school if the parents object to the religious orientation or beliefs of all schools within a reasonable distance from their home. Parents who qualify for this exemption have no obligation under the compulsory education law to provide their children with any education, but in practice almost all of them home educate.[696]

Liefaard et al., in an analysis of this legal situation in the Netherlands, argue that little attention has been paid by the legislator to the child's right to (quality) education.[697] They point out that, according to the CRC, not only does the child have a right to quality education (art. 28 and 29), but also a right to participate in decisions relating to education (art. 12) and a right to the protection of their own religious beliefs. In this sense, the Dutch "exemption" rule contradicts international children's rights.[698] They conclude that, if these rights are taken into consideration, home-schooling could be in line with the CRC.[699]

From a philosophical perspective, Merry & Karsten examine the case of home-schooling in the Netherlands. They argue that "by effectively removing one's children from school, parents express their educational preferences in ways that appear to directly challenge the paternalistic role that states typically assume".[700] In the Netherlands, home-schooling is "certainly marginalized"[701], and

> much strong resistance arises from the belief that compulsory attendance laws safeguard children's interests by ensuring an adequate level of education necessary for functioning in society and contributing to its economic stability.[702]

The article continues without further discussion of the empirical reality of home-schooling in the Netherlands. Instead it analyzes the position of home-schooling in liberal democratic societies, questioning whether to allow home-schooling would lead to more or less liberty (although the liberty of choice of children themselves is not part of the consideration). They argue strongly in favour of the legalization of home-schooling, because "parents are best placed to know what is best for their own children" and therefore they should be free to choose their

696 Ibid: 307.
697 Liefaard et al. (2016: 380).
698 Ibid: 383.
699 Ibid: 386.
700 Merry & Karsten (2010: 498).
701 Ibid: 499.
702 Ibid: 505.

education, including home-schooling. The only exception is that the state should interfere if there is clear evidence that a child's wellbeing being contravened.[703]

Verplaetse, lastly, provides an ethical evaluation of home-schooling in Belgian Flanders and the Netherlands, which is interesting because home-schooling is legal in Belgium. He argues that, ethically speaking, home-schooling can be allowed, provided that state control makes sure that it provides the children with an "open future", meaning that children learn in such a way that leaves many of their future options open. The guiding principle is that children may develop to be very different from their parents. Therefore, education should prepare a child for a large range of options, for example, with respect to job opportunities and lifestyles. Home-schooling that promotes only the religion of the parents, for example, harms this principle and should be state sanctioned.[704] State inspection is necessary.[705]

In sum, most authors seem to agree that current Dutch legislation provides insufficient protection either for parents who want to home-school and/or for children whose right to education is not guaranteed. Authors seem to agree that home-schooling could be legal and in conformity with children's (international) rights, provided some changes are made, such as an inspection of the quality of home-schooling. Empirical research, however, has shown that Dutch home-schooling parents are not open to the option of state inspection of the quality of the education they provide, beyond giving advice.[706] In light of the current research, it is important to note that:

- empirical information about home-schooling in the Netherlands is limited
- no research takes the child's perspective into consideration nor includes children
- most of the research, and certainly the empirical research, focuses solely on the group of children whose parents are exempted from sending them to school because of their religious or philosophical convictions (CEA art. 5(b)). It therefore excludes other children in the Netherlands who are home-schooled.

Roma children

Although the issue of Roma children being out of school is often mentioned in the research on Roma in the Netherlands, it is not mentioned in studies on children out of school. It is rather in studies on Roma in the Netherlands that Roma children not going to school is indicated as one of the many issues that

[703] Ibid: 510-11.
[704] Verplaetse (2012: 87-89).
[705] Ibid: 89-90.
[706] Blok & Karsten (2008: III-V).

state and municipality authorities encounter when interacting with Roma families. I will give a brief overview of the available research and the specific findings as regards education for Roma children.

Terlouw (2014) discusses the right to education for Roma children on the European level. Based on a literature study, she indicates how Roma children are structurally discriminated against in their access to education. More than half of Roma in Europe have never been to school and more than 50% of Roma are illiterate. Whenever children do participate in education, they are often separated from other students, put in special classes and sent to special education schools, for children with special needs.[707] She continues to discuss jurisprudence on the European level as regards Roma children and education, which puts a positive obligation on states to stop both direct and indirect discrimination through segregation in education.[708]

In addition to limited academic research, Dutch municipalities and the Dutch state have commissioned several research projects and implemented different policies for the integration of the Roma. The type of research, that will be discussed below, is meant to help civil servants on the municipality level, and the SAO in particular, to deal with the issue of Roma children who are out of school. Therefore, this research is mostly practical and of limited academic value, as methodology is often lacking and there is limited reference to sources.

Van der Ree et al. indicate that part of the issue is the distrust between parents and school management. Many parents have negative experiences with Dutch school education in the past, including experiences of exclusion and discrimination.[709] Roma children on the other hand behave "differently" due to their different cultural background, whereby their behaviour is often perceived by teachers as problematic.[710] Roma children usually start attending school at age 5 (compared to most children in the Netherlands who start at age 4), at which time they are "behind" in their mastery of the Dutch language compared to other children, they have lower development of fine motor skills and a lower ability to concentrate.[711] In secondary education, gypsy[712] children are characterized by low self-esteem, extreme fear of failure, high sensitivity in relation to their background, and they have difficulty to work independently.[713] There is a high level of absenteeism and some abandon school altogether around the age of 13–14. Van der Ree et al. interpret the absence of these children as a sign that they are not happy in school and/or that Dutch school education

707 Terlouw (2014: 4-5), see also Rodrigues & Matelski (2004: 28).
708 Terlouw (2014: 4-5).
709 Van der Ree et al. (2001: 7-8), see also Rodrigues & Matelski (2004: 27-28).
710 Van der Ree et al. (2001: 8).
711 Ibid: 9. However, the source(s) of this information is unknown.
712 The authors refer to "gypsy" as a general category and understand Roma as a subcategory of gypsy people.
713 Ibid: 10.

does not match the possibilities and needs of these parents and children.[714] Furthermore, they indicate three practical reasons for absenteeism: 1) parents have to travel for work for longer periods and take the children with them; 2) Roma families lack an education tradition; parents are uneducated and there is a culture of distrust towards institutions and rules; 3) forced by the fact that no "appropriate" school can be found for these children.[715]

Sollie et al. argue that Roma are excluded, yet also exclude themselves from the larger society around them. Roma make a distinction between Roma and *gadje*: the society around them, which they are not a part of.[716] There is an attitude of "us versus them" and a distrust of (state) institutions. This leads Roma to exclude their children from (state) school education.[717] Internally, Roma live their lives according to their moral code called *Marime*, which is passed on orally through generations. The highest authority and judge of the Roma is the *kris romani,* while practical leadership of the community is at the hands of the *rom baro*.[718] The authors estimate that there are around 30,000–35,000 Roma living in the Netherlands.[719] Due to their low level of education and discrimination, there are few employment opportunities for Roma. Many live in poverty and some resort to criminal behavior, which leads to a further negative stigma in the eyes of the larger society, which in its turn has consequences for school attendance of Roma children.[720]

A report by the project "Monitor Racism and the Extreme Right", about the discrimination of Roma and Sinti in the Netherlands, estimates that there are around 6,000 Roma in the Netherlands.[721] Under the heading of "education", the research findings are similar to those mentioned before. Additional information is that some Roma parents keep children at home sometimes to help with household chores.[722] The researchers also found that "Roma […] children are regularly refused admittance to schools they want to attend", and that "the mistrust of Roma […] is so great in some areas of the Netherlands that schools ask for prior assurance that a child will not cause any problems […] it becomes more and more difficult for Roma […] to find a school where their children are welcome".[723]

Lastly, the KPC group has published a report of primary education for "caravan inhabitants, Roma and Sinti", which includes a quantitative survey of

714 Ibid: 11-12.
715 Ibid: 14.
716 Sollie et al. (2013: 28-29, 35). Bhopal & Myers in this context speak about "an uncrossable borderline between Gypsy culture and non-Gypsy culture" (2008: 1, 35).
717 Sollie et al. (2013: 35), see also Rodrigues & Matelski (2004: 28).
718 Sollie et al. (2013: 40-43, 47-48).
719 Ibid: 31.
720 Ibid: 49-51.
721 Rodrigues & Matelski (2004: 8).
722 Ibid: 27.
723 Ibid: 43.

17 schools (including a survey among their students in the target group (n=282, n Roma=50)), and one qualitative discussion with professionals in schools and one SAO. It shows that parents of Roma children have a low level of education, with 46% having attended no or only primary school and only 6% having enjoyed education after secondary school (no parent went to higher professional education (*HBO*) or university).[724] Contrary to the assumption in other research, the report shows that 96% of Roma children started primary education at age 4 and only 4% started at age 5.[725] 52% of Roma children indicate that they have many learning difficulties (*leerproblemen*) and 18% have many behavioural problems.[726] While 71% indicated to be absent not more than 2 days per months, 28% were indicated to be absent more than 3 days per month, of whom 4% more than 10 days per month.[727] Most schools do not report this to the SAO/municipality.[728] Roma children were relatively well motivated for school[729], whereby the children were usually (much) more motivated for school education than their parents.[730] In some areas, school performance of gypsy children seems to be lower than average, while in some areas children seem to score similar to the national average, in particular in higher grades.[731] Of 35 students who were given a binding recommendation by the primary school concerning the level of secondary education they could attend, the recommendations significantly placed Roma children in much lower levels of secondary education than the average child living in the Netherlands:

Advice (from low to high level)	gypsy children[732]	national average[733]
PRO (for children with low IQ)	23%	0.8%
VMBO b/k/g	46%	23.4%
VMBO-t	17%	27.8%[734]
HAVO	11%	28.2%[735]
VWO	–	19.7%

724 Timmermans (2016: 15). It has to be noted, however, that 26% of children filled in "other" when asked about their parents' highest level of education.

725 Ibid: 16.

726 Ibid: 18-19.

727 Ibid: 20.

728 Ibid: 41.

729 0% had no motivation, 20% had limited motivation, 51% had average motivation, and 20% were highly motivated. Ibid: 24.

730 Ibid: 27.

731 Ibid: The test "language for toddlers" shows similar results for Roma and non-Roma (ibid: 29-30), a test on technical reading shows that gypsy chidren score lower in lower classes while higher in higher grades (Ibid: 30-31), on the tests of "reading and understanding" and vocabulary gypsy children score significantly below average (ibid: 32-34).

732 Ibid: 36. Again, the authors use the term "gypsy" as the broader category incorporating Roma, Sinti and caravan inhabitants.

733 Rijksoverheid (no date (c)).

734 Of which 5.3% was advised "VMBO-t+HAVO".

735 Of which 6.1% was advised "HAVO+VWO".

Academic research on Roma in the Netherlands indicates that parents often have to be motivated or forced by authorities to enroll their children in school, that children are often absent and they do not leave school education with a qualifying degree (*startkwalificatie*).[736] Another study groups the presence of Roma in Dutch schools together with the discussion about immigrants in the Netherlands and argues that coercive methods used by Dutch authorities to secure integration/assimilation are based on institutional discrimination, based on a denied history of racism, which is counterproductive to the quality of education received by immigrant children, including Roma.[737] Lastly, in a cultural anthropological analysis of Roma in the Netherlands, Jorna argues that Dutch authorities should try to understand the Roma culture from the inside out instead of from an external perspective.[738]

In general, as regards the Roma child's right to education, it can be noted that there is a significant overlap in the available research, both in terms of methodology (qualitative interviews with a few (around 20) respondents combined with a literature study) and outcomes. It is striking that there is very little research on Roma in the Netherlands that involves the Roma themselves. Instead, professionals are taken as sole, or near sole, respondents.[739] Bhopal & Myers argue, in relation to Gypsy culture in the UK, that:

> the representations that are made of [Gypsies] tend to reflect an imaginary sense of the Gypsy which is configured, in general, from a non-Gypsy perspective. In many ways this is a hugely confused perspective.[740]

There are three studies in the Netherlands that did include Roma themselves as respondents and discussed education, to my best knowledge. One is the "monitor inclusion", which unfortunately is not accessible online (anymore).[741] Second is the follow-up research, which included 13 qualitative interviews with 20 Roma/Sinti participants. The authors indicate that, within the Roma/Sinti community, increasing importance is attached to education and going to school becomes more and more normalized, which creates a ripple-effect for other Roma children in terms of increased school attendance.[742] This includes enrollment in preschool and primary school, yet it is limited on the level of professional and higher education.[743] In addition, respondents indicate that Roma children are discriminated against in primary education. For example

736 Wijkhuijs & Sollie (2014: 81).
737 Vasta (2007: 713-15, 728, 732-36).
738 Jorna (2014).
739 Wijkhuijs & Sollie (2014: 75); Rodrigues & Matelski (2004: annex I); van der Veen et al. (2011: 15-16); Jorna (2014: 78).
740 Bhopal & Myers (2008: 1).
741 See: Kennisplatform Integratie & Samenleving (n.d.) https://www.kis.nl/publicatie/monitor-inclusie-nulmeting.
742 Seidler et al. (2015: 45).
743 Ibid: 45-48.

they receive recommendations for lower levels of follow-up education than their test scores warrant and there is prejudice and stigma among education professionals.[744] Lastly, they indicate that boys and girls attend school equally, thereby contradicting the view of professionals who argue that school attendance in secondary education is less among Roma girls than Roma boys.[745]

Third is the 2011 study by the Trimbos Institute which analysed the school attendance of Roma girls in secondary education and interviewed girls together with one parent, in a total 27 interviews, 12 of which were with girls who were often or always absent from school.[746] Among the girls who did not attend school, the three who had quit school were married and had children or were pregnant. Other girls did not attend school because the school closed, because their families were evicted from their homes due to debts/statelessness, or because of conflicts with students/teachers.[747] The children often started their school careers being "behind" in their Dutch language level, since they only spoke Romanes at home and in their community.[748] Among the girls who were absent, motivation to study seemed low because their future perspective was to become a married housewife and mother, a view shared by their mothers.[749] To avoid enforcement by authorities, mothers called the school to report that their children were sick.[750] The girls who attended school had ambitions to work and earn money at least until they would marry and were supported by their mothers.[751] The parents of girls who attended school were more open to interaction with non-Roma society.[752] Most of the absent girls did not enjoy school, while most of the school-attending girls did.[753] None of the girls experienced structural attention for cultural diversity in the school curriculum, yet many received occasional questions from teachers about Roma culture.[754]

5.2.4. UN HUMAN RIGHTS BODIES REPORTING ON THE CHILD'S RIGHT TO EDUCATION IN THE NETHERLANDS

Because the Netherlands, both as a state as well as represented by Dutch NGOs and CSOs, is very involved in the UN human rights reporting cycles and these

744 Ibid: 49.
745 Ibid: 51-52.
746 Van der Veen et al. (2011: 45).
747 Ibid: 45-46.
748 Ibid: 47-48.
749 Ibid: 48-49, 52.
750 Ibid: 52, 60-61.
751 Ibid: 49, 53.
752 Ibid: 54.
753 Ibid: 56.
754 Ibid: 60.

processes seem to be taken quite seriously, it is relevant to present the discussion on the child's right to education in the Netherlands as it appears in these evaluative cycles.

In general, according to the reporting to the UN human rights bodies, almost all children in the Netherlands in the age of compulsory education attend school education.[755] Concerns are raised about children out of school, specifically if this occurs based on discriminatory grounds (referring to discrimination of children with disabilities). As may be expected, these concerns are mostly based on available research (as discussed under §5.2.3) and are therefore based on a limited understanding of the situation of children out of school in the Netherlands, due to the limited definition of *thuiszitters*.

Children out of school

In the last reporting cycles to the UN various Human Rights Bodies, "children out of school" were discussed mostly in relation to the exclusion of disabled children from school education. Several NGOs, CSOs and UN rights committees have expressed concerns about the discrimination of children with disabilities by schools.[756] The organizations are concerned about "children who are not accepted at schools or sent away because of their disability or chronic illness" and "children with a disability who do not receive reasonable accommodation, such as adapted exams or study materials".[757] Because of this, according to the Netherlands Institute for Human Rights, "many children with disabilities are at home instead of in school".[758] The Dutch Ombudsman for Children argues that this is the (only) group out of school children.[759]

The Dutch government replied that, particularly to tackle this problem, in 2014 they introduced the "Appropriate Education Act" ("*Wet Passend Onderwijs*"). Under this act, "all schools are [legally] obliged to provide for pupils with specific educational needs who apply for admission".[760] NGOs are critical of this act in the sense that it does not "provide a right to be included in mainstream settings, nor does it provide a right to adequate support in order to receive a qualitatively good education" for children with disabilities.[761]

755 In 2015, 99% of 14-year olds attended fulltime education, and 98% of 16-year olds (Ministry of Education, Culture and Science (no date)). See also United Nations (1996: paras. 350-355) *Core document forming part of the reports of States Parties: Netherlands (European part of the Kingdom).*

756 The Netherlands Institute for Human Rights (2015a); Kruseman et al. (2016: 44-45).

757 The Netherlands Institute for Human Rights (2015a: 5).

758 Ibid.

759 Dutch Ombudsman for Children (2014: para. 8(I)).

760 Committee on the Rights of the Child (2014a: para. 276); Committee on the Rights of the Child (2015b: para. 33); Committee on Economic, Social and Cultural Rights (CESCR) (2016a: para. 32).

761 Kruseman et al. (2016: 44).

They argue that, in spite of the Appropriate Education Act, 15,000 children[762] are not receiving any education at all, because "there is no adequate option for them in the educational system, or [they] are considered 'uneducable' and are officially exempted from school attendance in favour of enrolment in day care settings".[763]

In their list of issues, both the Children's Rights Committee and the CESCR ask the Netherlands to provide data on children out of school[764], to which in reply the Netherlands sent no, or incomplete and outdated data.[765]

Finally, in their concluding observations, the Children's Rights Committee was concerned with the lack of data on children out of school and with the fact that it is unclear under the Appropriate Education Act where the child would go whose educational needs the school cannot meet.[766] They recommend to "adopt a human-rights based approach to disability" which is inclusive for children with disabilities, learning and behavioural difficulties, and to "take measures to address the root causes of school dropouts by adopting targeted policies to support and reinstate such children in the education system".[767]

Home-schooling

Home-schooling is left almost completely out of the discussion of the child's right to education in the Netherlands. The only recent occurrence is during the last CRC consideration of the report of the Netherlands when Mr. Gurn of the Country Task Force remarked that "given the increase in home schooling in the Netherlands, [I wonder] how the State was able to guarantee the quality of such education".[768] In reply, Ms. Berg of the Dutch delegation argued that:

> the government had a policy on homeschooling but did not promote the practice. The main reason for homeschooling in the Netherlands was religious conviction. Children that were homeschooled sat the same standard tests as all other children.[769]

---

762 Referring to the limited understanding of *thuiszitters* combined with those exempted from the legal obligation to attend school (see §5.2.2).

763 Kruseman et al. (2016: 45). It has to be noted that here they count children with unpermitted absenteeism and children whose parents were exempted from the obligation to send children to school.

764 Committee on the Rights of the Child (2014b: part III, paras. 4-5); Committee on Economic, Social and Cultural Rights (CESCR) (2016b: para. 29).

765 Kingdom of the Netherlands (2015: annex 1); Committee on Economic, Social and Cultural Rights (CESCR) (2017a: para. 79).

766 Committee on the Rights of the Child (2015c: para. 40).

767 Ibid: paras. 41, 51.

768 Committee on the Rights of the Child (2015a: para. 49).

769 Committee on the Rights of the Child (2015b: para. 6). This information seems to be false and there is no indication as to where Ms. Berg got this information.

In their concluding observations, the Children's Rights Committee expresses its concern over the "lack of monitoring of the quality of home-schooling" and recommends to "monitor the quality of home-schooling and ensure that such children do not lag behind on their peers in regular schools".[770]

Roma children

Although on a national level school attendance of Roma children is recognized as an issue, and the lack of schooling for Roma children and girls in particular is considered a violation of the child's right to education[771], the issue is not mentioned in most of the reporting to UN human rights bodies, either by the state, the NGOs/CSOs nor by the respective committees.

Only in relation to the Convention on the Elimination of all Forms of Racial Discrimination do NGOs and CSOs discuss the position of the Roma community[772], indicating that, in the Netherlands, Roma are not recognized as ethnic minorities and, as a consequence, their emancipation is pursued through general policies.[773] NGOs & CSOs argue that "considering [the Roma's] vulnerable position, greater efforts are required to create equal opportunities"[774], that Roma have been systematically excluded from employment opportunities[775], and that there is high occurrence of truancy and school drop-outs.[776]

The CERD asks for "information on the situation of Roma [...] particularly in relation to [...] education".[777] During the consideration of reports, country rapporteur Mr. Diaconu reiterated this question.[778] The Dutch government indicated that, since 2011 they had launched a program to tackle and prevent the exploitation of Roma children, which included a national Roma strategy, and in 2013 they noted "an improvement in primary school attendance but a persistently high dropout rate from secondary schools". They also argued that "Roma [...] themselves [bear] responsibility for safeguarding their cultures and languages".[779] In their concluding observations, the Committee recommends that the State party:

> take specific measures in favour of Roma, Sinti and Travellers, including by creating better opportunities in the labour market, combating discrimination in education

[770] Committee on the Rights of the Child (2015c: paras. 50-51).
[771] See §5.2.3.
[772] The focus is on Roma, Sinti and Traveller communities. This chapter will only focus on Roma.
[773] De Kroon et al. (2015: 18); the Netherlands Institute for Human Rights (2015b: 14).
[774] De Kroon et al. (2015: 18-19).
[775] De Kroon et al. (2015: 32); the Netherlands Institute for Human Rights (2015b: 14).
[776] The Netherlands Institute for Human Rights (2015b: 14, 20).
[777] Committee on the Elimination of All Forms of Racial Discrimination (CERD) (2015a: art. 2(e)).
[778] Committee on the Elimination of All Forms of Racial Discrimination (CERD) (2015b: art. 15).
[779] Committee on the Elimination of All Forms of Racial Discrimination (CERD) (2015c: art. 31-34).

and housing and tackling the problems faced by Roma regarding registration status and statelessness.[780]

The state reported that, in general, everyone in the Netherlands is protected by law from discrimination. "The government strongly rejects every form of discrimination [...] Discrimination is at odds with the notion of citizenship: it creates obstacles to people's involvement in society and impedes them from taking part in, and investing in, their community".[781] Under the Universal Periodic Review, general recommendations were made such as for the Netherlands to "intensify its efforts to eliminate discrimination against migrants and other minority women, who still face multiple forms of discrimination with respect to education, health, employment and social and political participation".[782]

5.2.5. FIELD RESEARCH FINDINGS: THE CHILD'S RIGHT TO EDUCATION IN THE NETHERLANDS

On the subject of the child's right to education in the Netherlands, it is clear that to go to school is the norm, and most children who are aged 5–18 and who do not have a qualifying diploma are in school. The estimated 2% of children who are out of school are either excluded by external actors (parent(s), school, state) and not allowed to go to school or they exclude themselves by refusing to go to school.

What all children out of school in the Netherlands seem to have in common is that they all fall outside of what is "normal". In research conversations with both children and adults the distinction between "normal" and "crazy" was made time and time again.[783] For children, attending regular education is normal. When you do not go to school, and to a lesser degree when you attend special education, you are *different* or even *crazy* in your own eyes and those of your peers/society.

On the adult level, the same discussion takes place. Parents whose children are out of school encounter social stigma. If your child is not in school, you are not normal. You might even be failing as a parent in the eyes of society.

780 Committee on the Elimination of All Forms of Racial Discrimination (CERD) (2015d: art. 19-20).

781 Committee on the Elimination of All Forms of Racial Discrimination (CERD) (2013: art. 15).

782 Human Rights Council (2012: art. 98.64, stated by Azerbaijan). See also recommendations by Nicaragua, Iran and Ukraine.

783 The case study did not include many situations of children who were physically very ill for longer periods (such as through, for example, cancer). Although they might also be "different", it is unlikely that they, or their parents, would be considered "crazy" in the public opinion.

On the other hand, many of these parents turn their backs – to different degrees – to what they call "society" or "the system".[784] In some cases their disapproval of the regular education system, which is part of "the system", is a reason to choose to keep their children at home. In some other cases, this attitude follows after a conflict with school or with authorities in general. The debate between the different parties involved about what is best for the child, at the core is often about: who here is crazy? Is it the mother who wants to educate her child at home, the father who wants to protect his daughter from the school norms that do not fit in his culture, or is it society who forces the child into a straitjacket through school education, where the child loses its individuality?[785]

Figure 4. I received this image from a mother who homeschool's her children. A similar vision on home-schooling vs. school education was often expressed by home-schooling parents.

Although the child is the subject of this discussion, it is seldom heard. In fact, what I found in this case study is that it is a very clear example of what happens when different legal orders are in conflict. Different people and institutions claim some kind of authority over the child, to decide on her/his behalf what is best for the child as regards her/his education. Although sometimes the child might indicate that s/he does not want to go to school, or the opposite, that s/he wants to go to school, children are usually not the ones who take the decisions.[786] When looking at the landscape of authorities over the child's education in the Netherlands, the following image emerges:

784 For similar findings in research on homeschooling see: Winstanley (2009: 358), Kapitulik, B.P. (2011). On Roma, see §5.2.3 last subsection.

785 See chapter 2 for a discussion about the division between "normal" and "crazy", as discussed by Foucault.

786 Since this case study focused on *thuiszitters*, homeschooling and Roma children, it did not include what are usually called "truants", mostly 16 or 17-year olds who decide they do not want to or have to go to school. These children would not self-identify as *thuiszitter*. In these cases, quite possibly children (and adults) do see children themselves as decisionmakers.

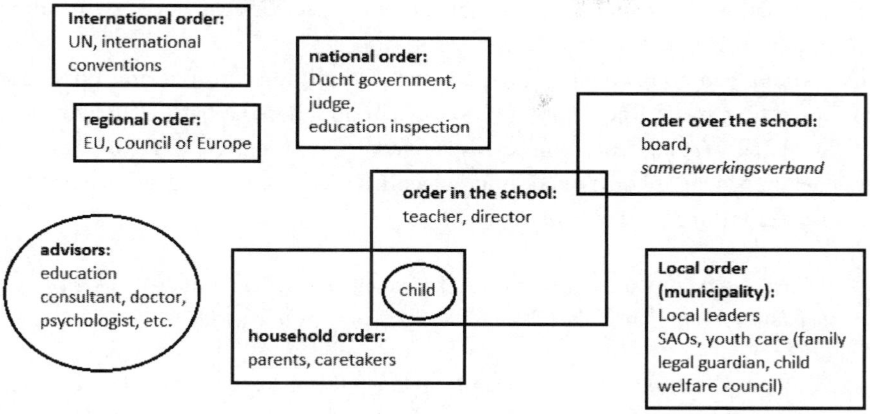

In situations where all these authorities agree with each other, normally the child's right to education is realized, with a little side note that, in this case, too, the child's right to participate in the decision about her/his education is not always respected. In the usual situation, this means that the parents enroll a child at age 4 in a primary school, the school accepts the enrollment and the child goes to school. When authorities agree that perhaps another form of education would be better for the child, this transition usually goes well.

However, the trouble starts when different authorities disagree. Conflicts arise between different authorities about what is best for the child, at the start usually between school and the parents. When the conflict grows, more and more parties get involved, and it becomes a conflict between many different authorities. The doctor says A, school says B, municipality says C, youth care says D, parents say E. These conflicts often occur among this group, and regardless of who is right or wrong, the child always loses.

Another striking finding of the field research was that all parents whose children were out of school who participated in the research (n=18) turned out to have certain features in common:

a) For all parents, the best interest of their child was the primary motivation for their actions. They would go to great lengths to give their children what they thought was the best education, in some cases preferring to spend some days in prison rather than send their child to a school which they believed would harm the child.
b) All parents themselves had negative to very negative (school) education experiences. This included both parents who kept their children out of school, as well as parents who tried to get their children into school. These experiences differed in degree (from a few years to a complete education period, from "a feeling of not fitting into the system" to serious forms of

physical and psychological abuse). Parents described their own education experience as awful, terrible, etc.

c) Parents had ambivalent feelings towards (certain) authorities and possessed a fighting spirit. They engaged in activism, fought legal battles, lived in fear of being arrested, in some cases moved to another country (for example Belgium, where home-schooling is legal). These battles were experienced as very emotional and exhausting.

Interview #28. A 43-year old mother (L.) of son A. 18 years old, who has a physical and psychological disability. She talks about his period in primary school.

A: In the classroom, A. would literally sit under the table, sometimes the whole day. I noticed he did not want to go to school anymore, because he literally started hitting me. And then I had to see how to get him to school. So difficult! And such a child becomes stronger…

Q: How was that?

A: Literally taking him under my arm. Put him on the back of the bike and meanwhile he's hitting your back, and he would swing sideways so you couldn't cycle anymore. Then I got him to school, then you'd stand on the school playground, and he would literally cling onto the drain pipe. And all children would go in and then I'd have to see how to get those hands loose and take him under my arm and put him down [in the classroom].

After A. has switched schools a few times, the mother decides to keep him home and homeschool. The SAO starts a legal case and the judge sentences L. to a suspended fine, on the grounds of child abuse. The education counselor cannot find an appropriate school, and L. continues to homeschool. A second court case follows with the possibility to remove A. from the home.

A: And that could not happen, because no one takes an adolescent with autism in their home. He will not go to a foster family, he will end up in youth detention. And he would not survive that…so that couldn't happen. So, the second court case, on judgment day he was in hiding […] we have always lived with suitcases packed in a safe space. I would have left everything behind. If they would have tried [to remove him from the home] and if I saw it coming in time, we continuously lived with that fear, we would have run. Eventually to another country, but it's very hard. There are very few countries that accept Dutch refugees. There was no good plan, I did not have any reserves, no financial means […] only those suitcases ready, something arranged for the stuff that would be left behind, leave by car, we'd quickly have to leave that behind, just like bank cards, bank accounts, we would have to leave it all behind and continue with a fake passport […] We have always lived that way, with the fear of having to run.

The meaning of the child's right to education

All children who participated in the research, indicated that the "right to education" in reality in the Netherlands means that you have to go to school.

Many thought that this was stupid, because a right should mean that you are allowed to get education. Children experience mandatory school attendance as something that is forced upon them, even those who like going to school. Often they have to do things which they do not understand why they have to be done that way, and sometimes they simply do it because the teacher says so.[787]

Figure 5. Anna (10): "Right to education is that you are allowed to go to school (but if you don't go you must then you MUST"

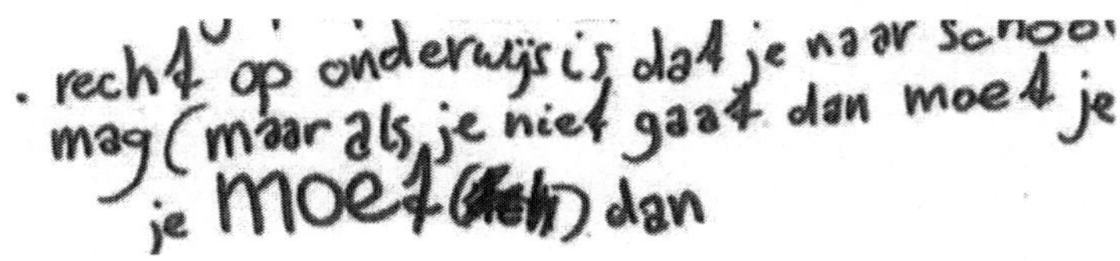

For children who do not function well in the regular school system, the obligation to attend all school classes can be dramatic, because it sometimes forces them to go to school even while they are completely stranded there cognitively, socially and/or emotionally.

All participants to the study argued that a right to education is important, that it is something that children have a right to, and that compulsory education is not the same as a right to education. They also acknowledge that a right has to be accompanied by a duty. Based on these conversations, according to the participants to the study, the best way to protect the right to education in the Netherlands seems to be:

- to end compulsory school attendance
- to install a right for children to education
- to install a duty to learn for children

Education in this scenario is a right that children should be able to claim. The state, schools and parents would have the duty to offer educational opportunities. Education does not necessarily need to take place in the school; the best educational environment for the education depends on what is best for the individual child.[788] Children of all school ages are increasingly capable of joining this discussion and voicing their opinions, as became clear during the research interviews. At the end of the day, it is about the education of the children and

---

787 A similar finding is presented by the Platform 2032 study. During the LAKS (student organization) student congresses, in 2015, ideas were collected from 294 from different schools. The report states that: "Students indicate that they want to know *why* they are learning what they are learning. They need a reflection on actuality, background and developments in the world" (Platform Onderwijs2032 (2016: 25)).

788 As was also concluded in the research by the Kinderombudsman. See Stam & Vreeburg-van der Laan (2013)).

they are the experts of their experiences.[789] All participants advocated for education adapted to the child, whereby "appropriate education" should refer not only to cognitive competence, but also to various forms of intelligence and the development of the child.[790]

The duty to study would lie with children, in exchange for a (right to) appropriate education. All children who participated in the research indicated that they like to learn. Almost all of them also indicated that it is annoying to be forced to do something of which you do not understand why you have to do it. A right to education should therefore also include that, for children, the aim of education should be clear.

Interview 30, an 11-year old girl who is in 7th class in a regular primary school. Together, we start counting and we find out that, per year, she takes about 72 tests.

Q: So, after every chapter you get a test. Why is that?
A: Well, for example […] you get three reports per year, and in one period you have three tests for geography and then, some get a 9, some a 6 and then they calculate the average mark and that is shown on your report.
Q: But what is it for?
A: I don't know either.
[…]
Q: So for all these tests, you don't really know what it's for, except that you get a mark on your report?
A: [starts laughing] Yes.
Q: Why do you find that funny?
A: Well, I am realizing only now that I don't know why I take a test! And even today I took one for geography! [continues laughing]

Is education necessary?

Although most participants argued that education is important for children, some did not. Some children and parents think that learning happens naturally and that the organization/institution of education is not necessary.

However, it is also clear that it is very difficult to function in the Dutch society without a certain level of education, as demonstrated, for example, by a Roma mother who was largely illiterate and now regretted not having received more education (Interview 55).

Interview 21, an 11-year old boy who is out of school. Over the years he has been in and out of school. He has trouble accepting authority and his parents are strongly opposed to forcing children to learn.

---

789 See also chapter 4 on research with children and taking their views seriously.

790 Gardner describes 8 forms of intelligence, a study that is very popular in the Netherlands (1983).

> I think it's a shame that education is mandatory. Because monkeys do not have education, and they just follow their instinct and all goes well [...] you do not necessarily need money [...] you can go fishing, find food or pluck apples. Or sow seeds.
> *This boy could not do any other multiplication than the table of 1.*

What kind of education do children have a right to?

In terms of what the education would look like that children should have a right to, many participants had ideas about how education could be improved.

Children who participated in this study argued that, in their education, there should be a balance between what they want to do and learn and what children need for when they grow up. Language and calculation are important to learn, but not always fun, so there has to be a balance and you have to add fun things, like playground time. Children also offered ideas on how to make the language/calculation lessons more fun, for example by combining a calculation class with a dance class ("if there's a sum, and the answer to the sum is 74, that's this [dance move 1], and something else, another number, 13 is for example this [dance move 2] and so it can become a dance").

Figure 6. A 10-year old girl:

"If I myself was allowed to decide about school then…
– starts at 11:00 until 16:30
– learning in a fun way (like dancing and movies)
– colourful building
– you can decide on your own courses (languages and calculation mandatory)"

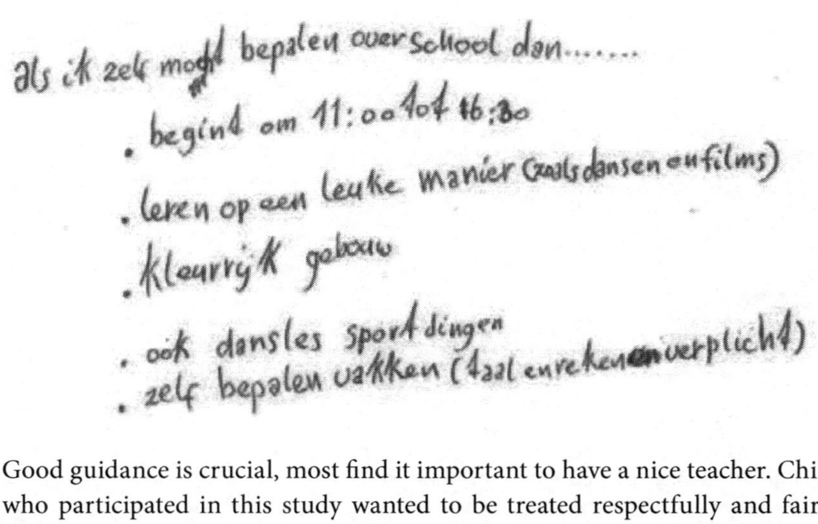

Good guidance is crucial, most find it important to have a nice teacher. Children who participated in this study wanted to be treated respectfully and fairly, to have someone to go to if they have a question, to be listened to, and to discuss conflicts. In terms of the content, they felt that they should be told the reason they have to learn a certain subject, and it should be more connected to the daily reality of children. In addition, they should be allowed to work at their own pace.

Lastly, what was most important about education according to children in this study was the social aspect. You can learn only when you feel safe and you only feel safe if you are comfortable in the group (class). It is not necessary to be friends with everyone, but you do want other children to be nice to you. This is the aspect of education that concerns students the most; who sits where in the classroom, who is nice, who is behaving badly, who is in love with whom, who is popular, etc. This aspect, meanwhile, is very underrepresented in Dutch education as part of the curriculum, as noticed by parents and professionals.[791]

Figure 7. Drawing by a 10-year old girl, who attends regular education.

"This is our school…all kinds of children with all kinds of colours […] When you are at school I feel very happy there because I have many friends around me there, who I can play with […] and if you feel alone and you are at school, you don't really feel alone anymore because there are so many children around you. [If I were bullied I would] still want to go to school because, I would rather be bullied than be home alone with a little brother or all alone. Because, it is almost never the case that the whole school bullies you. There is always someone who you can talk to."

791 See also the report of the national education inspectorate about the school year 2014/2015 (Insepectie van het Onderwijs (2016: 15)). They write: "Most schools teach civic education and thereby follow the legal minimum. However, they do not usually guard the quality of this education. Only a handful of schools evaluates the quality and few schools have insight into the social and societal competences that their students acquire. The inspectorate keeps concluding that civic education in school is not well planned, that concrete learning goals are lacking, and that it is unclear how education corresponds to the needs of students.

Experiences of children out of school

It is exactly this element of school education, the social element, that children out of school who participated in this study miss the most, except for children who have such negative experience with the social aspect of school (mostly through bullying) that they would rather stay home than be involved with other students. However, even those children mostly do have a wish to return to school/society.

> *Interview 42. A 14-year old boy who is slowly reintegrating into school.*
> My mother has considered [home-schooling] for me, but she did not choose it because she thinks social is very important [...] I do understand her. I think she might be right, but I don't want to admit it.

> *Interview 11. A 6-year old girl who is home-schooled. She has never been to school and is very positive about her education. When I end the conversation, the following happens:*

> Q: Ok, then I think this is it, thank you very much.
> A: It's just that, I find it quite stupid ... people think that I do not have friends, but we do have them because of course also other children are home-schooled.
> Q: Who thinks that you do not have friends?
> A: Well... I do not have many. Well. I don't care so much.
> Q: Do you think you have fewer [friends] than children who go to school?
> A: Yes I think so.
> Q: That may be a shame, or not?
> A: Not VERY bad.
> Q: No. But who thinks you do not have friends?
> A: Dekkers ... [she's referring to Sander Dekker, the state secretary of education)
> Q: Yes?
> A: At least, I believe so.
> Q: Why do you think that?
> A: I don't know.
> Q: Have you ever met him?
> A: No.

> *Interview 29, an 18-year old girl who was home-schooled after having gone to school on and off for about 6 years, argued that lacking classmates was an advantage of home-schooling:*
> No more fuss with other people [...] after [the suicide] of my father, I turned inward a bit and I feel like: if I do not interact with others, they cannot hurt me anymore.

When parents decide that children are not going to school anymore, this often comes as a surprise to children, who are told "you are not going to school anymore". Those who are out of school and are not home-schooled, are quite bored.

They sit at home, watch tv and wait for adults to find a solution to the conflict.[792] In some cases, the waiting lasts years. When schools decide that the child is no longer welcome, this is usually the result of a longer conflict with the parent. Several children who participated in the research indicated that they did not understand why they were not welcome in school anymore, and probably it had something to do with the fact that at school "they do not like my mother so much, I think".

Parents can protest to this situation with the national committee appropriate education. However, the committee's advice is non-binding, and "appalling behaviour of the parent" is considered a legitimate reason to unenroll the child. In other words, if your parent is in a conflict with the school, as a child you can be unenrolled, provided that the school makes sure that another school enrols the child.[793]

The group of children out of school includes children who are ill and therefore cannot attend school. Although schools have a legal obligation to make sure that these children receive education[794], in practice it seems that different schools handle this situation very differently. Some schools go to great lengths to make sure that the child still receives education, for example by organizing home visits from teachers and peers, organizing for the child to follow classroom education through use of a webcam, etc. Other schools do not do anything at all. Schools generally do not seem to be aware of their legal obligation in this matter, and often rely on the parent to organize their sick child's education.[795]

Home-schooling

Although home-schooling is illegal according to Dutch law, some parents decide to home-school their children. In these cases, they look for loopholes in the law and they try to obtain one of the legal exemptions to the obligation to send their children to school (CEA). One way to do so is through the exemption based on religious/philosophical beliefs. In this case, parents have to convince the municipal SAO in a letter that they object to the direction of the education in schools in their home area. It seems that some families indeed apply for this exemption based on their strong religious convictions (a professional told me about a family who have this exemption because, according to their religion, their children are not allowed to see any images such as you would find in any regular schoolbook. The children are home-schooled using homemade material). However, in most cases it seems that this legal article is used by parents who believe that home-schooling is the best form of education for their children, to obtain an exemption from the obligation to send their children to school.

792 See also §5.2.3.
793 See Onderwijsgeschillen (n.d.).
794 See §5.3.2.
795 See also §5.2.2.

> *Facebook page "home-schooling information for whom is interested", message on 16 April 2016:*
> My son is now 2,5. I keep reading here about exemption on the basis of religion/philosophical beliefs. But I don't have any "special" belief, I'm concerned with a) the way of education, and b) that I believe that 1 on 1 I can truly teach him more/let him experience more/explore than in such a class with 20 children and 1 teacher [...] is it possible at all to get an exemption in such a situation, or do I have to make up a philosophical belief?
> First replies:
> Surely you have a good life philosophy. Have a look at holism for example. Reading your post, this seems to be a match.
> You know, before I studied it more, I too thought about it more or less like you. Once I started writing the objections that I have to the management of the schools in my area it became clear that it really is my life philosophy.

Other parents choose to home-school their children because they feel forced to do so by circumstances. Their motivations are diverse; some feel forced by the fact that the child is, for example, unhappy in school, while others see the school education their child receives and feel that they could do this better at home. More often than not, there has been a conflict between parent(s) and school for a longer period and motivations are difficult to disentangle.

Children who are home-schooled are usually happy about the content of their education or at least not less happy than children in school. The great advantage of home-schooling is its flexibility; sometimes they can study what they find interesting, they can work at their own pace, they do not have to start early in the morning and the studying hours are less because it is more efficient studying at home than at school. They can play often and usually have stuffed animals close at hand. Some children enjoy getting a lot of attention from their parents.

The experience of home-schooling seems to become less positive as children grow older, because some elements of school education, and secondary education in particular, seem difficult to translate into a home setting, such as physical education, chemistry experiments, making music together, all forms of cooperative education, debating, presenting and school projects like a school musical or school theatre. Becoming independent from your parents seems more difficult if your parent is also your teacher and you are together so often. Lastly, participants indicate that the knowledge/skills level of the parents does not always suffice, that parents do not have certain knowledge and/or cannot explain certain things.

In some cases, instead of parents being the teachers, children are home-schooled through "distance education" (*afstandsonderwijs*), by means of educational material and external teachers who either can be contacted through email/skype, or who visit the home.

In some cases, schools see home-schooling as (part of) a temporary solution which is adjusted to the needs of the child, for different reasons. They may therefore keep the child enrolled and not report her/his absence to the municipality, or they may even cooperate in a "Miep Ziek" contract. This is a legal/financial construction through which parents, school and national education inspectorate (sometimes also the *samenwerkingsverband*) enter into a contract whereby a part of the financial sum the school receives to educate the student who is enrolled in the school is used to buy home-schooling material and also, in some cases, to pay private tutors.[796]

Roma children

During the field research, in line with the fact that "Roma children" are generally not part of the discussion on children out of school in the Netherlands, I found that most education professionals and politicians did not have much knowledge about this group, except for those working specifically with Roma as target group.[797]

For Roma children who participated in this study, going to school can make them feel like they have to choose between the Roma and the Dutch culture. When at school, Roma culture seizes to exist and vice versa. Some therefore choose to self-identify as Dutch, like Milosh (25): "Dutch people are a little more normal, I think, [they have] the same [Christian] faith, same look and feel". Others sometimes experience a loss of their own culture through school.[798]

Interview 53, a 9-year old Roma boy who is in special education

A: I learn reading, calculation, language, spelling, telling time, and traffic.
Q: You said that you do not learn your own language at school, only Dutch. Do you think you should be taught in your own language? Or Dutch only?
A: Yes.
Q: Why?
A: I also need to learn my own language. Because for 5 years I was in the group [removed out of home by state authorities] and there we only speak Dutch. And then I could only speak Dutch and [now I live home again] I have to speak Bosnian, our language, again.
Q: And that is difficult?
A: A little. I understand everything but I cannot really say things back.
Q: and so all those years you had no..
A: …not one word.

---

796 NRC (2013a & 2013b), Tweede Kamer (2013).

797 Of the participants, 2 educational specialists, 2 national politicians, the education inspector and 2 scientists specialized in education had not even heard of a potential issue with the Roma child's right to education.

798 See also v.d. Veen et al., who indicate that Roma are hardly represented in the curriculum and education material, and Roma children often feel that in respect of culture, "at school they are often in between their parents and the teachers" (2012: 44).

Although these children often like school, they do not always see its use. It seems that the cultural difference between home and school in some cases leads to children choosing not to attend school.

> *Interview 10, a 44-year old Roma mother who in her youth decided not to attend school anymore.*
> Mostly because I was a Roma, I thought, I will never get a diploma and I will never get a job [...] [people] see Roma as good-for-nothings, thieves and no own country, and those things. No one who will give me a job. I will not put in effort for a diploma, and then, a diploma for on the wall.

Professionals who participated in the research confirmed that Roma encounter serious discrimination and inequality in terms of opportunities.[799] In addition, Roma children are often placed disproportionately in special education[800], which influences their motivation to go to school.

Parents have not enjoyed education themselves and do not always see its use, or they do not have the skills to organize education for their children, for example due to illiteracy. Another group of parents keep children at home, to work and contribute to the family income, or because it would be inappropriate for girls of a certain age to attend school. Some schools refuse to enroll Roma children or simply assume that soon these children will stop showing up. At the municipality level, although much has been invested at times to stimulate integration, at other times nothing was done. Parents usually are not aware of the applicable (Dutch) rules and do not have the skills and knowledge of the Dutch legal/education system to protest, neither do they usually know the difference between regular and special education. What is especially striking is that in the interviews with both Roma and professionals, it seemed that there is a difference between Roma children and ethnic-Dutch children who are out of school in how much more effort is usually made by different authorities (parents, municipality (SAO) and school) when Dutch children are not attending school (although of course there are exceptions).

> *Interview 7, a municipality employee*
> [In our municipality] there were zero [Roma] children going to school until 2008 [...] a certain fatigue had emerged in relation to trying to integrate [the Roma][801] again and again, so halfway the nineties these efforts faded out.

Finally, for Roma children, like for most children out of school in the Netherlands, their situation seems to be caused often by a combination of

---

799 They add that this is influenced by the low education level of the Roma.

800 Of all children I met during this field research, 7 were in special education, 1 in regular education and 1 was being homeschooled. See also Timmermans (2016: 33).

801 In the original transcript, the participant was talking about "them". Professionals in general, when discussing Roma, were talking about "us" and "them".

unfortunate circumstances. Some Roma families are living in very poor circumstances, whereby their focus is short-term survival.[802] For Roma children, some of these personal/family issues can influence their learning focus.

Figure 8. Letter by a 9-year old Roma boy who is in special primary education.

He argues that they have many problems, and because he has understood that I will share my research findings with state authorities, wants to share these issues. He writes a letter for the mayor: "I want my father not to be wanted [as a criminal]. And my mother is with 5 children and she has no money. And that we can go somewhere on holiday."

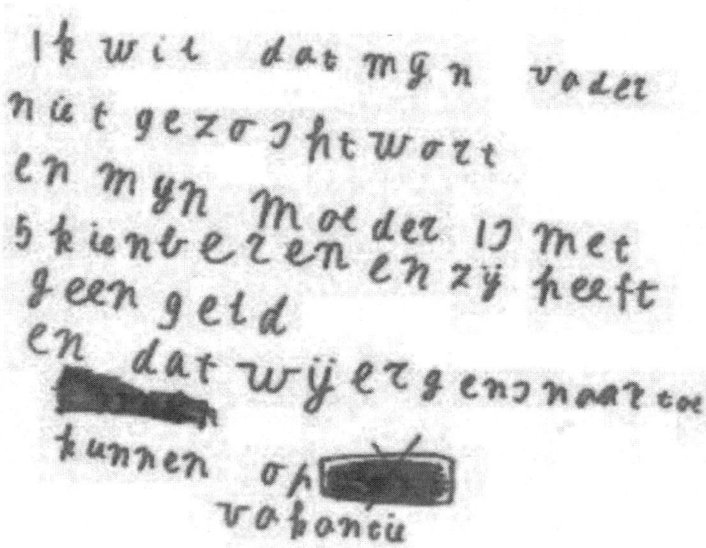
Ik wil dat myn vader
niet gezocht wort
en myn moeder is met
5 kienteren en zy heeft
geen geld
en dat wyergensnaartoe
[redacted] kunnen op
vakancie

5.2.6. LAW IN THE NETHERLANDS

In general, there are two sides to the rule of law in the Netherlands. On the one hand, law has a very strong authoritative position and, on the other hand, the law gives much space to individual or group autonomy. It is with the latter that the people in this study are mostly concerned as regards education, while the authoritarian limits of the law are mostly seen as a given.

Law has a very strong connotation in the Netherlands and seems to be generally experienced as an authority that has ultimate control over what people are and are not allowed to do. The whole social fabric seems to be, to a large extent, built up in terms of rules and enforcement, with space for autonomy only within the boundaries that are set by the law. This process of learning to abide rules starts at an early age, when parents and teachers tell children what to do and what not to do, including punishment for children who transgress the rules.

[802] Geurts (2010: 2.2.1) calls this a "group-directed logic of survival".

In this way, the idea of a powerful sovereign ruling over the individual, and that the individual always has to ask what they are and are not allowed to do, is strongly developed in people living in the Netherlands.

> *Interview 4, a 4-year old girl who attends regular school education*
> What you learn at school is that you have to be good, that you're not allowed to steal, that it's not good when you do something you're not allowed to do [...] If you're not good you have to always give a kiss. And screaming and punching [is also not allowed]. Then you have to go upstairs and you're never allowed to come back down, only when it gets dark. You're not allowed to kick either.

On the other hand, the Dutch state legal order creates much space for autonomy within its structure, especially for adults, including a large space for political debate. Since most people and authorities are law-abiding, almost everyone in the Netherlands seems to accept the basic norm of the Dutch legal order without question. Discussion addresses, rather, the interpretation of the law and its practical implementation (in education, for example, the question "what is appropriate education?" has been an important subject of debate in relation to the 2014 Appropriate Education Act), as well as potential amendments to legislation. Therefore, in the conversations for this case study, you see that most people wanted to discuss what quality education should be like in their view, rather than discuss the law. This includes, for example, home-schooling parents, who, while sometimes actively lobbying for the legalization of home-schooling on the political level, never considered home-schooling their children illegal. Thus, while certain conduct discussed in this chapter might seem illegal to the lawyer, it usually was not seen that way by the actors involved.

Those who resist this Dutch social order, tend to try to exclude themselves from what they refer to as "the system". They try to turn away from the established social order (as in, the way in which most people do things) and create as much autonomy as possible – within the boundaries of the state law – over their own (household) order. This often brings them into conflict with the state and other legal orders (school, municipality), and excludes them from society in some sense, because in the Netherlands those who do not conform to the regular social order are usually frowned upon.

Often this opposing of the social order is a choice of the parents, who choose to do so also on behalf of the child, thereby excluding the child (at least in part) from the regular order – which in the Netherlands is almost equal to excluding the child from society at large. Within the household, in most of these cases, children are still subjected to the authority of the parents, which becomes more encompassing as their legal power is shared less with other authorities (school, teacher, state). Alternatively, some households apply the idea of opposing any form of authority to the household legal order and stimulate ultimate autonomy in the child (in home-schooling, this particular form of education of children –

in the broad sense – is called "unschooling").[803] A child in these cases will not be forced to do anything against their will.

Lastly, it should be noted that, even within "the system", as regards education, the Dutch state legal order does create much space for autonomy for adults. Not only does the state provide high level free education for all, but also a strong protection of individual social and political rights. In education this is expressed by the fact that adults are free to start their own school, with very limited state conditions and control and will receive government funding to do so. Many parents who search for more autonomy resort to sending their children to many of the less authoritarian-structured schools, such as the Steiner, Montessori, Jenaplan and/or Democratic schools, which are all state-funded through the system of "independent schools". For children, recently the state legal order is starting to provide more autonomy, at least in the form of participation rights. A child of age 12, for example, has the right to be informed about, and participate in decisions about, her/his own medical treatment (since 1995)[804], to give or withhold consent to an adult who wants to adopt her/him (since 1997)[805], and to be heard in relation to the decision of who has legal parental authority over the child, in case of a divorce (since 1997).[806]

However, this case study has shown that children are mostly excluded from decisions made about their education and are lucky if their opinion is heard at all, by any or all of the adults involved.[807]

5.3. LEGAL ORDERS AND THE CHILD'S RIGHT TO EDUCATION IN THE NETHERLANDS

In this third section, I will dissect the different legal orders related to the child's right to education in the Netherlands, according to the theoretical framework as described in chapters 1 and 3. This means that every potential legal order involved will be analyzed, if applicable, according to three different potential forms of law:

A: Formal written law: *Rules found in official, formal legal texts, created by the legislature and open and available to the public.*

---

803 See, for example, Petrovic & Rolstad (2017) who argue that "to the extent that traditional schooling is a project of massification – increasingly dominated by a neoliberal ethos in our contemporary times – as opposed to emancipation, unschooling should be seen as its antithesis, providing an option for parents seeking a truly democratic education".

804 Civil Code Book 7: Particular Contracts (*Burgerlijk Wetboek 7*) (art. 450).

805 Civil Code Book 1: Law of Persons and Family Law (*Burgerlijk Wetboek 1: Personen- en Familierecht*) (art. 228).

806 Civil Code Book 1: Law of Persons and Family Law (art. 251a (4)).

807 See also §5.3.7 and §5.3.8.

B: Law for the community: *Rules created by the legislator, known by the subjects of the legal order.*
C: Hidden law: *non-public rules created by the legislature, known only to a specific group of people*

5.3.1. INTERNATIONAL LEGAL ORDER

A. *Formal written law*

The Netherlands is a party to the following international human rights instruments, which include provisions relating to education:

Treaty	**status**	**year**	**relevant articles**
Universal Declaration of Human Rights (UDHR) (1948)	–	1948	18, 26
International Covenant on Civil and Political Rights (1966)	Ratified	1978	18(4)
International Covenant on Economic, Social and Cultural Rights (ICESCR) (1966)	Ratified	1978	10, 13
International Convention on the Elimination of All Forms of Racial Discrimination (ICERD) (1969)	Ratified	1971	5, 7
Convention on the Rights of the Child (CRC) (1989)	Ratified	1995	2, 3, 5, 12, 13, 14, 23, 28, 29, 30
Convention on the Rights of Persons with Disabilities (2006)	Ratified	2016	4, 24

In short, according to the international human rights instruments ratified by the Netherlands, the child living in the Netherlands has a right to free, compulsory primary education and, in general, to quality education which promotes the development of the child in a spirit of peace, dignity, tolerance, freedom, equality, and solidarity.[808]

To understand international law as regards the issues around children out of school in the Netherlands, this right to education has to be read in combination with other rights, such as the right to freedom of religion and the rights of persons with disabilities. Therefore, in this subsection I will discuss certain themes that have come to the fore in this case study in terms of the applicable formal written international law, namely:

1) right to education, right to freedom of religion & right to participation
2) right to education, rights of persons with disabilities & right to non-discrimination

[808] 1948 Universal Declaration of Human Rights (UDHR) (art. 26 (1) and (2)); 1966 International Covenant on Economic, Social and Cultural Rights (ICESCR) (art. 13); 1969 International Convention on the Elimination of All Forms of Racial Discrimination (ICERD) (art. 5, 7), 1989 Convention on the Rights of the Child (CRC)(art. 28, 29).

3) right to education, minority rights & right to non-discrimination
4) right to education, children out of school and the obligation of States Parties

These four themes are the most relevant, as they directly relate to debated state law in the Netherlands.

1. Right to education, right to freedom of religion & right to participation

Most international human rights instruments include a right to education, as well as a right to freedom of religion/belief. However, until the establishment of the Convention on the Rights of the Child (CRC) in 1989, it seems not to have been a concern that there might be a tension between these rights for children and the rights of their parents.

The Universal Declaration of Human Rights, for example, states that everyone has the right to "freedom of thought, conscience and religion; this right includes freedom to change his religion or belief"[809], which includes "theistic, non-theistic and atheistic beliefs, as well as the right not to profess any religion or belief"[810], and that "everyone has the right to education".[811] However, the UDHR also states that "parents have the prior right to choose the kind of education that shall be given to their children".[812] These rights are reiterated in for example the ICCPR, which states that:

> The States Parties to the present Covenant undertake to have respect for the liberty of parents and, when applicable, legal guardians to ensure the religious and moral education of their children in conformity with their own convictions.[813]

These instruments do not reflect upon what should happen if the child were to have a different religious belief than the parents and would for example want to attend another school than the (religious) school chosen by parents.

The 1989 CRC establishes individual rights for children more clearly, stating that "State Parties shall respect the right of the child to freedom of thought, conscience and religion"[814], and that "States Parties shall respect the rights and duties of the parents and, when applicable, legal guardians, to provide direction to the child in the exercise of his or her right in a manner consistent with the evolving capacities of the child".[815] This article can be read together with the child's right to participation:

---

809 UDHR (art. 18(1)).
810 UN Human Rights Committee (1993: para. 2) *CCPR General Comment No. 22: Article 18 (Freedom of Thought, Conscience or Religion).*
811 UDHR (art. 26(1)).
812 Ibid: art. 26(3).
813 1966 International Covenant on Civil and Political Rights (ICCPR) (art. 18(4)).
814 CRC (art. 14(1)).
815 Ibid: art. 14(3).

> States Parties shall assure to the child who is capable of forming his or her own views the right to express those views freely in all matters affecting the child, the views of the child being given due weight in accordance with the age and maturity of the child. For this purpose, the child shall in particular be provided the opportunity to be heard in any judicial and administrative proceedings affecting the child, either directly, or through a representative or an appropriate body [...][816]

It seems therefore that, since the CRC, the child has the right to be heard in matters relating to her/his own education, and her/his view should be given due weight in accordance with the age and maturity of the child, when it comes to decisions on the child's right to education.

In the 2015 report of the UN Special Rapporteur on freedom of religion or belief[817], the Rapporteur focused on the rights of the child and her/his parents in the area of religion or belief. In this rapport, the Rapporteur writes:

> Every individual child is a rights holder in his or her own capacity, not just through membership in a family or community. Moreover, the interests of parents and children are not necessarily identical, including in the area of freedom of religion or belief. There can be situations in which the rights of the child must be safeguarded also against his or her parents. One example is the infliction of harmful practices, such as female genital mutilation or child marriage, sometimes carried out in the name of culture, tradition or religion.[818]

According to the rapporteur, "the status of the child as rights holder must always be respected and should, inter alia, be reflected in the manner in which parents provide guidance and direction to the child."[819] Although some might fear that this can set a precedence for the state to interfere in the family, especially when the family has certain religious beliefs which are different from majority/state religion, on behalf of the child, the Rapporteur argues that this fear is ungrounded and parental rights are sufficiently protected in the CRC and elsewhere.[820] The requirement to respect the child's "evolving capacities", is explained as follows: while the direction that parents may give their children in religious education is particularly far-reaching for infants or young children who are totally dependent on regular support[821], more mature children may themselves decide whether to participate in religious community practices.[822] In school, no child should ever be forced to participate in such practices against her/his will.[823]

816 Ibid: art. 12(1) and (2).
817 United Nations General Assembly (2015).
818 Ibid: para. 14.
819 Ibid: para. 23.
820 Ibid: para. 28-34.
821 Ibid: para. 40.
822 Ibid: paras. 46, 54.
823 Ibid: para. 48.

Most importantly, the Rapporteur writes that, while the CRC combines the recognition of the child as rights holder with respect for the rights and duties of parents in directing the child in the exercise of their rights[824], there are situations where the state can and should interfere on behalf of the child's right against the wishes of the parent, and one of these rights is the child's right to education.[825] The child, for example, has the right to access to sexual and reproductive information, regardless of whether the parents' consent.[826] In the case of state protection of children's rights against parental rights, to remove the child from the family should always be a last resort.[827] The Rapporteur recommends states to generally interpret the rights of children and parental rights in the area of freedom of religion or belief to be positively interrelated, unless state intervention is necessary to protect the child from neglect, domestic violence or harmful practices[828], which includes infringement of the child's right to education.[829] Such intervention must "always be enacted with empirical and normative diligence".[830]

2. Right to education, rights of persons with disabilities & right to non-discrimination

Since all children have a right to education according to the various human rights instruments, this of course includes children with disabilities. According to the right to non-discrimination as stated in the CRC, State Parties have to respect this right without discrimination on grounds of the child's (or her/his parents') disability.[831] To this end, children with disabilities should have effective access to education and States Parties are recommended to "undertake a comprehensive review of all domestic laws and related regulations in order to ensure that all provisions of the [CRC] are applicable to all children, including children with disabilities".[832] Yet the question remains what kind of equal treatment in terms of education these children should receive, considering that they may differ in mental and/or physical capacities compared to the majority of children in their peer groups.[833]

---

824 Ibid: para. 58.

825 Ibid: para. 59.

826 Ibid: paras. 59, 62, referring to Committee of the Rights of the Child (2003) *General comment no. 4 on adolescent health and development in the context of the Convention on the Rights of the Child.*

827 Ibid: paras. 60-61.

828 Ibid: para. 76.

829 Ibid: paras. 59, 62.

830 Ibid: para. 79(f).

831 CRC (art. 2a). See also Committee on Economic, Social and Cultural Rights (1994) *General Comment No. 5: Persons with Disabilities* (para. 15).

832 Committee on the Rights of the Child (2007) *General Comment No. 9 (2006) The rights of children with disabilities* (para. 17).

833 For a discussion on research on this subject, see §5.2.3.

In the CRC, it is stated that assistance should be extended to the disabled child to meet her/his special needs and to thereby "ensure that the disabled child has effective access to and receives education".[835]

The Convention on the Rights of Persons with Disabilities adds that with a view of realizing the child's right to education without discrimination, "States Parties shall ensure an inclusive education system at all levels".[836] In ensuring these rights, States Parties will ensure that:

> Persons with disabilities are not excluded from the general education system on the basis of disability, and that children with disabilities are not excluded from free and compulsory primary education, or from secondary education, on the basis of disability.[837]

To this end, children with disabilities should receive the support required to facilitate their effective education.[838] Practically, this includes support such as transportation to and from school[839], teacher training, availability of necessary

834 Source: http://interactioninstitute.org/illustrating-equality-vs-equity/, accessed 2 April 2019.
835 CRC (art. 23 (3)).
836 2007 Convention on the Rights of Persons with Disabilities (CRPD) (art. 24(1)).
837 Ibid: art. 24(a).
838 Ibid: art. 24(d).
839 Committee on Economic, Social and Cultural Rights (1994) *General Comment No. 5: Persons with Disabilities* (para. 23).

equipment and support in schools[840], facilitating the learning of Braille and other alternative modes of communication[841], and sign language.[842]

In the long term, the Committee on the Rights of Persons with Disabilities has indicated that the state's obligation resulting from the Convention "to undertake to take measures to the maximum of its available resources [...] achieving progressively the full realization of these [economic, social and cultural] rights"[843], is "not compatible with sustaining two systems of education: a mainstream education system and a special/segregated education system".[844]

3. Right to education, (Roma) minority rights & right to non-discrimination

The right to non-discrimination, as mentioned above, also applies in particular to children living in the Netherlands who do not have a Dutch background, including non-nationals and children of different ethnicity[845], thereby including a prohibition on discrimination in education against Roma. An obligation rests on states to identify and redress any discrimination in education, and to disaggregate education data "by the prohibited grounds of discrimination".[846] This also includes a positive obligation on states to take "positive measures to ensure that education is culturally appropriate for minorities".[847]

The Committee on the Elimination of Racial Discrimination in General Recommendation XXVII writes, specifically on the discrimination against Roma that states should:

a) adopt and implement national strategies and programmes and express determined political will and moral leadership, with a view to improving the situation of Roma and their protection against discrimination by state bodies, as well as by any person or organization.[848]
b) support the inclusion in the school system of all children of Roma origin and to act to reduce drop-out rates, in particular among Roma girls, and, for these purposes, to cooperate actively with Roma parents, associations and local communities.[849]

---

840 Ibid: para. 35.
841 CRPD (art. 3a).
842 Ibid: art. 3b.
843 CRPD (art. 4(2)).
844 Committee on the Rights of Persons with Disabilities (2016: para. 40).
845 Committee on Economic, Social and Cultural Rights (1994: para. 34).
846 Ibid: para. 37.
847 Committee on Economic, Social and Cultural Rights (1999: para. 50)). *General Comment No. 13: The Right to Education.*
848 Committee on the Elimination of Racial Discrimination (2000: para. 2) *General Recommendation XXVII on Discrimination Against Roma.*
849 Ibid: para. 17.

c) prevent and avoid as much as possible the segregation of Roma students, while keeping open the possibility for bilingual or mother-tongue tuition.[850]
d) consider adopting measures in favour of Roma children, in cooperation with their parents, in the field of education.[851]
e) act with determination to eliminate any discrimination or racial harassment of Roma students.[852]
f) take the necessary measures to ensure a process of basic education for Roma children of travelling communities, including by admitting them temporarily to local schools, by temporary classes in their places of encampment, or by using new technologies for distance education.[853]
g) include in textbooks, at all appropriate levels, chapters about the history and culture of Roma, and encourage and support the publication and distribution of books and other print materials as well as the broadcasting of television and radio programmes, as appropriate, about their history and culture, including in languages spoken by them.[854]

4. Right to education, children out of school and the obligation of States Parties

Under international law, primary education is compulsory for every child and there is a subsequent obligation for State Parties to guarantee this right.[855]

The Committee on Economic, Social and Cultural Rights in their general commentary no. 13 have specified which obligations this puts upon states, namely three levels of obligations: "to respect, protect and fulfil".[856] More precisely,

> States have obligations to respect, protect and fulfil each of the "essential features" (availability, accessibility, acceptability, adaptability) of the right to education. By way of illustration, a State must [...] protect the accessibility of education by ensuring that third parties, including parents and employers, do not stop girls from going to school; fulfil (facilitate) the acceptability of education by taking positive measures to ensure that education is culturally appropriate for minorities [...] and of good quality for all.[857]

850 Ibid: para. 18.
851 Ibid: para. 19.
852 Ibid: para. 20.
853 Ibid: para. 21.
854 Ibid: para. 26.
855 UDHR (art. 26(1)), ICESCR (art. 13(a)); CRC (art. 28(a)).
856 Committee on Economic, Social and Cultural Rights (1999: para. 46).
857 Ibid: para. 50.

- "availability" refers to making available necessary material conditions for education, such as functional educational institutions, buildings, materials, and providing qualified teachers
- "accessibility" refers to making education available to everyone equally, without discrimination. It also includes physical (including distant learning through modern technology) and economic accessibility
- "acceptability" means that the form and substance have to be acceptable (relevant, culturally appropriate, good quality) in the first place to students and, in appropriate cases, to parents
- "adaptability" means that education has to be flexible so that it can adopt the needs of students and changing societies.[858]

In considering all these elements, the best interest of the student needs to be the primary consideration.[859]

B. Law for the community

Almost all participants (except the youngest) were familiar with the idea of the "right to education", which most argued was a right for children to develop themselves, according to their individual needs, talents and/or interests. When asked whether children in the Netherlands have this right, participants usually started discussing what this right should entail, for example which specific courses should or should not be part of the school curriculum, whether or not it includes home-schooling, etc. Some children remarked that there is a discrepancy between "having a right", which means that you are allowed to do or have something, versus the obligation to attend school.[860] Some of the participants included a right to play and/or to have fun into the right to education.

Most of the participants did not identify this right as international law, but rather saw it as a given, a universal truth: "all children have a right to education" or a normative opinion or belief:

Interview 51, a national education inspector.

Q: What is the meaning of the child's right to education?
A: I think that children have an autonomous right to develop and to become who they are. Who they want to become [...] the vehicle to this purpose, I think, is education.

858 Ibid: para. 6.
859 Ibid: para. 7.
860 See also §5.2.5: the meaning of the child's right to education.

While in some sense the child's right to education is recognized by almost all in the Netherlands as applying to children living in the Netherlands, it is not so much understood as a law, but rather as something that simply *is*. The participants generally did not discuss the right to education in a legal sense, for example by discussing it as a rule they would have to comply with, wondering who made the rule, how/where it could or would be enforced, etc. In this sense then, the international legal child's right to education is not law for the community in the Netherlands.

Figure 9. Drawing by a 7-year old boy who attends regular school.

"Right to education: it has to be safe, good breaks, and every child has the right to a teacher. You also have a right to a school playground with play equipment. That is important because the child should be able to play."
In the drawing we see, from top left to bottom right: a school playground without play equipment, a safe school building with a steady roof, a playground with equipment, an unsafe school building of which the roof collapses, a safe school playground (tree does not fall), an unsafe school playground (tree falls over), a classroom with a teacher, a classroom without a teacher.

5.3.2. THE REGIONAL (EUROPEAN) LEGAL ORDER

A. *Formal written law*

Rules found in official, formal legal texts, created by the legislature and open and available to the public.

On the level of the regional (European) legal order, there are two separate legal orders: the European Union (EU) and the Council of Europe (CoE). Each of these orders have different corresponding courts and laws (see below). Because the people in the Netherlands do not seem to see these as separate legal orders, and the EU is also connected to the CoE in the sense that the European Convention on Human Rights is law for the EU, I will discuss both these orders in this section.

Legal order	(relevant) formal written law	Legislator	Court	Relevant article(s)
European Union	2000 Charter of Fundamental Rights of the European Union	European Commission & European Parliament	Court of Justice of the European Union (CJEU)	14
Council of Europe	Conventions:	Council of Europe	European Court of Human Rights (ECtHR)	
	1950 European Convention on Human Rights (ECHR) – Protocol I		European Court of Human Rights (ECtHR)	2, 14
	1996 Revised European Social Charter		n.a.	15, 17
	1992 European Charter for Regional or Minority Languages		n.a.	7, 8
	1998 Framework Convention for the Protection of National Minorities		n.a.	12–14
	Recommendations:			
	2000: on the education of Roma/Gypsy children in Europe		n.a.	1, 3, 5, 6, 8–10, 12
	2009 on the education of Roma and Travellers in Europe		n.a.	
	2012: on ensuring quality education		n.a.	6, 10–13, 16–29

According to these legal instruments, all children have a right to education, enjoyed without discrimination on any grounds.[861] This right includes:

- the possibility to receive compulsory education;[862]
- a right for parents to ensure the education and teaching of their children in conformity with their religious and philosophical beliefs;[863]
- a right for children with disabilities to be provided education in regular education where possible, or otherwise in specialized institutions;[864]
- a right of children to obtain the education they need for the full development of their personality and of their physical and mental capacities;[865]

---

861 2000 Charter of the fundamental rights of the European Union (hereafter: Charter) (art. 14); ECHR (art. 2, 14).

862 1950 European Convention on Human Rights (ECHR) (art. 2). The Charter adds "pedagogical convictions" (art. 14(2)).

863 Charter (art. 14(3)).

864 1996 European Social Charter (Revised). (art. 15(1)).

865 Ibid: art 17(1), see also **Council of Europe (2012)** Recommendation CM/Rec (2012)13 of the Committee of Ministers to Member States on ensuring quality education (art. 6).

- a right for children to free primary and secondary education as well as encouragement to regular attendance at schools;[866]
- a right to education in one's minority language[867], history and culture.[868] However, the Netherlands has opted in their 1998 Declaration to adopt a more limited application with regards to the "Romanes language", which only obliged the state to have the Romanes language "among the objectives of education and training provided within [the country]".[869]

Furthermore, the Council recommends that the education for Roma children should receive special attention, for example through providing distance education to accompany those who "lead an itinerant or semi-itinerant lifestyle"[870], to ensure better communication with parents, including between parents and schools, and to this end use mediators from the Roma community if necessary[871] to design the curriculum and teaching material "so as to take into account the cultural identity of Roma children", including Roma history and culture, yet this should not lead to the establishment of separate curricula and/or separate classes[872], to ensure through education policies the non-discriminatory access to quality education for Roma children and ensure that Roma children are effectively accepted in school.[873] In particular, "educational authorities should set up assessment procedures that do not result in risks of enrolling children in special-education institutions based on linguistic, ethnic, cultural or social differences".[874] Access to compulsory education for Roma children should be subject to the same criteria as the majority population.[875] Development of educational policy should involve consultation of the Roma community.[876]

Lastly, in the 2012 Recommendation on ensuring quality education, the Council specifies compulsory education and its obligations on states:

---

866 1996 European Social Charter (Revised) (art. 17(2)).

867 1992 European Charter for Regional or Minority Languages (art. 8(b-c)); 1995 Framework Convention for the Protection of National Minorities (art. 12, 14).

868 1992 European Charter for Regional or Minority Languages (art. 8 (g)); 1995 Framework Convention for the Protection of National Minorities (art. 12). See also **Council of Europe (2009)** Recommendation CM/Rec (2009)4 of the Committee of Ministers to member states on the education of Roma and Travellers in Europe.

869 Council of Europe (1998); 1992 European Charter for Regional or Minority Languages (art. 7(3, 5)), (art. 18).

870 Council of Europe (2000) Recommendation No R (2000) 4 of the Committee of Ministers to Member States on the education of Roma/Gypsy children in Europe (art. 1, 3).

871 Ibid: art. 5.

872 Ibid: art. 10; Council of Europe (2009: art. 5, 6).

873 Council of Europe (2009: art. 1(b-d)).

874 Ibid: art. 6.

875 Ibid: art. 11.

876 Ibid: "principles of policies" (art. 1, 2).

> Without exception, all school-age children should have the right and the obligation to take part in quality education [...] all parents or legal guardians should have the right and the duty to enroll their children in the system. Where parents or legal guardians fail to enroll their children in school, public authorities should have the responsibility and the means to ensure the children's rights to quality education.[877]

In this recommendation, they further broaden the concept of inclusive education to "those who are unable to make successful use of mainstream education programs for diverse reasons, which range from lack of proficiency in the language(s) of instruction or substantial differences in previous educational curricula to severe mental or physical disability".[878]

Court rulings

Since much of European law is further explained in court proceedings, I want to quickly share some court interpretations of the child's right to education insofar relevant for this case study.

No cases on the child's right to education have been brought before the CJEU. In ECtHR cases, we can observe that the court in general has been of the opinion that the child's right to education is of much greater importance than the rights of parents to decide about the upbringing and education of their children, whether or not this is based on parents' religious and/or philosophical beliefs.

To illustrate:

- Cases in which parents sued states arguing that their child should be exempted from compulsory sex-education, due to their religious or philosophical beliefs, were ruled inadmissible because sex-education was considered to protect the child's health and/or would protect them from sexual abuse.[879]
- In cases where the school imposes educational content that goes against the religious or philosophical beliefs of the parents, this is considered a violation of ECHR art. 2 by the court only when this education provides a clear, compulsory and direct teaching of a particular religion or philosophical belief, or clear, compulsory and direct disrespect of the parents' religion or philosophical beliefs.[880]
- As regards home-schooling and a subsequent exemption of the obligation to send their children to school due to religious reasons, the court ruled in

877 Council of Europe (2012: art. 12).

878 Ibid: art. 26, 27.

879 See: AR. and L.R. v. Switzerland (2017); Jimenez Alonzo et Jimenez Merino v. Spain (2000).

880 See: Mansur Yalçin and others v. Turkey (2014); Lautsi and others v. Italy (2011); Appel-Irrgang and others v. Germany (2009); Hasan and Eylem Zengin v. Turkey (2007); Keller v. Germany (1998); Valsamis v. Greece (1996); Efstratiou v. Greece (1996).

a case of Christian parents in Germany who sued the German state for not allowing them to home-school their children, that their application was inadmissible.[881] The court argued that according to the German authorities:

> "not only the acquisition of knowledge but also integration into and first experiences of society are important goals in primary-school education. The German courts found that those objectives could not be met to the same extent by home education, even if it allowed children to acquire the same standard of knowledge as provided by primary-school education", and that the parents "were free to educate their children after school and in the weekends".

Interestingly, the case was also filed on behalf of the children, however the court held that "the applicant children were unable to foresee the consequences of their parents decision to opt for home education because of their young age. As it would be very difficult for the applicant children to take an autonomous decision for themselves at that age", and therefore considered the case as an application by the parents.

- As regards inclusive education (the maximum inclusion of all children in regular rather than special education), the court notes that:

> With regard to pupils with special needs, the Court accepts that the choice between having a single type of school for everyone, highly specialised structures or unified structures with specialist sections is not an easy one and there does not appear to be an ideal solution. It involves a difficult exercise in balancing the various competing interests.'[882] Therefore, 'a wide measure of discretion' must be left to the appropriate authorities, who should take parental convictions into consideration.[883]

- In this respect, segregation of Roma children into separate school buildings or classes has repeatedly been ruled both a violation of the right to non-discrimination and a violation of the child's right to education. In general, for children to attend special education is only warranted if this aims at their integration into regular education.[884]
- In terms of the right to inclusion for disabled children, the ECtHR has ruled in several cases that while "there is an increasing body of opinion which holds that, whenever possible, disabled children should be brought up with normal children of their own age [...] this policy cannot apply to all handicapped children". Therefore, "a wide measure of discretion" must be left to the appropriate authorities, who should take parental convictions into consideration, yet "it cannot be said that the second sentence of article 2 (P1–

---

881 Konrad v. Germany (2006).

882 D.H. and others v. The Czech Republic (2006).

883 Klerks against the Netherlands (1995). See also: Dahlberg and Dahlberg v. Sweden (1994).

884 Lavida and others v. Greece (2013); Sampani and others v. Greece (2012); D.H. and others v. The Czech Republic (2006).

2) requires the placing of a child with a serious [..] impairment in a regular school [...] rather than in an available place in a special school".[885]

- In terms of support of students with special needs in school, the committee[886] evaluates whether proper procedures have been followed (in terms of assessment of needs), yet argues that "it is not the Commission's task to assess the standard of teaching provided by schools".[887]
- In cases of exclusion of children from school, again the court assesses primarily whether due process has been followed, including whether or not the exclusion measure was proportionate to the situation. If a child is removed from school, the state is responsible for protecting the child's right to education.[888]
  - It is interesting to note here that a legitimate reason for the exclusion of a child from school was the fact that his parents did not show up to a meeting with the principal concerning re-admission. Here then the rights of the child were not separated from the actions of the parents.[889]

B. Law for the community

Rules created by the legislator, known by the subjects of the legal order.

Only one of the participants mentioned European law. It seems therefore that European law is not law for the community in the Netherlands. This may be confirmed by, and/or be the cause of, the fact that there have only been two cases brought before the ECtHR regarding the child's right to education in the Netherlands, one in 1995 and one in 1965.[890]

5.3.3. ROMA LEGAL ORDER

Initially I thought, based on literature study, that the Roma legal order might be a separate legal order legislating over Roma children's right to education. However, in this case study, no data was found that confirmed this hypothesis. It seemed instead that Roma children who participated in the study were more ruled over in the household legal order. In some cases, the legislator was the oldest male in the family, but this was often part of the (physically close) household. In general, the caretaker with (most) authority over the Roma children seemed to be a person that was physically close, so literally within the household.[891]

---

885 Klerks against the Netherlands (1995). See also: Dahlberg and Dahlberg v. Sweden (1994).

886 Before November 1st, 1998, admissibility of cases before the ECtHR was decided by the European Commission of Human Rights.

887 S.P. v. The United Kingdom (1997).

888 Memlika v. Greece (2015); Ali v. The United Kingdom (2011).

889 Ali v. The United Kingdom (2011).

890 Klerks against the Netherlands (1995), X. v. the Netherlands (1968).

891 It has to be noted that the sample of Roma respondents was relatively small, so that it is still open to further research to see if this finding applies to all or most Roma in the Netherlands.

5.3.4. STATE LEGAL ORDER

A. *Formal written law*

Several national laws address the child's right to education in the Netherlands, even though there is no legal right to education for children. To give an overview, these are all Dutch state laws and orders related to primary and secondary education, insofar as they are relevant to the current case study:

Law	Relevant articles	Content
1848 Constitution	23, 93	General organization of education (legislation, finances); legal status of international and regional law
1963 Secondary Education Act (SEA)[892]	1, 2, 3b, 4, 6a-6c, 6f, 7, 10, 10a, 10b, 10b1–10b3, 10d, 10e, 11b, 12–15, 17a, 17b, 18, 24b, 26, 27, 27b, 27c, 48, 70, 75a, 77, 84, 85b1, 86, 108, 118a,	Qualification of school employees, school transport, school safety, content and quality of secondary education, complaints procedure, political organization schools and their trans-school political bodies, admission and expelling of students, control and enforcement, financial considerations
1969 Compulsory Education Act (CEA)[893]	1, 2, 3.1, 4, 4a, 4b, 5, 5a, 6, 7, 8, 11, 12, 13, 13a, 13b, 14, 15, 16, 16a, 19, 21, 21a, 22, 26, 27.	Regulation of the obligation to enroll children in school and for children to attend lessons.
1981 Primary Education Act (PEA)[894]	1, 4, 4c, 8, 9, 9a, 9b, 14 18a, 39, 40, 40a, 43, 58, 63, 69, 70, 120, 125, 165, 180, 180a, 185.	Qualification of school employees, school transport, school safety, content and quality of primary education, complaints procedure, political organization schools and their trans-school political bodies, admission and expelling of students, control and enforcement, after school care, financial considerations, founding an independent school, school buildings
1982 Law on the Expertise Centers (LEC)[895]	1, 2, 4, 5a, 9, 11, 13, 14, 14a, 14c, 14f, 15, 18, 18a, 19, 23, 28a, 39, 40, 40a, 40b, 41, 41a, 42, 42a, 45, 46, 47, 47a, 47b, 49, 60, 61, 70, 71, 117, 129, 165, 166, 166a.	Organization of special education (primary and secondary level).
1985 Order on nomadic population under PEA (ONPPEA)[896]	A2, B1, B2, B3, B5, B10, B12, B13, B16, B16a, B16b, B16c, B17, C1, C2, C3, C9, C10, C11, 13, C19.	Education for children of parents who live a nomadic life, because they work in a circus, on a fair or as sailors.

892 *Wet op het Voortgezet Onderwijs (WVO).*
893 *Leerplichtwet (LPW).*
894 *Wet op het Primair Onderwijs (WPO).*
895 *Wet op de expertise centra.*
896 *Besluit trekkende bevolking WPO.*

Law	Relevant articles	Content
1985 Order on Exemption CEA Nomadic Population (OECEANP)[897]	1–3	Exemption from CEA for parents of children who live a nomadic life.
1993 Order on the organization of the SEA (OOOSEA)[898]	2–4, 6, 9, 13, 14, 15, 15a, 15b, 15d, 26b-26d, 26h-26j, 27, 28, 28a, 31–36	Similar to SEA yet with more details on content of educational program in secondary education, and more details on enrollment/unenrollment including the position of special needs students.
2015 Civil Code Book 1: Law of Persons and Family Law[899]	25(1), 247	Legal authority over the child

Constitution

According to the constitution, the government has constant concern for education. Everyone is free to provide education, provided the quality of education is subject to government control. There should be enough schools for all children to receive public education. Both types of schools (public and independent) will be financed by the state.[900] In addition, according to the Dutch constitution: "Provisions of treaties and of resolutions by international institutions which may be binding on all persons by virtue of their contents shall become binding after they have been published."[901] Therefore international and regional (European) law is in principle binding in the Netherlands. However, the Supreme Court has ruled that individuals cannot present a rights claim based on either the ICESCR or the CRC in a Dutch court, in contrast to claims based on the ECHR.[902]

1963 Secondary Education Act (SEA), 1981 Primary Education Act (PEA), 1993 Order on the organization of the SEA (OOSEA)

The SEA and PEA are quite similar and therefore will be discussed together. Both laws organize the content, conditions and financing of primary/secondary education and its enforcement. Relevant for the current case study are:

- <u>Aim of education</u>: Education is based on the idea that students grow up in a multicultural society, stimulates active citizenship and social integration,

[897] *Besluit vrijstelling leerplicht trekkende bevolking.*
[898] *Inrichtingsbesluit W.V.O.*
[899] *Burgerlijk Wetboek 1: Personen- en Familierecht.*
[900] Constitution of the Netherlands, art. 23.
[901] Ibid: art. 93.
[902] Zoontjens (2003: 9-11).

and aims for students to have knowledge of, and meet, different backgrounds and cultures of their peers.[903] Primary education is aimed at emotional and rational development, development of creativity and obtaining necessary knowledge of social, cultural and physical skills.[904] Secondary public education is aimed at the development of the student with attention for religious, philosophical and societal values such as are found in the Dutch society, with attention for differences in values.[905] For secondary education, law establishes the program content for all levels.[906]

- Language: Education will be organized so that there is special attention for combatting those who fall behind, specifically those who fall behind in mastering the Dutch language.[907] Languages taught are Dutch and English (always), German and French (optional), Frisian (optional only in the province of Friesland).[908] Teaching may be through Dutch, Frysian or other local language which is the used language in the area of the school. Partially, teaching may be through English, German or French.[909] In primary education, for students with a non-Dutch cultural background, other languages can also be used in part for teaching.[910]
- School safety: every school is obliged to have a regulation regarding safety at school, with someone who is responsible for its execution. "Safety" refers to the social, psychological and physical safety of the students, mostly in relation to bullying.[911]
- Special needs: education aims to provide individual guidance, attuned to the needs of the student with special needs.[912] For children with disabilities a "development perspective" is established together with parents every year.[913] In primary education, for children with disabilities, adjusted aims of education can be applied[914], and children with special needs can be exempted from the central exam.[915]

---

903 PEA (art. 8(3)); SEA (art. 17).

904 PEA (art. 8(2).

905 SEA (art. 42(1)).

906 SEA (art. 6f, 7, 10, 10a, 10b, 10b1, 10b2, 10b3, 10d, 11b, 12-15); OOSEA (art. 26b- 26d, 26h-26j, 27, 28, 28a, 31-36); 2006 Decision core aims first three years of secondary education (*Besluit kerndoelen onderbouw VO*); 2014 Decision experiments continuous educational line VMBO-MBO 2014-2022 (*Besluit experimenten doorlopende leerlijnen vmbo-mbo 2014-2022*).

907 PEA (art. 8(11)); SEA (art. 6c).

908 PEA (art. 9); SEA (art. 6a).

909 In secondary education, this may also include other languages which are the subject of the teaching (SEA (art. 6a(a), 11e).

910 PEA (art. 9, 13, 13a, 14).

911 PEA (art. 4c); SEA (art. 3b).

912 PEA (art. 8(4)); SEA (art. 10e, 17b)

913 PEA (art. 40a); SEA (art. 26).

914 PEA (art. 9(9)).

915 PEA (art. 9b(4)).

- Illness: education is organized in such a way that students who have to stay at home or in a hospital because of illness, can enjoy sufficient education.[916] To this end, the school[917] can be supported by an education facility in the hospital and/or the school advisory service (*schoolbegeleidingsdienst*).[918]
- Transportation: any child who needs transport to and from school can apply to the municipality for funding for this transport, and will receive this under certain conditions of necessity.[919]
- Students who are behind in their mastery of the Dutch language can receive extra Dutch education, before attending primary school (*voorschoolse educatie*) and/or during primary school in addition to regular school hours. The former needs to be organized by the municipality according to the law, while the latter is optional for the municipality and schools to organize. Participation is conditional upon the permission of the parents.[920] The goal of this program is to prevent segregation and stimulate integration. In addition, the municipality is responsible for dividing these children among the different schools within the municipality.[921]
- Finances: public and independent schools are financed by the state.[922] Schools get paid per student.[923] The ministry may decide to provide extra financial means that support the education (participation).[924]
- Finances and position of special needs students: all schools are included in a regional *Samenwerkingsverband*. This organ is responsible for certain elements of support for special needs students: they establish a support plan, distribute the financial means for extra support for students with special needs among the schools in their area, and they decide in what type of school (special, special needs, regular) this student is best placed.[925] Municipalities get a yearly sum for extra Dutch education for students who are behind in their mastery of the Dutch language.[926] School advisory services (*schoolbegeleidingsdiensten*) receive financial support from the Ministry for their activities with students who are out of school due to illness.[927] In primary education, school authorities receive money annually from the

916 PEA (art. 8(10)); SEA (art. 6b).
917 Officially it is the "school legal person".
918 PEA (art. 9a); SEA (art. 18).
919 PEA (art. 4); SEA (art. 4).
920 PEA (art. 165).
921 PEA (art. 165, 166, 167, 167a, 168). In relation to secondary education, the municipality has a similar, yet more loose assignment to prevent segregation (SEA (art. 118a).
922 PEA (art. 69); SEA (art. 77). For more details, see 1985 Decision financing PEA (*Besluit financiering WPO)*, 1985 Decision financing SEA (*Bekostigingsbesluit WVO*).
923 PEA (art. 120, 121); SEA (art. 84, 85b1, 86, 108).
924 PEA (art. 70).
925 PEA (art. 18a, 120(4)); SEA (art. 10e(4), 17a); OOSEA (art. 15d).
926 PEA (art. 168a), see also "students who are behind in their mastery of the Dutch language" below.
927 PEA (art. 180); SEA (art. 18).

Ministry for "school guidance".[928] In secondary education, school authorities can apply to the Ministry for this type of financial support.[929]

- Enrollment: children can be enrolled in primary education as of age 4[930] and have to be enrolled in writing by their parents.[931] In secondary education, children can enroll either based on the educational report and school recommendation provided by the primary school if they have reached the age of 14 in primary education[932], or if they were previously enrolled in a secondary education of similar or higher level.[933] If neither of these conditions apply, the inspectorate may allow an exception.[934]
  The school authority decides whether or not a child is admitted, yet this decision cannot be influenced by legal residency until the age of 18.[935] The school authority decides whether or not the child needs extra support because of a disorder or disability. If the school decides to refuse the child because of her/his special needs, the school is responsible for finding another school that is ready to enroll the child, unless there is no place available for the child, or the school authority asks the parents to declare that they will respect/support the foundation of the school and the parents refuse.[936] They have to do so together with the *Samenwerkingsverband*.[937] In secondary education, this also requires the advice of at least two experts.[938] Children can also be refused on the grounds of religious or philosophical beliefs, unless there is no other school in the area for the child and unless the school is "exclusively for internal students".[939] An independent primary school can refuse a child when parents did not submit sufficient data (documents).[940]
- Unenrollment: children leave primary school when deemed by the school authority to be sufficiently prepared for secondary education, provided the parents agree, or at the latest at the end of the school year during which they turned 14.[941] The school authority can decide to expel the child for a

928 PEA (art. 180a).
929 SEA (art. 70, 75a).
930 PEA (art. 39(1-3)).
931 PEA (art. 40(2), 40b), SEA (art. 27b).
932 PEA (art. 42); 2014 Exam Decision Primary Education (*2014 toetsbesluit PO*); OOSEA (art. 3, 6).
933 OOSEA (art. 6, 9).
934 OOSEA (art. 3(4), 4).
935 PEA (art. 40(1)); SEA (art. 27(1), 27(2c)); OOSEA (art. 2).
936 PEA (art. 40(3-5)); SEA (art. 27(2b-2d).
937 See "finances and position of special needs students" above.
938 OOSEA (art. 15a). "Experts" refers to social workers, pedagogues, psychiatrists, psychologists, and/or doctors.
939 PEA (art. 58); SEA (art. 48); 2009 Regulation learning plus arrangements secondary education (2009 *Regeling leerplusarrangementen VO*) which provides financing particularly for children living in poverty.
940 PEA (art. 63(4)).
941 PEA (art. 39(4)).

maximum of one week.[942] In secondary education, schools can unenroll students provided that, if they are still subject to the CEA, they find another school that is willing to enroll the student.[943]

- Complaints procedure: parents and employees can submit complaints, such as on discrimination, to the complaints committee of the school.[944] In case of a dispute about enrollment/unenrollment, or the established development perspective, parents can file a complaint with the national dispute committee. They will judge within 10 weeks and schools are to follow their decisions.[945] In secondary education, in addition, parents and students can object to this decision in writing to the school authority.[946]

1982 Law on the Expertise Centers (LEC)

The law on special education is in many ways similar to the laws on primary and secondary education.

According to this law, special education and secondary special education is education for children who need mainly an orthopedagogical/orthodidactical approach.[947] This form of education is meant for children who are a) deaf, b) hard of hearing, c) have serious speech impairments, d) are visually impaired, e) are physically disabled, f) have been suffering from long-term illness, with or without physical disability, g) are seriously impaired in their capacity to learn, h) are "very difficult to raise/educate" (*zeer moeilijk opvoedbaar*, sometimes also translated as "socially maladjusted"), i) are in schools connected to pedological institutes (for children with complicated learning, behaviour or emotional problems), j) have multiple disabilities.

Education for these children is divided over four different forms of education:

- Cluster 1: visually impaired children, or those with multiple disabilities of which visual is one
- Cluster 2: children who are deaf, hard of hearing, have speech impediments, or those with multiple disabilities of which audio is one
- Cluster 3: children with a physical disability, long-term ill children with a physical disability, children who are seriously impaired in their capacity to learn

942 PEA (art. 40(1), 40c); OOSEA (art. 13).
943 SEA (art. 27(1)); OOSEA (art. 14).
944 PEA (art. 14); SEA (art. 24b, 27(4)).
945 PEA (art. 43); SEA (art. 27c); OOSEA (art. 15b).
946 OOSEA (art. 15).
947 LEC (art. 2(1)).

- Cluster 4: long-term ill children without physical disability, children who are very difficult to raise/educate, children in schools connected to pedological institutes.[948]

Education for these children has to be adapted to the development possibilities of the child. If possible, it aims to bring children to following education in regular primary and/or secondary schools.[949] Like primary and secondary education, special education is based on the idea that students grow up in a multicultural society, stimulates active citizenship and social integration, and aims for students to have knowledge of, and meet, different backgrounds and cultures of their peers.[950] Parents can request for the child who follows special secondary education to take exams at a regular school for secondary education.[951]

Enrollment: children can be enrolled in special education from age 4, except for children who are deaf / hard of hearing, who can enroll at age 3.[952] Children can enroll in special secondary education based on the advise of a previous school authority, or if they have reached the age of 14 in special primary education.[953] In both situations the *samenwerkingsverband* has to indicate that the child is allowed to enroll in special education.[954] For this purpose, a special (research) committee is in place.[955] An inspector of the education inspectorate can state that this process has led to a wrongful placement of a student, in which case the school has to unenroll the student.[956]

Unenrollment: children unenroll from special primary education when the school advisory board thinks they are ready for secondary special education or when they have reached 14 years of age. Children leave secondary special education at the latest when they have reached age 20.[957] Contrary to regular education, the school has the right to unenroll a student when this student is in a cluster 1 or 2 institution and the school has unsuccessfully searched for an appropriate place in another school for 8 weeks.[958] Schools for children residing in a special institution (*inrichting*), e.g. a special institution for care of

948 LEC (art. 2(2-4)).
949 LEC (11(1, 3)). For an indication of the specific content of special education, see LEC (art. 13, 14, 14a, 14c, 14f, 15, 16.)
950 LEC (art. 11(4)).
951 LEC (art. 47).
952 LEC (39(1)).
953 LEC (art. 9(3)).
954 LEC (art. 40).
955 LEC (art. 41).
956 LEC (art. 42).
957 LEC (art. 9(4).
958 LEC (art. 40(18).

the disabled, youth care or youth health care[959], are allowed to remove these students as soon as they are no longer residing in the institution.[960]

The schools can also provide extra support to children in regular education who would otherwise (without this extra support) be in special education.[961]

In terms of transportation[962], school safety[963], illness[964], language[965], complaint procedure[966], support in case of illness[967], role of *Samenwerkingsverbanden*[968], other rules regarding enrollment and unenrollment[969], expelling a student[970], development perspective[971], refusal to enroll students based on religious/philosophical reasons[972], financing[973] and school guidance[974], the rules are the same as, or very similar to, these regulations for children in regular education.

1985 Order on Nomadic Population Primary Education Act (ONPPEA) & 1985 Order on Exemption CEA Nomadic Population (OECEANP)

Two orders have been adopted by the Dutch government in relation to education for Nomadic people. These orders apply to children whose parents live a nomadic life. They distinguish between two groups of the nomadic population: those who work on a fair or in a circus (group a), and those who are sailors (group b)., The Dutch state has special legislation for the education of these children.

The parents referred to in group a, the circus and fair group, are exempted from the legal obligation to enroll their child in a school from March to October if they are travelling with their children while working on a fair or in a circus, unless there is less than 5 kilometers distance between the caravan of the child and the riding school for the nomadic population.[975] For these riding schools, special rules apply. While the aims of education are the same as those for non-

959 LEC (art. 71c(1-2)).
960 LEC (art. 40(18)).
961 LEC (art. 9).
962 LEC (art. 4).
963 LEC (art. 5a).
964 LEC (art. 11(6)).
965 LEC (art. 13, 18 – with the exception that those who have great difficulty learning, or learning impairments due to multiple handicaps, do not have to study languages (art. 13(5)).
966 LEC (art. 23, 45).
967 LEC (art. 18a, 166).
968 LEC (art. 28a).
969 LEC (art. 40, 42a).
970 LEC (art. 40a).
971 LEC (art. 41a).
972 LEC (art. 60).
973 LEC (art. 70, 71, 117, 129,
974 LEC (art. 165, 166a).
975 OECEANP (art. 1, 2); CEA (art. 5a). For more information on these riding schools, see: Stichting rijdende school (n.d.) www.rijdendeschool.nl/. Around 200 children are in these schools.

nomadic children, many of the legal protections do not apply, such as for example the requirements for safety in school[976] and the availability of a national dispute committee.[977] Although schools for nomadic children have to provide guidance for special needs students[978], there are no other regulations nor financial means for children with special needs, including children who are out of school due to illness and children who are behind in their mastery of the Dutch language.[979] The school authority can decide whether or not the child is accepted without having to refer to another school, and there is no connection to a *samenwerkingsverband* and, therefore, the Appropriate Education Act does not apply.[980]

The schools are riding with a circus and/or fair during March to October, and have a fixed position during November to February.[981] These schools provide primary education for children age 4 to maximum 14 years old[982], and they are subject to quality control by the national education inspectorate.[983] The schools are financed by the Ministry only if they can show that they will have at least 20 students, upon application.[984]

For group b, parents who are sailors can be exempted from the obligation to send their children to school while the children are between the ages of 3,5–7 years old and are sailing with them.[985] Their education is organized by the "school for sailing children", which has a fixed main location on shore and can potentially have other fixed locations on shore.[986] The education inspectorate can give permission to other nomadic children to be enrolled in the school for sailing children.[987]

The same conditions apply to the school for sailing children as those that apply to group a schools, except that there can be a difference in age of the children and the duration of the school term.

1969 Compulsory Education Act (CEA)

The 1969 Compulsory Education Act (CEA) lays out the obligations of parents and children to enroll children in school and attend, including the measures enforcement for the municipality and in particular the School Attendance

976 PEA (art. 4c); ONPPEA (art. A2).
977 PEA (art. 43); ONPPEA (art. A2).
978 PEA (art. 8); ONPPEA (art. A2).
979 PEA (art. 9, 9a, 9b, 40a, 4, 18a, 120, 168a, 180, 180a); ONPPEA (art. A2).
980 PEA (art. 14, 40(1), 40(2), 40b, 40(3-5), 58).
981 ONPPEA (art. B1).
982 ONPPEA (art. B2, B10).
983 ONPPEA (art. B5).
984 ONPPEA (art. B13, B16, B16b, B16g, B16l, B17, B18, B20-22).
985 CEA (art. 5a); ONPPEA (art. C2).
986 ONPPEA (art. C1). In practice, this school prepares "education packages" for parents to "homeschool" their children on board, yet children may also attend the school buildings (*ligplaatsonderwijs*). See: Stichting Landelijk Onderwijs aan Varende Kinderen (LVOK) https://www.lovk.nl/home/.
987 ONPPEA (art. C2(2)).

Officer (SAO). According to the CEA, the parental[988] obligation to enroll their child in a school begins on the first school day of the month when the child turns 5 years old[989], and ends either:

i. when the child has obtained a qualifying degree (*startkwalificatie*): namely, an MBO degree level 2–4, HAVO, VWO, HBO or WO diploma[990], and has followed either 12 full years of schooling[991], or is at the end of the schoolyear during which s/he has become 16 years old[992],
ii. when the child has obtained a certificate or diploma for practical education (*praktijkonderwijs*)[993],
iii. when the child has followed the "job market oriented" or "day-care" graduate profile of secondary special [needs] education[994],
iv. when the child has become 18 years old.[995]

The obligation to ensure school attendance, of all lessons, is solely the parents' responsibility for children between 5–12 years old[996], while it is shared between the parents and the child for ages 12 until the end of the enrollment obligation.[997] There is extra emphasis on the child's responsibility to attend school from ages 16–18.[998]

Parents can be exempted from these obligations, if:

a) the child is not fit to be accepted into a school or institution on physical or psychological grounds, based on a recent declaration to this purpose by a qualified doctor, pedagogue or psychologist[999],
b) parents object to the direction of the education in schools or institutions within reasonable distance from their home, provided that the child has not visited any of these schools in the previous schoolyear[1000],

988 In this discussion I will use the term "parent" for clarity, while in the law in fact it speaks of the "person who has authority over the child". For this reason, it is possible for a judge to give partial (or complete) authority over the child to a government actor and thereby overrule a parental decision for example as regards the child's education.
989 CEA (art. 3.1).
990 Ibid: art. 1, 4a(b).
991 Ibid: art. 3.1(a).
992 Ibid: art. 3.1(b).
993 Ibid: art. 4a(2).
994 Ibid: art. 4a(2).
995 Ibid: art. 4b.
996 Ibid: art. 2(1), 4.
997 Ibid: art. 2(1), 2(3), 4.
998 Ibid: art. 4c.
999 Ibid: art. 5(a), 7.
1000 Ibid: art. 5(b), 8.

c) the child is enrolled in a school in a foreign country and visits this school regularly[1001]
d) if the parents and child lead a nomadic life[1002],
e) in special circumstances, where it can be shown that the child enjoys sufficient education in a different way.[1003]

These types of exemptions can be given by the municipality upon application.[1004]

In addition, parents (and the child starting at age 12) can be exempted from the obligation to make sure that their child visits the school, if:

f) the school is closed or there is no education activity[1005],
g) visiting the school is forbidden by general, binding rules[1006],
h) the child has been temporary expelled as a measure of discipline[1007],
i) the child is hindered in her/his ability to visit school due to sickness, provided the parents inform the school leader within two days of the beginning of the sickness[1008],
j) the child is unable to visit the school due to obligations following from religious or philosophical beliefs, provided the parents inform the school leader within two days in advance[1009],
k) the family can go on holiday outside of school holidays only, due to the profession of one of the parents, provided the school leader has given permission to do so, and for a maximum of 10 days per schoolyear[1010],
l) the child is hindered from visiting the school or institution due to other serious circumstances, provided the school leader has given permission if it concerns absenteeism for less than 10 schooldays. In case of more absenteeism, the SAO has to give permission.[1011]

As regards enforcement, this is the job of the municipal SAO (*leerplicht-ambtenaar*)[1012], while the national education inspectorate (*inspectie van*

1001 Ibid: art. 5(c).
1002 Ibid: art. 5a.
1003 Ibid: art. 15. This seems to create a possibility for homeschooling, yet "special circumstances" is not defined further, nor is this article discussed in literature (see §5.2.3).
1004 Ibid: art. 6.
1005 Ibid: art. 11(a).
1006 Ibid: art. 11(b).
1007 Ibid: art. 11(c).
1008 Ibid: art. 11(d), 12. If the child does not live with the parents anymore, the child her/himself has to inform the school leader (art. 13b).
1009 Ibid: art. 11(e), 13. If the child does not live with the parents anymore, the child her/himself has to inform the school leader (art. 13b).
1010 Ibid: art. 11(f), 13a.
1011 Ibid: art. 11(g), 14.
1012 Ibid: art. 16.

het onderwijs) is charged with controlling the quality of education.[1013] The municipality has to check with their basic population registration whether all children who fall under the CEA are enrolled in a school (or exempted from this obligation)[1014], whereas school leaders have to report children who are absent without permission for at least 16 hours during four consecutive weeks, to the municipality and the Ministry of Education.[1015] The SAO opens an investigation and tries to motivate the people involved to adhere to their obligations. If they find that the parent, or the child of age 12 and older, is in violation of the CEA they can start legal proceedings. Parents can be sentenced to maximum one month in prison or a fine of maximum € 4,150. Children can be sentenced to community service (*taakstraf*) and a fine of maximum € 4,150 can also be imposed. After one violation by the parents which resulted in a conviction, in case of a second violation the case is transferred to child welfare services (*Kinderbescherming*).[1016] A school leader who violates the law in relation to reasons k) and l) mentioned above, who does not report absentees adequately, or who provides false information can receive a fine from the Ministry of Education of € 10,000 per violation, with a maximum of € 100,000 per school year.[1017]

2015 Civil Code Book 1: Law of Persons and Family Law

According to the Dutch civil code, parents have legal authority over the child, which includes a duty to care.[1018] A parent who does not act responsibly by providing education for their children can have her/his parental authority taken away by a judge.[1019] However, in these cases it has to be proven that there is an "immediate danger to the cognitive development of the child".[1020]

B. *Law for the community*

Rules created by the legislator, known by the subjects of the legal order.

Participants in the study referred relatively little to national law when discussing the child's right to education. As discussed under §5.2.6, participants were more likely to discuss their views on good/quality education rather than to reflect on the law.

1013 Ibid: art. 16a.
1014 Ibid: art. 19.
1015 Ibid: art. 21, 21a.
1016 Ibid: art. 22, 26.
1017 Ibid: art. 27.
1018 2015 Civil Code (art. 1:247).
1019 Ibid: art. 1:255.
1020 For an overview of relevant cases, see Zoontjens (2014).

The best-known law to participants is the Compulsory Education Act, in the sense that most adult participants seemed to be aware that parents were legally obliged to send their children to school and that there were legal consequences if they did not. Some children also argued that they had to go to school because of the state, although most felt this obligation coming from their parents rather than the state.

It is important to note that while, since 2014, according to state law schools who refuse the enrollment of a child in their school, or decide to unenroll a child, have to find another school for the child, none of the parents or children were aware of this law.

C. *Hidden law*

One potential hidden state law as regards the child's right to education is the "Miep Ziek" law (see §5.2.5: home-schooling).[1021] This is an unwritten hidden law, which in written form would state something like:

> in cases where the child is not able to attend school for a longer period, and/or there is no school able to provide appropriate education, the national education inspectorate may enter into a contract with the SAO, school and the parents, whereby the child is administrated as enrolled in the school, yet stays at home and receives home-schooling. The financial (state) compensation for this student, received by the school, will be used for the home education of the child, for which the school will be responsible.

This is a hidden law because, although the government has instigated this practice by the state institution of the national education inspector[1022], it is not a formal written law. Although it has been reported in the media[1023], it is not widely known to the Dutch people, nor is it clear which children exactly can apply for this procedure and how.[1024] Parents and children who are involved in these kinds of constructions are asked not to share this information.[1025] When an education lawyer tried to use the legal process to make this information public, under the Freedom of Information Act (*Wet Openbaarheid van Bestuur*), the

1021 See also NRC (2013a & 2013b); Tweede Kamer (2013).

1022 Ministry of Education, Culture and Science (2014).

1023 NRC (2013a & 2013b).

1024 Zoontjens, who is an expert in Dutch education law, argued (when we met to discuss this case study) that this is not a hidden law but simply the Dutch inspectorate filling in the formal legal norm stated in the PEA (art. 8(10)) and SEA (art. 6b), which state that "education will be organized in such a way that students who have to stay at home or have due to illness or who have to be admitted into a hospital, will receive sufficient education in an adequate manner". However, it is not at all clear that these "Miep Ziek" contracts apply only to children who have to stay at home due to their illness. In fact, I have encountered situations where this was not necessarily the case, and I have also encountered situations where children did have to stay home due to illness and could not get this type of contract.

1025 Slump (2014: 3).

government refused to share the contracts because this would harm the privacy of the parties involved. They were however willing to share a model contract.[1026]

5.3.5. MUNICIPALITY LEGAL ORDER

Municipalities in the Netherlands do not create law, but they are subordinate to the state legal order and, as such, are charged with applying state law and policy. However, the many municipalities do differ in how they apply state law and, in this respect, have quite some discretion.

Although there is therefore no "law" on the municipal level, it was clear from the case study that the application of the SAO differed greatly per municipality. The main differences which came to the fore in the case study were:

- In some municipalities it was much easier for parents to obtain a legal exemption from the obligation to send their children to school than in other municipalities.
- Municipalities were quite free in how to approach Roma children who were out of school. Some did not do anything at all, some organized special classes for Roma girls, some were strict on enforcement and would sometimes resort to taking parents to court if they did not send their children to school.
- There was a large variety in the flexibility and willingness of SAOs to be flexible and arrange solutions for children who were out of school. While some would either solve the case by taking no action, granting an exemption to the obligation to send a child to school, and/or resort to indictment of the parents, others would go to great lengths to find solutions together with the different actors involved.
- A new enforcement mechanism that was just started to be used as an experiment by municipalities in relation to Roma parents who refused to send children to school, was to issue a fine which would accumulate for every day that the child was not in school (a so-called municipal *last onder dwangsom*). The idea was that this measure, which was usually applied by municipalities to situations where civilians or corporations change things to the public infrastructure illegally (say, they build a shed without a permission)[1027], would have a quicker effect compared to a court case which in some cases could take a year or more.

Speaker at State-organized study day on Program Approach Exploitation Roma Children:
We also notice that the threshold is sometimes different [per municipality] when considering Roma. When a child with blue eyes and blond hairs is absent three times, SAO interferes. With Roma, you are happy if they are absent only three times.

1026 Ministry of Education, Culture and Science (2014).

1027 General Administrative Law Act (*Algemene Wet Bestuursrecht*) (afdeling 5.3.2); Gemeente Moerdijk (2011).

5.3.6. SCHOOL LEGAL ORDER

Individual schools often are legal orders, with their own rules and enforcement. As one SAO argued:

> In [internal] school affairs, school decides. [...] schools often have their own rules, their school rules. So, what you see is that for a child who is absent due to *luxeverzuim* (the family going on holiday outside of the school holidays), one school may say, OK your parents chose for you to be absent, you cannot retake the test. One time, a child in this manner had missed 4, 5 tests in one week [...] the only thing I can say is: go back to school and talk to the board. It really is a school affair. [...] I cannot say: school, you are not allowed to do that. In that sense, schools are small islands.

Each school usually publishes their internal school rules in written, formal documents.[1028]

Of the participants to the study, some children argued that the school decides the content of their education, but most seemed to situate the rules and enforcement in school on the level of the classroom legal order.

Parents, teachers and SAOs referred to school laws insofar as relevant to their case(s). They mentioned that the school decides the content of education, and that the school regulates the inclusion/exclusion of students in their school, especially when they have sufficient students. This means that they decide whether or not to enroll certain students, whether students should attend special education, whether students have to change classes and whether or not sick children receive education.

Interestingly, although according to national law the *samenwerkingsverband* has quite a significant role in these decisions, this was mentioned only by one participant.

5.3.7. CLASSROOM LEGAL ORDER

No reference was made to formal written laws of the classroom, which may not exist, so I can only discuss the law for the community.

In general, children who attend school, and who are home-schooled, argue that their teacher decides what they have to do in school. The most important classroom rule cited was that "you have to learn". If children do not show the expected behaviour, enforcement happens through often quite elaborate systems of punishment, which involve several steps of escalation (including warnings, the teacher getting angry, yellow and red cards, having your name recorded on the school board, being sent out of the classroom, the writing of a certain sentence

1028 See for example: De Rotonde (n.d.); De Meerwaarde (n.d.).

(such as "I should not speak while the teacher is speaking") a certain number of times). Most of the participants did not question this authority of the teacher, although they did sometimes argue that some punishments were too harsh or that a certain teacher was mean, screamed too much, etc. Two children argued that they generally disliked being told that they "must" do something and had trouble dealing with that in a classroom setting.

> *Interview 6, a boy of 9-year old who attends regular education.*
> Sometimes learning is very annoying. But then you do it anyway because the teacher tells you that you must. If you don't you will receive punishment, for example you have to sit in the hallway or stay inside during the break. I think it is actually logical that you get punished, because if you don't listen you are supposed to get punished.

5.3.8. HOUSEHOLD LEGAL ORDER

For most children, the household legal order (which only contained law for the community) seemed crucial in the protection/violation of their right to education. In most cases, parents decided whether or not the children were allowed to attend school. For those who were not attending school, parents decided whether the child received education at home or not. Parents also decide which type of education they find appropriate for the child, including whether or not they will receive special educational support, and which school the child will attend. It is also generally up to parents to decide whether or not to have their children tested for certain mental or physical disabilities. Whether or not the child is heard in these decisions, seems generally up to the discretion of the parents.

In general, the authority of the parents concerning the education of their children is quite strong, unquestioned by children, and questioned only to a limited degree by other authorities. Whenever schools or state authorities disagree with the parents, this can result in conflicts between these different authorities whereby parents insist on their authority over their child's education, including situations in which professionals are threatened by parents.

It is often in regard to these situations that children end up out of school, and their right to education is violated.

5.3.8 AUTONOMOUS CHILD

Some of the children decide themselves not to go to school anymore. They either go to the school building but skip most classes or stay at home. Of the 9 participants who indicated to have experienced this, 8 indicated that the reason for not wanting to go to school was that they did not feel safe and/or they did not feel at home or at ease in school. A feeling of unsafety was mostly caused by bullying.

In general, children in the Netherlands are not very autonomous with regard to their education. Adults of the different legal orders usually decide for them, and often children's opinions are not even heard nor taken seriously.

Interview 42, a 14-year old boy who is temporarily staying home from school and has autism.

A: Parents have power over you and school does too. For example, a teacher gives weak arguments about what you have to do. It's also very dependent on age. I have quite a few people [around me] who think they are better than [me] just because they are older. I have quite a few teachers who are quite dumb, they don't know what they are talking about and still everyone says they are right because they are older...I can object, and sometimes even if I am right people do not admit that I am right, because [I'm] younger. I don't like that, I don't like injustice.
Q: So, to be a child in that sense is some kind of a handicap?
A: Yes exactly. Just like for example having a black skin colour, being Moroccan, those things [...]
Q: Also, when you have autism?
A: Then certainly. Some people think that autism is that you are crazy and in a wheelchair. People do not exactly know what it is. That's hard to deal with.
Q: How do you notice that?
A: People have prejudices about autism. For example sometimes at school, if I don't go to school because I have to rest, or I come a few minutes late, I'm not really punished, there is no consequence for me and people think it is because I have autism [...] I prefer if there is no difference because [...] it's important to me that everyone is equal.
Q: So, if you stay at home for a day, they should call your parents and say: you have to send your child to school because it is subject to compulsory education?
A: Yes, actually, yes. And whether I agree or not, but I want to be given the chance to argue why I am or am not there. [...] I don't want to be made into an exception.

A few children on the other hand were quite autonomous in relation to their education. However, as discussed under §5.2.5, children out of school in the Netherlands – who are the focus of this case study – are mostly found in situations of a plurality of issues, for themselves in terms of mental/physical issues, as well as in the household. In these complicated circumstances, it seems like leaving the choice completely up to children as regards their education often harms the child right to education. For example, I encountered a case of an 11-year old boy whose parents told him he only had to learn things if he wanted to. Because he had a combination of Asperger Syndrome and atychiphobia (fear of failure), this resulted in the child not trying out new things and therefore learning very little.

5.4. CONCLUSION

For most children in the Netherlands, the child's right to education in practice seems to be well respected and most children in the Netherlands receive a high level of free education. Interestingly, this education is supposed to be aimed at growing up in a multicultural society, stimulating active citizenship and social integration, and for students to have knowledge of, and meet, different backgrounds and cultures of their peers.[1029] However, whenever a child, or the situation that the child grows up in, is different from "normal", this protection of the child's right to education starts showing serious cracks and issues, both in the formal state law as well as in practice.

One of these "not normal" situations relates to the religious/philosophical beliefs of the parents. As shown under §5.1.1, the relationship between education and religion has historically been the subject of much political debate. This still shows in both state legislation and policy, in the sense that in Dutch law and policy the religious/philosophical beliefs of the parents are deemed more important than the child's right to education (and the child's right to her/his own religious/philosophical beliefs). These parental beliefs are a legal reason for the state to exempt parents (and their children) from compulsory education, without protecting the child's right to education at all, both in state law and in practice. It is uncertain whether children whose parents have this exemption receive any education at all and, if they do, what the quality of this education is.[1030] In short, if as a child your parents have religious/philosophical objections against schools in your area, you do not have a right to education in the Netherlands. Children can also be refused by schools based on the religious/philosophical belief of the school that does not match the belief of the parent/child.[1031]

Another "not normal" situation concerns children with special needs due to physical or mental disabilities or illness. In these cases, parents can also be exempted from the obligation to send their child to school, which under state law is the end of the child's right to education.[1032] When these children do stay within the school education system, on the one hand, there are many measurements to provide them with extra support, while on the other hand they enjoy less legal protection compared to "regular" children. Since the 2014 Appropriate Education Act, schools can only refuse to enroll, or unenroll a student because they cannot give appropriate guidance, if they find another school in the area that can provide the appropriate education needed for the child. However, there are exceptions to this rule, namely if there is no place available for the child, or if the parents do not respect/support the foundation

---

1029 See §5.3.4: A: Formal written law.

1030 See §5.2.3: homeschooling.

1031 See §5.3.4: A: Formal written law.

1032 See §5.3.4: A: Formal written law.

of the school (again related to "religious/philosophical beliefs"). In cases where parents disagree with the school, when they are of the opinion that their child should not go to another school, parents can go through a complaint procedure. However, if the parents are considered wrong by all authorities involved, yet they still refuse to send their child to another school, the child often ends up at home (with or without legal exemption for the parent to the obligation to send the child to school). Although according to state law this should lead to enforcement by the state towards the parent – provided no exemption is granted – this does not always happen in practice, and the procedure can take a long time.

Children who attend cluster 1 or 2 special education or who are residing in a special institution enjoy less protection of their right to education under state law compared to children in regular education, in the sense that schools are allowed to unenroll these children without finding them a place in another school (the "Appropriate Education Act" does not apply). Children who are unable to attend school due to illness, are supposed to receive education from the school in which they are enrolled, unless the parents have obtained an exemption to compulsory education. In practice however, it seems that not many schools are aware of this legal obligation, nor is it enforced by the state and/or municipalities. Therefore, many sick children are effectively deprived of their right to education.

A third "not normal" situation concerns parents who do not want their children to attend school but want to home-school instead. Although this is not legal under Dutch law, parents seem to be successful at obtaining exemptions to compulsory education, which gives them the freedom to do whatever they want with the children in terms of education. In these cases, there is no guidance, no financial support and no quality or other control by the state. A related situation is when parents have a general distrust of state authority, society, and what they call "the system" and therefore do not want their children to attend school. While they may opt for home-schooling instead, they may not provide the child with any education at all. These parents are often able to obtain a legal exemption to compulsory education for their child, for example by using the religious/ philosophical beliefs pretext.[1033]

A fourth "not normal" situation concerns Roma children. Of all not-normal situations, the situation of Roma children constitutes the gravest violation of the child's right to education by the Dutch state. Although many measures and financial means have been implemented to create a comprehensive approach to the "Roma issue", the regular violation of the Roma child's right to education is the consequence of serious discrimination of this ethnical minority. When Roma

1033 Although you could argue that the distrust of the general social order and consequent dislike of schools in the area is a philosophical belief, Dutch judges have not excepted this as falling under parental philosophical belief (cases 16-427 189-09, 16/244340-10, 16-274251-11, 23-002874-15, 475451/10/2990. See overview cases: Hopman, M. (2016) "Rechtszaken en overige uitspraken over recht op onderwijs in Nederland" (*"Court cases and other judgments about the right to education in the Netherlands"*)).

children are out of school, some municipalities or schools do not do anything. Schools sometimes refuse to enroll Roma children, or unenroll them without providing an alternative school enrollment, for which there are no consequences. Communication between municipality and Roma families often occurs via written letters, while many of these parents are illiterate. Roma children who do attend school are overrepresented in special education and in general in lower levels of education. Sometimes they are put in special Roma school classes. There is no place for Roma culture and/or the Romanes language in Dutch education. Roma are not involved in creating policy for including Roma children in regular education. Education data is not disaggregated by ethnicity. All of these Dutch legal and policy measurements concerning Roma go against international and European laws and recommendations.

Lastly, a "not normal" group out of school children that has not been involved in the field research for this case study is the children of circus workers, fair workers (group a) and/or sailors (group b). It has to be noted that, according to Dutch state law, these children are exempted from compulsory education, either for 8 months per year (group a) or completely until the age of 7 (group b). Children in group a can receive education in riding schools during those 8 months. Yet education in these riding schools is subject to much less protection compared to regular schools. For example, the requirements for safety in the school do not apply, there are no regulations or financial means for children with special needs, and the Appropriate Education Act does not apply. In this sense, the right to education for these children is also violated by the Dutch state.

In general, the Dutch state leaves a lot of authority over children to parents, including an almost complete ultimate authority in relation to the child's education. In other words, almost complete autonomy is granted to the household legal order in this matter. The guiding principle seems to be the idea that children are the property of the parents, and that the state has no right to "go beyond the front door", as has been argued in political debates.[1034] Consequently, the state in many cases opts to not protect the child's right to education in case this goes against the wishes of the parents. To a lesser degree, the child's right to education is not protected when this goes against the wish of a school, for example if they do not want to enroll a Roma child or if they refuse the child based on her/his religious beliefs. In this sense, it seems that the Dutch state acts against international and European law, which both view the child as an individual rights bearer and consistently position the child's right to education above parental rights to decide about the child. Under international and European law, the Dutch state can and should interfere to protect the child's right to education, even when this goes against the wishes of the parents.[1035]

1034 See De Telegraaf (2014), NOS (2016).

1035 See §5.3.1 and §5.3.2.

5.5. UPDATE: THE CHILD'S RIGHT TO EDUCATION IN THE NETHERLANDS, MAY 2016- JULY 2020

What has happened regarding the child's right to education in the Netherlands since the data collection for this case study? This paragraph will discuss relevant legal and political developments between May 2016 and June 2020.[1036]

On the international level, there is no change in formal written law, nor does there seem to be much change in political perspective. While the Netherlands recommended to Czechia[1037] and Romania[1038] at the human rights council in Geneva to "step up efforts to improve the position of Roma people [...] for example in terms of ensuring access to education", there is no mention of Roma in their own reporting to the Human Rights Council.[1039]

For the upcoming evaluation cycle by the Committee on the Rights of the Child (the Dutch state report is due in September 2020) civil society organisations reported on:

- Excessive regional differences regarding quality of support and care for children, including their right to education[1040]
- The fact that in spite of the Appropriate Education Act, the number out of school children is not going down[1041]
- The relative high number of children with a disability who are out of school[1042], and the lack of inclusivity in regular schools for children with disabilities[1043]

While there was no mention of home-schooling nor of Roma in these reports, the Committee has invited the Dutch state to report on:

- Measures taken to eliminate disparities between municipalities regarding children's access to education[1044]
- The criteria for determining the exemption of children with disabilities from compulsory education on physical or psychological grounds[1045], measures

1036 Since no follow-up field research has been conducted, this paragraph will be based on literature study as well as the study of legal documents, political transcript and media articles.
1037 The Netherlands (2017).
1038 The Netherlands (2018).
1039 Human Rights Council (2017).
1040 De Kinderombudsman (2019: 2-3), see also §5.3.5.
1041 De Kinderombudsman (2019: 3); Kinderrechtencollectief (2019: 28).
1042 Netherlands Institute for Human Rights (2019: 13-14);
1043 Kinderrechtencollectief (2019: 28).
1044 UN Committee on the Rights of the Child (2019: paras. 12(a) under the heading of "non-discrimination", 25(a)).
1045 Ibid (2019: para. 20).

taken to prevent absenteeism from schools of children with disabilities, children with learning and behavioural difficulties and dropouts[1046]

- Data on children not attending or dropping out of school, including children being home-schooled and children exempted from compulsory education[1047]
- The implementation of the Appropriate Education Act, including the results achieved in reducing the number of children, including highly gifted and high-achieving students, who are out of school or who have received exemptions from compulsory education.[1048]
- Progress achieved in:
  - Reducing school dropout rates and supporting such children to be reinstated in the education system[1049]
  - Monitoring the quality of home-schooling to ensure that such children do not lag behind their peers in regular schools[1050]

On the European level, nothing relevant changed to the formal written law. There has been one relevant court case regarding home-schooling at the ECtHR: a case where German parents kept their children at home for the purpose of home-schooling and complained, when the state interfered, of a violation of their right to respect for private and family life.[1051] In this case, the court argued that:

> enforcement of compulsory school attendance, to prevent isolation of the applicants' children and ensure their integration into society, was a relevant reason for justifying the partial withdrawal of parental authority [by the German state]. It further finds that domestic authorities reasonably assumed – based on the information available to them – that children were endangered by the applicants not sending them to school and keeping them in a "symbiotic" family system.[1052]

Following this line of reasoning, it seems that the current Dutch law which allows for parents to be exempted from the obligation to send the children to school could possibly be against the EHRM, since in those cases children are isolated, not integrated into society and kept in a "symbiotic" family system. However, one could also argue that this ruling only indicates that under the ECHR a state would be justified to interfere in these kinds of situations, yet is not obliged to do so.

1046 Ibid (2019: para. 20(b)).
1047 Ibid (2019: paras. 48 (a-d)).
1048 Ibid (2019: para. 25).
1049 Ibid (2019: para. 25(b)).
1050 Ibid (2019: para. 25(c)).
1051 ECHR (art. 8); Wunderlich v. Germany (2019).
1052 Wunderlich v. Germany (2019: para. 51).

On the national level, it seems that it will be difficult for the Dutch state to answer the questions asked by the UN Committee on the Rights of the Child. Regarding the formal written law, the government still has not changed the national law to incorporate the child's right to education. Although they have been planning to change the compulsory education act since at least 2015, this has not yet happened either.[1053] The only minor relevant change made to the education law has been the law on "more space for new schools" (*Meer ruimte voor nieuwe scholen*), whereby it has become easier for a group of people (e.g. parents) to establish an independent school that receives government funding.[1054]

Parlementarian Peter Kwint (Socialist Party (SP)) proposed an amendment to the compulsory education act to go with the 2020 amendment whereby the possibility for parents to be exempted from the obligation to send their children to school based on their religious/philosophical convictions[1055] would be taken out. He argued that the new possibilities for parents to start schools which adhere to their religious or philosophical convictions leaves this option unnecessary.[1056] However, the minister of education advised against this amendment, arguing that this proposal exceeded the scope of this new law under discussion[1057], and a majority in parliament voted against the amendment.[1058]

It does seem like there is more interest/awareness on the political level for the child as an individual rights bearer, also in the field of education, as well as for the fact that children have participation rights. For example, in 2016 the Primary and Secondary education councils, the council of Dutch municipalities and the Dutch ministries of education, health and justice entered into an agreement (*Thuiszitterspact*), agreeing to follow the ambition that no child would be out of school in 2020 for longer than 3 months. Part of the approach was to give the child a central position, including involving the child in finding a solution where possible.[1059] Another example is that a "right to be heard" as well as a "right to learn" are regularly mentioned in the discussion on how the education law should be amended.[1060] In January 2020 the the Ministers of education, health and justice write in a letter on appropriate education and children out of school: "Listen to, and talk with, the child instead of about the child. We see that this

---

1053 The latest is that the Minster of education mentioned in a meeting in 2019 that he is working on an amendment to the national education law regarding homeschooling (Tweede Kamer (2019a)).

1054 2020 Law more space for new schools (*Wet meer ruimte voor nieuwe scholen).*

1055 CEA art 5(b); 8, see also §5.3.4 (A).

1056 Wet meer ruimte voor nieuwe scholen (2019) Nr. 16: Amandement van dhr. Kwint.

1057 Minister voor basis- en voortgezet onderwijs en media (2019).

1058 Tweede Kamer (2019b).

1059 PORaad et al. (2016: para. 3).

1060 See for example Tweede Kamer (2019c: 5-6); Dullaert (2019); LAKS (2019); Tweede Kamer (2020a: 5-6); Tweede Kamer (2020b).

happens too little and this is unacceptable".[1061] The minister of education has indicated on several occasions to want to translate this principle into new law, yet has still to realize a proposal.[1062] However, meanwhile, the number of children out of school in the Netherlands (counted according to the Dutch government definition of children out of school)[1063], is still increasing every year.[1064]

As parlementarian v. Meenen pointed out during the last political discussion on this topic: while the government has indicated to want to establish a right to learn for all children, nothing has happened yet. In his words: "I'm running out of patience, because in the meantime the number of children out of school is growing as well as the number of children that are excluded from compulsory education [...] I am asking the Minister again: why is it taking so long? Literally generations of children are lost."[1065]

Regarding the Roma, municipal, school, classroom and household legal order no update can be given, because no new qualitative studies have been published regarding these subjects to the best of my knowledge.

1061 Tweede Kamer (2020a: 5).

1062 See for example in 2019 when the minister of education indicated to be preparing a law that would arrange for an obligation for local authorities to determine which actor has deciding power in case of a conflict between different authorities regarding the best option for realizing the child's right to education (Tweede Kamer (2019c: 7-9). See §5.2.5 regarding the necessity of this law). See also Tweede Kamer (2020a and 2020b) for other promises of legal proposals related to children out of school.

1063 See §5.2.2 for a discussion about the (in)adequacy of this statistic.

1064 Tweede Kamer (2020).

1065 Tweede Kamer (2020b: 8-9).

CHAPTER 6

THE CHILD'S RIGHT TO EDUCATION IN THE CENTRAL AFRICAN REPUBLIC

Figure 10. A 14-year old girl, who is in the second class of high school (5ème) in a city in the Center-South of the CAR, shows her writing ability (name has been changed).

6.1. INTRODUCTION

The Central African Republic (CAR) is a true contender for the label of "worst country in the world". The country has been rated as having the lowest human development[1066], and as being both the poorest[1067] and the unhappiest country in the world.[1068] Regarding the child's right to education, the country has been ranked the worst country in terms of children's rights[1069], having the lowest

1066 United Nations Development Program (UNDP) (2016).

1067 See Gregson, J. (2017). Over 2015, the GNI per capita in CAR was $ 330, according to the World Bank (2017) "Central African Republic". Available at: http://data.worldbank.org/country/central-african-republic).

1068 Helliwel, J., Layard, R. & Sachs, J.D. (2017).

1069 KidsRights Foundation (2017).

opportunities for youth development[1070] and having the lowest education achievement in the world.[1071]

When I first arrived in the Central African Republic and started asking people about the CAR child's right to education, a common initial reaction would be: "In the CAR, the right to education does not exist." In a way, the question itself seemed almost ridiculous. In my view, there are three ways in which we can understand why people argue that the right to education does not exist in the CAR. First, there is a very large discrepancy between formal (international and national) law on the right to education and the reality in the CAR. Second, it is doubtful whether there are any laws and/or rights in the CAR at all. Third, even if there are rights, it is particularly doubtful if these apply to children.

To understand the situation in the CAR as regards the child's right to education, the chapter will start with explaining the empirical findings as regards the daily situation in the CAR with regard to education. This section will give a general impression of the situation, based on interviews, observations and literature (§6.2). Second, the question will be discussed what laws apply, with statutory law of different legal orders divided up into formal written law, law for the community and hidden law.[1072] To answer this question, the interviews will be analyzed for references to laws and/or legal orders, according to the criteria for law as indicated in chapters 1 and 3 (§6.3). Section 6.4 will present an analysis of law for children as concerns education in the CAR, which includes a literature review whereby the findings of this case study are placed in a broader context of law in the CAR (§6.4). Lastly, the chapter will end with an update of developments in the CAR since the data collection for this case study (2017) (§6.5).

6.1.2. METHODOLOGY

In line with the described methodology in chapter 4, in preparation for the field research, the following possible legal orders related to the case study were identified:

Legal order	**Legislator (sovereign)**	**Relevant legal community**
International legal order	United Nations	All residents of the CAR (including non-CAR nationality)
Continental legal order	African Union	All residents of the CAR (including non-CAR nationality)
State legal order	CAR government	All residents of the CAR (including non-CAR nationality)

1070 The Commonwealth (2016).

1071 United Nations Development Program (UNDP) (2016).

1072 See §1.4.

Legal order	Legislator (sovereign)	Relevant legal community
NGO national legal order	NGO / cluster education	All residents of the CAR (including non-CAR nationality)
Religious legal order (Christian or Muslim)[1073]	Religious leader(s)	All members of a certain religion in a particular area (village or larger area)
Municipality legal order	Local government (mayor)	All residents of the relevant municipality
Village legal order	Village chief	All residents of the relevant village
School legal order	Principal / board	Teachers, students of the school (and possibly their caretakers)
Classroom	Teacher	Students of the classroom
Family	Caretaker (Father / mother / older sibling / nanny / other family member / foster parent)	Children of the family

Based on this initial scheme, I spent 3 months in the CAR (divided over two periods in August-September and November-December 2016). During this period, I engaged in 87 qualitative interviews with the following participants:

Primary workplace / role	Child	Parent / tuteur	Teacher / school director	APE[1074]	NGO / UN employee	Education inspection	Politician	Religious leader[1075]	TOTAL
TOTAL	31	23	12	2	10	5	6	5	92[1076]

During these interviews, one question was posed as the central research question of the discussion, namely: "what is the meaning of the child's right to education in the CAR?" Although it was explained to participants that this question was really the only question that the researcher wanted to discuss, after several interviews per target group, certain themes kept coming up in discussion and after an initial number of interviews (about 6 or 7), a list was drafted per group

1073 According to data of the US government, 51% of CAR people are Protestants, 29% Roman Catholic, 10% Muslim, 4.5% other religious groups and 5.5% have no religious beliefs (see Bureau of Democracy, Human Rights and Labor (2014)).

1074 The "APE" is the *"assosciation des parents d'élèves"*. Normally, there is an APE for every school. Their responsibilities differ and are often unclear, ranging from collecting school fees, paying teachers, stimulating school attendance, taking care of the school property, to controlling the school, the teachers, etc.

1075 These include both Christian and Muslim religious leaders.

1076 The total here is 92, because of double roles that some people fulfill; one NGO director was a former education inspector and former teacher, one religious leader is also working for an NGO, etc.

of recurring themes, so that these themes were continuously brought up in all subsequent interviews (see attachment 1).

In addition to the formal interviews, data was supplemented by:

a) *Informal, recorded discussions*
I engaged in 51 informal conversations, which I recorded with the permission of the participant. These conversations were more spontaneous discussions about the subject of the research, which I used to test certain theories or to discuss specific subjects (such as the use of the *chicotte*[1077] or the role of corruption). These discussions were held with the following people:

Primary workplace / role	Child	Parent / tuteur	Teacher / School director	APE	NGO / UN employee	Education inspection	Politician	Religious leader	Lawyer	(non-political) Employee min edu / affaires sociales	Researchers	**Student**	TOTAL
TOTAL	14	4	9	1	7	1	3	8	1	3	4	2	57[1078]

b) *Observations*
I recorded 24 observations, including observations in 10 different classrooms. For an overview, see attachment 2.

c) *Questionnaire*
In cooperation with UNICEF, we sent out a questionnaire through the "Ureport" system.[1079] Through text messaging, 5 questions about personal experience with primary education in the CAR were answered by 2,984 young people, generally aged 12–35.[1080] The questions were:

1077 A wooden stick with rubber bands attached, used for corporal punishment. See figure 13.

1078 Again, among these people are people who fulfill double roles, when both these roles were of importance to the discussion; for example, three religious leaders were also teachers. The total amount of informal, recorded discussions is 51.

1079 Other than helping me by sending out the questions per text message, UNICEF CAR has not been involved in the research in any way and can therefore not be held accountable for any of its outcomes.

1080 Unfortunately, the Ureport does not provide completely clear data on the participants. Thus, what we can say that of all Ureporters (23,462) 1% is of age 0-14, 27% of age 15-19, 41% of age 20-24, 19% of age 25-30, 5% of age 31-34 and 7% is 35+. 66% is male, 34% is female (UNICEF (n.d.) "UReport République Centrafricaine". Available at: https://centrafrique.ureport.in/ureporters/.

Original	**Translation**
1. Mon école fondamentale est/était... 1) Une école privée 2) Une école publique 3) Je ne suis jamais allé à l'école	1. My primary school is/was... 1) a private school 2) a public school 3) I have never been to school
2. A l'école fondamentale je suis/j'étais chicoté... 1) Quelques fois 2) Chaque mois 3) Chaque semaine 4) Chaque jour 5) Jamais	2. In primary school I am/was hit with the *chicotte*... 1) a few times 2) every month 3) every week 4) every day 5) never
3. A l'école fondamentale je vois/j'ai vu quelqu'un dans ma classe être chicoté... 1) Quelques fois 2) Chaque mois 3) Chaque semaine 4) Chaque jour 5) Jamais	3. In primary school I see/saw someone in my class being hit with the *chicotte*... 1) a few times 2) every month 3) every week 4) every day 5) never
4. Pendant mon éducation, j'ai eu d'expérience avec la corruption dans la classe... 1) 1 fois 2) 2–5 fois 3) Souvent 4) Jamais 5) Jamais, mais j'ai entendu parler	4. During my education I have had experience with corruption in the classroom... 1) 1 time 2) 2–5 times 3) often 4) never 5) never, but I have heard about it
5. J'ai payé pour avoir une bonne note, par argent ou par des actions sexuelles... 1) 1 fois 2) Quelques fois 3) Souvent 4) Jamais	5. I have paid to get a good mark, by money or by sexual actions... 1) 1 time 2) a few times 3) often 4) never

6.2. THE CHILD'S RIGHT TO EDUCATION IN CAR: GENERAL FINDINGS

Before getting into the legal analysis of the CAR legal orders involved in the child's right to education in the CAR, I will first present the general research findings, starting with what "education" means in the CAR context (§6.2.1), followed by a brief analysis of access to education (§6.2.2) and of the quality of education (§6.2.3) This section is meant to give an overview of the daily reality of CAR children as regards education, before we look at the legal factors influencing the situation. All information in this section is based on research data from the field research for this case study, unless indicated otherwise in footnotes. Since the data for this case study relies heavily on the field research data, more so than in the two other cases in this thesis[1081], for every statement made, I have indicated specific interviews as sources.[1082]

6.2.1. EDUCATION FOR CHILDREN IN THE CAR

In the CAR, there are two places where the child can receive education: at home and in school. At home, family members teach children practical things related to the household (to cook, to clean) and/or to employment (to hunt, to cultivate, etc.). Social norms and customs are also taught at home.[1083] In school, the curriculum entails some practical skills (such as personal hygiene) but is mostly oriented towards the teaching of formal knowledge and skills (mostly literacy and calculus).[1084] School education is seen as very important by most *Centrafricains* (both adults and children).[1085] However, many children in the CAR only receive education at home or even no education at all.[1086] For the current chapter, in line with the children's rights article[1087], I will mainly focus on school education.

6.2.2. ACCESS TO EDUCATION

Although there is little data available, it is clear that many children in the CAR are not in school. According to 2010 survey data, 73% of the children between the ages of 6–11 attended primary education and 18% of the children between ages 12–18 attended secondary education.[1088] However, these data do not show how many children are in school, because in the CAR many children of ages 12–18 attend primary school. According to less detailed but more recent data of UNESCO, the number of out of school children steadily decreased from 331,029

1081 This is because there is no recent academic research on (the child's right to) education in the CAR, and the subject itself depends greatly on the daily experience of people involved (rather than formal written law, which plays a larger role in relation to the right to nationality). General literature on the CAR, insofar relevant, will be discussed under §6.4.2.

1082 For an overview of all interviews, see attachment 2.

1083 Interviews 8, 9, 10, 12, 15, 22, 23, 28, 35, 36, 39, 56, 60, 61, 64, 65, 83. See also Bah-Gayn de Gaulle, who defines education (which he is researching in a CAR context) as "the means to transfer [the cultural universe of habits, religious customs and morals that form the distinct feature of society] from one generation to the next" (1984: 11).

1084 Interviews 62, 74; observations 6, 9, 10, 13-16, 18-20, 22, 24.

1085 Interviews 1-3, 5, 8, 9, 12, 18-21, 30, 32, 35-37, 39, 40, 46, 47, 49, 50, 54, 56-58, 61, 66-70, 72, 73, 82, 83.

1086 Interviews 1, 2, 4-7, 10-12, 14-16, 21, 22, 24-29, 38, 42-45, 47-49, 51-54, 56, 57, 59, 60, 65, 70, 71, 80, 87, 93, 120, 121.

1087 CRC art. 28, 29.

1088 Institut Centrafricain des Statistiques et des Études Économiques et Sociales (ICASEES) (2012: 203-08).

in 2006 to 206,651 in 2012.[1089] However, since both reports apply to the situation before the latest armed conflict in 2013, data is not necessarily applicable to the current situation.

During my field research, it was clear that many children were not in school, for different reasons. The reasons participants mentioned are:

- Inability to afford school fees[1090]
- Armed conflict (not safe to go to school and/or the school is closed)[1091]
- General absence of (functioning) schools[1092]
- Children stay away from school to avoid getting hit by the teacher[1093]
- Low quality of education (in public schools)[1094]
- Having to do other things (work, household chores)[1095]
- Lack of motivation, not seeing the use of school[1096]

Often several of these reasons were combined – for example, because the family has trouble affording school fees and they see little effect of the education enjoyed by the child (because of its poor quality), the child starts working instead of going to school.

1089 See: UNESCO (n.d.) *Central African Republic.* Available at: http://uis.unesco.org/country/CF.

1090 Including inability to afford necessary school materials (books, notebooks, etc). Interviews 1, 4-7, 10, 12, 14-16, 21, 22, 24, 25, 27-29, 38, 42-45, 47-49, 51, 53, 54, 56, 57, 59, 60, 70, 71, 80, 81, 120, 121, 127, 128. See also: Banque Mondiale (2008: 44).

1091 Interviews 2, 4-6, 10-12, 14-16, 25, 26, 38, 52-54, 60, 87, 93. See also World Bank Group (2017:6-7); OCHA (2016d); Jesuit Refugee Service (2016) "Central African Republic: Living in the factory". Available at: http://en.jrs.net/news_detail?TN=NEWS-20161220074535; Human Rights Watch (2017).

1092 Interviews 10, 13, 16, 42, 43, 45, 53, 56. Even when there are school buildings, teachers might not show up to teach (interviews 1, 3, 5, 6, 7, 8, 11, 16, 18, 22, 35, 37, 46, 49, 50, 53, 60, 65, 69, 72, 79, 80, 84, 87; observation 22). According to the 2016 survey, among the 10 largest localities in each commune (whereby the CAR is divided up into 179 communes), 44% have a public primary school (Groupe de la Banque Mondiale (2017)). The lack of schools seems most urgent when considering secondary schools (ibid: 15-16).

1093 Interviews 36, 41, 60, 62, 65, 75, 81.

1094 Interviews 1, 4, 5, 10, 11, 14, 16, 26, 36, 37, 49, 57, 60, 61, 64, 65, 73, 74, 76, 82, 83, 85, 86, 97. This is in accordance with observations 6, 9, 10, 14, 15, 16, 18, 20, and 22.

1095 Interviews 4, 8, 10, 11, 14, 16, 18, 24, 28, 43, 45, 57, 64, 80, 82.

1096 Interviews: 1, 2, 4, 9, 22, 24, 36, 37, 88.

6.2.3. QUALITY OF EDUCATION

Figure 11. A girl shows proudly that she has learned to write "I go to school" in English (she said this sentence in Sango)

Most participants argued that the quality of education in the CAR, especially in public education, is very poor. They also argued that the quality of education has steeply diminished over the years.[1097] Although there is little data available, this observation seems to be confirmed by research on literacy in the CAR; according to UNESCO data, 64% of people between the ages of 15–24 were illiterate in 2015, which is a steep increase since 2000 (when it was 39%).[1098] Even though more and more children go to school[1099], the quality of education is diminishing.

Using the same dataset, it can be estimated (very) roughly that about 29% of children who attend primary school do not learn how to read and write.[1100] Of the 32 children that I interviewed, 23 children answered the question whether they could write a simple sentence such as "my name is…" (which they were asked to demonstrate).[1101] Most children in public school could not write a simple sentence, and all children in private school could.

1097 Interviews 1, 3, 4, 5, 7, 10, 11, 14, 16, 26, 36, 37, 49, 57, 60, 61, 64, 65, 73, 74, 76, 82, 83, 85, 86, 97. This is in accordance with with observations 6, 9, 10, 14-16, 18, 20, and 22. See also: UNESCO (2010): pp. 15-16.

1098 UNESCO (n.d.).

1099 Again, there is little data available. According to UNESCO, the number of out of school children steadily decreased from 331,029 in 2006 to 206,651 in 2012 (UNESCO n.d.).

1100 According to the dataset, about 36% of people of ages 15-24 in the CAR in 2015 know how to read and write. Assuming they learned this in school, and the 15-24-year olds were in school around 2006, when 65% of primary school aged children were enrolled in school, this amounts to 65%-36% = 29% who were in school but do nt know how to read and write.

1101 If simply asked, the children would often say that they could, whereas if asked to demonstrate, they sometimes changed their answer saying that they actually could not. Some children said they could write, but they wrote incomprehensible gibberish. The sample includes children in both primary and secondary education. Children who were in school < 1 year and those who were < 8 years old were excluded from the sample. The average age of the children in the sample is 13.1 years.

Public school		Private school	
Able to write	Unable to write	Able to write	Unable to write
4	12	7	0

There are many factors that can be found in CAR classrooms that influence the quality of education, of which the most important ones will be discussed below: (1) malnutrition, (2) availability and quality of educational material, (3) the position and quality of the teachers, (4) corporal punishment and (5) corruption in the classroom.

1. Malnutrition

In the CAR, a large part of the population suffers from malnutrition, mostly because the regular CAR diet lacks necessary vitamins and minerals.[1102] Almost 41% of children under 5 years old have stunted growth[1103] and CAR children eat 1.3 meals a day on average.[1104] Research has shown that stunting during infancy has a strong adverse effect on cognitive function in late childhood. These children perform significantly less well in school.[1105] Some participants mentioned children being hungry as a problem for education.[1106]

2. Availability and quality of educational material

A general lack of educational material, and specifically of qualitative material, has been indicated as limiting the quality of education in the CAR.[1107] First, many schools have a shortage of basic learning materials such as books, chalkboards, notebooks and pens, buildings, desks and chairs.[1108] Outside of schools there is also very little learning material. There are (almost) no books, no street signs, no flyers, no market signs, etc.[1109] Some children claimed that even though they were able to read and write before when they were in school, by

1102 According to research by the World Food Programme, 60% of CAR households have insufficient food consumption due to a too limited diet. In addition, many children are said to suffer from intestinal worm infections, which worsens malnutrition. See World Food Program (2015). See also World Food Program (2016. 25); Groupe de la Banque Mondiale (2017:30-39).

1103 World Health Organization (2016: 85).

1104 World Health Organization (2016: 28).

1105 See, among others: Berkman et. al. (2002); Mendez & Adair (1999) Africa Progress Panel (2012: 8).

1106 Interviews 36, 86, 87.

1107 Interviews 14, 29, 51, 53, 60, 65, 80, 81, 98. See also: République Centrafricaine Education Cluster (2015: 12); FMSI (2013).

1108 Interviews 4, 7, 14, 17, 25, 29, 47, 52, 53, 54, 57, 60, 70, 80, 85, 87, 93, 120, 121.

1109 See also Diambomba, M. (1998: 27-31).

now they had forgotten[1110], which makes sense when reading and writing skills cannot be put into practice.

Some of the learning material available in schools is of questionable quality. Most children use a small chalkboard and chalk during the reading/writing lessons[1111], which means that what is learned will be erased immediately after the exercise. Buildings, desks and chairs are of poor quality and shared by many, chalkboards are broken.[1112] Lastly, there are only two official schoolbooks available: the French and mathematics books called "Ma Semaine". Both books are in French (while the national language is Sango). The content of the mandatory material does not seem to match CAR reality. For example, the stories in the French book are often about things that do not exist in (most of) the CAR, such as how to take the train, the desert, tv programs (see image below).[1113]

Figure 12. examples in textbooks that very few CAR children are familiar with (such as tv programs, camels, trains).

3. *The position and quality of teachers*

In the CAR, the position of the teacher is generally quite precarious. There are three main categories of teachers:

1) Qualified teachers (*enseignant titulaires*): teachers who have been appointed by the state as qualified teachers and are therefore on the state's payroll. They

1110 Interviews 6, 12, 16, 21, 24, 37, 38.
1111 Observations 6, 13-16, 22.
1112 Observations 6, 13-16, 22.
1113 These pictures are taken from the French "Ma Semaine" books for classes CM1, CP and CE1.

have usually followed a certain education over a period of two years in one of the country's pedagogical centres.

2) Intern or volunteer teachers (*contractuelles* or *vacataires*): teachers who are enrolled in teachers' education and/or who have completed teachers' education, but for some reason they are not "integrated" by the state. In other words, they are not on the state payroll even though they are teaching in schools.
3) Teacher-parent (*maîtres-parents*): teachers who are recruited by the community among the local population. They sometimes get some teacher education through for example NGO programs. They are paid by parents, sometimes through the APE.

In public schools, none of these teachers are paid well and/or regularly. Not only are their salaries often below the international poverty line[1114], but more often they are not paid at all. For the teachers who are on the state payroll, it is extremely difficult to get their salaries unless they live close to a bank – and there are hardly any banks in the country. In addition, often there is no money available, when the state is out of cash.[1115] Payment by NGOs usually happens over a short period (an education project may last for 6 months) and the *maitres-parents* are dependent on the monthly contributions of parents and/or children.

Most of the teachers in the CAR of either category are generally said to have low teaching skills. They do not completely master the things that the students are supposed to learn (such as French spelling) and they lack necessary didactics and pedagogics.[1116] For example, during a typical reading lesson, the teacher will read out the words written on a chalkboard. A child is then asked to come and read the text to the rest of the class. Instead of truly reading the words, the children learn the text by heart and pretend to "read" it themselves by repeating the words of the teacher.

1114 Teachers paid by NGOs (*contractuelles* or *vacataires*) earn about $ 50 per month, and teachers who have a family are paid well below the international poverty line, which is set by the world bank at $1.90 per person per day. School directors/*enseignants titulaires* get paid almost $ 100 per month, *maitres-parents* are paid between $ 3.5- $ 35 per month.

1115 According to a survey in 2016, only 1 out of every 10 commune capitals has "some form of banking system, which is either a bank agency or a local credit mutual" (out of a total of 179 communes). See: Central African Republic (2017: 13). This means that teachers have to either send someone to the nearest city, a dangerous and expensive journey that takes several days to weeks, hoping that they come back with the salary, or they travel themselves, leaving the class without a teacher. Interviews 4, 6, 7, 11, 14, 16, 17 22, 23, 27, 36, 47, 48, 49, 51, 52, 54, 57, 60, 65, 70, 75, 78, 80, 84, 85, 86, 87, 96, 120, 121; observation 12. See also Groupe de la Banque Mondiale (2017): p. 12.

1116 Interviews 1, 3, 7, 16, 17, 20, 22, 27, 50-52, 57, 60, 61, 64, 65, 74, 80, 81, 84, 92; observations 6, 16, 18. See also: République Centrafricaine (2002): p. 18.

Figure 13. Observation 6: reading lesson in a classroom on an IDP site.

The correct spelling and grammar of this text would be: "Les criquets sont *de* retour du nord du Cameroun. *Ils* sont dans nos villes, dans nos cultures. *Ils* parcourent en volant des distances énormes *puis* ils se posent et dévorent presque *tout*: les fruits des arbres, le mil, les arachides, le riz, le plastique et même la laine sur le dos des moutons".

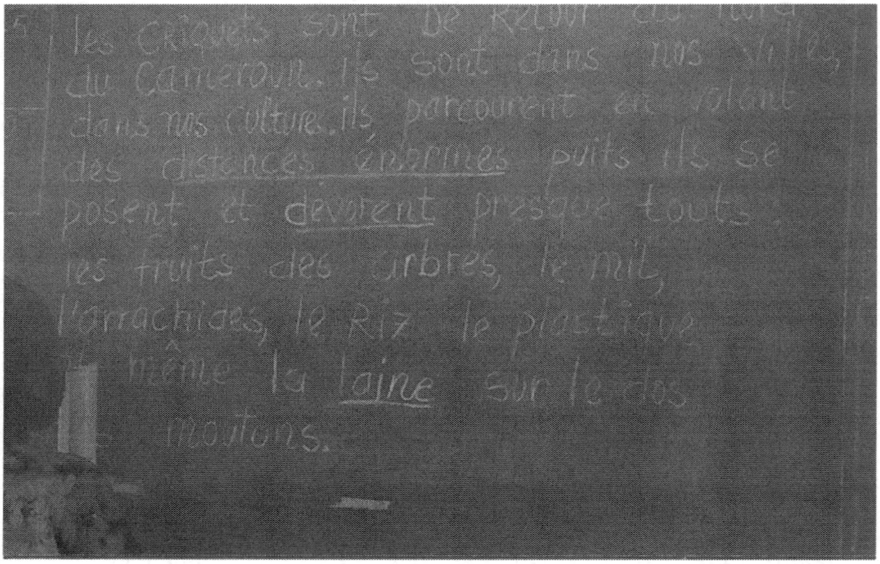

Both of these factors, the poor level of teacher education and the poor payment of teachers, heavily influence the quality of education in the CAR. It makes the profession of teaching especially unpopular. This in turn results in a great shortage of teachers and consequently overcrowded classrooms.[1117] Many schools in the CAR have so many students and so few teachers, that students to be divided up into classes of 200[1118], and the school day has to be divided up so that class A has lessons in the morning (7.00 – 11.00) and class B has lessons in the afternoon (11.00 – 15.00).[1119]

1117 Interviews 4, 7, 10, 14, 16, 17, 22. According to the *National Commune Monography Survey*, local authorities indicate that the main challenges for primary schools are the insufficient number of teachers or the lack of teacher qualifications. See: Groupe de la Banque Mondiale (2017): p. 15.

1118 Interviews 14, 27, 43, 51, 55, 60, 85, 92; observations 14, 15, 16, 22. Official numbers show a teacher:student ratio of about 1:80. However, it has to be noted that these numbers do not necessarily give an accurate picture, because this usually concerns an average per school (x amount of students / x amount of teachers), which is a calculation that does not take into account the fact that the lower classes (CI, CP) are much more crowded than the higher classes in primary school (CM1, CM2). During our observations, these higher classes usually contained about 30 students. In the lower classes, I have observed several classrooms with 150-200 students.

1119 Interviews 1, 7, 37, 78, 80; observation 16.

4. *Corporal punishment*

Although the use of punishment in relation to school or classroom rules will be discussed under §6.3, it is worth noting here that corporal punishment (here defined as any form of hurting the child physically meant as a punishment)[1120] is a common practice in the CAR classrooms.[1121]

The most common instrument used to inflict corporal punishment is the "*chicotte*", a wooden stick with rubber bands attached (see picture).[1122] The use of the *chicotte* is widespread; according to the UReport questionnaire, 88% of 2,984 participants have been hit with the *chicotte* in primary school, of which 11% endure it on a daily basis. In addition, 91% says they have seen their classmates getting hit with the *chicotte* in primary school, of which 36% witnessed this form of physical punishment on a daily basis.

Figure 14. A chicotte on a table in a CM1-CM2 classroom.

Total been hit	Total never been hit
88%	12%

[1120] Or, as used in academic writings: the use of physical force with the intention of causing a child to experience physical pain, for the purpose of correction or control of the child's behavior. This is an adapted definition of Straus's definition. See Straus (2000: 1110).

[1121] Interviews 1, 2, 3, 4, 5, 8, 16, 17, 19, 21, 24, 31, 32, 35, 36, 39, 40, 41, 45, 46, 48, 49, 50, 53, 54, 58, 59, 65, 78, 80, 81, 82, 92; observations 10, 14, 15, 16, 22, questionnaire.

[1122] Interviews 1, 2, 3, 4, 5, 8, 16, 17, 19, 21, 24, 31, 32, 35, 36, 39, 40, 41, 45, 46, 48, 49, 50, 53, 54, 58, 59, 65, 78, 80, 81, 82, 92; observations 10, 14, 15, 16, 22.

In primary school, I was hit with the chicotte...

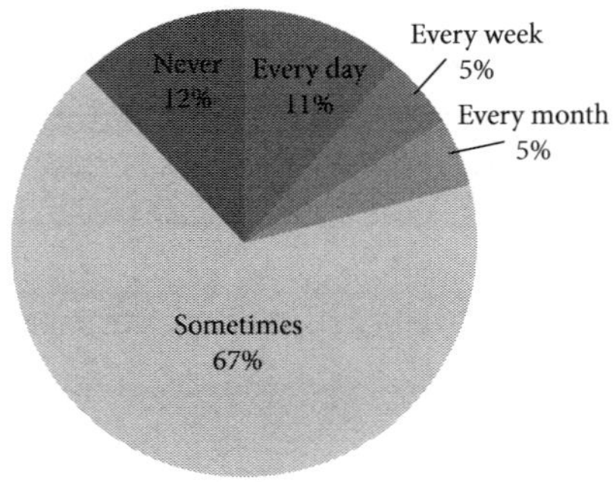

In primary school, I see/have seen someone in my class get hit with a chicotte...

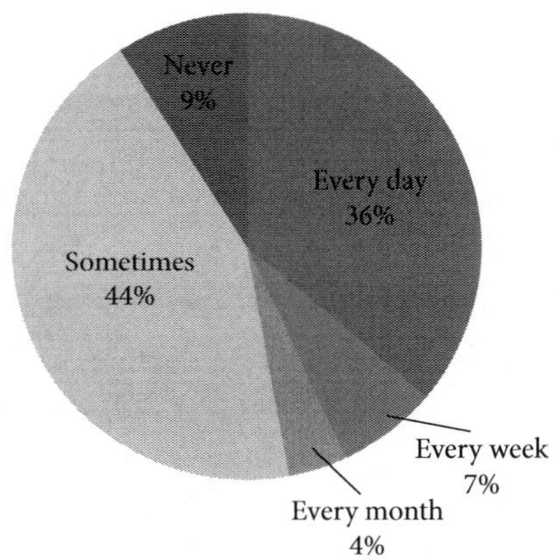

Total seen hit	Total never seen hit
91%	9%

Different ways of using the *chicotte* in the classroom are:

- The teacher hits the child on the body (mostly the buttocks, legs and/or back)[1123]
- The teacher hits the child on the body while the child is in a difficult position (for example upside-down against the wall)[1124]
- The teacher orders other children to (help to) hit their fellow student[1125]

Hitting with the *chicotte* often leads to scarring. When the teacher uses her/his full force, this form of punishment can have serious health consequences such

1123 Interviews 1, 8, 18, 35, 36, 41, 48, 58, 59, 78, 82.
1124 Interviews 35, 36, 41, 58.
1125 Interviews 8, 35, 36, 41, 78, 82.

as hyperventilation, blindness, infection, and even death.[1126] Other forms of corporal punishment include when children are hit with other objects such as sticks and/or rulers, when children are made to stand outside in the burning sun for a period of time and/or when children have to stand upside-down against the wall for a period of time.

Opinions on the use of the *chicotte* in school vary greatly among CAR people, both among children and among adults. These views were expressed by participants[1127]:

View	No. of adults	No. of children
1. The chicotte should not be used because it teaches violence to children	5	2
2. Corporal punishment should be used when children do not know the response to a question	2	6
3. Children should not be asked or even forced to hit each other	-	2
4. The chicotte should not be used because it does not work	4	3
5. The chicotte should not be used because children will not come back to school	5	2
6. The chicotte is necessary to install discipline (to make sure that children follow the rules)	5	6
7. The chicotte should be used to motivate the students	3	2
8. The chicotte should not be used because it is dangerous	5	7
Total votes against the use of the chicotte in the classroom	**66%**	**53%**

5. *Corruption in the classroom*[1128]

A great influence on the quality of education is the corruption found in CAR classrooms. Instead of learning for exams, students can pass exams by paying the teacher, either with money or sex.

In general, there are two forms of corruption found in CAR classrooms: corruption according to the marketplace model (marks for sale) and the extortion model (when the teacher forces the student to pay, as a condition for education).

1) Marketplace model:
   a. Marks for sale
   b. Exam answers for sale

1126 Interviews 1, 5, 16, 22, 35, 36, 40, 41, 45, 70, 72, 80. Several children reported their classmates having to go to the hospital; one child reported the death of a classmate. See also NewStatesman (2015) and Malone (2008).

1127 Interviews 1, 2, 3, 14, 16, 18, 21, 31, 36, 39, 40, 41, 43, 45, 46, 48-50, 51, 59, 60, 62, 64, 65, 75, 78, 80-82, 92, 107.

1128 Interviews 2, 3, 4, 5, 6, 10, 16, 18, 21, 22, 24, 25, 34, 35, 36, 40, 42, 43, 45, 46, 49, 53, 60, 64, 65, 73, 86-88.

2) Extortion model:
   a. No teaching unless the teacher gets paid
   b. If you do not pay, the teacher will make you fail the exam and you will have to repeat the class

The whole practice of corruption is quite tricky, because students can get in trouble for both engaging and not engaging in the practice. Sometimes teachers might be insulted if you offer them money, sometimes they might be glad, sometimes they might even punish you for not wanting to sleep with them. Both paying and not paying can get you in trouble. Seeing as there is a limit of the number of students who can continue to the next school year, sometimes this means that a student who did not pay will therefore fail the exams (even if they know the answers).

Interview 5. A 14-year old girl, who lives on an IDP site in a town in the center of the CAR. She is in class CM2 of a private school.

A: When you study, and you have your mark, if someone comes who gives money to take your mark, they will take your mark and give it to the one who has given money. So, in the end, if you have passed the exam, they take your mark and give it to someone else. And if you go and protest, it's a problem. When the student wants to reclaim his mark, and the parents of the student come too to claim the mark, it will turn into a fight. If that happens, it's over, the teacher will not favour you, he will not count on you anymore, he will abandon you in the classroom. Next, the teacher will create problems so that they can send you away from school and send you elsewhere.

Q: Did that happen to you?

A: Not to me, but it happened to my close friends. It made me very sad.

One of the consequences of paying with sexual activities, in addition to diminishing the value of school diplomas and exam results, is that it spreads HIV/AIDS.[1129] This is said to contribute to the shortage of teachers.[1130]

Seeing as corruption in education is a taboo subject, no certainty can be given about its occurrence. However, an indication may be given by the questionnaire we sent:

1129 UNAIDS estimates that in 2015 about 3.7% of CAR people between ages 15-49 is infected with HIV/AIDS (2017). According to the world bank / PNUD estimation in 2008, about 13% of all teachers have HIV/AIDS and about 70 teachers a year were dying from the disease. However, in 2008 the percentage of people between ages 15-49 that were infected was still 10.7%, so the number of infected teachers has probably gone down since then (Banque Mondiale (2008): p. 3).

1130 See The Guardian (2001).

Question 1 (1,157 participants): During my education, I have had experience with corruption in the classroom…

once	14%
2–5 times	51%
often	19%
never	15%
I have heard about it	2%

Question 2 (892 participants): I have paid to have a good mark, with money or with sexual activities…

once	11%
a few times	6%
often	4%
never	79%

84% of the participants had direct experience with corruption in the classroom. 21% admits to having paid themselves to get a good mark at least once, either by money or by sexual activities.[1131]

6.3. CAR LEGAL ORDERS AND THE CHILD'S RIGHT TO EDUCATION

The field research resulted in a somewhat different field of possible legal orders than originally expected (see §6.1.2). The following possible legal orders related to the child's right to education in the CAR will be discussed below, in terms of their formal written law (A), law for the community (B) and hidden law (C).[1132]

Field research resulted in the following overview of potentially relevant legal orders, as concerns the child's right to education in the CAR:

1131 However, as the participants are people who can read and write in French and who own a mobile phone (to be able to answer the questionnaire), they can be assumed to be the "better off" students – the real occurrence of corruption in classrooms might therefore in fact be higher. On the other hand, even if the first 3 questions of this questionnaire were specifically about primary education, the connotation of "during my education" includes all levels of education and thus goes a little beyond the scope of this research, which focuses on primary and secondary education.

1132 See chapter 1.

Legal order	Legislator (sovereign)	Relevant legal community
International	United Nations, African Union, International donors	All residents of the CAR (including non-CAR nationality), in particular NGOs and CAR government
National	CAR government, Education cluster, NGOs operating on a national level	All residents of the CAR (including non-CAR nationality). In particular teachers, parents, students.
Religious	Religious leader(s)	All members of a certain religion in a particular area (village or larger area)
Local	Local government (mayor or village chief)	All residents of the relevant municipality
School	School director, APE	Teachers, students of the school (and possibly their caretakers)
Classroom	Teacher	Students of the classroom
Household	Caretaker (father / mother / older sibling / *tuteur* / other family member)	Children within the household
Autonomous child	Child	Child

6.3.1. THE INTERNATIONAL AND REGIONAL LEGAL ORDER

A. *Formal written law*

The Central African Republic is a party to the following international and regional legal instruments:

Treaty	Status	Year	Relevant articles
Universal Declaration of Human Rights (UDHR) (1948)	–	1960	5, 26
International Convention on Economic, Social and Cultural Rights (ICESCR) (1966)	Accession	1981	13
African (Banjul) Charter on Human and Peoples' Rights	Ratified	1986	4, 5, 17(1), 20, 23(1), 28
Convention on the Rights of the Child	Ratified	1992	6, 19, 28, 29, 30, 32
United Nations Convention against Corruption (2003)	Ratified	2006	5
African Union Convention for the Protection and Assistance of Internally Displaced Persons in Africa (Kampala Convention)	Ratified	2010	9.2
Convention against Torture and Other Cruel, Inhuman or Degrading Treatment (1984)	Accession	2016	1, 2

By signing these documents, the CAR government has promised to:

- Grant every CAR child the right to education[1133], including internally displaced children on sites (IDP sites)[1134]
- Provide access to primary education for all[1135]
- Make all public education free of charge[1136]
- Make primary education compulsory to all[1137] and take measures to encourage regular attendance and reduce drop-out rates[1138]
- Develop secondary education and make it accessible to all children[1139]
- Make sure that no one shall be treated cruelly or in a degrading manner (including punishment)[1140]
- Direct education to the full development of the person, in a spirit of understanding, tolerance and friendship and peace[1141]
- Direct education to the development of respect for the child's own cultural identity, its language and (national) values[1142]
- Actively prevent corruption[1143]

According to the CAR government, in their 2011 report to the UNCRC[1144], "in the hierarchy of norms, international treaties are in second place, just after the Constitution and before domestic legislation" (para. 19)).

Reporting to the UN Committee on the Rights of the Child

In 2011, the CAR government submitted their second periodic report to the Committee on the Rights of the Child.[1145] In the report, they write: "the Central African Republic offers greater opportunities to children, whose situation has improved over the past decade in the areas of health, education and

1133 1981 African Charter on Human and People's Rights (Banjul Charter) (art. 17); 1966 International Covenant on Economic, Social and Cultural Rights (ICESCR) (art. 13); 1989 Convention on the Rights of the Child (CRC) (art. 28-29).
1134 2009 African Union Convention for the Protection and Assistance of Internally Displaced Persons in Africa (Kampala Convention) (art. 9.2(b)).
1135 CRC (art. 28.1(a)).
1136 ICESCR (art. 13.1); 1948 Universal Declaration of Human Rights (UDHR) (art. 26(1)).
1137 UDHR (art. 26 (1)); CRC (art. 28.1(a)).
1138 CRC (art. 28.1(e)).
1139 CRC (art. 28.1(b)).
1140 Banjul Charter (art. 5); 1984 Convention against Torture and Other Cruel, Inhuman or Degrading Treatment or Punishment (Convention against Torture) (art. 1,2); CRC (art. 19.1, 28.2); UDHR (art. 5).
1141 UDHR (art. 26(2)); CRC (art. 29.1(a-d)).
1142 CRC (art. 29(c)).
1143 2005 United Nation Convention against Corruption (UNCAC) (art. 5).
1144 Committee on the Rights of the Child (2016a).
1145 Ibid.

protection".[1146] "the overall objective [CAR] has set itself is to create conditions that enable Central African children to enjoy equal opportunities to develop fully as they start out in life".[1147] To this end, through legal reform, "[t]he State guarantees children and adults access to education, culture and vocational training, while parents have an obligation to provide for the education and instruction of their children up to at least the age of 16. Education is free of charge in public schools for all levels of education".[1148]

Specifically, on the subject of education[1149], the government writes that their target is for all children to receive a full education by 2015, which will be indicated by the net school enrollment rate, the school completion rate and the literacy rate.[1150] To achieve this goal, the only measurement taken is the publication of school fees in public schools, in an Order of the Ministry of Education, which sets the school fee for primary education at 600 CFA and for secondary education at 1,500 CFA.[1151]

In 2016, the Committee issued a List of Issues, asking for additional, updated information on measurements taken to:

- eliminate all forms of violence against children, including sexual abuse and corporal punishment[1152]
- guarantee free and universal education[1153]
- prevent attacks on schools and their use by armed forces[1154]

In addition, the Committee asked for budget information over the past three years in the education sector[1155], the number of cases of abuse and violence against children[1156], the number of investigations into alleged cases of sexual violence[1157] and percentages of school enrollments in primary and secondary schools.[1158]

In its reply in 2016, the CAR government wrote that, in general, they have established several projects to inform the people about the harmful effects and consequences of violence against children, plus a joint rapid response

1146 Ibid (para. 5).
1147 Ibid (para. 8).
1148 Ibid (para. 14).
1149 Ibid (section VII).
1150 Ibid (para. 196).
1151 Ibid (para. 218).
1152 Committee on the Rights of the Child (2016b (para. 4).
1153 Ibid (para. 6).
1154 Ibid (para. 6).
1155 Ibid (para. 14).
1156 Ibid (para. 15b).
1157 Ibid (para. 15c).
1158 Ibid (para. 17).

and enforcement unit to deal with cases of sexual violence against women and children.[1159] On the subject of education, the following measures have been taken:

- the minister of education has issued memorandums with the orders to exempt all final-year primary school people from IDP and refugee camps from the payment of examination fees, and they are restoring education after the crisis[1160]
- several administrative and political measurements are taken to prevent attacks on schools[1161]
- during the school year 2015–2016, 1999 temporary learning and child protection spaces were established at 32 refugee/IDP sites, which provided educational activities in which almost 30,000 children participated. Training was provided to 356 parent-teachers[1162]

In 2017, the Committee issued its concluding observations.[1163] They write that the CAR should adopt its domestic legislation, among others by explicitly prohibiting corporal punishment in all settings.[1164] They urge the CAR government to take measures to: provide free primary education to all children[1165], to increase enrollment and decrease dropout rate[1166], invest in school infrastructure, improve number of teachers and school staff, train teachers including *maîtres-parents*[1167] and to continue to cooperate with UNICEF, UNESCO and others to achieve these goals.[1168]

B. *Law for the community*

When discussing international law for the community as regards children's education in CAR, it is hard to distinguish between written and unwritten law for the community. This is mostly because it is unclear if the community has a clear idea what the written law says in this case. None of the participants referred directly to any of the conventions, and many referred to either "children's rights" or "human rights".[1169] Some participants (both adults and children) did not answer when asked about rights or started talking about something else.

1159 Committee on the Rights of the Child (2016c: para. 33).
1160 Ibid (para. 1.7a).
1161 Ibid (para. 1.7b).
1162 Ibid (para. 1.7d). Under para. 1.9 different data on the same subject are provided, without mentioning the applicable time period.
1163 Committee on the Rights of the Child (2017).
1164 Ibid (paras. 7, 36-39).
1165 Ibid (para. 61a).
1166 Ibid (para. 61b).
1167 Ibid (para. 61c).
1168 Ibid (para. 61e).
1169 Interviews 4, 8-10, 12, 14-21, 24, 28, 29, 32, 34, 37, 39, 40, 42, 43, 45, 47-49, 51, 55, 57, 59-62, 64, 65, 75, 80-83, 86, 87, 92.

In general, of the participants who did engage in conversation on the topic, the idea that children have rights seemed to be contested. It was sometimes perceived as something imposed by Western powers and surely as something that did not mean much in a CAR context. Many seemed ambivalent about its status as proper law. Of all the participants who had heard of children's or human rights, only 24% seemed to understand it as a proper legal entitlement, even if it is permanently violated in the CAR context.

> *Interview nr. 62. An employee of the Ministry of Education.*
> The first question is, do children have rights? In the context of the CAR. I personally think that we have to relativize that concept, compared to the Western world. Traditionally, in the CAR context, we think that the child does not have rights, only duties. S/he has to go to the field, to fish, to help the adults with the work. When s/he will attain a certain age, s/he will have rights. Today, there are changes. The youth asks for their rights. They are influenced by European ideas, human rights et cetera. Whether that is an advantage or an inconvenience, we still have to analyse.

B1. Written law for the community

In general, almost all people in the CAR have heard of the child's right to education; even if its exact meaning is not always clear (see also below). International staff does not really claim any position for children's rights, arguing that they mean little in the CAR context.[1170]

> *Interview 11. An employee of an NGO, working on the national level.*
> I think the right to education doesn't really exist here [...] education is seen as a privilege almost. A lot of the needs that arrive are life-saving, and like health, wash and sanitation, food is always prioritized in situations of crisis. And especially here in the CAR with the amount of displacements. But even in the more rural areas I think the right to education is overlooked and other tasks are prioritized when it comes to children [...] if you are put in crisis, education is completely overlooked.

Of the 24 Central African participants who had some idea of what a right to education means (mostly adults), 14 argue that the child's right to education does not exist in the CAR.[1171] As this 13-year old child explains, what does it mean to have a right to education if you cannot register for school because you cannot afford the school fees? Do only the children who go to school have this right?

> *Interview 24. A 13-year old girl, who has been out of school since age 11. She lives in a town in the South-East.*
>
> A: The children have the right to go to school. But for us, it is difficult. There are some children that have that right, but for us it is difficult because they do not

[1170] Interviews 11, 16, 17, 61, 84.

[1171] Interviews 4, 24, 42, 43, 45, 47, 51, 52, 57, 60, 62, 86, 87, 92.

prepare the return to school, the clothes, the notebooks. To go to school, you have to be clean, you have to…

Q: Who is it that does not prepare?
A: Our parents. Our family.
Q: Why do they not do so?
A: I don't know […] my parents did not want to support me and I did not have the possibility either to get money to buy school supplies.
Q: And after, what do you do?
A: I do nothing […] I think I will try to return to school this year.
Q: How?
A: I pray to God and maybe if he can help me to give me some money that could help me to buy the notebooks and pens to go to school.

Three others that mentioned international law or rights seem to think of it more as a foreign power.[1172] They argue that they are not allowed to engage in corporal punishment "because of human rights", and, since it is something illegal in the eyes of a foreign power, therefore they lie saying that they do not engage in this kind of behavior when asked about the practice by a Caucasian, western researcher[1173]:

Interview 80. A school director in a town in Southeastern CAR.

Q [after reading school rules]: For example, here it says that all corporal punishment is forbidden. So, imagine there is a teacher who uses it…?
A: There, we have forbidden it. Sometimes we intervene, and we pull the ears.
Q: You pull the ears of the teachers?
A: Yes. If that doesn't work, we say no, the corporal punishment is forbidden. […]
Q: But in that case, I see quite a few chicottes here, no?
A: Where??!
Q [points at the desk next to her]: There for example, just next to us?
A: No, that is for last year […]
Q: But there was one too in the classroom where I was [just before the interview]
A: OK, that's there for…we don't use it.
Q: OK. I have a little trouble believing that [laughs and the director starts laughing too. MH explains anonymity again]
A: But it is forbidden, forbidden!
Q: By whom?
A: They talk about, about what…human rights.
Q: So, it is forbidden by human rights?
A: Yes.
Q: But you are not in agreement with that? Why do you think it is forbidden by human rights and you use it anyway?
A: Yes, because it is forbidden because one time, there was a case in Bangui [of a teacher who hit the child so hard s/he died]. That's why it is forbidden now. […]

1172 Interviews 75, 80, 92.
1173 This occurred more in relation to national law, see §6.3.2.

Q: But why do you still use it?
A: We use it? But yes, sometimes you can use it, the chicotte does also settle certain things. Sometimes they arrive too late. We start at 7, but they start arriving at 7.40 ... tomorrow they will repeat it. You have to [scare] them a little. S/he will say: tomorrow I arrive on time. [The teacher] said he will hit me, so tomorrow I will come on time. [...] who comes late, we give them 2 strikes. In that way, it influences the others too, it is already time, I have to run!
Q: And do you tell [the students] also to hit each other?
A: No, it is only the teacher. We cannot tell one to hit the other. That, it's forbidden.

B2. Unwritten law for the community

There is no unwritten international law for the community; the public international law is written by definition (in conventions). Yet it is worth noting that many children have an idea about what their right to education means – an idea that influences their behavior – while they do not know that this law has not actually been created by a sovereign. It seems to be a false belief in a non-existent international law. However, as the source of this (idea of a) right was not clear, it could also refer to a local understanding of the child's right to education resulting from a local legislator.

10 of the 16 children who claimed to know about the child's right to education gave it a different meaning.[1174] They all emphasized their individual responsibility and added tasks they had to perform in relation to the family.

Interview 8. An 11-year old girl who is in class CP2 of a public school. She lives on an IDP site in a town in the centre of the CAR.
For me, the child's right to education in the CAR, tells us not to move around randomly, so that the parents are not bothered a lot, when they have to come and find us. The right tells me to go to school, to study, so that I can support my parents [...] the right allows me to eat and respect the parents of my parents. When they send me to do a job, I have to do it and return, without staying on the road and amusing myself.

C. Hidden law

As far as I have been able to find, there is no hidden international law in the CAR as regards education. However, it may be worth noting that, even if it is not law-based, the international community, and international donors in particular, do decide on the CAR policy on education to a large degree. Seeing as the CAR Ministry of Education hardly has any budget – which is not even enough to pay its employees (teachers) –[1175] international donors have quite

1174 Interviews 8, 9, 10, 12, 19-21, 32, 37, 59.
1175 Interviews 7, 11, 22, 27, 52, 53, 61, 62, 74. Several participants remarked that for 2016 the national budget was only 4% of the total government budget.

some decision power concerning education policy. A special role is reserved here for the former colonial power France. There is a "*conseiller technique*", an advisor to the Minister of Education who works at the Ministry of Education and who is paid by the French government (and follows instructions from Paris). Although it was clear that this position is not exactly ceremonial, investigating the precise political power that comes with it would require more time and resources than were available to me at this moment.

> *Interview 62. An employee of the Ministry of Education.*
> Primary and early secondary education (fondamental 1 [F1] and fondamental 2 [F2])[1176] has always been the political interest that has received the help of the donors. I am against that approach. We cannot favour education in F1 and F2 and leave out the technical and superior education. It is those politics…all the donors, UNICEF, the French embassy etc., they are all focussed on F1 and F2. Technical education, professional education, university…nothing. Here are the consequences.

6.3.2. THE NATIONAL LEGAL ORDER

A. *Formal written law*

CAR national law has several articles relevant to the child's right to education.

First of all, the relevant articles of the 2015 Constitution state that[1177]:

- Everyone has the right to corporal integrity. No person shall be subjected to torture, rape, abuse or cruel, inhuman, degrading or humiliating treatment[1178]
- The state and other public collectivities have the duty to create preconditions and public institutions that guarantee the education of children[1179]
- Everyone has the right to access sources of knowledge. The state guarantees each citizen acces to instruction, to culture and to professional training. Education of youth shall be provided by public or private institutions[1180]
- Parents are obliged to provide for the education of their children until at least the age of 16[1181]
- The State and other public authorities have an obligation to establish and ensure the proper functioning of public institutions for the education of young people. Education is free in public schools for the various levels of education

1176 Fondamental 1 stands for primary school, which is 6 years of schooling. Fondamental 2 stands for early secondary school, which is the first 4 years of high school.

1177 2015 *Constitution de la République Centrafricaine* (hereafter 2015 Constitution).

1178 Ibid (art. 3).

1179 Ibid (art. 6).

1180 Ibid (art. 7).

1181 Ibid (art. 7).

The 2010 penal law[1182] provides several articles prohibiting violence against children, either in the form of beating and/or sexual abuse:

- Anyone who has intentionally injured or beaten a child under the age of 15 years will be punished with imprisonment of one to five years and a fine of 100,002 to 600,000 francs[1183]
- Any indecent assault which is consummated or attempted, without violence, on the person of a child shall be punished with imprisonment of one month and one day to five years, and a fine of 100,002 to 800,000 francs. The term of imprisonment shall be two to five years if the female child, who is eighteen years of age and is not emancipated by marriage, is a pupil of a school and the perpetrator of the act is in service in this establishment[1184]
- Every indecent assault consummated or attempted on the child under the age of 15 is considered rape. If the perpetrators have authority over the child, if they are teachers, or of a school where the child is a student, the penalty will be increased by one degree[1185]
- Any erotic attraction of an adult to a child constitutes the offense of pedophilia. Anyone who has been guilty of pedophilia shall be punished with imprisonment of two to five years and a fine of 100,002 to 2,000,000 francs. In the case of a second offense, the penalty shall be doubled, and the offender shall be subject to the additional penalty provided for in Article 21 paragraph 3 of this Code[1186]
- Submitting a person to torture, cruel, inhuman, or degrading treatment is punished with forced labor.[1187] This offense is punishable by hard labor in perpituity when commited: against a minor under the age of 18 years; by a person who is a depositary of public authority or entrusted with a public service mission in the course of or in connection with the performance of his duties or his mission; with the use of force. The penalty incurred is twenty years of hard labor when the offense is committed against a minor under the age of eighteen years by any other person having authority over the minor[1188]

The 1997 law on education[1189]states that:

- Education is a national priority; every citizen has a right to education. Access to instruction, to culture and to professional formation is guaranteed to children and adults[1190]

1182 *Loi no. 10.001 portant Code pénal centrafricain* (hereafter Penal Code).
1183 Ibid (art. 74).
1184 Ibid (art. 86).
1185 Ibid (art. 87).
1186 Ibid (art. 110).
1187 Ibid (art. 118).
1188 Ibid (art. 119).
1189 *Loi no. 97.014 portant orientation de l'éducation* (hereafter 1997 education law).
1190 Ibid (art. 1).

- The CAR has to develop structures for non-formal education[1191], of which literacy is a part[1192]
- Going to school is compulsory from age 6 to age 15[1193]
- Teaching in primary school (F1) has as its mission to guarantee a basic general and practical education to all children. It must be integrated into the environment. Teaching in F1 has as its objectives, the mastering of ... language, literature, writing, calculation. It has to develop in the child its intellectual, manual and physical capacities, a business spirit. It has to transfer moral and civic values, to favor the education in family life and to orient the child towards the working world[1194]
- The classes in primary school will be called première année fondamentale – cinquième année fondamentale, instead of course préparatoires (CP) – cours moyen 2 (CM2)[1195]
- Lower high school (F2) is also oriented towards inserting the children in an active and working life[1196]
- The classes in lower high school (F2) will be called 6è année fondamentale – 9è année fondamentale instead of 6ème-3ème[1197]
- Sango and French are the two languages of instruction. The teaching of, and in, Sango is introduced into the curriculum of primary school in the year 2000[1198]
- The right to education includes for students the obligation to accomplishe the tasks inherent to their studies, to attend and to respect the school rules, to consider the treatment of furtniture and buildings, which as national collective property have to be protected[1199]
- Teaching staff has to: help students with their work, to follow their studies, in particular through the obligatory school booklet; participate in training; be members of the school board[1200]
- Every village has a local community which speaks about the educational activities in the village (APE). They can recruit a teacher called "*maître-parent*"[1201]
- The APEs, territorial-, communal-, and village collectivities, as well as the local representatives of administrations have to participate in pre- and post-school activities[1202]

1191 Ibid (art. 5).
1192 Ibid (art. 36).
1193 Ibid (art. 6).
1194 Ibid (art. 12).
1195 Ibid (art. 13).
1196 Ibid (art. 16).
1197 Ibid (art. 18).
1198 Ibid (art. 42).
1199 Ibid (art. 50).
1200 Ibid (art. 51).
1201 Ibid (art. 64).
1202 Ibid (art. 75).

Lastly, the Ministry of Education published a decree (*note circulaire*) in 2016[1203], indicating that enrollment for public primary schools should cost 1,800 CFA[1204] per year for the first child and 800 CFA[1205] per year for every following child. This sum consists of:

- 250 CFA MASCA[1206]
- 250 CFA schoolbooks
- 300 CFA sports
- 1000 CFA APE (which is used to pay *maitres-parents* and other school necessities, such as school building maintenance etc.)

For the student in CM2 (the last class of high school) this goes up to 2,450 CFA to include a school identity[1207], high school preparation and CEF1.[1208] Secondary school (F2) officially costs 2,500 CFA[1209] per child per year.

B. *Law for the community*

To understand CAR national law for the community and CAR national hidden law, considering the CAR child's right to education, it is important to understand who decides what about education on a national level. These decisions include both policy and legal decisions. Generally, political relations on the national level and their connection to the local level can be represented as follows:

1203 2016 Decision on the determination of registration fees for Basic 1, 2, General Secondary education and Technical education and withdrawal of diplomas (*Decision: Portant Fixation des Frais d'Inscription au Fondamental 1, 2, Secondaire General et Technique et du Retrait des Diplomes*).

1204 Almost 3 US dollars.

1205 $ 1.30.

1206 This is a mandatory insurance that every student in the CAR has to pay together with their school fees. The MASCA costs 250 CFA per year. The objective of the insurance is to ensure that, in the case of an accident during school time, children get the necessary medical care. For example, the cost for medication and casts if they break a leg will be paid for by this insurance. However, it seems that in practice the insurance almost never pays for anything. Because the insurance company is state-owned, this money in a way is more like an extra taxation (Interviews 75, 80, 81, 84, 127, 128. See also the Commission Education Sociale, Culture, Jeunesse et Sports (2003a; b), which indicates, as an issue of the educational system, the lack of payment by the MASCA to parents whose children have been injured (b 9), and UNESCO (2010: 4)).

1207 During my research I have never come across this "school identity", it was not mentioned by anyone I spoke to, so in fact I am not quite sure what it is.

1208 CEF1 is a school diploma for whomever has finished primary school successfully. However, the existence of this diploma was never mentioned during the research by any of the participants.

1209 A little over 4 US dollars.

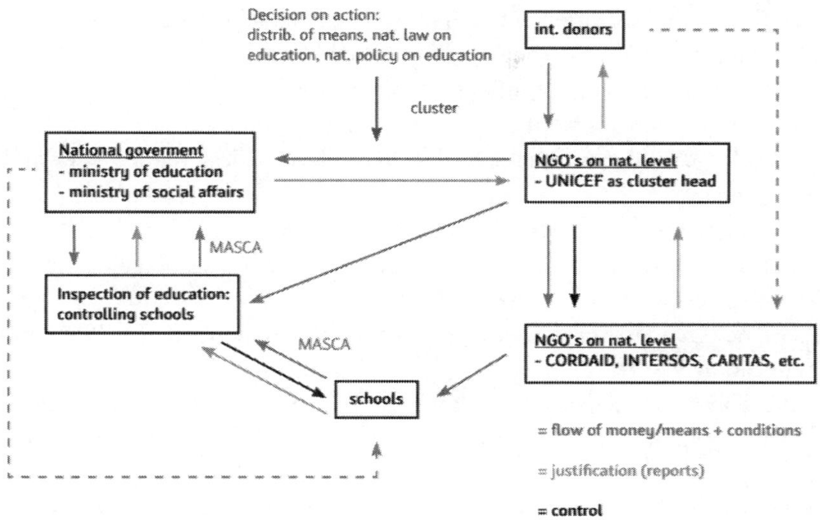

B1. Written law for the community

People in the CAR are aware of the existence of state law and sometimes refer to it, but they usually do not know its content – including government officials. Of the 20 participants that mentioned national law[1210] (mostly after I explicitly asked them), 9 – of whom 3 were government officials – had false beliefs about the content[1211], such as they argued that, according to state law, the language of education is French[1212], whereas in fact, according to the 1997 education law, Sango and French are the two languages of instruction and "the teaching of, and in, Sango is introduced into the curriculum of primary school in the year 2000".[1213] They also argued that education is not obligatory according to state law[1214], whereas in fact it is according to both the 2015 constitution (art. 7) and the 1997 education law (art. 6 and 50). Others had very limited knowledge of the law and could not say more than "the child has a right to education according to CAR law"[1215], or "the *chicotte* is forbidden according to the national law on education".[1216]

National formal written law that is definitely not law for the community, as it was not mentioned by any (or only one) of the participants, are:

1210 Interviews 4, 14, 16, 17, 22, 42, 43, 52, 53, 60, 62, 75, 80-82, 90, 91, 96, 104, 109.
1211 Interviews 14, 16, 17, 22, 52, 53, 62, 96, 109.
1212 Interviews 52, 62, 96.
1213 1997 education law (art. 42).
1214 Interviews 4, 16, 62.
1215 Interviews 22, 75, 81.
1216 Interviews 22, 42, 43.

- The obligation of parents to provide education for their children until age 16[1217] and the obligation of children to attend school from age 6 to age 15[1218]
- The fact that education should be free in public schools[1219]
- The prohibition to beat a child less than age 15[1220]
- The prohibition for adults in general, and teachers in particular, to have sex with children, in particular with children of less than age 15 and/or students[1221]
- The state's promise to develop structures for non-formal education[1222]
- The law stating that education has to be oriented towards preparing the child for the working world in the CAR[1223]
- The new names for classes in F1 and F2, introduced in the 1997 law on education[1224]
- The fact that Sango and French are the two official languages of instruction.[1225] All participants thought this was French only.

The authority of state law, in the eyes of the population, combined with the limited knowledge of the content of national formal written law, is a source of (abuse of) power for government officials. In general, this is an issue in the CAR, with the different law enforcement groups (police, *gendarmerie*, army (FACA)) forcing people to pay fines for the violation of non-existent laws. Sometimes people actually believe that they have to pay, such as the police officers who came to the IDP site in the capital to collect obligatory fees for the "*droit de bouger*" ("the right to move") – one of the displaced told me about how stupid they [people living on the IDP site] were that they had not realized that they should pay this.[1226] Others however are more cynical, such as one of my taxi drivers who said the police regularly stopped him to fine him for something, calling them "ordinary thieves". However, the aggressive treatment by law enforcement officers, combined with threats and the arms they carry, often causes people to pay anyway.[1227]

1217 2015 Constitution (art. 7).
1218 1997 education law (art. 6).
1219 2015 Constitution (art. 7). This was mentioned by one participant (interview 42).
1220 Penal code (art. 74).
1221 Ibid (art. 87, 110). This was mentioned by one participant (interview 16).
1222 1997 education law (art. 5, 36).
1223 Ibid (art. 12, 16).
1224 Ibid (art. 13, 18). In fact, all classes in schools are still referred to by the old, French names that were officially changed by this article.
1225 Ibid (art. 42).
1226 Interview 109.
1227 On Friday November 25th, 2016, there was a radio emission of the national Radio Ndeke Luka, a program during which they asked their audience to phone in if they had ever had the experience of a law enforcement group (either the police, gendarmerie or the FACA) that stopped them, asked for their documents, and upon showing all the necessary documents, still obliged them to pay money for imaginary missing documents. Many people called

In relation to education, this came to the fore in interviews also, as even people who have knowledge of the national written law do not have much faith in its rule. They argue, for example, that even though there are texts that forbid sexual relations between the teacher and the student, nobody respects those texts.[1228] Several explained that there is no system of national legislation; the laws are not known to the people, they are not publically accessible. Even for the people who are able to read they are inaccessible, because they are not published online and they do not exist in the national language (Sango), only in French.[1229] Finally, if a case does come before the judge, you cannot be sure what law s/he will apply and the outcome of the case might depend mostly on who pays the judge most and/or the socio-political position of the defendant.[1230]

It is indeed true that, although I was able to find the penal code and the text of the constitution online (but not easily), I could not find the education law anywhere. In my effort to find this text, I searched online; I searched in the general library of the university in Bangui, as well as in the library of the law faculty of the same university; I asked several government officials (both working at the national and local level, including all education inspectors). The only person finally able to provide me with the text of this law was an NGO employee working at the national level. The document I received was sometimes difficult to read (see image below).

Interview 16, an employee of an NGO, working on education on the national level.

A: There is a law on education that was adopted in 1992.
Q: Do you have it?
A: I can, if you would like me to, I can send it by email.

E-mail received 25 August 2016

"As promised, I have searched for the original, signed version of the law in question, but I have not been able to find it back. Maybe you can find it on the internet. Sorry."

---

in to tell their stories. I personally experienced this on several occasions. Even though they charged me with statements about the penal code I knew to be untrue, the level of intimidation combined with facing a group of armed, aggressive men while being alone in a dark street, easily compels you to pay whatever they ask. In this case, indeed, what is the difference between a law enforcer and a thief?

1228 Interview 16.

1229 Interviews 16, 22, 52, 90, 91.

1230 Interviews 16, 22, 52, 73, 90, 91, 104. See also Lombard who writes that "In the research project I led on the topic of access to justice in CAR [...] every single person interviewed described the state judicial sector as wholly corrupt" (2016a: 193).

Figure 15. Screenshot of the PDF received of the CAR national education law.

TITRE 2 : DE LA VIE SCOLAIRE ET UNIVERSITAIRE

CHAPITRE 1 - DU DROIT A L'EDUCATION

Art. 6 - La scolarité est obligatoire de six à quinze ans.

l'Etat favorise la création d'établissements scolaires sur toute l'étendue du territoire national, là où les conditions démographiques sont réunies.

Art. 7 - Le droit à l'éducation implique la participation de toute la Collectivité.

Art. 8 - La nation se fixe comme priorité, l'éducation de base et comme objectifs d'améliorer la scolarisation des filles et de parvenir à terme à la scolarisation pour tous.

CHAPITRE II - DE L'ORGANISATION DE LA SCOLARITE

Art. 9 - La scolarité est organisée en niveaux d'enseignement

- l'éducation de la petite enfance
- l'enseignement fondamental 1
- l'enseignement fondamental 2
- l'enseignement secondaire général et la formation technique et professionnelle
- l'enseignement supérieur

It is however the case that CAR people do seem to view their national government as a legitimate authority and source of law.[1231] Therefore there might be a great potential for state law to influence the lives of CAR citizens – if only they would know its content.

Interview 22. An education inspector (chef secteur) in a town in the center of the CAR

A: There are girls who want to continue their studies. So, they dress in a certain way. They show themselves. Sometimes that's what attracts the teacher.
Q: That is against the law, or not?[1232]
A: Yes. But it is a double-edged knife.

[1231] See also Lombard (2016), discussing the behavior of rebel groups in northern CAR; "though legal categories generally went unenforced and were maybe even unenforceable in their north-eastern CAR context […], they were nevertheless an important element of how rebel group members understood themselves and justified their undertakings" (136). More in general, she argues that "in CAR, 'the state' – as a form, as an ideal type – is the focus of people's utopian dreams, and these desires are intensified rather than undermined by its continual failure to live up to them" (108).

[1232] Earlier in the interview, the respondent indicated that he knew the national law on education.

Q: Why?
A: Because if there is sexual harassment, it is not just the teacher, it is the girl too. Because of her behavior.
Q: So, both are to blame?
A: Exactly.
Q: She is harassing the teacher?
A: OK.
Q: No matter what age?
A: Surely. We often think of 6eme, the children who are often 12 years old. But it is a little difficult, because a child of 12 cannot execute a sexual harassment. Those are the ones of 18 years old, who are blocked in their studies but forces themselves to continue. So it starts there, the way of dressing.
Q: And imagine a girl of 16 years old, or…from what age is the child to blame?
A: At the moment, even the girls of 7–10 years old who see their older sisters dress up, they think it really is a better way to dress. If the parents don't pay attention in the family, the girls will follow.
Q: That is hard for the teacher?
A: It all depends. Say for example that a girl has the habit to go to school with a shirt […] [the teacher's] task is to reproach the girl […] if there is already a sexual thought on his mind, he can let himself go. Both are wrong, both are in error.
Q: No matter what age the girl has?
A: No, those who have attained the age of puberty do this, before they don't. I don't know the age of puberty, those of age 14…who have discovered their private parts. But the teachers are to blame when they are the ones who approach the girls. Because they are attracted by a certain behavior…they are obliged to make advances.

Interview 53. An education inspector (chef secteur) in a large town in Western CAR.

A: For us [inspectors], being responsible for national education, when we take a teacher who has hit, hurt or worried a child he has to pass before a judge.
Q: So imagine you find a teacher who has hit [chicoté] a child, what do you do?
A: Well, just to scare [the child] that can happen, pull the ears or whipping the buttocks, etc. But in any case the punishments in the form of torture and the punishments with severe injuries, the parents complain in front of the judge, we support that […] the small punishments continue, they make the students sit on their knees […] but not to hurt the child.
Q: But to whip (chicotter) the child, that doesn't hurt?
A: Yes, that hurts, but that's why we have forbidden that on a national level.
Q: Yes, but you were just talking about whipping the buttocks.
A: That is acceptable ("ça va"), but it hurts so that's why we say you should not punish the children anymore.
Q: Yes, but you just said that it is still a big problem.
A: Yes, but I tell you that because it is the reality of the terrain. Even if it is forbidden, there are teachers who continue to use the chicotte. However, during our yearly meetings with the teachers, every trimester we remind them. And when the inspector comes, they hide the chicotte […] we have to work on educating them ("sensibilisation").

Lastly, on the role of national formal written law in CAR society, it might be telling that although all participants were asked what they would do if they were the CAR president or minister of education, only one said something about the law.[1233]

B2. Unwritten law for the community

Another legislator in national law concerning children's education seems to be the NGOs or, more specifically, the education cluster lead UNICEF. Several participants indicated to national laws on education that, according to them, were "UNICEF laws", such as the obligation of parents to send their children to school, the prohibition on the use of the chicotte or the prohibition on letting children repeat a grade more than once.[1234]

This is particularly confusing in relation to the prohibition on the use of the chicotte. Many people argue that the use of the *chicotte* is forbidden, but the source of this prohibition is unclear.[1235] Sources mentioned are the (state) national law on education[1236], the school regulations which were decided on a national level[1237], or by a meeting of "the general states" ("*états generaux*")[1238], the school regulations in general[1239], a government decision[1240], UNICEF[1241], a decree ("*note circulaire*")[1242], or human rights / children's rights.[1243] It is very well possible that the person's belief in the source of a certain law influences the respect they have for the law – if they even perceive it as law at all.

Do NGO(s) actually create law on a national level? This is hard to determine, especially because, if such rules are created, they are unwritten rules. It is at least certain that they have a lot of political power, and they do spread their messages over the CAR's towns and villages through the practice of "*sensibilisation*" (a form of collectively informing and/or education people, in some sense comparable to the role of the herald in the middle ages – although the emphasis of *sensibilisation* is more on providing information/education than on declaring the law). Several participants argued that they use this practice to convince parents to send their children to school, often together with education inspectors.[1244] However, this does not seem to be a practice of declaring law.

1233 Interview 36.
1234 Interviews 47, 53, 55, 92, 96.
1235 Interviews 4, 7, 14, 17, 22, 42, 43, 51, 52, 55, 60, 62, 80-82, 92.
1236 Interview 14, 22, 42, 43.
1237 Interviews 4, 17.
1238 Interview 52.
1239 Interview 62.
1240 Interview 51.
1241 Interviews 55, 92.
1242 Interview 81.
1243 Interviews 60, 80, 82.
1244 Interviews 13, 17, 51, 52, 81; observation 13.

In addition to NGOs being the ones who control most of the money (see §6.3.1(C)), their position of political power is influenced by the fact that the CAR government employees have a very bad reputation with NGOs. Some NGO workers are not sure whether their colleagues in the government are sufficiently motivated to improve CAR education (allegedly some employees of the ministry of education only show up at work about 30 minutes per week) and they lack the necessary governance skills. This is another reason it often seems to be the NGOs who make the final decisions.[1245]

Lombard (2016) indicates that in the CAR, there is

> opacity and unertainty that surround who is ultimately in charge. Is it the UN mission? The French? Central African politicians? Perhaps there are complicated technical-legal answers to those questions, but on a day-to-day basis their answers are impossible to determine.[1246]

Interview 11. An employee of an NGO, working on the national level.

Q: So, who would you say is governing the education decisions on a national level?

A: It's definitely the NGOs. Definitely. I think there is a power relation, because humanitarian agencies have all of the money. But more and more I see the Ministry of Education being implicated, being involved in decisions, and they're often put at the forefront, for example if we're doing big events [...]

Q: So in a way you are almost the minister of education?

A: Yes I would say in a way [...] the power between [NGO] and the Ministry of Education is incomparable.

Q: Interesting, it is so un-democratic in a way.

A: It is, but then [NGO], they have all the expertise. Even the strategic document of the recovery plan, it is entirely developed by [NGO]. The Ministry of Education has 1 or 2 focal points, but the whole process is very much led by [NGO]. Because there are very clear deadlines and deliverables that need to be met with a certain quality of the work, and it's clearly known that the Ministry of Education won't be able to acquire the standard if they do it alone.

Q: The standard of the donors?

1245 Interviews 11, 27, 52, 129; observations 3, 19. Interestingly, according to academic research, in many African countries the political power of NGOs seems to be limited by government restrictions (see for example Bratton (1987); v.d. Borgh & Terwindt (2014)). The fact that this seems to be different in the CAR, at least concerning education, might be explained by what Lombard refers to as "wholesale outsourcing"; 'Previously, concessions were primarily granted for resource extraction, but now, through foreign aid, all government prerogatives have been turned into concessions as well, amounting to the wholesale outsourcing of the country's sovereignty" (2016a: 9). Lombard further describes the dynamic between donors and Central African politicians [and INGOs, I would add], as follows: "what brings everyone together is the idea of the state [...] and yet everyone involved knows that this is at best a stage set, which allows people to put on a performance while ducking in and out behind the scenery to conduct other business with varying degrees of openness" (64-65).

1246 Lombard (2016a): p. 217.

A: Exactly. [...] the fact that the humanitarian organizations take such a, have such a ... it almost takes away the responsibility of the government in providing access to education for the population. It almost takes away their credibility.

C. *Hidden law*

Although it is a taboo subject, it is no secret that the CAR suffers greatly from corruption on all levels of society.[1247] On the level of the government, too, we find many different forms of corruption that directly or indirectly influence education in the CAR.[1248] There seem to be three general occurrences of corruption on the government level (in relation to education):

1) Money that is supposed to be for education disappears
2) Nepotism: when government jobs are given to family members or friends of those in power (for example positions within the education inspection)
3) Favors-for-money, such as teachers paying government officials to look the other way when for example they are sent to teach in a certain town and they do not want to go

Similarly, the NGOs also seem to suffer from corruption, in the forms of 1) money that is supposed to be for education disappears; and 3) favors-for-money.[1249] For example, when a field office is handling money transferred down to them by NGOs on the national level, which they received to build a school, pay teachers, etc. The NGO field office may report back to the national level saying that they built a school, but in fact they have not done the work – or only in part – and kept the money in their pocket.

However, for both the government and NGOs operating on a national level, it seems that the instances of corruption – even if they are many, and insofar as I was able to research – are not rule-based. The instances of corruption are more the private initiatives of individuals or particular deals between two individuals. Since it is customary, therefore, the practice does not seem to be based on a hidden law.

Interview 60. A former education inspector, who now works for an NGO in the Center-West of CAR.

A: For example, a teacher who does not want to be assigned, they have to go and talk to the education inspector, to ask him whether she can stay here, and this can be done through money or prostitution. [...] on a higher level, the nominations of

1247 See, among others: Gan Business Anti-Corruption Portal (2016); Transparency International (n.d.) "Central African Republic". Available at: https://www.transparency.org/country/CAF; Freedom House (2017).

1248 Interviews 16, 17, 22, 27, 36, 42, 43, 52, 60, 65, 73, 80, 104.

1249 Interviews 7, 11, 16, 17, 43, 52, 62, 65, 84.

the headmasters, they are sometimes nominated because they pay. Not because of their capacities. Or they can be nominated because of their political positions. Such as for example the education inspectors.

Q: Concretely, what does it mean, for example are the reports of the inspection adapted to the preferences of the Ministry?

A: Yes, yes. For example, if the number of teachers [in the area] is insufficient, one cannot say concretely I need a teacher. One cannot say the truth because it is the minster who has nominated you. [...] one cannot critique.

Q: So, what do you do?

A: We don't tell the truth. We camouflage things.

Interview 64. A religious leader and head of an NGO, working on a national level, in a city in the Center-South.

A: In the context of NGOs, often I have had to send back people who asked me to give them a percentage of the sum received. I wonder sometimes whether the head [of the organization] is aware. To give an example, recently we gave a sum of money so that certain people could be given accommodation, and the person in charge of this, of the organization took a percentage before giving it to the people in need. [...] After, they were fired. When we discover this kind of activities, we automatically involve the people involved.

Q: It occurs often.

A: That's it.

Q: In general, I don't arrive at getting this kind of information. You know other NGOs too?

A: [name of another NGO]. It is important to know that in most cases of corruption it is the employees who are corrupted and not the NGO itself. It is important to make the difference. But certainly, if we discover it, we fire them immediately. For a long time, we identify and we denounce the corruption. We give "a kick in the ant's nest" ("un coup de pied dans la fourmilière"). There is also the problem of incompetency. Certain employees of NGOs are incompetent because they have received their position through a political election by a member of the family, the ethnicity...

6.3.3. THE RELIGIOUS LEGAL ORDER

Generally, it seems that religion – any kind of religion – does not constitute a legal order in the CAR, or at least not concerning education. None of the participants, with one exception (see below), referred to religion as a decisional power in their lives. Religious leaders themselves indicated that their role was not to rule but to advise. When asked how they influenced the child's right to education, for example among their followers, they would argue that their only role is to give advice ("*conseil*") to for example parents or children.[1250]

1250 Interviews 15, 23, 64, 65, 81, 89, 95, 96, 127, 128.

The one exception I encountered was in a town in the centre of the CAR, where the Islamic religious leader preached to parents not to send their girls to school, arguing that this would be forbidden according to the holy scriptures.[1251] However, all other Islamic religious leaders I spoke to argued that this one Imam was wrong and that girls in fact should go to school; that it says so in the Quran and that this is how they advise their followers.[1252]

6.3.4. THE LOCAL LEGAL ORDER

Like the religious legal order, the local legal order does not seem to really exist or at least have an influence in the CAR. I have certainly not encountered any formal written law on the local level and no participant referred to local law.

There are local leaders in CAR society, most notably the mayors and the village chiefs and perhaps we can also count the local NGO leaders under this heading. However, all these parties identified themselves as giving advice to the people rather than legislating and/or enforcing anything.[1253] This might have been different in the past, when perhaps village chiefs had more authority, as some participants mentioned. However, none of the local leaders identified themselves as authorities and neither did participants indicate a local leader as having authoritative power over them in relation to education.

Interview 28. Chief of a small village in the Center-South of the CAR, where there has not been a school for the past couple of years. At the time of the interview (August 2016), school was supposed to start again in September.

Q: Why do you not ask the literate parents to teach the children, each a few hours per week?
A: They cannot accept to teach if we don't pay them.
Q: But what if they would just teach half a day per week?
A: That would be good, but it is not possible. They have to go fishing. If they don't go, how will they feed their children?

1251 Interviews 9, 10.

1252 Interviews 15, 23, 65.

1253 Interviews 7, 9, 10, 11, 13, 14, 15, 17, 22, 28, 47, 53, 55, 57, 70, 79, 80, 81, 84, 93. There was one exception to this, namely I encountered a mayor who argued that she obliged all children in the village to go to school. She argued that she would send the *gendarmerie* to the mines to collect the children and send them to school. She would also fine the parents if children were not in school. Due to this policy, she said, now 100% of the children between ages 6-18 of the village were in school (interview 56). However, it is hard to take this very seriously, first of all, because there was only one school with two classrooms and two teachers in the village - classrooms which were overcrowded as it was, with children no older than 12 (observations 14 and 15). Secondly, her own secretary denied the story, saying it was a lie (interview 57).

Q: I have trouble believing that teaching for only 4 hours a week will make the difference between eating and not eating.
A: I cannot command them. If they don't want to, can you force them?
Q: You are the chief, do you not have that power?
A: I have power, but I cannot force people.
Q: So what kind of power do you have in relation to education?
[...]
A: Before, the young people were receiving the village chief. Nowadays, after the arrival of human rights, if you ask them to do something, they don't accept it. When they don't accept it, you have no right to take it by force.

One last exception worth mentioning is one town where, at the time I was there for research (August 2016), an armed group (UPC, which is part of the ex-Seleka armed groups) was running a development program in the town, which included education. They ran a school which provided education for both children (during daytime) and adults (evenings and weekends). Teachers' salaries and other expenses were paid for by the armed group's leader, the General Ali Darass (also a sought war criminal), and when I visited the school it seemed like one of the better functioning schools in the country.[1254] Unfortunately, I did not have the opportunity to investigate the case more to see in what way it was law-based.

6.3.5. THE SCHOOL LEGAL ORDER

A. *Formal written law*

Most schools in the CAR have a document with school rules. These differ per school, but generally they state rules about at what time students and teachers have to be present in the morning, sometimes about clothes to wear (uniform or simply "clean clothes"), a prohibition on stealing and fighting and a prohibition on the use of corporal punishment by the teacher.[1255]

1254 Interviews 23, 93, observation 25.
1255 Interviews 4, 17, 51, 52, 62, 75, 80; observations 16, 22.

Figure 16. Example of school rules in a local public school.

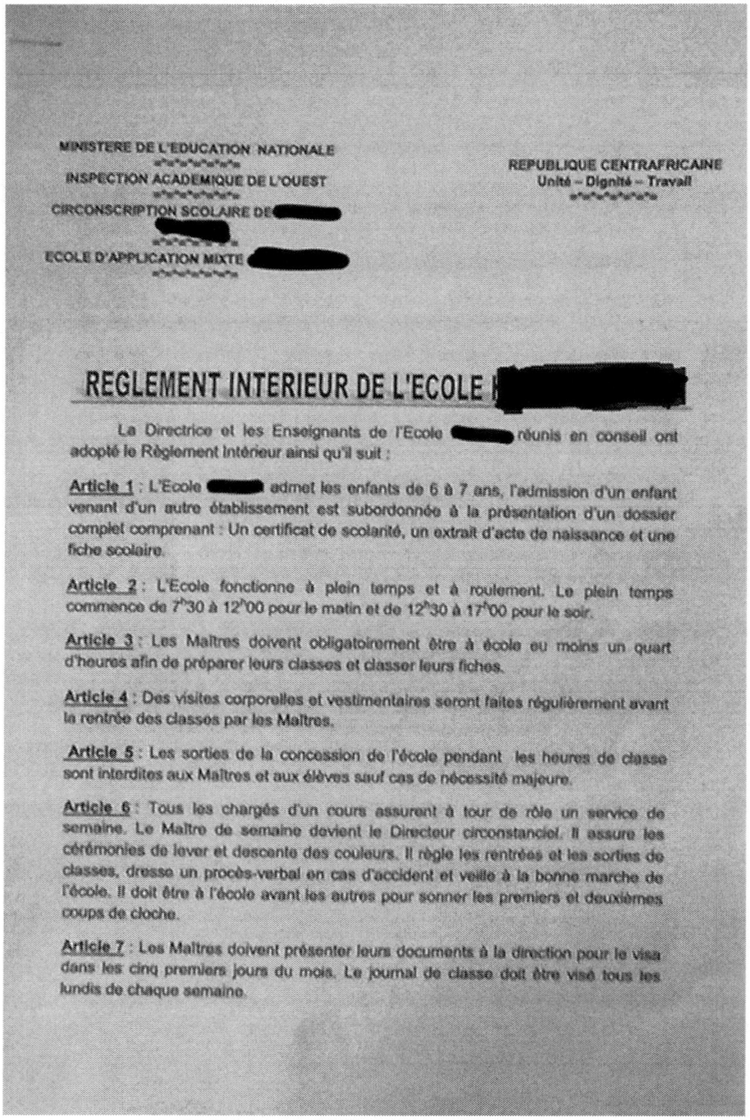
MINISTERE DE L'EDUCATION NATIONALE
INSPECTION ACADEMIQUE DE L'OUEST
CIRCONSCRIPTION SCOLAIRE DE [redacted]
ECOLE D'APPLICATION MIXTE [redacted]

REPUBLIQUE CENTRAFRICAINE
Unité – Dignité – Travail

REGLEMENT INTERIEUR DE L'ECOLE [redacted]

La Directrice et les Enseignants de l'Ecole [redacted] réunis en conseil ont adopté le Règlement Intérieur ainsi qu'il suit :

Article 1 : L'Ecole [redacted] admet les enfants de 6 à 7 ans, l'admission d'un enfant venant d'un autre établissement est subordonnée à la présentation d'un dossier complet comprenant : Un certificat de scolarité, un extrait d'acte de naissance et une fiche scolaire.

Article 2 : L'Ecole fonctionne à plein temps et à roulement. Le plein temps commence de 7h30 à 12h00 pour le matin et de 12h30 à 17h00 pour le soir.

Article 3 : Les Maîtres doivent obligatoirement être à école au moins un quart d'heures afin de préparer leurs classes et classer leurs fiches.

Article 4 : Des visites corporelles et vestimentaires seront faites régulièrement avant la rentrée des classes par les Maîtres.

Article 5 : Les sorties de la concession de l'école pendant les heures de classe sont interdites aux Maîtres et aux élèves sauf cas de nécessité majeure.

Article 6 : Tous les chargés d'un cours assurent à tour de rôle un service de semaine. Le Maître de semaine devient le Directeur circonstanciel. Il assure les cérémonies de lever et descente des couleurs. Il règle les rentrées et les sorties de classes, dresse un procès-verbal en cas d'accident et veille à la bonne marche de l'école. Il doit être à l'école avant les autres pour sonner les premiers et deuxièmes coups de cloche.

Article 7 : Les Maîtres doivent présenter leurs documents à la direction pour le visa dans les cinq premiers jours du mois. Le journal de classe doit être visé tous les lundis de chaque semaine.

It is unclear who or what the source of these rules is, but it seems that these documents come from the national level and that they have been developed by NGOs operating on the national level.[1256]

1256 Interview 17.

B. *Law for the community*

B1. Written law for the community

The situation in the school legal order seems to be quite similar to the situation of the national legal order, in particular concerning the role of the formal written law. Only few students and teachers seem to be aware of the formal written law within the school, and it does not seem to carry much weight. For example, one day when I came into a classroom to observe the lesson, the teacher had the school rules on her table and gave them to me to read. Article 10 stated that corporal punishment was forbidden. While I was reading the document in the classroom, she was walking through the classroom with a stick, beating students who did something wrong. After the lesson she came to see me, to ask about my research and mostly to inquire whether I knew things that she, as a teacher, could do better.[1257]

B2. Unwritten law for the community

The amount of school fees required for subscription (both at the beginning of the school year as well as the required monthly fee, both in public and private schools) could possibly be considered to be part of the unwritten school law for the community. The fee differs per school and is set either by the director, the teacher and/or the APE. It is collected by these parties, and it is something the relevant legal community (students and/or caretakers) knows about because it is orally transmitted information.[1258] However, this probably is more of a market transaction rather than a "law" – with the seller setting price X for product Y. No participant related the subject of school fees to law, nor did they refer to, or seem to know of, the Ministry's decree that sets a fixed amount for enrollment in public education.[1259]

6.3.6. THE CLASSROOM LEGAL ORDER

The classroom seems to be perceived as a legal order by most students, with the teacher as the sovereign. Children are able to mention rules that the teachers impose on them, including punishments if the rules are transgressed. These rules seem to be all orally transmitted, so there is no A or B1 law. There does not seem to be non-public C law in the classrooms either. The transactions around the buying/selling of marks seem more like market transactions than law-based

---

1257 Observation 16.

1258 Interviews 5, 6, 14, 19, 39, 42, 47, 51, 55, 60, 68, 70, 75, 80, 110-124.

1259 Ssee §6.3.2 (A).

actions. It is possible that there are unwritten classroom laws that apply only to a select group of students, which are not known to all students – for example, if students of a specific ethnic background are exempted from the unwritten classroom rules as described below. However, I have not encountered any concrete example of such a non-public law in my field research.

B2. Unwritten law for the community

The law (or rule) most mentioned by participants is the fact that you are not allowed to make mistakes in your schoolwork. Therefore, if the teacher asks you to read something, or write something, or make a calculation, and you make a mistake, you are doing something illegal.[1260] The most common punishment for this offense is for children to be hit with the *chicotte*.[1261]

However, it has to be questioned whether this actually counts as "law". As Hart writes, when comparing the gunman, who is saying "Hand over those notes" to a bank clerk, to the legislator:

> the gunman does not issue to the bank clerk [...] *standing orders* to be followed time after time by classes of persons. [...] We must therefore suppose that there is a general belief on the part of those to whom the general orders apply that disobedience is likely to be followed by the execution of the threat not only on the first promulgation of the order, but continuously until the order is withdrawn or cancelled. This continuing belief in the consequences of disobedience may be said to keep the original orders alive or 'standing' [...].[1262]

In addition, Hart argues that "the word 'obedience' often suggests deference to authority and not merely compliance with orders backed by threats."[1263] The question therefore is if students indeed feel an obligation to follow the rules of the teacher, even if there is no immediate, direct threat of being hit. On the one hand, this does not seem to be the case because there are many students who decide on their own accord to exit the classroom, specifically not to endure any (more) corporal punishment.

The practice seems to be perceived by some more as a kind of terror – perhaps like a dictator reigning by terror (which does not exclude it necessarily from being law):

> *Interview 36. A 20-year old girl who recently got her high school diploma (BAC) at a public school, in a city in the Center-South of the CAR:*

1260 Interviews 18, 21, 31, 36, 37, 40, 47, 50, 59, 60, 68, 83, 92.

1261 Interviews 18-21, 24, 31, 36, 37, 39-41, 45, 47, 49, 50, 59-61, 68, 78, 80, 83, 92, 107.

1262 Hart (1961/2012: 22-23). See also the argument about the distinction between the social norm and legal norm as set out in chapter 1 of this thesis.

1263 Ibid: 51.

A: When the teacher poses a question to the classroom, and the class cannot manage to find an answer, he starts to point at students, pointing, if he still doesn't find a response, he starts letting students come to the front of the class. One by one, one by one, and if through bad luck one of them finds the answer, he can give the chicotte to all who are in front. Those who don't know. Sometimes he will order the student who had the [correct] response to hit her/his fellow students.
Q: So you have also hit your fellow students?[1264]
A: No, I haven't, or yes, maybe I have done that, but I have already forgotten about it [laughs]
Q: Yes? Does it embarrass you?
A: Yes.
Q: Why does it embarrass you?
A: Because a person, completely like me, the way in which I hit, I try to put myself in her/his place and if someone hits me in that way it doesn't do me good. What I don't want others to do to me, I shouldn't do that to others either.
Q: So why did you do it?
A: Because it was an order of the teacher. If I didn't, he would have hit me. And if you don't hit hard, your fellow student, the teacher will hit everyone. Hard.

On the other hand, it might be that students do feel an obligation to obey the classroom unwritten law if indeed they view the teacher as a sovereign, as someone who is the legitimate author of their actions (at least in part). To argue that legal enforcement is too harsh is not a denial of the legal power of the sovereign, it is rather an acknowledgment of the existence of a certain law and a certain legal enforcement, even if one disapproves of the type of enforcement from a normative perspective. As a legislator, the teacher may install the law "every student must know the correct answer to the question asked in the class". Students may recognize the legitimate authority of the teacher as legislator, and therefore this (and other) rule(s) are laws. However, students may not agree with the enforcement measures executed as punishment for illegal behavior. The violent behavior of the teacher may limit the student's belief in the authority of the teacher as a legislator in the longer run, because the student loses the respect required for personal authority.[1265] However, the student still respects the authority of the teacher as legislator based on what Weber calls "rational grounds"; they believe they owe obedience not to the teacher as an individual, but to the impersonal order of the school and the classroom.

This observation is supported by the fact that participants do indicate several classroom rules, of which the most commonly cited were:

1264 Because the respondent indicated earlier in the interview that she was a good student.
1265 What Weber (1978: 216-18) calls "charismatic authority".

- You are not allowed to make mistakes in your schoolwork[1266]
- You are not allowed to fight or hurt others[1267]
- You are not allowed to chat/make noise (*bavarder*) in the classroom[1268]
- You have to arrive on time for class[1269]

Other rules were mentioned only by 3 participants or less and therefore seem to apply more to individual classrooms, such as a prohibition on pregnancy, having to greet your parents, or having to respect the teacher.[1270] In addition to the *chicotte*, quite a few other methods of enforcement/punishment were mentioned by participants, of which the most common were:

- Advice (*conseil*) by the teacher (mostly not seen as a punishment but a way of enforcement nonetheless)[1271]
- Having to sit on your knees for a period of time[1272]
- Being sent home[1273]

Positive enforcement was not mentioned by participants at all in the context of obedience to rules, but it was observed regularly during classroom observations by the researcher. Means of positive enforcement included a lot of singing and dancing. For example, when a student gives a correct answer, the teacher asks the class "and, is it good?" and the class responds "yes, it's good, it's beautiful!" (*Et, c'est bien? – Oui, c'est bien, c'est joli!).*[1274]

Interview 5. A 14-year old girl who is in class CM2 of a private school.

Q: Do you think that, generally, the teacher has the right to hit the students if they do something that is not good?

A: The teacher has the right to punish, but not in the way which we just discussed [chicotte]. When a student has done something, one can give him work to do. Not to chase after him during the class and hitting him.

1266 Interviews 18, 21, 31, 36, 37, 40, 47, 50, 59, 60, 68, 83, 92.
1267 Interviews 18, 31, 39, 40, 45.
1268 Interviews 18, 19, 21, 24, 31, 36, 41, 45, 54, 70.
1269 Interviews 18, 40, 49, 80, 82, 83.
1270 Interviews 20, 21, 39, 40.
1271 Interviews 19, 20, 24, 32, 54, 55.
1272 Interviews 31, 41, 48, 49, 55, 70, 71.
1273 Interviews 31, 32, 39, 40, 45, 49.
1274 Observations 6, 16, 18.

6.3.7. THE HOUSEHOLD LEGAL ORDER

In CAR households, it seems that the only candidate for law is the unwritten law for the community. There is no formal written law (there are hardly any written documents at all), and there seems to be nothing to hide from the rest of the household community, so there is no C hidden law.

B2. Unwritten law for the community

It seems that CAR children and caretakers present different views on the household as a legal order. In relation to education, only 29% of children argued that their caretakers decide whether they go to school or not, whereas 71% of the caretakers interviewed argue that they are the ones who decide whether the child goes to school or not. The caretakers do this either through violence ("if my child does not listen, I use the *chicotte*"), or through advising the child (*conseil*).[1275] A possible unwritten law for the household community could be "the child has to go to school" or the opposite "the child is not allowed to go to school". These were the only two possible household laws found during the research in relation to education.

Whether this is indeed law for the household community seems questionable and might differ per household. In the case of the caretaker as adviser, the caretaker is not the legislator since the decisionary power lies with the child, and there are no legal consequences of going against the advice. In the case of enforcement through violence, whether this is indeed legal enforcement depends on how the child perceives the situation: is it random violence of someone trying to force you to do something or is it the legal enforcement of a legitimate law? Both situations seem to occur in the CAR.

A factor influencing the possible status of the caretaker as legislator seems to be the situation of the household. There seem to be four different types of household situations for children[1276];

1) Children live without family, either because they have been abandoned by their family or because they are orphans and there is no family around.
2) Children live with a family that is indifferent to them; they are allowed to live in the same house as long as they don't bother anyone. They receive little care and have to find their own food.

1275 Interviews 1, 2, 4, 5, 9, 13, 15, 16, 18, 20, 23, 25, 32, 34, 36, 39, 40, 46, 47, 49, 50, 54, 55, 66, 69, 72, 80, 82, 83; observation 17.

1276 Interviews 1-6, 8-10, 12-16, 18-21, 23, 28, 32, 33, 36, 38, 39, 43, 45, 49-51, 55, 57, 60, 62, 64, 65, 68, 71, 73, 75-78, 80-82, 89. These four obviously are ideal types in the Weberian sense of the term.

3) Children are perceived as part of the family's workforce; they work together with their caretakers, for example on the field or in the mines. Any money they make, they hand over to their caretakers.
4) Children are cared for by the family, without having to give anything in return. Caretakers feel that "if you have put a child on Earth, you have to take care of it". Therefore, they try to do what they can to educate, feed and support the children.

Of these four types of child-family relations, only families of the third and the fourth type are involved in the decision whether children go to school. Families of the third type, who perceive children as part of the family's workforce, do not want the child to go to school. Families of the fourth type either prohibit or encourage the child to go to school, depending on what the family finds most useful for the child.

During childhood, CAR children often move through different family situations. For example, a child might be cared for as a baby, then start contributing to the family income by working in the mines for a few years, then live on the street for a while, before they move to the household of different family members. This process of moving around different households is greatly influenced by poverty, armed conflict and disease.[1277]

Most likely the instability of households for children makes them more autonomous; knowing that you often cannot count on your family to help you, as you cannot even know for how long they are going to be around, means that you have to take care of yourself (see more below).

6.3.8. THE AUTONOMOUS CHILD

At the end of the day, CAR children for the most part seem to be autonomous, in the sense of *autos-nomos*: making law for one's self. As has been shown under §6.3.7, some CAR children live without a family and, as a consequence, they have to take care of themselves. But even for the ones who do share a household with caretakers, few of them seem to think of the caretakers as legislators.

As has been mentioned, most children argue that they themselves decide whether they go to school (71%). This is confirmed by teachers and education inspectors who observe that children are often left to themselves, especially when the family cannot afford school fees.[1278] These children have to go around searching money for school fees, asking all the adults they know for money, working for money or, in the case of girls, finding a boyfriend who will pay for them.[1279] Although some children are heavily influenced by their families in

1277 Interviews 1, 6, 14, 33, 36, 37, 38, 41, 44, 50, 55, 75, 76, 77, 78.

1278 Interviews 4, 7, 42, 43, 47, 48, 49, 53, 54, 57, 81; observation 12.

1279 Pregnancies are also a reason for girls to drop out of school. According to WHO data, 23% of CAR women between ages 15-19 has given birth (World Health Organization (2016: 105).

taking this decision, they still argue it is they who decide, and they do indeed sometimes act against the wishes of their family.

Interview 18. An 8-year old boy in a town in the South-East.

Q: Do you go to school every day, or not, when there are no holidays?
A: I don't go all days, sometimes my grandmother tells me to go to the [agricultural] field [to work].
Q: Ok. So, who decides if you go to school or not?
A: It's my grandmother who often tells me to join her to the field.
Q: And what do you think about it?
A: I see the bad [side]. And sometimes if she asks me to accompany her to the field, I do a little smart trick, to go to school.
Q: So what do you do?
A: I leave the house early in the morning, I wash myself [fais la toilette] and I am the first at school.
Q: Before your grandmother gets up?
A: Yes.
Q: And after, does she punish you, or is it OK?
A: There are no punishments.
Q: In the end, is it you who can decide to go to school or not?
A: Yes.
Q: OK. So why do you get up so early? Because if your grandmother says you have to go to the field, and you say no, you don't go. Right?
A: Sometimes I refuse to go to the field and I leave for school.
Q: So sometimes you do go to the field? Why?
A: It's when she takes the chicotte and she wants to hit me, it's in that moment that I have gone to the field.

Several children argued that even though their caretakers had different preferences, they went to school anyway, even when threatened with violence.[1280] So in these cases, it is only when there is a direct threat of violence that the will of the caretaker was enforced upon the children, much like a thief forcing the bank clerk to hand in money by threatening her/him with a gun, rather than a legislator ruling over the addressee of the law.

Interview 32. A 14-year old girl who lives in a town in Eastern CAR.

Q: Who decides if you go to school or not?
A: Me.
Q: And if you say in the morning I am not going to school, do you not go?
A: No. My father will hit me with the chicotte.
Q: So, it's your father who says you have to go to school or is it you who chooses to go?
A: It's me who chooses to go to school.

1280 Interviews 6, 8, 18, 39, 45.

Other examples of the autonomous position of the child that came to the fore in the research were participants' observations that children themselves decide to go to school (they enroll themselves, they themselves are responsible for finding the money required for enrollment)[1281], or when participants argued that the child itself is responsible when they choose to have sex with the teacher in return for good marks.[1282]

6.4. LAW IN THE CAR

On the 27th of September 2016 the current President of the CAR, Faustin-Archange Touadéra, gave a speech at the US Brookings Institute.[1283] In this speech, he told the audience he had:

> committed myself, once in office [since March 2016], to build a country of peace, of security, a country that's concerned with the search of cohesion and justice... where corruption would be the main enemy of the government...in summary, I have committed myself to building rule of law in my country.

He claimed that this project had been successful, when saying that:

> the government has set up a court system that has become functional all over the country so that justice can be rendered effectively and close to the citizens. And government authority is functional all over the country with help of the international community [...] different forms of aid [have] brought back peace and constitutional legitimacy.

Unfortunately, these statements seem to be quite far from the truth. In this section, I will first argue that there is almost no law for children concerning their right to education (§6.4.1). Secondly, I will argue that the argument is not limited to the child's right to education but that it in fact tells us a lot about the (non-) existence of legal orders, and the consequent absence of the rule of law, in the CAR (§6.4.2). I will end the section with a general reflection on CAR society, qualifying it as a society of autonomous individuals (§6.4.3).

1281 Interviews 19, 21, 24, 29, 31, 32, 34, 36, 37, 40, 43, 45, 48, 50, 55, 57, 60, 81; observation 20.

1282 Interviews 22, 36.

1283 See Hopman, M. (2017c) "Speech of Touadera, president of the CAR,27 sept in the US + discussion". Available at: http://kinderrechtenonderzoek.nl/speech-of-touadera-president-of-the-car-27-sept-in-the-us-discussion/?lang=en.

6.4.1 CONCLUSION: LAW ON EDUCATION FOR CHILDREN IN THE CAR

As has been shown at length under §6.3, it is doubtful whether in the CAR there is any law for children at all concerning their (right to) education. When the data of §6.3 is combined, the following scheme of possible law in this context emerges:

Legal order	Legislator (sovereign)	Relevant legal community	Type of law found				
			A	B1	B2	C1	C2
International	United Nations, African Union, International donors	All residents of the CAR (including non-CAR nationality), in particular NGOs and CAR government	x / –	x / –	–	–	–
National	CAR government, Education cluster, NGOs operating on national level	All residents of the CAR (including non-CAR nationality). In particular teachers, parents, students	x / –	x / –	x / –	–	–
Religious	Religious leader(s)	All members of a certain religion in a particular area (village or larger area)	–	–	–	–	–
Local	Local government (mayor or village chief)	All residents of the relevant municipality	–	–	–	–	–
School	School director, APE	Teachers, students of the school (and possibly their caretakers)	x / –	x / –	–	–	–
Classroom	Teacher	Students of the classroom	–	–	x	–	–
Household	Caretaker (father / mother / older sibling / *tuteur* / other family member)	Children within the household	–	–	x / –	–	–
Autonomous child	Child	Child	–	–	–	–	–

On the level of international and national law, we do find written, formal laws (A), but it is questionable in what sense these actually count as "law". Theoretically, state law is created by the CAR state sovereign, an artificial person that has been authorized to create law by the CAR legal community.[1284] International

1284 See §1.3. However, state laws might be at least to some degree written by expats. See The World Bank Group (2012: 23) "Often, these laws are drafted by international consultants dispatched to CAR".

laws apply to the CAR legal community, because the CAR state sovereign has signed and ratified these international conventions. However, it is clear that the CAR legal community in fact does not know who the sovereign/source of this international laws is.[1285] In this sense, perhaps there is no recognition of the basic norm, of the international legal sovereign as legislator, involved. Even though there seems to be a general recognition of the CAR government as sovereign, the local community does not know if, and if so which, laws are made by this sovereign and therefore there is no recognition of these national and international laws as law. While the people in the CAR seem to recognize the CAR government as legislator (thereby recognizing the basic norm), they do not know state laws and do not generally expect its enforcement.

Lastly, formal, written law is supposed to be "open and available to the public"[1286], which, as has been shown, is not exactly the case when it comes to written, formal law on education in the CAR.[1287]

Similarly, when we look for international and/or national law for the community, knowledge of the law seems to be very limited within CAR society, including among CAR legislators. Whenever someone does mention a law, what they believe is the law, it seems to be more a matter of coincidence whether the rule mentioned is in fact the result of a legislative act of a sovereign, as there are so many false beliefs about the content of the law.[1288]

Within the school, regarding the school legal order, we see the same general pattern. Documents exist with written, formal school rules, but the source of these rules is questioned and they are not necessarily publicly accessible, nor known by the students.[1289]

A clear exception seems to be the legal order of the classroom. The teacher is seen as a legal authority by most students, and s/he creates and enforces law over the students. Although the enforcement practices are regularly perceived as too harsh and unjust (though not by all), and students might adhere to the classroom law more out of fear for punishment than out of respect for the law (besides, the most important classroom law is "you are not allowed to make mistakes", a law that is extremely difficult to adhere to because students simply do not always know the correct answers to the teacher's questions, as they are in school to learn these answers), they are still recognized as law.[1290]

However, on the whole, it seems that CAR children are mostly autonomous concerning education. They do not feel that anyone makes any law for them; not the government, not the NGOs, not the religious leaders, or the village chiefs –

1285 See §6.3.1 B and 6.3.2 B2.
1286 See §1.4.4.
1287 See §6.3.2 B1.
1288 See §6.3.1 B and §6.3.2 B.
1289 See §6.3.5. For example, one list of school rules presented to me was a handwritten piece of paper kept in the director's office (observation 22).
1290 See §6.3.6.

with the exception of the teacher in the classroom. Even when frequently facing (threats of) violence, mostly by their caretakers, they take their own decisions, such as whether to go to school or not.[1291]

6.4.2. LITERATURE REVIEW: THE GENERAL (NON) EXISTENCE OF LEGAL ORDERS IN THE CAR

It seems that the (non)existence of law on education for children in the CAR can be understood in a broader context of general lawlessness in the country, on all levels of society. Although it cannot simply be concluded from my field research that law is virtually nonexistent in the CAR, other research on law in the CAR does seem to convey a similar image to that presented in relation to law on education for children in this thesis, namely, the image of autonomous actors who take their individual decisions and who change course only when they are influenced in their decision by third parties either through advice or through violence. CAR citizens, although they are aware of the existence of "legal institutions" (courts, government, the state) and "legal enforcement" (police, gendarmerie, army) in their country, with few exceptions, do not have law. Although a general discussion on legal orders in the CAR is generally beyond the scope of this chapter, this last paragraph will shortly present some findings by other researchers on law in the CAR, which may provide a context for, and explain some of, the findings of the case study.

The national level

On the level of the national legal order, the CAR is generally known as a "failed state" or "phantom state"[1292], meaning that, even though the CAR has a government and a more or less defined territory, government governance of the territory is often minimal or absent. In Smith's words:

> Not only does the state fail to meet [*Centrafricain's*] expectations in providing public goods; it metes out extortionist and coercive abuse to a majority while purveying a sovereignty rent to a minority in power. Thus, the Central African state is for most citizens a painful absence *and* a hurtful experience.[1293]

This is not a recent development; it is, rather, a continuum of different forms of non-legal social organization that have existed in the CAR for as long as we know. According to some researchers, in the pre-colonial times, the people lived in "locally-oriented groupings in which powers of coercion were shared among

1291 See §6.3.7 and §6.3.8.
1292 International Crisis Group (2007:1); Carayannis & Lombard (2015: 3); Smith (2015a: 17).
1293 Smith (2015a: 17).

all residents rather than hierarchically with a governing class".[1294] Others argue that, for the Nzakara, Zanda and Gbandi ethnicities, CAR pre-colonial society used to be organized according to patrilineage, with men dominating women and children as heads of the family, while for the other ethnicities power was shared more between men and women.[1295] In any case, they agree that there were no relations of political power outside of the family.

During French colonization,

> [i]n the absence of an effective tribunal system, the much-feared "*gardes régionnaux*" – soldiers drawn from throughout the French colonies – incarnated the law and enforced policies, often with the aid of their *chicottes* [...] Though the colonial system had a legal code, which was particularly well-developed from the 1920s onward, this system existed only on the books. In practice, the power held by isolated officials was almost entirely personal in nature [..] they could hide many of their activities [...] under the anodyne conventions of bureaucratic report-writing.[1296]

After independence, things by and large do not seem to have changed radically.[1297] As de Vries & Glawion write: "From colonial times to today, rulers have [...] never controlled their sovereign territory".[1298] No CAR government to date has been able to establish an independent judiciary.[1299] Courts, which are scarcely dispersed over the country, are generally out of order.[1300] If they are functional, cases brought before tribunals are generally not adjudicated according to law (national or otherwise), but according to who pays most to the judge or who is related most closely to the judge.[1301] According to Marchal, the dysfunction of the court system has become aggravated in recent years, after recent fighting "saw the destruction of legal records and flight of legal personnel from the country".[1302]

Law enforcement officers are equally distrusted by the population, because they are perceived as not serving justice but rather engaging in corruption and

1294 The World Bank Group (2012: 13).

1295 Bigo (1988: 16).

1296 The World Bank Group (2012: 16).

1297 On the political climate during the governance of Dacko (1960-1965), Bigo writes that "no one believes in the 'nation of the Central African Republic' (*nation centrafricaine*)".

1298 De Vries. & Glawion (2015: 14). A possible exception here might be some elements of Bokassa's reign – according to Bigo, famers in the CAR in the beginning complied to "operation Bokassa". Farmers had to sow cotton in all fields, and if they would not succeed to (which often happened), they would be threatened with prison sentences. However, the population worked hard to attain these goals only during one or two harvests, and then went back to their traditional ways and rhythm (Bigo (1988: 61)).

1299 Smith (2015a: 38).

1300 The World Bank Group (2012: 18-19).

1301 Ngoumbango Kohetto (2013: 113); Marchal (2015: 71); The World Bank Group (2012: 37).

1302 Marchal (2015: 11).

extortion.[1303] The CAR government hardly operates as a legislature.[1304] Some argue that, in line with general concessionary politics, even the task of legislating is outsourced to external actors.[1305] As Ngoumbango Kohetto writes:

> in fact, the laws enacted in the "metropole" correspond to the needs and realities of Western society and are generally incompatible with the situation in the Central African Republic [...] the jurisdictions are perceived as foreign. The law [...] is like an external instrument.[1306]

Or, in the words of Smith:

> CAR's ruling elite has transacted the country's sovereignty wholesale and no longer piecemeal [...] a country which has descended into chaos by dint of outsourcing its state attributes in the first place is digging itself deeper into a hole with the altruistic help of the outside world.[1307]

International law does not seem to mean much in the country either, in spite of the physical presence of foreign peacekeeping forces, which can be seen from the fact that even the perpetrators of the worst violations of human rights, such as the mass killing of civilians[1308], do not suffer any legal consequences of their actions.[1309]

The local level

On the local level, conflict resolution is traditionally the domain of the village chief. However, it seems that this has never been much of a legal arrangement,

---

1303 Marchal (2015: 58): "In July 2010, President Bozizé made a speech saying that the CAR police was 'full of bandits' and that people should not trust them". See also Knoope & Buchanan (2017: 11); The World Bank Group (2012: 37); §6.3.2 B1.

1304 Marchal (2015 70); Bierschenk & de Sardan (1997: 467).

1305 According to Bigo, at least in 1988 and since independence, the CAR politicians are no more than the puppets of the French government (Bigo (1988: 86)).

1306 Ngoumbango Kohetto (2013: 211). See also Lombard & Batianga-Kinzi (2014: 9).

1307 Smith (2015b: 117).

1308 A very striking recent example is the attack of an armed group on the camp for internally displaced people in the town of Kaga Bandoro on October 12th, 2016, a camp which was situated directly next to a UN MINUSCA camp which houses 70 police officers and 200 soldiers. Although the armed group only consisted of about 60 soldiers, they "shot, stabbed, or burned to death the civilians, including at least four women, five children, three older people, and four people with disabilities. The casualty numbers are most likely higher because some victims were buried quickly. In addition to field research, Human Rights Watch, using satellite imagery analysis, identified at least 175 destroyed homes in the neighborhoods around the camp and 435 destroyed huts in the camp itself." Human Rights Watch (2016). See also: MINUSCA Human Rights Division (2016).

1309 Although a Special Criminal Court has been established, to date perpetrators of such crimes live in the CAR with impunity. See Mudge, L. (2017a; 2017b); Knoope. & Buchanan-Clarke (2017: 11).

but rather the chief has been sought out for his wisdom, to end conflict by giving advice to opposite parties on how to reconcile.[1310] As Bigo writes:

> The chief does not command, he has the function of a mediator, and uses his prestige to convince the opposite parties of his words and wisdom [...] the role of the chief is to be a mediator, a creator of peace [...] he has no decisional power [...] he has no authority.[1311]

Although the French administrators attempted to bestow more of a position of local authority upon these chiefs (responsible for enforcement of national (French) law), this project seems to have largely failed.[1312] The current role of the village chief is still one of a mediator/judge who tries to help parties in conflict to find a solution to their dispute – provided the villagers choose to present the conflict to the chief.[1313] This form of dispute resolution is not law-based. The chief is not a legislator, nor does s/he refer to laws as a (Western) judge or legal mediator would. Neither does the chief have the power to enforce her/his decisions.[1314] Rather, as has been argued in relation to the right to education, the role of the chief is to give advice on how to proceed.[1315] The same holds true for the role of religious leader and the local medicine man, who may also be sought out by people for the sake of advice, in conflict resolution or other issues.[1316]

The household, clan or family do not seem to take on any legal role either. Whether they have done so in the past or whether this has never been the case is hard to tell. Some researchers suggest that perhaps in the past there used to be customary law. However, these days – if they ever existed – seem to be over.[1317]

Historical exception: Bokassa?

One potential exception to this general rule seems to occur in CAR society, in the form of the historical figure of former president Bokassa, who at least in the eyes of a part of the population seems to have been recognized as ruling over the country. Bigo explains that the way for someone to rule over autonomous people, at least in the CAR, is by the exercise of personal power. On the CAR national level, former president Bokassa is the personification of this personal power. While Bokassa initially (after taking the presidency by force) follows and

---

1310 Ngoumbango Kohetto (2013: 427); Bierschenk& de Sardan (1997: 444); Bigo (1988: 19).
1311 Bigo (1988: 19, 21-22).
1312 The World Bank Group (2012: 17-18); Knoope & Buchanan-Clarke (2017:11, 14); Bierschenk & de Sardan (1997: 445); Bigo (1988: 29).
1313 Ngoumbango Kohetto (2013: 427, 436); The World Bank Group (2012: 18, 22, 39).
1314 The World Bank Group (2012: 41).
1315 See §6.3.4.
1316 Bierschenk & de Sardan (1997: 450); The World Bank Group (2012: 41, 50).
1317 Marchal (2015: 61); The World Bank Group (2012: 13).

adjusts national law[1318], he quickly starts accumulating all the political power onto his own person, for example by assigning himself several ministerial posts, and by judging cases (in the sense of dispute resolution) on national radio, for which he rarely used the formal, written law. In this way, he shapes his national rule according to the traditional role of the CAR village chief.[1319]

Westerners seem to fail to understand this form of political power. According to Bigo:

> Only the belief in the state, as a judicial, abstract category that directs our mentalities and our social imagination (but not necessarily that of the *Centrafricains*), permits us to cover [up] the African "realities". [The belief in states] cannot function (in the sense of using a language and permitting an interpretation) except for under the condition that it leaves intact the ideas of "representation", the distinction of "governing/governed", and that of the "state and civil society". However, [...] it is possible to think differently of the social relations and of the form of the exercise of power, by dismissing the false [...] explanations in terms of "representative of a social group that is institutionally supported", or as "head of state of a state/nation that is still under construction"! The logic of the exercise of personal power passes by other forms than those of the institutionalization [...] the power exercised by those leaders is a weak power, quasi powerless, that compensates its weakness by a staging of his own violence [...][1320]

It seems therefore that this form of political power is not legal power, because what is lacking here is the law. There are no valid legal norms that have been created by the sovereign (or, if there are, they last only for a very short period of time and there seems to be no way to measure their validity at any given point in time). Perhaps what Bigo discovers in studying Bokassa is that there can be political power, even on a national level, without institutionalized rules, without law. Bigo argues that the arbitrariness of Bokassa's judgments results in:

> the destruction of any idea of law and public space in the CAR: for a law to have the force of law, it must be known, public. But, if it depends completely on the will of Bokassa, it is clear that the people do not know what they should or shouldn't do.[1321]

A society of autonomous individuals

In general, researchers notice a lack of social cohesion in CAR society.[1322] On the local level we find, as Marchal puts it, a general "inability of the social bonds

1318 Bigo (1988: 106-108).
1319 Bigo (1988: 108-112).
1320 Bigo (1988: 101).
1321 Bigo (1988: 113).
1322 Marchal (2015: 61); Knoope & Buchanan-Clarke (2017: 12).

to produce a clear situation that makes sense of the position of everyone".[1323] Knoope & Buchanan-Clarke attribute this to collective trauma:

> the country's society exhibit signs of collective trauma, such as high levels of distrust and suspicion among and between citizens at the individual and community level.[1324]

However, it seems that this autonomy and the related nonexistence of law goes further back into the history of CAR society. And perhaps it is not necessarily "wrong", although we automatically tend to morally judge any society that is described as lacking social cohesion. As Ngoumbango Kohetto puts it:

> Traditionally, conflict resolution would take place with violence, followed by peaceful negation procedures. The "judge" was no other than the political authority that personified the totality of power, and his role was rather to consolidate the parties, to help them find a solution. The Western jurist refuses to see judges in those instances, and advocates the establishment of a "true justice", that of the Whites.[1325]

This radical autonomy of the individual matches much better with the idea of conflict resolution by a non-legal mediator, who advises parties in a conflict on what to do, thereby recognizing the autonomy of the individuals involved, who, at the end of the day, make their own decisions. It also explains the failure of the (Western?) system of national laws and tribunals; if you do not recognize any law made for you, nor the authority of anyone making law for you, and you are an autonomous individual who finds her/himself forced to go to a court, it makes sense to pay off the judge so that you can get what you want.

It also makes sense for the CAR society to have such a low level of social cohesion, since it is one of the poorest and most violent countries in the world and resources are extremely scarce. Within society there is an atmosphere of mutual distrust and expectation of corrupt behaviour and dishonesty.[1326] As Posner argues, conforming to (social) norms without external enforcement will only happen if people expect, and care for, a future payoff for doing the "right" thing. Without this expectation or enforcement, cooperation is impossible.[1327] I will give an example of how this comes to the fore in CAR society: I am a CAR teacher and I want to go and teach today, because I want to work to get money. Now, I have been told that I will get paid once the school fees are paid by the students. This means that, in the future, at the end of the month, I might get a reward for teaching. However, I am not exactly certain if the students will pay, because they are very poor and maybe they do not have the money. You can

1323 Marchal (2015: 61).
1324 Knoope & Buchanan-Clarke (2017: 12).
1325 Ngoumbango Kohetto (2013: 427).
1326 Knoope & Buchanan-Clarke (2017: 12).
1327 Posner (2000: 11-27).

imagine the frustration of this position, not knowing whether I will actually get paid for my work at the end of the month. This will likely influence my behaviour at work; I might not prepare as well as I could, I might sometimes come in late or not show up at all (for example because I had the opportunity to work in the field and earn some money right away). The student, on the other hand, at the end of the month, has to decide whether to pay or not. They will pay to get taught. But since her/his teacher did not always show up, and was not well prepared, what guarantee is there that the teacher will show up next month? In this case, is it wise to pay? A similar thing happens in the CAR in the relationship between the citizens and the government; knowing that at least a large part of the government is corrupt and that the government does not provide basic services such as health care and education, what interest is there for the citizens to cooperate with the government – for instance, to pay taxes – unless they are forced to do so through violence? And, considering it the other way around, knowing that the citizens (and the international community) do not expect much from the government and that there are no consequences for government leaders if they distort funds to their personal bank accounts, what incentive is there for them to keep their pre-election promises and take care of the CAR citizens? Why would they even legislate?

Based on my field research, I recognize the observation by some researchers, on the lack of social cohesion in the CAR, in terms of political/legal organization. People do cooperate on a daily basis in the CAR, but what happens today is often not a guarantee for what will happen tomorrow. Almost everyone in CAR has a "high discount rate", meaning that they do not care enough about pay-offs in the future, but they would rather take an immediate profit.[1328] In line with the prisoner's dilemma, even if a CAR citizen would know they will get a double profit in the future, they might still choose the lower profit right now because of their dire immediate need. Theoretically, a society of autonomous individuals might live together in peace and prosperity. As Posner writes:

> In a world with no law and rudimentary government, order of some sort would exist. [...] The order would appear as routine compliance with social norms and the collective infliction of sanctions on those who violate them, including stigmatization of the deviant and ostracism of the incorrigible [...] The order, with all its benefits, would come at a cost. Robust in times of peace, it would reveal its precariousness at moments of crisis.[1329]

Collective infliction of punishment, or "popular punishment", is indeed a common practice in the CAR. Whenever a "crime" is committed (such as theft or witchcraft), people tend to take justice into their own hands by engaging in

1328 Ibid: 17-18.
1329 Ibid:3.

violent popular punishment.[1330] However, peace times are rare in the CAR, which has been involved in an on-and-off war for at least 20 years by now, and peace and security generally do not last long in the country (including colonial times).[1331] Therefore, the non-legal situation in the CAR might be best described by a Hobbesian view. According to Hobbes, a society where people have not authorized a sovereign to make law for them would be a warzone. Because all people want to survive and because they desire the same things which they cannot both enjoy, people become enemies. Therefore, for their own preservation, they will always try to subdue or to destroy the other. In such a society, according to Hobbes, the only way for anyone to secure themselves would be to try to be the master of all men – and some, because they take pleasure in "contemplating their own power in the acts of conquest", will go further than their personal security requires. At the end of the day, in such a society, people therefore have to live in perpetual fear of each other:

> Hereby it is manifest that during the time men live without a common power to keep them all in awe, they are in that condition which is called war; and such a war, as is of every man, against every man. For war consisteth not in battle only, or the act of fighting; but in a tract of time, wherein the will to contend by battle is sufficiently known: and therefore the notion of time, is to be considered in the nature of war, as it is in the nature of weather. For as the nature of foul weather, lieth not in a shower or two of rain, but in an inclination thereto of many days together: so the nature of war consisteth not in actual fighting, but in the known disposition thereto, during all the time there is no assurance to the contrary. […] In such condition, there is no place for industry, because the fruit thereof is uncertain: and consequently no culture of the earth; no navigation, nor use of the commodities that may be imported by sea; no commodious building; no instruments of moving, and removing such things as require much force; no knowledge of the face of the earth; no account of time; no arts; no letters; no society; and which is worst of all, continual fear, and danger of violent death; and the life of man, solitary, poor, nasty, brutish, and short.[1332]

It is probably clear by now that this description of a society without law, as Hobbes envisioned it in the 17th century, is not far from the actual situation in the CAR. As a priest, who has been living and working in the CAR for over 20 years, said in one of my interviews:

> Since about 20 years, the mentality of people in the CAR has changed. Traditional values, such as solidarity within the family and patriotism, have largely disappeared. What used to be traditional authority does not weigh much nowadays. What remains, is an authority that imposes itself on different levels, through violence […] In this way, young people internalize violence, they grow up with this model. In CAR

1330 Lombard & Batianga-Kinzi (2014).

1331 See §6.1 and §6.4.2 above.

1332 Hobbes, T. (1651/1996: 88-89).

society it is everyone to themselves; either you impose your will on someone else, and when you cannot, you suffer to their dominance ("on s'impose où on peut et on subit où on ne peut pas s'simposer").[1333]

6.5. UPDATE: THE CHILD'S RIGHT TO EDUCATION IN THE CENTRAL AFRICAN REPUBLIC, 2017–2020

In general, it is difficult to give a comprehensive update on the child's right to education in the CAR since very little reliable data exists and/or is publically available, and I have returned to the CAR only once in 2017 to share my research results with the local community. Almost all the online information available are documents published by NGO and government actors operating on a national level and there is little information available from the local level, due to the lack of research or online forums, quality independent press who publish online, etc.[1334]

On the whole, the situation in the country seems much the same in some areas while some positive changes can be observed in other areas.

On the international level there still seems to be a serious disconnect between the relevant actors in the CAR and the reality in the country. In their 2017 report to the UN Committee on Economic, Social and Cultural Rights, the CAR government reported on international and national law applicable to education in the CAR[1335], as well as strategies / institutions they have planned to establish.[1336] They also write that the education budget for 2017 has been increased to 24% of public expenditure[1337], yet it is hard to measure whether that is true, and if so, where the money went[1338] (there still are regular reports of the few government employed teachers not getting paid).[1339] According to the report, the majority of difficulties encountered in realizing the right to education ("difficulties" that are not further specified), is attributed to "the ongoing security crisis"[1340], with one mention of "the failure to respect the principle of free primary education in all areas of the country".[1341] In their concluding observations, the Committee

1333 Interview 61. A religious leader and director of an NGO field office, in Western CAR.
1334 One positive excemption here is Radio Ndeke Luka, who have really upgraded the online news publications on their website. See www.radiondekeluka.org.
1335 Committee on Economic, Social and Cultural Rights (2017b: paras. 91-96, 124-126).
1336 Ibid (paras. 97-121, 127-133).
1337 Ibid (para. 123).
1338 UNESCO (2020: 23) reports 13% in 2016.
1339 E.g. Education cannot wait (2019); Radio Ndeke Luka (2020a).
1340 Ibid (paras. 225-226).
1341 Ibid (para. 227).

recommends that the state give priority to education and the educational system in its peace and reconciliation activities.[1342]

The 2018 analysis of the education sector by UNESCO reports quantitative data, such as the number of children in schools and financial information, and is completely silent on the quality of education.[1343] Their data indicate a steep increase in the amount of children going to school between 2011–2017 (+59% in primary school, +7% in secondary school)[1344], as well as an increase in student/teacher ratio in primary schools (from 92 per teacher in 2011 to 100 per teacher in 2017).[1345] Aside from being quantitative, since the data in this report is provided by the education inspection, due to the high level of corruption and difficult circumstances it is unlikely that the data is very reliable.[1346]

On the national level a similar disconnect can be observed. In their strategy document for 2019–2021 the Cluster Education is mostly concerned with how to organize emergency education in times of crisis[1347], and the same measurements as taken in the past are continued (e.g. creating temporary learning spaces, educating parent-teachers, distributing books, "capacity building" at the level of the Ministry).[1348] There is no mention of the issue of corruption or of corporal punishment. Ironically, they write:

1342 Committee on Economic, Social and Cultural Rights (2018: para. 40).

1343 Quality of education is mentioned, yet only in terms of actions taken and/or in quantatitve terms. The paragraph on improvement of the quality of education discusses: 1) interventions aimed at getting more children in school; 2) number of teacher-parents educated to teach in temporary learning spaces; 3) number of school buildings reconstructed; 4) distribution of (French language) textbooks for French and mathematics (UNESCO 2018: 56-58).

1344 UNESCO (2018: 76).

1345 UNESCO (2018: 66).

1346 See §6.3.2 (C).

1347 For an interesting analysis and critique of emergency education in the CAR, see Murseli (2019).

1348 Strategie Cluster Education (2019). I was very disappointed to find that none of my research findings and recommendations have had any effect on this level of policy development. This while my study is the only academic study on education for children in the CAR, and while I actively informed the cluster members (NGOs and CAR ministry of Education) about the findings of my study, including meetings with several of the main actors. Perhaps the fact that they did not use the study is not surprising, since the outcomes of the study were not in their interest. In the popular scientific report that presented the study results (Hopman et. al. (2017)), recommendations made all would require a quite radical change of strategy compared to previous years. For example, it was recommended to focus on quality of education rather than of quantity, to engage in longterm education projects rather than shortterm, to engage/ organize national dialogue on the subjects of corruption and corporal punishment in education, etc. (2017: 67). The excuse of the country being in crisis, which implies a temporary problem, does not apply to a country that has been in a constant crisis for at least 25 years. The strategy document does include a short paragraph (9.7) called "innovations" where the clusters "encourages" its "partners" to make use of innovations available, and to think of other innovations, such as education over radio or to teach in Sango. However, this is not part of the strategy of the cluster but left to its partners.

> quality education saves lifes by providing physical protection against the dangers of exploitation in an environment of crisis. When a student finds himself in a safe learning environment, he has less risk of being sexually or economically exploited [...][1349]

This may however tell us only something only about those NGO/government actors interested in reporting on the international level/online, which may not tell us much about what local actors are doing regarding the right to education in the CAR, including on the national level. In this regard, there are some positive indications. One is a research brief which indicates that Dr. Moukadas Noure, the Minister of Education, has taken measures to combat corruption related to the high school exams (*baccalaureate*), and intervention that had actual effect.[1350] This was also confirmed by the observations of one of my local contacts. It also seems that the Minister has developed an "innovative radio education programme"[1351] and "test cash transfer programmes"[1352], both measures that we recommended based on the outcome of our study.[1353]

At the more local level, very limited information is available. It seems that there is still a great problem regarding the employment and consequent by the state of qualified teachers. For this reason, teachers have been on strike since January 2020, a situation for which to date no solution has been found.[1354] Local authorities seem to have sometimes been successful in realizing quality education, such as in the case of the rebel group that had effective control over Ndélé who governed favourably towards public education, thereby creating very good learning results.[1355] I could not find any information regarding corporal punishment in schools.

1349 Strategie Cluster Education (2019: 7).

1350 Glawion & Le Noan (2018: 1), see also Radio Ndeke Luka who report in 2019 that he percentage of students who passed the test was only 10,24% in 2019 – indicating that the correction process has improved (2019b). Prof. Moukadas Noure was also involve in my study and wrote the foreword to the popular scientific report presenting the research results (Hopman et al. (2017b)).

1351 Fondation Hirondelle (2020); Radio Ndeke Luka (2019a).

1352 Education cannot wait (2019); Fondation Hirondelle (2020).

1353 See Hopman et al. (2017b: chapter 7).

1354 See also Gouvernement de la Centrafrique (2020); Radio Ndeke Luka (2020a).

1355 Glawion & Le Noan (2018).

CHAPTER 7
THE CHILD'S RIGHT TO NATIONALITY IN THE TURKISH REPUBLIC OF NORTHERN CYPRUS

Figure 17. A house in the UN buffer zone, Nicosia.

DEFINITIONS

In this chapter, the following terminology will be used:
"Cyprus" refers to the total island of Cyprus
"Turkish Republic of Northern Cyprus", or "TRNC", refers to the internationally unrecognized state that controls the north side of Cyprus and claims independent statehood.[1356]

[1356] As an anaphora, I will refer to the TRNC as a state, not using the inverted commas, or the term "so-called", usually applied to the TRNC in international documents. This is not so much a political statement, as simply a measurement to improve the readability of the chapter

"Republic of Cyprus", or "RoC" refers to the internationally recognized state, and member of the European Union, that controls the south side of Cyprus.
"South Cyprus" refers to the territory governed by the RoC.
"Turkey" or "Turkish Republic" or "TR" refers to the internationally recognized state Turkey.
As regards the population of Cyprus, a distinction will be made between:

1. TRNC nationals: anyone with a TRNC nationality
2. RoC nationals: anyone with a RoC nationality
3. TR nationals: anyone with a TR nationality
4. TC(s): Turkish Cypriot(s), referring to people who have Turkish Cypriot ethnicity. Because it is difficult to determine who exactly belongs to this group, in this chapter this term will refer to those people who identify themselves as TCs (taking into consideration that people often identify with different social/ethnic groups. Someone who self-identifies as TC will often also identify as "Cypriot" and/or as "Turkish-speaking Cypriot"). Additionally, the term will be used when discussing literature in which it is used.
5. GC(s): Greek Cypriot(s), referring to people who have Greek Cypriot ethnicity. Because it is difficult to determine who exactly belongs to this group, in this chapter this term will refer to those people who identify themselves as GCs (taking into consideration that people often identify with different social/ethnic groups). Additionally, the term will be used when discussing literature in which it is used.
6. TRNC population: all people living in the TRNC (northern part of Cyprus)
7. RoC population: all people living in the RoC-controlled area (southern part of Cyprus)
8. Immigrants: anyone who comes to Cyprus as a student, tourist, migrant worker, (foreign) soldier, and/or illegal visitor, who does not have TRNC or RoC nationality
9. Among immigrants in the TRNC we identify the following sub-categories:
   a. International students on a student visa and their families,
   b. Tourist-residents: people who live in the TRNC on the legal status of a tourist visa, who have renewed their tourist visa at least once by means of exiting and re-entering the country in the same week and who have an intention to stay and live in the TRNC
   c. Legal migrant workers and families: non-TRNC nationals who come to TRNC to work, on a work permit issued by their future employer. Their

and hopefully the understanding of the situation of children living in the northern part of Cyprus.

spouses and children often join them, with spouses usually residing in the TRNC on a residency permit

d. Illegal migrant workers: non-TRNC nationals who come to TRNC to work, either without a work permit (in which case they normally would enter on a tourist visa and possibly fall under "tourist-residents") or who had a work permit yet overstayed this permit by staying and working in the TRNC after the work permit expired.

7.1. INTRODUCTION

The last case study of this PhD thesis concerns the child's right to nationality in the Turkish Republic of Northern Cyprus (TRNC). I initially got the idea to do research on the TRNC because I once went there while on vacation in (southern) Cyprus, with no prior knowledge of the conflict, and learned about the conflict during my stay. When I tried to read some literature about the children's rights situation in this unrecognized state, it turned out that there was hardly any information at all, particularly in English.[1357] Of the potential children's rights (CRC) articles to focus on, I chose the child's right to nationality (art. 7), because that seemed to be the most prominent children's rights violation in the TRNC, as will be explained below.

To sketch the relevant context, in this introduction, a brief history of Cyprus (§7.1.1) will be followed by a short introduction to the child's right to nationality (§7.1.2) and an introduction to what is known about children's rights in the TRNC (§7.1.3). Lastly, in the introduction, the methodology applied to the case study will be specified (§7.1.4). The chapter will continue with a general presentation of the research results of the case study (§7.2), followed by a specific analysis of the different legal orders and its laws as regards the child's right to nationality in the TRNC (§7.3). The chapter ends with an upate on the situation in the TRNC regarding the child's right to nationality 2018–2020 (§7.4).

Please note that the research for this case study was done together with a team of students, and I am very grateful for the involvement in this case study of M. Aktas, A.E. Borne, C. Bruchi, F. Pircher, R. Nys and N. Trip, and all the volunteer students who helped with transcribing the interviews.

1357 To illustrate: searching google scholar for "Children's rights Turkish Republic of Northern Cyprus" gives 18,600 results, of which only one seems to have a specific children's rights focus, while "children's rights in the Netherlands" gives 185,000 results.

7.1.1. CYPRUS: A BRIEF HISTORY

It is almost impossible to provide a complete and politically neutral representation of the history of Cyprus, since the debate about its history is a component of the current conflict.[1358] However, an attempt at a summary of historical moments that were key to the current situation of the TRNC child's right to nationality, is provided below.

Historically, Cyprus has been included in four different empires: the Greek, the Venetian, since 1571 the Ottoman empire, and in 1878 British rule took over the Island.[1359] At the time, the people living on the island mostly had a Greek or Turkish background.[1360] Calls for, first, *enosis* (unification of Cyprus with Greece) and, later, *taksim* (partition of Cyprus and the union of such parts with their respective motherlands (Turkey and Greece)) were heard among Greek Cypriot and Turkish Cypriot groups, respectively.[1361] Tensions rose in the 1950s, sometimes resulting into violence.[1362] Both sides set up organized armed groups.[1363] In 1959 the British withdrew in order to make room for an independent Cypriot state.[1364]

The constitution of the Republic of Cyprus was drafted by representatives from the "guarantor powers": Turkey, Greece and Great Britain, together with representatives from the Greek Cypriot and Turkish Cypriot community.[1365] Through international treaties, the *London-Zürich agreements*, it was agreed that: a) the guarantor powers would protect the Cypriot state, b) it was forbidden for any of the guarantor powers to take control of the island, and c) there should be a Cypriot governmental system aimed at ensuring peace and collaboration between the Turkish and Greek Cypriots.[1366] In 1960, the constitution was signed in the Cypriot capital Nicosia, which required every citizen of Cyprus to belong either to one of the two ethnic groups or to another religious group:

1358 As Bryant & Papadakis write: "like the island itself, history in Cyprus has been divided [...] [which] led to binary scholarship on the recent history of the island" (2012: 1).

1359 Yilmaz (2005: 76-78); Michael (2009: 7); Anastasiou (2008: 5); Fransman (2011: 903).

1360 It is unclear what the relationship was exactly between these groups. Some have argued that, until the rise of nationalism in the 1960s, Turkish and Greek Cypriots "did not necessarily conceive of each other as distinct communities in ethnic or national terms" (Navaro-Yashin (2012: 11); Anastasiou (2008: 49)). However, others have questioned this interpretation of history (Loizos (2012: 200-202)).

1361 Solsten (1993: xxi); Michael (2009: 8-14, 23); Anastasiou (2008: 8, 77).

1362 Sözen (2004: 62); Hatay (2017: 15); Anastasiou (2008: 86-93).

1363 Michael (2009: 21, 23); Bryant & Papadakis (2012: 5).

1364 Palmer (1986: 431).

1365 Sözen (2004: 62).

1366 Palmer (1986: 430); 1960 Treaty of Guarantee Signed at Nicosia on 16 August 1960; Michaels (2009: 25).

Article 2, Constitution of the Republic of Cyprus
(1) the Greek Community comprises all citizens of the Republic who are of Greek origin and whose mother tongue is Greek or who share the Greek cultural traditions or who are members of the Greek-Orthodox Church;
(2) the Turkish Community comprises all citizens of the Republic who are of Turkish origin and whose mother tongue is Turkish or who share the Turkish cultural traditions or who are Muslims;
(3) citizens of the Republic who do not come within the provisions of paragraph (1) or (2) of this Article shall, within three months of the date of the coming into operation of this Constitution, opt to belong to either the Greek or the Turkish Community as individuals, but, if they belong to a religious group, shall so opt as a religious group and upon such option they shall be deemed
to be members of such Community [...]
(7) (a) a married woman shall belong to the Community to which her husband belongs.
(b) a male or female child under the age of 21 who is not married shall belong to the Community to which his or her father belongs, or, if the father is unknown and he or she has not been adopted, to the Community to which his or her mother belongs.

Political/legal power was divided between the two main communities; the president was to be Greek and the vice-president Turkish[1367], 70% of the House of Representatives was to be elected by the Greek community and 30% by the Turkish community[1368], etc. Hereby, "nationalism [..] crept into the constitution, legitimizing the complete cultural segregation of the two communities and formalizing the concept of ethnic purity within the political framework of Cypriot society".[1369]

The Republic of Cyprus became a member state of the United Nations in 1960.[1370] However, neither Turkish Cypriots nor Greek Cypriots were completely satisfied with the outcome of the negotiations.[1371] In 1963 the Republic of Cyprus collapsed when the Greek Cypriot President proposed to change the constitution in a manner that was perceived to be reducing the Turkish Cypriot's influence in government.[1372] Political cooperation between the two communities came to an end, and the Turkish Cypriots refused / were refused continued political participation.[1373]

Tension and violence continued to mount between the communities, which was the reason for a United Nations peace-keeping force to be established, the UNFICYP, in 1964.[1374] The UN facilitated peace talks between the communities,

1367 1960 Constitution of the Republic of Cyprus (art. 1).
1368 Ibid (art 62).
1369 Anastasiou (2008: 62).
1370 1960 UN Security Council Resolution 155.
1371 Anastasiou (2008: 95).
1372 Nejatigil (1990: 5A.60.6); Michaels (2009: 26-27); Anastasiou (2008: 95).
1373 Nejatigil (1990: 5A.60.6); Michaels (2009: 27).
1374 1964 UN Security Council Resolution 186; Michaels (2009: 27).

which did not lead to a sustainable solution.[1375] In 1975 the Provisional Cyprus Turkish Administration was created.[1376]

In July 1974, the Republic of Cyprus faced a coup d'état by *enosis* supporters which led to another crisis. Concerned about the possibility of *enosis*, the Turkish military (from Turkey) seized a third of the island, claiming to be acting in the interest of the Turkish Cypriots.[1377] Following more violence, a ceasefire and a dividing line indicating the partition of the island were agreed upon in August 1974. The following year, it was agreed that each "side" was to exchange remaining populations; Turkish Cypriots were to go to the north, to the newly founded Turkish Federate State of Cyprus, and Greek Cypriots to the south, which remained the Republic of Cyprus.[1378]

In 1983, the northern authorities declared the independent state of the "Turkish Republic of Northern Cyprus" (TRNC).[1379] However, this was considered an illegal act and a violation of the territorial integrity of the Republic of Cyprus by the international community, and consequently the TRNC was not recognized as an independent state by any other state except Turkey.[1380] The TRNC was placed under a heavy economic embargo by the EU and the UN, which made it depend on economic aid from Turkey (in addition to military partnership).[1381] To this day, the Republic of Cyprus remains the only internationally recognized government in Cyprus.

Within the TRNC, the demographics of the population has experienced significant changes since Turkey's intervention in 1974. This is mainly due to the influx of Turkish citizens and others immigrating to the TRNC. These immigrants can be categorized into three different groups:

1. First wave in 1974–1980 (mostly 1974 and 1975): Turkish families, mostly with an agricultural background, from poor regions in Turkey, migrated to Northern Cyprus with the help of the Turkish government. These families were given houses, nationality of the Turkish Federate State of Cyprus, and often businesses to run upon arrival. This group is commonly known as "settlers".[1382]
2. Second wave in the 1980s: mostly semi-skilled migrant workers from Turkey who migrated in search of jobs. This allowed for a growing industry and

1375 Michael (2009: 29, 45-47).
1376 Nejatigil, Z. M. (1990: 5A.60.7); Michaels (2009: 42).
1377 Yilmaz (2005: 84); Palmer (1986: 437); Michaels (2009: 32); Anastasiou (2008: 9, 65, 99-100).
1378 United Nations Peacekeeping Force in Cyprus (1975); Michael (2009: 48).
1379 Hatay (2017: 15).
1380 1983 United Nations Security Council Resolution 541.
1381 Navaro-Yashin (2012:8); Michaels (2009: 43); Mehmet (2010: 8, 10); Talmon (2001); Günçavdi & Küçükç (2009).
1382 Interviews 3, 14, 16, 23, 24, 28, 2951, 59, 71, 75, 134, 135; Hatay, M. (2017: 17-19); Navaro-Yashin (2012:57, 117); Michael (2009: 44, 95-97).

economy in the TRNC. These persons were not given the TRNC nationality directly.[1383]

3. Third wave in 1990s – today: with a growing construction sector and increase in universities, this wave included persons of different nationalities, although the majority still has a Turkish background. Families migrate to join different sectors, varying from businessmen and university students to construction workers. It is often difficult or even impossible for this group to obtain TRNC nationality.[1384]

Since 1974, the RoC and the TRNC authorities have continued to hold peace talks, although they have yet to reach a solution.[1385] Several projects and attempts towards reunification and cooperation have taken place. Examples of these are a joint sewage system for the whole island in 1980, which was considered to be unsuccessful[1386], and the Annan Plan in 2004. This plan invited people from both communities to vote on a two-state federal republic and thus reunification of the island. The plan was eventually accepted by the majority of Turkish Cypriots, but it was rejected by the majority of Greek Cypriots.[1387] The most memorable and successful agreement reached to date has been the opening of the borders between the two states in 2003[1388], yet to date all peace talks have failed and a solution for the Cypriot people does not seem to be at hand.[1389]

7.1.2. THE CHILD'S RIGHT TO NATIONALITY

According to the 1989 CRC, every child has the right, from birth, to acquire a nationality (art. 7.1), and State Parties will ensure the implementation of this right "in accordance with their national law and their obligations under the relevant international instruments in this field, in particular where the child would otherwise be stateless" (art. 7.2).[1390]

According to the 1954 Convention relating to the Status of Stateless Persons, a "stateless person" means a person who is not considered as a national by any State under the operation of its law. Since the TRNC is an unrecognized,

---

1383 Interviews 24, 71, 75, 134; Hatay, M. (2017: 17, 20).

1384 Interviews 2, 46, 61, 71, 122, 124, 129, 135, 137; Hatay, M. (2017: 17, 20-23).

1385 For a detailed history and analysis of the Cypriot peace talks, see Michael (2009).

1386 Yilmaz (2005: 89).

1387 Dogan (2013: 67), Michael (2009: 145-189).

1388 2004 European Union Council Regulation 866/2004 ("Green Line Regulation").

1389 United Nations Security Council (2018); Stefanini (2018), Michael (2018); Hatay (2017: 1).

1390 The right to nationality can also be found in the 1948 Universal Declaration of Human Rights (UDHR), art. 15(1) and the 1966 International Covenant on Civil and Political Rights (ICCPR), art. 24.

or "quasi" state[1391], anyone who has only TRNC nationality can be considered stateless.[1392]

Since "in our modern world, nationality often operates as a legal or practical gateway to the enjoyment of other rights"[1393], the consequences of statelessness for children are detrimental. As the Institute on Statelessness and Inclusion (ISI) writes:

> to be stateless as a child can stunt opportunity, erode ambition and destroy the sense of self-worth. That we, the adults who set the rules for inclusion and exclusion, allow this to occur is [...] shameful [...] there is a captivating universality to this problem which is evident in listening to the questions or testimonies of stateless children: wherever they are in the world and whatever the cause of their plight, there is a common experience of loss and frustration [...] Childhood statelessness should be entirely preventable. It is never a child's "fault" if they are left without nationality, nor is it ever in the child's best interest to be stateless.[1394]

As de Groot & Vonk write, nationality is an "empty notion", nationality in itself does not entail specific rights and/or duties for individuals or states, but rather "acquires substantial meaning as a result of legal consequences which national [and international, I would add] legal systems connect with it".[1395]

More concretely, children need nationality for:

- Safe and legal border crossing, travel opportunities
- Educational opportunities
- Access to health care, social welfare protections and other critical economic and social rights facilities
- The ability to enjoy and depend on family life
- Access to (future) employment
- Security and protection from exploitation and abuse
- Non-deportability, or the lifelong guarantee of a right to entry and to indefinite residence in the country of one's nationality

1391 See, for example, Kolstø (2006).

1392 This point is up for discussion, similar to the discussions on nationality for Palestinians and Sahrawi. On the Sahwri, the researchers of the Institute on Statelessness and Inclusion (2014: 121-122) argue that "While the so-called Polisario Front, which has established itself as a government-in-exile, has proclaimed the independent statehood of the Sahrawi Arab Democratic Republic (SADR), this has only been recognised by a few dozen governments and it is not apparent that a Sahrawi nationality exists at present." For a general discussion on the Palestinian and Sahwri cases, see Institute on Statelessness and Inclusion (2014).

1393 Institute on Statelessness and Inclusion (2016: 5).

1394 Institute on Statelessness and Inclusion (2017).

1395 De Groot & Vonk (2015: 36).

- Social security, since non-citizens are particularly vulnerable to the hostility of nationals, convenient targets for marginalization, scapegoating and stigma[1396]

If children are not considered "members" of any state under international law, it is very difficult, if not impossible, to determine who is responsible for the protection of their rights. This is particularly the case for children living in unrecognized states, since it seems that their state of residence falls outside of the scope of international law.

In addition to the right to a (any) nationality, the right to nationality is usually understood to include a right to the nationality that someone is entitled to, based on the principles of preservation of identity (CRC art. 8) and, most importantly, non-discrimination (CRC art. 2).[1397] According to a report of the UN Human Rights Council, "where a child is precluded from obtaining a nationality on discriminatory grounds, this amounts to arbitrary deprivation of nationality".[1398] In other words, when children are not able to obtain a nationality because of their race, color, descent, national or ethnic origin, this is a form of arbitrary deprivation of nationality and therefore a violation of the child's right to nationality.[1399]

On the other hand, international law does seem to allow for discrimination based on nationality in the 1969 International Convention on the Elimination of All Forms of Racial Discrimination (ICERD), which allows for "distinctions, exclusions, restrictions or preferences made by a State Party to this Convention between citizens and non-citizens".[1400] However, the UN Special Rapporteur on the Rights of non-citizens points out that "the Convention [..] does not pre-empt the rights of non-citizens enumerated in other international instruments," since

> In its concluding observations and comments on several States parties' reports ICERD has reflected its continuing concern about various forms of discrimination against non-citizens, including discriminatory requirements for entry and residence and for citizenship.[1401]

In short, according to international law, every child has the right to a nationality, and a right to preserve his or her identity, including nationality. In addition, the

---

1396 Bhabha, J. (2017); UNHCR 2015: 2, 17-21). However, existing research in this field explores statelessness in the context of recognized states, so that the consequences of "statelessness" through membership of an unrecognized state may be quite different.

1397 De Groot & Vonk (2015: 46, 51).

1398 United Nations General Assembly (2015: para. 8).

1399 United Nations General Assembly (2009: para. 26); Committee on the Elimination of Racial Discrimination (2002: paras. 13-17).

1400 1969 International Convention on the Elimination of All Forms of Racial Discrimination (ICERD) (art. 1(2)).

1401 Economic and Social council, commission on human rights (2003: paras. 20-22).

state in whose territory they live is supposed to protect their rights, such as the right to education and the right to healthcare, irrespective of their nationality. No one, including states, is allowed to discriminate according to a child's nationality, although there is some ambiguity.

7.1.3. CHILDREN'S RIGHTS IN THE TRNC

Little is known about the children's rights situation in the TRNC. Because the TRNC is not recognized as a state, it cannot sign and ratify the 1989 CRC. The TRNC does not officially report on the children's rights situation on the island. Neither the Republic of Cyprus government nor the Turkish Republic, in their reporting to the UN Committee on the Rights of the Child, include children living in the TRNC. They are also not mentioned by the NGOs that submitted shadow reports to these states.[1402]

As concerns the child's right to nationality, children in the TRNC do not show up in statistics, such as statistics on stateless people of the world.[1403] Even the researchers of the ISI, in their extensive reports, do not discuss the case.[1404]

In general, for the estimated 80,000 children living on the Northern part of the island[1405], it is unclear whether their rights are taken into consideration by administrative and legislative bodies, including the UN, the European Union, the Council of Europe, the TR, RoC and TRNC governments and, lastly, the local administrative and legal bodies in the RoC and TRNC. While there is some research on the Cyprus conflict[1406], as well as the legal situation of the TRNC under national/international law[1407], there is a lack of research in terms of the concrete situation of children living in the TRNC. Therefore, it is impossible to

1402 Of all 5 NGO reports to the CRC, by Child Helpline International (2011), Global Initiative to End All Corporal Punishment of Children (2011), Hope for Children (2012), the International Disability Alliance (IDA) (2011), and Pancyprian Coordinating Committee for the Protection and Welfare of Children (PCCPWC) (2011), only 1 mentions the Turkish Cypriot children on the side of the TRNC, and they do so only in the sense that they "are concerned by the fact that collecting data and information for the situation of children all over Cyprus is not yet possible due to the continuation of the division of the island and the lack of government control over the occupied areas. The political situation is such that, for the moment, prevents any action on the matter."

1403 See UNHCR (2013).

1404 See Institute on Statelessness and Inclusion (2014, 2017).

1405 There is much obscurity concerning population data in Cyprus in general and the TRNC in particular, due to political interests. Hatay (2007) refers in this context to a "war of numbers". This number is based on the statistics of all people in TRNC with TRNC nationality, 18% are < 18 years old, and the estimated total population of the TRNC is 415,000 (for a more elaborate consideration of the TRNC population see §7.2.1). I took 18% of 415,000 = 79,420.

1406 See, for example, Anastasiou, H. (2008), Hatay, M. & Papadakis, Y. (2012), Michael (2009).

1407 See for example Dogan (2013), Ioannides (2017), Isachenko (2012), Kolstø, P. (2006), Kyris (2012), Mehmet (2010).

tell from a literature study whether, and if so how, the rights of children living in the TRNC are protected.

7.1.4. METHODOLOGY

The main question for this case study was the question "what is the meaning of the child's right to nationality in the TRNC?" In line with the described methodology in chapter 4, in preparation for the field research, the following possible legal orders related to the case study were identified[1408]:

Legal order	Legislator (sovereign)	Relevant legal community
International	United Nations	States: Republic of Cyprus (RoC), Turkey, possibly TRNC Organizations: NGOs, EU offices Individuals: RoC and TR nationals, possibly TRNC nationals, possibly TRNC residents
Regional	a) European Union b) Council of Europe	States: Republic of Cyprus (RoC), Turkey, possibly TRNC Organizations: EU-based NGOs, EU offices Individuals: RoC and TR nationals, possibly TRNC nationals, possibly TRNC residents
National	TRNC, Republic of Cyprus, Turkey	All residents of the TRNC (including non-TRNC nationality), TRNC, RoC and TR authorities
School	School management	Potential students of the school (and possibly their caretakers)
Household	Caretaker (father / mother / family member)	Children within the household
Autonomous child	Child	Child

A team of 6 researchers, consisting of PhD candidate Marieke Hopman and 5 Bachelor students, worked on the case study for a year. The students received extensive training, including a coaching trajectory, in qualitative field research in general, and the specific methodology for qualitative research of this research project (see chapter 4) in particular. In total, the team spent 9 weeks in the TRNC, divided over 3 periods, during which we collected 185 interviews and observations.

To understand the meaning of the child's right to nationality in the TRNC, we triangulated information from 4 different main sources (see below). Statements are included only if they were made by at least 3 different participants and confirmed by at least 2 different main sources, unless indicated otherwise.

The following four main sources provided our information for this chapter:

1408 For an explanation see §7.3.

1. *Formal interviews*

We carried out 87 formal interviews, asking respondents what they thought was the meaning of the child's right to nationality in the TRNC. Of these participants, 52% were male, and 48% were female. Interviews usually took around 45 minutes, although some were quite a bit longer or shorter. People were interviewed in eight different places in the TRNC, including cities and villages, and in one place in South Cyprus. Interviews were conducted with:

Role	Child	Parent / family member	Young adult (age 18–28)[1409]	Politician / government employee	Journalist / lawyer / researcher	Teacher	NGO employee	other[1410]	**TOTAL**
In TRNC	22	31	10	13	5	10	4	2	**97**[1411]
In RoC/other	–	–	1 (NL)	1 (RoC)	1 (RoC)	–	1 (RoC)	–	**4**

Insofar as we know, the participants of formal interviews living in TRNC had direct, first-hand experience with one or more of the following residency statuses:

Residency status	TRNC national	RoC national	TRNC student visa	TRNC tourist visa (tourist resident)	TRNC work permit	Illegal migrant worker
In TRNC	53	16	10	4	16	2

2. *Informal interviews*

We also engaged in 78 recorded informal interviews about the child's right to nationality in the TRNC. These conversations were more spontaneous

1409 Only includes young adults who were not parents. Young people were included as a target group of participants, because we quickly found out that children, and especially young children, did not know enough about the abstract legal concept of nationality to be able to discuss the subject much. However, young people who had very recently been children themselves, could now look back to their childhood and reflect on what it (had) meant for them.

1410 This includes one person with a work permit who did not have children and a religious leader.

1411 The total here is 94 (99), because of double roles that some people fulfill; some government employees are also parents, etc.

discussions about the subject of the research, where the researcher for example tested certain theories or discussed specific subjects. This includes for example when we returned to a family we had met before, to see how their situation had developed. 72% of these participants were male, 28% were female. These discussions were held with:

Role	Child	Parent / family member	Young adult[1412] (age 18–28)	Politician / government employee / journalist / lawyer	Teacher	NGO employee	other[1413]	**TOTAL**[1414]
In TRNC	5	18	10	17	6	3	11	**70**
In RoC/other	–	–	–	5	–	1 (RoC), 2 (bufferzone)	–	**8**

Insofar as we know, the participants of informal interviews living in TRNC had direct, first-hand experience with one or more of the following residency statuses:

Residency status	TRNC national	RoC national	TRNC student visa	TRNC tourist visa (tourist resident)	TRNC work permit	Illegal migrant worker
In TRNC	43	10	9	-	5	4

3. *Observations*

During our time in Cyprus, we recorded several observations related to the research subject, such as encounters with the police and visits to the Ministries of Interior both in TRNC and RoC.

4. *Literature research*

We studied various kinds of books, articles, reports, and legal documents relevant to the research subject.

1412 Only includes young people who were not parents.

1413 This includes several spontaneous discussions with people about whom we did not exactly know their position/profession.

1414 The total here is 78, because of double roles that some people fulfill; some government employees are also parents, etc.

7.2. THE CHILD'S RIGHT TO NATIONALITY IN THE TRNC: GENERAL FINDINGS

Before getting into the legal analysis of the legal orders involved in the child's right to nationality in the TRNC, I will first present the general findings of the case study, starting with an overview of people living in the TRNC (§7.2.1), a description of how to obtain the main nationalities available for children living in the TRNC (TRNC, RoC, TR) (§7.2.2), an overview of the rights that children living in TRNC have access to, based on their nationality (§7.2.3), and three exemplary cases (§7.2.4). The section will end with a short reflection on the meaning of law in the TRNC (§7.2.5).

The information presented in these sections is based mostly on the field research data, supplemented with other sources (the latter will be indicated in footnotes).

7.2.1. WHO LIVES IN THE TRNC?

The demographics of the TRNC population are highly contested by all parties involved in the conflict. Because the RoC constitution divides political powers between the two communities of Cyprus, which at the time was based on the ratio between the two populations (about 70% Greek, 30% Turkish), demography is a political tool. Hatay refers in this context to a "war of numbers".[1415] Nevertheless, we will cautiously try to provide an overview of the TRNC population count:

Within the TRNC, we estimate that around 418,000 people are currently living in the TRNC.[1416] Of this population, it is estimated that 215,000 have TRNC nationality, of whom around 38,000 are children.[1417] 160,000 people living in the TRNC are foreign students or workers (and their families), 20,000 are tourists[1418] and around 20,000 are military personnel and their families.[1419] There are estimated to be in total 70,000 families with work permits, of whom 54,500 have TR nationality and 15,500 have other nationalities.[1420] There are almost 93,000 foreign students (without TRNC nationality), of whom approximately 58,000 have TR nationality.[1421] It must be noted that these statistics exclude people living in TRNC without a legal residency permit.

1415 Hatay (2007: 4).

1416 Hatay (2017: 29), combined with information from our interviews.

1417 Hatay (2017: 29-31): excluding the 15,000 with TRNC nationality who do not live in the TRNC. Of all TRNC nationals, 190,000 are eligible to vote because they are over 18.

1418 It is unclear whether this number includes children.

1419 Hatay (2017: 32) estimates 30,000 but based on our experience in the field that seems quite high, at least while we were in the TRNC.

1420 Hatay estimates that these are in total 65,000, of whom 51,000 have TR nationality and 14,000 have other nationalities. Since this number excludes children out of school, we expect this to be higher (Hatay (2017: 35-36)).

1421 Hatay estimates that these are in total 88,000, of whom 55,000 have TR nationality and 30,000 have other nationalities. Since this excludes the families of these students, we also expect this number to be higher. Hatay (2017: 36).

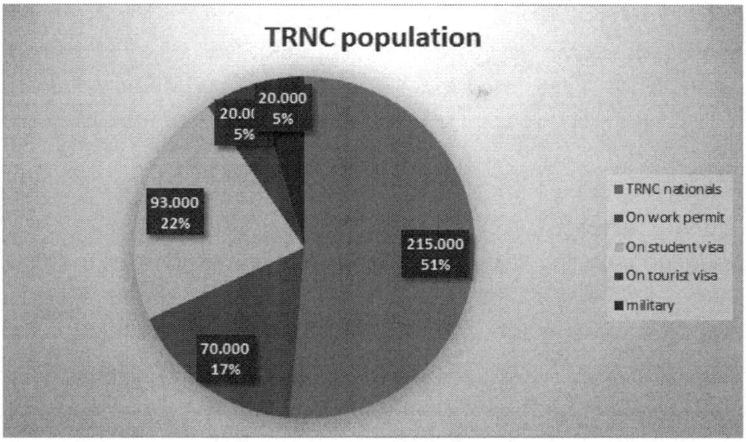

For the population of the TRNC, there are three main nationalities that people have: TRNC, RoC and TR (most people have a combination of these). People who do not have TRNC nationality need to have one of the following TRNC residency documents to reside in the TRNC legally[1422]:

- Residency permit
- Student visa
- Tourist visa
- Work permit
- Business permit
- White ID[1423]
- Membership of the Turkish military

Obtaining either one of these permits (except the tourist visa) costs money and renewing them annually costs money again. What people have to pay seems a bit arbitrary, as it seems to differ per person, but it seems that most

[1422] "Legally" here means according to TRNC law. According to the RoC, anyone who lives in Cyprus without a RoC nationality or a RoC residency document (including EU passport) resides in Cyprus illegally (United Nations (2014: para. 23)).

[1423] The "white ID" is supposed to be a kind of residency document that people may apply for after they have lived in the TRNC for a sufficient time. According to the Permanent Residence Permit Law No 51/2015, people may apply for a white ID if they are a) on a work permit and/or on a permit to set up a business for 6 years, b) have purchased a house for at least € 125,000 and have guaranteed income, c) are married to a TRNC citizen, or d) were born in TRNC or have been living in TRNC for at least 6 years as a minor. The law does not specify which rights holders of the white ID are entitled to. However, during our field research we have not found anyone who had this ID. The few participants (12) who mentioned the white ID argued that, with the white ID, a person has the same rights as a TRNC national except for political participation rights. 2 participants argued that it was either a political proposal but it was never realized or that it used to exist but perhaps not anymore. In TRNC media, it does seem like this ID exists and that it is the subject of political debate (Vamık (2016), Kibris Manşet (2015), Tas (2018), Yenidüzen (2015)). See also Hatay (2017: 23).

people pay between 400–800 TL per year per person (€ 76 – 153).[1424] For these families who often have very low or no income, this is a lot of money. For the TRNC state, who do not have a lot of income due to an international economic embargo and a failing tax system[1425], selling permits is an important source of revenue.

When one parent is in the TRNC using one of these documents, the family (spouse and children under 18 years old) usually get permission from TRNC authorities to come and live in the TRNC for the duration of the validity of the residency document. When the document expires, they all have to leave. In practice, people sometimes overstay. Those who overstay have to pay a daily fine which is equivalent to the daily minimum wage.[1426] In our research, we focused on international students, tourist-residents (those who continuously prolong their tourist visas with the intention to stay), people with work permits and people without residency documents, because, for these groups, there was the strongest indication of potential violations of children's rights.

Below you will find a short description of the different families with permits that we focused on in the case study. It is important to know that, in all cases, what we understood from the research participants is that children are not registered on the permits. If children overstay, therefore, there are no consequences. However, when they become 18 years old, they either have to apply for a permit themselves (or for TRNC nationality) or they have to leave the country.

Families on student visas

Although the TRNC is very small compared to most countries, there are 16 universities, which allegedly host 88,000 international students.[1427] In addition to TRNC and TR students, most of these students are from non-EU countries, mostly Africa (Nigeria, Zimbabwe), Central Asia and the Middle East.[1428] It is interesting for them to study in TRNC because it is relatively cheap and easy to get a visa. For some, a reason to study in TRNC is because it is part of Europe and sometimes only upon arrival they find out that they will not be able to enter the rest of Europe.[1429] Unless they are students from the EU or other exempted countries[1430], they cannot cross to the south unless they are able to obtain a visa to the RoC/EU.[1431] Therefore, they find themselves stuck in the northern part of the island.

1424 These prizes are calculated using the exchange rate from the time of the last field research period (April 2018), which is before the downfall of the Turkish Lira in August 2018.

1425 Mehmet (2010: 12, 16).

1426 See also 1982/2016 TRNC Foreigners and Immigration Act (art. 19).

1427 Hatay (2017: 36).

1428 See also Güsten (2014).

1429 See also Obioma (2016).

1430 In addition to EU nationals, people with nationalities from the following countries are allowed to cross: USA, Canada, Australia, Switzerland, Israel, Moldova, and Serbia.

1431 2004 European Union Council Regulation 866/2004 ("Green Line Regulation").

Some of these students arrive with children, some have their families brought over at a later stage, and some students have children while they are in the TRNC. Student visas need to be renewed every year and can be renewed for as long as the person is registered as a student at a TRNC university. Renewing the visa costs money for students, as they have to pay for health checks, police checks, etc. For children of parents on a student visa born in TRNC, it can be difficult to obtain any nationality because there are no embassies or consulates in the TRNC except the Turkish embassy. Since they cannot travel to the RoC, they have to either travel to Turkey to visit their embassy/consulate there (provided there is one in Turkey), or they have to pay someone to obtain the necessary documents in the south (which is not always allowed) or in the country of origin. Similar problems occur when passports or other identity documents of children expire.

Families on tourist visas

Nationals of almost every country can travel to TRNC and obtain a tourist visa upon arrival.[1432] Tourist visas are usually valid for 90 days. Some families however, and these seem to be mostly Turkish families, use the tourist visa as a more permanent residency document. These families have to do "exit and entry" every 3 months to renew their tourist visa. Although they are not allowed to work, most of these people work without a legal permit. Because of their tourist status, it is more difficult or sometimes not possible for these families to claim most of their basic rights such as health care, education, etc. in the TRNC.

Families on work permits

In the TRNC there are many families who reside in the TRNC on a work permit. To obtain a work permit, the employer needs to invite the foreign worker to the TRNC and arrange a temporary permit before arrival ("pre-permit"), which can be changed into a one-year permit once the employee has arrived in TRNC. This work permit has to be renewed every year, and the employee has to pay for certain documents (health checks, police checks, etc.) that s/he has to submit. Employees on a work permit are usually allowed to bring their families.[1433]

Families without legal residency permits

Some families are residing in the TRNC without a legal residency permit. Obviously, these people are not easy to find or to approach for research

1432 Two exceptions to this rule are nationals of Nigeria and Armenia. See: Deputy Prime Ministry and Ministry of Foreign Affairs (n.d. (a)).

1433 2006 TRNC Law on Work Permits for Foreigners No 63/2006; 2006/2012 TRNC Regulation of Foreigner's Work Permits.

interviews. From the few that we did speak to, combined with what we learned from researchers, journalists and politicians who looked into the issue as well as literature research, it seems that these families enter the TRNC on a valid permit (tourist visa, student visa, work permit or other), yet they overstay once these expire. In some cases the employer may have cancelled the work permit without telling the employee, because of the relatively high cost of the permit compared to hiring an illegal worker (in which case the employee only has the choice to either leave the TRNC forever, or at least until they are able to pay the fine that has been building up without their knowledge, or to stay in the TRNC without a permit). In other cases, families may not have been able to keep the job which they came for, or they never got a work permit in the first place. Most illegal workers can be found in low-wage, low-skilled jobs, such as construction and the hotel and catering industry.[1434]

7.2.2. WHICH NATIONALITY CAN A CHILD LIVING IN TRNC OBTAIN?

Children born in TRNC in most cases are eligible for one of three nationalities: Turkish (TR), TRNC and/or Republic of Cyprus (RoC). All three of these nationalities are obtained through a *jus sanguinis* system, meaning that these nationalities are obtained if the child is registered as the legal child of a parent with one of these nationalities. During our case study, we focused on these three nationalities.

For the parents who had other nationalities than these three, we did not encounter any problems with obtaining nationality for these children, except for difficulties with obtaining identity documents because of the lack of embassies/consulates in TRNC. It is possible that, if two parents both have a nationality of a state where nationality is transferred through a *jus soli* system, i.e. the acquisition of nationality of the state where the child is born, this would leave the child born in TRNC potentially stateless, but we did not encounter any such cases.

Obtaining TRNC nationality

TRNC nationality is obtained either at birth or through naturalization.

A child born to at least one parent who has TRNC nationality will automatically also obtain TRNC nationality according to TRNC law.[1435] This includes children born in other countries. Parents can have TRNC nationality

1434 Göyknüklü (2012: 86).

1435 1993 Turkish Republic of Northern Cyprus Citizenship Law No 52/1993/2005; 1983 Constitution of the Turkish Republic of Northern Cyprus (art. 63).

if they had a parent with TRNC nationality or if they had RoC nationality or citizenship of the Turkish Federate State of Cyprus before 15 November 1983.[1436] In practice, this state law seems to be applied consistently[1437], and the majority of the TRNC population is aware of this law.

A second way for children to obtain TRNC nationality is through naturalization. According to TRNC law, there are three ways for adults to become naturalized: by marriage (one can apply after having been married to a TRNC citizen for one year), by investment or publicity (one who invests in certain designated sectors or who actively promotes TRNC internationally) or by legally residing in TRNC for at least 5 years (additional conditions apply, such as the person has to have expressed the intention to settle in TRNC and needs to have sufficient income). Once the parent has been naturalized, children under the age of 18 should also be naturalized.

In the cases of naturalization by investment, publicity or residency, the law only provides for the possibility of *application* for citizenship if certain conditions are satisfied, yet it leaves the question whether or not this person will acquire TRNC nationality up to the Council of Ministers.

> **Turkish Republic of Northern Cyprus Citizenship Law No 52/1993/2005, art. 8(1):**
> Any alien person wishing to acquire citizenship ***may*** acquire citizenship of the Turkish Republic of Northern Cyprus by decision of the Minister provided he satisfies the following conditions [...]

The law even provides for the option to waive these conditions in cases where, for example, it concerns "persons who are likely to perform extraordinary services in science, politics and cultural sectors"[1438], or even "persons to whom the Council of Ministers deems it necessary to grant citizenship"[1439], a discretion that among others is said to be used by politicians to grant mostly Turkish migrants nationality in return for votes.[1440]

1436 1993 Turkish Republic of Northern Cyprus Citizenship Law No 52/1993.

1437 We encountered one case where this law was not applied, namely in the case of the son of a TRNC father and a TR mother. His parents were divorced, he lived with his father in TRNC since age 10, yet, when he applied, he did not get TRNC nationality (Interview 100). Since we did not encounter any other cases nor could we research the case in more detail, this seems to be an exception.

1438 Turkish Republic of Northern Cyprus Citizenship Law No 52/1993/2005 (art. 9(1)(B)).

1439 Ibid (art. 9(1)(C)).

1440 Michael (2009: 93, 97); Hatay (2017: 4-6).

Figure 18, taken from a newspaper article.

Shortly before the 2018 elections, new TRNC citizens received a text message from the TRNC Minster of Foreign Affairs. The text reads: "Dear Brother/Sister[1441], I hope your citizenship contributes to our community and country. Regards, Tahsin Ertuğruloğlu UBP[1442] Lefkoşa MP Candidate No:9" (Haber Kibris (2017)).

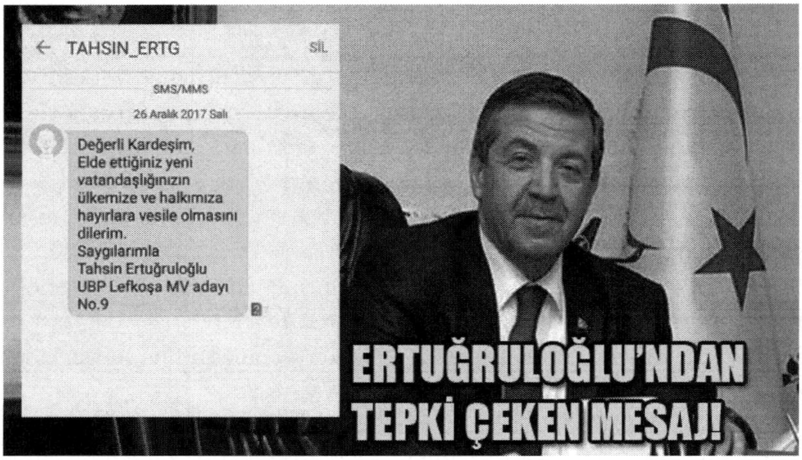

In practice, naturalization happens though an inconsistent and non-transparent process. To obtain nationality through naturalization, it is necessary for the applicant to know someone in the government (this is called a "*torpil*"), who will help to push the application through, although even having *torpil* is no guarantee for a successful application. In this way, people who have never visited the TRNC can be made citizens, while people who have lived and worked in the TRNC for many years, including their children who are born in TRNC, cannot obtain the nationality, to the great frustration of a large part of the TRNC population. People who have resided in the TRNC legally for more than 5 years are usually not allowed to apply for TRNC nationality (they are turned away by the employees of the Ministry of Interior) or after application their papers get lost or they are put on a waiting list. To apply, people have to submit several documents again, such as police reports and health checks, which they have to pay for and so this process, too, is a source of income for the TRNC state.

A popular belief is that one needs to have at least 10 work permit stamps, proving that they have worked legally in the TRNC for 10 years, to be able to get TRNC nationality (see §7.3.3.1 for a discussion).

When a parent is naturalized, their underage children obtain TRNC nationality automatically.[1443] However, in practice this application process can take quite some time, and some evidence suggests that the law is not applied to children born from previous marriages in the case of naturalization through marriage.

1441 There are no feminine/masculine words in Turkish.

1442 UBP is National Union Party, which was the ruling party before the 2018 elections.

1443 1993 Turkish Republic of Northern Cyprus Citizenship Law No 52/1993: art. 9(2).

Figure 19. An image that circulated on Facebook at the end of 2017, shortly before the 2018 elections.

It shows E.T. who received a TRNC ID card. The accompanying text reads: "The last day before entering the electoral ban, the beloved extraterrestrial character E.T. was also made a citizen of the TRNC. Hüseyin Özgürgün, the prime minister, gave the distinction of the completed citizenship process as a result of the additional affair of Muhaceret.[1444] He said that E.T. was loved all around the galaxy and that he would take important steps towards introducing the Galata to the TRNC. E.T. said that he would eliminate the problem of direct transportation to the TRNC[1445] with the cooperation of the bicycle and aviation federations and said he was happy to be in North Cyprus. On the other hand, the opposition is talking about whether E.T. will do military service in accordance with citizenship. Celebrate our independent sovereign proud republic."

Obtaining RoC nationality

RoC nationality is obtained in three ways: either at birth, by virtue of registration or through naturalization.

A child born to at least one parent who has RoC nationality will also obtain RoC nationality according to RoC law.[1446] This includes children born in other countries, provided their birth is registered in the prescribed manner within 2 years after the birth.[1447]

1444 Referring to the affair that the prime minister was said to have, upon which the woman, who had only been to the TRNC as a tourist, received TRNC nationality. See: Havadis Kibris (2017), Kibris Son Dakina (2017).

1445 Referring to the international embargo on direct transportation to the TRNC.

1446 1967/2000 Republic of Cyprus Citizenship Law (hereafter: RCCL) (sect. 3(-1, 2)); 2002/2017 Republic of Cyprus Civil Registry Law of 2002 (hereafter: RCCRL) (sect. 109 (-1, 2)).

1447 RCCL (art. 3(2)(b)).

There are two exceptions:

1) If the person was born abroad between 16 August 1960 and the date of entry into force of the RoC citizenship law in 1999, and the RoC parent was the mother, unless the person applies to the Minister after they are 21 years old[1448]
2) If any one of the parents has entered into or is staying in Cyprus illegally, meaning that they entered Cyprus through the TRNC and/or live in the TRNC without official permission of the RoC government ("unless the Council of Ministers otherwise orders").[1449]

A second way for children to obtain RoC nationality is through registration. Relevant for this case study is that someone who marries a RoC citizen and resides with their spouse in Cyprus for at least 3 years can obtain RoC nationality, however this does not apply 1) to children who are not the children of the RoC spouse and 2) to spouses who entered into and/or live in Cyprus illegally.[1450] Second, the RoC Minister may give RoC nationality through registration of the child (<18 years old) of a parent who has RoC nationality if a request is made by the parent or guardian of the child.[1451]

A third way for a child to acquire RoC nationality is through naturalization. A person can obtain RoC nationality through naturalization if they stayed in the RoC for the full 12 months preceeding the application, as part of an overall stay of 7 years.[1452] In addition, the Council of Ministers has the discretionary power to reduce this period, especially if it concerns a person of "Cypriot origin" (meaning a person born in Cyprus at the time when her/his parents usually resided in Cyprus).[1453] The law does not explicitly state what happens to children in case their parents obtains RoC nationality through naturalization – most likely parents can then apply for RoC nationality through registration on behalf of their children.

In practice, children living in TRNC are only able to obtain RoC nationality if they either have two RoC parents, if they deny having a father in the case that their mother has the RoC nationality, or if they can make a credible threat to sue the RoC state in the European Court of Human Rights. If they do obtain RoC nationality, it serves as a travel document and a nationality in relation to foreign countries, yet it does not bestow upon the person citizenship rights in the RoC (see also §7.2.3).

1448 RCCL (sect. 3(3)); RCCRL (sect. 109 (3)).

1449 RCCL (sect. 3(1)); RCCRL (sect. 109 (3)).

1450 >RCCRL (sect. 110(2)(d)). The RCCL does not state explicitly that this regulation does not apply to the children of the spouse, yet it states that "the Minister may cause the minor child of any citizen of the Republic to be registered as a citizen of the Republic upon application [...]" (sect. 5(3)).

1451 RCCRL (sect. 110 (3)); RCCL (sect. 5(3)).

1452 RCCRL (sect. 111, Third table, sub article 1); RCCL (sect. 6).

1453 RCCRL (sect. 110 (1), Third Schedule art. 2).

Obtaining TR nationality

According to TR state law, TR nationality is obtained either at birth or after birth.

Every child born to a TR parent obtains TR nationality. However, if the child is born out of wedlock to a TR father and a mother of another nationality, it can only acquire TR nationality "if the principles and procedures ensuring the establishment of descent are met".[1454]

TR nationality can also be acquired after birth. This can only be applied for by someone who is of the age of majority (18). The following are methods of acquisition of TR nationality after birth:

- A person who has been a resident of Turkey for 5 years, in addition to some other conditions (health, speaking Turkish, etc). Adhering to these conditions gives someone a right to apply for TR nationality; yet acquisition still depends on the decision of the council of ministers.[1455]
- A person who has "rendered outstanding services", for example in science or sports, can receive TR nationality based on a Council of Ministers decision.[1456]
- A person who has been married to a TR national for at least 3 years can apply for TR nationality[1457]

In these cases, if the parent who has guardianship over the child acquires TR nationality, the child will also acquire TR nationality on the same day, provided the spouse approves. If both parents acquire TR nationality, the children will also acquire TR nationality.[1458]

Lastly, people who acquired TRNC nationality at birth (through a TRNC parent), can acquire TR nationality if they "express in writing their wishes to become a Turkish citizen".[1459] However, anyone who acquired TRNC nationality after birth will have to go through the TR naturalization process like any other foreigner.[1460]

In practice, it seems that children living in TRNC who do not have a TR parent and who are TRNC nationals can indeed apply for a TR identity document with the TR embassy and receive this relatively easily. However, participants indicated that this is a travel document and not a full TR citizenship. All these "TR travel documents" state the same place of birth (in Turkey) and a specific number by which the TR authorities can recognize it as a TR travel document.

1454 2009 Turkish Citizenship Law, Law No: 5901 (art. 7).
1455 Ibid: art. 11.
1456 Ibid: art. 12.
1457 Ibid: art. 16.
1458 Ibid: art. 20 (2 and 3).
1459 Ibid: art. 42 (1).
1460 Ibid: art. 42 (2).

7.2.3. ACCESS TO RIGHTS

In the TRNC, which rights are accorded to children are related to which group of the population they belong to. Distinctions are made based on nationality and ethnicity. Below I will shortly indicate which rights can be accessed by which groups.

International rights

On the international level, the non-recognition of the TRNC has several consequences for children living in the TRNC and their rights.

1) **Right to non-discrimination** (CRC pre-amble and art. 2): in principle, children with TRNC nationality are excluded from the international community based on their nationality, while the claim of all states who signed the CRC is that "everyone is entitled to all the rights and freedoms set forth therein, without distinction of any kind, such as race, […] language, religion, political or other opinion, national or social origin, property, birth or other status" and that "the child should be fully prepared to live an individual life in society, and brought up in the spirit of the ideals proclaimed in the Charter of the United Nations, and in particular in the spirit of peace, dignity, tolerance, freedom, equality and solidarity".
2) **Right to education that is directed to the development of the child's personality, talents and mental and physical abilities to their fullest potential** (art. 29(a)): What is missing most according to children themselves is that no matter how hard they try to become very good in sports, arts or other disciplines, they do not have the right to compete in international tournaments. Another limitation to their development is the fact that they know that they live in an internationally unrecognized country which is under an international economic embargo, so that possibilities for economic growth and development are severely limited. Both these factors limit children's motivation and dreams.
3) **Right to education that is directed to the preparation for responsible life in a free society, in the spirit of understanding, peace, tolerance, friendship of all peoples, ethnic and national groups** (art. 29(d)): There are signs that children living in TRNC who are not Turkish Cypriots do not have the right to take part in peace-building activities. This is because UN agencies are in Cyprus on the invitation of the Republic of Cyprus and so they have to cooperate with the RoC government, which does not wish for these children to be included.

Interview 69, a politician in TRNC:
I live in a society which is not recognized by international organizations or anything. And that's pretty bad because we have lots of young people especially which have lots of potential, of what they like to do, and they cannot express themselves freely. They know that they have a limit on what they want to achieve.

In general, some adult participants in the research indicated that they notice the lack of international rights and protection by the international community of children's rights. They argue, for example, that TRNC politicians are aware that there is no control of rights protection/violation and that this means that there is no accountability. However, it seems that, even though the TRNC is excluded from the international control mechanism, and in general from the international political, economic and legal realm, international law does have significance in TRNC, including in children's rights. Politicians and political employees often argued that something needed to be done, because it was either in accordance with, or contrary to, children's rights – sometimes explicitly referring to the international Convention. TRNC state law, too, refers to international law in several places.

Regional (EU) rights

The EU is quite involved in the TRNC, since the accession of Cyprus to the EU. They provide financial and material support to schools in the north and scholarships to study in the EU for individual applicants. Although many people are aware of this type of support, it is confusing to them, as they also know that the EU has an embargo on trade with North Cyprus[1461], that European countries do not recognize the TRNC and that with their TRNC passport they cannot travel through Europe (except to the UK). Most people do not think that they could claim any protection of their rights on the regional European level.

Children's rights in Cyprus

In Cyprus, what right a child can claim very much depends on her/his nationality and ethnicity (where the parents are from). Below are the rights that our participants indicated were violated for some groups of children in the TRNC.

Right to non-discrimination[1462]

Many children experience discrimination in Cyprus. There seems to be a hierarchy of power and belonging[1463], and the lower you are, the more you are discriminated against. Of people living in TRNC, Turkish Cypriots are discriminated against by Greek Cypriots; Turkish people are discriminated against by Turkish Cypriots; non-Turkish migrants are discriminated against by Turkish people; and African (black) people are discriminated against by almost everyone.

1461 Talmon (2001).

1462 1989 Convention on the Rights of the Child (CRC)(preamble, art. 2); 1948 Universal Declaration of Human Rights (UDHR) (art. 7); 1966 International Covenant on Economic, Social and Cultural Rights (ICESCR) (art. 2); 1966 International Covenant on Civil and Political Rights (ICCPR) (art. 20, 24, 26); 1969 International Convention on the Elimination of All Forms of Racial Discrimination (ICERD); 1979 Convention on the Elimination of All Forms of Discrimination against Women (CEADW).

1463 See also §7.2.5.

Although of course not everyone discriminates and many people of all ethnicities are friendly to each other, children experience a lot of discrimination. For example: Turkish Cypriots are favored by teachers and the police; TRNC nationals get better treatment in hospitals; Turkish speaking students get better treatment than non-Turkish speaking students. On the bus, people do not want to sit next to black people and some Turkish people do not let their children play with black children.[1464]

> *Interview 61, a 15-year old boy who got TRNC nationality after his Turkish father went through the naturalisation process (using torpil).*
>
> Even if I'm right, because I come from Turkish background, [my opponent] would be able to find a way to escape if I get into a fight with a local Cypriot boy, because maybe his father or one of his relatives is a policeman and they would be able to find a way to get themselves to be the right person. Even if I'm right I wouldn't be able to find a way of proving myself right.
>
> *Interview 104, a 16-year old Filipino girl who came to TRNC with parents who are working in TRNC on work permits.*
>
> Here [in TRNC] you experience "you do not belong here".

Right to equal treatment and equal opportunities[1465]

Generally, within the TRNC, children whose parents are TRNC nationals enjoy better opportunities and get treated better than children from non-TRNC nationals. This happens for two reasons. First, because North Cyprus is relatively small, everyone knows everyone. There is a strong culture of favoritism; you get things done because you know people (as the Cypriots say: "I see you, you see me"). Because government jobs are only available for TRNC nationals, this is an advantage for TRNC nationals, who are therefore much more likely to know people in power. A child whose family has good connections will receive more opportunities, such as a privilege when confronted with the police, help when searching for a job, access to better schools, etc.

Second, TRNC nationals are generally richer and live in more favorable socio-economic circumstances than non-TRNC nationals, which allows them to afford better treatment and create better opportunities for their children. This is for several reasons: first, TRNC nationals have access to the better paid jobs, such as government jobs. Unlike non-TRNC nationals, TRNC nationals are allowed to have their own companies and they can get bank loans. They often do not have to pay rent or mortgages because they own their houses (some of

1464 See also Hatay (2017: 2-4), Webster & Timothy (2006), Stevens (2016).

1465 1989 CRC (preamble, art. 2, 28, 31(2)); 1948 UDHR (art. 7, 23); 1966 ICESCR (art. 6, 7, 9, 11), 1966 ICCPR (art. 26); 1969 CEARD.

which are Greek Cypriot houses given to them by the TRNC government) and they do not have to pay a yearly sum to renew their work permit, student visa and/or residency permit. If they have financial trouble, TRNC nationals can get financial support from the TRNC social services, non-TRNC nationals cannot. TRNC parents get pensions whereas non-TRNC do not. This puts TRNC parents in a much better financial position than non-TRNC parents. Meanwhile, both TRNC and non-TRNC have to pay taxes. Because of their better financial position, TRNC nationals are able to afford much better quality education and healthcare for their children (who often go to better quality private schools and hospitals).

Later in life, TRNC children are greatly advantaged compared to non-TRNC children in having access to college education through scholarships, lower subscription fees and even different exams for TRNC nationals.

Table 4: Institutionalized causes for difference in treatment & opportunities for children of TRNC and non-TRNC nationals

Allowed to TRNC nationals	Allowed to non-TRNC nationals
Access to better paid jobs such as government jobs	Not allowed to work for government, often work low-wage jobs
Allowed to have their own companies	Not allowed to have their own companies (unless with special permission)
Allowed to get a bank loan	Not allowed to get a bank loan (unless with special permission)
Mostly own their own houses, often given to them by the TRNC government	Pay rent, not allowed to buy houses
Do not have to pay to renew any documents	Have to pay yearly sum to renew work/ residency permit or student visa
Can get financial support from TRNC social services	Cannot get financial support from TRNC social services
Get state pensions	Do not get state pensions
Get scholarships, lower subscription fees and more points on exams in regard to college education	Have more trouble getting scholarships and entering college

Interview 13. A father, migrant worker who has been working in TRNC for 18 years, of which 14 years he had a work permit (before 2005 work permits were not mandatory). He acquired the TRNC nationality, after two unsuccessful applications, 6 months before the interview. His 2 children and wife are still in the process to receive TRNC nationality.

A. […] because we are from outside, like we are working people and my wife is not working, therefore I am working only myself and I cannot give this opportunity [to go to a private school] to my children.

Q: Okay. These opportunities, what are they? That are related to nationality?

A: Everything is interconnected because, for example, house rents are increasing these days. I started with the rents that are high, now most of my salary is going to his rent, therefore I can't really spend on the education of my children. But most of the TRNC citizens are owning a house therefore they can spend on education more. [...] If it was our own house, that money could stay apart so therefore we could send our children to better schools, private schools.

Right to healthcare[1466]

No child living in TRNC, whether they have RoC nationality or not, is entitled to healthcare in RoC. In TRNC, it seems that all children have a right to healthcare, no matter their residency status. However, children whose parents are in TRNC on a tourist visa, student visa or whose work permit has been expired, receive shorter and lower quality healthcare, for which they generally have to pay more.

Interview 103. A 16-year old high school student who has been in TRNC for 2.5 years. His parents are in TRNC on student visas.

Q: Do you know if there is any difference between people that have TRNC and you? Like are you allowed to do certain things that they are not allowed or vice versa?
A: At school it is the same [...] [However,] I got a problem, maybe for two months, I was too ill and I was dying, I thought "I am dying".[...] So I went to the hospital – my friend had the same problem – I went to the hospital and I said "it is my problem". They checked that. [...] My friend was better than me, and my situation was so bad, was worse. They just said "no you are ok, you can go", and they did not give me a report to give to school, but they gave it to him. And he slept more than two weeks at the hospital, and I had to go to school every day with that pain, it was...
Q: So, when you were at the hospital, do you think that your friend was treated better because he has a TRNC nationality?
A: Yes. I think that. Because I am speaking with [the hospital employee] using Turkish language, and he is replying by using English, and his English language was worse than mine.
Q: Why would he answer you in English?
A: I don't know, because he knew that I'm not Cypriot, so I think he thought that I can't speak Turkish.
Q: Has this happened before? That you think that the TRNC nationals get treated better?
A: No before that I thought it is same. At school we are like brothers.

Some parents indicate that, because they have no insurance (for example because they are staying in TRNC on a tourist visa), they cannot take their children

1466 1989 CRC (art. 3(3), 24); 1948 UDHR (art. 25); 1966 ICESCR (art. 12); 1969 CEARD (art. 5).

to the hospital. These children are either refused by the hospital or it is very expensive to get treatment, which these parents cannot afford.

Right to education[1467]

According to the 1983 TRNC constitution, every child has the right to compulsory education until the age of 15 and to free education until the age of 18. Many teachers and school directors seem to promote this right actively. For example, if parents are not able to afford fees for school books or uniforms, teachers sometimes raise this money or pay for this themselves. However, there are some concerns about the right to education for non-TRNC nationals:

- Some public schools ask high school fees (around 500 TL) to allow children of parents who are non-TRNC nationals, who are not on a work permit, to attend.
- Children whose parents are in the TRNC on a tourist visa or whose parents do not have legal permission to live in the TRNC need official approval from the ministry of education to be able to attend public school. This adds an extra hurdle to attend schools, especially if families are scared to be deported.
- Children whose parents are in the TRNC on a tourist visa regularly miss school because they have to exit and enter the country every 3 months (or sometimes more often).
- When schools are full, the children who are last to subscribe get refused. In practice, this means that children who arrive newly in the TRNC (for example with their parent who has a work permit or student visa), are more likely to be refused access to education.
- If non-TRNC children do not attend school, usually the TRNC authorities do not do anything about this, unless they are alerted by someone. And even if they are alerted, they do not seem to do much.
- The quality of education for non-TRNC nationals, who often attend public school for financial reasons, is much lower than for TRNC nationals, who often attend private schools. This is shown clearly by the fact that public schools, where school days last from 8:00–13:00h, provide much less education than private schools.
- Some non-TRNC children have been excluded from school trips, sports club trips and from activities in the municipality because of their nationality.

[1467] 1989 CRC (art. 28, 29); 1948 UDHR (art. 26); 1966 ICESCR (art. 13, 14); 1969 CEARD (art. 5).

Right to cross the border/checkpoints between North and South Cyprus[1468]

Every child who has at least one of the following is allowed to cross to the South side, with (written) permission of their parents:

- a European identity document or visa
- an identity document from certain allowed countries
- one "original Cypriot" parent (who had Cypriot nationality before 1974)

All other children will be stopped by the RoC police. This includes children who were born and raised in the TRNC, children who have TRNC nationality, children of international students on a TRNC student visa and all tourists from other countries other than those mentioned above.

> *Interview 108, a teacher at a public school*
> We have Greek friends [...] Sometimes we organize chess meetings here, in Nicosia, it is no problem. They come. But when it is [in the south], we have problem of the kids who are from Turkey, who have Turkish passports [...] If we organize for this school to go to south side, there will be not more than 10 students that can go! We have this joke every time!
>
> *Interview 50, a Zimbabwean father, who is in TRNC with his family, on a student visa.*
>
> I can't [go to the south side], because I have a stamp from this side. Even if my visa is valid for the south side, they said you came in from Ercan [the TRNC airport] so you can't come through. You have a student permit for the north.

Other concerns related to children's rights in the TRNC

- In the TRNC, some parents reported being unable to get a birth certificate for their newborn child because they did not have a passport.
- The TRNC has no juvenile justice system and no juvenile prison.
- A few children told us about serious child abuse in the government institutions run by TRNC authorities (not SOS children's village, but the state facilitations).
- Right to identity: many young people in TRNC seem confused about their identity, because of the identity politics of both TRNC, RoC and TR

1468 Although the right to freedom of movement is not in the CRC, because many children felt very hindered in the enjoyment of their rights, especially because many of their classmates could cross whereas they could not, I decided to include this "right". In any case, it does connect to the right to non-discrimination, since who can and cannot cross is based on nationality. For right to freedom of movement, see: 1948 UDHR (art. 13); 1969 CEARD (art. 5).

governments. They are confused whether they are Turkish, Turkish-Cypriot, Cypriot, Turkish-speaking Cypriot, etc.

- Right to protection[1469]: it seems that children who come into the country with their parents on a work permit, tourist visa or residency permit, are not properly registered, and are not known to the relevant authorities. They may be registered by the border police, but this information may then be unknown by, for example, the Ministry of Education. These children overstay their permits without any consequence. Therefore, if these children would, for example, disappear, be seriously abused, not attend school, etc. it is unlikely that anyone would notice.

7.2.4. EXEMPLARY CASES

To illustrate these issues outlined above, the following presents some examples of cases that we encountered during our research:

Case 1

Can is a Turkish migrant worker who came with his wife to the TRNC from Turkey in 2007. Before his arrival he received a work permit, which he has renewed every year since his arrival. After 10 years, he thinks that he has the right to apply for citizenship. His 17-year old daughter will receive TRNC nationality if he gets it. Therefore, Can pays for and collects all necessary paperwork (health report, police report, etc.). However, after he submits all this to the Ministry of Interior, when he comes back two months later to check on his application, they say that they lost his forms. According to Can, this happens because he has no *torpil*. Soon his daughter will turn 18 and then she will have to leave the country, unless she finds a way to obtain a student visa or a work permit.

Case 2

Aya, a 17-year old girl, wants to study in the UK after high school. Her mother is a Cypriot, born in Cyprus before 1974. Her father is Turkish. Her parents met in 1977 at a Turkish university. They then moved to TRNC and got married there. According to the Republic of Cyprus law, anyone with one RoC parent has a right to RoC nationality. Aya wants to apply for RoC citizenship so that with an European Union (EU) citizenship she can study in the UK without having to pay non-EU citizens' tuition fees. Therefore, Aya travels to the RoC and hands in all necessary documentation at the Ministry of Interior. However, because she has a Turkish father, when she comes back two months later to check on her application, they say the application is still pending, which is what they will keep telling her every time she goes back, until she gives up.

1469 1966 ICESCR (art. 10).

Case 3

Onur is the father of Ali (aged 11). He is a migrant worker from Turkey. Four years ago, Onur came to the TRNC with his wife and two children, because he could not find a job in Turkey. The family entered on a 3-month tourist visa. In TRNC, Onur got a job as a construction worker. He works long days and earns little money, while his wife stays home with the children. Ali does not go to school, because the school asks a 500 TL fee for children who are on a tourist visa, and his parents cannot afford this. He sometimes goes out to sell roses. Every three months, the family has to travel to Turkey and back to TRNC to renew their tourist visa. The focus of the family is mostly on finding food and rent for the next month, they do not really have any future plans.

Interview 46, with Ali.

Q: Who decides if you sell flowers?
A: I love selling.
Q: So, it's your choice?
A: Yes [...] I came here and saw that everyone was selling so I wanted to do it as well [...]
Q: And when you sell flowers, what do you do with the money?
A: I am saving it in a little pot.
Q: What are you saving it for?
A: To pay our debt.
Q: What debt?
A: Before we were buying something from grocery store, so we were buying it but not paying it [...]
Q: And you say everyone is selling flowers, what do you mean everyone?
A: My friends, everyone is selling.
Q: And are they not going to school?
A: The half is going to school and selling flowers, the other half is just selling flowers.

7.2.5. LAW IN THE TRNC

In general, "law" has a very strong connotation for people living in TRNC. People often refer to things being allowed or not allowed according to law, by which they mean TRNC state law, and to a lesser degree RoC state law, TR state law and European / international law. TRNC state law has a strong position in TRNC society. It is experienced as a power larger than the individual, to which there is no alternative or control. It is experienced as "all or nothing"; due to non-recognition, a person living in TRNC who is in conflict with TRNC state law has nowhere else to go.

However, law also has an instrumental role that reinforces social inequality through nepotism. To understand the role of law in the TRNC, it is essential to understand the underlying social fabric of TRNC (and in general of Cypriot) society. In Cyprus, nationality and ethnicity are part of the basic fabric of social action, including political and legal action.[1470] Based on nationality and ethnicity it is decided where you belong in society and, consequently, what rights you have. This form of segregation of social groups, and attribution of legal rights and privileges accordingly, is both incorporated in formal written state law (for example, the TRNC law on education applies only to "citizens")[1471], as well as in the application of formal laws (for example all people in TRNC have a right to free healthcare, but Turkish Cypriots generally receive better quality healthcare than Turkish people). This is not just the case within TRNC society, but also in the relationship between GCs and TCs.

There is a strong social hierarchy in Cyprus, and the higher you are in this hierarchy, the more rights and privileges you have[1472]:

In RoC, Europe and the world

1	RoC nationals	1. GCs 2. TCs

In TRNC

2	TRNC nationals	1. TCs 2. Turkish people 3. Other
3	Legal migrants in TRNC	1. Turkish people 2. Other
4	International students	1. Turkish students 2. Other
5	Tourist residents	1. Turkish people 2. Other
6	Illegal migrants	1. Turkish people 2. Other

1470 See also Anastasiou (2008: 6): "Since the nineteenth century, the multiplicity of divisive and explosive events that marred the history of the Island have been grounded in and motivated by a pervasive single factor: the phenomenon of ethnocentric nationalism", and, further: "one cannot grasp or appreciate the full scope and nature of the Cyprus problem unless one approaches and scrutinizes it from the vantage point of a critical understanding of the nationalist mind" (7).

1471 1986 TRNC Law on National Education No 17/1986.

1472 Whereby it could be added that within and among these categories there is also a distinction between people who are well connected and those who are not, so that a Turkish person who is befriended with a TRNC minister might get more privileges than a TC who does not have these connections. However, for a TC and Turkish person with the same connections, the TC would get the better treatment.

The distribution of nationality is connected to the unequal treatment of people with different ethnicities. It works two ways: you only have access to certain nationalities based on your ethnicity and your (political and social) position and you only have access to certain rights based on your nationality. This, too, is not just the case within TRNC society, but also in the relationship between the Republic of Cyprus and the TRNC.[1473]

In general, which law is applied and in what manner depends on the position of the person in the social hierarchy. This in turn has a significant influence on the role of formal written law in TRNC society. Although, as I mentioned, law has a very strong connotation for people living in TRNC, due to the connection between law and social hierarchy both in the letter of the law as well as in its application, people still perceive the law as arbitrary. They feel that, although law is powerful, it changes often and means something different depending on your position in the social hierarchy.

This also explains why there are several false beliefs about the content of the state law; people believe that the acts of authorities must be based on rules, so they try to determine what must be in the law (formal or informal) based on their interactions with state authorities.

As a researcher, it was difficult to find consistent patterns in people's encounters with law and state authorities, which made it difficult to discern forms of state law other than formal written law (namely, law for the community (B) and/or hidden law (C)[1474], which together make up what, in the context of TRNC, I will call "informal law"). When I brought this issue up on two separate occasions with two different local research assistants, they recognized this immediately:

> *Interview 203, a young Turkish Cypriot woman.*
> This is very much Cyprus life: there are no rules, or: different rules for different people. Which pretty much means no rules, because the rules are arbitrary.

> *Interview 204, a young Turkish Cypriot man.*
> Welcome to TRNC! There is no structure. It's all random. It's a random country of randomness.

At first, I thought that there were two parallel systems of state law that only slightly overlapped: formal state law on the one hand and informal law on the other hand, much like how the economy is divided into formal and informal economy. In TRNC, the informal economy has been argued to be "as high as 60 percent of the total economy".[1475] In this case formal state law would apply

1473 For more details and references, see section §7.2.3 "access to rights", under discrimination.
1474 See §7.3.
1475 Mehmet (2010: 12).

to everyone in principle, except for a person who has friends in high places, to whom informal law would apply.

Figure 20. Initial impression of the system of TRNC state law

However, I realized that, in fact, access to the informal law is incorporated into formal law, so that formal law includes many gateways to informal law – gates that only open for certain people. This means that access to "informal state law", or other rules that apply, is obtained through state law and in some sense these informal rules are a part of formal TRNC state law. Formal state law can be read as "this law applies, unless..." or "this law applies to most people, unless you are friends with the right person".[1476]

For example, the TRNC nationality law states that people can apply for TRNC nationality through naturalization if they adhere to certain conditions, yet the law also states that the Council of Ministers can give TRNC nationality to whomever they deem fit to obtain it.[1477] The TRNC criminal code, under its general principles, directly states that "nothing in this law shall affect [...] the power of the Turkish Republic of Northern Cyprus to pardon, remove, abbreviate, or postpone any or all of the sentences of any sentence given or to be given".[1478]

1476 I personally had the chance to put this theory to the test when I was stopped by the police and given a fine for an alleged traffic offense for the second time (foreigners are easily identified based on the different license plates on rental cars). On both occasions I became angry with the police officers because both times I did not believe that I had done anything illegal (although of course I did not know TRNC formal traffic law). The first time, my anger proved to have no result and I simply had to pay a fine of € 150 for bumping into the pavement – an action which damaged nothing else but my car. When I protested, they simply took my driver's license and told me that I could get it back by either paying or starting a court case which would probably take months, during which time I would not be allowed off the island. The second time, when I was fined for changing lanes in front of traffic lights, I mentioned to the police officer that a TRNC minister was a very close friend and that he would certainly not be happy to hear about this officer fining me for nothing (I took the liberty of writing down the officer's name). I never had to pay this fine.

1477 See §7.2.2.

1478 1962/2014 TRNC Criminal Law (chapter 1 general articles: art. 2(e)).

Figure 21. TRNC formal state law as a gate to informal law – accessible only to some.

Although some of the formal state law has been taken out in the RoC due to harmonization with EU law, this same system is applied in the RoC at least in relation to the acquisition of nationality (see more below). Nevertheless, an attempt at establishing all the laws of the different legal orders in relation to the child's right to nationality in the TRNC will be given below.

7.3. TRNC LEGAL ORDERS AND THE CHILD'S RIGHT TO NATIONALITY

To understand the legal situation for children residing in the TRNC as regards their right to nationality, we have to study a very complicated web of legal orders. The case is not in any way straightforward, not only because of the arbitrariness built into TRNC state law, but also because there are several state legislators claiming authority over the same people and over the same territory. This results in conflicting legal orders and conflicting laws. This is a situation that results out of political strife, where children are caught in the middle, consequently suffering a loss of protection of their basic rights.

One of the difficulties in untangling the web of legal orders concerning children living in the TRNC is the difficulty in determining who constitutes the relevant legal community of a certain legal order. For example, it is unclear if, and if so how, international law protects the rights of children living in the TRNC. Since any type of human rights are usually protected through conventions which are signed by states, whereby states are held ultimately responsible for the protection of the rights of their people (and "their people", in its turn, could be taken to mean "their nationals"), it is unclear how "universal" children's rights are protected for children living in the TRNC. A related issue is that it is similarly difficult to establish which state is the relevant authority for the people living in the TRNC (whose jurisprudence do they belong to?). Third, it is difficult to determine the informal laws of the TRNC, RoC and TR, since there sometimes seems to be no consistent pattern in how the law is applied and/or what people are told about the law by employees of the different ministries involved.

To start the process of untangling the different legal orders involved in the child's right to nationality in the TRNC, we identified several legal orders, namely the international, regional (European), national (TRNC, RoC and TR), local (municipality), corporate, school, household, and autonomous child. After our first explorative field trip, we distinguished the orders to focus on (see scheme §7.1.4). We excluded the local level because, whatever decisions they made on these levels in relation to the child's right to nationality seemed to follow directly from decisions by state authorities, so that the local level was more executive of state legal power rather than legislative in itself. Similarly, we excluded the corporate level as a legal order, since they were perceived and perceived themselves as either complying with (TRNC) state law or as acting illegally (for example when employing migrant workers without work permits). Lastly, we included the autonomous child because it was so important in the CAR case study that we wanted to see to what degree children make law for themselves when it comes to their right to nationality.

The analysis of the different laws of these different legal orders in relation to the child's right to nationality in the TRNC will be done according to the three forms of statutory law[1479]:

A) Formal written law: rules found in official, formal legal texts, created by the legislature and open and available to the public.
B) Law for the community: rules created by the legislator, known by the subjects of the legal order.
   B1: Written law for the community: when the relevant community knows the formal, written law.
   B2: Unwritten law for the community: either law of a legal order that has no formal written law (B2i), or unwritten law for the community that contradicts formal written law (B2ii).
C) Hidden law: non-public rules created by the legislature, known only to a specific group of people
   C1: Written (formal) hidden law
   C2: Unwritten hidden law

1479 See chapter 1.

7.3.1. THE INTERNATIONAL LEGAL ORDER

A. *Formal written law*

Because the application of international law is generally mediated through states and, in the case of children living in the TRNC, it is unclear which authorities are supposed to be the state party that applies international law to the lives of these children, all three candidate-addressees for international law as regards children living in TRNC (RoC, TR and TRNC) are discussed below.

The following international conventions and treaties, relevant for the child's right to nationality and subsequent rights in the TRNC, apply to these potential addressees:

Convention \ state	**Republic of Cyprus**	**Turkey**	**TRNC**
1989 UNCRC	Ratification/ Accession: 1991	Ratification/ Accession: 1995	– (formalized in state law: 1996)
1948 Universal Declaration of Human Rights	Admission to the UN: 1960	Admission to the UN: 1945	- (formalized in state law: 1996)
1954 Convention relating to the status of stateless persons	–	–	–
1961 Convention on the reduction of statelessness	–	–	–
1966 International Covenant on Civil and Political Rights	Ratification/ Accession: 1969	Ratification/ Accession: 2003	– (formalized in state law: 2004)
1966 International Covenant on Economic, Social and Cultural Rights	Ratification/ Accession: 1969	Ratification/ Accession: 2003	– (formalized in state law: 2004)
1969 International Convention on the Elimination of All Forms of Racial Discrimination	Ratification/ Accession: 1967	Ratification/ Accession: 2002	–
1979 Convention on the Elimination of All Forms of Discrimination against Women	Ratification/ Accession: 1985	Ratification/ Accession: 1985 (reservation with regard to passing of nationality by women withdrawn in 2000)	– (formalized in state law: 1996)
1990 International Convention on the Protection of Rights of All Migrant Workers and Their Families	–	Ratification/ Accession: 2004	–

Turkish Republic of Northern Cyprus

Is international law, law for the TRNC (and its population)?

The international legislator has adopted many resolutions stating that the Republic of Cyprus is the sole sovereign power over the territory of Cyprus, although it has to be noted that, in these resolutions, "the Republic of Cyprus" refers to the constitutional government of the RoC, which consists (theoretically) of both Greek and Turkish Cypriots.[1480]

Upon the declaration of the "Federated Turkish State" in North Cyprus in 1975, and the declaration of the independent state "Turkish Republic of Northern Cyprus" in North Cyprus in 1983, the UN Security Council considered these "attempts to create" legally invalid and condemned the declaration, including its further secessionist activities.[1481] In 1983 they specifically called upon "all States not to recognize any Cypriot State other than the Republic of Cyprus". The TRNC is considered a legally invalid state by the international legal community and are therefore excluded from signing any international treaty or convention.

Although the TRNC authorities and population know that they are excluded from the international legal order (and in this sense they are not part of the addressees of international law, meaning that it is not formal written law for them), the TRNC authorities have nevertheless formalized international law. The 1989 UN Convention on the Rights of the Child, for example, is unilaterally ratified by copy-pasting the whole text of the Convention into TRNC state law[1482], which they have done with several other international legal instruments (see scheme above). In addition, different TRNC laws refer to international law. For example, the Constitution in art. 13 on the status of Aliens, states that "The rights and liberties referred to in this Constitution may be restricted by law in respect of aliens, in accordance with international law", the Citizenship law states that

> The grant of citizenship to children born in the Turkish Republic of Northern Cyprus after the 15th November 1983 of a father or mother who is not a citizen of the Turkish Republic of Northern Cyprus, shall be regulated by law *in accordance with the provisions of international law* [my italics, MH].[1483]

The constitution has an article on "the Ratification of International Agreements".[1484] In this sense then, international law has turned into formal written law in the TRNC.

1480 UN Security Council, resolutions 155, 186, 353, 360, 367.

1481 UN Security Council, resolutions 367, 541 and 550.

1482 1996 TRNC Law Concerning the Confirmation of the Convention on the Rights of the Child, No. 6/1996.

1483 1993/2005 Turkish Republic of Northern Cyprus Citizenship Law No 52/1993/2005 (art. 67 (3)(c)).

1484 1983 Constitution of the Turkish Republic of Northern Cyprus (art. 90).

Republic of Cyprus

The Republic of Cyprus has signed and ratified several international conventions, thereby committing themselves to upholding the rights contained in these conventions for each child residing in their jurisdiction.

Does this include children living in TRNC? According to international law, a state has jurisdiction over all persons, property and activities in its territory, and over its nationals anywhere in the world.[1485] The Republic of Cyprus on the one hand seems to claim jurisdiction over North Cyprus. In their UN Human Rights Common Core Documents, the RoC claims jurisdiction over the whole of Cyprus[1486] and designates all people living in Cyprus as their population, except for "approximately 160,000–170,000 settlers transferred from Turkey in order to alter the demographic structure of Cyprus [...][1487] as well as the Turkish occupation forces".[1488] It is unclear whether this includes second and third generation Turkish migrants, whether it includes Turkish people who chose to move to northern Cyprus after the initial wave of Turkish migrants in 1974–75, and whether it includes migrants from other countries and their children, who migrated to North Cyprus after 1974. The RoC population does include Turkish Cypriots living in the north, who the RoC claims "were forced by their leadership to move to the area occupied by Turkish troops".[1489]

Since 2003 (shortly before joining the EU), the RoC in their UN reporting argued to have adopted "several packages of measures for the benefit of the Turkish Cypriots that have led to tangible economic and other benefits to that community", including free medical care and other social benefits. They argued that Turkish Cypriots "have the opportunity to acquire, access and make full use of their rights as citizens of the Republic of Cyprus".[1490] However, these remarks are taken out of the core document from the 2014 version onwards.

On the other hand, in their UN reporting, the RoC denies responsibility for the persons, properties and actions in North Cyprus, arguing that "the Government of the Republic of Cyprus is prevented by armed force from exercising its authority and control and ensuring implementation and respect

---

1485 Oxman, B.H. (2007).

1486 United Nations (2014): HRI/CORE/1/Add.28/Rev.1 (para. 1); HRI/CORE/CYP/2007, paras. 1-4; HRI/CORE/CYP/2009, paras. 1-4; HRI/CORE/CYP/2011, paras. 1-4; HRI/CORE/CYP/2012, paras. 1-4; HRI/CORE/CYP/2014, paras. 7-9.

1487 These numbers change; it concerned 109,000 settlers in 1993; 118,000 in 2007; 150,000–160,000 in 2009; 160,000-170,000 in 2011, 2012, 2014 and 2017.

1488 United Nations (2014) HRI/CORE/1/Add.28/Rev.1, para. 8; HRI/CORE/CYP/2007, para. 16 (118,000 settlers, 35,000 Turkish troops); HRI/CORE/CYP/2009, para. 17 (150,000-160,000 settlers, 35,000 Turkish troops); HRI/CORE/CYP/2011, para. 17 (160,000-170,000 settlers, 40,000 Turkish troops); HRI/CORE/CYP/2012 (160,000-170,000 settlers, 40,000 Turkish troops); HRI/CORE/CYP/2014, para. 23 (160,000-170,000 settlers, 40,000 Turkish troops).

1489 United Nations (2014) HRI/CORE/1/Add.28/Rev.1, para. 8.

1490 United Nations (2014) HRI/CORE/CYP/2009, para. 11; HRI/CORE/CYP/2011, para. 123; HRI/CORE/CYP/2012, para. 118.

of human rights in the occupied area".[1491] Since 2014, the core document only includes information and data concerning South Cyprus.[1492]

From the external perspective, the jurisdiction and related responsibility of the RoC over the northern parts of Cyprus, including protection of human rights, seem to be reiterated by different human rights committees in their concluding observations. The Children's Rights Committee, in all three of the concluding observations the RoC has received to date, notes that:

> the State party, as a consequence of events that occurred in 1974 and that resulted in the occupation of part of the territory of Cyprus, is not in a position to exercise control over all of its territory and consequently cannot ensure the application of the Convention in areas not under its control. However, it remains a matter of concern to the Committee that no information on children living in the occupied territories could be provided.[1493]

Although the issue of human and children's rights in North Cyprus is usually otherwise ignored by the different committees, due to a lack of information on the situation in the North, in some cases the Republic of Cyprus is directly held responsible for human rights in the North. For example, in 2016, the CESCR recommended that "the State party take effective measures to ensure that people in Cyprus can freely visit cultural heritage sites in both the southern and the northern parts of the island." In their otherwise lengthy reply to the observations of the committee, the Republic of Cyprus ignored this observation.

The Human Rights committee on the other hand, in their last observations in 2015[1494], seem more conservative in attributing responsibility for human rights protection of people living in North Cyprus to the Republic of Cyprus, seemingly limiting themselves to the human rights of people in South Cyprus, or insofar as they travel to South Cyprus. The committee does raise many concerns regarding the discrimination of Turkish Cypriots in the southern part of the island, such as:

- The Office of the Commissioner of Administration (the Ombudsman) does not have Turkish-speaking staff and reports generated by the office are not published in Turkish[1495]
- RoC nationality laws are applied "in a discriminatory manner in relation to individuals from particular groups, particularly children of Turkish Cypriots [...]"[1496]

1491 United Nations (2014) HRI/CORE/1/Add.28/Rev.1, para. 31; HRI/CORE/CYP/2007, para. 64; HRI/CORE/CYP/2009, para. 68; HRI/CORE/CYP/2011, para. 72; HRI/CORE/CYP/2012, para. 67; HRI/CORE/CYP/2014, para. 54.

1492 United Nations (2014) HRI/CORE/CYP/2014, para. 5; HRI/CORE/CYP/2014/Add.1/Rev.1;.

1493 Committee on the Rights of the Child (1996; 2003a; 2012a).

1494 Human Rights Committee (2015).

1495 Ibid: para. 5.

1496 Ibid: para. 6.

- Concerns about reports of a rise in incidents of racially motivated verbal and physical abuse by right-wing extremists and neo-Nazi groups against Turkish Cypriots[1497]
- "certain restrictions on crossing the Green Line – notably the State party's policy concerning the passage of Turkish settlers and their descendants who were born in occupied areas – unduly interfere with the enjoyment of the right to the freedom of movement conferred upon all residents of the island by article 12 of the Covenant"[1498]
- Concerns about allegations that a significant number of Turkish Cypriots were unable to vote during the European Parliament elections held on 25 May 2014, because their correct residential addresses had not been entered in the Government's database[1499]
- Concerns about the small number of Turkish Cypriots in the State party's civil service, including the police force and the judiciary, due to economic, linguistic and cultural barriers[1500]

Recommendations made by the committee are, among others, that:

> The State party should take immediate steps to ensure Turkish Cypriots have the same rights and obligations as all other Cypriot citizens, both in law and in fact, to vote and stand for elections so as to be in full compliance with articles 25 and 26 of the Covenant[1501],

and

> The State party should take adequate measures to ensure that the nationality laws are applied indiscriminately on the basis of clearly defined criteria. It should ensure that applicants have access to information concerning the requirements of citizenship and that they receive a decision on their application for citizenship within a reasonable period of time.[1502]

In the reply by the RoC, concerning Turkish Cypriots, they only reply to the last concern mentioned above, as follows:

> After the withdrawal of the Turkish Community from the organs of the State in 1963 following a decision of its leadership, the Constitutional provisions providing that the Public Service shall be composed as to thirty per cent of Turks, have been rendered temporarily ineffective. In light of that, *the official language of the State*

1497 Ibid: para. 7.
1498 Ibid: para. 17.
1499 Ibid: para. 22.
1500 Ibid: para. 23.
1501 Ibid: para 6.
1502 Ibid: para. 22.

> *currently used, is mainly the Greek language.* In addition, following the coup and the Turkish invasion of 1974, and the subsequent occupation of one third of Cyprus territory, as well as the illegal proclamation of a pseudo state in the occupied part of the Republic of Cyprus, United Nations Security Council Resolutions 541 (1983) and 550 (1984): (a) Deplore the declaration by the Turkish Cypriot authorities of the purported succession of part of the Republic of Cyprus, and (b) Reiterate the call upon all States not to recognise the purported state of the "Turkish Republic of Northern Cyprus" set up by secessionist acts and calls upon them not to facilitate or in any way assist the aforesaid secessionist entity. Accordingly, *the Turkish Cypriots' unwillingness to participate in the Republic of Cyprus' public service is mainly due to the relevant guidance and instigation by their leadership, as well as, to their decision to live and work, under an illegal entity*, condemned by the United Nations and the International Community. For these reasons any candidate wishing to compete with other candidates for any post in the Public Service mainly must meet the requirement of "very good knowledge of the Greek language". Obviously, Turkish Cypriots can compete with other candidates for a post in the Public Service, provided they meet the relevant requirements/qualifications of the post, including the language requirement. It is, of course, a different matter when Turkish Cypriots apply to any organ of the State, or resort to domestic Courts using the Turkish language [my italics, MH].[1503]

In short, the RoC does understand itself as addressed by and subjected to international law, including the 1989 Children's Rights Convention and several other international legal instruments that reiterate the principle of non-discrimination in the attribution of human (children's) rights. The question is whether the RoC understands itself as addressed by international law in relation to the population of the TRNC. In this respect, the RoC seems to present an inconsistent position. On the one hand, they claim jurisdiction over Cyprus, and over the whole population of Cyprus. On the other hand, they exclude from their jurisdiction the part of the population of Cyprus that moved from Turkey to North Cyprus since 1974 and possibly their children and grandchildren. They do include "Turkish Cypriots" living in the North, without defining this group, and they do not mention migrants who migrated to the North from other countries since 1974. They also deny responsibility for the persons, properties and actions in the North, due to the armed force that is preventing them from exercising their authority and control. In conclusion, everyone living in the North is left out of their reporting to UN organs.

The international legislator, of which of course the RoC is a part as a member state of the UN, seems to go along with this interpretation of obligations under

1503 Human Rights Committee (2018: para. 10). They do also state that "However, in order to facilitate any Turkish Cypriot wishing to compete to posts in the Public Service, special provisions were introduced in the relevant legislations, making the knowledge of the Turkish language, at the corresponding level of knowledge with the Greek language, available. For example, such provisions exist in the Scheme of Service for the entry posts in the Foreign Service, i.e. the posts of Attaches, and for Offices at the Press and Information Office, inter alia" (para. 11).

international law, insofar as there is a situation of *force majeure*, in the sense that RoC cannot be held responsible for what happens in the part of the territory that they do not control. On the other hand, the RoC's denial of responsibility seems to go further than *force majeure* whenever they choose not to take responsibility for, for example, collecting data on children's rights in the North, or when they are blocking Turkish Cypriots living in the North, who can travel to the South, from voting. In that sense, at least the committees on international law seem to view the RoC as having legal jurisdiction over the whole population of Cyprus, which is a responsibility which can only be excused temporarily, as long as insofar as *force majeure* is truly the case.

It can therefore be said with certainty that the RoC is legally obliged to apply international law to and to uphold human rights (including children's rights) for people while they are in the South, including Turkish Cypriots. Insofar as they deny RoC nationality to children on discriminatory grounds (because they have one Turkish parent or because they live in the North), they are violating international law.[1504] The same could be argued for arbitrarily denying children living in the North (including those with RoC nationality) other rights on the south side that are accorded to people living in the south, such as right to free healthcare, education, etc.[1505]

Lastly, it may be interesting in this context to mention that the Federal Republic of Germany (West Germany) took full responsibility for all people living in Germany (East and West), irrespective of how they entered the German territory.[1506] Like the RoC, The Federal Republic of Germany continued to apply the original constitution of a united Germany throughout the separation of East and West Germany. However, for Germany, this translated into active protection of the rights of people living in Germany, plus people of German descent and their children, plus people who were naturalized and received DDR nationality in the DDR (east Germany).[1507] They included all people who received DDR nationality because they did not recognize the DDR as an independent state, based on the argument that the German people did not choose to secede by "a free exercise of the right of self-determination".[1508] The argument could be made that in Cyprus, too, the people in the North did not choose to be separated from the RoC. In fact, in the 2004 referendum, the people expressed their wish to be part of a federal RoC and, therefore, the RoC authorities have a responsibility in relation to the rights of people living in the North. It seems that there is a unique historical-political situation in Cyprus, where the RoC government claims a territory – a claim that is recognized as legitimate by the international

1504 De Groot & Vonk (2015: 46).

1505 Although the Embassy of the RoC in Washington D.C. still states that "medical care is provided to Turkish Cypriots in public hospitals free of charge", this has not been the case.

1506 1949 Basic Law for the Federal Republic of Germany, specifically art. 116.

1507 1953 Gesetz über die Angelegenheiten der Vertriebenen und Flüchtelinge.

1508 See ruling in the Teso case: Teso-Beschluß GDR-Citizenship (1987).

community as well as by international and regional law –, but not (a large part of) the people who are currently living in the territory.

Turkey

Turkey, too, has signed and ratified several international conventions, thereby committing itself to upholding the rights contained in these conventions for each child residing in their jurisdiction.[1509]

Does this include children living in TRNC? As has been mentioned, according to international law, a state has jurisdiction over all persons, property and activities in its territory, and over its nationals anywhere in the world.[1510] Turkey does not claim North Cyprus as its territory, which suggests that it would only have jurisdiction over its nationals residing in the TRNC.[1511] The relation of Turkey towards the TRNC seems relatively similar to some former colonial powers to their former colonies (for example the relationship of France to the Central African Republic); although they recognize the TRNC as an independent state and treat it as such, they do feel an extra responsibility and/or some sense of ownership/authority. Practically, this is expressed in large sums of aid or development money, which comes not completely free from certain political conditions and/or pressure, plus the presence of military personnel. The discourse of the TRNC-TR relationship is that of the "motherland" (TR) and the "daughter" (TRNC). The 1983 TRNC constitution refers to Turkey as the "motherland", yet it also argues that the "absolute right to sovereignty" rests with the Turkish Cypriot people.[1512]

Figure 22. Graffiti in Lefkosa, TRNC.

1509 United Nations (2001).

1510 Oxman, B.H. (2007).

1511 United Nations (2001: paras. 1-7).

1512 1983 Constitution of the Turkish Republic of Northern Cyprus (preamble, art 3). Greece is also the "motherland" of the RoC (Ioannides (2017: 631)).

Many of the participants in our research complained about the TR having too much political power over the TRNC, through pressuring TRNC politicians. Regular protests take place against this in the TRNC, such as protests against Turkish influence in the areas of education and religion.[1513]

Looking at the perspective of the international community, Cyprus is not mentioned in the concluding observations on human rights in Turkey[1514], except for a comment on human rights violations perpetrated by Turkish troops. This does not address recent cases.[1515] Perhaps it could be argued that Turkey has effective control over the territory of North Cyprus, due to their military presence. However, under international law, authority over a territory by another state is only assumed if:

- the territory is "actually placed under the authority of the hostile army[,]" and "authority has been established and can be exercised"[1516];
- the state in power "exercises the functions of government in such territory"[1517]; and
- the occupier's authority is "to the exclusion of the established government".[1518]

It seems to me that the TRNC is not under the authority of Turkey according to these criteria. The mere presence of military troops does not amount to responsibility for human rights in the area (in Cyprus alone, in addition to the Turkish, there is a British[1519] and Greek[1520] military presence). In addition, although Turkey certainly has a strong political influence, it does not exercise the functions of government to the exclusion of the TRNC government. Therefore, under international law, I do not think that Turkey can be held responsible for the protection of the rights of children living in the TRNC, except for – to a limited extent – the children with Turkish nationality residing in the TRNC.

1513 See also Bozkurt (2014), who argues that, after the collapse of the 2004 Annan plan, Turkey positioned itself as "the IMF of Northern Cyprus". It seems that this is damaging TR-TRNC relations. For example, after the 2018 TRNC elections, the media reported an "appointment crisis", during which the new TRNC prime minister tried to make an appointment with the ministers of the TR, yet did not get a reply from Ankara for a long time. See: Karashan (2018), Haber Turk (2018).

1514 Committee on the Protection of the Rights of All Migrant Workers and Members of Their Families (2016); Committee on the Rights of the Child (2001; 2012b); Committee on Economic, Social and Cultural Rights (2011); Committee on the Elimination of Racial Discrimination (2016).

1515 Human Rights Committee (2012: para. 11).

1516 Hague Regulations, Art. 42.

1517 Fourth Geneva Convention, Art. 6.

1518 >U.S. v. List; Samson (2012).

1519 See Army (n.d.); Cyprus Mail Online (2018).

1520 See Psyllides (2017), Squires (2017).

The international legal community

A last optional addressee for international law, in particular children's rights protection, for the children in the TRNC is the international legal community. Although children's rights are often claimed to be "universal", and it is often said that all children have rights under international law, this does not necessarily seem to be the case for the children in the TRNC, as is shown by, for example, the exclusion of the TRNC from any rights convention, the lack of reporting on children's rights, the lack of international NGOs that protect children's rights in the TRNC[1521], and the exclusion of TRNC children from opportunities in the international community (such as bicommunal peace-building activities, education scholarships).

The international community could protect the rights of children living in the TRNC better in one (or more) of the following ways:

1. Invite the TRNC government to join the international legal community at least until the Cyprus conflict has been resolved, so as to ensure the protection of children's rights in North Cyprus.
2. Instate a mandate for the UN Commissioner for Human Rights, or the Committee on Children's Rights to research and report on the children's rights situation in the TRNC (such as is done for the "Occupied Palestinian Territory").[1522]
3. Invite the RoC and/or TR to report more fervently on the children's rights situation in the TRNC. Although, since this already happens in relation to the RoC (see above), a request that is consistently ignored, it is unlikely that would have an effect. Perhaps the TRNC can write its own report and submit it through the TR or ROC as an annex to their report.
4. To recognize the TRNC as a member state, in other words, to recognize the TRNC as an international state and member of the UN (and then invite the TRNC government to sign and ratify the UNCRC).
5. The international legislator could use its political and legal position in relation to Turkey, as a UN member state, to argue that, by entering Cyprus through a military option in 1974 they breached article 2(4) of the UN Charter, and force them to pull out or else annul their membership of the UN

1521 The only international NGO operating in this field in the TRNC is SOS Children's Village. Children's rights organizations operating in the RoC exclude children who live in the North from almost all of their efforts and activities.

1522 However, the position of Palestine is based on UN General Assembly resolution 3,236, which recognizes that "the Palestinian people is entitled to self-determination" and that "the Palestinian people has been prevented from enjoying its inalienable rights", including "the right to national independence and sovereignty" (1974 UN General Assembly resolution 3236). No such recognition by the international legislator exists for the Turkish Cypriots.

(alike the South Africa-Namibia ICJ advisory opinion in 1971).[1523] However, this may have made sense in 1974 or shortly after, yet it seems unlikely to be legally sound today since, at the moment, the Turkish military presence in Cyprus is based on the invitation by the TRNC authorities.
6. Put much more political pressure on the RoC to engage in peace talks and work towards reunification, especially since they claim jurisdiction over the whole island, while in 2004 they voted (and the RoC authorities actively campaigned) against reunification.
7. Provide financial means for (I)NGOs working on children's rights in TRNC.

In the current situation, because of the considerations mentioned above, it seems that, from the perspective of formal written international law, a legal vacuum has come into existence when considering international law and in particular the rights of children in the TRNC.

B. Law for the community

Rules created by the legislator, known by the subjects of the legal order.

The TRNC population – with the exception of the younger children – are very much aware of the fact that the TRNC is not a part of the international community. Although most people do have ideas about international laws, and in particular international children's rights as normative imperatives – rights that the children *should* have – they generally do not understand these as legal rights applicable to children living in the TRNC. In some cases, international law may be applied, but only insofar as a TRNC politician and/or judge decides to do so. There is no legal obligation.

> *Interview 32, an employee of the TRNC government:*
> TRNC is out of international law. I wish it was different. But sometimes in the courts, during trials for instance for children, they sometimes, the heads of courts make reference to international agreements. So, the judge, himself or herself, if the law doesn't prevent it, they try to refer to the international agreements, in case of the individual trials or whatever. But only if the TRNC law doesn't prevent him from doing it.

C. Hidden law

There seems to be no hidden international law for children in the TRNC.

1523 International Court of Justice (ICJ) (1971); Reisman (1984: 644-45).

7.3.2. THE REGIONAL (EUROPEAN) LEGAL ORDER

On the level of the regional (European) legal order, there are two separate legal orders: the European Union (EU) and the Council of Europe (CoE). Each of these orders have different corresponding courts and laws (see below). Because the people in Cyprus do not see these as separate legal orders, and the EU is also connected to the CoE in the sense that the European Convention on Human Rights is law for the EU, I will discuss both of these orders in this section.

Legal order	(relevant) formal written law	Legislator	Court	Member state
European Union	2000 Charter of Fundamental Rights of the European Union	European Commission & European Parliament	Court of Justice of the European Union (CJEU)	RoC
Council of Europe	See below	Council of Europe	European Court of Human Rights (ECtHR)	RoC, Turkey

A. *Formal written law*

Rules found in official, formal legal texts, created by the legislature and open and available to the public.

European Union

For the EU, the question arises to whom EU formal written law applies in relation to North Cyprus. In this case, only the RoC is a Member State of the EU so EU law can only apply to the RoC. Does that include children in North Cyprus?

According to the EU website:

> Despite joining the EU as a de facto divided island, the whole of Cyprus is EU territory. Turkish Cypriots who have, or are eligible for, EU travel documents are EU citizens. EU law is suspended in areas where the Cypriot government (Government of the Republic) does not exercise effective control. Cyprus has two official languages: Greek and Turkish; only Greek is an official EU language.[1524]

In this sense, the position of the EU sovereign seems to echo the position of the RoC; they want to govern the territory but not the people living in the territory – with the difference that the EU does include the people living in the North who

[1524] European Union (no date) *About the EU: Cyprus*. Available at: https://europa.eu/european-union/about-eu/countries/member-countries/cyprus_en.

have RoC nationality as EU citizens (inc. EU citizenship rights). However, since EU law is "suspended" for North Cyprus, this excludes both the EU and the RoC having any responsibility for the rights of children living in North Cyprus.[1525] In this way, the rights stated in the European Charter, such as that "everyone is equal before the law" (art. 20), the prohibition on discrimination based on "race…ethnic or social origin…language…membership of a national minority" (art. 21) and the rights of the child (art. 24) do not apply to children living in the TRNC.

It can even be argued that the EU exacerbates the rights situation for children living in the North, at least in a legal sense, not only because of the EU Green Line Regulation, which prohibits most people (including children) living in the North from entering the RoC unless they have an EU nationality and/or a RoC visa[1526], but also because they have given the RoC a position in which they can veto any EU measures that might be profitable to children living in North Cyprus. According to Kyris,

> the status of EU membership appears to have boosted the confidence of the Greek Cypriots as independent actors and has, therefore, reduced motivation for cooperation towards the achievement of a settlement. For example, the Greek-Cypriot controlled government of RoC have used their veto power to stop EU from developing trade links with Turkish Cypriots […].[1527]

The European Court of Justice, in addition, has been successfully used by Greek Cypriots to severely limit trade from the TRNC to European countries, based on the argument that the movement and phytosanitary certificates issued by the TRNC authorities could not be recognized (because the TRNC is an unrecognized entity).[1528] This situation has been called "short-sighted" by the World Bank.[1529]

EU law directly influences the children living in the North who have RoC nationality mostly in terms of future perspectives. By being considered EU citizens, these children know that they will be able to travel freely within the EU, study within the EU for a reduced (EU) student fee, reside and work in EU countries, etc. This creates a great inequality between children in North Cyprus, even within classrooms, because, while some of them are preparing for studying abroad, to visit the RoC, travel abroad, others know that they will never get the

---

1525 See also: 2003 Treaty of Accession – Act concerning the conditions of accession of the Czech Republic, the Republic of Estonia, the Republic of Cyprus, the Republic of Latvia, the Republic of Lithuania, the Republic of Hungary, the Republic of Malta, the Republic of Poland, the Republic of Slovenia and the Slovak Republic and the adjustments to the Treaties on which the European Union is founded (Protocol No 10 on Cyprus).

1526 2004 European Union Council Regulation 866/2004 ("Green Line Regulation") (art. 2).

1527 Kyris (2012: 92).

1528 Talmon (2001), Shaelou (2010: 32-34).

1529 As quoted by Shaelou (2010: 7).

same opportunities. This is an inequality based on nationality (potentially in conflict with the EU law on non-discrimination).

On the other hand, the EU has also positively influenced the situation for children living in North Cyprus. There is an EU aid programme for "the Turkish Cypriot community", which is the result of a decision by the European Council.[1530] Over the period 2006–2018, the EU allocated nearly 52 million Euro to "projects in support of the Turkish Cypriot community".[1531] It is also possible to imagine that, without the EU ambitions of both RoC and TR, the TRNC might have been even more isolated today – for example the borders might still have been closed.

Council of Europe

Both the RoC and Turkey are member states of the Council of Europe. As members, they have consented to / signed the following rights instruments:

Convention \ state	**Republic of Cyprus**	**Turkey**	**TRNC**
1950 European Convention on Human Rights (ECHR)	Ratification	Ratification	–
1963 Protocol No. 4 to the Convention for the Protection of Human Rights and Fundamental Freedoms	Ratification	Signature	–
2000 Protocol No. 12 to the Convention for the Protection of Human Rights and Fundamental Freedoms	Ratification	Signature	–
2000 European Convention on Nationality	–	–	–

This means that both Turkey and RoC are legally obliged to secure the rights following from these conventions and protocols "to everyone within their jurisdiction".[1532] This includes the right to non-discrimination[1533] and the right to freedom of movement.[1534]

Do the people living in North Cyprus fall under the jurisdiction of the RoC and/or Tukey? In addition to the discussion of this question in relation to international law (see §7.3.1), the following can be added in relation to the Council of Europe legal order.

1530 Council Regulation (EC) No 389/2006 of 27 February 2006 establishing an instrument of financial support for encouraging the economic development of the Turkish Cypriot community and amending Council Regulation (EC) No 2667/2000 on the European Agency for Reconstruction.

1531 See European Commission (n.d.). For a lengthy analysis of European integration of Cyprus, see Shaelou (2010).

1532 European Convention on Human Rights (ECHR) (art. 1).

1533 Ibid (art. 14); 2000 Protocol No. 12 to the Convention for the Protection of Human Rights and Fundamental Freedoms (art. 1).

1534 1963 Protocol No. 4 to the Convention for the Protection of Human Rights and Fundamental Freedoms (art. 2).

CoE perspective

In general, the CoE explains the meaning of "jurisdiction" as "primarily territorial" and supposed to be exercised "normally throughout the State's territory".[1535] However, an exception may be made if a territory is under the effective control of another state.[1536] In the several court cases before the ECtHR that concern responsibility for human rights violations in Northern Cyprus, Turkey was the defendant in all cases. In all these cases, the ECtHR has ruled that Turkey has effective control over the TRNC, both through its military presence as well as through the TRNC authorities which are understood as a "subordinate local administration".[1537] Turkey is therefore responsible.[1538]

However, upon a closer examination, it seems that the court, especially in recent cases, may apply this formulation mostly as a gateway, to a certain degree, to discuss the responsibility of TRNC authorities – for which Turkey is held ultimately responsible. Although the court does not recognize the TRNC authorities nor judges them under the ECHR, it seems that the responsibility of Turkey is an indirect way for the ECtHR to address potential human rights violations by the TRNC. In *Turkey v. Cyprus*, for example, the court on the one hand decided based on ECtHR jurisprudence (*Loizidou*) that the TRNC is a subordinate government of the TR, while at the same time discussed TRNC law, the court system, police and practices of the TRNC authorities to determine whether the rights of people in the North have been violated.[1539] This happens throughout the ECtHR cases that involve northern Cyprus.[1540]

At the end of the day, since 1974, the ECtHR has consistently held Turkey responsible for the human rights violations in the TRNC, even if committed

[1535] Council of Europe (2017: para. 2).

[1536] Ibid: paras. 4-6.

[1537] Ibid: paras. 4-6.

[1538] The key cases here are Loizidou v. Turkey (1995) and Cyprus v. Turkey (1999; 2014).

[1539] Council of Europe (2017: throughout the whole report). Mr. F. Busuttil and Mr. C.L. Rozakis, in their partly dissenting opinions, disagree with this approach. Mr. Busuttil argues that in line with the Loizidou judgment, this "can only mean that the legal and judicial systems established by the TRNC, and presently in force in northern Cyprus, emanate from an unlawful regime which is incapable of generating legality". Mr. Rozakis argues that, in line with the Loizidou judgment, "the authorities in the northern part of Cyprus [...] are, as a *fictio juris*, Turkish authorities. No distinction may be made between the Turkish authorities operating on the Turkish mainland and those operating in the occupied territory of the Republic of Cyprus" and continues to argue that the TRNC/TR legal authorities cannot be considered impartial.

[1540] See for example Güzelyurtlu and others v. Cyprus and Turkey (2017) where it is stated that "the "TRNC" authorities [...] have criminal jurisdiction over individuals who have committed crimes on the whole island of Cyprus" (para. 188). In this case both RoC and TR had to pay damages for not cooperating in the investigation of a murder case; Kyriacou Tsiakkourmas and other v. Turkey (2015); Olymbiou v. Turkey (2009); Case of individual Greek Cypriots against Turkey in relation to damages (inc. loss of land) related to the 1974 invasion: Joannou v. Turkey (2017).

by the TRNC authorities, leading to the first time ever a state was ordered to pay damages to another state. In 2014, the ECtHR decided that, for the rights violations of the family of missing persons (who went missing as a consequence of the 1974 war) and the violations of the rights of Greek Cypriots living in the Karpas regions in the TRNC between 1974–1994 (when the application was made), Turkey had to pay the RoC € 90,000,000 (which the RoC had to distribute to the effected individuals).[1541]

RoC perspective

From the perspective of the RoC, the RoC, in an official letter to the CoE in 1973, indicated that under "nationals" it understands:

> persons having at 1 December 1968 acquired or being entitled to acquire, citizenship of the Republic of Cyprus, in accordance with the provisions of Annex D to the Treaty of Establishment, or those who acquire that citizenship in accordance with the Republic's Nationality Act, 1967.

Under territory, the territory of Cyprus is referred to. This declaration is still applicable today.[1542] Hereby it seems that the RoC authorities take responsibility for only the RoC nationals living in Northern Cyprus, but not the other people. This can also be seen from the fact that, among their complaints in *Cyprus v. Turkey*, they listed "the situation of Turkish Cypriots in Northern Cyprus" as one of the issues.[1543] They also deny any responsibility for the unrecognized TRNC authorities, and attribute responsibility for human rights violations in Northern Cyprus to Turkey, who they claim have "overall and exclusive control".[1544] Interestingly, they add that:

> if Turkey were not to be held responsible for conditions in Northern Cyprus, no other legal person could be held responsible and the effectiveness of the Convention system and the public order of Europe would be undermined.[1545]

Turkish Perspective

From the perspective of Turkey, it is clear that Turkey does not concern itself at any point in time responsible for the rights of people living in the TRNC, because in the view of Turkey the TRNC is an independent state. In all ECtHR

1541 Cyprus v. Turkey (2014).

1542 Council of Europe (1972) Declaration contained in a letter from the Permanent Representative of Cyprus, dated 3 March 1972, registered at the Secretariat General on 3 March 1972 "Interpretation of the terms: "nationals" and "territory"".

1543 Cyprus v. Turkey (1999: para. 19).

1544 Ibid: paras. 43, 93.

1545 Ibid: para. 94.

cases, they argue that they lack jurisdiction over the territory of the TRNC.[1546] This is a position that in earlier proceedings led them to refuse to even engage in the court proceedings that addressed Northern Cyprus. They also argue that the RoC authorities are not the legitimate legislators in relation to Cyprus, because the RoC is a bi-communal state that cannot legitimately function without Turkish Cypriots in its constitutional organs.[1547]

A critical note

As a researcher, I find the position of the ECtHR in relation to recent cases regarding North Cyprus problematic. This is not only because it contributes to inequality between the communities living in Cyprus, but mostly because, these days (and at least since 2004) the position of Turkey in relation to the TRNC is akin to that of a former colonial power. Even if it may have been the case during the Turkish invasion, or even many years after, that the TRNC was indeed a subordinate administration of Turkey, at some point the position of the "occupying power" towards the country that they invaded changed. Even if the relationship between TR and TRNC is considered problematic by many, it cannot be argued that the TR has full control in any way, and it can even be discussed in what sense the TR has more control over TRNC compared to the control of Greece over the RoC and the UK over Cyprus.

In general, it cannot be argued that, because the colonial powers once illegally invaded and occupied many African countries, that these days the national governments of African countries are still "subordinate administrations" of the occupying countries. This is not the case even if these former colonial powers have military troops in the country in question (the UK still has two military bases in Cyprus). It seems that the relationship between the occupying power and local administration has to be subject to regular re-evaluation according to set criteria, as it seems that, with time, these relationships can change. It seems also, unfortunately, that the ECtHR does not allow for this possibility as it still continues to refer to the 1995 *Louizidou* case in all its considerations of the responsibility of Turkey for human rights violations in the TRNC, without any question of a re-evaluation of the TR-TRNC relationship.

A similar objection can be made to the EU's position in relation to the TRNC. It seems that the EU requires the TRNC to cut all ties with the TR, yet they have no solution for how the people in TRNC should live if they do so. Aside from serious financial issues, the TR currently acts as a mediator between the international community and the TRNC. Without the TR, people in TRNC could not receive any mail (because of the embargo, you cannot send mail

1546 Ibid: paras. 22, 40, 92.

1547 Ibid: para. 27.

directly to the TRNC), could not export any products (or through RoC against high taxation rates), would not have a currency (they use Turkish Lira), would not have telecommunications (they use the TR country code +90), etc. Also, if the Turkish military were to leave, it is uncertain what would happen to the people currently living in, and/or working in, what before 1974 were Greek Cypriot properties. It is quite likely that GCs would come to reclaim what they feel they own and it is not unlikely that this confrontation would in some cases be violent. For all this, the EU does not offer any alternatives (nor does any other international actor, for that matter).

B. Law for the community

B1. Written law for the community

People living in the TRNC, except for younger children, are very much aware that they have EU rights only when they have RoC nationality, and this is one of their motivations to (try to) obtain RoC nationality.

C. Hidden law

C2. Unwritten hidden law

It is worth noting that the EU does engage in supporting children living in the TRNC, for example by providing grants to TRNC schools, organizing events in the TRNC and providing scholarships for "Turkish Cypriot" students[1548] to study in the EU.[1549] Although these are political policy decisions that do not have the character of a general rule (and therefore are not law), it does seem that there might be a general, unwritten rule underlying these decisions. It is impossible to tell what this rule would be – and perhaps it should better be called a political idea instead of a law – but the EU since 2004 does consistently seem to apply the idea that "people living in the TRNC (should) have (limited) EU rights".

Another potential candidate for an unwritten hidden law is the basic rule according to which human rights violations that happen in Northern Cyprus are judged by the ECtHR: it seems that they are judged according to the rule:

1548 Although they give no definition of Turkish Cypriot, from the Frequently Asked Questions – pages on the EU scholarship website, it seems that students can apply on the condition that they a) are born in Cyprus or have a parent who was born in Cyprus, b) have TRNC nationality, and c) currently live in the TRNC. See The European Union Scholarship Programme for the Turkish Cypriot Community (n.d.).

1549 See also Shaelou (2010: 5).

Since:

a) everyone has human rights
b) without Turkish responsibility over Northern Cyprus, the people living, or owning property, in TRNC could not claim their rights on a supranational level
c) Turkey invaded Cyprus illegally in 1974, according to international law
d) The TRNC is an unrecognized state and not a party to the Council of Europe

Therefore: The ECtHR needs to hold TR responsible for all human rights violations occurring in the TRNC.

However, this may be more of a moral consideration rather than a legal rule, although in some sense, in applying the rule (and finding a legal formulation to do so), the court makes it into a legal rule.

Interview 22. A 31-year old politician.

A: After the Annan plans, in 2004, they said we would start with [..] direct flights, free travel, free trade […] But it did not happen of course […] One of my friends […] has a really good definition of what [Turkish] Cypriots are: abandoned children of the Mediterranean.
Q: How are you abandoned?
A: We are abandoned by Europe […] Especially by Europe as they left us by ourselves.

7.3.3. THE STATE LEGAL ORDER

7.3.3.1. Turkish Republic of Northern Cyprus

From the perspective of international law, one could argue that the TRNC does not have state law because it is not a state.[1550] However, because we are concerned with the rights of children living in North Cyprus, the internal perspective is important and, as I have already indicated under §7.2.5, TRNC law is definitely state law for people living in TRNC.

[1550] Yet, there are also contradicting indications, such as when the ECtHR refers to TRNC "law", or when the British authorities argued in a case against a TC who wished to obtain UK nationality, that he was "the holder of a valid TRNC travel document issued by the North Cypriot authorities in your name. As a holder of a TRNC passport you are considered to be a national of North Cyprus and as such recognized as a citizen of North Cyprus and therefore entitled to all the benefits accruing to any citizens laid down by the Constitution of 12 March 1985 […] The Secretary of State is satisfied that North Cyprus is a fully functioning democracy with respect for human rights […] these rights are provided by law […]" (as quoted by Navaro-Yashin (2012:104)).

A. Formal written law

As has been explained at length under §7.2.2, according to TRNC formal written law, children can obtain TRNC nationality either at birth, if they have at least one parent who has TRNC nationality, or through naturalization in case their parents become naturalized. The child's right to nationality is protected through the formalization of the CRC into TRNC state law.

In addition, the TRNC 1983 constitution provides for a right to non-discrimination and excludes favoritism:

> Every person shall be equal before the Constitution and the law without any discrimination. No privileges shall be granted to any individual, family, group or class.[1551] The organs and the administrative authorities of the State are under an obligation to act in conformity with the principle of equality before the law and not to make any discrimination in their actions.[1552]

According to the same constitution, all people living in TRNC have a right to health[1553], protection against hunger[1554] and a right to education[1555], which is compulsory until age 15 and free until age 18[1556], including the obligation for the state to "give the necessary assistance, through scholarships or otherwise, for the purpose of enabling successful pupils who lack financial means to receive the highest level of education".[1557]

B. Law for the community

B1. Written law for the community

Interestingly, in the TRNC, many of the TRNC population are convinced that they know the content of formal written state law, while they actually have false beliefs about its content. In fact, they are so convinced about their knowledge of the state law, that, as a researcher, I often started doubting whether we had maybe missed something in our legal doctrinal research. However, the source of this knowledge of TRNC state law seems to be hearsay, the media and/or encounters with TRNC authorities, who tend to give false information about the content of the state law[1558], rather than actual legal doctrinal research.

1551 1983 Constitution of the Turkish Republic of Northern Cyprus (art. 2).
1552 Ibid (art. 8).
1553 Ibid (art. 45).
1554 Ibid (art. 56).
1555 Ibid (art. 59).
1556 Ibid (art. 59 (5)).
1557 Ibid (art. 59(7)).
1558 A practice that is employed both in RoC and TRNC, as you will also see under §7.3.3.2.

On the other hand, people who strongly argue that rule X or Y is "the law in TRNC", can also be understood to refer to unwritten state law for the community, or hidden law, which may be "the law" rather than formal written state law (often this distinction is not made by participants to the research, who simply refer to "what the law says"). For example, several respondents argued that, if a parent has TRNC nationality, the child automatically gets TRNC nationality at birth, which is a correct belief according to a written formal state law and therefore this would be written law for the community. However, there is also a large number of false beliefs in state law for obtaining TRNC nationality by birth, for example that:

- A child obtains TRNC nationality at birth only if s/he has two parents who have TRNC nationality
- A child can obtain TRNC nationality at birth only if the father has TRNC nationality
- A child born in Cyprus can get TRNC nationality at age 18, at that time the parents get it too
- A child born in TRNC of parents who were born in the TRNC can get TRNC nationality

These are all false beliefs in TRNC state law, because it is not in TRNC formal written state law nor practiced by the authorities as such.

While the state law of acquisition of TRNC nationality at birth through a parent who is a TRNC national is still relatively well known, the range of ideas about what the state law says about obtaining TRNC nationality through naturalization becomes much broader, and it is hard to find any consistency so that it may be hard to speak of any "community" when we try to find "law for the community". This variety may be attributed to the fact that nationality law is usually complex and abtract, combined with the fact that people in Cyprus are generally not quick to say "I don't know", and lastly the fact that TRNC law changes often. On the other hand, many of these beliefs result from information obtained from TRNC officials, when the Ministry of Interior told a citizen that they could (not) apply for TRNC nationality for (legal) reason X or Y.

Interview 51. Employee of the TRNC Ministry of Interior.

Q: How can you get a TRNC nationality [by naturalization]?
A: It used to be: if you live here for 10 years. [checks with colleagues] They're trying to make a new law: you have to be born here and have lived here for 10 years.
Q: How does it work now?
A: You can't [become naturalized]. Apparently. If you know someone, you can get it.
Q: Through *torpil*?
A: Exactly. [...]
Q: So even if I have a work permit for 20 years, and my children are born here...?
A: You can't; only if you know someone.

Similar confusion exists concerning the child's right to education and healthcare, in particular under what conditions children without TRNC nationality are allowed free public education and healthcare.

B2. Unwritten law for the community

Although it is mostly difficult to find a pattern in the many beliefs people in TRNC have with regard to the content of TRNC state law, and therefore it is not always easy to distinguish unwritten law for the community from false beliefs in state law (the difference being whether the law is indeed the result of a legislative act by the legislator), there are a few candidate unwritten laws that relate to the child's right to nationality:

- Most people think that you need to have stamps in your Work Permit (WP) proving 10–12 years of legal residency and work in TRNC to get TRNC nationality. Although not everyone in this situation gets the nationality, it seems at least that people after so many years on a WP are usually allowed to apply. We have encountered cases where people indeed received nationality, even without *torpil*.
- Another unwritten law seems to be that children do not need to have any kind of residency permit, but that they can overstay any permit as long as they like. In formal written law there is no mention of children and their need for residency permits.

The rule that people are more likely to obtain TRNC nationality through naturalization if they have friends in high places (*torpil*, see §7.2.2) is not an unwritten law, because this rule is in fact part of formal written law in TRNC, which leaves the decision about who becomes naturalized up to the council of ministers and whomever they "deem it necessary" to give nationality, thereby leaving it up to personal preference of the Ministers.

Interview 32. An employee of the TRNC government.

Q: I would like to know what happens if you are born here but your parents are not TRNC citizens?

A: […] We have a citizenship law, but it changes frequently. Even today, it is on the agenda to change it, so they are discussing to change it. […] [the law] says for the people, we are talking about the people who don't have TRNC citizenship, for the people who live here and work here at least 10 years […] they may get a citizenship. It doesn't say they will directly get citizenship, you *may* get citizenship. […] And [my Turkish migrant friends], they have been 10, 20 years and they don't get citizenship. But there are people, from Turkey for instance, who get citizenship just in one day, not even one day, because there is a provision in the article which says the important people, due to their service for the country they get citizenship directly. And they just give them the identity card directly. For instance, one journalist in Turkey and one businessman let's say, who took citizenship of Cyprus but don't even live in Cyprus. [...]

Q: I would like to know who decides if you are important enough to get the citizenship?

A: Authoritarian state! This is my opinion [laughs]. I'll take it back.

Q: I'd like to remind you again that no one will know what you said to us.

A: Since I am working for the government, it is not good if someone knows it. The state is doing this and the people in the government, the representatives of the Ministry of Interior. You are asking the official procedure right?

Q: Official and in practice. I would like to know what it's like.

A: The official procedure is this: so you apply for citizenship at the Ministry of Interior, they look at your documents and then they take documents to the Council of Ministers, the Cabinet. And it is the Cabinet who decides what to do. The government decides what to do. If you are a child of two parents who are both TRNC citizens, they don't take you to the Cabinet. You are directly a TRNC citizen. But in other cases, if you are from other countries, the decision is given in the cabinet. [...] Depends if you have relatives. Let's say you are a football player and they know you well, they may make you a citizen and, in that case, they may make your mother and father a citizen as well. But it is always maybe. [...] In practice we don't make Vietnamese people or far away countries' citizens or other people, but we make Turkish immigrants citizens. Because we are under the control of Turkey [...]

Q: So you have to make them a TRNC citizen?

A: No have to, not for all of them. You may make them.

Q: But the Turkish political pressure makes it more likely for the Cabinet to decide...

A: I don't want to say it like this [laughs] so I don't want to give such an answer because I work for the government. But yes, you can say it. I can give you a political answer: in the media and in the public sphere, we have a misconception that Turkish immigrants are being made citizens because of the demand from Turkey. There is perception in North Cyprus, in the public sphere and in the media, that Turkish immigrants are being made immigrants because of the demand from Turkey. [...] During the rightist or liberal governments, they are more ready to make Turkish immigrants citizens. But the leftist governments can resist to this.

Q: And if I remind you again that no one will be able to trace you to what you said, do you think I could get a more personal answer?

A: My worldview is a left one and I believe this is my home country and I don't consider it true or a good thing that the other countries demand something from us and we do it. So, we shouldn't accept these demands from other countries, we should govern ourselves. So, no other countries should impose its views upon me, regardless of their relation, giving aids to us, financial aid or whatever... so you may be a liberal or you may be a leftist, but you should resist this, the demands from other countries upon our country.

C. Hidden law

The only hidden law that we found was a written hidden law (C1), a decree sent out by the Ministry of Education to all schools in TRNC in 2010, which indicated that schools should not accept children whose parents were not in the TRNC on a legal residency permit, thereby going against formal written state law which grants a right to education and makes education mandatory until age 15 for all children. This hidden law is not a public decree, it was only addressed to the headmasters of schools and what we understand from some teachers, it was quite secretive and not even shared with all teachers. It cannot be found in the online repository of laws and decrees of the TRNC. When we received this copy, we were explicitly asked not to reveal our source.

This hidden law may explain why some teachers or school administrators argued that they were not allowed to accept non-legal resident children into their schools.

Figure 23. Written hidden law in TRNC: a decree from the Ministry of Education.

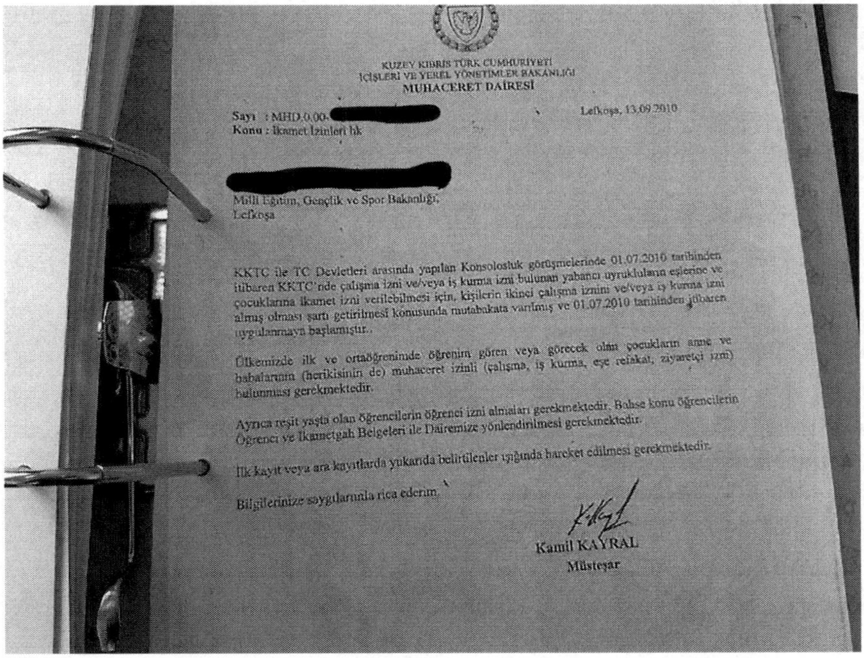

KUZEY KIBRIS TÜRK CUMHURİYETİ
İÇİŞLERİ VE YEREL YÖNETİMLER BAKANLIĞI
MUHACERET DAİRESİ

Sayı : MHD.0.00-[redacted]
Konu : İkamet İzinleri hk.

Lefkoşa, 13.09.2010

[redacted]

Milli Eğitim, Gençlik ve Spor Bakanlığı,
Lefkoşa

KKTC ile TC Devletleri arasında yapılan Konsolosluk görüşmelerinde 01.07.2010 tarihinden itibaren KKTC'nde çalışma izni ve/veya iş kurma izni bulunan yabancı uyrukluların eşlerine ve çocuklarına ikamet izni verilebilmesi için, kişilerin ikinci çalışma iznini ve/veya iş kurma izni almış olması şartı getirilmesi konusunda mutabakata varılmış ve 01.07.2010 tarihinden itibaren uygulanmaya başlamıştır..

Ülkemizde ilk ve ortaöğreniminde öğrenim gören veya görecek olan çocukların anne ve babalarının (herikisinin de) muhaceret izinli (çalışma, iş kurma, eşe refakat, ziyaretçi izni) bulunması gerekmektedir.

Ayrıca reşit yaşta olan öğrencilerin öğrenci izni almaları gerekmektedir. Bahse konu öğrencilerin Öğrenci ve İkametgah Belgeleri ile Dairemize yönlendirilmesi gerekmektedir.

İlk kayıt veya ara kayıtlarda yukarıda belirtilenler ışığında hareket edilmesi gerekmektedir.

Bilgilerinize saygılarımla rica ederim.

Kamil KAYRAL
Müsteşar

7.3.3.2 The Republic of Cyprus

A. Formal written law

As was discussed under §7.2.2, there are three ways for children to obtain RoC nationality: by birth (through one RoC parent), by naturalization and by registration. Exceptions are made if one of the parents of the child entered Cyprus through the North or lives in the North "illegally".

According to the RoC constitution, everyone is equal before the law[1559], and everyone has the right to the rights and freedoms in the constitution without discrimination based on their community, race, [...] religion, language, [...] political or other beliefs, national or social origin, birth, [...] unless the express provision of the Constitution defines the opposite.[1560]

B. Law for the community

B1. WRITTEN LAW FOR THE COMMUNITY & B2: UNWRITTEN LAW FOR THE COMMUNITY

Knowledge of the TRNC population of RoC formal written law follows much the same pattern as their knowledge of TRNC formal written law; there are many diverse beliefs about what is law in the RoC. These beliefs are based on hearsay, information from the media and information obtained from RoC authorities.

Generally, people think that, according to RoC formal written law, children have the right to RoC nationality if they can prove that they are Cypriot. This means that they have at least one parent who has RoC nationality (because they, or their parents, were Cypriot citizens before 1974). However, they think that, in practice, the RoC does not apply this formal written law and actually applies a discriminatory policy whereby children of "mixed marriages", in particular one RoC and one TR parent, cannot obtain RoC nationality. Some people living in the TRNC believe that this policy is based on the unwritten RoC law that states that "If a mixed (RoC/TR) couple is married in the TRNC, their marriage is illegal and the RoC does not recognize this marriage. Therefore, they cannot pass on their RoC nationality to their children." They believe this is the unwritten state law for mixed marriages, because this is what they are often told when they apply at the RoC Ministry. Their application does not get rejected; instead they are put on a waiting list and told that their application is "pending", but they never receive the nationality. However, the couples who, for this reason, get married somewhere outside of TRNC find that this does not help their children. This is a false belief in an unwritten law.

A way to get around the formal written law for a child of a mixed marriage whose mother is a RoC national is to state that the father is unknown. Because the RoC does not have access to registration of TRNC marriages or birth certificates, children can pretend that their father is unknown, for example by saying that their mother was a prostitute. Some people in the North argue that they have used this option successfully. However, this is more of a loophole in the formal written law rather than an unwritten law.

1559 1960 Constitution of the Republic of Cyprus (art. 28(1)).

1560 Ibid (art. 28(2)).

C. Hidden law

At first, I thought, based on our interviews and observations, that the employees of the RoC Ministry of Interior must have knowledge of a hidden law – either written or unwritten – which they apply, which states something like:

"Make sure that any child who has Turkish ("settler")[1561] connections, either by blood or through birth place, does not receive RoC nationality unless it cannot be avoided. This can be done by:

1. Arguing that the marriage was illegal, if they have a "TRNC marriage certificate"
2. Arguing that they have an illegal birth certificate if they have a "TRNC birth certificate"
3. Arguing that their parents entered the island illegally and/or are living in the TRNC illegally

In these cases, instead of rejecting their file, take it and tell them that they are on a waiting list."

However, ater I found out that there is indeed written hidden RoC law[1562]: a 2007 decision of the Council of Ministers which is published only in Greek, published in the official Gazette but not available online, which states that of the following specific criteria, at least one must be fulfilled in order to enable the claimant to obtain nationality under article 109(3) of the RoC nationality law, to grant Cypriot citizenship to a person with one parent who has or used to have the nationality of the RoC, even if the other parent's entry in or stay in Cyprus is illegal:

1) Children born on or before 20/07/1974
2) Children whose foreign parent is not a Turkish national but a national of another country (a European citizen or a national of other countries with whom the reciprocity regime applies)
3) Children whose parents' marriage took place abroad anytime or in Cyprus before 20/07/1974
4) Children whose Turkish Cypriot father / mother had relations with a Turkish citizen regardless of the events of 1974 (due to studies or employment outside Cyprus)

1561 Everyone from Turkish ethnicity living in North Cyprus is usually considered a "settler" by the RoC.

1562 Because it is written and published in the official Gazette, of course one could argue that it is not hidden law at all. I do think it is hidden law from the perspective of the Turkish Cypriot population, to whom this law is not made available. In addition, as discussed further in this section, there seems to be an underlying hidden law that contradicts this written hidden law.

5) Children whose parents live in the mixed village of Pyla[1563]

However, even this law is not applied, since we met people whose parents of mixed marriages were married in Turkey (criteria 3) and/or whose RoC/TR parents met while studying in Turkey (criteria 4), yet these children were not able to obtain RoC nationality either. It seems, therefore, that the unwritten hidden law identified in the first paragraph is indeed applied by the employees of the RoC Ministry of Interior. When sharing the results of this research, several RoC government employees confirmed this suspicion, arguing that it was a necessary measure to make sure that the demograpy of the island is not altered by Turkey who is sending Turkish settlers, whereby the Greek Cypriots would soon be the minority on the island.

Another hidden law seems to be (we found a few cases and saw some proof of this) that children of mixed marriages can get RoC nationality if the parents 1) can make a credible threat that otherwise they will start a court case at the ECtHR or 2) they have enough time, money and patience to go through the whole RoC court system. What seems to happen is that in the latter cases, first lower level court cases are started in the RoC, for which the court dates are continuously postponed by the RoC authorities as long as the RoC formal written law allows. Then the cases are taken up by the Supreme court, where again the hearing is postponed as long as possible. All together this can take about 10 years. In the end, right before the Supreme Court has to make a ruling, the parents get a call from the Ministry that the passports for the children are ready. In the former case, when someone makes a credible threat to go to the ECtHR, a similar phone call follows.

Lastly, it is said that people from the TRNC with the right connections in politics and by paying a sufficient sum of money could obtain RoC nationality. However, we also spoke to people who tried this method and lost a lot of money to no avail, so it is not certain whether this is indeed based on some unwritten hidden law.

7.3.3.3. Turkey

As indicated before, Turkey takes the position that TRNC is an independent state and therefore they generally do not legislate in relation to TRNC. They do engage in several agreements and development programs.[1564] Since the people we interviewed generally did not express any concerns in relation to TR nationality or other rights they wanted (their children) to obtain through the TR, and because there were no TR authorities in Cyprus except for the embassy, we do not have much data.

1563 2007 Decision of the Council of Ministers: Criteria of the Cabinet for the registration of persons having a Cypriot parent and a foreign parent who has entered or stayed illegally in Cyprus, 14.02.2007, No. Decision 65,067,, as quoted in the 2015 report of the Commissioner for Human Rights and Administration (Tsiartis et al. (2015: para. B(9)).

1564 See Deputy Prime Ministry and Ministry of Foreign Affairs (no date(b)).

A. Formal written law

As explained under §7.2.2, any child who has one TR national as a parent can obtain TR nationality. In addition, whoever acquires TRNC nationality at birth can acquire TR nationality upon application.

B. Law for the community

In this case, again, it is difficult to determine a law for the community, as people have varying beliefs about the acquisition of TR nationality. Regarding obtaining TR nationality at birth, some say that this happens through one TR parent, some say only if there is a TR father. From the cases that we have encountered, it seems that one TR parent is enough, but parents do have to go to the embassy to apply for/get the nationality.

It is clear that Turkey distributes TR passports for travel purposes to Turkish Cypriots.[1565] However, the people in TRNC are not clear on the conditions nor about in which cases it concerns a proof of TR nationality, or only a travel document. It seems that everyone with a TRNC nationality can obtain a TR travel document at the embassy (and this seems to be an unwritten public law), and children of at least one TR parent can get TR nationality.

7.3.4. SCHOOL LEGAL ORDER

In terms of the children's access to school, it seemed that individual public schools took quite some liberty in making up rules in relation to the admission procedure. This included deciding who to allow access (specifically, with which kind of nationality and/or permit), and in relation to the amount of school fees asked. Generally, public schools are supposed to be free. But since they do not get any or very little financial budget from the Ministry of Education, many schools "illegally" hold their own treasury with income from school fees. This process seems to be different for every school, therefore we cannot say more about the laws involved as they will differ from school to school.

7.3.5. HOUSEHOLD LEGAL ORDER

In relation to the child's right to nationality, most of this is decided by the state and, to a lesser degree, international law, since "nationality" is a state-legal concept. However, there are choices that parents make on behalf of their children, for example whether or not to apply for TR or RoC nationality (and

1565 See also Navaro-Yashin (2012: 107).

required legal documentation such as birth certificates). However, even if in the eyes of some children their parents made these choices for them, it seemed that, for the parents, this was not so much a choice as a weighing of the options presented to them by state law. Therefore, it does not seem like there really is household law in this case.

7.3.6. THE AUTONOMOUS CHILD

Children in our research, especially the younger ones, often did not know the meaning of the concept of "nationality". It was something too abstract for them to grasp. If we would ask whether they had an identity card or passport, some would say they did not know while others would say "yes, from Cyprus" and they were not be able to distinguish between TRNC and RoC documents. When asked whether they could travel, they would mention countries they would want to travel to in the future, not thinking that there might be limits on where they would be allowed to go.

For the older children, starting at around age 14 and 15, they seemed to be mostly aware of their nationalities and what opportunities that gave them (or not), but they did not seem to feel autonomous in any way in relation to their nationality. Nationality was more of an external fact in their lives, which they had to live with as well as they could; simply "the cards that were dealt to them".

7.4. CONCLUSION

Since the divison of the island Cyprus in 1974, it is unclear whether children living in the North have any rights at all and, if they do, who is supposed to protect their rights. In this case study, the answer to questions about the rights of children in the TRNC in general and the child's right to nationality in particular, greaty depends on the perspective one takes.

From the perspective of the international community, although on the one hand children's rights are claimed to be "universal"[1566], the state-centric organization of international law on the other hand creates a legal vacuum for children living in unrecognized states. While the TRNC is not able to sign/ratify the CRC due to its non-recognition, neither Turkey nor the RoC claim jurisdiction and subsequent responsibility for children living in the TRNC. It is unclear whether on the UN level either of these two states are considered responsible. Specifically, as regards the child's right to nationality, it does seem that Turkey and the RoC can be held responsible insofar as they violate the child's right to obtain their respective nationalities, through discriminative measures or other ways of arbitrary

[1566] Since it, as an instrument, falls under the 1948 Universal Declaration of Human Rights (CRC (1989: preamble)). The UN SDGs, similarly, aim to "leave no one behind" (UNDP (2018)).

deprivation of nationality. The RoC mostly seems to discriminate against children who have one parent who is a RoC national and who live in Northern Cyprus. These children are often not allowed RoC nationality, whereby the RoC is violating international law. Meanwhile, children who only obtain TRNC nationality can be considered stateless from the international legal perspective. Therefore, although all children are supposed to have a right to nationality under international law, in fact the international legal system makes these children stateless by not recognizing their nationalities, thereby severely limiting their enjoyment of rights such as education, freedom of movement, among other rights.[1567]

From the regional (European) perspective, it seems that the Council of Europe holds Turkey responsible for the rights of children living in the TRNC, by reasoning that the initial Turkish invasion in 1974 was illegal and therefore Turkey is responsible for all consequences of this invasion, which they seem to understand to include anything done by the TRNC authorities today. However, there has not been a case before the ECtHR that concerned the rights of children living in the TRNC as its subject, so therefore we cannot be sure whether this line of reasoning would indeed assign Turkish responsibility to all children's rights violations in the TRNC. As I have argued under §7.3.2 (A), the relationship between TR and TRNC is rather comparable to a former colonial power to its now independent former colony. Therefore, I believe the ECtHR has to re-evaluate the relationship between the occupying power and local administration, according to fixed criteria, because these relationships change over time and therefore its ruling from 1995 in the *Louizidou* case is not necessarily still applicable. The European Union, on the other hand, while not claiming responsibility for the rights of children in Northern Cyprus, does actively protect some of these rights through the aid program for the Turkish Cypriot community, although it is not involved with regard to the right to nationality.

From the state legal perspective, it is clear that, to understand state law relating to the child's right to nationality from all three main states potentially legislating over the nationality of the child living in TRNC (TRNC, RoC, TR), it is important to understand that, for all these three states, there is a clear distinction between formal written law, law for the community and hidden law. In the TRNC, while formal written law is usually followed as concerns obtaining TRNC nationality by children of at least one TRNC national parent, laws on obtaining nationality through naturalization only provide for the possibility of application for citizenship, which has to be decided by the Council of Ministers. The TRNC does not (really) regulate obtaining nationality through naturalization. It seems that, on this subject, there is no unwritten law for the community, nor hidden law. In the RoC, while formal written law makes it possible for every child of at least one parent who is a RoC national to obtain RoC nationality, they do have a provision to exclude children of whom at least one parent entered Cyprus via the TRNC or

1567 See §7.2.3.

who lives in the TRNC. These applications are also subject to consideration by the Council of Ministers. There is a formal written decree whereby exceptions are made to the exclusion of children of a parent who entered/lives in TRNC, yet these rules are not followed either and, in general it seems that unless a child living in TRNC has two RoC parents, they cannot obtain RoC nationality. Turkey, lastly, does follow its formal written law in allowing every child who has at least one TR national parent to obtain TR nationality. In addition, according to an unwritten law for the community[1568], anyone with a TRNC nationality can obtain a TR passport for travel purposes, although this travel document is not the same as the proper conferral of nationality.

Since the child's right to nationality is very much a legal concept regulated on the level of the state (and perhaps at the international level), in this case there were no really relevant "lower" level legal orders such as the household or the school which made law in relation to the child's right to nationality for children living in the TRNC.

7.5. UPDATE: THE CHILD'S RIGHT TO NATIONALITY IN THE TRNC: JANUARY 2018 – JULY 2020

Since data collection ended quite recently and we only shared our research results in November 2018, some formal changes have occurred, yet it seems that not much has changed on a day-to-day basis (yet).

On the international level there has been no development regarding the position of the international community and international legal bodies in relation to the TRNC. The Cyprus problem is still a subject of discussion at the UN level, but no progress has been made regarding the peace process.[1569]

Regarding the RoC, there has been some development. First, in their 2018 reply to the list of issues, the RoC indicated that the ratification of the 1954 Convention on Refugees and Stateless Persons was pending upon Parliament, and that steps were taken for the ratification of the 1961 Convention on the Reducation of Statelessness.[1570] To date, this has not lead to ratification by the RoC of either convention.[1571]

Second, in 2018–2019 during the Universal Periodic Review at the UN Human Rights Council, the RoC did not write anything about the right to nationality in

[1568] At least I have not been able to find this in written form.

[1569] The last development reported being that UN secretary Guterres met with both GC and TC leaders and had "frank and focused" informal discussions. However, nothing was agreed on nor was any follow-up established (United Nationsl Secretary General (2019)). See also Security Council Report (2020).

[1570] Committee on the Elimination of Discrimination against Women (2018: para. 60).

[1571] United Nations Treaties Collection (2020).

their state report.[1572] The issues of access to nationality for children of Turkish Cypriot origin and accompanying discrimination were again discussed[1573], as they were in 2015.[1574] During the working group discussion, while the RoC argued that "legislation [does] not include discriminatory provisions against any ethnic group or non-European nationals"[1575], Germany[1576], Ireland[1577], the United Kingdom[1578] and the Netherlands[1579] raised concerns. To this, the RoC replied that

> "all Turkish Cypriots, irrespective of where they lived, were holders of Cypriot birth certificates, identity documents and passports. The Government had had to adopt emergency measures to counter the influx of illegal settlers, including the adoption of criteria concerning the granting of Cypriot nationality to them and their descendants"[1580], and that "all the cases concerning the granting of Cypriot nationality were examined on humanitarian grounds".[1581]

However, Germany, Ireland, the Netherlands, Argentina, the United Kingdom and the USA all recommended that the RoC take measure to ensure non-discriminatory application of nationality law, within a reasonable timeframe.[1582] Of these recommendations, the RoC accepted to ensure equal treatment for all applying for Cypriot nationality and to take measures to ensure that nationality laws are applied universally on the basis of clearly defined criteria.[1583] Yet they do not accept to automatically apply nationality law in an efficient, non-discriminatory and transparent matter irrespective of the nationality of the applicant[1584], and they do not accept the recommendations on granting nationality to children of mixed (TR/TC) marriages:

> Cyprus takes note of recommendations […] concerning the procedures for granting nationality to children of mixed marriages between members of the Turkish Cypriot community and Turkish citizens who are illegally residing in the northern part of the territory of the Republic of Cyprus, which is under military occupation since 1974. These children can in no way be considered as stateless.[1585]

1572 UN Human Rights Council (2018a).
1573 In cooperation with the Institute for Statelessness and Inclusion, we submitted a report to the Human Rights Council regarding the right to nationality and the subsequent access to human rights based on nationality, ethnicity and residency in the RoC. See: Hopman et al. (2018b).
1574 Human Rights Council (2018b: para. 16).
1575 Human Rights Council (2019a: para. 60).
1576 Ibid: para. 64.
1577 Ibid: para. 73.
1578 Ibid: para. 130.
1579 Ibid: para. 88.
1580 Ibid: para. 132.
1581 Ibid: para. 134.
1582 Ibid: paras. 139.96-139.101.
1583 Human Rights Council (2019b: para 31).
1584 Ibid: paras 32, 33.
1585 Ibid: paras. 34, 35.

In that sense, change seems unlikely since the RoC indicates to not to want to comply with international human rights law in this respect.

Turkey has also recently (January 2020) undergone its universal periodic review under the UN Human Rights Council. In its state report, Turkey did not mention Cyprus at all.[1586] Neither was Cyprus mentioned in the summary of stakeholders' submissions.[1587] During the working group discussion, there was no mention of the right to nationality. Recommendations in relation to the Cyprus conflict were made by Cyprus, Greece and Armenia and regarded solely human rights issues related to the 1974 war (e.g. information on missing persons).[1588] None of these recommendations were accepted by Turkey.[1589]

At the European level, there have been no relevant legal and/or political developments.

On the state level in the TRNC, according to my local contacts, nothing much has changed.[1590] The 2018 government has changed again (as happens regularly), and the new government is again promising to change nationality law, but has not yet offered a concrete legal proposal.

In the RoC, one interesting development has been that for the first time, a court case regarding RoC nationality for a child of a TC mother (with RoC nationality) and TR father has been completed and reached a decision in the RoC administrative court.[1591] The case concerned a person who had applied for RoC nationality in 2004, to which no reply had been received. In 2015, s/he initiated legal action, whereupon her lawyer received a letter from the Deputy Director of the Ministry of Interior, stating that since she did not meet the criteria set in the 2007 Council of Ministers decision[1592] her application was "placed on waiting list No. 688 in order to be considered favorable in case of extension of the criteria of the Council of Ministers". According to the applicant, the 2007 Council of Ministers decision is based on criteria that discriminate on the grounds of ethnic origin and therefore violates the principle of equal treatment as enshrined in the 1960 Constitution as well as in international human rights law.

The judge rejected the application, arguing that according to the 2002 RoC Civil Registry Law, art. 109, a person cannot obtain RoC citizenship if entry or stay in Cyprus of any one of the parents of that person was illegal, unless the Council of Ministers otherwise orders. This law therefore leaves disgression for the executive power to make an exception to this rule if they please, and

1586 Human Rights Council (2019c).

1587 Human Rights Council (2019d).

1588 Human Rights Council (2020: paras. 46.5-46.11).

1589 Ibid (paras. 47-49). Turkey stated that they don't accept any recommendation by Cyprus because they do not recognize Cyprus nor accept its claim to represent the whole island (ibid: para. 47).

1590 I inquired with 9 local contacts.

1591 Case Hancer v. Republic of Cyprus Ministry of Interior (2020).

1592 See §7.3.3.2 (C).

the applicant did not deny illegal entry and/or stay in Cyprus of her parent(s). Regarding the principles of international law, the judge seems to argue that while the conditions for acquisition and deprivation of citizenship can be determined by EU member states, and are subjected to judicial review in light of EU law which also recognizes international law in case of citizens of the union, this does not apply since the applicant is not a citizen of the EU.[1593] The applicant is sentenced to pay the defendant (RoC Minsitry of Interior) € 1.500.

In Turkey there have been no relevant developments on the state level.

Regarding the more local school, household and autonomous child orders my local contacts indicate that nothing has changed (yet).

[1593] The judge refers here to art. 48 of the case of Rottman v. Freistaat Bayern at the European course of Justice (2010).

CHAPTER 8
REFLECTION & CONCLUSION

LOOKING BACK & LOOKING FORWARD

In this chapter I will answer, and reflect on, the first part of the main question for this PhD research, namely:

Can violations of children's rights in different cultural, social and political contexts be better understood if analyzed within a legal pluralist framework, taking into account the child's perspective and the relations of power corresponding to the different legal orders surrounding children? And, consequently, how can this understanding be used to improve the concrete situation of children?

This question consists of several sub-questions that each merit individual reflection, namely:

1) Is it possible to understand children's rights violations if analyzed within a legal pluralist framework (as developed in this thesis)?
   a. Can this be done, taking into account the child's perspective?
   b. Can this be done, taking into account the relations of power corresponding to the different legal orders surrounding children?
2) If it is possible, in general, to understand children's rights violations if analyzed within a legal pluralist framework (as developed in this thesis), is this possible for children's rights violations in different cultural, social and political contexts?
3) If all this is possible, does it lead to a better understanding of children's rights violations than when analyzed
   a. From non-legal pluralist framework
   b. Without taking into account the child's perspective
   c. Without taking into account the relations of power corresponding to the different legal orders surrounding children
4) How can this understanding be used to improve the concrete situation of children?

All these questions I will attempt to answer based on the data as presented in previous chapters, as well as a reflection on the theoretical framework and methodology in relation to the three case studies of this thesis. Questions 1–3 will be answered in this chapter, question 4 will be answered in chapter 9. In terms of structure, each paragraph will answer a different sub-question. Where relevant (§8.1, 8.3.1 and 8.3.2), the general answer, in light of the complete research, will be followed by specific answers per case study.

8.1. UNDERSTANDING CHILDREN'S RIGHTS VIOLATIONS, ANALYZED WITHIN A LEGAL PLURALIST FRAMEWORK

In chapters 1–4 of this thesis, a theoretical framework and accompanying methodology were developed for a potentially better understanding of children's rights violations. The hypothesis in these chapters was that, to study children's rights violations through a framework of legal pluralism, whereby the existence of the different legal orders and its statutory laws would be analyzed as relating to a specific children's right in a specific area, would lead to an understanding of the legal factors involved in the violation/protection of that right. This framework would have to consist of a clear definition of law (chapter 1), and a theory on and method for how to empirically find the different laws of different legal orders (chapters 3 and 4). In addition, it was hypothesized that it would be important to take the child's perspective into account in data collection (chapters 2 and 4), and that analysis would have to take into account the power relations corresponding to the different legal orders surrounding children (chapters 1, 3 and 4).

In chapter 1, it was stated that law has to be understood as a social fact. We only notice that there is a law, because someone (an individual or a group of people) has created a rule that we (the legal community) perceive as law, only because we understand this individual or group that created the rule to be authorized to create laws. The recognition of the legislator, according to the basic norm, is therefore crucial for the understanding of law as law. Likewise, the sovereign only exists because of the recognition of the legal community of the sovereign as sovereign.[1594] That is to say that the sovereign exists and has its power only because it is recognized as such by the relevant community. Haugaard's example made this especially clear:

> what distinguishes the actual Napoleon from the "napoleons" who are found in psychiatric institutions is not internal to them but the fact the former (unlike the latter) had a substantial ring of reference which validates his power.[1595]

1594 §1.1, 1.3.

1595 Haugaard (2008: 122).

A legal norm was argued to be different from a social norm in two ways: first, in a legal situation you cannot stop being a member of the legal community of a legal order when you have done something illegal, from the internal perspective of that order and, second, there is a power inequality between the sovereign and the subject of the legal order.[1596]

Lastly, a conceptual framework for the understanding and study of statutory law was introduced, wherein a distinction was made between A) formal written law, B) law for the community and C) hidden law.[1597]

	formal written law (A)	law for the community (B)	hidden law (C)
Written	+	B1	C1
Unwritten	–	B2	C2
Public	+	+	–

In chapter 2, it was shown how in society, from an adult perspective, children are perceived as being different from adult human beings. Compared to the "normal" adult, who is rational and well behaved, the child is unreasonable, immoral and unsociable – much like a madman.[1598] For this reason, the child cannot be granted political freedom or autonomy, and has to be socialized, until s/he has not overcome this condition of childhood.[1599] This binary distinction between children and adults is the basis for all law for children and the basis for children's rights which, in many ways, are different from (adult) human rights.[1600]

In chapter 3 it was shown that, when looking at law from the child's perspective, what is law for the child really depends on whoever the child believes is authorized to make law for her/him and whether this person, or group of people, does indeed create law.[1601] Based on this axiom it is clear that, from the child's perspective, law can be found in different legal orders surrounding the child, such as the household and the school, and potentially does not even include state law.[1602] Looking at law through children's eyes therefore automatically leads to a legal pluralist understanding of law.[1603]

In chapter 4, a methodology was developed to be able to find all law applicable to, and relevant for, the understanding of the protection/violation of a specific child's rights in a specific socio-legal context. It was stated here that, in addition to legal doctrinal research to find formal written international and

1596 §1.2.
1597 §1.4.
1598 §2.1, 2.2.1.
1599 §2.2.2, 2.2.3.
1600 §2.3.
1601 §3.2.
1602 §3.2, 3.4.
1603 §3.3.

state law, it is necessary to engage in qualitative research with both legislators and addressees of the law of each (potential) legal order related to the child's right under research.[1604] The participants in the research should therefore include the children themselves. However, it was indicated that research has shown that doing research with children is not easy and that adult researchers have a tendency to "know better" and to be biased towards information obtained from children. It is therefore important to truly listen to children, to allow them to participate in several phases of the research if possible, and to allow them as much agency in the research process as possible.[1605] This, of course, comes with specific ethical considerations, such as that the child has to be enabled to give informed consent to participate in the research (ideally without needing the consent of the parent), has to be guaranteed confidentiality and anonymity, and the researcher and participant should be positioned as equals insofar as possible.[1606]

To practically realize this, a concrete method for qualitative research with children was developed, the so-called "micro-research", which uses inquiry-based science instruction and Socratic dialogue as the foundation for its approach.[1607] Practically, a researcher who wants to understand the legal orders surrounding a child's right, in a specific socio-legal context, has to identify possible legal orders and then, for each order, try to identify which forms of law (formal written law, law for the community and/or hidden law) may apply. Formal written law can be mostly found through legal doctrinal research and literature study; law for the community and hidden law have to be found through empirical legal research. In addition, empirical legal research is necessary to test whether indeed all relevant legal orders have been identified. Data has to be analyzed according to the theoretical framework as developed in chapters 1 and 3.[1608]

All this was the theoretical answer to the question of how to better understand children's rights violations. Yet the question remains whether this approach indeed lead to understanding children's rights violations. I will answer this question per case study.

8.1.1. THE CHILD'S RIGHT TO EDUCATION IN THE NETHERLANDS

In the first case study on the child's right to education in the Netherlands, I followed the methodological approach which suggested to focus on specific target groups that were particularly at risk for violations of their right to

1604 §4.2.
1605 §4.2.1 – 4.2.3.
1606 §4.2.4.
1607 §4.3 – 4.4.
1608 §4.4.

education.[1609] In this case, I identified as target groups: children out of school (*thuiszitters*), homeschooled children and Roma children.

It worked particularly well in this case study to approach the subject from the child's perspective. As was shown in chapter 5[1610], when we look at the subject through children's eyes, we get a very different perspective on the matter than when we look at the subject through adults' eyes – including politicians and professionals. The main issue here was that professionals and politicians had developed a way to measure the number of children whose right to education was potentially violated in a very bureaucratic way that excluded the lived experiences of children. In quantitative terms, this meant that less than 10,000 children were indicated as potentially having their right to education violated, while this research showed that, when looking through children's eyes, this number should include all children who are not in school for longer periods and not just those who are registered in a certain way. According to my estimation, this should amount to between 50,000–60,000 children per year. The government also argues that 619 children are homeschooled (those whose parents are exempted due to 5(b) of the Compulsory Education Act). However, I have shown that it is not certain whether all these 5(b) children receive any education and that there are many more children receiving homeschooling that are not in this 5(b) group.[1611] For children of all three focus groups, insofar as they were (sometimes) out of school, it showed that their experiences in relation to education were quite similar, in particular as regards social exclusion.[1612]

Regarding the legal pluralist approach to the case study, I believe that this approach contributied to the understanding of the violation of the child's right to education in the Netherlands. First, it showed the relationship between international, regional and national formal law and how national formal law in some respects violates the international/regional child's right to education.[1613] Second, it showed that, while people in the Netherlands were aware of the child's right to education, they did not really identify this as an international or regional law. In general, people were not aware of European law on this subject at all.[1614] Third, it showed that, while generally (state) law has a very strong authoritative position in the Netherlands, most people do not really know its content as regards (the right to) education.[1615] Fourth, in terms of the power relations between different legal orders, the case study showed that the household legal order has a very strong authoritative position over children who are out of school. For all three focus groups, it is usually parents who decide if the child

1609 See §4.4.1.
1610 §5.2.1 & 5.2.2.
1611 §5.2.1.
1612 §5.2.1.
1613 §5.3.1 – 5.3.3.
1614 §5.3.1 & 5.3.2.
1615 §5.2.6 & 5.3.4.

receives any education and whether it is at home or in school. This authority is questioned or challenged relatively little by other authorities and/or children themselves, so that often the parents are ultimately responsible for the violation of the child's right to education.[1616] In terms of the power relations between different legal orders, it is clear that the center of legal power[1617] for children out of school in the Netherlands mostly lies within the household legal order.

The application of the methodology in the qualitative interviews did not work too well in this case study. This may not be necessarily due to the theoretical framework and methodology, but rather to a lack of training and experience on the part of the researcher. As it was my first time applying this methodology, I found that, as a researcher, I was providing too little structure. People would want to talk about the content of education, and I did not want to direct the discussion very much as prescribed by the conversation method.[1618] The question "what is the meaning of the child's right to education?" does not necessarily lead to a discussion of legal orders involved, but in many cases it resulted in a discussion about what type of education (including didactics and pedagogy) is the best education. Basically, and with the benefit of hindsight, I recognize that I did not sufficiently keep in mind the theoretical framework and did not sufficiently steer the conversations in the direction of laws involved.[1619] I did remedy this in some of the conversations, while in others it was just simply not something that participants wanted to discuss. In the end, I feel that, although generally I had sufficient data to understand the violations of the child's right to education in the Netherlands from a legal pluralist perspective, it would have been better to have more, or higher quality, data. Another concern is that I feel I did not involve a sufficient number of Roma participants, since I underestimated how difficult they were to reach, and I also was quite intimidated by professionals telling me that it was dangerous to talk to Roma or to visit them in their houses. I was warned not to do this by some professionals, who told stories of aggression involving guns, which initially held me back from approaching Roma families.

Looking back after completing two more case studies, and having gained a lot more experience, these are two points that I would have done differently if I were to do the case study again. In this respect, I also learned from the amount of scrutiny that the research report was under.[1620] On the positive side, I was able to transfer these learning experiences into the two subsequent case studies.

1616 §5.3.7.
1617 See §3.3.4, discussing Pospisil.
1618 §4.4.
1619 §4.4.2.
1620 See chapter 9.

8.1.2. THE CHILD'S RIGHT TO EDUCATION IN THE CENTRAL AFRICAN REPUBLIC

In the second case study on the child's right to education in the Central African Republic (CAR), the preparation of the field research was quite different from the first case study, as there was very little information available about education in the CAR. I was therefore not able to identify clearly the groups of children particularly at risk for violations of their right to education before the field research phase. Instead, I decided to travel to the CAR and determine who were children most at risk for violations of their right to education in the field. Although I started by looking at children in hospitals and in orphanages, I very soon came to realize that, in fact, for all children living in the CAR there was a high risk of violation of their right to education. Subsequently, I decided to let go of trying to identify focus groups and instead had a more open, inclusive attitude towards the children I would encounter anywhere while travelling around the country.

Analyzing children's rights violations within a legal pluralist framework worked very well in this case study. As indicated in chapter 6, it was a challenge to find any law related to the child's right to education in any of the potential legal orders. This I think is in itself a very valuable, and unexpected, finding. Although it may go beyond the scope of the current thesis, I even think that this finding of the CAR being a society in which, in the first place, everyone is an individual, autonomous actor – much like in a Hobessian state of nature[1621] – can potentially give great insights into the how and why of the perpetual violent conflict in the CAR. The legal pluralist approach led to several other research findings relevant to the understanding of the protection/violation of the child's right to education in the CAR, namely:

1) that mostly children themselves are autonomous concerning their education[1622]
2) that the classroom seems to be the only social order experienced as a legal order by children[1623]
3) that there are potential issues with the power balance between the state and NGOs as potential legislators, as well as between the state and the international community as a whole (including international law, which seems to be experienced by some people in the CAR as something external to the CAR and imposed by Western powers)[1624]

[1621] §6.4.
[1622] §6.3.8.
[1623] §6.3.6.
[1624] §6.3.1 & 6.3.2.

4) that local orders (religious and local legal orders) are not so much legal orders, but rather are present community leaders who have an advising role in the community[1625]

Incorporating the child's perspective worked very well in this case study, perhaps even better than in the Dutch case study, probably because in the CAR the children were more autonomous and had more insight into their situation. The most valuable data in this case study came from children, who were the most honest participants. Although I initially was quite shocked to hear from very young children about the physical and sexual violence in the classrooms, and I may have worried for a while whether it would be ethically OK to ask them questions about these subjects without providing any psychological help, I soon realized that these were Western and paternalistic ideas on my part. The children were in fact very willing to talk about these subjects. They often brought it up themselves and seemed happy and empowered by the fact that their experiences were considered interesting to a researcher. The research conversation also provided them with a platform to talk about issues that otherwise they may not have been able to share. Several children were very eager to tell me details of their experience of violence and abuse (such as in the example below). When some children did not want to address these issues, they were capable of indicating this and we could change the subject of the conversation.

Interview 6, a young girl (around age 15) who lives in a camp for internally displaced persons.

Q: [at the end of the interview] Is there something else that I forgot [to ask]?
R: Yes.
Q: You think I forgot a question?
R: You have forgotten a very important subject. This is the subject of young girls and the Séléka [armed group], they have […] abused the girls, by use of force.
Q: Do you want to tell me about that?
R: When we returned to school, the Séléka had gone out and they took a number of girls with them into the bush, and after at that moment, I want to claim this, those Séléka, they took out their arms, and I ran to return to the school, and I could not find one teacher. […]

Talking to children in this case was also particularly useful because of the very honest information they gave, compared to adults who would sometimes lie (in particular in relation to corruption)[1626], or would be unaware of the reality on the ground for children as regards their education.

1625 §6.3.3 & 6.3.4.
1626 See §6.3.2 (C).

8.1.3. THE CHILD'S RIGHT TO NATIONALITY IN THE TURKISH REPUBLIC OF NORTHERN CYPRUS (TRNC)

The third case study was quite different from the other two, because nationality is a very state-legal concept. It constitutes a kind of membership of a state and therefore is the subject of state level legislation in the first place, rather than of legal orders closer to the child. Consequently, the child's perspective was less relevant, as young children often did not know what "nationality" meant or why they did or did not have a certain nationality. However, speaking with children of around age 14 or 15 and older was still very relevant, because around that age they seemed to have acquired an understanding of concepts such as nationality and ethnicity and what this meant for their lives. The consequences of nationality, such as travel options, studying abroad and crossing to the south side of Cyprus, also became clearer to children around these ages.

In this case, there was also very little information available about the subject in literature and I decided to determine groups of children specifically at risk for having their right to nationality violated once I was in the field. Soon enough, these turned out to be: children of mixed marriages, children with only TRNC nationality, children of parents on a TRNC student visa, children of parents on a TRNC tourist visa, children of parents on a TRNC work permit, and children of illegal migrant workers.[1627]

The legal pluralist approach to the study was relevant to this case study, albeit in a different manner than the first and second case studies. Although the legal orders that are closer to the child (in this case the school and household legal order)[1628] do not legislate directly on nationality, they do have an influence in different ways. Schools have rules whereby, based on the child's nationality/residency status, they either do or do not admit the child to the school. It is also based on nationality/residency status that the school fees are determined.[1629] The household did not really make law, but parents did make choices on behalf of (future) children that may influence their nationality, such as deciding where to give birth, where to get married and where to live.[1630]

The most added value of the use of the legal pluralist approach in this case, however, was that it gave a clear framework wherein it was possible to consider the different legal orders of the "states" involved (Republic of Cyprus, TRNC and Turkey). It provided the framework within which to discuss these different legal orders, without getting into difficulties with the issue of whether or not TRNC state law can indeed be considered law, as would be an issue for a more legal doctrinal scholar. In this sense, any case of children's rights in the TRNC or any

1627 §7.2.1 & 7.2.2.
1628 §7.3.3.4 & 7.3.3.5.
1629 §7.3.3.4.
1630 §7.3.3.5.

other unrecognized state could not possibly be adequately researched without a legal pluralist framework. The discussion of the power relations between the different legal orders, also involving the international and regional legal orders in relation to the three potential state legal orders, was crucial for an understanding of the child's right to nationality in the TRNC. For example, it could be shown that while the international legal order excludes the TRNC, stating that the Republic of Cyprus is the only legitimate authority on the island of Cyprus, at the same time the RoC is not held responsible for the rights of children living in the North. Therefore, a legal vacuum of some sorts is created from the perspective of the international legal order, while the regional legal order, and in particular the Council of Europe, seems theoretically to hold Turkey responsible for children's rights in the TRNC, although they have not legislated nor ruled on the subject. This, in its turn, is influenced by the fact that cases on Northern Cyprus are only brought before the ECtHR by the RoC, which does not start court cases on violations of the rights of children living in the North (whose rights to nationality in some cases are violated by the RoC).[1631]

Since a group of five bachelor students of Maastricht University were involved in this case study, who also engaged in field research including qualitative interviews, this case study showed that it is possible for the theoretical and methodological framework presented to be used by other researchers. The student researchers did some reading and received one day of training before travelling to TRNC, and they were subsequently coached in the field. Although, of course, the quality of the research conversations was a little bit lower initially than if it had been executed by more experienced researchers – as will always be the case when involving inexperienced students – this gradually improved, and it should also be balanced against the larger quantity of research conversations and research output obtained in this way, which otherwise would have been impossible.

8.2. UNDERSTANDING CHILDREN'S RIGHTS VIOLATIONS IN DIFFERENT CULTURAL, SOCIAL AND POLITICAL CONTEXTS

If it is possible, in general, to understand children's rights violations if they are analyzed within a legal pluralist framework (as developed in this thesis), is this possible for children's rights violations in different cultural, social and political contexts?

The three case studies chosen were all situated in very different cultural, social and political contexts. While the first two focused on the same right

[1631] §7.3.1 – 7.3.3.3.

(education) in different contexts, the latter focused on a different right (nationality). The sample of three case studies is obviously very small and therefore this question can only be answered very tentatively. The theoretical and methodological framework should be tested in more and different cases and in relation to different children's rights articles to answer it completely.

Based on these first three cases, it is interesting to note that the theoretical and methodological framework worked well for obtaining and analyzing valuable data, to arrive at an understanding of the violation/protection of a specific child's right, in three very different cultural, social and political contexts. In all three cases, the power relations between the different legal orders (including an absence thereof in the case of the CAR) was an important factor in understanding the child's right's protection/violation, as described above. Also, it is important to note that in each of the case studies, the understanding of these protections/violations was coupled with a more general understanding of the role of law in these respective societies, based on the research data.

One thing that worked less well in the different contexts was to incorporate the perspective of younger children, since this was less useful in the last case study. I do not believe that this is due to the cultural, social or political context of the TRNC but rather it has to do with the right under research (nationality) being too abstract for young children to relate to.

Ideally, the theory and methodology presented in this thesis would be tested, and perhaps refined, more in different case studies, in different socio-legal cultures, as well as focusing on different rights of children, to be really able to answer whether it does indeed lead to acquiring a valuable understanding of children's rights/violations in those particular contexts. Yet, so far, the results are generally promising.

8.3. A "BETTER" UNDERSTANDING OF CHILDREN'S RIGHTS VIOLATIONS?

The last sub-question necessary to reflect upon before being able to answer the main question of the thesis, is whether the approach taken in this thesis does indeed lead to a *better* understanding of child's rights violations, compared to if the same case studies would have been analyzed

a. From non-legal pluralist framework
b. Without taking into account the child's perspective
c. Without taking into account the power relations corresponding to the different legal orders surrounding children

I propose that to understand "better" in this context can be in two senses: 1) a more accurate, precise, in-depth understanding of the factors related to the protection/violation of a certain children's right in a specific socio-legal context; 2) an understanding of the factors related to the protection/violation of a certain children's right in a specific socio-legal context that is useful for interventions on behalf of the child and the protection of her/his rights.

8.3.1. A MORE ACCURATE, PRECISE, IN-DEPTH UNDERSTANDING OF THE FACTORS RELATED TO THE PROTECTION/VIOLATION OF A CERTAIN CHILDREN'S RIGHT

Did the approach proposed in this thesis lead to a more accurate understanding of these factors? First of all, the scope of the research has been limited to the legal factors, so that it is likely that other relevant factors were left out (see more below). However, it also has to be noted that "legal factors" has been given a broad meaning in this study, including all the rules of all the different legal orders surrounding the child in relation to her/his right, so that it includes all rules made by a person with legal authority, considered by the relevant community as binding.

In relation to the first case study, the question whether the approach led to a more accurate understanding of the factors involved in the violation/protection of the child's right to education in the Netherlands for children out of school is relatively easy to answer, because we can compare it to other research on the same, or a similar, subject. Here we see that the current study in some respects (who to include in the category of "children out of school"[1632], what are the causes for the violation of the child's right to education in terms of the roles of different authorities involved[1633], what is the situation of children who are homeschooled in the Netherlands[1634], what is the role of the power relations between the different legal orders involved in relation to the protection/violation of the child's right to education[1635]) provides new information that had not been found in other studies before.[1636] While admittedly a large part of the analysis involves legal doctrinal research (mostly in the relationship between international, regional and state law)[1637], which seems important especially because of the role of law in Dutch society[1638], and perhaps in more classical legal research

1632 §5.2.1 & 5.2.2.

1633 §5.3.

1634 §5.2.1 & 5.2.5.

1635 §5.2.1, 5.2.2, 5.2.4, 5.2.5, 5.3.

1636 §5.2.3.

1637 §5.3.1, 5.3.2, 5.3.4.

1638 §5.2.6.

the child's perspective could also have been labelled "the *de facto* situation", I think this would have left out the very important issue of the struggle between the different legal orders creating rules for the child in relation to education. I found that it is especially in these situations of conflict between different legal orders (parents, school, state) that children end up without any education.[1639] Another very important factor is that new information was found in this study because the child's perspective was taken as central, whereas, in other research this was usually left out.[1640] This gave a different and, in my view, more accurate representation of several important factors involved in the protection/violation of the child's right to education, such as the role of parents. The role of the parents is often left out of the discussion on the child's right to education in the Netherlands, because when parents are interviewed they usually blame the school and the state; when the school is interviewed they usually blame the school management and the state; and when the state is interviewed they usually blame the schools.[1641] Therefore the adult discourse on this subject has been excluding both the autonomy of children and the strong authoritative role of the parent in these situations, thereby leaving a large gap in the understanding of the factors involved in the protection/violation of the right to education for children out of school. Lastly, I have to say that, in relation to the issue of Roma children and their right to education, I feel that I did not find sufficient data to come up with important, accurate, and in-depth new insights. However, I don't think that is because of the theoretical and methodological approach of the study but rather because of the insufficient number of participants from the Roma community in the study.[1642]

Concerning the second and third case study, CAR and TRNC, the question whether a more accurate understanding was arrived at is much more difficult to answer, because we cannot compare it to other scientific research on the respective topics. Therefore I can only answer this question by imagining what I would have found if I would have used a different approach, for example a more legal doctrinal approach or a more anthropological approach.

In the CAR case, a legal doctrinal approach would have been almost useless, since it would be very far removed from the lived reality of people in the CAR in whose lives formal, written law plays almost no role at all. In this sense, at least to understand the legal factors involved in the violation/protection of the child's right to education, the legal pluralist approach is essential, which in any case incorporates the legal doctrinal approach. Whether completely different approaches to the CAR case study would have had more accurate results, I find very difficult to answer at this point, due to a lack of other studies on the topic.

[1639] §5.4.

[1640] §5.2.3.

[1641] Based on my own interviews with adults in this case study, literature research and analysis of political interventions to date which are aimed at schools, municipalities and/or state laws.

[1642] As discussed under §8.2.1.

The third case study in the TRNC cannot be compared to any other existing research on the topic. As argued under §8.2.3, a legal doctrinal approach would not have presented a framework in which it would have been (easily) possible to analyze the power relations between the different "state" legal orders of the RoC, TR and TRNC, which are all three relevant for understanding the factors that protect/violate the child's right to nationality in the TRNC. In addition, without considering smaller legal orders (schools, households), the consequences of nationality and the related discrimination would most likely have gone unnoticed, while a legal doctrinal study of the formal written law – which may have been left out of a more sociological study – was necessary to understand the position of the different state legal orders and the meaning of the right to nationality under international law. In general, I feel that we acquired a good understanding of the situation, based on the reactions of locals to our research findings. However I have to say that, perhaps, one problem with the approach in this case was that we were looking for patterns of laws to determine what unwritten laws would be, while most people held different beliefs about what the law was, resulting from different experiences with legal authorities.[1643] It also seemed that authorities applied different rules at different times, but it was very difficult to find any patterns in this behavior.[1644] In those instances, through the current approach, one could not conclude more than that different rules are applied by different people working for the same authorities, to different people with the same circumstances or applied even differently to the same people at different times. What was missing for a more in-depth understanding here was to find why exactly different rules were applied to different people, or to the same people at different times. In the case of people applying for RoC nationality, we found a hidden law that offered some explanation[1645], but in the TRNC we did not find any such hidden law. While I am convinced that there must be some reason based on which the employees, of for example the TRNC Ministry of the Interior decide whether or not to accept a certain application, through our current approach we unfortunately could not find these underlying reasons, although I am not sure whether another approach would have found an answer.

Lastly, in general, what is lacking in the theory and methodology as developed in this thesis, is that non-legal social norms are excluded from the analysis. Therefore, even if we have a better understanding of the legal factors related to the protection/violation of the child's right, do we really have a better understanding of all relevant factors related to this protection/violation? On the one hand, the approach in this thesis gives a clearly delineated overview of all the law involved in the protection/violation of a child's right, and it has been

1643 See §7.2.5, 7.3.

1644 §7.3.3.1 – 7.3.3.3.

1645 §7.3.3.2 (C).

important to limit the scope of the research, not only to make it doable within the timeframe of a PhD project, but, more importantly, because it was the first time for this type of approach to be applied to the study of children's rights and thus it had to be spelled out, applied and reflected upon carefully.

On the other hand, this means that non-legal social norms are left out of the picture, while these are sometimes very important to the lived realities of children, and they can be very important reasons why a child's right is being protected/violated. These can be, for example, family tradition, cultural reasons, moral reasons. For example, a child may want to attend school but also feel morally obliged to work and thereby contribute to the family income. This may not be a legal requirement, but it is an important factor in the consideration of the child nonetheless. Similar non-legal factors that were revealed in these case studies were, for example, the discussion about whether "social development", including "belonging" is part of the education curriculum in the Netherlands and whether, for children who are out of school, this could be a reason to send them to school – as many of these children and parents indicated feeling some social pressure for children to go to school. In the CAR case, both the discussion of the use of the *chicotte* (whip) and the sexual relations between students and teachers were subjects of moral discussion in society. Some felt that the whipping was in the best interest of the child to help them to study, and some felt that young girls would seduce their teachers to get a better grade rather than it being a case of being abused by their teachers. In the TRNC case, reasons for certain nationality laws were related to social pressure, either external (from Turkey or the peace negotiations) or internal (from internal pressure groups). The treatment of children of migrant workers and children of international students, for example, was often the result of strong anti-foreigner sentiments among the Turkish Cypriot population, whereby a large part of this treatment was not necessarily based on law.

All these non-legal social norms that are influential in the protection/violation of the children's rights under research, had to be largely left out of the PhD thesis. Although I usually mentioned them, I did not have the theoretical and methodological framework to really research them. These non-legal social norms are, in my opinion, an important part of the story, and it is necessary to understand them in addition to the legal norms involved, to create a more complete picture on the basis of which interventions on behalf of children can be developed. I intend to develop the current framework and methodology further in my future research so that these non-legal social norms can be incorporated.

8.3.2. AN UNDERSTANDING OF THE FACTORS RELATED TO THE PROTECTION/VIOLATION OF A CERTAIN CHILD'S RIGHT THAT IS USEFUL FOR INTERVENTIONS ON BEHALF OF THE CHILD AND THE PROTECTION OF HER/HIS RIGHTS

In general, I believe that the approach to children's rights research as presented in this thesis leads to an understanding of these factors that is useful for intervention aimed at the protection of the child's right. This is for several reasons. First, the legal pluralist approach addresses all different law and legal orders that are related to the current situation that the child is in, so that there is a clear overview of current laws that each intervention would have to take into account. Second, because children themselves are heard in this approach, this gives a much more realistic view of the actual situation that children find themselves in, including more reliable information for intervention. As indicated under §8.2.1–8.2.3, this is mostly true for the research on the child's right to education and somewhat less true for the research on an abstract right such as the right to nationality. Third, because the current approach discusses the power relations between the different legal orders involved, this gives valuable information for a potential intervention, such as where to focus on. An intervention can usually not address all actors and all factors involved at the same time, and therefore to know where the center of legal power[1646] lies is very important. Fourth, because all kinds of actors of all different legal orders are involved in the research, they are already made aware of the subject, involved in thinking about it, and are much more likely to acquire knowledge of the research findings, which in itself could be considered a kind of intervention (see also chapter 9). Fifth, the current approach brings together formal written law and law as it is understood, followed and/or applied by the relevant community, including a discussion of the role of law in each of the communities. This is crucial information for any potential intervention. In a situation where state law has no significance, it hardly makes sense to intervene by amending state law, while in societies where state law does have a strong position this could be a useful intervention.

In the Dutch case study, the current approach led to many useful insights for possible interventions. So far, political interventions that attempt to protect children that are out of school have been mostly aimed at schools, such as the introduction of the 2014 Appropriate Education Act which was supposed to end children being out of school[1647], which by now has been largely discredited and even called a "failure" in the press.[1648] At the time of the data collection for this

1646 See §3.3.4.

1647 Ministry of Education, Culture and Science (2018: 3).

1648 See, among others: Kneyber (2017), NOS (2018). In his most recent discussion on appropriate education the Minister of education writes that "appropriate education, in my view, certainly

case study (2015–2016), policymakers seemed to have been largely blind and deaf to the voices of children themselves and to the fact that the role of the parent is often crucial in the protection/violation of the child's right to education. In this respect, politicians were largely led by existing research and a strong political lobby by parents. The political debate had mostly been about protection of parental authority rather than the right of the child.[1649] Based on the current research, which provides a different perspective than most of the existing research, it can be easily predicted that interventions on the state level aimed at schools, without taking the voice and potential autonomy of the child, as well as the role of the parents in violating the child's right to education and a potential limitation of the legal authority of the household legal order into consideration, is not going to solve the issue of children out of school. Nor is it going to make sure that all children in the Netherlands, whether they are in or out of school, receive the education that they have a right to. From a parental perspective, this research has shown that the best way to protect a child's right to education is to cooperate with other legal orders rather than to create conflict. From the municipality perspective, this research has shown that to have an idea of the situation of the child as regards her/his education, whether in or out of school, it is crucial to also hear the voice of the child her/himself and that this is possible with children even of very young ages.

In the CAR case study, the legal pluralist approach to this case study resulted in several important insights for intervention. First, the insight that mostly children themselves are autonomous concerning their education[1650], means that interventions aimed at protecting the child in terms of education are potentially more effective when they are aimed at children directly rather than at their parents, the latter which is currently a common practice. Second, the insight that the classroom seems to be the only social order experienced as a legal order by children[1651] stresses its potential and importance for the civic education of children. It is possible to imagine that less violent education, which simultaneously creates a positive, cooperative classroom order, could prepare future generations for a more peaceful, cooperative and (legally) organized way of living together. Based on the research results, creating such classrooms would merit significant investments. Third, findings relating to the power balance between the state and the NGOs, as well as between the state and

has not failed […] at the same time, I do see that improvements are necessary" (Ministry of Education, Culture and Science (2018: 1)). He continues: "In appropriate education the child should be central, not the system […] first off, I want to give much more ownership to teams of teachers, school leaders and parents" (ibid: 1, 11-12). He mentions the role of parents when indicating that, in some cases, parents expect too much of a school. The balance between demands of parents and the possibilities of the school to meet these demands "require a conversation" (ibid: 6). The child her/himself is not mentioned at all in the 18-page letter.

1649 See §5.2.2 and chapter 9. It seems that this has now changed: see §6.5.

1650 §6.3.8.

1651 §6.3.6.

the international legal order[1652], raise questions as regards the responsibility of different actors involved and, in particular, the role of the international community in relation to the child's right to education in the CAR. Fourth, the insight that local orders (religious and local legal orders) are not so much legal orders but rather present community leaders who have an advising role in the community[1653] means that perhaps these leaders can be empowered in different ways as regards the child's right to education. It may for example be useful to provide them with education or to provide them with the means to create education opportunities for their community. Payment of teachers could also be organized through these leaders, as they generally have a trusted position. On the other hand, it cannot be expected that these leaders use their authority to oblige children to go to school, as this is not their position.

In the TRNC case study, the research findings are very useful for intervention in general, because of a current complete lack of information on children's rights in Northern Cyprus. In general, there is almost no research on the TRNC and, in particular, none on children's rights in the TRNC. Therefore, anyone who wants to intervene to protect the rights of children living in the TRNC is operating in the dark.

Because there is no comparison, it is hard to tell whether the legal pluralist approach necessarily provides the best information for intervention on behalf of children compared to other approaches in this case. On the one hand, it seems that it has been a relevant approach, since it provided much needed accurate data on the legal factors protecting/violating the child's right to nationality and subsequent rights violations based on nationality/residency status.[1654] At the same time, the case of the child's right to nationality in the TRNC is significantly influenced by political will. While, in the first two case studies usually everyone agrees that all children have a right to education and the question is more how to achieve this goal, not everyone agrees that all children living in the TRNC have a right to nationality. The discussion revolves mostly around who has to be considered illegal, both from the external perspectives of international and regional law as well as the RoC, Turkish and TRNC perspectives. Another question is the issue of political responsibility, so that, while most seem to agree with the international standard of the child's right to nationality as a general norm, Turkey and the RoC do not take the responsibility for protecting this right, while the TRNC cannot protect this right as the TRNC nationality is not an internationally recognized nationality.

Therefore it seems that, especially in this case, information about the non-legal norms involved is crucial for interventions on behalf of the children in the TRNC. While the analysis of the legal factors can support external intervention,

---

1652 §6.3.1 & 6.3.2.

1653 §6.3.3 & 6.3.4.

1654 See §8.2.3.

for example by reporting rights violations under international law at the UN human rights level, it is unlikely that this will really influence the situation of children living in the TRNC. It is possible (but not very likely) that the RoC will have to amend its national law and practice to give RoC nationality to all children of one RoC parent, including mixed marriages, but this will not help the children living in the TRNC who do not have a RoC parent. The underlying issue, of which the issues around the right to nationality seem to be a sign rather than a cause, is the culture of discrimination in Cyprus, both on the north and the south side.[1655] That is the most important issue that an intervention should address. As long as a general will to exclude particular children exists on all political levels (from international to within TRNC), and there is no, or insufficient, will to protect the rights of certain groups of children living in the TRNC, they will not receive protection of their rights through any intervention based on legal considerations. While the current research provided important information for anyone interested in the rights of children living in the TRNC, research into the culture of discrimination in Cyprus, its causes, prevalence, and how this potentially can be changed, needs a different theoretical and methodological framework than a legal pluralist framework.

[1655] §7.2.5.

CHAPTER 9
RESEARCH IMPACT

(HOW) CAN THIS UNDERSTANDING BE USED TO IMPROVE THE CONCRETE SITUATION OF CHILDREN?

Figure 24. Quote from a research participant in the TRNC (picture taken from field research notebook).

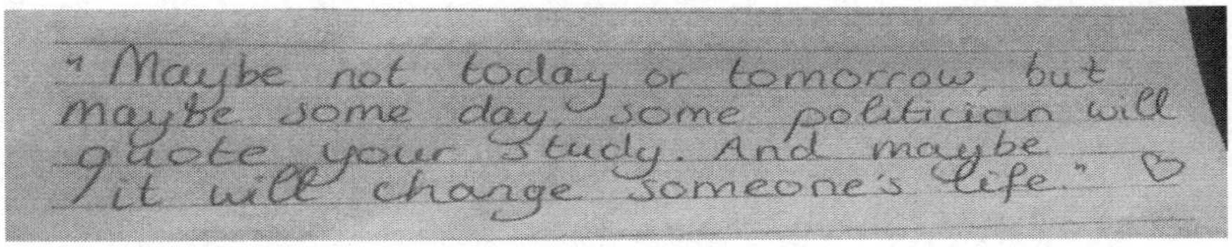

9.1. INTRODUCTION

In this chapter I will answer the second part of the main question of this thesis: If violations of children's rights in different cultural, social and political contexts can be better understood if analyzed within a legal pluralist framework, taking into account the child's perspective and the power relations corresponding to the different legal orders surrounding children, (how) can this understanding be used to improve the concrete situation of children?

Within the range of different reasons to do research, from purely theoretical curiosity to wanting to solve an issue directly, this study fits in the category of "use-inspired basic research", namely research that has as its purpose both a quest for fundamental understanding, as well as a consideration for use.[1656] While the question whether the study has indeed provided fundamental understanding was answered in the previous chapter, in this chapter I want to answer the question whether the study has indeed provided understanding and insight that is useful for improving the concrete situation for children. In the context of this study, there are two elements to this question: on the one hand, does the study indeed provide this type of information, in terms of its content?

1656 Stokes (1997: 73).

On the other hand, if it does, does it contribute to improving the situation for children, rather than only on a theoretical level (and if so, how?).

9.2. USEFUL INFORMATION

As regards this first question, I think that this can be answered relatively easily. In general, it seems to me that any study that provides a good understanding of a social issue, and in particular any study that provides a better understanding of the issue than already exists in the literature, provides information that is useful for improving the concrete situation being researched. The only condition probably depends on the choice of the research subject and whether this choice is motivated towards a morally justifiable end.[1657] What constitutes a morally justifiable end is of course debatable, however, this study seems to adhere to the stricter, as well as the broader, criteria set by different authors. For example, Dyson argues that "science works for evil when its effect is to provide tools for the rich, and works for good when its effect is to provide necessities for the poor".[1658] Care argues that research should be aimed at the protection of basic human needs, diminishing the extreme disparity standards of living between people and remedying the inadequacy of humanitarian aid. The researcher has to put the responsibility for others above one's self-realization.[1659] In Kovac's more moderate view, to put the responsibility for the basic needs of others above one's self-realization should be a moral ideal in science rather than a moral rule, since Care's position that, for competent individuals (i.e. researchers), heavy sacrifice is morally required, is unrealistic for scientists.[1660]

For all of these three different ideas about morally justifiable ends of research, the protection of the basic rights of children fits well into any definition. Therefore, as long as the current study does indeed provide (sufficiently) accurate understanding in relation to its subject, and this is ideally also an understanding that can be of use for intervention on behalf of the protection of the child's right – which I believe it does, as has been argued under §8.4 – the answer to the first question is a positive one.

9.3 SOCIAL IMPACT

The second question, whether the study does indeed contribute to improving the lives of children and, if so how, is a much more difficult question that leads us to

1657 Kovac (2007: 164).

1658 Dyson (1993), as quoted in Kovac (2007: 164).

1659 Care (1987), as discussed in Kovac (2007: 164-65).

1660 Kovac (2007: 168).

the debates on the social impact of research. To be able to answer this question, below I will first discuss the activities undertaken during the research process to try to have a social impact. In the following subsection, I will discuss whether or not these measures were effective, including a reflection on the role of research in relation to social impact.

9.3.1. SOCIAL IMPACT ACTIVITIES

To start, I will first present an overview of all the research activities and output that were part of this PhD research. All activities took place between April 2015 and January 2019. The first three months represented the first crowdfunding period[1661], which I conducted in addition to other employment. The PhD started on July 1, 2015 and ended in January 2019. Activities that were not related to the PhD (such as, for example, my position and work as a PhD representative) are left out of the overview, as well as fundraising activities (through teaching, project management, consultation, etc.) insofar as they were not directly related to children's rights.

To present the concrete social impact activities, I chose to use the scheme developed for this purpose by the Dutch science organizations (see next page).[1662]

In general, the research process consisted of several elements which were relevant to its social impact:

1. choice of research topic[1663]
2. crowdfunding campaign, which involved the bystander community from the start
3. research approach: participative methodology of all stakeholders involved
4. communication throughout the research process (mostly case study 2 and 3)
5. involving local/target community in communication and research
6. actively sharing research results with relevant communities

In terms of communities involved, there were three distinct groups:

1) academics who are working on similar or related topics
2) "bystanders": people in society who were interested in the research topic, yet who did not belong to the "core community"
3) "core community": the community that is the subject of the research

---

1661 The whole PhD research was financed through crowdfunding and other forms of fundraising. Funds were collected initially by the Tilburg University Alumni Fund, then, after I moved the project to Maastricht University, by the Universiteitsfonds Limburg / Children's rights Research Fund. See: Universiteitsfonds Limburg (n.d.) "Children's Rights Research Fund". Available at: https://www.ufl-swol.nl/en/fonds/childrens-rights-research-fund/.

1662 KNAW et al. (2016: 25).

1663 See §9.2.

		Quality Domains	
		Research Quality	Relevance to society
Assessment Dimensions	Demonstrable products	1. research products for peers 2 peer reviewed journal articles 1 peer reviewed book chapter 1 PhD thesis 14 academic presentations (invited speaker) 1 academic seminar organized Education: 5 students involved in last case study (MaRBLe project), 2 masterclasses on children's rights, 1 research project on refugee children's right to education in the Netherlands (PREMIUM), 2 project weeks on children's rights in two different high schools, 8 "study hours" on children's rights with NGO team	4. Research products for societal target groups 3 popular scientific reports (two of which in two different languages) 1 UN Human Rights Committee (UPR) report 1 Quiz 4 blogs on external websites 165 blogs on project website (www.childrensrightsresearch.com, total 19.115 views, 96 reactions) 13 vlogs 21 newsletters 13 research presentations for popular audience 4 practical discussions of CAR research results with groups of (CAR) teachers 1 theater play developed (about CAR case), performed around 20 times 37 media interviews (23 printed articles, 3 online articles, 11 radio interviews) 2 written expert testimonies in court 1 Expert testimony at UN Minorities Forum 388 updates on Facebook research page (477 followers) 3.199 tweets, 1952 followers (over 2 accounts)
	Demonstrable use of products	2. Use of research products by peers – The "Lipstick Law" article (2017) features in the top-10 of best read articles of the Journal of Legal Pluralism and Unofficial Law (#7, 1277 views)	5. Use of research products by societal groups – All popular scientific reports have been "sold out" too quickly for demand (250 NL, 156 CAR, 250 TRNC) – Total of € 27.943,16 received in private donations, of approximately 250–300 donors – 1 high school student's review of the CAR theater play – Parliamentary questions asked about NL case study – Recommendations by 6 countries to the Republic of Cyprus regarding respecting the right to nationality in a non-discriminatory manner at the Universal Periodic Review of the UN Human Rights Council

	Demonstrable marks of recognition	3. Marks of recognition from peers – A grant proposal for follow-up research has been awarded € 788.000, from NWO/WOTRO and organizations involved (2019) – Selected for KNAW Faces of Science (2018) – Winner UM Action Research Award (2017) – Awarded Edlab/MaRBLe grant for TRNC case study (2017) – Awarded SWOL research grant for TRNC case study (2017) – Education: very positive reviews by students	6. Marks or recognition by societal groups – 22 invitations from organizations to come and present research results (3 NGOs, 5 Ministry of Education (2 NL, 2 CAR, 1 TRNC), 2 municipalities, 3 institutions, 5 embassies, 4 Country representatives in Geneva), 11 country representatives and EU delegation informed individually about research results in between sessions in Geneva.[1664] – General: very positive replies from target communities, including several presents received out of gratitude (mostly in TRNC and CAR). Also some hate mail (mostly from Dutch parents and Greek Cypriots) – Nominated for VIVA 400, category "world improver" (2018) – Winner Tilburg University Science Slam (2016)

1664 All advocacy activities in Geneva were performed by student-researcher Ambra Borne.

9.3.2. IMPACT?

Of course, it is relatively easy to list the social impact activities and at least we can say that, during this research project, something happened and there has been some concrete output. However, the most important question is, does this output in the end lead to social change for children? Throughout the research, I have been struggling with this question, especially when faced with serious children's rights violations. Most of the time, it seems simply impossible to know how/if the research has any impact. After all, after sharing the research results with the relevant actors, it is up to them to use the findings for their own political purposes. However, I did learn some lessons which can potentially serve for the research to have (more) social impact, which I will share below. Second, I will try to answer the question whether this particular research project has had social impact.

Lessons learned

First, what worked really well in terms of awareness raising was to have a community of bystanders involved in the research project from the very beginning. In this case, what worked particularly well was to ask these people to make a donation. I noticed that quite a few of the initial donors, including people that I do not know personally, kept following the research project over the years. I suspect that this is related to the fact that they made a contribution and they liked to keep track of what happened with their money. Transparency, in terms of successes and failures, finances, activities, etc., I believe has been important in this respect (based on the very positive replies and high level of engagement that I encountered whenever I would share stories of struggles, successes and budget issues). Regular, open and honest communication with followers of the project (both the bystanders and the target community members) has been key in this respect.

Second, it also worked well to involve stakeholders from all different legal orders as participants in the research. By making stakeholders active participants, rather than passive recipients of research data, quite likely caused them to be interested in the research results and, also, through the methodology (Socratic dialogue and inquiry-based learning) were prompted to engage in critical thinking on the topic. A good example here is provided by an interview with a politician in the first case study:

> *Interview Nr. 26, a politician working on education in the Netherlands on the national level*
>
> Q: What is the meaning of the child's right to education in the Netherlands?
> A: [discusses the child's right to education in the Netherlands in the context of conflicts between parents and schools]
> Q: You're saying: it's the right of the parent?

A: For young children, that is.
Q: Is that different at a later stage, when children are older?
A: Well, see, as long as children are under the legal authority of their parents, the parent has to be able to act on behalf of the child. So, until age 18 [...]
Q: So, you are saying, it is the right of the parent, as legal authority over the children.
A: Yes...yes, you could say, it should actually be with the child. The child has the right to education. But, yes...education has to be given to the child, not to the parent [...]
Q: So, what is the right to education? Whose right is it then?
A: Well, I...This honestly is the first time that I am thinking about this [...] but I would say: it is the right of the child.

In this case, by being "forced" during the research conversation to reflect on the meaning of the child's right to education, the politician gained a new insight where s/he started looking more from the child's perspective. This insight was translated into action when, during the following parliamentary debate on home schooling, s/he started by arguing that "in my view, the right to education belongs to the child. The child has a right to education; it does not belong to the parent or whomever, but the child."

In general, in all three case studies, often research participants would be eager to hear more about the research results and, thereby, an important part of the relevant stakeholders at least took note of the research outcomes. In the third (TRNC) case study, research participants included journalists, which was very useful because not only did they know a lot about the subject and about the society, but involving them in the research also meant that they were (more) interested in the research results and likely to share the results in the media.

Third, it also worked well when I wrote and printed popular scientific research reports on the different case studies and went back to the target communities to share these reports and to discuss the results in media, during general presentations and in discussions with special interest groups. At the very least this created awareness, much more than if I would have published only academic output and/or would have only published the reports online.

Lastly, it was important to try to find means to reach the target community, in particular the more local parties such as the children and parents, through means of communication that would reach them. This seemed to be very different per cultural context – for example, since hardly anyone in the CAR had an internet connection, radio was the preferred mode of communication, while in TRNC the media was a good way to reach people. Although this may seem obvious, I have seen several examples of NGOs not taking this into account and thereby, for example, producing an awareness video for people who did not have access to internet/computers.

On the other hand, an aspect that did not work well was that there was quite a bit of backlash in the form of negative reactions (hatemail, phone calls, blog posts, etc.), especially in relation to the first case study. Although on the one hand, this means that the research did not go unnoticed, on the other hand I worried a lot about whether this might actually have a negative impact on the children involved. Especially the backlash coming from Dutch parents who want to keep their children out of school was worrisome. One parent, for example (not someone who had participated in the research), emailed on May 26th, 2016:

> I find that you are acting out of evil. As if the world is not broken enough by civilization and compulsory education, you deliver the final blow to what is left of freedom. Compulsory education is incompatible with freedom of choice, dictatorial and incompatible with family law. You are contributing to the destruction of the earth, mostly because education aims to destroy family ties, to infect children by others including abuse by caretakers, which often leaves its marks. Your attitude fits the VVD [political party] and youth care, corrupt gang of child traffickers and paedophiles.

This is not one exceptional email; I received several similar messages from different people. At that time, I never expected this type of reaction, and I worried greatly about the children of these parents and the possible negative effect the research may have had on their lives. On social media, too, the report was heavily discredited by some people, mostly based on false statements, such as "not one child who is homeschooled was interviewed", but also some more serious critiques of the methodology and the opinion that the researcher had been biased/prejudiced. On the other hand, there were also many positive replies to the report, from academics, professionals and children themselves.

Negative feedback reappeared again in relation to the third case study, yet this time I was prepared and had given more thought to how to prevent this from negatively impacting children in the TRNC. In this case, negative feedback came – as expected – mostly from Greek Cypriots. On some occasions, we would have meetings with RoC political actors who would become very angry with us and, after the publication of a blog with part of the research results, this also resulted in quite some negative comments on social media. However, in this case I did not worry that this would do harm to children living in the TRNC, or at least not more harm than if the research would not have been published, since the conflicts surrounding this issue take place on a more meta- (international and national) level, rather than in their direct, daily surroundings of children, such as the household or the school.

A third difficulty was to safeguard the sometimes vague line between researcher and activist, especially in the result-sharing phase. It has at times been very tempting to advise political decision makers beyond the direct research results, beyond what one could conclude as a researcher, on how to protect children's rights better. There are many things that a researcher cannot always write down, for example because there is not enough data to prove a certain statement which the researcher nevertheless believes to be true and important. In addition, many people have the tendency to ask a researcher: what should we do? What do you recommend? Of course, the researcher can give a scientific answer to this question, as Weber describes[1665], by taking a certain normative standard (i.e. the children's rights convention) and tell a decisionmaker: if you want to realize the child's right to education, then, based on the research data, it seems that political action A or B would be most effective at achieving this goal. However, it is sometimes difficult to keep it very clear in mind which arguments are 100% scientific and which arguments carry an element of personal, subjective experience or thought (if these can be separated at all). Throughout the research process, I have tried to keep Weber's guidelines in mind, although Weber wrote them at a time before social media and the active media engagement of researchers. In conclusion, I think I have succeeded in keeping the distinction between researcher and activist, although I expect it will always be difficult and new dilemmas will always arise. The important thing here, in my view, is to keep in mind to present only research data, and only data which is sufficiently certain (i.e. a sufficient number of people have confirmed a certain statement) to a wider audience. A researcher can present this research data in a passionate fashion and can add subjective perspectives in terms of how certain research outcomes personally affect her/him, yet the researcher should stick to presenting research data only. The absolute risk to be avoided, in my view, is to present personal opinions or suspicions as scientific fact.

Did this research project have a social impact?

As discussed at length in the literature on the social impact of research, it is difficult to measure the social impact of any research. One reason is because "the lag between research and impact may be decades"[1666], but also because we have not yet found a definitive answer on how to do this. Bohnmann, in his literature survey of academic publications on social impact, argues that "there is not yet an accepted framework with adequate data sets, criteria, and methods for the evaluation of societal impact".[1667] He lists four main problems with the measurement of social impact:

1. Causality problem: it is not clear what impact can be attributed to what cause
2. Attribution problem: it is not clear what portion of impact should be accredited to a certain research or to other inputs
3. Internationality problem: international research and development is virtually impossible to attribute

[1665] See §4.1.4.
[1666] Smith (2001: 528).
[1667] Bornmann (2013: 219).

4. Evaluation timescale problem: premature impact measurement may overemphasize short-term benefits[1668]

Taking into account the difficulty in measuring research impact, and the fact that the research is relatively new I will try to present some concrete impact that I think the research has had, subdivided per case study.

The child's right to education in the Netherlands

I think that the most important point taken from the Dutch case study by stakeholders involved, and in particular political actors, has been the importance of the child perspective / the child's right to participate in decisions about her/his life as regards education. As discussed in chapter 5, the research showed that when looking at the case of children out of school through children's eyes, this sheds quite a different light on the matter and could lead to a better understanding of the issue, as well as more effective interventions. The concrete impact of this can be seen, for example, in the "*thuiszitterspact*", an agreement between the Primary and Secondary education councils, the council of Dutch municipalities, and the Dutch ministries of education, health and justice, which was published and signed on June 13th, 2016 and in which I was involved as an advisor to the Ministry of education. The pact includes the ambition to make sure that in 2020 no child would be out of school longer than for 3 months, whereby the approach was to:

> give the child a central position: continuously, solutions have to be sought from the perspective of the child's right to an appropriate [education] offer. Parents, and where possible the child her/himself, have to be involved from the beginning in the realization of an appropriate offer.[1669]

Regional initiatives followed the national initiative in creating regional pacts, including the above-mentioned formulation, though not always.[1670] Lately, both the right for the child to be heard as well as a right to learn are regularly mentioned in the discussion on how the education law should be amended.[1671] It is of course not possible to tell whether this approach to put the child and her/his right in a central position is a direct consequence of this research, but, at least, it is likely that there was some influence in this sense.

1668 Ibid.: 219.

1669 PORaad et al. (2016: para. 3) "Thuiszitterspact", available at: https://www.rijksoverheid.nl/documenten/publicaties/2016/06/13/thuiszitterspact.

1670 E.g. Regionaal thuiszitterspact West-Brabant (2017); Regionaal thuiszitterspact Noord-Kennemerland (2017: 4); Thuiszittersaanpak regio Lekstroom (2017).

1671 See §5.5.

Another direct impact was the fact that a politician working on education on the national level (Ms. Ypma) submitted written questions to the government, based on the research report[1672], to which the state secretary of education answered in writing.[1673] However, in his replies, the state secretary (Mr. Dekker) argued that he would react to the report more in depth in his next report on children out of school, which unfortunately he did not do in the end. No one followed up and neither Mr. Dekker nor Ms. Ypma still work on education at the national political level today.

A more uncertain impact is related to the media interviews that I did, which were certainly read by many because they often invoked reactions on social media, and the presentations/discussions I held with professionals on the municipal level. For example, I was invited as a keynote speaker for a conference on children out of school for professionals working in the Amsterdam region. During the workshop, following the presentation, I could hear professionals thinking about and discussing the presentation/research, and therefore I do hope that there has been some positive impact. A blog on the possibility to change "compulsory education officers" into "right to education officers" also invoked many reactions.[1674]

In a more long-term sense, however, it is still difficult to tell what the impact of the research will be. Since 2017 there is a new Minister of Education (Arie Slob), who is from a Christian political party (*ChristenUnie*). His party is a known proponent of homeschooling. The government still registers children out of school from an adult perspective[1675] and state legislation on the subject has not changed. The ambition to no longer have children out of school longer than three months in 2020 has not been achieved. To the contrary, the number of children out of school in the Netherlands (counted according to the Dutch government definition of children out of school)[1676], is still increasing every year.[1677]

Lastly, until now it has not been successful to get attention for the subject of Roma children out of school. The media, which was very interested in "*thuiszitters*" and homeschooling, did not have an interest in this topic, regardless of how much I tried to convince them of the importance of the subject. On the national political level there was also little interest.

The child's right to education in the Central African Republic

Whether the research in the Central African Republic had any social impact is even more difficult to assess. Before this research, there was (almost) no research

1672 Tweede Kamer (2016a).
1673 Tweede Kamer (2016b).
1674 Hopman (2016c) "De leerrechtambtenaar: concrete uitwerking". Available at: http://kinderrechtenonderzoek.nl/de-leerrechtambtenaar-concrete-uitwerking/.
1675 See §5.2.2 & §5.5.
1676 See §5.2.2 for a discussion about the (in)adequacy of this statistic.
1677 Tweede Kamer (2020).

on the topic. From this fact, and the importance attached by people in the CAR to education for children, it can be assumed that the research would serve some purpose, assuming that a research on the topic would be executed in a valid manner.

Direct reactions to the research report, when I went back to distribute it, were extremely positive. People would start reading it, page by page, right upon receiving a copy. The fact that I went back to share the research results in itself was greatly appreciated by the people who had participated in the research and with whom I had a chance to share the research results personally. I unfortunately did not have nearly enough copies of the report to meet the demand (mostly because there are no printing possibilities in the CAR, meaning that I had to take copies of the report in suitcases on the airplane). I even tested the popularity of the report by giving one to a street vendor in Bangui, who promptly had sold it the next day. In the poorest country of the world, a report like this being sold so quickly seemed to me like clear proof of interest and positive appreciation. I also remember several CAR locals who visited my presentation(s) of the research results and complemented me in a surprised manner, arguing that they did not expect a white girl to understand their culture so well. I never received any negative feedback from the target community (except for one NGO that did not want me to publish about the physical abuse in classrooms). I also never paid anyone to attend the very well-attended research presentations, whereas I knew from NGOs and political organizations that they always paid people to attend and that otherwise no one would come.

One very direct impact the research had was that, during my second research stay, I met a young woman on a refugee site who spoke very good French. She had finished public primary and high school, yet she could not start her studies at the university because she lacked the financial means. I ended up employing her as a research assistant and, while I had many great research assistants over the years, she was definitely the best. When I left, I introduced her to an NGO which I knew was looking for local employees. Today, she still works at the NGO and is also finishing her third year of BA law studies at the university of Bangui. In addition, she informed me that after we had been talking about the study, she knows several families who as a result decided to send their children to school.

Another indirect impact is an INGO which was designing an intervention program for education in the CAR, and which read my research report and called me for input regarding their intervention program – which seemed like a great program. Unfortunately, I have not been able to trace the further developments/impact of this program.

One last potential positive outcome are the discussions I had with the minister of education, prof. Moukadas Noure. The minister is currently successful in ridding the high school exam process of corruption, and is also setting up education for children via the radio, as well as a new payment system for teachers.[1678] While these were all recommendations resulting from our study,

[1678] See §6.5.

it is of course difficult to tell whether this study was actually influential in this respect.

Concerning several other discussions, presentations and consultancies of organizations, politicians and groups of teachers, I can only hope that this had some positive impact.

The child's right to nationality in the TRNC

The impact of this case study is also very difficult to determine, especially because it has been finished only recently. While there has been some impact on the formal written level, it seems like there is not that much actual change for children living in the TRNC.[1679]

Part of the social impact activities for this case study included sharing the results at the international (UN) level, which resulted in 6 countries of the Human Rights Council Working Group recommending to the RoC to take measures to ensure non-discriminatory application of nationality law within a reasonable timeframe.[1680] However, the RoC in their replied that they do not want to grant nationality to children of mixed (TR/TC) marriages[1681], so this does not seem to lead to any actual change to the lives of children – at least in the short term.

At the local level, the research was met with a lot of interest and enthusiasm, including a lot of local media attention. Everyone we met and who heard about why we were in the TRNC wanted to help in some way. Since the TRNC is a very close and small society, we therefore very easily reached many politicians, journalists and other stakeholders. A presentation of the research results in the Home for Cooperation was also well attended. I was personally surprised at how positively the Turkish Cypriots reacted to our conclusion that, even though they feel and are discriminated against by Greek Cypriots, they themselves also discriminate against many groups of non-Turkish Cypriots in the TRNC. Instead of protesting this, they all agreed, arguing that they had never realized that but that it was true.

However, whether this actually will make a difference and whether they will start treating non-Turkish Cypriot children differently, both on an institutional and interpersonal level, is unclear and hard to tell. There was definitely some level of awareness raised which was not there before, in relation to children's rights, and in particular the rights of non-Turkish Cypriot children living in the TRNC. In the RoC, however, research results were met with less enthusiasm and interest, and it seemed that, generally, none of the relevant RoC actors that we spoke to (excluding some of the international actors from embassies) were willing to give/protect the rights of children living in the TRNC and certainly not to those who were not Turkish Cypriots.

1679 See §7.5.

1680 Ibid: paras. 139.96-139.101.

1681 See §7.5.

On the level of the international community, there seemed to be a lot of interest. However, here the question is whether this will actually have an impact, because it is a politically unpopular position to defend anything related to the TRNC, which will most likely invoke a negative reaction by both the RoC and Greece. The question will be whether states choose to stand up for the rights of children living in the TRNC, even though they live in an internationally unrecognized state.

9.4. CONCLUSION

Throughout the research it has been a struggle wondering whether or not the research actually had any positive social impact. To a large extent, we cannot know what impact the research will really have on the concrete lives of children, nor can we steer the political process more than by providing information.[1682] The task of the researcher is to provide the relevant data in relation to children's rights violations/protections, to make sure that they are accessible to relevant stakeholders as much as possible and at most to suggest possible interventions. When this process is completed, the researcher leaves and then it is up to all relevant stakeholders either to take action or to remain passive. This cannot be the responsibility of the researcher.

> Not everything that is faced can be changed, but nothing can be changed until it is faced.
> – James Baldwin

> Do not take lightly small good deeds,
> Believing they can hardly help;
> For drops of water one by one
> In time can fill a giant pot.
> – Dilgo Khyentse Rinpoche, from the "Sutra of the Wise and the Foolish"

> Marieke, [...] you know what to do. Just continue what you started. Be a witness, be a voice.
> – Former UN special representative, Prof. Dr. Jan Pronk, in reply to a blog post "Coming back from CAR again"

> Maybe not today or tomorrow, but maybe some day, some politician will quote your study. And maybe it will change someone's life.
> – Research participant in the TRNC

1682 I mean here "political actors" in a broad sense, including parents who decide over children, NGO employees, etc.

BIBLIOGRAPHY

ACADEMIC ARTICLES, BOOKS AND BOOK CHAPTERS

Admiraal, W., Westhoff, G. & de Bot, K. (2007) "Evaluation of bilingual secondary education in the Netherlands: Students' language proficiency in English", *Educational Research and Evaluation* 12(1): 75–93.

Adelson, J., Green, B. & O'Neill, R. (1969) "Growth of the idea of law in adolescence", *Developmental Psychology* 1(4): 327–332.

Akengin, H. (2008) "A Comparative Study on Children's Perceptions of the Child Rights in the Turkish Community of Turkey and Northern Cyprus", *Education* 129(2): 224–238.

Alderson, P. (2000) 'Children as Researchers: The Effects of Participation Rights on Research Methodology', in Christensen, P. & James, A. (eds.) *Research with Children: Perspectives and Practices.* London: Routledge.

Alderson, P. (2001) "Research by Children", *International Journal of Social Research Methodology* 4(2): 139–153.

Alderson, P. (2008) *Young Children's Rights: Exploring Beliefs.* London: Jessica Kingsley Publishers.

Allen, R. (2009) 'Ethical Dimensions of Youth Justice', in Holm, S., Kenway, I. & Gunning, J. (eds.), Ethics, Law and Society. Farnham: Ashgate.

Allott, A.N. (1977) "The People as Law-Makers: Custom, Practice and Public Opinion as Sources of Law in Africa and England", *Journal of African Law* 21: 1–23.

Allott, A.N. (1984) "What is to be Done with African Customary Law?: The Experience of Problems and Reforms in Anglophone Africa From 1950", *Journal of African Law* 28 (1–2): 56–71.

Anastasiou, H. (2008) *The Broken Olive Branch: Nationalism, Ethnic Conflict, and the Quest for Peace in Cyrus. Volume One: The Impasse of Ethnonationalism.* New York: Syracuse University Press.

Anderson, J. & Claassen, R. (2012) "Sailing Alone: Teenage Autonomy and Regimes of Childhood", *Law and Philosophy* 31: 495–522.

Archard, D. (1993) *Children: Rights and Childhood.* Didcot: Taylor & Francis.

Areeda, P.E. (1996) "The Socratic Method", *Harvard Law Review* 109(5): 911–22.

Ariès, P. (1962) *Centuries of childhood: a Social History of Family Life.* New York: Vintage Books.

Aristotle (350 B.C./1932) *Politics.* Cambridge: Harvard University Press.

Allen, G. (2008) 'Research ethics in a culture of risk', in Farrell, A. (ed.) *Ethical research with children.* London: Open University Press.

Barnes, B. (1988) *The Nature of Power.* Cambridge: Polity Press.

Baxter, J. & Eyles, J. (1997) "Evaluating qualitative research in social geography: establishing 'rigour' in interview analysis", *Transactions of the Institute of British Geographers* 22(4): 505–525.

Beazley, H., Bessell, S. Ennew, J. & Waterson, R. (2009) "The right to be properly researched: Research with children in a messy, real world", *Children's Geographies* 7(4): 365–378.

Bennion, F.A.R. (2001) *Understanding Common Law Legislation: Drafting an Interpretation.* Oxford: Oxford University Press.

Bentham, J. (1782/1970) *Of Laws in General.* London: Athlone Press.

Berkman, D.S., Lescano, A.G., Gilman, R.H., Lopez, S.L., and Black, M.M. (2002) "Effects of stunting, diarrhoeal disease, and parasitic infection during infancy on cognition in late childhood: a follow-up study", *Lancet* 359(9306): 564–571.

Bhopal, K. & Myers, M. (2008) *Insiders, outsiders and others: Gypsies and identity.* Hertfordshire: University of Hertfordshire Press.

Bierschenk, T. & de Sardan, O. (1997) "Local powers and a distant state in rural Central African Republic", *The Journal of modern African studies* 35(3): 441–468.

Biesta, G. (2012) *Goed onderwijs en de cultuur van het meten: ethiek, politiek en democratie ("Good education and the culture of measuring: ethics, politics and democracy").* Den Haag: Boom Lemma Uitgevers.

Bigo, D. (1988) *Pouvoir et Obéissance en Centrafrique ("Power and Obedience in the Central African Republic").* Paris: Karthala.

Bishop, S.L. (2008) *Legal Oppossitional Narrative: A Case Study in Cameroon.* Lanham: Lexington Books.

Block, S.D., Oran, H., Oran, D., Baumrind, N. & Goodman, G.S. (2010) "Abused and neglected children in court: Knowledge and attitudes", *Child Abuse & Neglect* 34(9): 659–670.

Boekholt, P.Th.F.M. & de Booy, E.P. (1987) *Geschiedenis van de school in Nederland: vanaf de middeleeuwen tot aan de huidige tijd ("History of the school in the Netherlands: from the Middle Ages to current times").* Assen/Maastricht: Van Gorcum.

Bogdal, K.M. (2014) "Hoe Europea zijn zigeuners uitvond: over een schaduwzijde van moderniteit" (*"How Europe invented its gypsies: about the shadowside of modernity"*), *Justitiële Verkenningen* 40(5): 9–22.

Boostrom, R. (1991) 'The nature and functions of classroom rules" *Curriculum Inquiry* 21(2): 193–216.

Bornmann, L. (2013) "What is societal impact of research and how can it be assessed? a literature survey", *Journal of the Association for Information Science and Technology* 64(2): 217–233.

Bozkurt, U. (2014) "Turkey: from the 'Motherland' to the 'IMF of Northern Cyprus'?", *The Cyprus Review* 26(1): 83–105.

Bratton, M. (1987) *The Politics of Government-NGO relations in Africa: Working Paper No. 456.* Nairobi: Institute for Development Studies, University of Nairobi.

Brocklehurst, H. (2009) 'Childhood in conflict: can the real child soldier please stand up?', in Holm, S., Kenway, I. & Gunning, J. (eds.), *Ethics, Law and Society.* Farnham: Ashgate.

Bruinsma, F (2003) *Dutch Law in Action.* Nijmegen: Ars Aequi Libri.

Bryan, L.A. & Keys, C.W. (2001) "Co-Constructing Inquiry-Based Science with Teachers: Essential Research for Lasting Reform", *Journal of Research in Science Teaching* 38(6): 631–645.

Bryant, R. & Papadakis, Y. (2012) "Introduction: Modalities of Time, History and Memory in Ethnonational Conflicts", in: Bryant, R. & Papadakis, Y. (eds.) *Cyprus and the Politics of Memory: History, Community and Conflict.* New York: I.B. Tauris & Co Ltd.

Buruma, Y. (2007) "Dutch Tolerance: On Drugs, Prostitution, and Euthanasia", *Crime and Justice* 35(1): 73–113.

Campbell, R. & Wasco, S.M. (2000) "Feminist approaches to social science: Epistemological and methodological tenets", *American journal of community psychology* 28(6): 773–791.

Cane, P. & Kritzer (eds.) (2010) *The Oxford Handbook of Empirical Legal Research.* Oxford: Oxford University Press.

Carayannis, T. & Lombard, L. (2015) 'Introduction', in Carayannis, T. & Lombard, L. (2015) (eds.) *Making Sense of the Central African Republic.* London: ZED Books.

Care, N. S. (1987) *On sharing fate.* Philadelphia: Temple University Press.

Carter, B. & Coyne, I. (2018) "Participatory Research: Does It Genuinely Extend the Sphere of Children's and Young People's Participation?", in: Coyne & Carter (eds.) *Being Participatory: Researching with Children and Young People.* New York: Springer International Publishing.

Cherney, I. & Perry, N.W. 'Children's Attitudes Towards their Rights: An International Perspective', in Verhellen, E. (ed) *Monitoring Chidren's Rights.* Leiden: Martinus Nijhoff Publishers.

Christensen, P. & James, A. (2008) 'Introduction: Researching Children and Childhood Cultures of Communication',

in Christensen, P. & James, A. (eds.) *Research with Children: Perspectives and Practices.* London: Routledge.

Clark, J. & Linder, C. (2006) *Changing Teaching, Changing Times: Lessons from a Sout African Township Science Classroom.* Leiden: Sense Publishers.

Clery, E. (1998) "Homeschooling: the meaning the homeschooled child assigns to the experience", *Issues in Educational Research* (8): 1–13.

Cotterrell, R. (2009) 'Ehrlich at the edge of Empire: Centres and peripheries in legal studies', in Hertogh, M. (ed.) *Living Law: Reconsidering Eugen Ehrlich.* Oxford: Hart Publishing.

Coyne, I. & Carter, B. (2018) "Participatory Research in the Past, Present and Future", in: Coyne & Carter (eds.) *Being Participatory: Researching with Children and Young People.* New York: Springer International Publishing.

Cremin, T., Glauert, E., Craft, A., Compton, A. & Stylianidou, F. (2015) "Creative Little Scientists: exploring pedagogical synergies between inquiry-based and creative approaches in Early Years science", *Education* 3(13): 404–419.

Danby, S & Farrell, A. (2005) 'Opening the research conversation', in Farrell, A. (ed.) *Ethical research with children.* London: Open University Press.

Darbyshire, P., MacDougall, C. & Schiller, W. (2005) "Multiple methods in qualitative research with children: more insight or just more?", *Qualitative research* 5(4): 417–436.

David T., Tonkin, J., Powell, S. & Anderson, C. (2005) 'Ethical aspects of power in research with children', in Farrell A (ed.) *Ethical research with children*. London: Open University Press.

Davies, B. (1984) "Children through their own eyes", Oxford Review of Education 10(3): 275–292.

Davies, M. (2010) 'Legal Pluralism', in Cane, P. & Kritzer, H. (eds) *The Oxford handbook of empirical legal research*. Oxford: Oxford University Press.

de Boer, A., Pijl, S.J. & Minnaert, A. (2010a) "Regular primary schoolteachers' attitudes towards inclusive education: a review of the literature", *International Journal on Inclusive Education* 15(3): 331–353.

de Boer, A., Pijl, S.J. & Minnaert, A. (2010b) "Attitudes of parents towards inclusive education: a review of the literature", *International Journal on Inclusive Education* 15(2): 165–181.

de Graaf, N.D., De Graaf, P.M. & Kraaykamp, G. (2000) "Parental Cultural Capital and Educational Attainment in the Netherlands: A Refinement of the Cultural Capital Perspective", *Sociology of Education* 73(2): 92–111.

de Groot, G.-R. & Vonk, O. W. (2015) *International Standards of Nationality Law: Texts, Cases and Materials*. Oisterwijk: Wolf Legal Publishers.

de Sousa Santos, B. (2002) *Toward a New Legal Common Sense: Law, Globalization, and Emancipation*. Cambridge: Cambridge University Press.

de Sousa Santos, B. (2006) "The Heterogeneous State and Legal Pluralism in Mozambique", *Law & Society Review* 40(1): 39–75.

Dewey, J. (1938/1997) *Experience and Education*. New York: Touchstone.

Diambomba, M. (1998) "Les déterminants du rendement scolaire des élèves de CP et de CM1 en République Centrafricaine" («*The indicators of school results of students in class CP and CM1 in the Central African Republic*»), *Cahiers québécois de démographie* 27(1): 13–42.

Dogan, N. (2013) "Ramifications of the ICJ Kosovo Advisory Opinion for the TRNC", *Ankara Bar Review* (1): 59–80.

Dorjee, T., Baig, N. & Ting-Toomey, S. (2013) "A social ecological perspective on understanding "honor killing": an intercultural moral dilemma", *Journal of Intercultural Communication Research* 42(1): 1–21.

Dyson, F. (1993) "Science in trouble", *The American Scholar* 62: 513–522.

Edmond, G. & Hamer, D. (2010) 'Evidence Law', in Cane, P. & Kritzer (eds.) *The Oxford Handbook of Empirical Legal Research*. Oxford: Oxford University Press.

Ehrlich, E. (1920/1986) *Gesetz und lebendes Recht: vermischte kleinere Schriften („Law and living law: missing smaller writings")*. Berlin: Duncker & Humblot.

Ehrlich E. (1936/1975) *Fundamental Principles of the Sociology of Law*. New York: Arno Press.

Ehrlich, E. & Isaacs, N. (1922) "The Sociology of Law", *Harvard Law Review* 22: 130–145.

Erikson, E.H. (1950/1987) *Childhood and Society*. London: Paladin Grafton Books.

Estes, R.J. & Winer, N.A. (2001) The Commercial Sexual Exploitation of Children in the U.S., Canada and Mexico. Philadelphia: University of Pennsylvania.

Farrell, A. (2008) 'Ethics and research with children', in Farrell, A. (ed.) *Ethical research with children*. London: Open University Press.

Favali, L. & Pateman, R. (2003) *Blood, Land, and Sex: legal and political pluralism in Eritrea*. Bloomington: Indiana University Press.

Fekkes, M., Pijpers, F.I.M., Frederiks, M., Vogels, T. & Verloove-Vanhorick, P. (2006) "Do Bullied Children Get Ill, or Do Ill Children Get Bullied? A Prospective Cohort Study on the Relationship Between Bullying and Health-Related Symptoms", *Pediatrics* 117(5): 1569–1574.

Fisher, C.B. (2010) "Adolescent and Parent Perspectives on Ethical Issues in Youth Drug Use and Suicide Survey Research", *Ethics & Behavior* 13(4): 303–332.

Flyvbjerg, B. (2006) "Five Misunderstandings About Case-Study Research", *Qualitative Inquiry* 12: 219–245.

Fortin, J. (2009) *Children's Rights and the Developing Law*. Cambridge: Cambridge University Press.

Foucault, M. (1961/2001) *Madness and Civilization*. London: Routledge.

Foucault, M. (1975/1995) *Discipline and Punish*. New York: Random House.

Fransman, L. (2011) *Fransman's British Nationality Law*. Haywards Heath: Bloomsbury Professional.

Fundudis, T. (2003) "Consent Issues in Medico-Legal Procedures: How Competent Are Children to Make Their Own Decisions?", *Child and Adolescent Mental Health* 8(1): 18–22.

Gaither, M. (2008) *Homeschool: An American History*. New York: Palgrave MacMillan.

Gardner, H. (1983) *Frames of mind: the theory of multiple intelligences*. New York: Basic Books.

Geurts, K. (2010) *'Met één achterste kan je niet op twee paarden zitten': Handboek leerlingbegeleiding twee ("'with one behind you cannot sit on two horses': Handbook student guidance two")*. Antwerpen: Uitgeverij Plantyn.

Glenn, H.P. (2010) *Legal Traditions of the World*. Oxford: Oxford University Press.

Graham, A., Powell, M.A. & Taylor, N. (2015) "Ethical research involving children: Putting evidence into practice", *Family Matters* 96: 23–28.

Griffiths, J. (1986) "What is legal pluralism?", *The journal of legal pluralism and unofficial law* 24: 1–55.

Griffiths, J. (2003) "The social working of legal rules", *Journal of Legal Pluralism and Unofficial Law* 48: 1–84.

Grisso, T. (1997) "The Competence of Adolescents as Trial Defenders", *Psychology, Public Policy, and Law* 3(1): 3–32.

Günçavdi, Ö. & Küçükç, S. (2009) "Economic Growth Under Embargoes in North Cyprus: An Input-Output Analysis", *Turkish Studies* 10(3): 365–392.

Hart, H.L.A. (1961/2012) *The Concept of Law*. Oxford: Oxford University Press.

Hart, R.A. (2008) 'Stepping Back from 'The Ladder': Reflections on a Model of Participatory Work with Children', in Reid, A., Jensen, B.B., Nikel, J. & Simovska, V. (eds.) *Participation and Learning: Perspectives on Education and the Environment, Health and Sustainability*. New York: Springer.

Hartog, J. & Oosterbeek, H. (1988) "Education, Allocation and Earnings in the Netherlands: Overschooling?", *Economics of Education Review* 7(2): 185–194.

Harvey, K. (2018) "Being Participatory", in: Coyne & Carter (eds.) *Being Participatory: Researching with Children and Young People.* New York: Springer International Publishing.

Hatay, M. & Papadakis, Y. (2012) "A Critical Comparison of Greek Cypriot and Turkish Cypriot Official Histiographies (1940s to the present)", in: Bryant, R. & Papadakis, Y. (eds.) *Cyprus and the Politics of Memory: History, Community and Conflict.* New York: I.B. Tauris & Co Ltd.

Haugaard, M. (2008) 'Power and Legitimacy', in Mazzotti, M. (ed), *Knowledge as Social Order: Rethinking the Sociology of Barry Barnes.* Farnham: Ashgate Publishing Limited.

Haugaard, M. (2010) "Power and Social Criticism: Reflections on Power, Domination and Legitimacy", *Critical Horizons* 11(1): 51–74.

Hegel, G.W.F. (1820/1991) *Elements of the Philosophy of Right.* Cambridge: Cambridge University Press.

Helwig, C. (1997) "The Role of Agent and Social Context in Judgments of Freedom of Speech and Religion", *Child Development* 68(3): 484–495.

Hendrick, H. (2008) 'The Child as a Social Actor in Historical Sources: Problems of Identification and Interpretation', in Christensen, P. & James, A. (eds.) *Research with Children: Perspectives and Practices.* London: Routledge.

Hertogh, M. (2009) 'From 'Men of Files' to 'Men of the Senses': A Brief Characterisation of Eugen Ehrlich's Sociology of Law', in Hertogh, M. (ed.) *Living law: Reconsidering Eugen Ehrlich.* Oxford: Hart Publishing.

Hewitt, J. (2007) "Ethical components of researcher – researched relationships in qualitative interviewing", *Qualitative health research* 17(8): 1149–1159.

Hobbes, T. (1651/1996). Leviathan. Cambridge: Cambridge University Press

Hopman, M.J. (2017a) "Lipstick law, or: the three forms of statutory law", *The Journal of Legal Pluralism and Unofficial Law* 49(1): 54–66.

Hopman, M.J. (2019) "A new model for the legal pluralist study of children's rights, illustrated by a case study on the child's right to education in the Central African Republic", *The Journal of Legal Pluralism and Unofficial Law* 51(1): 72-97.

Ioannides, I. (2017) "Cyprus and EU enlargement to the Western Balkans: a balancing act", *Southeast European and Black Sea Studies* 17(4): 631–647.

Isachenko, D. (2012) *The Making of Informal States: Statebuilding in Northern Cyprus and Transdniestria.* New York: Palgrave MacMillan.

James, A. (2011) "To Be (Come) or Not to Be (Come): Understanding Children's Citizenship", *The Annals of the American Academy* 633: 167–179.

James, A. & Prout, A. (eds.) (1997/2005) *Constructing and Reconstructing Childhood: Contemporary Issues in the Sociological Study of Childhood.*

Jenks, C. (1996) *Childhood.* London: Routledge.

Johnston, M. & Lubomudrov, C. (1987) "Teachers' level of moral reasoning and their understanding of classroom rules and roles", *The Elementary School Journal* 88(1): 64–77.

Jorna, P. (2014) "Tussen eigenheid en aanpassing: over cultuur en integratie van Nederlanse Roma en Sinti" ("Between authenticity and assimilation: on culture and integration of Dutch Roma and Sinti"), *Justitiële Verkenningen* 5: 72–85.

Kalmijn, M. & Kraaykamp, G. (2003) "Dropout and Downward Mobility in the Educational Career: An Event-History Analysis of Ethnic Schooling Differences in the Netherlands", *Educational Research and Evaluation* 9(3): 265–287.

Kapitulik, B.P. (2011) *Resisting schools, reproducing families: gender and the politics of homeschooling.* Massachusetts: University of Massachusetts, Open Access Dissertations.

Kant, I. (1779/1996) 'Metaphysics of Morals', in Gregor, M.J. (ed.) *Practical Philosophy: the Cambridge Edition of the Works of Immanuel Kant.* Cambridge: Cambridge University Press.

Kant, I. (1781/1996) 'Critique of Practical Reason', in Gregor, M.J. (ed.) *Practical Philosophy: the Cambridge Edition of the Works of Immanuel Kant.* Cambridge: Cambridge University Press.

Kant, I. (1792/1996) 'On the Relation of Theory to Practice in the Right of a State', in Gregor, M.J. (ed.) *Practical Philosophy: the Cambridge Edition of the Works of Immanuel Kant.* Cambridge: Cambridge University Press.

Kant, I. (1795/1996) 'Toward Perpetual Peace', in Gregor, M.J. (ed.) *Practical Philosophy: the Cambridge Edition of the Works of Immanuel Kant.* Cambridge: Cambridge University Press.

Karnieli-Miller, O., Strier, R. & Pessach, L. (2009) "Power relations in qualitative research", *Qualitative health research* 19(2): 279–289.

Kelsen, H. (1934/2002) *Pure Theory of Law.* New Jersey: The Lawbook Exchange Ltd.

Kelsen, H. (1945/2007) *General Theory of Law & State.* New Jersey: Transaction Publishers.

Khoury-Kassabri, M. & Ben-Arieh, A. (2008) "Adolescents' Approach toward Children's Rights: Comparison among Christian, Jewish, and Muslim Children in Jerusalem", *Journal of Social Issues* 64(4): 881–901.

Kitzinger, J. (1997) 'Who are you kidding? Children, power, and the struggle against sexual abuse', in James, A. & Prout, A. (eds.) *Constructing and Reconstructing Childhood.* London: Falmer Press.

Kolstø, P. (2006) "The sustainability and Future of Unrecognized Quasi-States", in *Journal of Peache Research* 43(6): 723–740.

Koster, M., Pijl, S.J., Nakken, H. & van Houten, E. (2010) "Social Participation of Students with Special Needs in Regular Primary Education in the Netherlands", *International Journal of Disability, Development and Education* 57(1): 59–75.

Kovac, J. (2007) "Moral Rules, Moral Ideals, and Use-Inspired Research", *Science and Engineering Ethics* 13(2): 159–169.

Kvale, S. (2006) "Dominance through interviews and dialogues", *Qualitative inquiry* 12(3): 480–500.

Kusters, W. (2014) *Filosofie van de Waanzin* ("Philosophy of Madness"). Rotterdam: Lemniscaat.

Kyris, G. (2012) "The European Union and the Cyprus problem: a story of unlimited impetus", *Eastern Journal of European Studies* 3(1): 87–99.

Lazar, S (2005) 'Citizens Despite the State: Everyday Corruption and Local Politics in El Alto, Bolivia', in Haller, D & Shore, C. (eds.) *Corruption: Anthropological Perspectives*. London: Pluto Press.

Leeman, Y. & Volman, M. (2001) "Inclusive education: recipe book or quest. On diversity in the classroom and educational research", *International Journal of Inclusive Education* 5(4): 367–379.

Leman, P. (2011) "African Oral Law and the Critique of Colonial Modernity in The Trial of Jomo Kenyatta", *Law & Literature* 23(1): 26–47.

Levine, R.A. & New, R.S. (2008) *Anthropology and Child Development: A Cross-Cultural Reader. New Jersey: Wiley-Blackwell.*

Liebel, M. (2008) 'Citizenship from below: Children's rights and social movements', in Invernizzi, A. & Williams, J. (eds) *Children and citizenship*. New York: SAGE Publications Ltd.

Liefaard, T., Doek, J. & Verkroost, D. (2016) "Vrijstelling van school en de rechten van het kind: Vrijstelling op grond van artikel 5 sub b Leerplichtwet bezien vanuit het kinderrechtenperspectief" ("*Exemption from schooling and the rights of the child: Exemption based on article 5 sub b Act on Compulsory Education, seen through a children's rights perspective*"), *Nederlands Juristenblad* (6): 380–386.

Limber, S.P., Kask, V., Heidmets, M., Hevener Kaufman, N. and Melton, G.B. (1999) "Estionian Children's Perception of Rights: Implications for Societies in Transition", *The International Journal of Children's Rights* 7(4): 365–383.

Lindahl, H. (2013) *Fault Lines of Globalization: Legal Order and the Politics of A-Legality*. Oxford: Oxford University Press.

Lipman, M. (2003) *Thinking in education*. Cambridge: Cambridge University Press.

Lipman, M., Sharp, A.M & Oscanyan, F.S. (1977) *Philosophy in the Classroom*. Philadelphia: Temple University Press.

Lister, R. (2008) 'Unpacking Children's Citizenship', in Invernizzi, A. & Williams, J. (eds) *Children and citizenship* ew York: SAGE Publications Ltd.

Lister, R., Smith, N., Middleton, S. & Cox, L. (2003) "Young people talk about citizenship: empirical perspectives on theoretical and political debates", *Citizenship studies* 7(2): 235–253.

Lockyer, A., Invernizzi, A. & Williams, J. (2008) 'Education for citizenship: Children as citizens and political literacy', in Invernizzi, A. & Williams, J. (eds) *Children and citizenship* ew York: SAGE Publications Ltd.

Loizos, P. (2012) 'Correcting the Record: Memory, Minority Insecurity and Admissible Evidence', in: Bryant, R. & Papadakis, Y. (eds.) *Cyprus and the Politics of Memory: History, Community and Conflict*. New York: I.B. Tauris & Co Ltd.

Lombard, L. (2016a) *State of Rebellion: Violence and Intervention in the Central African Republic*. London: Zed Books.

Lombard, L. & Batianga-Kinzi, S. (2014) "Violence, Popular Punishment, and War in the Central African Republic", *African Affairs* 114(454): 52–71.

Maclean, M. (2010) 'Families', in Cane, P. & Kritzer (eds.) *The Oxford Handbook of Empirical Legal Research*. Oxford: Oxford University Press.

MacNaughton, G. & Smith, K. (2005) 'Transforming research ethics: The choices and challenges of researching with chidlren', in Farrell, A. (ed.) *Ethical research with children*. London: Open University Press.

Marchal, R. (2015) 'Being Rich, Being Poor: Wealth and Fear in the Central African Republic', in Carayannis, T. & Lombard, L. (eds.) *Making Sense of the Central African Republic.* London: ZED Books.

Marcus, A., Riggs, R., Horning, A., Rivera, S., Curtis, R. & Thompson, E. (2011) "Is Child to Adult as Victim is to Criminal?", *Sexuality Research and Social Policy* 9: 153–66.

Marmor, A. (2006) "How law is like chess", *Legal Theory* 12: 347–371.

Mayall, B. (2001) "The sociology of childhood in relation to children's rights", *The International Journal of Children's Rights* 8: 243–259.

Mayall, B. (2008) 'Conversations with Children', in Christensen, P. & James, A. (eds.) *Research with Children: Perspectives and Practices.* London: Routledge.

Mayes, S., Roberts, M.C., Boles, R. E. & Brown, K.J. (2006) "Children's knowledge of household safety rules", *Children's Health Care* 35(3): 269–280.

Matthews, G.B. (1982/1995) *Filosofie van de kinderjaren* (original title: "Philosophy and the Young Child"). Rotterdam: Lemniscaat.

McDowell, L. (1994) "Social Justice, Organizational Culture and Workplace Democracy Cultual Imperialism in the City of London", *Urban Geography* 15(7): 661–680.

Mead, M. (1928) *Coming of age in Samoa: A Psychological Study of Primitive Youth for Western Civilisation.* New York: William Morrow & Company.

Mehmet, O. (2010) *Sustainability of Microstates: The Case of North Cyprus.* Salt Lake City: The University of Utah Press.

Meloni, F., Vanthuyne, K. & Rousseau, C. (2015) "Towards a relational ethics: Rethinking ethics, agency and dependency in research with children and youth", *Anthropological Theory* 15(1): 106–123.

Melton, G.B. (1980) "Children's Concepts of their Rights", *Journal of Clinical Child Psychology* 9(3): 186–190.

Melton, G.B. (1982) "Children's Rights: Where are the Children?", *American Journal of Ortopsychiatry* 52(3): 530–538.

Melton, G.B. & Limber, S.P. (1992) 'What Children's Rights Mean to Children', in Freeman, M. & Veerman, P. (eds.) *The Ideologies of Children's Rights.* Norwell: Kluwer Academic Publishers.

Mendez, M.A. & Adair, L.S. (1999) "Severity and Timing of Stunting in the First Two Years of Life Affect Performance on Cognitive Tests in Late Childhood", *The Journal of Nutrition* 129(8): 1555–1562.

Morrow, V. (2005) 'Ethical issues in collaborative research with children', in Farrell, A. (ed.) *Ethical research with children.* London: Open University Press.

Merry, M.S. & Karsten, S. (2010) "Restricted Liberty, Parental Choice and Homeschooling", *Journal of Philosophy of Education* 44(4): 497–513.

Merry, S.E. (1988) "Legal Pluralism", *Law & Society Review* 22: 869–896.

Michael, M.S. (2009) *Resolving the Cyprus Conflict: Negotiating History.* New York: Palgrave MacMillan.

Minner, D.D., Levy, A.L. & Century, J. (2010) "Inquiry-Based Instruction – What Is It and Does It Matter? Results from a Research Synthesis Years 1984 to 2002", *Journal of Research in Science Teaching* 47(4): 474–496.

Mokhele, P.R. (2006) "The teacher–learner relationship in the management of discipline in public high schools" *Africa education review* 3(1–2): 148–159.

Moore, S.F. (1973) "Law and social change: the semi-autonomous social field as an appropriate subject of study", *Law & Society Review* 7: 719–746.

Mullender, A., Hague, G., Imam, U.F., Kelly, L., Malos, E. & Regan, L. (2002) *Children's Perspectives on Domestic Violence.* Thousand Oaks: SAGE Publications.

Murseli, H. (2019) "L'éducation en situation de conflit en République centrafricaine: les Espaces Temporaires d'Apprentisage en question", *Cahiers de la recherche sur l'éducation et les savoirs* 18: 73–93.

Navaro-Yashin, Y. (2012) *The Make-Believe Space: Affective Geography in a Postwar Polity.*

Nelken, D. (1984) "Law in action or living law? Back to the beginning in sociology of law", *Legal studies* 4: 157–174.

Nejatigil, Z. M. (1990) 'The Legal System of the Turkish Republic of Northern Cyprus', in: Redden, K. R. (ed.) *Modern Legal Systems Cyclopedia.* Buffalo: William's Hein & Co.

Nolasco, C.A.R.I., Vaughn, M.S. & del Carmen, R. (2010) "Toward a New Methodology for Legal Research in Criminal Justice, *Journal of Criminal Justice Education* 21(1): 1–23.

Ngoumbango Kohetto, J. (2013) *L'accès au droit et à la justice des citoyens en République centrafricaine («Access to law and justices for the citizens of the Central African Republic»).* Université de Bourgogne: HAL.

Nuijten, M., & Anders, G. (2007) *Corruption and the Secret of Law: A Legal Anthropological Perspective.* Hampshire: Ashgate.

O'Kane, C. (2000) 'Facilitating children's views about decisions which affect them', in Christensen, P. & James, A. (eds.) *Research with Children: Perspectives and Practices.* London: Routledge.

O'Kane, C. (2008) 'The Development of Participatory Techniques: Facilitating Children's Views about Decisions Which Affect Them', in Christensen, P. & James, A. (eds.) *Research with Children: Perspectives and Practices.* London: Routledge.

Oomen, B. (2002) *Chiefs in South Africa: law, power and culture in the post-apartheid era.* Leiden: Leiden University Press.

Oomen, B. (2015) "Law is Again", *Recht der Werkelijkheid* 36: 104–109.

Opertti, R., Brady, J. & Duncombe, L. (2009) "Moving forward: Inclusive education as the core of Education for All", *Prospects* 39: 205–214.

Oxman, B.H. (2007) 'Jurisdiction of States', *Max Planck Encyclopedia of Public International Law.*

Palmer, S. (1986) "The Turkish Republic of Northern Cyprus: Should the United States Recognise it as an Independent State", *Boston University International Law Journal* 4: 423–450.

Parra,J. (2011) "Stateless Roma in the European Union: Reconciling the doctrine of sovereignty concerning nationality laws with international agreements to reduce and avoid statelessness", *Fordham International Law Journal* 34: 1666–1694.

Peterson-Badali, M., Abramovtich, R. & Duda, J. (1997) "Young children's legal knowledge and reasoning ability', *Canadian Journal of Criminology* 39(2): 145–170.

Petrovic, J.E. & Rolstad, K. (2017) "Educating for autonomy: Reading Rousseau and Freire toward a philosophy of unschooling", *Policy Futures in Education* 15(7–8): 817–833.

Piaget, J. (1926/1959) *The Language and Thought of the Child*. London: Routledge.

Piaget, J. (1932/1960) *The Moral Judgment of the Child*. Glencoe: The Free Press.

Pijl, S.J. (2010) "Preparing teachers for inclusive education: some reflections from the Netherlands", *Journal of Research in Special Education Needs* 10(1): 197–201.

Plato (381 B.C./2012) *The Republic*. West Sussex: Capstone Publishing Ltd.

Plato (385–370 B.C./1961a) 'Laches', in Hamilton, E. and Cairns, H. (eds.) *The Collected Dialogues of Plato (The Collected Dialogues of Plato*. Princeton: Princeton University Press.

Plato (385–370 B.C./1961b) 'Laws', in Hamilton, E. and Cairns, H. (eds.) *The Collected Dialogues of Plato (The Collected Dialogues of Plato*. Princeton: Princeton University Press.

Plato (385–370 B.C./1961c) 'Symposium', in Hamilton, E. and Cairns, H. (eds.) *The Collected Dialogues of Plato (The Collected Dialogues of Plato*. Princeton: Princeton University Press.

Popper, K.R. (1962) *Conjectures and Refutations: The Growth of Scientific Knowledge*. New York: Basic Books.

Posner, E.A. (2000) *Law and Social Norms*. Cambridge: Harvard University Press.

Pospisil, L. (1967) "Legal Levels and Multiplicity of Legal Systems in Human Societies" *The Journal of Confict Resolution* 9(1): 2–26.

Pospisil, L. (1974) *Anthropology of law: a comparitive theory*. New Haven: HRAF Press.

Powell, M.A. & Smith, A.B. (2009) "Children's participation rights in research", *Childhood* 16(1): 124–142.

Powell, M.A., Graham, A., McArthur, M., Moore, T., Chalmers, J. & Taplin, S. (2020) "Children's participation in research on sensitive topics: addressing concerns of decision-makers", *Children's Geographies* 18(3): 325–338.

Quas, J.A., Cooper, A. & Wandrey, L. (2009a) 'Child Victims in Dependency Court', in Bottoms, B.L., Najdowski, C.J. & Goodman, G.S. (eds.) *Children as Victims, Witnessess, and Offenders: Psychological Science and the Law*. New York: The Guilford Press.

Quas, J.A., Wallin, A.R., Horwitz, B., Davis, E. & Lyon, T.D. (2009b) "Maltreated Children's Understanding of and Emotional Reactions to Dependency Court Involvement", *Behavioral Sciences and the Law* 27: 97–117.

Raz, J. (1979/2009) *The Authority of Law*. Oxford: Oxford University Press.

Redding, R.E. (1993) "Children's Competence to Provide Informed Consent for Mental Health Treatment", *Washington and Lee Law Review* 50: 695–751.

Reisman, W.M. (1984) "Editorial Comments: Coercion and Self-Determination: Construing Article 2(4)", *American Journal of International Law* 78(3): 642–645.

Richards, H. & Emslie, C. (2000) "The 'doctor' or the 'girl from the University'? Considering the influence of professional roles on qualitative interviewing", *Family Practice* 17(1): 71–75.

Roberts, H. (2008) 'Listening to Children: and Hearing Them', in Christensen, P. & James, A. (eds.) *Research with Children: Perspectives and Practices.* London: Routledge.

Rohaan, E.J., Taconis, R. & Jochems, W.M.G. (2010) "Reviewing the relations between teachers' knowledge and pupils' attitude in the field of primary technology education", *International Journal of Technology and Design Education* 20: 15–26.

Rousseau, J.J. (1754/2002) 'The Second Discourse: Discourse on the Origin and Foundations of Inequality Among Mankind', in Dunn, S. (ed.) *The Social Contract and The First and Second Discourses.* New Haven: Yale University Press.

Rousseau, J.J. (1755/1994) *Discourse on Political Economy and The Social Contract.* Oxford: Oxford Univesrity Press.

Rousseau, J. J. (1762/1977) *Du contrat social.* Paris: Éditions du Seuil.

Rousseau, J.J. (1762/1979) *Emile: or On Education.* New York: Basic Books.

Ruijs, N.M., Van der Veen, I. & Peetsma, T.D.T. (2010) "Inclusive education and students without special educational need", *Educational Research* 52(4): 351–390.

Rutter, M., & Rutter, M. (1993). Developing minds: Challenge and continuity across the life span. New York: Basic Books.

Schapiro, T. (1999) "What Is a Child?", *Ethics* 109(4): 715–738.

Sacco, R. (1995) "Mute Law", T*he American Journal of Comparative Law* 48: 455–467.

Saywitz, K.J. (1989) 'Children's conceptions of the legal system:"Court is a place to play basketball"', in Ceci, S.J., Ross, D.J. & Toglia, M.P. (eds.) *Perspectives on children's testimony.* New York: Springer.

Saywitz, K., Jaenicke, C. & Camparo, L. (1990) "Children's knowledge of legal terminology", *Law and Human Behavior* 14(6): 523–535.

Schneider, J., & P. Schneider (2005) 'The Sack of Two Cities: Organized Crime and Political Corruption in Youngstown and Palermo', in Haller, D & Shore, C. (eds.) *Corruption: Anthropological Perspectives.* London: Pluto Press.

Schuman, H. (2007) "Passend onderwijs – pas op de plaats of stap vooruit?" (*"Appropriate education – taking a pause or a step forward?"*), *Tijdschrift voor orthopedagogiek* 46: 267–280.

Scott E.S. & Grisso, T. (1997) "The Evolution of Adolescence: A Developmental Perspective on Juvenile Justice Reform", *The Journal of Criminal Law and Criminology* 88(1): 137–189.

Scott, J. (2008) 'Children as respondents: the Challenge for Quantitative Methods, in Christensen, P. & James, A. (eds.) *Research with Children: Perspectives and Practices.* London: Routledge.

Searle J.R. (2011) *Making the Social World.* Oxford: Oxford University Press.

Searle, J.R. (1995) *The Construction of Social Reality.* New York: The Free Press.

Shaelou, S.L. (2010) *The EU and Cyprus: principles and strategies of full integration.* Leiden: Martinus Nijhoff Publishers.

Shaw, M.N. (1997) *International Law.* Cambridge: Cambridge University Press.

Shore, C. (2005) 'Culture and Corruption in the EU: Reflections on Fraud, Nepotism and Cronyism in the European Commission' in Haller, D & Shore, C. (eds.) *Corruption: Anthropological Perspectives.* London: Pluto Press.

Siems, M.M. & Sthigh, D.M. (2012) "Mapping Legal Research", *The Cambridge Law Journal* 71(3): 651–676.

Skolnick, A. (1975) "'The Limits of Childhood: Conceptions of Child Development and Social Context", *Law and Contemporary Problems* 39 (3): 38–77.

Smetana, J.G. (1988) "Adolescents' and parents' conceptions of parental authority", *Child development* 59(2): 321–335.

Smetana, J.G. (1995) "Parenting styles and conceptions of parental authority during adolescence", *Child development* 66: 299–316.

Smetana, J.G. & Asquith, P. (1994) "Adolescents' and parents' conceptions of parental authority and personal autonomy", *Child development* 65(4): 1147–1162.

Smith, K. (2011) "Introducing Governable Subjects: images of Childhood Old and New", *Childhood* 19(1): 24–37.

Smith, R. (2001) "Measuring the social impact of research: Difficult but necessary", *British Medical Journal* 323(7312): 528.

Smith, S.W. (2015a) 'CAR's History: The Past of a Tense Present', in Carayannis, T. & Lombard, L. (eds.) *Making Sense of the Central African Republic.* London: ZED Books.

Smith, S.W. (2015b.) 'The Elite's Road to Riches in a Poor Country', in Carayannis, T. & Lombard, L. (eds.) *Making Sense of the Central African Republic.* London: ZED Books.

Smith, K. (2013) 'A Rights-based approach to observing and assessing children in the early childhood classroom', in Swadener, B.B., Blanchet-Cohen, N., Lundy, L. & Habashi, J. (eds.) *Children's Rights in Education: International Perspectives.* Bern: Peter Lang.

Sollie, H., Wijkhuis, V., Hilhorst, W., van der Wal, R & Kop, N. (2013) *Aanpak multi-problematiek bij gezinnen met een Roma-achtergrond ("approach multi problems with families with a Roma background").* Den Haag: Boom Lemma Uitgevers.

Solsten, E. (1993). *Cyprus: a Country Study.* Washington D.C.: U.S. Government Printing Services.

Sommer, D., Pramling Samuelsson, I. & Hundeide, K. (2010) *Child Perspectives and Children's Perspectives in Theory and Practice.* Basingstoke: Springer Nature.

Sözen, A. (2004) "A Model of Power-Sharing in Cyprus: From the 1959 Londen-Zürich Agreements to the Annan Plan" *Turkish Studies* 5(1): 61–77.

Spee-van der Wekke, J., Meulmeester, J.F., Radder, J.J. & Verloove-Vanhorick, S.P. (1998) "School absence and treatment in school children with respiratory symptoms in The Netherlands: data from the Child Health Monitoring System", *Epidemiology & Health* 52(6): 359–363.

Sperling, J. (2010) *'Moet jij niet naar school?' Een onderzoek naar de juridische aspecten van thuisonderwijs vanuit Nederlands en rechtsvergelijkend perspectief* (*'Dont you have to go to school?' A study on the legal aspects of home education from a Dutch and comparative law perspective).* Rotterdam: Erasmus Universiteit Rotterdam.

Spyrou, S. (2002) "Images of 'the Other': 'the Turk' in Greek Cypriot children's imagination", *Race Ethnicity and Education* 5(3): 255–272.

Stevens, P.A.J. (2016) *Ethnicity and Racism in Cyprus: National Pride and Prejudice?.* Hampshire: Palgrave Macmillan.

Stokes, D.E. (1997) *Pasteur's Quadrant: basic science and technological innovation.* Washington D.C.: Brookings Institution Press.

Storimans, Th. (2006) "Geschiedenis en achtergronden van de wettelijke leerplicht" (*"History and backgrounds of the legal duty to study"*), *Justitiële Verkenningen* 32(6): 9–21.

Straus, M.A. (2000). "Corporal Punishment and Primary Prevention of Physical Abuse", *Child Abuse & Neglect* 24(9): 1109–14.

Sunier, T. (2004) "Naar een nieuwe schoolstrijd?" (*"Towards a new school struggle?"*), *BMGN-Low Countries Historical Review* 119(4): 552–576.

Talmon, S. (2001) "The Cyprus Question before the European Court of Justice", *European Journal of International Law* 12: 727–750.

Tamanaha, B.Z. (1993) 'The folly of the 'social scientific'concept of legal pluralism", *Journal of Law and Society* 20:192–217.

Tamanaha, B.Z. (2008) "Understanding Legal Pluralism: Past to Present, Local to Global", *Sydney Law Review* 30: 375–411.

Tamanaha, B.Z. (2011) "A Vision of Social-Legal Change: Rescuing Ehrlich from "Living Law"" (2011) *Law & Social Inquiry* 36(1): 297–318.

Tangen, R. (2008) "Listening to children's voices in educational research: some theoretical and methodological problems", *European Journal of Special Needs Education* 23(2): 157–166.

Tapp, J.L. & Levine, F.J. (1974) "Legal socialization: Strategies for an Ethical Legality", *Stanford Law Review* 27(1): 1–72.

Terlouw, A. (2014) "De weg naar (het recht op) school voor Romakinderen" (*"the road to (the right to) school for Roma children"*), *Nijmegen Migration Law Working Paper Series 2014/05.*

Thapar-Björkert, S. & Henry, M. (2007) "Reassessing the research relationship: Location, position and power in fieldwork accounts", *International Journal of Social Research Methodology* 7(5): 363–81.

Thomas, G. (2013) "A review of thinking and research about inclusive education policy, with suggestions for a new kind of inclusive thinking", *British Educational Research Journal* 39(3): 473–490.

Thomas, N. & O'Kane, C. (1998) "The ethics of participatory research with children", *Children & society* 12 (5): 336–348.

Thornberg, R. (2008) "School children's reasoning about school rules", *Research Papers in Education* 23(1): 37–52.

Thornberg, R. (2009) "'The moral construction of the good pupil embedded in school rules", *Education, citizenship and social justice* 4(3): 245–261.

Torbeyns, J., van der Noortgate, W., Ghesquière, P., Verschaffel, L., van de Rijdt, B. & van Luit, J.E.H. (2002) "Development of Early Numeracy in 5- to 7-Year-Old Children: A Comparison Between Flanders and The Netherlands", *Educational Research and Evaluation* 8(3): 249–275.

Tisak, M.S. (1986) "Children's conceptions of parental authority", *Child Development* 57(1): 166–176.

Traag, T. & van der Velden, R.K.W. (2011) "Early school-leaving in the Netherlands: the role of family resources, school composition and background characteristics in early school-leaving in lower secondary education", *Irish Educational Studies* 30(1): 45–62.

Trubek, D.M. (1972) "Max Weber on Law and the Rise of Capitalism", *Faculty Scholarship Series*. Yale Law School: paper 4001.

Turley, J. (1986) "Introduction: The Hitchhiker's Guide to CLS, Unger and Deep Thought", *Northwestern University Law Review* 81: 593–620.

Twining, W. (2009) *General Jurisprudence: Understanding Law from a Global Perspective.* Cambridge: Cambridge University Press.

Unger, R.M. (1987) *Politics, a Work in Constructive Social Theory.* Cambridge: Cambridge University Press.

Urinboyev, R. & Svensson, M. (2013) "Living law, legal pluralism, and corruption in post-Soviet Uzbekistan", *The Journal of Legal Pluralism and Unofficial Law* 45(3): 372–390.

v.d. Borgh, C. & Terwindt, C. (2014) *NGOs under Pressure in Partial Democracies.* London: Palgrave Macmillan.

van Bijsterveldt, S. (2013) "Een vergeten episode uit de schoolstrijd: de ontdekking van 'openbaar' en 'bijzonder' onderwijs" (*"A forgotten episode of the school strife: the discovery of 'public' and 'independet' education"*), *Tijdschrift voor Religie, Recht en Beleid* 4(3): 16–32.

van Daalen, E. & Mabillard, N. (2018) "Human Rights in Translation: Bolivia's law 548, working children's movements, and the global child labour regime", *The International Journal of Human Rights*: 1–19.

van der Veen, I., Smeets, E. & Derriks, M. (2010) "Children with special educational needs in the Netherlands: number, characteristics and school career", *Educational Research* 52(1): 15–43.

van Gestel, R. (2008) *Wetgeven is Vooruitzien [Legislating is looking ahead].* Den Haag: Boom Juridische uitgevers.

van Klink, B. (2009) 'Facts and norms: The unfinished debate between Eugen Ehrlich and Hans Kelsen', in Hertogh, M. (ed.) *Living Law: Reconsidering Eugen Ehrlich.* Oxford: Hart Publishers.

van Waas, L. (2008) *Nationality Matters: Statelessness under International Law.* Mortsel: Intersentia.

VanderStaay, S.L., Faxon, B.A., Meischen, J.E., Kolesnikov, K.T. & Ruppel, A.D. (2009) "Close to the Heart: Teacher Authority in a Classroom Community", *CCC* 61(2): W262–82.

Vansieleghem, N. & Kennedy, D. (2011) "What is Philosophy *for* Children, What is Philosophy *with* Children – After Matthew Lipman?", *Journal of Philosophy of Education* 45(2).

Vasta, E. (2007) "From ethnic minorities to ethnic majority policy: Multiculturalism and the shift to assimilationism in the Netherlands", *Ethnic and Racial Studies* 30(5): 713–740.

Verplaetse, J. (2012) "Als men zich op school niet thuis voelt. Thuisonderwijs in Vlaanderen en Nederland ethisch getoetst" ("If one does not feel at home at school. An ethical test of homeschooling in Flanders and the Netherlands"), *Ethiek & Maatschappij* 11(3): 80–92.

von Benda-Beckmann, F. & von Benda-Beckmann, K. 'The social life of living law in Indonesia', in Hertogh, M. (ed.) *Living law: Reconsidering Eugen Ehrlich*. Oxford: Hart Publishing.

Walker, N.E., Brooks, C.M. & Wrightsman, L.S. Nancy (1999) *Children's Rights in the United States: In Search of a National Policy*. New York: Sage Publications, Inc.

Warmbrunn, W. (1968) *The Dutch Under German Occupation, 1940–1945*. Palo Alto: Stanford University Press.

Warnke, A.M. (1999) "Vagabonds, Tinkers, and Travellers: Statelessness among the East European Roma", *Indiana Journal of Global Legal Studies* 7(1): 335–367.

Warren, S. (2009) 'Let's do it Properly: Inviting Children to be Researchers', in Lewis A. & Lindsay, G. (eds), *Researching Children's Perspectives*. London: Open University Press.

Warren-Leubecker, A., Tate, C.S., Hinton, I.D. & Ozbek, I.N. (1989) 'What do Children Know about the Legal System and When Do They Know It? First Steps Down a Less Travelled Path in Child Witness Research', in Ceci, S.J., Ross, D.F. & Toglia, M.P. (eds.) *Perspectives on Children's Testimony*. New York: Springer.

Water, T. (2018) "Ethical Issues in Participatory Research with Children and Young People", in: Coyne & Carter (eds.) *Being Participatory: Researching with Children and Young People*. New York: Springer International Publishing.

Watts, M., Alsop, S., Gould, G. & Walsh, A. (1997) "Prompting Teacher's Constructive Reflection: Pupil's Questions as Critical Incidents", *International Journal of Science Education* 19(9): 1025–1037.

Weber, M. (1904/1949) *The Methodology of the Social Sciences*. Glencoe: The Free Press.

Weber, M. (1922/1978) *Economy and Society: An outline of interpretive sociology*. Berkeley: University of California Press.

Weber, B. (2011) 'Evidence of language contact in the Parliament Rolls of Medieval England: Nothwithstanding-constructions as a case of Nachbau', in Svenja Kranich (ed) *Multilingual Discourse Production: Diachronic and Synchronic Perspectives*. Amsterdam: John Benjamins Publishing Company.

Webster, C. & Timothy, D.J. (2006) "Travelling to the 'Other Side': the Occupied Zone and Greek Cypriot Views of Crossing the Green Line", *Tourism Geographies* 8(2): 162–181.

Wijkhuijs, V. & Sollie, H. (2014) "Multi-probleemgezinnen met een Roma achtergrond: waarom verloopt hun integratie moeizaam?" (*"Roma multi-problem families in the Netherlands: what hinders their integration?"*), *Journal of Social Intervention: Theory and Practice* 23(1): 72–90.

Winstanley, C. (2009) "Too cool for school? Gifted children and homeschooling", *Theory and Research in Education* (7): 347–362.

Woodhead, M. & Faulkner, D. (2008) 'Subjects, Objects or Participants? Dilemmas of Psychological Research with Children', in Christensen, P. & James, A. (eds.) *Research with Children: Perspectives and Practices*. London: Routledge.

Woodhouse, B.B. (1994) ""Out of Children 's Needs, Children 's Rights": The Child's Voice in Defining the Family", *Brigham Young University Journal of Public Law* 8(2): 321–341.

Woodman, G.R. (1989) "Constitutions in a World of Powerful Semi-Autonomous Social Fields", 8(1): 1–19.

Wright, J.P. & Cullen, F.T. (2001) "Parental efficacy and delinquent behavior: Do control and support matter?", *Criminology* 39: 677–706.

Yilmaz, M. (2005) "Cyprus Conflict and Question of Identity", *Review of International Law and Politics* 1 (4): 76–78.

Ziegert, K. (2009) 'World Society, Nation State and Living Law in the Twenty-First Century', in Hertogh, M. (ed.) *Living Law: Reconsidering Eugen Ehrlich*. Oxford: Hart Publishing.

Zoontjens, P.J.J. (2003) *Het beweeglijk recht op onderwijs* (*"the dynamic right to education"*). Den Haag: Boom Juridische Uitgevers.

Zoontjens, P.J.J. (2014) 'Leerplicht en de handhaving daarvan' (*"Compulsory education and its legal enforcement"*), in Michiels, F.C.M.A. & Muller, E.R. (eds.) *Handhaving. Bestuurlijk handhaven in Nederland*. Deventer: Kluwer Juridische Uitgevers.

MEDIA

ANP (2015) "Leraren kritisch over passend onderwijs" *("teachers critical about appropriate edcuation")*, *Nu.nl*. Available at: https://www.bnr.nl/nieuws/wetenschap/10314989/puinhoop-bij-passend-onderwijs, accessed 12 November 2018.

Ball, J., and Ackerman, S. (2013) "NSA Loophole Allows Warrantless Search for US Citizens' Emails and Phone Calls", *The Guardian*. Available at https://www.theguardian.com/world/2013/aug/09/nsa-loophole-warrantless-searches-email-calls, accessed 18 December 2018.

Blok, H. (2004) "Thuisonderwijs is prima alternatief" (*"Homeschooling is a fine alternative"*), *NRC*. Available at: https://www.nrc.nl/nieuws/2004/01/08/thuisonderwijs-is-prima-alternatief-7668925-a416364, accessed 28 October 2018.

Cyprus Mail Online (2018) "Britain, Cyprus and the use of the British bases", *Cyprus Mail Online*. Available at: https://cyprus-mail.com/2018/04/14/use-british-bases-cyprus/, accessed 1 October 2018.

De Telegraaf (2014) "Dekker wil af van Thuisondewrijs" (*"Dekker wants to get rid of homeschooling"*), *Telegraaf*. Available at: https://www.telegraaf.nl/nieuws/903944/dekker-wil-af-van-thuisonderwijs, accessed 23 November 2018.

Güsten, S. (2014) "Students Flock to Universities in Northern Cyprus", *The New York Times*. Available at: https://www.nytimes.com/2014/02/17/world/europe/students-flock-to-universities-in-northern-cyprus.html, accessed 22 September 2018.

Haber Kibris (2017) "Ertuğruloğlu'ndan tepki çeken mesaj!" (*"Message from Ertuğruloğlu!"*), *Haber Kibris*. Available at: https://haberkibris.com/ertugruloglundan-tepki-ceken-mesaj-2017–12–26.html, accessed 24 September 2018.

Haber Turk (2018) "Randevu krizi aşıldı, KKTC Başbakanı Anakara'ya davet edildi" (*"Appointment crisis avoided, TRNC Prime Minister invited to Ankara"*), *Haber*

Turk. Available at: https://www.haberturk.com/randevu-krizi-asildi-kktc-basbakani-ankara-ya-davet-edildi-1865694, accessed 1 October 2018.

Havadis Kibris (2017) "Ortalık karıştı!" (*"It's confused!"), Havadis Kibris*. Available at: https://www.havadiskibris.com/ortalik-karisti/, accessed 24 September 2018.

Karashan, S. (2018) "Türkiye ve KKTC arasında randevu krizi" (*"Appointment crisis between Turkey and the TRNC"*), *DHA*. Available at: https://www.dha.com.tr/dunya/turkiye-ve-kktc-arasinda-randevu-krizi/haber-1567861, accessed 1 October 2018.

Karpazali, E. (2013) "Turkey & North Cyprus: a troublesome mother-daugther relationship", *World Bulletin*. Available at: https://www.worldbulletin.net/filebox/turkey-north-cyprus-a-troublesome-mother-daughter-relationship-h113124.html, accessed 1 October 2018.

Keultjes, H. (2016) "Bijna tienduizend leerlpichtige kinderen thuis", *Algemeen Dagblad*. Available at: https://www.ad.nl/binnenland/bijna-tienduizend-leerplichtige-kinderen-thuis~ab487eee/, accessed 7 November 2018.

Kibris Manşet (2015) "Kimler Beyaz Kimlik Alacak?" (*"Who will get white identity?"), Kibris Manşet*. Available at: www.kibrismanset.com/guncel/kimler-beyaz-kimlik-alacak-h122807.html, accessed 22 September 2018.

Kibris Son Dakina (2017) "Sevgiliye Vatandaşlik Hediye!" (*"Valentine Citizenship Gift!"), Kibris Son Dakina*. Available at: https://www.kibrissondakika.com/torpil-disinda-nasil-aciklanabilirr/, accessed 24 September 2018.

Kneyber, R. (2017) "Er gaat veel fout bij 'passend onderwijs', en de overheid heeft geen idee", *Trouw*. Available at: https://www.trouw.nl/samenleving/er-gaat-veel-fout-bij-passend-onderwijs-en-de-overheid-heeft-geen-idee~a5238f31/, accessed 13 February 2019.

Kuiper, R. & Bouma, K. (2015) "Duizenden kinderen zitten 'volstrekt onnodig' thuis", *De Volkskrant*. Available at https://www.volkskrant.nl/nieuws-achtergrond/duizenden-kinderen-zitten-volstrekt-onnodig-thuis~b9e91cfe/, accessed 7 November 2018.

Kuiper, R. (2016) "Passend onderwijs rammelt nog: zorgleerling krijgt niet overal dezelfde begeleiding" (*"Appropriate education is still shaky: student in need of care does not get the same support everywhere"*), *De Volkskrant*. Available at: https://www.volkskrant.nl/nieuws-achtergrond/passend-onderwijs-rammelt-nog-zorgleerling-krijgt-niet-overal-dezelfde-begeleiding~b965eadf/, accessed 12 November 2018.

Michael, P. (2018) "Substantial and effective work needed before new Cyprus talks", *Cyprus Mail Online*. Available at: https://cyprus-mail.com/2018/09/11/substantial-and-effective-needed-before-new-cyprus-talks/, accessed 13 September 2018.

NOS (2015) "Zorgen in kamer over passend onderwijs" (*"Chamber worried about appropriate education"*), *NOS*. Available at: https://nos.nl/artikel/2055366-zorgen-in-kamer-over-passend-onderwijs.html, accessed 12 November 2018.

NOS (2016) "Dekker kan door met plan voor strengere regels thuisonderwijs" (*"Dekker can continue with stricter rules hoemschooling"*), *NOS*. Availabe at: https://nos.nl/artikel/2093188-dekker-kan-door-met-plan-voor-strengere-regels-thuisonderwijs.html, accessed 23 November 2018.

NOS (2018) "Aantal leerlingen dat thuiszit daalt niet" (*"Number of children out of school is not decreasing"*), *NOS*. Available at: https://nos.nl/artikel/2218153-aantal-leerlingen-dat-thuiszit-daalt-niet.html, accessed 13 February 2019.

NRC (2013a) "Thuisonderwijs via geheime constructies" (*"Homeschooling through secret constructions*), *NRC*. Available at: https://www.nrc.nl/nieuws/2013/06/07/thuisonderwijs-via-geheime-constructies-1257450-a592327, accessed 12 November 2018.

NRC (2013b) "'Miep is ziek', zo noemt de inspectie het" (*"Ann is ill, that's what the inspection calls it*"), *NRC*. Available at: https://www.nrc.nl/nieuws/2013/06/07/miep-is-ziek-zo-noemt-de-inspectie-het-1257367-a1287047, accessed 12 November 2018.

Obioma, C. (2016) "The ghosts of my student years in northern Cyprus", *The Guardian*. Available at: https://www.theguardian.com/world/2016/jan/16/chigozie-obioma-booker-nominee-haunted-student-years-northern-cyprus, accessed 22 September 2018.

Psyllides, G. (2017) "Edek suggests increasing Greek troops", *Cyprus Mail Online*. Available at: https://cyprus-mail.com/2017/07/22/edek-suggests-increasing-greek-troops/, accessed 1 October 2018.

Radio Ndeke Luka (2019a) *RCA: Education par la radio, une première expérience lancée dans le pays*. Availalble at: https://www.radiondekeluka.org/actualites/education/34985-rca-education-par-la-radio-une-premiere-experience-lancee-dans-le-pays.html, accessed 23 July 2020.

Radio Ndeke Luka (2019b) *RCA: le taux de réussite au premier tour du baccalauréat 2019 s'élève à 10,24%*. Available at: https://www.radiondekeluka.org/actualites/education/34259-rca-le-taux-de-reussite-au-premier-tour-du-baccalaureat-2019-s-eleve-a-10–24.html, accessed 23 July 2020.

Radio Ndeke Luka (2019c) *RCA: Baccalauréat 2019, la mise en garde de Moukadas Nour*. Available at: https://www.radiondekeluka.org/actualites/education/33977-rca-baccalaureat-2019-la-mise-en-garde-de-moukadas-nour.html, accessed 23 July 2020.

Radio Ndeke Luka (2020a) *Centrafrique: grogne des enseignants contractuels et vacataires au ministère des Finances et du budget*. Available at: https://www.radiondekeluka.org/actualites/education/35818-centrafrique-grogne-des-enseignants-contractuels-et-vacataires-au-ministere-des-finances-et-du-budget.html, accessed 23 July 2020.

Rutten, K. (2016) "Puinhoop bij passend onderwijs" (*"A mess at appropriate education"*), *BNR*. Available at https://www.bnr.nl/nieuws/wetenschap/10314989/puinhoop-bij-passend-onderwijs, accessed 12 November 2018.

Slump, K. (2010) "Column: Mijn bijzondere klasje", *Balans Magazine*. Available at https://www.balansdigitaal.nl/wp-content/uploads/2017/07/Mijn-bijzondere-klasje.pdf, accessed 28 October 2018.

Slump, K. (2014) "Het Onderwijs(voor)recht", *Advies Onderwijsrecht*. Available at: www.adviesonderwijsrecht.nl/inc/uploads/2014/09/Het-onderwijsvoorrecht-K.J.-Slump-september-2014.pdf, accessed 12 February 2019.

Squires, N. (2017) "Turkey will only withdraw troops from Cyprus if Greece does the same, Turkish president Erdogan warns", *The Telegraph*. Available at: https://www.

telegraph.co.uk/news/2017/01/13/turkey-will-withdraw-troops-cyprus-greece-does-turkish-president/, accessed 1 October 2018.

Stefanini, S. (2018) "Two Votes, one last chance for Cypriot reunification", *Politico.* Available at: https://www.politico.eu/article/cyprus-reunification-two-votes-one-last-chance/, accessed 13 September 2018.

Tas, M. (2018) "'Beyaz kimlik' geliyor" (*"white identity is coming"), Diyalog.* Available at: https://www.diyaloggazetesi.com/kibris/beyaz-kimlik-geliyor-h63437.html, accessed 22 September 2018.

The Guardian (2001) "Spread of Aids in schools blamed on staff", *The Guardian.* Available at: https://www.theguardian.com/world/2001/aug/24/aids.schools, accessed 10 April 2017.

The Guardian (2015) "The NSA Files", *The Guardian.* https://www.theguardian.com/us-news/the-nsa-files, accessed 3 February 2015.

Trouw (2016) "Aantal leerplichtige thuiszitters gedaald" (*"Number of children out of school who are subject to compulsory education decreased"), Trouw.* Available at https://www.trouw.nl/home/aantal-leerplichtige-thuiszitters-gedaald~a1e2e6fa/, accessed 7 November 2018.

UN NEWS CENTRE (2015) "UN warns Central African Republic is becoming largest forgotten humanitarian crisis". Available at: https://news.un.org/en/story/2015/04/497142, accessed 27 April 2015.

Vamık, A. (2016) "Beyaz Kimlik almayana vatandaşlık yok!" (*"White identity no citizenship!"), Gündem Kibris.* Available at: https://www.gundemkibris.com/mansetler/beyaz-kimlik-almayana-vatandaslik-yok-h167650.html, accessed 22 September 2018.

Waterman, S. (2013) "Documents on Secret Court Rulings for NSA Operations to be Released", *The Washington Times.* Available at www.washingtontimes.com/news/2013/sep/10/documents-secret-court-rulings-nsa-operations-be-r/, accessed 18 December 2018.

Yenidüzen (2015) "Beyaz Kimlik Dönemi!" (*"White identity period!"*), *Yenidüzen.* Available at: www.yeniduzen.com/beyaz-kimlik-donemi-57824h.htm, accessed 22 September 2018.

ONLINE ARTICLES

't Carillon (no date) *Onze schoolregels.* Available at: https://www.bscarillon.nl/over-de-school/regels-en-afspraken/onze-schoolregels/1941, accessed 21 November 2018.

Atlantic Hospitality (n.d.) "Guest Room Cribs – Commerical Baby Cribs". Available at: http://atlantichospitalityinc.com/guest_room_cribs.html, accessed 24–08–2015.

Army (n.d.) "Deployments: Cyprus". Available at: https://www.army.mod.uk/deployments/cyprus/, accessed 1 October 2018.

Bullock, J. (2010) "Momnesia Mondays". Available at: www.mommybknowsbest.com/momnesia-mondays-2, accessed 24–08–2015.

Centraal Bureau voor de Statistiek (CBS) (2015) "Aantal kinderen in Nederland daalt" (*"Number of children in the Netherlands decreasing*"). Available at https://www.

cbs.nl/nl-nl/nieuws/2015/48/aantal-kinderen-in-nederland-daalt, accessed 1 November 2018.

De Meerwaarde (no date) "Schoolregels". Available at: https://www.demeerwaarde.nl/Algemeen/Algemene_informatie/Fraaie_school/Schoolregels, accessed 21 November 2018.

De Rotonde (no date) "Schoolregels – dit ben ik als leerling". Available at: https://www.derotondebreda.nl/onze-leerlingen/schoolregels, accessed 21 November 2018.

Doench, L. (2016) "Internet meme demolition derby: Medicating Calvin & Hobbes Edition". Available at: http://groundedparents.com/2016/02/19/internet-meme-demolition-derby-medicating-calvin-hobbes-edition/, accessed 14 February 2019.

Douglas, L. (2016) "The Elusive Pursuit of Equity". Available at: http://secondlineblog.org/2016/11/the-elusive-pursuit-of-equity/, accessed 16 November 2018.

Education cannot wait (2019) "Press release". Available at: https://www.educationcannotwait.org/the-government-of-central-african-republic-education-cannot-wait-and-a-wide-coalition-of-donors-and-partners-launch-us77–6-million-education-programme-for-900000-children/, accessed 15 July 2020.

European Commission (n.d.) "Aid Programme for the Turkish Cypriot community". Available at: https://ec.europa.eu/info/funding-tenders/funding-opportunities/funding-programmes/overview-funding-programmes/aid-programme-turkish-cypriot-community_en, accessed 14 January 2018

Fondation Hirondelle (2020) "Education by radio: a pilot-project launched in CAR with Radio Ndeke Luka". Available at: https://www.hirondelle.org/en/our-news/1047-education-par-la-radio-une-experience-lancee-en-centrafrique-avec-radio-ndeke-luka, accessed 15 July 2020.

Google search (2017a) "Health Central African Republic". Available at: https://scholar.google.nl/scholar?q=health+central+african+republic&btnG=&hl=en&as_sdt=0%2C5, accessed 25 April 2017.

Google search (2017b) "Education Central African Republic". Available at: https://scholar.google.nl/scholar?q=education+central+african+republic&btnG=&hl=en&as_sdt=0%2C5, accessed 25 April 2017.

Hopman, M. (2016a) "Rechtszaken en overige uitspraken over recht op onderwijs in Nederland" (*"Court cases and other judgments about the right to education in the Netherlands")*. Available at: http://kinderrechtenonderzoek.nl/rechtszaken-en-overige-uitspraken-over-recht-op-onderwijs-in-nederland/, accessed 2 November 2018.

Hopman, M. (2016c) "De leerrechtambtenaar: concrete uitwerking". Available at: http://kinderrechtenonderzoek.nl/de-leerrechtambtenaar-concrete-uitwerking/, accessed 23 January 2019.

Hopman, M. (2017c) "Speech of Touadera, president of the CAR,27 sept in the US + discussion". Available at: http://kinderrechtenonderzoek.nl/speech-of-touadera-president-of-the-car-27-sept-in-the-us-discussion/?lang=en, accessed 27 July 2017.

Jesuit Refugee Service (2016) "Central African Republic: Living in the factory". Available at: http://en.jrs.net/news_detail?TN=NEWS-20161220074535, accessed 20 June 2017.

Kennisplatform Integratie & Samenleving (n.d.) https://www.kis.nl/publicatie/monitor-inclusie-nulmeting, accessed 6 November 2018.

Kombos, C. (2018) "Developments in Cypriot Constitutional Law: the year 2016 in Review". Available at: www.iconnectblog.com/2017/12/developments-in-cypriot-constitutional-law-the-year-2016-in-review/, accessed 10 October 2018.

LAKS (2019) "De Maartnieuwsbrief". Available at: https://www.laks.nl/de-maartnieuwsbrief/, accessed 13 July 2020.

Malone, N. (2008) "How Many Lashes Can One Man Take?". Available at: www.slate.com/articles/news_and_politics/explainer/2008/11/how_many_lashes_can_one_man_take.html, accessed 12 April 2017

Ministerie van Onderwijs, Cultuur en Wetenschap (no date) "Geschiedenis" *("history")*. Available at: https://www.rijksoverheid.nl/ministeries/ministerie-van-onderwijs-cultuur-en-wetenschap/organisatie/geschiedenis, accessed 17 October 2018.

Mudge, L. (2017b) "Justice Needed for Lasting Peace in Central African Republic: Prosecute Those Responsible for Grave Crimes". Human Rights Watch, available at: https://www.hrw.org/news/2017/06/20/justice-needed-lasting-peace-central-african-republic, accessed 6 August 2017

NewStatesman (2015) "What actually happens when you get flogged". Available at: www.newstatesman.com/politics/2015/02/what-actually-happens-when-you-get-flogged-death, accessed 12 April 2017.

Nicolatos, M. M. (no date) "Austerity measures and economic crisis. The Case of Cyprus: A Judge's approach". Available at: www.supremecourt.gov.cy/Judicial/SC.nsf/All/F474B9EC2A7494D2C2257CC500387A2B?OpenDocument, accessed 10 October 2018.

No Author (2015a) "Akward and Strange Things Kids Say and Do". Available at: https://www.facebook.com/childrenarestrange, accessed 21–08–2015.

No Author (2015b) "I Used to Believe…the childhood beliefs site". Available at: www.iusedtobelieve.com, accessed 21–08–2015.

Onderwijsgeschillen (n.d.) "Verwijdering leerling van school" *("unenrollment student from school")*. Available at: https://onderwijsgeschillen.nl/thema/verwijdering-leerling-van-school#redenen, accessed 12 November 2018.

Rijksoverheid (n.d.) "Gedoogbeleid softdrugs en coffeeshops". Available at: www.rijksoverheid.nl/onderwerpen/drugs/gedoogbeleid-softdrugs-en-coffeeshops, accessed 03–02–2015.

Rijksoverheid (n.d. (a)) "Wanneer hoeft mijn kind niet naar school?" (*"When does my child not have to go to school?")*. Available at https://www.rijksoverheid.nl/onderwerpen/leerplicht/vraag-en-antwoord/wanneer-hoeft-mijn-kind-niet-naar-school, accessed 4 November 2018.

Rijksoverheid (n.d. (b)) "Doelen passend onderwijs" *("aims appropriate education")*. Available at https://www.rijksoverheid.nl/onderwerpen/passend-onderwijs/doelen-passend-onderwijs, accessed 12 November 2018.

Rijksoverheid (n.d. (c)) "Schooladvies en heroverweging schooladvies" *("schooladvise and reconsideration school advise")*. Available at https://www.onderwijsincijfers.nl/kengetallen/po/leerlingen-po/prestaties-schooladvies, accessed 12 November 2018.

Rijksoverheid (n.d.(d)) "Oprichten nieuwe school" (*"Founding a new school"*). Available at: https://www.rijksoverheid.nl/onderwerpen/vrijheid-van-onderwijs/oprichten-nieuwe-school, accessed 14 February 2019.

Rockwell, B. (2014) "He Did What? 17 Hilarious Strange Kid Habits". Available at: www.popsugar.com/moms/Weird-Things-Kids-Do-28044686#photo-28044686, accessed 21–08–2015.

Samson, E. (2012) "Israel, Gaza, and the End of "Effective Control". Available at: http://opiniojuris.org/2012/04/26/israel-gaza-and-the-end-of-effective-control/, accessed 13 February 2019.

SOS Children's Villages International (2015) "General information on Northern Cyprus". Available at: https://www.sos-childrensvillages.org/where-we-help/europe/northern-cyprus, accessed 8 October 2015.

Stichting Landelijk Onderwijs aan Varende Kinderen (LVOK) https://www.lovk.nl/home/, accessed 8 November 2018.

Stichting rijdende school (n.d.) www.rijdendeschool.nl/, accessed 8 November 2018.

The European Union Scholarship Programme for the Turkish Cypriot Community (n.d.) Available at: www.abburs.eu/en/, accessed 13 February 2019.

The Organisation for Economic Co-operation and Development (2017) "Netherlands". Available at: https://data.oecd.org/netherlands.htm, accessed 17 October 2018.

Transparancy International (n.d.) "Central African Republic". Available at: https://www.transparency.org/country/CAF, accessed 13 February 2019.

UNAIDS (2017) "Central African Republic". Available at: www.unaids.org/en/regionscountries/countries/centralafricanrepublic, accessed 10 April 2017.

UNESCO (n.d.) "Central African Republic". Available at: http://uis.unesco.org/country/CF, accessed 4 April 2017.

UNICEF (n.d.) "UReport République Centrafricaine". Available at: https://centrafrique.ureport.in/ureporters/, accessed 12 April 2017).

UNICEF (2014a) "With 15 million children caught up in major conflicts, UNICEF declares 2014 a devastating year for children". Available at: www.unicef.org/media/media_78058.html, accessed 17 January 2015

United Nations Human Rights Office of the High Commissioner (n.d.) "Status of Ratification: Interactive Dashboard". Available at: http://indicators.ohchr.org/, accessed 13 February 2019.

United Nations Treaties Collection (2020a) "Chapter V. Refugees and Stateless Persons. 3. Convention relating to the rights of stateless persons. Status at: 17–07–2020. Available at: https://treaties.un.org/Pages/ViewDetailsII.aspx?src=TREATY&mtdsg_no=V-3&chapter=5&Temp=mtdsg2&clang=_en, accessed 17 July 2020.

United Nations Treaties Collection (2020b) "Chapter V. Refugees and Stateless Persons. 4. Convention on the reduction of statelessness. Status at: 17–07–2020. Available at: https://treaties.un.org/Pages/ViewDetails.aspx?src=TREATY&mtdsg_no=V-4&chapter=5&clang=_en, accessed 17 July 2020.

Universiteitsfonds Limburg (n.d.) "Children's Rights Research Fund". Available at: https://www.ufl-swol.nl/en/fonds/childrens-rights-research-fund/, accessed 15 February 2019.

Unlock the Law (2015) "Rules of the Game of Thrones – What are the Laws of Westeros?". Available at: www.unlockthelaw.co.uk/News/rules-of-the-game-of-thrones-what-are-the-laws-of-westeros/22862938.html, accessed 18–08–2015.

Urban Dictionary (n.d.) "Crazy", available at: https://www.urbandictionary.com/define.php?term=Crazy, accessed 11 February 2019.
Urban Dictionary (n.d.) "Sick", available at: https://www.urbandictionary.com/define.php?term=sick, accessed 11 February 2019.
World Bank (2017) "Central African Republic". Available at: http://data.worldbank.org/country/central-african-republic, accessed 2 April 2017.
Zenios, S. (2017) "EU borders: walking backwards from Northern Ireland to Cyprus", *LSE*. Available at: http://blogs.lse.ac.uk/politicsandpolicy/northern-ireland-cyprus-borders/, accessed 23 September 2018.

OTHER

Gouvernement de la Centrafrique (2020) Réunion du Premier Ministre, Firmin NGREBADA avec le collectif des enseignants vacataires 1 July 2020 [video]. Availalble at: https://www.facebook.com/watch/?v=661768558015310, accessed 15 July 2020.
Hopman, M.J. (2014a) *Childhood and Children's Rights: Including a case study of the practice of child combatants in Rwanda and the Netherlands.* Amsterdam: University of Amsterdam (MA thesis).
Hopman, M.J. (2014b) *Research proposal: "Looking at law through children's eyes".* Available at: http://kinderrechtenonderzoek.nl/wp-content/uploads/2014/09/Research-proposal-MH-29dec.pdf, accessed 11 February 2019.
Hopman, M.J. (2014c) *Budget PhD.* Available at: http://kinderrechtenonderzoek.nl/wp-content/uploads/2014/09/Budget-PHD-Hopman.docx, accessed 25 April 2017.
United Nations Secretary General (2019) *UN Secretary-General's Statement on Cyprus.* Available at: https://www.un.org/sg/en/content/sg/statement/2019–11–25/un-secretary-general%E2%80%99s-statement-cyprus, accessed 21 July 2020.

REPORTS

Africa Progress Panel (2012) *A Twin Education Crisis is Holding Back Africa: Millions are not in school, millions more are failing to learn.* Available at: www.africaprogresspanel.org/policy-papers/a-twin-educationcrisis-is-holding-back-africa1/, accessed 20 June 2017.
Australian Government, National Health and Medical Research Council & Australia Research Council (2007/2018) *National Statement on Ethical Conduct in Human Research. Available at:* https://nhmrc.gov.au/about-us/publications/national-statement-ethical-conduct-human-research-2007-updated-2018#toc__95, *accessed 11 February 2019.*
Banque Mondiale (2008) *Le Système éducatif Centrafricain: Contraintes et marges de manœuvre pour la reconstruction du système éducatif dans la perspective de la réduction de la pauvreté («The education system in the CAR: constraints and room for maneuer for the reconstruction of the educational system in the perspective of*

poverty reduction»). Washington: Banque internationale pour la reconstruction et le développement/Banque mondiale.

Bhabha, J. (2017) "The importance of nationality for children", in *The World's Stateless Children*. Available at: www.institutesi.org/worldsstateless17.pdf, accessed 17–8–2017.

Blok, H. & Karsten, S. (2008) *Vervangend onderwijs aan kinderen van ouders met een richtingbezwaar* (*"Replacement education for children of parents with a direction based objection"*). Amsterdam: SCO-Kohnstamm Instituut.

Blok, H., Triesscheijn, B. & Karsten, S. (2010) *Vervangend onderwijs aan kinderen van ouders met een richtingbezwaar; aanvullend onderzoek ("Replacement education for children of parents with a direction based objection: complementary study")*. Amsterdam: SCO-Kohnstamm Instituut.

Bureau of Democracy, Human Rights and Labor (2014) *International Religious Freedom Report for 2014: Central African Republic*. Available at: www.state.gov/j/drl/rls/irf/religiousfreedom/index.htm?year=2014&dlid=238196, accessed 27 June 2017.

Centraal Bureau voor de Statistiek (CBS) (2008) *Gezondheid en zorg in cijfers 2008 ("health and care in numbers 2008")*. Available at: https://www.cbs.nl/nl-nl/publicatie/2008/47/gezondheid-en-zorg-in-cijfers-2008, accessed 1 November 2018.

Central African Republic (2017) *2016 National Commune Monograph Survey*. Available at: http://documents.worldbank.org/curated/en/154771488193937523/Central-African-Republic-2016-National-commune-monography-survey, accessed 13 February 2019.

Child Helpline International (2011) *Session 59 – Recommendations under the Convention on the Rights of the Child Prepared by Child Helpline International and "Hope for Children" - September 2011*.

Commission Education Sociale, Culture, Jeunesse et Sports (2003a) *Diagnostic de l'éducation*. Available at: http://dialogue.national.free.fr/dn_commissions_education_diag.htm, accessed 20 June 2017.

Commission Education Sociale, Culture, Jeunesse et Sports (2003b) *Les recommendations fortes*. Available at: http://dialogue.national.free.fr/dn_commissions_education_recomfort.htm, accessed 20 June 2017.

De Kinderombudsman (2019) "The Netherlands – Input for List of Issues prior to reporting", available at: https://tbinternet.ohchr.org/Treaties/CRC/Shared%20Documents/NLD/INT_CRC_IFN_NLD_36876_E.pdf, accessed 13 July 2020.

de Kroon, E., Panis, F. & Tas, M. (2015) *Joint parallel report to the nineteenth to twenty-first Periodic Reports of the Netherlands on the International Convention on the Elimination of all Forms of Racial Discrimination (CERD)*. Nederlands Juristen Comité voor de Mensenrechten (NJCM), on behalf of 28 NGOs&CSOs. Available at: https://tbinternet.ohchr.org/_layouts/treatybodyexternal/Download.aspx?symbolno=INT%2fCERD%2fNGO%2fNLD%2f21177&Lang=en, accessed 28 October 2018.

de Vries, L. & Glawion, T. 2015. *Speculating on Crisis: The Progressive Disintegration of the Central African Republic's Political Economy*. Den Haag: Clingendael.

Department of Health, Social Services and Public Safety (2012) *Code of Practice on Protecting the Confidentiality of Service User Information*. Available at: https://www.health-ni.gov.uk/publications/code-practice-protecting-confidentiality-service-user-information, accessed 11 February 2019.

Dullaert, M. (2019) *De Kracht om door te zetten: hoe kunnen we de impasse rondom thuiszitten doorbreken?* Available at: https://www.tweedekamer.nl/downloads/

document?id=845d11ee-11c3-4166-8833-bb6399d504c4&title=De%20kracht%20om%20door%20te%20zetten.%20Hoe%20kunnen%20we%20de%20impasse%20rondom%20thuiszitten%20doorbreken_.pdf, accessed 13 July 2020.

Dutch Ombudsman for Children (2014) *Ombudsperson report on children's rights in The Netherlands NHRI Report.* Available at: https://tbinternet.ohchr.org/Treaties/CRC/Shared%20Documents/NLD/INT_CRC_NGO_NLD_17975_E.pdf, accessed 27 October 2018.

Economic and Social council, commission on human rights (2003) *Prevention of Discrimination: The rights of non-citizens. Final report of the Special Rapporteur, Mr. David Weissbrodt, submitted in accordance with Sub-Commission decision 2000/103, Commission resolution 2000/104 and Economic and Social Council decision 2000/283.* E/CN.4/Sub.2/2003/23.

FMSI (2013). *Universal Periodic Review (UPR) for the Central African Republic: 17th session (Oct-Nov 2013).* Geneva.

Freedom House (2017) *Central African Republic.* Available at: https://freedomhouse.org/report/freedomworld/2017/central-african-republic, accessed 7 June 2017.

Gan Business Anti-Corruption portal (2016) *Central African Republic Corruption Report.* Available at: www.business-anti-corruption.com/country-profiles/central-african-republic, accessed 7 June 2017.

Glawion, T. & Le Noan, A.-C. (2018) *Education Insecurity in the Central African Republic: Case study of the rebel-held city Ndélé – Research brief August 2018.* Available at: https://www.giga-hamburg.de/sites/default/files/md_pdf/GlawionLeNoan2018_ResearchBrief_EducationInsecurityinNdeleCAR.pdf, accessed 15 July 2020.

Göyknüklü, C. (2012) *Human Rights of Migrant Workers in North Cyprus.* Lefoşa: Turkish Cypriot Human Rights Foundation.

Global Initiative to end all corporal punishment of children (2011) *Briefing from Global Initiative to End All Corporal Punishment of Children: Briefing for the Committee on the Rights of the Child Pre-Sessional Working Group – October 2011*: Cyprus (third/fourth report). Available at: https://tbinternet.ohchr.org/_layouts/treatybodyexternal/Download.aspx?symbolno=INT%2fCRC%2fNGO%2fCYP%2f60%2f8493&Lang=en, accessed 13 February 2019.

Gregson, J. (2017) *The World's Richest and Poorest Countries.* Available at: https://www.gfmag.com/global-data/economic-data/worlds-richest-and-poorest-countries, accessed 20 June 2017.

Groupe de la Banque Mondiale (2017) *République Centrafricaine: Enquête Nationale sur les Monographies Communales 2016.* Available at: http://documents.worldbank.org/curated/en/806401487659549915/pdf/112939-WP-p160717-FRENCH-PUBLIC-ABSTRACT-SENT-IDU-Submission-from-Johannes-GHoogeveen.pdf, accessed 20 June 2017.

Hart, R.A. (1992) *Children's Participation: from tokenism to citizenship.* Florence: UNICEF International Child Development Centre.

Hatay, M. (2007) *Is the Turkish Cypriot Population Shrinking?: An Overview of the Ethno-Demography of Cyprus in the Light of the Preliminary Results of the 2006 Turkish-Cypriot Census.* Oslo: International Peace Research Institute.

Hatay, M. (2017) *Population and Politics in north Cyprus: an overview of the ethno-demography of north Cyprus in the light of the 2011 census*. Oslo: Peace Research Institute Oslo & Nicosia: Friendrich-Ebert-Stiftung (Foundation).

Haveman, R. H. (2012) *Rule of Law Quick Scan Rwanda*. The Hague: HiiL. https://www.hiil.org/wp-content/uploads/2018/09/Rule-of-Law-Quick-Scan-Rwanda.pdf, accessed 18 December 2018.

Helliwel, J., Layard, R. & Sachs, J.D. (2017). *World Happiness Report 2017*. Available at: http://worldhappiness.report/wp-content/uploads/sites/2/2017/03/HR17.pdf, accessed 27 June 2017.

Heyma, A., van den Berg, E., Snoek, M., Knezic, D., Sligte, H. & Emmelot, Y. (2017) *Effect van een masteropleiding op leraren en hun omgeving ("effect of a Master education on teachers and their surroundings")*. Amsterdam: SEO Economisch Onderzoek.

Hope for Children (2012) *Country Report for the Protection of Children in Cyprus*. Nicosia: "Hope for Children" UNCRC Policy Center.

Hopman, M.J. (2016b). *(W)elk kind heeft recht op onderwijs?: Een onderzoek naar de betekenis van recht op onderwijs voor kinderen in Nederland, specifiek gericht op thuisonderwijs, thuiszitters en Roma kinderen ("Which child has the right to an education?: A research on the meaning of the child's right to education in the Netherlands, specifically focused on home schooling, children out of school and Roma children")*. Leiden: Defence for Children. Available at: http://kinderrechtenonderzoek.nl/wp-content/uploads/2014/09/Rapport-totaal-PDF.pdf, accessed 13 February 2019.

Hopman, M.J., Borne, A.E., Bruchi, C., Nys, R. Pircher, F. & Trip, N. (2018a) *Deleted off the map: the child's right to nationality in the Turkish Republic of Northern Cyprus*. Maastricht University (Turkish edition: Haridatan Sılınmek: Kurzey Kibris Türk Cumhuriyeti'nde Çocuğun Vatandaşlik Hakki). Availalbe at: http://kinderrechtenonderzoek.nl/report-trnc/?lang=en, accessed 13 February 2019.

Hopman, M.J., Borne, A.E., de Chickera, A. (2018b). *Joint Submission to the Human Rights Council at the 32nd Session of the Universal Periodic Review: Republic of Cyprus*. Available at: www.institutesi.org/UPR32_Cyprus.pdf, accessed 13 February 2019.

Hopman, M.J., Saragnet, D.C.B. & Dopani, P. (2017b) The child's right to education in the Central African Republic. Maastricht University (French edition: le droit de l'enfant à l'éducation en République Centrafricaine. Maastricht University). Available at: http://kinderrechtenonderzoek.nl/wp-content/uploads/2017/11/Childrens-raport-ENG-OK.pdf, accessed 13 February 2019.

Huisman, P.W.A. & Zoontjens, P.J.J. (2016) *Leerrechten als structurele grondslag voor wetgeving ("Learning rights as structural foundation for legislation")*. Rotterdam/Tilburg: NCOR- Nederlands Centrum voor Onderwijsrecht.

Human Rights Council (2012) *Report of the Working Group on the Universal Periodic Review: Netherlands*. A/HRC/21/15. Available at: https://documents-dds-ny.un.org/doc/UNDOC/GEN/G12/150/77/PDF/G1215077.pdf?OpenElement, accessed 28 October 2018.

Human Rights Watch (2013) *"Letting the Big Fish Swim": Failures to Prosecute High-Level Corruption in Uganda*. Human Rights Watch. Available at www.refworld.org/docid/526642344.html, accessed 18 December 2018.

Human Rights Watch (2016) *Central African Republic: Deadly Raid on Displaced People: UN Peacekeepers Should Offer Increased Protection*. Available at: https://www.hrw.org/news/2016/11/01/central-african-republic-deadly-raid-displaced-people, accessed 6 August 2017.

Human Rights Watch (2017). *No Class: When Armed Groups Use Schools in the Central African Republic*. Available at: https://www.hrw.org/sites/default/files/report_pdf/car0317_web.pdf, accessed 12 April 2017.

Inspectie van het Onderwijs (2010) *Het onderwijs in het schrijven van teksten: de kwaliteit van schrijfonderwijs in het basisonderwijs ("Education in tekst writing: the quality of writing education in primary education")*. Available at https://www.onderwijsinspectie.nl/binaries/onderwijsinspectie/documenten/rapporten/2011/02/16/het-onderwijs-in-het-schrijven-van-teksten/Het+onderwijs+in+het+schrijven+van+teksten+printversie.pdf

Inspectie van het Onderwijs (2016) *De staat van het onderwijs: onderwijsverslag 2014/2015 ("the state of education: education report 2014/2015)*. Available at https://www.onderwijsinspectie.nl/documenten/publicaties/2016/04/13/staat-van-het-onderwijs-2014–2015, accessed 12 November 2018.

Institut Centrafricain des Statistiques et des Études Économiques et Sociales (ICASEES) (2012) *Enquête par grappes à indicateurs multiples – MICS couplée avec la sérologie VIH, RCA, 2010: Suivi de la situation des enfants, des femmes et des hommes*. Bangui: ICASEES.

International Council on Human Rights Policy (2009) *When Legal Worlds Overlap: Human Rights, State and Non-State Law*. Geneva: ICHRP. Available at: www.ichrp.org/files/reports/50/135_report_en.pdf, accessed 3 February 2019.

International Crisis Group (2007) *Central African Republic Anatomy of a Phantom State*. Available at: https://www.crisisgroup.org/africa/central-africa/central-african-republic/central-african-republic-anatomy-phantom-state, accessed 13 February 2019.

International Disability Alliance (IDA) (2011) *Suggestions for disability-relevant questions to be included in the list of issues for Pre-sessional Working Group, CRC 60th Session*. Available at: https://tbinternet.ohchr.org/_layouts/treatybodyexternal/Download.aspx?symbolno=INT%2fCRC%2fNGO%2fCYP%2f60%2f8490&Lang=en, accessed 13 February 2019.

Institute on Statelessness and Inclusion (2014) *The World's Stateless*. Available at: www.institutesi.org/worldsstateless.pdf, accessed 16–8–2017.

Institute on Statelessness and Inclusion (2016) *Addressing the right to a nationality through the Convention on the Rights of the Child: a toolkit for civil society*. Available at: www.institutesi.org/CRC_Toolkit_Final.pdf, accessed 23 September 2018.

Institute on Statelessness and Inclusion (2017) *The World's Stateless Children*. Available at: www.institutesi.org/worldsstateless17.pdf, accessed 17–8–2017.

Jepma, I., Swart, B. & Vergeer, M. (2011) *Opstaan tegen het thuiszitten ("standing up against "thuiszitten")*. Sardes & Kohnstamm Instituut.

KidsRights Foundation (2017) *The KidsRights Index 2017*. Available at: https://kidsrights.org/sites/default/files/inline-files/The%20KidsRights%20Index%202017.pdf, accessed 27 June 2017.

Kinderrechtencollectief (2019) *Children's Rights in the Netherlands: Input to the list of issues of the UN Committee on the Rights of the Child, prepared by the Dutch NGO Coalition for Children's Rights*. Available at: https://tbinternet.ohchr.org/Treaties/CRC/Shared%20Documents/NLD/INT_CRC_NGO_NLD_35899_E.pdf, accessed 13 July 2020.

Kingdom of the Netherlands (2015) *Annexes 1–4 to the Response of the Kingdom of the Netherlands to the List of Issues (CRC/C/NLD/Q/4) in relation to the fourth periodic report submitted by the Netherlands under article 44 of the Convention on the Rights of the Child*. Available at: https://tbinternet.ohchr.org/Treaties/CRC/Shared%20Documents/NLD/INT_CRC_ARL_NLD_20334_E.docx, accessed 27 October 2018.

Kochenov, D. & Lindeboom, J. (2018) *QNI: Quality of Nationality Index*. Zürich: Ideos Publications Ltd.

KNAW, VSNU & NOW (2016) *Standard Evaluation Protocol 2015–2021: Protocol for Research Assessments in the Netherlands*. Available at: www.vsnu.nl/files/documenten/Domeinen/Onderzoek/SEP2015-2021.pdf, accessed 23 January 2019.

Knoope, P. & Buchanan-Clarke, S. (2017) *Central African Republic: a conflict misunderstood*. Capetown: The Institute for Justice and Reconciliation.

Kruseman, J., Hoekstra, L., Ooms, M. & Hesselman, M. (2016) *Joint Parallel Report to the Sixth Periodic Report of the Netherlands on the International Covenant on Economic, Social and Cultural Rights (E/C.12/NLD/6)*. Dutch section of the International Commission of Jurists (NJCM), on behalf of 21 NGOs & CSOs. Available at: https://tbinternet.ohchr.org/_layouts/treatybodyexternal/Download.aspx?symbolno=INT%2fCESCR%2fICO%2fNLD%2f25038&Lang=en, accessed 29 October 2018.

MINUSCA Human Rights Division (2016) *Special Report on Kaga-Bandoro Incidents: 12 to 17 October 2016*. Available at: https://minusca.unmissions.org/sites/default/files/minusca_report_kaga_bandoro_en.pdf, accessed 6 August 2017.

Mokkink, L.B., v.d. Lee, J.H., Grootenhuis, M.A., Offringa, M., v. Praag, B.M.S., Heymans, H.S.A. (2006) *Omvang en gevolgen van chronische aandoeningen bij kinderen ("size and consequences of chronic diseases for children")*. Available at https://www.zorgvoorhetziekekind.nl/media/files/Rapport_Mokkink_et_al.pdf.pdf, accessed 1 November 2018.

Mudge, L. (2017a) *Killing Without Consequence: War Crimes, Crimes Against Humanity and the Special Criminal Court in the Central African Republic*. Human Rights Watch, available at: https://www.hrw.org/report/2017/07/05/killing-without-consequence/war-crimes-crimes-against-humanity-and-special, accessed 6 August 2017;

National Research Council (1996) *National Science Education Standards*. Washington, D.C.: The National Academy Press.

Netherlands Institute for Human Rights (2019) *Report to the 84th session of the Committee on the Rights of the Child pre-sessional working group for adoption of the list of issues prior to reporting for the Kingdom of the Netherlands (5th and 6th report)*. Available at: https://tbinternet.ohchr.org/Treaties/CRC/Shared%20Documents/NLD/INT_CRC_IFN_NLD_36875_E.pdf, accessed 13 July 2020.

OCHA (2016d) *Aperçu des Besoins Humanitaires («Overview of Humanitarian Needs»).* Available at: https://www.humanitarianresponse.info/ system/files/documents/ files/rca_ocha_171123_hno_french.pdf, Accessed 2 April 2017.

Pancyprian Coordinating Committee for the Protection and Welfare of Children (PCCPWC) (2011) *Re: Implementation of the Convention on the Rights of the Child, Third and Fourth Periodic Reports of Cyprus (CRC/C/CYP/3–4), due 2008, submitted Aug.2009, to be discussed 2011).* Available at: https://tbinternet.ohchr.org/_layouts/treatybodyexternal/Download.aspx?symbolno=INT%2fCRC%2fNGO%2fCYP%2f60%2f8489&Lang=en, accessed 13 February 2019.

Platform Onderwijs2032 (2016) *Ons onderwijs2032: eindadvies ("our education2032: final advise").* Den Haag: Bureau Platform Onderwijs2032.

République Centrafricaine Education Cluster (2015) *Education Cluster Assessment on the State of Education in the Central African Republic: End of first semester – April 2015.* Available at: http://reliefweb.int/report/central-african-republic/education-cluster-assessment-state-education-central-african, accessed 20 June 2017.

Rodrigues, P.R. & Matelski, M. (2004) *Monitor racism & the extreme right: Roma and Sinti.* Amsterdam: Anne Frank House / Leiden University.

Sandberg, K. (2014) *25 years of the convention on the rights of the child: The genesis and spirit of the Convention on the Rights of the Child.* New York: United Nation's Children's Fund (UNICEF). Available at: https://www.unicef.org/crc/files/03_CRC_25_Years_Sandberg.pdf, accessed 2 February 2019.

Schenke, W., Heemskerk, I.M.C.C., Lockhorst, D., Bornhof, M. (2018) *Monitor Professionele ontwikkeling schoolleiders en bestuurders VO 2016–2017 ("Monitor professional development school leaders and directors, secondary education 2016–2017").* Amsterdam: Kohnstamm-Instituut.

Schoonheim, J. & Nieuwboer, J. (2015) *Het recht op inclusief onderwijs in de jurisprudentie* ("The right to inclusive education in case law"). In1school. Available at: https://www.in1school.nl/images/kennis-opinie/onderzoeken-in1school/Het%20Recht%20op%20Inclusief%20Onderwijs%20in%20de%20Jurisprudentie.pdf, accessed 12 February 2019.

Security Council Report (2020) *July 2020 Monthly Forecast: Cyprus.* Available at: https://www.securitycouncilreport.org/monthly-forecast/2020–07/cyprus-6.php, accessed 21 July 2020.

Seidler, Y., Weltevrede, A.M., Nieuwenhuys, M. & de Boom, J. (2015) *Eerste vervolgmeting naar de woon- en leefomstandigheden Roma en Sinti in Nederland ("First follow-up measure of the housing- and living circumstances of Roma and Sinti in the netherlands").* Rotterdam: Risbo BV / Erasmus Universiteit Rotterdam.

Sleeboom, I., Hermanns, J., Buysse, W. & Hilhorst, N. (2009) *Back to school: thuiszitters in de GGZ Kinderen en Jeugd Rivierduinen ("Back to school: thuiszitters in the GGZ [psychological health organization) children and youth Rivierduinen [north and middle of province "Zuid Holland"].* GGZ Kinderen en Jeugd Rivierduinen.

Stam, J. & Vreeburg- van der Laan, E.J.M. (2013) *Van leerplicht naar leerrecht ("from compulsory eduction to learning right").* Den Haag: De Kinderombudsman.

The Commonwealth (2016) *Global Youth Development Index and Report.* London: Commonwealth Secretariat. Available at: http://cmydiprod.uksouth.cloudapp.

azure.com/sites/default/files/2016-10/2016%20Global%20Youth%20Development%20Index%20and%20Report.pdf, accessed 27 June 2017.

The Netherlands Institute for Human Rights (2015a) *Submission for the 69th session of the Committee on the Rights of the Child concerning the 4th Periodic Report of the Kingdom of the Netherlands.* Available at https://tbinternet.ohchr.org/Treaties/CRC/Shared%20Documents/NLD/INT_CRC_NGO_NLD_20212_E.pdf, accessed 27 October 2018.

The Netherlands Institute for Human Rights (2015b) *Submission to the Eighty-seventh Session of the UN Committee on the Elimination of all forms of racial discrimination (CERD) on the Examination of the combined nineteenth to twenty-first Periodic Reports of the Netherlands.* Available at https://tbinternet.ohchr.org/Treaties/CERD/Shared%20Documents/NLD/INT_CERD_IFN_NLD_21037_E.pdf, accessed 28 October 2018.

Timmermans, R. (2016) *Onderwijs aan kinderen van woonwagenbewonders, Roma en Sinti: Monitor Primair Onderwijs (2014–2015).* KPC Groep. Available at: https://www.kpcgroep.nl/media/1337/monitor-owrs-rapport-2014–2015.pdf, accessed 12 November 2018.

Tsiartas, E., Kakotas, G., Georgiadis, N. (2015) *Έκθεση Επιτρόπου Διοικήσεως και Ανθρωπίνων Δικαιωμάτων αναφορικά με το χειρισμό, από το Τμήμα Αρχείου Πληθυσμού και Μετανάστευσης, αιτήσεων Τουρκοκυπρίων για απόκτηση κυπριακής υπηκοότητας* ("*Report of the Commissioner for Human Rights and Administration concerning the handling, by the Civil Registry and Immigration Department, of Turkish Cypriot applications for the acquisition of Cypriot citizenship*"). Available at: www.ombudsman.gov.cy/Ombudsman/ombudsman.nsf/All/D0AEEB68EDEEDC4EC2257F1C00241383/$file/2138_2009ka_25112015.doc?OpenElement, accessed 11 October 2018.

UNDP (2018) *What does it mean to leave no one behind?* Available at: www.undp.org/content/dam/undp/library/Sustainable%20Development/2030%20Agenda/Discussion_Paper_LNOB_EN_lres.pdf, accessed 13 February 2019.

UNESCO (2010) *World Data on Education 2010/11: République Centrafricaine.* Available at: www.ibe.unesco.org/fileadmin/user_upload/Publications/WDE/2010/pdf-versions/Central_African_Republic.pdf, accessed 20 June 2017.

UNESCO (2018) *Republique centrafricaine: Analyse du secteur de l'éducation.* Available at: https://unesdoc.unesco.org/ark:/48223/pf0000366412?posInSet=1&queryId=d47e49ee-494f-4413-8037-fa1d56afc054, accessed 15 July 2020.

UNHCR (2013) *Stateless Persons.* Available at: www.unhcr.org/protection/statelessness/546e01319/statistics-stateless-persons.html, accessed 17-8-2017.

UNHCR (2015) *I am here, I belong: the urgent need to end childhood statelessness.* Available at: https://www.unhcr.org/ibelong/wp-content/uploads/2015-10-StatelessReport_ENG16.pdf, accessed 13 February 2019.

UNICEF (2019a) *The state of the world's children 2019. Children, Food and Nutrition: Growing well in a changing world.* New York: UNICEF.

UNICEF (2019b) *Under-five mortality; September 2019.* Available at: https://data.unicef.org/topic/child-survival/under-five-mortality/, accessed 7 July 2020.

UNICEF (2019c) *Literacy: October 2019.* Available at: https://data.unicef.org/topic/education/literacy/, accessed 7 July 2020.

UNICEF (2019d) *Drinking water: June 2019.* Available at: https://data.unicef.org/topic/water-and-sanitation/drinking-water/, accessed 7 July 2020.

United Nations Development Program (UNDP) (2016) *Human Development Report 2016.* Available at: http://hdr.undp.org/sites/default/files/2016_human_development_report.pdf, accessed 12 February 2019.

United Nations General Assembly (2015) *Elimination of all forms of religious intolerance: Interim report of the Special Rapporteur on freedom of religion or belief.* A/70/286.

United Nations Peacekeeping Force in Cyprus (1975) *Report pursuant to Security Council resolution 370.* S/11789.

van Batenburg, Th.A., Dokter, N.S. & Mulder, B.F. (2006) *Leerplichtige leerlingen zonder onderwijs ("pupils subject to compulsory education without education").* GION: Gronings Instituut voor Onderozek van Onderwijs, Opvoeding en Ontwikkeling.

van der Ree, Y., van den Hurk, A & Timmermans, R. (2001) *Als niet kan wat moet, moet wat kan: handreiking ter bestrijding van het schoolverzuim onder woonwagen- en zigeunerkinderen ("If what is obligatory cannot be done, what can be done must be done: guidelines for combatting school absenteeism for caravan – and gypsy children").* 's-Hertogenbosch: KPC Groep.

van der Veen, C., de jonge, M.C., van Oorspronk, S. & Curie, K. (2011) *Roma en schoolverzuim: De situatie (waar, waarom en wat te doen) van schoolverzuim en – uitval bij Roma-meisjes in het voortgezet onderwijs in Nederland ("Roma and school absenteeism: The situation (where, why and what to do) of school absenteeism for Roma girls in secondary education in the Netherlands").* Utrecht: Trimbos-Instituut.

van Dorst, S. Th. (2011) *Onderwijsvormen en onderwijsvernieuwingen* ("*forms of education and renewals of education*"). Psychological Institute for Consultation, Education and Scientific Research. Available at: www.mdelfos.nl/2011%20Onderwijsvormen%20en%20-vernieuwingen.pdf, accessed 17 October 2018.

van Eekelen, J. (2010*) Thuiszitters, sneller terug naar school: Bevindingen dossieronderzoek thuiszitters 2010 (""thuiszitters", back to school more quickly: findings of file research thuiszitters 2010).* Arnhem: Ingrado.

Vanneste, Y. & Lanser, H. (2010) *Snel terug naar school is veel beter: landelijke handreiking voor een integrale aanpak van schoolziekteverzuim bij kinderen en jongeren* ("*Quickly back to school is much better: national guideline for a holistic approach of school absenteeism due to sickness of children and young people*"). Available at https://www.nji.nl/nl/Download-NJi/Publicatie-NJi/Handreiking_Schoolziekteverzuim.pdf, accessed 1 November 2018.

Verbeek, M., Knispel, A. & Nuijen, J. (2012) *GGZ in tabellen 2011.* Utrecht: Trimbos Instituut. Available at: https://www.trimbos.nl/docs/0dd9e8b1-4a0e-4a1b-91d2-03c2711886d8.pdf, accessed 12 February 2019.

Verhoef, J., Govers-Vreeburg, E.J.E. & Lubbersen, D.M.S. (2011) *Hoera! Ik ga weer naar school: Leerlingen met psychische of gedragsproblemen die thuiszitten ("Hurrah! I'm going to school again: Pupils with psychological or behavior problems who are out of school").* De Nationale Ombudsman.

Volman, M., Raban, A., Heemskerk, I., Ledoux, G., Kuiper, E. (2018) *Toekomstgericht onderwijs. Doelen en werkwijzen van innovatieve VO-scholen ("Future-oriented education. Goals and methods of innovative secondary education schools").* Amsterdam: Kohnstamm-Instituut.

Waddington, L. & Toepke, C. (2015) *Moving towards inclusive education as a human right.* In1school. Available at: www.in1school.nl/images/actueel/agenda/Legal_Opinion_Moving_Towards_Inclusive_Education.pdf, accessed 12 February 2019.

Walraven, M., van Eck, P., Damstra, G. (2017) *Past de ondersteuningsstructuur van het onderwijs aan zieke leerlingen? ("does the support structure of education for ill children fit?").* Oberon. Available at: https://www.rijksoverheid.nl/binaries/rijksoverheid/documenten/rapporten/2017/07/01/rapportage-ondersteuningsstructuur-onderwijs-zieke-leerlingen/Rapportage+Ondersteuningsstructuur+onderwijs+zieke+leerlingen.PDF, accessed 11 November 2018.

World Bank Group (2012) *Understanding access to justice and conflict resolution at the local level in the Central African Republic (CAR).* Available at http://documents.worldbank.org/curated/en/970091468192841525/text/782640WP0CAR0A0Box0377336B00PUBLIC0.txt, accessed 13 February 2019.

World Bank Group (2017) *The Central African Republic: National Recovery and Peacebuilding Plan 2017–21.* Available at: https://eeas.europa.eu/sites/eeas/files/car_main_report-a4-english-web.pdf, accessed 20 June 2017.

World Food Program (2015) *The Central African Republic: Going beyond providing food as part of our school meal programme.* Available at: https://www.wfp.org/stories/car-school-meals-programmes-go-beyondproviding-food, accessed 14 April 2017.

World Food Program (2016) *Enquête Nationale sur la Sécurité Alimentaire: République Centrafricaine, Décembre 2016.* Rome: ICASEES et le PAM. Available at: http://documents.wfp.org/stellent/groups/public/documents/ena/wfp290682.pdffgroupe, accessed 5 April 2017.

World Health Organization (2016) *Statistics 2016.* Available at: www.who.int/gho/publications/world_health_statistics/2016/en/, accessed 14 April 2017.

STATUTES AND LEGAL DOCUMENTS

INTERNATIONAL ORGANIZATIONS

United Nations

1948 Universal Declaration of Human Rights (UDHR)
1954 Convention relating to the status of stateless persons
1960 UN Security Council Resolution 155 S/4469
1960 Treaty of Guarantee Signed at Nicosia on 16 August 1960
1961 Convention on the reduction of statelessness
1964 UN Security Council Resolution 186 S/5575
1966 International Covenant on Economic, Social and Cultural Rights (ICESCR)
1966 International Covenant on Civil and Political Rights (ICCPR)
1969 International Convention on the Elimination of All Forms of Racial Discrimination (ICERD)
1974 UN Security Council Resolution 353
1974 UN Security Council Resolution 360

1974 UN General Assembly resolution 3236
1975 UN Security Council Resolution 367
1979 Convention on the Elimination of All Forms of Discrimination against Women (CEADW)
1983 United Nations Security Council Resolution 541 S/RES/451
1984 Convention against Torture and Other Cruel, Inhuman or Degrading Treatment or Punishment (Convention against Torture)
1984 United Nations Security Council Resolution 550
1989 Convention on the Rights of the Child (CRC)
1990 International Convention on the Protection of Rights of All Migrant Workers and Their Families
2005 United Nation Convention against Corruption (UNCAC)
2007 Convention on the Rights of Persons with Disabilities (CRPD)
International Court of Justice (ICJ) (**1971**) *Legal Consequences for States of the Continued Presence of South Africa in Namibia (South West Africa) notwithstanding Security Council Resolution 276 (1970), Advisory Opinion.*
UN Human Rights Committee (**1993**) *CCPR General Comment No. 22: Article 18 (Freedom of Thought, Conscience or Religion)*. CCPR/C/21/Rev.1/Add.4.
Committee on Economic, Social and Cultural Rights (**1994**). *General Comment No. 5: Persons with Disabilities.* E/1995/22.
Committee on the Rights of the Child (**1996**) *Consideration of reports submitted by States parties under article 44 of the Convention: Concluding observations: Cyprus.* CRC/C/15/Add.59.
United Nations (**1996**) *Core document forming part of the reports of States Parties: Netherlands (European part of the Kingdom)* HRI/CORE/1/Add.66.
Committee on Economic, Social and Cultural Rights (**1999**). *General Comment No. 13: The Right to Education.* E/C.12/1999/10.
Committee on the Elimination of All Forms of Racial Discrimination (**2000**) *General Recommendation XXVII on Discrimination Against Roma.* A/55/18, annex V.
Committee on the Rights of the Child (**2001**) *Consideration of reports submitted by States parties under article 44 of the Convention: Concluding observations: Turkey.* CRC/C/15/Add.152.
United Nations (**2001**) *Core document forming part of the reports of States Parties: Republic of Turkey.* HRI/CORE/1/Add.116.
Committee on the Elimination of All Forms of Racial Discrimination (**2002**) *General Recommendation XXX on Discrimination Against Non Citizens.* Available at: https://www.refworld.org/docid/45139e084.html, accessed 13 February 2019.
Committee on the Rights of the Child (**2003a**) *Consideration of reports submitted by States parties under article 44 of the Convention: Concluding observations: Cyprus.* CRC/C/15/Add.205.
Committee of the Rights of the Child (**2003b**) *General comment no. 4 on adolescent health and development in the context of the Convention on the Rights of the Child.* CRC/CG/2003/4.
Committee on the Rights of the Child (**2007**) *General Comment No. 9 (2006) The rights of children with disabilities.* CRC/C/GC/9.

United Nations General Assembly (**2009**) *Human rights and arbitrary deprivation of nationality: Report of the Secretary-General.* A/HRC/13/34.

Committee on Economic, Social and Cultural Rights (2011) *Consideration of reports submitted by States parties under articles 16 and 17 of the Covenant: Concluding observations of the Committee on Economic, Social and Cultural Rights: Turkey.* E/C.12/TUR/CO/1.

Committee on the Rights of the Child (**2012a**) *Consideration of reports submitted by States parties under article 44 of the Convention: Concluding observations: Cyprus.* CRC/C/CYP/CO/3–4.

Committee on the Rights of the Child (**2012b**) *Consideration of reports submitted by States parties under article 44 of the Convention: Concluding observations: Turkey.* CRC/C/TUR/CO/2–3.

Human Rights Committee (**2012**) *Concluding observations on the initial report of Turkey adopted by the Committee at its 106th session (15 October – 2 November 2012).* CCPR/C/TUR/CO/1.

Committee on the Elimination of All Forms of Racial Discrimination (CERD) (**2013**) *Consideration of reports submitted by States parties under article 9 of the Convention, Nineteenth to twenty-first periodic reports of States parties due in 2013: Netherlands.* CERD/C/NLD/19–21.

Committee on the Rights of the Child (**2014a**) *Consideration of Reports submitted by States parties under article 44 of the Convention, Fourth periodic reports of States Parties due in 2012: The Netherlands.* CRC/C/NLD/4.

Committee on the Rights of the Child (**2014b**) *List of Issues.* CRC/C/NLD/Q/4.

United Nations (2014) *Common core document forming part of the reports of States parties: Cyprus.* HRI/CORE/CYP/2014 (Earlier versions cited: HRI/CORE/1/Add.28/Rev., HRI/CORE/CYP/2007, HRI/CORE/CYP/2009, HRI/CORE/CYP/2011, HRI/CORE/CYP/2012).

Committee on the Elimination of All Forms of Racial Discrimination (CERD) (2015a) *List of themes in relation to the combined nineteenth to twenty-first periodic reports of the Netherlands (CERD/C/NLD/19–21).* CERD/C/NLD/Q/19–21. Available at: https://documents-dds-ny.un.org/doc/UNDOC/GEN/G15/126/08/PDF/G1512608.pdf?OpenElement, accessed 28 October 2018.

Committee on the Elimination of All Forms of Racial Discrimination (CERD) (2015b) *Consideration of reports, comments and information submitted by States parties under article 9 of the Convention (continued) Combined nineteenth to twenty-first periodic reports of the Netherlands.* CERD/C/SR.2375. Available at https://documents-dds-ny.un.org/doc/UNDOC/GEN/G15/186/69/PDF/G1518669.pdf?OpenElement, accessed 28 October 2018.

Committee on the Elimination of All Forms of Racial Discrimination (CERD) (2015c) *Consideration of reports, comments and information submitted by States parties under article 9 of the Convention (continued) Combined nineteenth to twenty-first periodic reports of the Netherlands (continued).* CERD/C/SR.2376. Available at https://documents-dds-ny.un.org/doc/UNDOC/GEN/G15/186/70/PDF/G1518670.pdf?OpenElement, accessed 28 October 2018.

Committee on the Elimination of All Forms of Racial Discrimination (CERD) (2015d) *Concluding observations on the combined nineteenth to twenty-first periodic reports of the Netherlands.*

Committee on the Rights of the Child (2015a) *Summary record of the 2003rd (Chamber A) meeting.* CRC/C/SR.2003. Available at: https://tbinternet.ohchr.org/_layouts/treatybodyexternal/Download.aspx?symbolno=CRC%2fC%2fSR.2003&Lang=en, accessed 27 October 2018.

Committee on the Rights of the Child (2015b) *Summary record of the 2003rd (Chamber A) meeting.* CRC/C/SR.2005. Available at: https://tbinternet.ohchr.org/_layouts/treatybodyexternal/Download.aspx?symbolno=CRC%2fC%2fSR.2005&Lang=en, accessed 27 October 2018.

Committee on the Rights of the Child (**2015c**) *Concluding observations on the fourth periodic report of the Netherlands.* CRC/C/NLD/CO/4.

Human Rights Committee (**2015**) *Concluding observations on the fourth periodic report of Cyprus.* CCPR/C/CYP/CO/4.

United Nations General Assembly (**2015**) *Impact of the arbitrary deprivation of nationality on the enjoyment of the rights of children concerned, and existing laws and practices on accessibility for children to acquire nationality, inter alia, of the country in which they are born, if they otherwise would be stateless: report of the Secretary-General.* A/HRC/31/29.

Committee on the Protection of the Rights of All Migrant Workers and Members of Their Families (**2016**) *Concluding observations on the initial report of Turkey.* CMW/C/TUR/CO/1.

Committee on Economic, Social and Cultural Rights (CESCR) (**2016a**) *Consideration of reports submitted by States parties under articles 16 and 17 of the International Covenant on Economic, Social and Cultural Right. Sixth periodic reports of States parties due in 2015: the Netherlands.* E/C.12/NLD6.

Committee on Economic, Social and Cultural Rights (CESCR) (**2016b**) *List of issues in relation to the sixth periodic report of the Kingdom of the Netherlands.* E/C.12/NLD/Q/6.

Committee on the Elimination of Racial Discrimination (**2016**) *Concluding observations on the combined fourth to sixth periodic reports of Turkey.* CERD/C/TUR/CO/4–6.

Committee on the Rights of Persons with Disabilities (**2016**) *General Comment No. 4 (2016) on the right to inclusive education.* CRPD/C/GC/4.

Committee on the Rights of the Child (**2016a**) *Consideration of reports submitted by States parties in application of article 44 of the Convention: Second periodic reports by States parties due in 1999: Central African Republic.* CRC/C/CAF/2.

Committee on the Rights of the Child (**2016b**) *List of issues in relation to the second periodic report of the Central African Republic. Addendum: Replies of the Central African Republic to the list of issues.* CRC/C/CAF/Q/2.

Committee on the Rights of the Child (**2016c**) *List of issues in relation to the second periodic report of the Central African Republic.* CRC/C/CAF/Q/2/Add.1.

Committee on Economic, Social and Cultural Rights (CESCR) (**2017a**) *List of issues in relation to the sixth periodic report of the Kingdom of the Netherlands, addendum: Replies of the Netherlands to the list of issues.* E/C.12/NLD/Q/6/Add.1.

Committee on Economic, Social and Cultural Rights (**2017b**) *Consideration of reports submitted by States parties under articles 16 and 17 of the International Covenant on Economic, Social and Cultural Rights: Initial report of States parties due in 1990 – Central African Republic.* E/C.12/CAF/1.

Committee on the Rights of the Child (**2017**) *Concluding observations on the second periodic report of the Central African Republic.* CRC/C/CAF/CO/2.

Human Rights Council (**2017**) *National report submitted in accordance with paragraph 5 of the annex to Human Rights Council resolution 16/21: Netherlands.* A/HRC/WG.6/27/NLD/1.

The Netherlands (**2017**) *Recommendation 115.173 to Czechia.* Available at: https://upr-info-database.uwazi.io/en/entity/cgnkc5axnz, accessed 13 July 2020.

Committee on Economic, Social and Cultural Rights (**2018**) Concluding observations concerning the initial report of the Central African Republic. E/C.12/CAF/CO/1.

Committee on the Elimination of Discrimination against Women (**2018**) List of issues and questions in relation to the eight periodic report of Cyprus: Addendum – Replies of Cyprus. CEDAW/C/CYP/Q/8/Add.1

The Netherlands (**2018**) *Recommendation 114.195 to Romania.* Available at: https://upr-info-database.uwazi.io/en/entity/tizp2nm3gy, accessed 13 July 2020.

Human Rights Committee (**2018**) *Concluding observations on the fourth periodic report of Cyprus: Addendum: Information received from Cyprus on follow-up to the concluding observations.* CCPR/C/CYP/CO/4/Add.1.

Human Rights Council (**2018a**) *National report submitted in accordance with paragraph 5 of the annex to Human Rights Council resolution 16/21.* A/HRC/WG.6/32/CYP/1.

Human Rights Council (**2018b**) *Compilation on Cyprus.* A/HRC/WG.6/32/CYP/2.

United Nations Security Council (**2018**) "Progress towards a settlement in Cyprus: Report of the Secretary-General". S/2018/610.

Committee on the Rights of the Child (**2019**) *List of issues prior to submission of the combined fifth and sixth periodic reports of the Netherlands*". CRC/C/NLD/QPR/5–6.

Human Rights Council (**2019a**) *Report of the Working Group on the Universal Periodic Review: Cyprus.* A/HRC/41/15.

Human Rights Council (**2019b**) *Report of the Report of the Working Group on the Universal Periodic Review: Cyprus – Addendum. Views on conclusions and/or recommendations, voluntary commitments and replies presented by the State under review.* A/HRC//41/15/Add.1.

Human Rights Council (**2019c**) *National report submitted in accordance with paragraph 5 of the annex to Human Rights Council resolution 16/21: Turkey.* A/HRC/WG.6/35/Tur.1.

Human Rights Council (**2019d**) *Summary of Statekholders' submissions on Turkey.* A/HRC/WG.6/TUR/3.

African Union

1981 African Charter on Human and People's Rights (Banjul Charter)

2009 African Union Convention for the Protection and Assistance of Internally Displaced Persons in Africa (Kampala Convention)

Council of Europe

1950 European Convention on Human Rights (ECHR)
1963 Protocol No. 4 to the Convention for the Protection of Human Rights and Fundamental Freedoms. European Treaty Series – No. 5. 16.IX.1963.
1992 European Charter for Regional or Minority Languages. European Treaty Series – No. 148. 5.XI.1992.
1995 Framework Convention for the Protection of National Minorities. European Treaty Series – No. 157. 1.II.1995.
1996 European Social Charter (Revised). European Treaty Series – No. 163. 03.V.1996.
2000 European Convention on Nationality. European Treaty Series – No. 166. 6.XI.1997.
2000 Protocol No. 12 to the Convention for the Protection of Human Rights and Fundamental Freedoms. European Treaty Series – No. 177. 4.XI.2000.
Council of Europe (1998) *Reservations and Declarations for Treaty No.148 – European Charter for Regional or Minority Languages: Declarations contained in a Note Verbale handed over by the Permanent Representative of the Netherlands at the time of deposit of the instrument of acceptance, on 2 May 1996 – Or. Engl.*
Council of Europe (2000) Recommendation No R (2000) 4 of the Committee of Ministers to member states on the education of Roma/Gypsy children in Europe
Council of Europe (2009) Recommendation CM/Rec(2009)4 of the Committee of Ministers to member states on the education of Roma and Travellers in Europe.
Council of Europe (2012) Recommendation CM/Rec(2012)13 of the Committee of Ministers to member States on ensuring quality education.

European Union

2000 Charter of the fundamental rights of the European Union (Charter). 2000/C 364/01, 18 December 2000.
2003 Treaty of Accession – Act concerning the conditions of accession of the Czech Republic, the Republic of Estonia, the Republic of Cyprus, the Republic of Latvia, the Republic of Lithuania, the Republic of Hungary, the Republic of Malta, the Republic of Poland, the Republic of Slovenia and the Slovak Republic and the adjustments to the Treaties on which the European Union is founded. 12003T/PRO/10.
2004 European Union Council Regulation 866/2004 ('Green Line Regulation'), 29 April 2004.
2006 Council Regulation (EC) No 389/2006 of 27 February 2006 establishing an instrument of financial support for encouraging the economic development of the Turkish Cypriot community and amending Council Regulation (EC) No 2667/2000 on the European Agency for Reconstruction.

STATE LAW

Central African Republic

1997 Law on education (Loi no. 97.014 portant orientation de l'éducation)

2010 Penal law (Loi no. 10.001 portant Code pénal centrafricain)

2015 Constitution (Constitution de la République Centrafricaine)

2016 Decision on fixation of registration fees for Basic 1, 2, General Secondary education and Technical education and withdrawal of diplomas (Decision: Portant Fixation des Frais d'Inscription au Fondamental 1, 2, Secondaire General et Technique et du Retrait des Diplomes)

Germany

1949 Basic Law for the Federal Republic of Germany

1953 Gesetz über die Angelegenheiten der Vertriebenen und Flüchtelinge ("*Law on the Affairs of the Expelled and the Refugees*")

Republic of Cyprus

1960 Constitution of the Republic of Cyprus

1967/2000 Republic of Cyprus Citizenship Law

2002/2017 Republic of Cyprus Civil Registry Law of 2002 (168(I)/ 2017)

2007 Decision of the Council of Ministers: Criteria of the Cabinet for the registration of persons having a Cypriot parent and a foreign parent who has entered or stayed illegally in Cyprus, 14.02.2007, No. Decision 65.067.

The Netherlands

1848 Constitution (*Grondwet*)

1963 Secondary Education Act (SEA) (*Wet op het Voortgezet Onderwijs*)

1969 Compulsory Education Act (CEA) (*Leerplichtwet)*

1981 Primary Education Act (PEA) (*Wet op het primair onderwijs)*

1982 Law on the Expertise Centers (LEC) (*Wet op de expertise centra*)

1985 Order on nomadic population under PEA (ONPPEA) (*Besluit trekkende bevolking WPO)*

1985 Order on Exemption CEA Nomadic Population (OECEANP) (*Besluit vrijstelling leerplicht trekkende bevolking*)

1985 Decision financing PEA (*Besluit financiering WPO)*

1985 Decision financing SEA (*Bekostigingsbesluit WVO*)

1992 General Administrative Law Act (*Algemene Wet Bestuursrecht*)

1993 Decision on the organization of the SEA (DOSEA) (*Inrichtingsbesluit W.V.O*)

2003 Dutch Opium Law (*Opiumwet*)

2006 Decision core aims first three years of secondary education (*Besluit kerndoelen onderbouw VO*)

2009 Regulation learning plus arrangements secondary education (2009 *Regeling leerplusarrangementen VO*)

2012 Appropriate Education Act (*Wet van 11 Oktober 2012 tot wijziging van enkele onderwijswetten in verband met een herziening van de organisatie en financiering van de ondersteuning van leerlingen in het basisonderwijs, speciaal en voortgezet speciaal onderwijs, voortgezet onderwijs en beroepsonderwijs (Wet Passend Onderwijs)*

2014 Decision experiments continuous educational line VMBO-MBO 2014–2022 (*Besluit experimenten doorlopende leerlijnen vmbo-mbo 2014–2022*)

2014 Exam decision Primary Education (*2014 toetsbesluit PO)*

2015 Civil Code Book 1: Law of Persons and Family Law (*Burgerlijk Wetboek 1: Personen- en Familierecht*)

2016 Civil Code Book 7: Particular Contracts (*Burgerlijk Wetboek 7: Bijzondere Overeenkomsten)*

2020 Law more space for new schools (*Wet meer ruimte voor nieuwe scholen*: *Wet van 1 juli 2020 tot wijziging van de Wet op het primair onderwijs, de Wet op het voortgezet onderwijs, de Wet op de expertisecentra, de Wet op het onderwijstoezicht en enkele andere wetten in verband met actualisering van de deugdelijkheidseisen, het daarmee samenhangende onderwijstoezicht en de vermindering van administratieve verplichtingen in het funderend onderwijs, alsmede reparatie van wetstechnische gebreken (acutalisering deugdelijkheidseisen funderend onderwijs))*

Turkey

2009 Turkish Citizenship Law, Law No: 5901

Turkish Republic of Northern Cyprus

1962/2014 TRNC Criminal Law

1982/2016 TRNC Foreigners and Immigration Act

1983 Constitution of the Turkish Republic of Northern Cyprus

1986 TRNC Law on National Education No 17/1986

1993/2005 Turkish Republic of Northern Cyprus Citizenship Law No 52/1993/2005

1996 TRNC Law Concerning the Confirmation of the Convention on the Rights of the Child, No. 6/1996

2006 TRNC Law on Work Permits for Foreigners No 63/2006

2006/2012 TRNC Regulation of Foreigner's Work Permits.

United States of America

Fisa Amendments Act of 2008: Foreign Intelligence Surveillance Act of 1978 Amendments Act of 2008 or FISA Amendments Act of 2008. Public Law No: 110–261 (07/10/2008).

COURT CASES

European Court of Human Rights

Case AR. and L.R. v. Switzerland (2017). *Application No. 22338/15,* 19 December 2017.
Case Ali v. The United Kingdom (2011) *Application No. 40385/06,* 11 January 2011.
Case Appel-Irrgang and others v. Germany (2009) *Application No. 45216/07,* 6 October 2009.
Case Cyprus v. Turkey (1999) *Application No. 25781/94,* 4 June 2011.
Case Cyprus v. Turkey (2014) *Application No. 25781/94: Judgment (just satisfaction),* 12 May 2014.
Case D.H. and others v. The Czech Republic (2006) *Application No. 57325/00,* 7 February 2006.
Case Dahlberg and Dahlberg v. Sweden (1994) *Application No. 18511/91,* 2 March 1994.
Case Efstratiou v. Greece (1996) *Application No. 24095/95,* 18 December 1996.
Case Güzelyurtlu and others v. Cyprus and Turkey (2017) *Application No. 36925/07,* 4 April 2017.
Case Hasan and Eylem Zengin v. Turkey (2007) *Application No. 1448/04,* 9 October 2007.
Case Jimenez Alonzo et Jimenez Merino v. Spain (2000) *Application No. 51188/99,* 25 May 2000.
Case Joannou v. Turkey (2017) *Application No. 53240/14,* 12 December 2017.
Case Keller v. Germany (1998) *Application No. 36283/97,* 4 March 1998.
Case Klerks against the Netherlands (1995). *Application No. 25212/94,* 4 July 1995.
Case Konrad v. Germany (2006) *Application No. 25504/03,* 11 September 2006.
Case Kyriacou Tsiakkourmas and other v. Turkey (2015) *Application No. 13320/02,* 2 June 2015.
Case Lautsi and others v. Italy (2011) *Application No. 30814/06,* 18 March 2011.
Case Lavida and others v. Greece (2013) *Application No. 7973/10,* 28 May 2013.
Case Loizidou v. Turkey (1995) *Application No. 15318/89,* 18 December 1996.
Case Mansur Yalçin and others v. Turkey (2014). *Application No. 21163/11,* 16 September 2014.
Case Memlika v. Greece (2015) Application No. 37991/12, 6 October 2015.
Case Olymbiou v. Turkey (2009) *Application No. 16091/90,* 27 October 2009.
Case S.P. v. The United Kingdom (1997) *Application No. 28915/95,* 7 February 2006.
Case Sampani and others v. Greece (2012) *Application No. 59608/09,* 11 December 2012.
Case Valsamis v. Greece (1996) *Application No. 21787/93,* 18 December 1996.
Case Wunderlich v. Germany (2019) *Application No. 18925/15,* 10 January 2019.
Case X. v. the Netherlands (1968) *Application No. 2648/65,* 6 February 1968.

Germany

Teso-Beschluß GDR-Citizenship (1987). BVerfGE 77, 137 2 BvR 373/83. Translation available at: https://law.utexas.edu/transnational/foreign-law-translations/german/case.php?id=569, accessed 13 February 2019.

Republic of Cyprus

Case Hancer v. Republic of Cyprus Ministry of Interior (2020) *Case no. 625/2015, ECLI: CY: DD: 2020: 292.* Available at: www.cylaw.org/cgi-bin/open.pl?file=/administrative/2020/202006-625-15.html, accessed 24 July 2020.

OTHER

Council of Europe (1972) Declaration contained in a letter from the Permanent Representative of Cyprus, dated 3 March 1972, registered at the Secretariat General on 3 March 1972 "Interpretation of the terms: "nationals" and "territory"". Available at https://www.coe.int/en/web/conventions/full-list/-/conventions/treaty/013/declarations?p_auth=1eTxshcv&_coeconventions_WAR_coeconventionsportlet_enVigueur=false&_coeconventions_WAR_coeconventionsportlet_searchBy=state&_coeconventions_WAR_coeconventionsportlet_codePays=CYP&_coeconventions_WAR_coeconventionsportlet_codeNature=10, accessed 14 January 2019.

Council of Europe (2017) *The Council of Europe's Brief Overview of relevant case-law of the Euoprean Court of Human Rights in light of ongoing work on Draft Law of Ukraine #3593-D1 "On the temporarily occupied territory".* Available at: https://rm.coe.int/native/168070248d, accessed 13 February 2019.

Deputy Prime Ministry and Ministry of Foreign Affairs (n.d.(a)) *Visa Regulations.* Available at: http://mfa.gov.ct.tr/consular-info/visa-regulations/, accessed 23 September 2018.

Deputy Prime Ministry and Ministry of Foreign Affairs (n.d.(b)) *Relations with Turkey.* Available at: http://mfa.gov.ct.tr/foreign-policy/relations-with-turkey/, accessed 14 October 2018.

Eerste Kamer (1993–1994) *Wijziging van de Leerplichtwet 1969 en enkele andere wetten ("Amendments of the Law on the Duty to Study 1969 and some other laws").* Kamerstuk 22900, Ondernummer 64.

European Union (n.d.) *About the EU: Cyprus.* Available at: https://europa.eu/european-union/about-eu/countries/member-countries/cyprus_en, accessed 2 October 2018.

Gemeente Moerdijk (2011) *Richtlijn dwangsommen.* Available at: https://decentrale.regelgeving.overheid.nl/cvdr/XHTMLoutput/Actueel/Moerdijk/CVDR107644.html, accessed 20 November 2018.

Minister voor basis- en voortgezet onderwijs en media (2019) *Brief van de minister voor basis- en voortgezet onderwijs en media, 27 September 2019.* Available at: https://www.eerstekamer.nl/behandeling/20190927/brief_regering_reactie_op/document3/f=/vl2jk7oocrnt.pdf, accessed 12 July 2020.

Ministry of Education, Culture and Science (n.d.) *Onderwijs in cijfers: Ontwikkeling van aantal deelnemers ("Education in numbers: development of the number of participants").* Available at https://www.onderwijsincijfers.nl/kengetallen/onderwijs-algemeen/leerlingen-en-studenten/aantallen-ontwikkeling-van-het-aantal-deelnemers, accessed 26 October 2018.

Ministry of Education, Culture and Science (2014) "beslissing op bezwaar", brief aan mr. K.J. Slump dd. 4 April 2014. Available at: https://www.adviesonderwijsrecht.nl/inc/uploads/2013/03/140404-Besluit-minOCW-inzake-WOB-Miep-Ziek.pdf, accessed 20 November 2018.

Ministry of Education, Culture and Science (2015a) "Begrippenkader schoolverzuim" (*Conceptual framework school absenteeism*"). Available at https://www.rijksoverheid.nl/binaries/rijksoverheid/documenten/brochures/2018/07/26/begrippenkader-schoolverzuim/Begrippenkader+schoolverzuim.pdf, accessed 1 November 2018.

Ministry of Education, Culture and Science (2015b) "Kamerbrief met reactie op onderzoeken passend onderwijs" (*letter to the second chamber with reaction to researches appropriate education*"). Available at https://www.rijksoverheid.nl/onderwerpen/passend-onderwijs/documenten/kamerstukken/2015/09/25/kamerbrief-met-reactie-op-onderzoeken-passend-onderwijs, accessed 12 November 2018.

Ministry of Education, Culture and Science (2016) "Kamerbrief over cijfers leerplicht en aanpak thuiszitters" ("*Parliamentary letter on numbers compulsory education and approach* thuiszitters"). Reference 876853. Available at https://www.rijksoverheid.nl/binaries/rijksoverheid/documenten/kamerstukken/2016/02/03/kamerbrief-over-cijfers-leerplicht-en-aanpak-thuiszitters/kamerbrief-over-cijfers-leerplicht-en-aanpak-thuiszitters.pdf, accessed 1 November 2018.

Ministry of Education, Culture and Science (2018) "Cijfers schoolverzuim en vrijstellingen funderend onderwijs" ("*Numbers school absence and exemptions founding education*"). Kamerbrief 19 February 2018. Reference no. 1285336.

PORaad, VORaad, VNG, Ministerie van Ondewijs, Cultuur en Wetenschap, Ministerie van Volksgezondheid, Welzijn en Sport & Ministerie van Veiligheid en Justitie (2016) "Thuiszitterspact". Available at: https://www.rijksoverheid.nl/documenten/publicaties/2016/06/13/thuiszitterspact, accessed 13 February 2019.

Regionaal thuiszitterspact West-Brabant (2017) Available at: https://www.rsvbreda.nl/images/Regionaal_thuiszitterspact_West-Brabant.pdf, accessed 13 February 2019.

Regionaal thuiszitterspact Noord-Kennemerland (2017). Available at: https://www.ppo-nk.nl/thoughts/743, accessed 13 February 2019.

Strategie Cluster Education (2019) "Republique Centrafricaine 2019–2021". Available at: https://www.humanitarianresponse.info/sites/www.humanitarianresponse.info/files/documents/files/strategie_eie_cluster_education_rca.pdf, accessed 14 July 2020.

Thuiszittersaanpak regio Lekstroom (2017) Available at: www.samenwerkingsverband-zuid-utrecht.nl/Nieuws/ArtMID/499/ArticleID/29/Thuiszittersaanpak-regio-Lekstroom, accessed 13 February 2019.

Tweede Kamer (1967) *Leerplichtwet 1968: Memorie van Toelichting Nr. 3*. Kamerstuk 9039, ondernummer 3.

Tweede Kamer (2013) *Aahangsel der handelingen: Vragen van de leden Jasper van Dijk en Smaling (beiden SP) aan de staatssecretaris van Onderwijs, Cultuur en Wetenschap over* thuisonderwijs via geheime constructies (ingezonden 12 juni 2013). Antwoord van Staatssecretaris Dekker. Nr. 2750. Available at: https://zoek.officielebekendmakingen.nl/ah-tk-20122013–2750.html, accessed 12 November 2018.

Tweede Kamer (2016a) *Vragen van het lid Ypma (PvdA) aan de Staatssecretaris van Onderwijs, Cultuur en Wetenschap over het onderzoek "(W)elk kind heeft recht op onderwijs? Een onderzoek naar de betekenis van recht op onderwijs voor kinderen in Nederland, specifiek gericht op thuisonderwijs, thuiszitters en Roma kinderen" (ingezonden 27 mei 2016).* 2016Z10407.

Tweede Kamer (2016b) *Vragen van het lid **Ypma** (PvdA) aan de Staatssecretaris van Onderwijs, Cultuur en Wetenschap over het onderzoek "(W)elk kind heeft recht op onderwijs? Een onderzoek naar de betekenis van recht op onderwijs voor kinderen in Nederland, specifiek gericht op thuisonderwijs, thuiszitters en Roma kinderen" (ingezonden 27 mei 2016). Antwoord van Staatssecretaris **Dekker** (Onderwijs, Cultuur en Wetenschap) (ontvangen 17 juni 2016).* 2863.

Tweede Kamer (2018) *Cijfers Schoolverzuim n vrijstellingen funderend onderwijs.* 26695 Nr. 121. Available at: https://www.tweedekamer.nl/kamerstukken/brieven_regering/detail?id=2018Z02829&did=2018D05755, accessed 13 February 2019.

Tweede Kamer (2019a) *Meer ruimte voor nieuwe scholen: behandeling wetsvoorstel, 12 September 2019.* Available at: https://www.eerstekamer.nl/behandeling/20190912/behandeling_meer_ruimte_voor/document3/f=/vl2fkatoyzzu.pdf, accessed 13 July 2020.

Tweede Kamer (2019b) *Stemming Meer ruimte voor nieuwe scholen.* Available at: https://www.eerstekamer.nl/behandeling/20191001/stemming_meer_ruimte_voor_nieuwe/document3/f=/vl2ylnstugo8.pdf, accessed 12 July 2020.

Tweede Kamer (2019c) *Brief van de ministers voor basis- en voortgezet onderwijs en media, van volksgezondheid, welzijn en sport en voor rechtsbescherming.* Available at: https://www.tweedekamer.nl/downloads/document?id=54636db1-a870-42e3-892e-0e5dc1d967d8&title=Stand%20van%20zaken%20thuiszitters.pdf, accessed 13 July 2020.

Tweede Kamer (2020a) *Brief van de ministers voor basis- en voortgezet onderwijs en media, van volksgezondheid, welzijn en sport en voor rechtsbescherming: Nr. 130.* Available at: https://www.tweedekamer.nl/downloads/document?id=ada82b88-9e76-434a-9969-f605514a6488&title=Thuiszitters%20in%20het%20funderend%20onderwijs%20.pdf, accessed 13 July 2020.

Tweede Kamer (2020b) *Verslag van Algemeen Overleg: Nr. 359.* Available at: https://www.tweedekamer.nl/downloads/document?id=d02a9494-d78a-4021-8b8c-b945b689283a&title=Verslag%20van%20een%20algemeen%20overleg%2C%20gehouden%20op%205%20februari%202020%2C%20over%20Onderwijs%20en%20Zorg.pdf, accessed 13 July 2020.

Wet meer ruimte voor nieuwe scholen (2019) *Nr. 16: Amandement van dhr. Kwint.*

SUMMARY

Athough all children are supposed to have rights, and children's rights are considered universal with the 1989 UN Convention on the Rights of the Child being the most ratified human rights convention to date, children's rights are grossly violated on a daily basis and on a global scale. This thesis aims to contribute to understanding why these rights violations happen and what can be done to improve the protection of children's rights. It does so by incorporating a child's perspective in the study of legal norms related to the realization/violation of children's rights.

For children, law is not necessarily limited to what is stated in state legal codes, of which they are generally unaware, rather it is what their parents or their teachers tell them. When looking at law through children's eyes, the rules of the household, the classroom, and other legal orders which they are members of, can in many instances be classified as law. This law, that we find when looking at law through children's eyes, has to be recognized as part of a complete picture of law influencing the protection and/or violation of children's rights.

To this end, in chapters 1–4 of this thesis, a theoretical framework and accompanying methodology have been developed for a potentially better understanding of children's rights violations. The hypothesis in these chapters was that, to study children's rights violations through a framework of legal pluralism, whereby the existence of the different legal orders and its statutory laws would be analyzed as relating to a specific child's right in a specific area, would lead to an understanding of the legal factors involved in the violation/protection of that right. This framework consists of a definition of law (chapter 1) and a theory on and method for how to empirically find the different laws of different legal orders (chapters 3 and 4). In addition, it was hypothesized that it would be important to take the child's perspective into account in data collection (chapters 2 and 4), and that analysis would have to take into account the power relations corresponding to the different legal orders surrounding children (chapters 1, 3 and 4).

In chapter 1, it was stated that law has to be understood as a social fact. We only notice that there is a law, because someone (an individual or a group of people) has created a rule that we (the legal community) perceive as law, only because we understand this individual or group that created the rule to be authorized to create laws. The recognition of the legislator, according to the basic norm, is therefore crucial for the understanding of law as law. Likewise, the sovereign only exists because of the recognition of the legal community of the sovereign as sovereign. That is to say that the sovereign exists and has its power only because it is recognized as such by the relevant community. Haugaard's example made this especially clear:

> what distinguishes the actual Napoleon from the "napoleons" who are found in psychiatric institutions is not internal to them but the fact the former (unlike the latter) had a substantial ring of reference which validates his power.[1683]

A legal norm was argued to be different from a social norm in two ways: first, in a legal situation you cannot stop being a member of the legal community of a legal order when you have done something illegal, from the internal perspective of that order and, second, there is a power inequality between the sovereign and the subject of the legal order.

Lastly, a conceptual framework for the understanding and study of statutory law was introduced, wherein a distinction was made between A) formal written law, B) law for the community and C) hidden law.

	formal written law (A)	**law for the community (B)**	**hidden law (C)**
Written	+	B1	C1
Unwritten	–	B2	C2
Public	+	+	–

In chapter 2, it was shown how, in society, from an adult perspective, children are perceived as being different from adult human beings. Compared to the "normal" adult, who is rational and well behaved, the child is unreasonable, immoral and unsociable – much like a madman. For this reason, the child cannot be granted political freedom, or autonomy and has to be socialized, until s/he has not overcome this condition of childhood. This binary distinction between children and adults is the basis for all law for children and the basis for children's rights which, in many ways, are different from (adult) human rights.

In chapter 3, it was shown that, when looking at law from the child's perspective, what is law for the child really depends on whoever the child believes is authorized to make law for her/him and whether this person, or group of people, does indeed create law. Based on this axiom, it is clear that, from the child's perspective, law can be found in different legal orders surrounding the child, such as the household and the school, and potentially does not even include state law. Looking at law through children's eyes therefore automatically leads to a legal pluralist understanding of law.

In chapter 4, a methodology was developed to be able to find all law applicable to, and relevant for, the understanding of the protection/violation of

1683 Haugaard (2008: 122).

a specific child's rights in a specific socio-legal context. It was stated here that, in addition to legal doctrinal research, to find formal written international and state law, it is necessary to engage in qualitative research with both legislators and addressees of the law of each (potential) legal order related to the child's right under research. The participants in the research should therefore include the children themselves. However, it was indicated that research has shown that doing research with children as an adult is not easy and that adult researchers have a tendency to "know better" and to be biased towards information obtained from children. It is therefore important to truly listen to children, to allow them to participate in several phases of the research if possible (such as data analysis), and to allow them as much agency in the research process as possible. This, of course, comes with specific ethical considerations, such as that the child has to be enabled to give informed consent to participate in the research (ideally without needing the consent of the parent), has to be guaranteed confidentiality and anonymity, and the researcher and participant should be positioned as equals insofar as possible.

To practically realize this, a concrete method for qualitative research with children was developed, the so-called "micro-research", which uses inquiry-based science instruction and Socratic dialogue as the foundation for its approach. Practically, a researcher who wants to understand the legal orders surrounding a child's right, in a specific socio-legal context, has to identify possible legal orders and then, for each order, try to identify which forms of law (formal written law, law for the community and/or hidden law) may apply. Formal written law can be mostly found through legal doctrinal research and literature study; law for the community and hidden law have to be found through empirical legal research. In addition, empirical legal research is necessary to test whether indeed all relevant legal orders have been identified. Data has to be analyzed according to the theoretical framework as developed in chapters 1 and 3.

Subsequently, the theoretical framework and methodology were put to the test in three empirical case studies:

- The child's right to education in the Netherlands (chapter 5)
- The child's right to education in the Central African Republic (CAR) (chapter 6)
- The child's right to nationality in the Turkish Republic of Northern Cyprus (TRNC) (chapter 7)

Each of these case studies includes empirical data from field research as well as data from literature research.

Finally, the third part of the thesis is the conclusion, which includes an answer to the main research question, divided over two chapters: first, a reflection on whether the theoretical framework and methodology as developed in this thesis do indeed lead to a better understanding of children's rights violations in different cultural, social and political contexts and, if so, in what way, (chapter 8) and, second, whether this understanding can indeed be used to improve the concrete situation of children (chapter 9).

ACKNOWLEDGEMENTS

While each PhD thesis is probably a group project to a certain extent in the sense that its success or failure often depends on the support by people other than the PhD candidate, this thesis in particular has been the result of an immense amount of support of a very large group of people. Without all this support, this research project and the resulting thesis would literally not have come into existence. So while I am the person obtaining the doctoral degree, I can take only limited credit for this whole project as it was so much a shared process that depended in large part on this support. I owe thanks to so many people, some of whom I don't even know by name (because of anonymous donations). Nevertheless, below I will attempt to provide a – necessarily incomplete – list of all who have contributed to this research project. Because I don't want to distinguish between the different people involved in terms of rankings, titles, anonymity, etc. the following acknowledgements will be in (more or less) chronological order and I will use first names only.

The project started in 2013, when I was doing (masters) research in Rwanda and emailed Rianne, because I decided then and there that I wanted to continue research on children's rights and pursue a PhD. Although we had never met, I'd read an interview with Rianne and thought she might be an inspiring supervisor and mentor. This intuition turned out to be very right. Rianne has been with me from the start working on this project, has experienced and stood by me during all its difficulties and hurdles, through academic as well as personal issues. Generally, she has been one of the rocks of this project. Rianne, thank you so much for EVERYTHING, both the academic and life lessons, and I'm so happy that we will continue to work together!

Other people who joined the project in the proposal phase were advisors Jan and Phil, who have both regularly contributed throughout the project, with their critical perspectives, questions and discussions, as well as practical advises in particular in relation to field research. Thank you both so much for your inspiration, time and commitment.

The second step was to find funding for the project, starting with a crowdfunding campaign. Of the Tilburg Univesrity Alumni Fund, I particularly have to thank Stephanie for setting up and supporting the campaign – thank you for your enthusiasm and for making it fun! The whole campaign was pretty much a group project, and I think almost all my friens and family helped in some way or other. In particular Jessica who wrote the beautiful campaign song

"How many teardrops", Michiel who helped with the recording and mixing, choirs Kwaya and a choir of ARtEZ students (thanks to Maarten and Maartje for setting this up), Marc and Laura for speaking during the kick-off presentation. Of course I am also eternally grateful to all the donors, around 200 at the time, who made the project possible with their donations.

In relation to the first case study on the child's right to education in the Netherlands, I am particularly grateful to the colleagues at Defence for Children – the Netherlands, whom I greatly enjoyed working together with and I am very proud of the report we published and the media buzz it created. Thanks in particular to Aloys, Laura, Tanja, Daniëlle and now Timo, for making sure the advocacy and research do not get lost, and that these children out of school will not be overlooked much longer.

Some time right before the CAR case study I was kindly adopted by Maastricht University, where colleagues I had never met before created the possibility for me to be a scholarship student and to finance my PhD through crowdfunding and other forms of fundraising. Thanks to Jos and Marlies for setting up this construction, and to Rianne, Fons and Saskia for being on the advisory committee of the Children's Rights Research Fund. A particular thank you to Hildegard who, as dean of the law faculty at the time, decided to take me in and also suggested her wonderful husband René as a second supervisor.

Thank you so much René, the second rock this project has been leaning on, for joining the project, being so flexible and incredibly friendly and a really great life coach. Your relativization of whatever I would get upset about has been most helpful, as well as your enthusiasm for the research and your love for footnotes and references. But most of all I thank you for your incredible kindness! I am so happy and excited to also keep working with you and Hidlegard in the future.

The second case study on the child's right to education in the CAR would not have been possible without the support of Père Luk of CARITAS. His support and friendship have been vital to the case study in many ways. Thanks to my research assistants Bonheur and Petruchka for doing great work, even into the late hours. Thanks to many friends who made my stay much more fun and also, on many occasions, much more safe, in particular: Edouard, Lina, Freddy, Eva, Celine, Bernard, Julien, Brise. Thanks to Timothy and Pauline for help with the translation of the research report and source material. A big thank you to the large group of students who volunteered to transcribe interviews on a Saturday (!).

The third case study on the child's right to nationality in the Turkish Republic of Northern Cyprus benefitted from the generous help of many people in Cyprus, who were so very kind and helped as translators, research assistants and informants. I will leave out their names for anonymity reasons. The case study was made possible financially because of contributions of many donors in a second crowdfunding campaing, as well as the SWOL and MaRBLe/EDLAB scholarships. In addition, part of the fundraising, research and reporting/analysis were conducted by – and would not have had the same quality without – the star MaRBLe student team: Ambra, Céline, Florentina, Nikki and Raphaela. Great job girls! Thanks also for Mehmet for his help with the translation of the report as well as Turkish sources. Thanks to the Institute on Statelessness, in particular Laura and Amal, for working together with us on sharing the research results. Thanks to Rik for the beautiful design of the report – may it be the first of many! And, again, thanks all students who volunteered to transcribe interviews.

Thanks for the (academic) feedback on different (draft) chapters from Rebecca, Louisa and Paul.

Thanks to the assessment committee: Fons, Teun, Nick and Ton, for reading the lengthy thesis in such short time. I look forward to our discussion on the subject matter, which hopefully will extend beyond this project into the future.

Thanks to my paranymphs Kila and Frank – thank you for helping in preparing the defense and, most of all, the party – can't wait to celebrate!

Lastly, thanks to all friends and family who have supported me throughout the project, who have been understanding and patient with my absence, passionate (but perhaps sometimes overbearing or boring) stories about injustices in the world, and who have at times had to worry about whether I would come back in one piece, yet supported me nevertheless. I hope you don't mind me not listing your names and all the joys you add to my life – I hope you know that I love you and will make sure to tell you in person!

A particular thank you to Mark, love of my life, who really did not have so much to do with the thesis, but certainly made and continues to make the process – and my life in general – much more easy and fun. Thank you for supporting the PhD by making me coffee, fruits, delicious meals and supplying the occasional candy.

Last but certainly not least, a special thank you to my parents to whom I have dedicated this thesis. They have always been supportive of this project and believed in me, even when I am certain that this was not always easy. Thank you mom and dad for letting me take my own path.

CURRICULUM VITAE

Marieke J. Hopman was born on 23 December 1988, in Heiloo, the Netherlands. She completed VWO high school in 2006, and studied childhood and educational studies for two years in Amsterdam. After quitting her studies and working fulltime as a projectleader on a project for disadvantaged youth in Amsterdam, in 2009 she started her BA in philosophy at Tilburg University. In 2013, she started her MA in philosophy at the University of Amsterdam. During her studies she worked as a teacher both in high school, at the university and on HBO level. During her MA she took her studies in the direction of children's rights, taking a few law courses and working on a thesis on the meaning of childhood, children's rights and child combatants in Rwanda and the Netherlands. In 2015, after a successful crowdfunding campaing, she started her PhD research "Looking at law through children's eyes", first at Tilburg University, then at Maastricht University. The first draft of the thesis was submitted in January 2019.

For her thesis work she has been awarded the following grants and/or prizes:

- Tilburg University Science Slam Award (2016)
- MaRBLe/EDLAB scholarship for MaRBLe/TRNC research project (2017)
- SWOL scholarship for MaRBLe / TRNC research project (2017)
- Nominated for VIVA 400, category "world improvers" (2017)
- Maastricht University Action Research Award (2017)
- Selected for KNAW Faces of Science (2018)

A follow-up to the current project, on the development rights of children living in areas of ongoing political conflict, has been awarded an NWO/WOTRO SDG grant in 2019.

ATTACHMENT 1

Lists of themes / questions for discussion during formal interviews for the CAR case study (with chapter 6)

a) Questions interviews right to education CAR: children

1. Quand je parle des droits des enfants à l'éducation en RCA, tu penses à quoi?
2. Tu as de l'éducation? (Tu apprends?)
   a. Non -> pourquoi pas? C'est qui qui décide? Tu en penses quoi?
   b. Oui: quelle sorte? Pourquoi? Qui décide? Tu en penses quoi?
3. Tu vas à l'école?
   a. Non -> Q2a -> Q4.
   b. Oui: Pourquoi? Qui décide? Tu en penses quoi?
      i. Tu es dans quelle classe?
      ii. Est-ce qu'il y a des règles dans l'école? Lesquelles? Quoi arrive si tu ne respectes pas les règles? Est-ce qu'il y a des conséquences?
      iii. Combien des élèves est ce qu'il y a dans ta classe?
      iv. J'ai entendu des histoires sur la corruption dans les écoles, est-ce que tu as d'expérience avec ça?
4. Est-ce que tu sais lire et écrire? Tu trouves ça comment /important?
   a. Oui -> Tu sais écrire ton nom? (montrer?)
5. Si tu pourrais décider sur le droit des enfants à l'éducation en RCA, tu ferais comment? Tu l'organiserais comment?
6. Est – ce qu'il y a quelque chose que j'ai oublié à demander sur le sujet?
7. Dessin
8. Formulaire de consentement

b) Questions interviews right to education CAR: parents / grand-parents (enfants=petits-enfants)

1. Quand je parle des droits des enfants à l'éducation en RCA, vous pensez à quoi?
2. Avez-vous eu de l'éducation? (Vous avez appris?)
   a. Non -> pourquoi pas? Qui a décidé? Vous en pensez quoi?
   b. Oui: quelle sorte? Pourquoi? Qui a décidé? Vous en pensez quoi?

3. Vous êtes allé à l'école?
   a. Non -> 2a
   b. Oui -> quelle sorte? Pourquoi? Qui a décidé? Vous en pensez quoi? Jusqu'au quelle classe?
4. Vos enfants ont d'éducation? Tous?
   a. Oui -> 2b, 5
   b. Non -> 2a, 6
5. Vos enfants vont a l'école? Tous?
   a. Non -> 2a
   b. Oui -> 2b
      i. Les écoles sont comment?
         1. Combien des élèves?
         2. Règles? La chicotte?
         3. Payer?
         4. Corruption?
6. Si vous pouviez décider sur le droit des enfants à l'éducation en RCA, vous feriez comment? Vous l'organiseriez comment?
7. Est-ce qu'il y a quelque chose que j'ai oublié de demander sur le sujet?
8. Formulaire de consentement

c) Questions interviews right to education for teachers / school management

1. Quand je parle des droits des enfants à l'éducation en RCA, vous pensez à quoi?
2. Vous avez eu de l'éducation? Quelle forme? Vous en pensez quoi / c'était comment?
3. Dans votre école:
   a. C'est une école publique ou privé?
   b. Vous enseignez quelle classe?
   c. Il y a combien des élèves dans la classe?
   d. Vous pensez quoi de l'éducation à votre école? (Qualité, motivation des élèves, ...)? Pourquoi?
   e. Est-ce qu'il y a des règles dans l'école / dans la classe? Lesquelles? Violence?
      i. Si l'enfant ne respecte pas les règles, on fait quoi? Est- ce qu'il y a des punitions? Lesquelles?
      ii. Vous utilisez la chicotte? Pourquoi (pas)?
      iii. On utilise la chicotte dans cette école? Pourquoi (pas)?
   f. J'ai entendu les histoires sur de la corruption dans les classes, vous avez d'expérience avec ça?
   g. Vous pensez quoi du matériel utilisé dans l'école Pourquoi?

4. Si vous pouviez décider sur le droit des enfants à l'éducation en RCA, vous feriez comment? Vous l'organiseriez comment? Pourquoi?
5. Vous avez un salaire? C'est combien? C'est payé régulièrement?
6. Est-ce qu'il y a quelque chose que j'ai oublié de demander sur le sujet?
7. Formulaire de consentement

d) Questions interviews right to education for education inspection / politicians / ONG / APE

1. Quand je parle des droits des enfants à l'éducation en RCA, vous pensez à quoi?
2. Vous avez eu de l'éducation? Quelle forme? Vous en pensez quoi / c'était comment?
3. Vous pouvez m'expliquer que vous faites quoi exactement comme emploi? (Quels responsabilités? Quelles relations de décision vis-à-vis parents, enseignants, directeurs d'écoles, inspection, ONGs, politique...?)
   a. Vous faites quoi pour réaliser le droit des enfants à l'éducation en RCA? Vous rencontrez quels obstacles?
   b. REGIONAL: vous avez la responsabilité pour combiens écoles? Quels sorts? Combiens enseignants, maitres parents, enfants?
   c. Est-ce que les enseignants, maitres parents, etc sont payé?
4. Pour les fonctionnes publique: Vous avez un salaire? C'est combien? C'est payé régulièrement + par qui?
5. Est-ce qu'il y a de la violence dans les écoles? Quels sorts?
   a. On utilise la chicotte dans les écoles? Pourquoi (pas)?
6. J'ai entendu des histoires sur la corruption, vous avez de l'expérience avec ça?
   a. Dans les classes
   b. ONGs?
   c. Inspection académique?
   d. APE?
   e. Gouvernement?
7. Si vous pouviez décider sur le droit des enfants à l'éducation en RCA, vous feriez comment? Vous l'organiseriez comment? Pourquoi?
8. Vous pensez qui du matériel utilisé dans l'école? Pourquoi?
9. Est-ce qu'il y a quelque chose que j'ai oublié de demander sur le sujet?
10. Formulaire de consentement

ATTACHMENT 2

Overview of interviews and observations (with chapter 6)

Interviews:

No.	m/f	age	role 1	class / position	private/public	residence	role 2
1	m	16	child	3eme	private	city	
2	f	14	child	5eme	public	city	
3	m	13	child	CM2	public	city	
4	m	36	NGO / UN employee	controller	–	large town	parent / tuteur
5	f	14	child	CM2	private	town (IDP site)	
6	f	15	child	CM2	public	town (IDP site)	
7	m	–	education inspection	chef secteur	–	town	
8	f	11	child	CP2	public	town (IDP site)	
9	f	12	child	5eme	private	town	
10	f	34	parent / tuteur	mother	–	town	
11	f	28	NGO / UN employee	–	–	city	
12	m	12	child	CP2 after summer?	public	village	
13	m	51	politician	village chief	–	village	parent / tuteur
14	m	–	teacher/ school director	maitre-parent	public (bache)	village (IDP site)	
15	m	39	religious leader	–	–	city	
16	f	–	NGO / UN employee	–	–	city	(non-political) employee min edu/ aff sociales
17	f	40	NGO / UN employee	–	–	city	
18	m	8	child	CP2	public	town	
19	f	8	child	CP2	public	town	
20	m	13	child	CM1	private	town	

No.	m/f	age	role 1	class / position	private/public	residence	role 2
21	f	18	child	CE2	public	town	
22	m	49	education inspection	chef secteur	–	town	
23	m	55	religious leader	–	–	town	
24	f	13	child	CM1	public	town	
25	m	45	parent / tuteur	father, grandfather	–	town	
26	m	42	NGO / UN employee	–	–	town	
27	m	-	NGO / UN employee	–	–	city	
28	m	61	politician	village chief	–	village	
29	m	38	teacher/ school director	–	public	village	
30	m	11	child	CM2	private	town	
31	m	12	child	CM1	private	town	
32	f	14	child	4eme	private	town	
33	f	9	child	C1	private	town	
34	f	23–25	parent / tuteur	mother	public	town	
35	m	11	child	CM1	public	town	
36	f	20	child	BAC	public	City (IDP)	
37	f	12	child	CM1	public	City (IDP)	
38	f	10	child	école d'art	public	City (IDP)	
39	m	17	child	terminale	private	city	
40	f	16	child	seconde S2	private	city	
41	f	8	child	CE1	private	city	
42	m	–	teacher/ school director	coordinator, inspection teacher	private	city	

No.	m/f	age	role 1	class / position	private/public	residence	role 2
43	m	43	teacher/ school director	directeur, prof uni	private	city	
44	f	30	parent / tuteur	mother	–	City (IDP)	
44	f	45	parent / tuteur	mother	–	City (IDP)	
44	f	35	parent / tuteur	mother	–	City (IDP)	
44	f	19	parent / tuteur	mother / child	–	City (IDP)	child
45	f	13	child	CM 2	public	village	
46	f	60	parent / tuteur	aunt	–	city	
47	m	39	APE	president	public	village	parent / tuteur
48	f	19	child	none, stopped CM1	public	village	
49	m	33	parent / tuteur	father	–	city	
50	f	27	parent / tuteur	mother	–	city	
51	f	40	teacher/ school director	director	public	large town	
52	m	37	NGO / UN employee	–	–	large town	
53	m	-	education inpection	chef secteur	–	large town	
54	m	12	child	CM2	public	village	
55	m	49	parent / tuteur	vader	–	village	
56	f	55	politician	mayor	–	village	
57	m	-	politician	secretary to the mayor	–	village	
58	f	9	child	CP2	public	large town	
59	m	13	child	CM1	public	large town	
60	m	43	NGO / UN employee	director	–	large town	education inspector, teacher
61	m	55	NGO / UN employee	coordinator	–	large town	religious leader

No.	m/f	age	role 1	class / position	private/public	residence	role 2
62	m	–	politician	–	–	city	
63	m	–	education inpection	chef secteur	–	city	
64	m	–	religious leader	–	–	city	
65	m	–	religious leader	–	–	city	
66	m	24	parent / tuteur	father	–	village	
67	f	11	child	C1	public	village	
68	f	27	parent / tuteur	mother	–	village	
69	f		parent / tuteur	father	–	village	
70	m	–	teacher/ school director	directeur school	public (onofficieel)	village	
71	f		parent / tuteur	moeder		village	
72	f		parent / tuteur	moeder		village	
73	m		parent / tuteur	vader		city	
74	m		politician	conseiller		city	
75	f		teacher/ school director	maitre-parent	private	town	
76	f		parent / tuteur	oma		town	
77	f		parent / tuteur	moeder		town	
78	f		teacher/ school director	maitre-parent	public	town	
79	m		APE	president	public	town	
80	m		teacher/ school director	directeur school, enseignant titulair	public	town	
81	m		teacher/ school director	directeur	private ECAC	town	
82	m	31	parent / tuteur	vader		town	
83	f	12	child	kind	public	town	

No.	m/f	age	role 1	class / position	private/public	residence	role 2
84	m	37	NGO / UN employee	chef projets COOPI		town	
85	m	–	teacher / school director	directeur PO + VO school	–	–	
86	m	–	student	higher education	private	city	
87	m	–	religious leader			city	NGO / UN employee
88	m	–	student	VO	private	city	
89	f	–	religious leader	soeur	–	village	
90	m	–	(non-political) employee min edu/aff sociales		–	city	
91	m	–	(non-political) employee min edu/aff sociales		–	city	
92	m	–	NGO / UN employee	coordinateur	–	town	
93	m	–	NGO / UN employee	coordinateur (armed group)	–	town	
94	m	–	parent / tuteur	–	–	town	
95	m	–	religious leader	–	–	town	teacher / school director
96	m	–	religious leader	–	private	town	teacher / school director, NGO / UN employee
97	m	–	religious leader	–	–	large town	NGO / UN employee
98	m	–	teacher / school director	director IDP site school	–	large town	die zei "boeken zijn corrupte deal"
99	m	–	researcher	phd	–	NL	
100	v	–	researcher	ass. Prof	–	NL	
101	v	–	researcher	ass. Prof	–	NL	
102	v	–	researcher	phd	–	NL	
103	m		NGO / UN employee	–	city	(in interv 1.1)	

No.	m/f	age	role 1	class / position	private/public	residence	role 2
104	m	–	lawyer	–	–	large town	
105	m	–	education inspection	–	–	large town	teacher / school director
106	v	–	NGO / UN employee	–	–	city	
107	m	–	religious leader	–	–	large town	
108	m	–	(non-political) employee min edu/aff sociales	–	–	city	
109	v	–	child	–	public	city	
110	v	–	child	–	public	village	
111	m	–	child	–	public	village	
112	v	8	child	–	public	village	
113	v	6	child	–	public	village	
114	v	5	child	–	public	village	
115	m	8	child	–	public	village	
116	v	5	child	–	public	village	
117	v	12	child	–	public	village	
118	m	–	teacher/ school director	–	public	village	
119	–	–	child	–	public	village	
120	m	–	APE	–	public	village	
121	m	–	teacher / school director	–	public	village	
122	v	–	parent / tuteur	–	public	village	
123	v	–	parent / tuteur	–	public	village	
124	m	–	parent / tuteur	–	public	village	
125	m	–	politician	–	–	city	

No.	m/f	age	role 1	class / position	private/public	residence	role 2
126	m	–	politician	–	–	city	
127	m	–	religious leader	–	private	town	teacher / school director
128	m	–	religious leader	–	private	town	teacher / school director
129	m	–	politician	–	–	city	
130	f	14	child	5eme		city	
131	f	14	child			city	
132	f	15	child			city	
133	f	16	child			city	

Observations:

No.	Date	Description	Place
1	8-8-2016	children being hit because of crying (making noise).	city
2	10-8-2016	visit site 1	town
3	12-8-2016	meeting cluster education	city
4	17-8-2016	visit site 2	town
5	17-8-2016	visit site 3	town
6	18-8-2016	observation site school	town
7	22-8-2016	visit site 4	city
8	28-8-2016	visit site 5	town
9	8-11-2016	observation private school	city
10	9-11-2-16	observation private school	city
11	10-11-2016	visite site 6	city
12	10-11-2016	visite site 7	city
13	24-11-2016	distribution school materials	village
14	24-11-2016	observation public school	village
15	25-11-2016	observation public school	village
16	26-11-2016	observation public school	large town
17	11-12-2016	child being hit bec of going home during school break	village
18	15-12-2016	observation public school	village
19	16-12-2016	observation ministry of education	city
20	20-12-2016	observation private school	town
21	20-12-2016	observation: payment APE – school director	town
22	21-12-2016	observation public school	town
23	27-11-2016	observation: library	large town
24	2-9-2016	Observation: school	town

Human Rights Research Series

The Human Rights Research Series' central research theme is the nature and meaning of international standards in the fi eld of human rights, their application and promotion in the national legal order, their interplay with national standards, and the international supervision of such application. Anyone directly involved in the defi nition, study, implementation, monitoring, or enforcement of human rights will fi nd this series an indispensable reference tool.
The Series is published together with the world famous Netherlands Network for Human Rights Research (formerly School of Human Rights Research), a joint eff ort by human rights researchers in the Netherlands.

 For previous volumes in the series, please visit http://shr.intersentia.com.

Published titles within the Series:

82. Mohammad Hadi Zakerhossein, *Situation Selection Regime at the International Criminal Court*
    ISBN 978–1–78068–618–9
83. Yi Zhang, *Advancing the Right to Health Care in China. Towards Accountability*
    ISBN 978–1–78068–677–6
84. Diana Itza Odier-Contreras Garduño, *Collective Reparations.Tensions and Dilemmas Between Collective Reparations and the Individual Right to Receive Reparations*
    ISBN 978–1–78068–705–6
85. Daphina Misiedjan, *Towards a Sustainable Human Right to Water. Supporting vulnerable people and protecting water resources*
    ISBN 978-1-78068-612-7
86. Benedicta Deogratias, *Trapped in a Religious Marriage*
    ISBN 978-1-78068-842-8
87. Kasim Balarabe, *Realising the Right to Water and Sanitation in Nigeria*
    ISBN 978-1-78068-901-2
88. Leonie Huijbers, *Process-based Fundamental Rights Review*
    ISBN 978-1-78068-887-9
89. Vincent Willem Vleugel, *Culture in the State Reporting Procedure of the UN Human Rights Treaty Bodies. How the HRC, the CESCR and the CEDAWCee use human rights as a sword to protect and promote culture, and as a shield to protect against harmful culture*
    ISBN 978-1-83970-006-4
90. Laura Íñigo Álvarez, *Towards a Regime of Responsibility of Armed Groups in International Law*
    ISBN 978-1-83970-004-0
91. Getahun A. Mosissa, *A Re-examination of Economic, Social and Cultural Rights in a Political Society in the Light of the Principle of Human Dignity*
    ISBN 978-1-78068-987-6
92. Veronika Flegar, *The Transformative Potential of a Vulnerability Focus in Basic Assistance Policies*
    ISBN 978-1-83970-039-2